ON IDEAS

ON IDEAS

Aristotle's Criticism of Plato's
Theory of Forms

GAIL FINE

CLARENDON PRESS · OXFORD

Oxford University Press, Walton Street, Oxford OX2 6DP
Oxford New York
Athens Auckland Bangkok Bombay
Calcutta Cape Town Dar es Salaam Delhi
Florence Hong Kong Istanbul Karachi
Kuala Lumpur Madras Madrid Melbourne
Mexico City Nairobi Paris Singapore
Taipei Tokyo Toronto
and associated companies in
Berlin Ibadan

Oxford is a trade mark of Oxford University Press

Published in the United States
by Oxford University Press Inc., New York

British Library Cataloguing in Publication Data
Data available

Library of Congress Cataloging in Publication Data
Fine, Gail.
On ideas: Aristotle's criticism of Plato's theory of forms /
Gail Fine.
Includes bibliographical references and indexes.
1. Aristotle. De ideis. 2. Plato—Influence. 3. Form
(Philosophy) 4. Universalism (Philosophy) I. Title.
B491.F63F56 1993 111'.2—dc20 92–29009

ISBN 0–19–823949–1
0–19–823549–6 (Pbk)

Printed in Great Britain
on acid-free paper by
Bookcraft Ltd Midsomer Norton, Avon

To My Parents
and
to Terry

PREFACE

THE *Peri ideōn* (*On Ideas*) is a short essay by Aristotle, which survives only in fragments preserved by the Greek commentator Alexander, in his commentary on Aristotle's *Metaphysics*. In this essay, Aristotle presents and criticizes arguments for the existence of Platonic forms, and sketches his alternative. It is an especially rich source for anyone who wants to understand Plato's theory of forms. For it characterizes forms, and sets out arguments for their existence, more systematically than Plato does or than Aristotle does elsewhere. Asking whether Plato is committed to these arguments and characterizations affords new insights into the dialogues. Attention to the *Peri ideōn* also illuminates Aristotle's understanding of and alternative to Plato. Nor is the work of purely historical interest. It is one of the first contributions to the continuing debate about the nature of universals, and it raises still-current questions about, for example, the range of universals and whether they can exist uninstantiated. Anyone interested in this debate should be interested in its origins.

I first became interested in the *Peri ideōn* when, as a graduate student at Harvard in the early 1970s, I took a seminar on it with Professor G. E. L. Owen. My interest in it deepened when I gave my own courses on it at Cornell. Initially I worked on the *Peri ideōn* piecemeal, analysing a given argument and tracing its Platonic roots. But I gradually became convinced that the first book of the *Peri ideōn* (which is my focus here) is an integrated whole, and so it seemed worth while to provide a connected discussion. This also seemed worth while because there was no systematic book length treatment of the *Peri ideōn* available in English.

Though the *Peri ideōn* is short, the present work is rather long. This is partly because the *Peri ideōn*'s arguments are cryptic, abstract, and indeterminate. To explain the various ways in which they can be read, and to trace the implications of these readings, takes some time. This is not to say that Aristotle must have had any particular determinate reading in mind; perhaps he deliberately phrased the arguments indeterminately in order to highlight a corresponding indeterminacy in Plato's texts. But even if this is so, we need to see precisely how the arguments Aristotle records are indeterminate, and we need to see what this shows us about Plato and about Aristotle's understanding of him.

Another reason for the relative length of my discussion is that the *Peri ideōn* cannot be properly evaluated or understood in isolation. For example, in order to see whether the arguments Aristotle records can fairly be ascribed to Plato, we need to look at the Platonic texts. In order to understand the point of Aristotle's criticisms, we need to look at other Aristotelian passages where they are developed more fully. Or again, short though the *Peri ideōn* is, it often considers the same few Platonic passages from different points of view, so I often need to follow suit. (In a letter to Mersenne Descartes says that '[r]epetitions may be offensive in some places, but they are elegant in others' (AT III 361/CSM III 180). I do not claim elegance, but the nature of the *Peri ideōn* makes some repetition necessary.)

Despite the length of my discussion, there are many omissions. For example, I do not provide a new text or edition of the *Peri ideōn*, nor do I discuss the second book of the *Peri ideōn*. I do not discuss in detail Platonists other than Plato, in order to see whether Aristotle might have them in mind, nor do I say much about Plato's late dialogues or so-called unwritten doctrines. There are many relevant aspects of Plato's and Aristotle's thought that I touch on but do not discuss in detail. Although I perhaps cannot justify all these omissions, I can explain my reasons for them.

Since Dieter Harlfinger has recently produced a new, and good, text of most of the *Peri ideōn*, based on a fresh examination of the manuscripts, it was unnecessary for me to produce yet another one. Nor was my aim to produce a critical edition of the *Peri ideōn*; what follows is more of a philosophical than a philological exploration (although I do not think there are firm boundaries here).

Although I do not discuss the second book of the *Peri ideōn*, the part I focus on (book 1) is self-contained. For example, as I explain in Ch. 2.7, its structure is neatly dilemmatic.

I shall argue that one central aim of *Peri ideōn* 1 is to illuminate Plato's theory of forms as it is described in the middle dialogues. (*Peri ideōn* 2, by contrast, claims to discuss Eudoxus' theory of forms; it also discusses some arguments about principles which, while they are relevant to Plato, are not so clearly concerned with the middle dialogues in particular.) This is not to say that other sources, such as the late dialogues or other Platonists, are irrelevant; and at some stages I consider some relevant passages in the late dialogues as well as other possible sources. But since the middle dialogues seem to be a chief target, and since exploring that target is already quite a large project, it seemed reasonable to limit myself primarily to it. Others might like to carry my project further by asking what light the *Peri ideōn* sheds on other sources.

To explore the arguments and assess their cogency, I need to take stands on a variety of topics in Plato and Aristotle. To defend all my views in detail would have made an already long and complicated book even longer and more complicated. But in Ch. 4 I indicate my views on some of the central issues. Although this account is not as detailed or as thoroughly defended as it perhaps should be, I hope that it at least provides a framework for what follows.

For my own part, it was only after much labour that the point of the

Peri ideōn and its sources in the dialogues became clear to me. But the effort revealed to me a richness and depth in the dialogues and in the *Peri ideōn* that I had not initially suspected. I hope that the light the *Peri ideōn* casts on Aristotle and on various Platonic passages proves as illuminating for others as it did for me.

An earlier version of Ch. 8 appeared as 'The One over Many', *Philosophical Review*, 89 (1980), 197–240; an earlier version of parts of Ch. 11 appeared as 'Owen's Progress: A Review of *Logic, Science, and Dialectic*', *Philosophical Review*, 97 (1988), 373–99. The present versions appear here by permission of Cornell University. An earlier version of Ch. 9 appeared as 'The Object of Thought Argument: Forms and Thought', in *Apeiron: A Journal for Ancient Philosophy and Science*, 21 (1988), 105–46; the present version appears here by permission of Academic Printing and Publishing. An earlier version of Ch. 13 appeared as 'Aristotle's Criticisms of Plato', J. Klagge and N. Smith (eds.), in *Methods of Interpreting Plato and his Dialogues*, *Oxford Studies in Ancient Philosophy*, Supplementary Volume (1992), 13–41. An earlier version of part of Ch. 14 appeared as 'Aristotle and the More Accurate Arguments', in M. Nussbaum and M. Schofield (eds.), *Language and Logos* (Cambridge University Press, 1982), 155–77. I gratefully acknowledge permission to use portions of these earlier articles. I am also grateful to the Casa Editrice Leo S. Olschki for permission to reprint Harlfinger's text of the *Peri ideōn*.

In writing this book, I have acquired a number of debts that I am pleased to record. I have been greatly influenced by G. E. L. Owen, both by his classes and by his published writings (now collected in *Logic, Science, and Dialectic*), and also by his unpublished manuscript on the *Peri ideōn* (on deposit in the Classics Library in Cambridge University). I thank Mrs Sally Owen for giving me permission to consult Owen's manuscript before it was available to the public.

Since 1975, I have had the great privilege of being a member of the Sage School of Philosophy at Cornell University. The friendliness, support, and stimulation that I have received from many colleagues and students has been remarkable. I should especially like to thank Sydney Shoemaker and Nicholas Sturgeon, both of whom provided encouragement as well as insightful comments, both written and oral, on various versions of various chapters; and Norman Kretzmann, who also provided encouragement, and who read and commented helpfully on most of a penultimate version.

In 1982–3, while on a National Endowment for the Humanities fellowship, I was a Visiting Fellow at Brasenose College, Oxford; and in 1987 I was a Visiting Fellow at Wolfson College, Oxford. I should like to thank the National Endowment for the Humanities for its generous financial support, and the Fellows of Brasenose College and Wolfson College for their hospitality. Much of this book was written while I was in Oxford on these and other occasions. I should like to thank a number of people I first came to know there for their helpful conversations and comments, as well as for their hospitality—especially John Ackrill, Julia Annas, Jonathan Barnes, Lesley Brown, and Michael Woods.

I am also grateful to Jennifer Whiting both for encouragment and also for many helpful and incisive comments, both written and oral, on various drafts of various chapters; to S. Marc Cohen for helpful written comments on Chs. 15 and 16; to Mark Crimmins for helpful comments on Ch. 2; to an anonymous referee for Oxford University Press, who provided detailed and insightful comments not just on one draft, but on two drafts; to Angela Blackburn, Frances Morphy, and Peter Momtchiloff of the Press, all of whom were extremely pleasant and supportive, and to Leofranc Holford-Strevens, both for expert copy-editing and for many helpful comments of substance. Many other people provided helpful comments on various articles, later versions of which are now chapters of this book; these people are acknowledged in the articles.

I am also grateful to the American Council of Learned Studies for a fellowship for 1990–1.

I should also like to thank Paul Matthewson for verifying references, Sigurdur Kristinsson for preparing the Index Locorum and Index Nominum, and Terry Irwin for preparing the General Index.

My greatest debt, both personal and professional, both in this project and in all else, is to Terry Irwin. To my enormous benefit, he has read and commented copiously (both in writing and in conversation) on virtually every draft of everything I have written ever since we first met at Harvard in 1971. Many of my ideas were first formulated in discussion with him; and everything I have done bears the mark of his help. He is also the best of husbands and the best of friends.

G.F.

CONTENTS

ABBREVIATIONS

Plato is cited by the standard Stephanus pagination. Aristotle is cited by the standard Bekker pages and lines. For Plato and Aristotle, I have used the editions in the Oxford Classical Texts, unless otherwise indicated. Barnes's revision of the Oxford Translation of Aristotle is cited as *ROT*. The Greek commentators on Aristotle are cited by page and line from the relevant volume of *Commentaria in Aristotelem Graeca* (= *CAG*).

I

Text and Translation

THE fragments of the *Peri ideōn* are preserved in Alexander's commentary on the *Metaphysics*. This commentary can be found in full in volume i of *Commentaria in Aristotelem Graeca*, edited by M. Hayduck and published in 1891. In 1975 Dieter Harlfinger published a new edition of parts of Alexander's commentary. His edition includes most of the fragments of the *Peri ideōn*,[1] as well as some connected passages from Alexander's commentary; it is based on a fresh examination of the manuscripts, including a manuscript (O) not available to Hayduck. I use Harlfinger's edition where it is available; elsewhere I use Hayduck's text.[2] References follow Hayduck's and Harlfinger's line-numbering, which is indicated by the numbers printed in the margin of the Greek text on pp. 2–11. In each line so numbered, a vertical rule indicates the beginning of the corresponding line in Hayduck's or Harlfinger's edition. No vertical rule is printed where the line-beginnings coincide.

There are two recensions of Alexander's commentary: the *recensio vulgata* (OAC) and the *recensio altera* (LF).[3] OAC is the more reliable, and unless otherwise noted I translate and discuss it. But since LF is often useful and illuminating, and I sometimes discuss it, I have included a text of the relevant portions of it.

The text and translation that follow include both more and less than the *Peri ideōn*. The *Peri ideōn* occupied two books, but since my focus is book 1, I have omitted book 2. In addition to book 1, I have included both some Alexandrian remarks that are interspersed with the *Peri ideōn* and also Eudemus' version of the Third Man Argument.

Recensio Vulgata

79 Πλεοναχῶς μὲν ταῖς ἐπιστήμαις πρὸς τὴν τῶν ἰδεῶν κατασκευὴν
προσεχρήσαντο, ὡς ἐν τῷ πρώτῳ Περὶ ἰδεῶν λέγει· ὧν δὲ νῦν μνημο-
5 νεύειν ἔοικε λόγων, εἰσὶ τοιοῦτοι. εἰ πᾶσα ἐπιστήμη πρὸς ἕν τι καὶ τὸ
αὐτὸ ἐπαναφέρουσα ποιεῖ τὸ αὑτῆς ἔργον καὶ πρὸς οὐδὲν τῶν καθ᾽ ἕκαστον,
εἴη ἄν τι ἄλλο καθ᾽ ἑκάστην παρὰ τὰ αἰσθητὰ ἀίδιον καὶ παράδειγμα τῶν
καθ᾽ ἑκάστην ἐπιστήμην γινομένων· τοιοῦτον δὲ ἡ ἰδέα. ἔτι ὧν ἐπιστῆ-
μαί εἰσι, ταῦτα ἔστιν· ἄλλων δέ τινων παρὰ τὰ καθ᾽ ἕκαστά εἰσιν αἱ
10 ἐπιστῆμαι· ταῦτα γὰρ ἄπειρά τε καὶ ἀόριστα, αἱ δὲ ἐπιστῆμαι ὡρισμένων·
ἔστιν ἄρα τινὰ παρὰ τὰ καθ᾽ ἕκαστα, ταῦτα δὲ αἱ ἰδέαι· ἔτι εἰ ἡ ἰατρικὴ
οὐκ ἔστιν ἐπιστήμη τῆσδε τῆς ὑγιείας ἀλλ᾽ ἁπλῶς ὑγιείας, ἔσται τις αὐτο-
υγίεια· καὶ εἰ ἡ γεωμετρία μή ἐστι τοῦδε τοῦ ἴσου καὶ τοῦδε τοῦ συμμέτρου ἐπιστήμη ἀλλ᾽ ἁπλῶς ἴσου καὶ ἁπλῶς συμμέτρου, ἔσται τι αὐτόισον
15 καὶ αὐτοσύμμετρον, ταῦτα δὲ αἱ ἰδέαι.

Οἱ δὴ τοιοῦτοι λόγοι τὸ μὲν προ-
κείμενον οὐ δεικνύουσιν, ὃ ἦν τὸ ἰδέας εἶναι, ἀλλὰ δεικνύουσι τὸ εἶναί τινα παρὰ
τὰ καθ᾽ ἕκαστα καὶ αἰσθητά. οὐ πάντως δέ, εἴ τινα ἔστιν ἅ εἰσι παρὰ τὰ καθ᾽
ἕκαστα, ταῦτά εἰσιν ἰδέαι· ἔστι γὰρ παρὰ τὰ καθ᾽ ἕκαστα τὰ κοινά, ὧν φαμεν καὶ
20 τὰς ἐπιστήμας εἶναι. ἔτι τε τὸ καὶ τῶν ὑπὸ | τὰς τέχνας ἰδέας εἶναι. καὶ γὰρ πᾶσα
τέχνη πρὸς ἕν τι ἀναφέρει τὰ γιγνόμενα ὑπ᾽ αὐτῆς, καὶ ὧν εἰσιν αἱ τέχναι, ταῦτα
ἔστιν, καὶ ἄλλων τινῶν παρὰ τὰ καθ᾽ ἕκαστά εἰσιν αἱ τέχναι. καὶ ὁ ὕστερος δέ,
πρὸς τῷ μηδὲ οὗτος δεικνύναι τὸ εἶναι ἰδέας, καὶ ὧν οὐ βούλονται ἰδέας εἶναι
κατασκευάζειν ἰδέας δόξει. εἰ γὰρ διότι ἡ ἰατρικὴ μή ἐστι τῆσδε τῆς ὑγιείας
80 ἐπι|στήμη ἀλλ᾽ ἁπλῶς ὑγιείας, ἔστιν αὐτό τις ὑγίεια, ἔσται καὶ ἐπὶ τῶν τεχνῶν
ἑκάστης. οὐ γὰρ τοῦ καθ᾽ ἕκαστα οὐδὲ τοῦδέ ἐστιν, ἀλλ᾽ ἁπλῶς ἐκείνου περὶ ὅ
ἐστιν, οἷον ἡ τεκτονικὴ ἁπλῶς βάθρου ἀλλ᾽ οὐ τοῦδε καὶ ἁπλῶς κλίνης ἀλλ᾽ οὐ
5 τῆσδε· ὁμοίως καὶ ἡ ἀνδριαντοποιητικὴ καὶ ἡ γραφικὴ καὶ | ἡ οἰκοδομικὴ δὲ
καὶ τῶν ἄλλων ἑκάστη τεχνῶν ἔχει πρὸς τὰ ὑφ᾽ ἑαυτήν. ἔσται ἄρα καὶ τῶν ὑπὸ
τὰς τέχνας ἑκάστου ἰδέα, ὅπερ οὐ βούλονται.

Χρῶνται καὶ τοιούτῳ λόγῳ εἰς κατασκευὴν τῶν ἰδεῶν. εἰ ἕκαστος τῶν
10 πολλῶν ἀνθρώπων ἄνθρωπός ἐστι καὶ τῶν ζῴων ζῷον καὶ ἐπὶ τῶν | ἄλλων

79. 4 προσεχρήσαντο (sc. Platonici; cfr. 80. 8, 79. 23, 80. 6 etc.) edd.: προσεχρήσατο OAC
10 ὡρισμένων C, coni. Bonitz, cfr. rec. alt.: ὡρισμένον OA   11 ἡ edd., rec. alt.: om. OAC
22 μηδὲ OA: μὴ καὶ C   24 διότι OA: μὴ ὅτι C   **80.** 1 αὐτό τις AC: αὐτότης O
1–6 ὑγιείας ἐστίν, αὐτό τις ὑγίεια ἔσται, καὶ . . . ἑκάστης (οὐ γὰρ . . . τὰ ὑφ᾽ ἑαυτήν), ἔσται
Brandis   8 καὶ OAC: δὲ καὶ Rose   εἰ OAC: εἰ γὰρ Ascl.   9 τῶν ζῴων OAC: τῶν
πολλῶν ζῴων Ascl.

Recensio Altera

Οἱ ἀπὸ τῶν ἐπιστημῶν ὁρμώμενοι λόγοι καὶ κατασκευάζοντες εἶναι ἰδέας **79**
πλεοναχῶς μὲν λαμβάνονται· ὧν δὲ νῦν μνημονεύει, εἰσὶν οὗτοι. εἰ πᾶσα
ἐπιστήμη πρὸς ἕν τι καὶ τὸ αὐτὸ ἐπαναφέρουσα ποιεῖ τὸ ἑαυτῆς ἔργον καὶ πρὸς
οὐδὲν τῶν καθ' ἕκαστα, οἷον ὁ γεωμέτρης πρὸς ἕν τι τρίγωνον καὶ οὐ | πρὸς 5
τόδε τι τὸ καταγεγραμμένον καὶ ὁμοίως αἱ ἄλλαι ἐπιστῆμαι, ἕτερόν τι ἂν εἴη
καθ' ἑκάστην αὐτῶν παρὰ τὰ αἰσθητὰ ἀίδιον καὶ παράδειγμα τῶν καθ' ἑκάστην
ἐπιστήμην γινομένων· τοῦτο δ' ἂν εἴη ἡ ἰδέα. πάλιν ὧν ἐστιν ἐπιστήμη, ταῦτα
ἔστιν· ἄλλα δὲ ταῦτα παρὰ τὰ καθ' ἕκαστα· τὰ γὰρ καθ' ἕκαστα ἄπειρα καὶ
ἀόριστα, αἱ δὲ ἐπιστῆμαι ὡρισμένων εἰσίν· ταῦτα ἄρα | εἶεν ἂν αἱ ἰδέαι. ἔτι εἰ ἡ 10
ἰατρικὴ οὐκ ἔστιν ἐπιστήμη τῆσδε τῆς ὑγιείας ἀλλ' ἁπλῶς ὑγιείας, ἔσται τις
αὐτοϋγίεια· καὶ εἰ ὁ γεωμέτρης οὐ τοῦδε τοῦ συμμέτρου ἢ τοῦδε τοῦ ἴσου
ἐπιστήμην ἔχει, ἀλλὰ ἁπλῶς ἴσου καὶ ἁπλῶς συμμέτρου, πρὸς ἃ τὰ ἄλλα
ἀναφέρων ἀποδείκνυσι τάδε τινὰ εἶναι, ἔστιν ἄρα τὸ αὐτόισον καὶ αὐτοσύμ-
μετρον· ταῦτα ἄρα ἰδέαι.

Τούτων οὖν τῶν τριῶν λόγων οἱ δύο οἱ πρῶτοι οὐ δεικνύουσιν, ὅτι εἰσὶν ἰδέαι, 15
ἀλλὰ ἄλλα τινὰ παρὰ τὰ καθ' ἕκαστα. οὐκ ἐξ ἀνάγκης δέ, εἰ ἄλλα τινὰ παρὰ τὰ
καθ' ἕκαστά ἐστι, ταῦτα ἰδέας εἶναι· ἔστι γὰρ τὰ καθόλου, ὧν φαμεν εἶναι τὰς
ἐπιστήμας. πρὸς τούτῳ δὲ δεικνύουσιν, ὅτι καὶ τῶν τεχνητῶν εἰσιν ἰδέαι. πᾶσα
γὰρ τέχνη πρὸς ἕν τι καὶ κοινὸν ἀναφέρουσα ποιεῖ | τὰ καθ' ἕκαστα, καὶ ὧν εἰσι 20
τέχναι, ταῦτα ἔστιν, οἷον τέχνη οἰκίας, καὶ ἔστιν οἰκία παρὰ τὰς καθ' ἕκαστα
οἰκίας. καὶ ὁ τρίτος δὲ λόγος οὐδὲ αὐτὸς δείκνυσιν εἶναι ἰδέας—εἰ γὰρ διότι ἡ
ἰατρικὴ μή ἐστι τῆσδε τῆς ὑγιείας | ἐπιστήμη ἀλλ' ἁπλῶς ὑγιείας ἐστίν, αὐτοϋ- **80**
γίειά τις ἔσται—ἀλλὰ καὶ ὧν οὐ βούλονται εἶναι ἰδέας, κατασκευάζει ἰδέας
εἶναι· ἑκάστη γὰρ τῶν τεχνῶν οὐ τοῦ καθ' ἕκαστα οὐδὲ τοῦδέ ἐστι τέχνη, ἀλλ'
ἁπλῶς ἐκείνου περὶ ὅ ἐστιν, οἷον τεκτονικὴ ἁπλῶς βάθρου καὶ ἁπλῶς κλίνης,
καὶ ἡ ὑφαντικὴ ὡσαύτως | καὶ ἡ ἀνδριαντοποιητικὴ καὶ ἡ γραφικὴ, καὶ ἁπλῶς 5
πᾶσα τέχνη τοῦ καθόλου καὶ οὐ τοῦδέ τινός ἐστι τέχνη· ἢ γὰρ ἂν ἓν σχῆμα καὶ
μέτρον ἁπλῶς κλίνης καὶ βάθρου ἐποίει· νῦν δὲ ποιεῖ πολλὰ διαφέροντα καὶ
τοῖς σχήμασι καὶ τοῖς μεγέθεσιν. εἴδη ἄρα οἱ τοιοῦτοι λόγοι καὶ ὧν οὐκ
ἐβούλοντο εἶναι ἰδέας ⟨κατασκευάζουσιν⟩.

Ἦν δέ τις καὶ τοιοῦτος λόγος κατασκευάζων εἶναι ἰδέας. εἰ ἕκαστος τῶν ἀνθρώ- 10
πων ἄνθρωπός ἐστι καὶ τῶν ἵππων ἵππος καὶ τῶν ἄλλων ὁμοίως, καὶ οὐδέν τι

---

79. 1 ὁρμώμενοι F: ὡρμώμενοι L   11 ἀλλ' L: οὐχ F   18 δεικνύουσιν L: δείκνυσιν F   τεχνητῶν F: τεχνιτῶν L   21 οἰκία L: ἡ οἰκία F   οἰκίας Hayduck: ὑγείας L:
om. F   **80.** 4 ἁπλῶς κλίνης–7 μέτρον (homoeot.) add. in marg. L   5 καὶ ἡ
ἀνδριαντοποιητικὴ καὶ ἡ γραφικὴ om. F   9 κατασκευάζουσιν suppl. Hayduck
80. 10–**82.** 9 om. F

ὁμοίως, καὶ οὐκ ἔστιν ἐφ' ἑκάστου αὐτῶν αὐτὸ αὐτοῦ τι κατηγορούμενον,
ἀλλ' ἔστι τι ὃ κατὰ πάντων αὐτῶν κατηγορεῖται οὐδενὶ αὐτῶν ταὐτὸν ὄν,
εἴη ἄν τι τούτων παρὰ τὰ καθ' ἕκαστα ὄντα ὃν κεχωρισμένον αὐτῶν ἀίδιον· ἀεὶ
γὰρ ὁμοίως κατηγορεῖται πάντων τῶν κατ' ἀριθμὸν ἀλλασσομένων. ὃ δὲ ἕν
15 ἐστιν ἐπὶ πολλοῖς κεχωρισμένον τε αὐτῶν καὶ ἀίδιον, | τοῦτ' ἔστιν ἰδέα· εἰσὶν
ἄρα ἰδέαι.

Τοῦτόν φησι τὸν λόγον κατασκευάζειν ἰδέας καὶ τῶν ἀποφάσεων καὶ τῶν
μὴ ὄντων. καὶ γὰρ ἡ ἀπόφασις κατὰ πολλῶν κατηγορεῖται μία καὶ ἡ αὐτὴ καὶ
κατὰ μὴ ὄντων, καὶ οὐδενὶ τῶν καθ' ὧν ἀληθεύεταί ἐστιν ἡ αὐτή. τὸ γὰρ οὐκ
ἄνθρωπος κατηγορεῖται μὲν καὶ καθ' ἵππου καὶ κυνὸς καὶ πάντων τῶν παρὰ τὸν
20 ἄνθρωπον, καὶ | διὰ τοῦτό ἐστιν ἓν ἐπὶ πολλῶν καὶ οὐδενὶ τῶν καθ' ὧν κατη-
γορεῖται ταὐτόν ἐστιν. ἔτι ἀεὶ μένει κατὰ τῶν ὁμοίων ὁμοίως ἀληθευόμενον· τὸ
γὰρ οὐ μουσικὸν κατὰ πολλῶν ἀληθεύεται (πάντων γὰρ τῶν μὴ μουσικῶν),
81 ὁμοίως καὶ τῶν οὐκ ἀνθρώπων τὸ οὐκ ἄνθρωπος· ὥστε εἰσὶ καὶ τῶν ἀποφάσεων
ἰδέαι. ὅπερ ἐστὶν ἄτοπον· πῶς γὰρ ἂν εἴη τοῦ μὴ εἶναι ἰδέα; εἰ γὰρ τοῦτό τις
παραδέξεται, τῶν γε ἀνομογενῶν καὶ πάντῃ διαφερόντων ἔσται μία ἰδέα,
5 γραμμῆς, ἂν οὕτω τύχῃ, καὶ ἀνθρώπου· οὐχ ἵπποι γὰρ | ταῦτα πάντα. ἔτι ἔσται
καὶ τῶν ἀορίστων τε καὶ τῶν ἀπείρων μία ἰδέα. ἀλλὰ καὶ τοῦ πρώτου καὶ τοῦ
δευτέρου· οὐ ξύλον γὰρ ὅ τε ἄνθρωπος καὶ τὸ ζῷον, ὧν τὸ μὲν πρῶτον τὸ δὲ
δεύτερον, ὧν οὔτε γένη οὔτε ἰδέας ἐβούλοντο εἶναι. δῆλον δὲ ὅτι οὐδὲ οὗτος ὁ
λόγος ἰδέας εἶναι συλλογίζεται, ἀλλὰ δεικνύναι βούλεται καὶ αὐτὸς ἄλλο εἶναι
10 τὸ κοινῶς κατηγορούμενον τῶν καθ' | ἕκαστα ὧν κατηγορεῖται. ἔτι αὐτοὶ οἱ
βουλόμενοι δεικνύναι ὅτι ἕν τι τὸ κοινῶς κατηγορούμενόν ἐστι πλειόνων καὶ
τοῦτό ἐστιν ἰδέα, ἀπὸ τῶν ἀποφάσεων αὐτὸ κατασκευάζουσιν. εἰ γὰρ ὁ
πλειόνων τι ἀποφάσκων πρὸς ἕν τι ἐπαναφέρων ἀποφήσει (ὁ γὰρ λέγων
"ἄνθρωπος οὐκ ἔστι λευκός, ἵππος οὐκ ἔστιν" οὐ καθ' ἕκαστον αὐτῶν ἴδιόν τι
15 ἀποφάσκει, ἀλλὰ πρὸς ἕν τι τὴν | ἀναφορὰν ποιούμενος τὸ λευκὸν ἀποφάσκει τὸ
αὐτὸ πάντων), καὶ ὁ καταφάσκων ἂν πλειόνων τὸ αὐτὸ οὐ καθ' ἕκαστον ἄλλο,
ἀλλὰ ἕν τι ἂν εἴη ὃ καταφάσκει, οἷον τὸν ἄνθρωπον κατὰ τὴν πρὸς ἕν τι καὶ
ταὐτὸν ἀναφοράν· ὁμοίως γὰρ ὡς ἡ ἀπόφασις καὶ ἡ κατάφασις. ἔστιν ἄρα τι ὂν
ἄλλο παρὰ τὸ ἐν τοῖς αἰσθητοῖς, ὃ αἴτιόν ἐστι τῆς ἀληθοῦς ἐπὶ πλειόνων τε καὶ
20 τῆς κοινῆς καταφάσεως, καὶ τοῦτό ἐστιν ἡ ἰδέα. τοῦτον δὴ τὸν λόγον φησὶν οὐ
μόνον τῶν καταφασκομένων ἀλλὰ καὶ τῶν ἀποφασκομένων ἰδέας ποιεῖν·
ὁμοίως γὰρ ἐν ἀμφοτέροις τὸ ἕν.

25 Ὁ λόγος ὁ ἀπὸ τοῦ νοεῖν κατασκευάζων τὸ εἶναι ἰδέας τοιοῦτός ἐστιν.
εἰ ἐπειδὰν νοῶμεν ἄνθρωπον ἢ πεζὸν ἢ ζῷον, τῶν ὄντων τέ τι νοοῦμεν
καὶ οὐδὲν τῶν καθ' ἕκαστον (καὶ γὰρ φθαρέντων τούτων μένει ἡ αὐτὴ

10 τι om. Ascl.   11 κατὰ Ascl., coni. Bonitz, cfr. rec. alt.: καὶ OAC   12 ταὐτὸν
ὄν OAC: ὂν ταὐτὸν Ascl.   τι τούτων OAC: τοῦτο Ascl.   ὄντα om. Ascl.   13 ἀεὶ γὰρ
ὁμοίως κατηγορεῖται πάντων OAC: ἐπεὶ καὶ ἀιδίων κατηγορεῖται καὶ πάντων Ascl.   14 τε
om. Ascl.   **81**.3 γε O: τε AC   5 καὶ τῶν ἀορίστων τε om. Bonitz, Hayduck
13–14 ἵππος οὐκ ἔστιν OAC: ἵππος οὐκ ἔστι λευκός e Sepúlveda coni. Bonitz
AC   26 εἰ ἐπειδὰν O Ascl.: ἐπειδὰν A   ἢ πεζὸν ἢ OAC: ἵππον Ascl.   20 δὴ O: δὲ

τούτων αὐτὸ ἑαυτοῦ κατηγορεῖται, ἀλλὰ ἄλλο τι κατὰ τούτων οὐδενὶ τούτων τὸ
αὐτὸ ὂν ἀλλ' ἕτερον ἀιδίως πάντων τῶν ἐξαλλαττομένων κατ' ἀριθμὸν κατη-
γορούμενον, ἕτερόν τι ὂν ἢ κεχωρισμένον—. ὃ δὲ ἕν ἐστιν | ἐπὶ πολλῶν καὶ 15
κεχωρισμένον αὐτῶν καὶ ἀίδιον, τοῦτ' ἔστιν ἰδέα· εἰσὶν ἄρα ἰδέαι.

Τοῦτόν φησι τὸν λόγον κατασκευάζειν, ὅτι εἰσὶ καὶ τῶν ἀποφάσεων ἰδέαι. καὶ
γὰρ ἡ ἀπόφασις κατὰ πολλῶν κατηγορεῖται μία καὶ ἡ αὐτὴ οὖσα κατά τε ὄντων
καὶ μὴ ὄντων, καὶ οὐδενὶ τῶν καθ' ὧν ἀληθεύεταί ἐστιν ἡ | αὐτή. τὸ γὰρ οὐκ 20
ἄνθρωπος ἀληθεύεται καὶ κατὰ τοῦ ἵππου καὶ κατὰ τοῦ κυνὸς καὶ πάντων τῶν
παρὰ τὸν ἄνθρωπον ὄντων τε καὶ μὴ ὄντων· κατά τε γὰρ ξύλου καὶ λίθου καὶ
κατὰ ἱπποκενταύρου καὶ κατὰ Χιμαίρης καὶ ἁπλῶς τῶν ἀνυποστάτων καὶ
αὐτοῦ τοῦ μηδαμῇ μηδαμῶς ὄντος καὶ ὁμοίως ἐπὶ πάντων ἀληθεύεται·
εἰσὶν ἄρα καὶ τῶν ἀποφάσεων ἰδέαι. ὅπερ ἐστὶν ἄτοπον. εἰ γὰρ τοῦτό τις παρα- **81**
δέξεται, τῶν ἀνομογενῶν πάντῃ ἐστὶ μία ἰδέα, γραμμῆς, εἰ τύχῃ, καὶ ἀνθρώπου
καὶ ἵππου· πάντα γὰρ ταῦτα οὐ κύνες καὶ οὐ ξύλα. ἀλλὰ καὶ τοῦ προτέρου καὶ
ὑστέρου· οὐ ξύλον γὰρ ὅ τε ἄνθρωπος καὶ τὸ ζῷον. δῆλον | δὲ ὅτι οὐδὲ οὗτος ὁ 5
λόγος ἰδέας εἰσάγει, ἀλλὰ δεικνύναι βούλεται καὶ αὐτὸς ἄλλο εἶναι τὸ κοινῶς
κατηγορούμενον τῶν καθ' ἕκαστα ὧν κατηγορεῖται. πρὸς δὲ τούτῳ καὶ ὧν οὐκ
ἐβούλοντο ἰδέας εἶναι—· τοῦ γὰρ πρώτου καὶ δευτέρου ἰδέαν οὐκ ἔλεγον εἶναι.

Ὁ λόγος ὁ ἀπὸ τοῦ νοεῖν κατασκευάζων εἶναι τὰς ἰδέας τοιοῦτός ἐστιν. | ὅταν 10
νοῶμεν ἄνθρωπον ἢ ἵππον ἢ πεζὸν ἢ ζῷον, ὧν τι νοοῦμεν καὶ οὐδὲν τῶν καθ'
ἕκαστα (καὶ γὰρ φθαρέντων τῶν καθ' ἕκαστα οὐδὲν ἧττον ἡ ἔννοια μένει τῶν

---

14 ὂν ἢ L: fort. ἂν εἴη καὶ Hayduck   22 Χιμαίρρης L   **81.** 11 ἡ Hayduck: εἰ L

ἔννοια), δῆλον ὡς ἔστι παρὰ τὰ καθ' ἕκαστα καὶ αἰσθητά, ὃ καὶ ὄντων
ἐκείνων καὶ μὴ ὄντων νοοῦμεν· οὐ γὰρ δὴ μὴ ὄν τι νοοῦμεν τότε. τοῦτο
82 δὲ εἶδός τε καὶ ἰδέα ἐστίν. φησὶ δὴ τοῦτον τὸν λόγον καὶ τῶν φθειρομένων τε καὶ
ἐφθαρμένων καὶ ὅλως τῶν καθ' ἕκαστά τε καὶ φθαρτῶν ἰδέας κατασκευάζειν,
οἷον Σωκράτους, Πλάτωνος· καὶ γὰρ τούτους νοοῦμεν καὶ φαντασίαν αὐτῶν
5 φυλάσσομεν καὶ μηκέτι ὄντων· φάντασμα γάρ τι | καὶ τῶν μηκέτι ὄντων
σώζομεν. ἀλλὰ καὶ τὰ μηδ' ὅλως ὄντα νοοῦμεν, ὡς ἱπποκένταυρον, Χίμαιραν·
ὥστε οὐδὲ ὁ τοιοῦτος λόγος ἰδέας εἶναι συλλογίζεται.

11 Ὁ μὲν ἐκ τῶν πρός τι κατασκευάζων ἰδέας λόγος τοιοῦτός ἐστιν. ἐφ'
ὧν ταὐτόν τι πλειόνων κατηγορεῖται μὴ ὁμωνύμως, ἀλλ' ὡς μίαν τινὰ
δηλοῦν φύσιν, ἤτοι τῷ κυρίως τὸ ὑπὸ τοῦ κατηγορουμένου σημαινόμενον
83 εἶναι ταῦτα ἀληθεύεται κατ' αὐτῶν, ὡς ὅταν ἄνθρωπον λέγωμεν Σωκράτην καὶ
Πλάτωνα, ἢ τῷ εἰκόνας αὐτὰ εἶναι τῶν ἀληθινῶν, ὡς ἐπὶ τῶν γεγραμμένων
ὅταν τὸν ἄνθρωπον κατηγορῶμεν (δηλοῦμεν γὰρ ἐπ' ἐκείνων τὰς τῶν
5 ἀνθρώπων εἰκόνας τὴν αὐτήν τινα φύσιν ἐπὶ πάντων σημαίνοντες), ἢ | ὡς τὸ μὲν
αὐτῶν ὂν τὸ παράδειγμα, τὰ δὲ εἰκόνας, ὡς εἰ ἀνθρώπους Σωκράτη τε καὶ τὰς
εἰκόνας αὐτοῦ λέγοιμεν. κατηγοροῦμεν δὲ τῶν ἐνταῦθα τὸ ἴσον αὐτὸ ὁμωνύμως
αὐτῶν κατηγορούμενον· οὔτε γὰρ ὁ αὐτὸς πᾶσιν αὐτοῖς ἐφαρμόζει λόγος, οὔτε
τὰ ἀληθῶς ἴσα σημαίνομεν· κινεῖται γὰρ τὸ ποσὸν ἐν τοῖς αἰσθητοῖς καὶ
10 μεταβάλλει συνεχῶς καὶ οὐκ ἔστιν ἀφωρισ|μένον. ἀλλ' οὐδὲ ἀκριβῶς τὸν τοῦ
ἴσου λόγον ἀναδεχόμενον τῶν ἐνταῦθά ἐστί τι. ἀλλὰ μὴν ἀλλ' οὐδὲ ὡς τὸ μὲν
παράδειγμα αὐτῶν τὸ δὲ εἰκόνα· οὐδὲν γὰρ μᾶλλον θάτερον θατέρου
παράδειγμα ἢ εἰκών. εἰ δὲ καὶ δέξαιτό τις μὴ ὁμώνυμον εἶναι τὴν εἰκόνα τῷ
παραδείγματι, ἀεὶ ἔπεται ταῦτα τὰ ἴσα ὡς εἰκόνας εἶναι ἴσα τοῦ κυρίως καὶ
15 ἀληθῶς ἴσου. εἰ δὲ τοῦτο, | ἔστι τι αὐτόισον καὶ κυρίως, πρὸς ὃ τὰ ἐνθάδε ὡς
εἰκόνες γίνεταί τε καὶ λέγεται ἴσα, τοῦτο δέ ἐστιν ἰδέα, παράδειγμα †καὶ
εἰκὼν† τοῖς πρὸς αὐτὸ γινομένοις. εἰς μὲν οὖν οὗτος λόγος ὁ καὶ τῶν πρός τι
κατασκευάζων ἰδέας, δοκῶν ἐπιμελέστερον καὶ ἀκριβέστερον καὶ προσε-
χέστερον ἅπτεσθαι τῆς δείξεως τῶν ἰδεῶν. οὐδὲ γὰρ τὸ κοινὸν εἶναί τι παρὰ τὰ
20 καθ' | ἕκαστα ἁπλῶς οὗτος ὁ λόγος δοκεῖ δεικνύναι, ὥσπερ οἱ πρὸ τοῦ, ἀλλὰ τὸ
παράδειγμά τι εἶναι τῶν ἐνταῦθα ὄντων κυρίως ὄν· τοῦτο γὰρ χαρακτηριστικὸν
εἶναι δοκεῖ τῶν ἰδεῶν μάλιστα.

28 δῆλον ὡς ἔστι παρὰ OAC: φανερὸν ὅτι ἔστι τι παρὰ Ascl.   καὶ¹ et ὃ om. Ascl.   29 οὐ
γὰρ δὴ–82. 1 ἐστίν OAC: οὐ γὰρ τοῦ μὴ ὄντος ἐστὶν ἰδέα καὶ εἶδος Ascl.   1 δὴ OAC: δὲ
Ascl.   2 τε¹ᵉᵗ² om. Ascl.   3 καὶ γὰρ OAC: καὶ γὰρ καὶ Ascl.   4 φάντασμα
. . . ὄντων (homeot.) om. AC   γάρ τι rec. alt., Ascl.: γὰρ O   5 τῶν O: ἐπὶ τῶν Ascl.
6 Χίμαιραν OAC: καὶ Χίμαιραν Ascl.   οὐδὲ ὁ τοιοῦτος λόγος OAC: οὐδ' οὗτος ὁ λόγος Ascl.
11 ἐκ OAC: καὶ coni. Bonitz   13 τῷ (cfr. 83. 2) A² Bonitz: τὸ OA¹C   **83.** 1 ἀληθεύεται OA¹C: ἀληθεύεσθαι A²   3 κατηγορῶμεν OAC: κατηγορούμεν Brandis   4 σημαί-
νοντες OAC: σημαίνειν Brandis   5 Σωκράτη O: Σωκράτην C: Σωκρα' A   15 αὐτόισον A (in ras.?): αὐτοῖσον C: αὐτοῖς O   15–16 παράδειγμα καὶ εἰκὼν OAC: καὶ εἰκὼν del.
Wilpert, Leszl: παραδειγματικὸν coni. Ross, *Select Fragments*

τοιούτων), δῆλον ἄρα ὡς ἔστι τι παρὰ τὰ καθ' ἔκαστα, ὃ καὶ ὄντων καὶ μὴ ὄντων
ἐκείνων νοοῦμεν· οὐ γὰρ δὴ τὸ μὴ ὂν νοοῦμεν τότε.
τοῦτο δὲ οὐδὲν ἂν εἴη ἕτερον ἢ ἡ ἰδέα ἄφθαρτος οὖσα. φησὶν οὖν Ἀριστοτέλης **82**
ὅτι κατὰ τοῦτον τὸν λόγον καὶ τῶν φθειρομένων καὶ ἐφθαρμένων καὶ ὅλως τῶν
καθ' ἔκαστά τε καὶ φθαρτῶν, οἷον Σωκράτους, Πλάτωνος (καὶ γὰρ τούτους
νοοῦμεν καὶ φαντασίαν αὐτῶν φυλάττομεν καὶ μηκέτι ὄντων· | φάντασμα γάρ 5
τι καὶ τῶν μηκέτι ὄντων σώζομεν) ἰδέα ἂν εἴη. ἀλλὰ καὶ τὰ μηδὲ ὅλως ὄντα
νοοῦμεν, οἷον ἱπποκένταυρον, Χίμαιραν· ὥστε οὐδὲ ὁ τοιοῦτος λόγος ὁ ἀπὸ τοῦ
νοεῖν ἰδέας εἶναι συλλογίζεται, ἀλλὰ τι ἕτερον παρὰ τὰ καθ' ἔκαστα. τούτῳ δὴ
καὶ τὸ καθόλου τὸ ἐν τοῖς καθ' ἔκαστα ἁρμόζει καὶ οὐκ ἐξ ἀνάγκης ἰδέαν
εἰσάγει.

Ὁ μὲν ἐκ τῶν πρός τι λόγος κατασκευάζων τὰς ἰδέας τοιοῦτός ἐστιν. ἐφ' ὧν 10
κατὰ πλειόνων τι κατηγορεῖται ἢ ὁμωνύμως ἢ συνωνύμως κατηγορεῖται. καὶ εἰ
συνωνύμως, ἢ κυρίως ἐκεῖνο λέγεται εἶναι
τὰ καθ' ὧν κατηγορεῖται, οἷον ἄνθρωποι Καλλίας καὶ Θεαίτητος, καθ' ὧν ὁ **83**
ἄνθρωπος κατηγορεῖται, ἢ οὐ κυρίως λέγεται εἶναι ἐκεῖνο τὰ καθ' ὧν
κατηγορεῖται· οὐ κυρίως γὰρ αἱ εἰκόνες Σωκράτους καὶ Πλάτωνος τὸ
ἄνθρωπος κατηγορῆται· οὐ κυρίως γὰρ αἱ εἰκόνες Σωκράτους καὶ Πλάτωνος
ἄνθρωποι | λέγονται. ἢ ὁμωνύμως, ὡς ὅταν τὸ καθ' οὗ κατηγορεῖται τὸ μὲν 5
κυρίως λέγηται ἐκεῖνο τὸ κατηγορούμενον, τὸ δ' οὐ κυρίως, οἷον ὅταν ὁ
Σωκράτης καὶ ἡ Σωκράτους εἰκὼν ἄνθρωπος λέγηται. τὸ γοῦν αὐτόισον
κατηγορεῖται κατὰ τῶν αἰσθητῶν ἴσων, καὶ λέγονται ταῦτα αὐτόισα. ἢ
ὁμωνύμως ἢ συνωνύμως ἄρα. συνωνύμως μὲν καὶ κυρίως αὐτόισα οὐκ ἂν
ῥηθεῖεν· τὸ | γὰρ αὐτόισον τὸ ἀληθῶς ἴσον σημαίνει· ῥεῖ δὲ τὸ ποσὸν ἀεὶ τῶν 10
αἰσθητῶν τῶν ἴσων. ἀλλ' οὐδὲ ὁμωνύμως αὐτόισα λεχθεῖεν, ὥστε εἶναι τὸ μὲν
κυρίως τὸ δ' οὐ κυρίως, καὶ τὸ μὲν ὡς παράδειγμα θατέρου τῶν ἴσων, τὸ δ' ὡς
εἰκών· τί γὰρ μᾶλλον τοῦτο ἐκείνου παράδειγμα, ἐκεῖνο δὲ εἰκών, ἐπεὶ κατ'
ἄμφω τὸ ποσὸν ὁμοίως ῥεῖ; λείπεται οὖν τὸ αὐτόισον κατηγορεῖσθαι αὐτῶν
συνωνύμως, οὐ κυρίως δέ· τὸ γοῦν αὐτόισον οὐ τῶνδε τῶν ἴσων τῶν αἰσθητῶν 15
κυρίως κατηγορεῖται ἀλλὰ ἄλλου παρὰ ταῦτα, οὗ εἰκόνες ὡς ὁμοιώματα τὰ
τῇδέ εἰσιν ἴσα· τοῦτο δ' ἔστιν ἡ ἰδέα. φησὶν οὖν ὅτι εἰ καὶ ἀκριβῶς οὗτος ὁ λόγος
κατασκευάζει τὰς ἰδέας ὡς οὐ καθόλου τι λέγων τὸ κατηγορούμενον, ἀλλ' ὡς
παράδειγμα καθ' ὃ τὰ κατ' ἐκεῖνο λεγόμενα εἰσιν,

---

82. 6 Χίμαιρραν L   12 ἐκεῖνο L: ἐκείνων F   83. 2 ὧν F: ὂν L   4 κατηγορή-
ται Hayduck: κατηγορεῖται LF   5 καθ' οὗ Hayduck: καθὸ LF   6 λέγεται LF
13 κατ' Hayduck: καὶ LF   14 αὐτῶν F: αὐτὸν L   19 ἐκεῖνο Hayduck: ἐκείνῳ LF

Τοῦτον δὴ τὸν λόγον φησὶ καὶ τῶν πρός τι ἰδέας
κατασκευάζειν. ἡ γοῦν δεῖξις ἡ νῦν ἐπὶ τοῦ ἴσου προῆλθεν, ὅ ἐστι τῶν πρός τι· τῶν
25 δὲ πρός τι οὐκ ἔλεγον ἰδέας εἶναι διὰ τὸ τὰς μὲν | ἰδέας καθ᾿ αὑτὰς ὑφεστάναι
αὐτοῖς οὐσίας τινὰς οὔσας, τὰ δὲ πρός τι ἐν τῇ πρὸς ἄλληλα σχέσει τὸ εἶναι
ἔχειν. ἔτι δὲ εἰ τὸ ἴσον ἴσῳ ἴσον, πλείους ἰδέαι τοῦ ἴσου ἂν εἶεν· τὸ γὰρ αὐτόισον
αὐτοῖσῳ ἴσον· εἰ γὰρ μηδενὶ ἴσον, οὐδὲ ἴσον ἂν εἴη. ἔτι δεήσει καὶ τῶν ἀνίσων
κατὰ τὸν αὐτὸν λόγον ἰδέας εἶναι· ὁμοίως γὰρ τῶν ἀντικειμένων ἔσονταί γε ἢ
30 οὐκ ἔσονται ἰδέαι· τὸ | δὲ ἄνισον ὁμολογεῖται καὶ κατ᾿ αὐτοὺς ἐν πλείοσιν εἶναι.
πάλιν δὲ ἐκοινοποίησε τὴν δόξαν ὡς πρὸς οἰκείαν οὖσαν αὐτὴν λέγων, διὰ τοῦ
εἰπεῖν "ὧν οὔ φαμεν εἶναι καθ᾿ αὑτὸ γένος", γένος λέγων ἀντὶ τοῦ ὑπόστασιν
καὶ φύσιν, εἴ γε τὸ πρός τι παραφυάδι ἔοικεν, ὡς ἐν ἄλλοις εἶπεν.

35 Ὁ δὲ λόγος ὁ τὸν τρίτον ἄνθρωπον εἰσάγων τοιοῦτος. λέγουσι τὰ | κοινῶς
κατηγορούμενα τῶν οὐσιῶν κυρίως τε εἶναι τοιαῦτα, καὶ ταῦτα εἶναι
84 ἰδέας. ἔτι τε τὰ ὅμοια ἀλλήλοις τοῦ αὐτοῦ τινος μετουσίᾳ ὅμοια ἀλλήλοις εἶναι,
ὃ κυρίως ἐστὶ τοῦτο· καὶ τοῦτο εἶναι τὴν ἰδέαν. ἀλλ᾿ εἰ τοῦτο, καὶ τὸ κατηγορούμενόν τινων κοινῶς, ἂν μὴ ταὐτὸν ᾖ ἐκείνων τινὶ ὧν κατηγορεῖται, ἄλλο τί
5 ἐστι παρ᾿ ἐκεῖνο (διὰ τοῦτο γὰρ γένος ὁ αὐτοάνθρωπος, | ὅτι κατηγορούμενος
τῶν καθ᾿ ἕκαστα οὐδενὶ αὐτῶν ἦν ὁ αὐτός), τρίτος ἄνθρωπος ἔσται τις παρά τε
τὸν καθ᾿ ἕκαστα, οἷον Σωκράτη καὶ Πλάτωνα, καὶ παρὰ τὴν ἰδέαν, ἥτις καὶ
αὐτὴ μία κατ᾿ ἀριθμόν ἐστιν.

Δείκνυται καὶ οὕτως ὁ τρίτος ἄνθρωπος. εἰ τὸ κατηγορούμενόν τινων
πλειόνων ἀληθῶς καὶ ἔστιν ἄλλο παρὰ τὰ ὧν κατηγορεῖται, κεχωρισμένον
αὐτῶν (τοῦτο γὰρ ἡγοῦνται δεικνύναι οἱ τὰς ἰδέας τιθέμενοι· διὰ τοῦτο
25 γάρ ἐστί τι αὐτοάνθρωπος κατ᾿ αὐτούς, ὅτι ὁ ἄνθρωπος κατὰ τῶν καθ᾿ ἕκαστα
ἀνθρώπων πλειόνων ὄντων ἀληθῶς κατηγορεῖται καὶ ἄλλος τῶν καθ᾿ ἕκαστα ἀνθρώπων ἐστίν)—ἀλλ᾿ εἰ τοῦτο, ἔσται τις τρίτος ἄνθρωπος. εἰ γὰρ
ἄλλος ὁ κατηγορούμενος ὧν κατηγορεῖται, καὶ κατ᾿ ἰδίαν ὑφεστώς, κατηγορεῖται δὲ κατά τε τῶν καθ᾿ ἕκαστα καὶ κατὰ τῆς ἰδέας ὁ ἄνθρω-
85 πος, ἔσται τις τρίτος ἄνθρωπος παρά τε τὸν καθ᾿ ἕκαστα καὶ τὴν ἰδέαν. οὕτως δὲ

24 δὲ om. Ascl.   ἰδέας·εἶναι OAC: εἶναι ἰδέας Ascl.   25 ἰδέας OAC: ἰδέας αὑτὰς
Ascl.   25 ὑφεστάναι–26 σχέσει om. C   25 αὑτοῖς om. Ascl.   27 ἰδέαι τοῦ
ἴσου ἂν εἶεν OAC: ἂν εἶεν τοῦ ἴσου ἰδέαι Ascl.   27 ἴσον² ... ἀνίσων OAC: ἢ Ascl.
29 γε ἢ OAC: καὶ Ascl.   33 ἐν ἄλλοις| 1096a21   34 τοιοῦτος OAC: τοιοῦτός ἐστι
Ascl.   84. 1 ἰδέας Ascl., Hayduck: τὰς ἰδέας coni. Bonitz: τὰ ἴσα OAC   ἔτι τε O Ascl.:
ἔτι AC   3 μὴ O: μὲν AC   4 ἐκεῖνο OA¹C: ἐκεῖνα A² edd.   6–7 Σωκράτη καὶ
Πλάτωνα O: Σωκράτην καὶ Πλάτωνα C: Σωκρα᾿ καὶ Πλάτωνι A   23 κεχωρισμένον OAC:
κεχωρισμένα A (varia lectio)   24 οἱ OC: ἢ A   26 πλειόνων–27 ἀνθρώπων
(homoeot.) om. C   27 ἔσται OA²C: ἔστι A¹   28 καὶ om. C   85. 1 τις τρίτος
(cf. 84. 27) O: τρίτος τις AC   τὸν O: τοὺς AC

ἀλλ᾽ οὖν πρός τί γε ἰδέας ποιοῦσιν· τὸ γὰρ ἴσον ἐφ᾽ οὗ νῦν ὁ λόγος προέβη τῶν 22
πρός τί ἐστιν· πρὸς ἴσον γὰρ τὸ ἴσον λέγεται. οἱ δὲ τὰς ἰδέας εἰσάγοντες οὐκ
ἐβούλοντο ἰδέας εἶναι τῶν πρός τι. ἔτι καὶ ἄλλο τι ἐκ τοῦ | τοιούτου λόγου 25
ἄτοπον αὐτοῖς συμβαίνει τὸ τῶν αὐτῶν πλείονας ἰδέας εἶναι· τὸ γὰρ αὐτόισον
αὐτοῖσῳ ἐστὶν αὐτόισον· εἰ γὰρ μηδενί, οὐδ᾽ αὐτόισον ἂν εἴη. ἔτι καὶ τῶν ἀνίσων
ἰδέας ποιεῖν· πολλὰ γὰρ καὶ κατ᾽ αὐτοὺς τὰ ἄνισα. εἰ γὰρ μὴ τῶν ἀνίσων εἰσὶν
ἰδέαι, οὐδὲ τῶν ἴσων· εἰ δὲ ἐκείνων, καὶ τούτων, καὶ ἔσονται τῶν στερήσεων
ἰδέαι, ὅπερ ἄτοπον, εἰ χρὴ ἄτοπον | εἰπεῖν τὸ ἀδύνατον. 30

Οἱ τὰς ἰδέας δεικνύντες λόγοι τρίτον εἰσάγουσιν ἄνθρωπον. ἔστι δὲ ὃ λέγει
τοιοῦτον.
ἐπειδὴ τὰ ὅμοια μετουσίᾳ τινὸς ὅμοια ἀλλήλοις εἰσί, τοῦτο ἔλεγον εἶναι τὴν 84
ἰδέαν. ὅμοιος δὲ ὁ αἰσθητὸς ἄνθρωπος τῷ αὐτοανθρώπῳ ἤτοι τῇ ἰδέᾳ. οὗτοι οὖν
μετουσίᾳ τινὸς παρ᾽ αὐτούς εἰσιν ὅμοιοι, καὶ ἔστιν οὗτος τρίτος ἄνθρωπος. εἰς ὃ
αἰσθητός, ἄλλος ἡ ἰδέα, καὶ ἕτερος ἤγουν τρίτος πρὸς | ὃν ἀναφερόμενοι οὗτοι 5
ὅμοιοι λέγονται εἶναι πάλιν, ἐπεὶ τὸ κατηγορούμενόν τινων κοινῶς, ἐὰν μὴ
ταὐτὸν ᾖ ἐκείνων τινὶ ὧν κατηγορεῖται, ἄλλο τί ἐστι παρ᾽ ἐκεῖνο. ἐπεὶ οὖν ὁ
ἄνθρωπος κατηγορεῖται κατὰ Σωκράτους καὶ Πλάτωνος καὶ τῆς ἰδέας ἤτοι τοῦ
αὐτοανθρώπου, καὶ οὐκ ἔστι τὸ κατηγορούμενον πάντη ταὐτὸν τῷ Σωκράτει
οὔτε τῷ Πλάτωνι οὔτε τῇ ἰδέᾳ· | εἰ γὰρ ἦν ταὐτόν, ἡ ἰδέα Σωκράτης ἂν 10
ὑπῆρχεν, ὡσαύτως καὶ ὁ Πλάτων, ἢ πάλιν Πλάτων ἢ Σωκράτης ἡ ἰδέα, ἢ ὁ
Σωκράτης καὶ ἡ ἰδέα Πλάτων.

Εἰ δε τοῦτο οὐκ ἔστιν, ἄλλος τίς ἐστι παρὰ τὰ καθ᾽ ἕκαστα καὶ τὴν ἰδέαν
ὁ κατηγορούμενος, καὶ οὗτός ἐστιν ὁ τρίτος ἄνθρωπος. εἰ δὲ πάλιν καὶ κατὰ τοῦ 85

27 καὶ κατ᾽ L: κατ᾽ F   83. 31–85. 4 om. F   84. 7 ἐκεῖνο L: ἐκεῖνα coni. Hayduck

καὶ τέταρτος ὁ κατά τε τούτου καὶ τῆς ἰδέας καὶ τῶν καθ᾽ ἕκαστα κατηγορούμενος, ὁμοίως δὲ καὶ πέμπτος, καὶ τοῦτο ἐπ᾽ ἄπειρον.

5 Ἔστι δὲ ὁ λόγος οὗτος τῷ πρώτῳ ὁ αὐτός· τοῦτο δὲ συμβαίνει αὐτοῖς, | ἐπεὶ ἔθεντο τὰ ὅμοια τοῦ αὐτοῦ τινος μετουσίᾳ ὅμοια εἶναι· ὅμοιοι γὰρ οἵ τε ἄνθρωποι καὶ αἱ ἰδέαι. ἀμφοτέρους δὴ τοὺς δοκοῦντας ἀκριβεστέρους εἶναι λόγους διήλεγξε, τὸν μὲν ὡς καὶ τῶν πρός τι κατασκευάζοντα ἰδέας, τὸν δὲ ὡς τρίτον ἄνθρωπον εἰσάγοντα, εἶτα ἐπ᾽ ἄπειρον αὔξοντα τοὺς ἀνθρώπους. ὁμοίως
10 δὲ καὶ τῶν ἄλλων ἕκαστον αὐξηθήσεται ὧν λέγουσιν ἰδέας εἶναι. | τῇ μὲν οὖν πρώτῃ τοῦ τρίτου ἀνθρώπου ἐξηγήσει ἄλλοι τε κέχρηνται καὶ Εὔδημος σαφῶς ἐν τοῖς Περὶ λέξεως, τῇ δὲ τελευταίᾳ αὐτὸς ἔν τε τῷ πρώτῳ Περὶ ἰδεῶν καὶ ἐν τούτῳ μετ᾽ ὀλίγον.

4 τοῦτο—αὐτοῖς om. Bonitz, Hayduck   8 αὔξοντα O: αὔξουσα AC   11 Εὔδημος] Wehrli, *Schule des Aristoteles*, viii, fr. 28   πρώτῳ Heitz, Rose, Wilpert, Ross: τετάρτῳ OAC, Brandis, Bonitz, Hayduck

τρίτου ἀνθρώπου καὶ τῆς ἰδέας καὶ τοῦ καθ' ἕκαστα κατηγορεῖται, καὶ τέταρτος ἔσται ἄνθρωπος, εἴπερ μὴ ἔστι τὸ κατηγορούμενον ταὐτόν τινι ὧν κατηγορεῖται, καὶ τοῦτο ἐπ' ἄπειρον.

85. 3 ᾧ L

They used the sciences in many ways to establish that there are ideas, as he says in the first book of *On Ideas*. And the arguments he seems to have in mind here (*nun*)[4] are the following (*toioutoi*):[5]

79. 5

I

If every science does its work by referring to some one and the same thing, and not to any of the particulars, then for each science there would be some other (*allo*) thing besides (*para*) the sensibles, which is everlasting and a paradigm of the things that come to be within that science (*tōn kath' hekastēn epistēmēn ginomenōn*). And this sort of thing (*toiouton*)[6] is the idea.

II

Further, the things the sciences are sciences of, these things are. And the sciences are of some other things (*allōn*) besides (*para*) the particulars; for these ⟨i.e. the particulars⟩ are indefinite (*apeira*) and indeterminate (*ahorista*), whereas the sciences are of determinate things (*hōrismenōn*). Therefore there are some things besides the particulars, and these things are the ideas.

79. 10

III

Further, if medicine is the science not of this health but of health without qualification, there will be some health itself.[7] And if geometry is the science not of this equal and of this commensurate but of equal without qualification and of commensurate without qualification, there will be some equal itself and some commensurate itself. And these things are the ideas.

79. 15

IV

Now these (*toioutoi*)[8] arguments do not prove what they set out to prove, that there are ideas; but they do prove that there are some things besides the particulars and sensibles. But it does not immediately[9] follow that if there are some things that are besides the particulars, they are ideas; for there are the common things (*ta koina*) besides the particulars, and we say that the sciences are in fact (*kai*)[10] of them.

V

Further, ⟨there is also the objection that if these arguments succeeded, they would prove⟩ that there are also (*kai*) ideas of the things falling

79. 20

under the crafts. For (I′) every craft also refers the things that come to be
by its agency (*hup' autēs*) to some one thing; and (II′) the things the
crafts are crafts of, these things are, and the crafts are of some other
things besides the particulars. And (III′) this last ⟨argument⟩,[11] in
addition to the fact that, like the other arguments, it does not prove that
there are ideas, will seem to establish that there are also ideas of things
for which they do not want ideas ⟨as well as of things for which they want
80 ideas⟩. For if, because medicine is the science not of this health but of
health without qualification, there is some health itself, then this will also
apply to each of the crafts. For none of them is of the particular or the
this either, but each is of the ⟨F⟩ without qualification that it is about.
For example, carpentry is of bench without qualification, not of this
bench, and of bed without qualification, not of this bed. And sculpture,
80. 5 painting, house-building, and each of the other crafts is related in a
similar way to the things that fall under it. Therefore there will be an idea
of each of the things that fall under the crafts as well ⟨as of the things
that fall under the sciences⟩, which they do not want.

The One over Many Argument (80. 8–81. 22)

They also use the following (*toioutos*) argument to establish that there are
ideas:

I

If each of the many men is a man, and if each of the many animals is an
80. 10 animal, and the same applies in the other cases; and if in the case of each
of these it is not that something is predicated of itself but that there is
something which is predicated of all of them and which is not the same as
any of them (*oudeni autōn tauton on*), then this is[12] some being besides
(*para*) the particular beings which is separated from them and everlasting. For it is in every case (*aei*) predicated in the same way of all the
numerically successive (*tōn kat' arithmon allassomenōn*) ⟨particulars⟩.[13]
And what is a one in addition to (*epi*) many, separated from them, and
80. 15 everlasting is an idea. Therefore there are ideas.

IIA

He says that this argument establishes that there are ideas both of negations and of things that are not (*kai tōn apophaseōn kai tōn mē ontōn*).
For one and the same negation is predicated of many things, including
things that are not, and it is not the same as any of the things of which it

is true. For not-man is predicated of horse and of dog and of everything besides man, and for this reason it is a one over (*epi*) many and is not the same as any of the things of which it is predicated. Further, it always remains, since it is true in the same way of similar things ⟨i.e. of the numerically successive particulars⟩. For not-musical is true of many things (of all those things that are not musical) in the same way, and similarly not-man is true of all those things that are not men. Therefore there are also ideas of negations.

80. 20

81

IIB

This is absurd. For how could there be an idea of not being? For if one accepts this, there will be one idea of things that are different in genus and different in every way, such as line and man, since all these are not-horses. And there will also be one idea of indeterminate and indefinite things (*tōn ahoristōn te kai tōn apeirōn*); and also of things of which one is primary, one secondary (for man and animal, of which one is primary, one secondary, are both not-wood), and of such things they did not want genera or ideas.

81. 5

III

And it is clear that this argument too does not validly deduce that there are ideas; rather, it too tends to prove that what is predicated in common is something other than the particulars of which it is predicated (*allo einai to koinōs katēgoroumenon tōn kath' hekasta hōn katēgoreitai*).

81. 10

IV

Further, the same people who want to prove that what is predicated in common of a plurality of things (*pleionōn*) is some one thing, and that it is an idea, establish this from negations. For if someone denying something of a plurality of things denies it by referring to some one thing (for someone saying 'man is not white, horse is not ⟨white⟩', does not deny something peculiar to them in each case but, by referring to some one thing, denies the same white of all of them), then someone affirming the same thing of a plurality of things will not be affirming something else (*allo*) in each case, but there will be some one thing he affirms—e.g. man—with reference to some one and the same thing. For as with negation, so with affirmation. Therefore there is some other being besides the being in sensibles, which is the cause of the affirmation that is both true of a plurality of things and also common; and this is the idea.

81. 15

81. 20

This argument, then, he says, produces ideas not only of things that are affirmed but also of things that are denied. For in both cases ⟨there is a reference to⟩ the one ⟨thing⟩ in the same way (*homoiōs*).

The Object of Thought Argument (81. 25–82. 7)

81. 25 The argument that establishes from thinking that there are ideas is the following (*toioutos*):

I

If, whenever we think of man, footed, or animal, we are thinking (*a*) of something that is (*ti tōn ontōn*) and (*b*) of none of the particulars (for the same thought remains even when they have perished), then clearly there is ⟨something⟩,[14] besides (*para*) the particulars and sensibles, which we are thinking of whether or not they are. For surely we are not 82 then thinking of something that is not. And this is a form (*eidos*)[15] and idea.

II

He says, then, that this argument also establishes that there are ideas of perishing and perished things, and in general of particular and perishable things, such as Socrates and Plato. For (*a*) we also think of them, and (*b*) we retain and preserve an appearance of them even when they no longer 82. 5 are.[16]

III

Indeed, we also think of things that in no way are (*ta mēd' holōs onta*), such as hippocentaur and Chimaera.

IV

So (*hōste*) neither does this (*toioutos*) argument validly deduce that there are ideas.

LF adds (82. 7–9):
So this (*toioutos*) argument from thinking too does not validly deduce that there are ideas, but ⟨it does validly deduce⟩ that there is something else besides the particulars. Now the universal[17] which is in the particulars (*to katholou to en tois kath' hekasta*) also fits this ⟨description—i.e. it is something besides particulars⟩, and it does not necessarily introduce an idea.

The Argument from Relatives (82. 11–83. 33)

The argument that establishes from (*ek*) relatives that there are ideas is 82. 11
the following (*toioutos*):

I

In cases where some same thing is predicated of a plurality of things
(*pleionōn*) not homonymously, but so as to reveal some one nature, it is
true of them either (*a*) because they are fully (*kuriōs*) what is signified by
the thing predicated, as when we call Socrates and Plato man; or (*b*) 83. 1
because they are likenesses of the true ones, as when we predicate man
of pictured ⟨men⟩ (for in their case we reveal the likenesses of man,
signifying some same nature in all of them); or (*c*) because one of them is 83. 5
the paradigm, the others likenesses, as if we were to call Socrates and the
likenesses of him men.

II

And when we predicate the equal itself of the things here, we predicate it
of them homonymously.[18] For (*a*) the same account (*logos*) does not fit
them all. (*b*) Nor do we signify the truly equals. For the quantity in
sensibles changes (*kineitai*) and continuously shifts (*metaballei*) and is not
determinate (*aphōrismenon*). (*c*) But neither do any of the things here 83. 10
accurately receive the account of the equal.

III

But neither ⟨can they be called equal non-homonymously⟩ by one of
them's being a paradigm, another a likeness. For one of them is not a
paradigm or a likeness any more than another.

IV

And indeed, if (*ei de kai*) someone were to accept that the likeness is not
homonymous with the paradigm, it always follows that these equals are
equals by being likenesses of what is fully and truly equal.

V

But if this is so, then there is something which is the equal itself and 83. 15
which is fully ⟨equal⟩, in relation to (*pros*) which, by being likenesses,
the things here both come to be and are called equal. And this is an idea,
being a paradigm †and likeness†[19] of the things that come to be in
relation to it.

VI[20]

This, then, is the one argument that establishes that there are ideas even (*kai*) of relatives (*pros ti*). It seems more carefully and more accurately and more directly to aim at the proof of the ideas. For this (*houtos*) argument does not, like the ones before it, seem to prove simply (*haplōs*)

83. 20 that there is some common thing besides the particulars, but rather ⟨it seems to prove⟩ that there is some paradigm of the things here which is fully. For this seems to be especially characteristic of the ideas.

VII

He says, then, that this argument establishes that there are ideas even (*kai*) of relatives. At least (*goun*), the present proof has been advanced on the basis of the equal, which is a relative. But they used to say that

83. 25 there are no ideas of relatives. For in their view the ideas subsist in themselves, being, in their view, kinds of substances, whereas relatives have their being in their relation to one another.

VIII

Further, if the equal is equal to an equal, there will be more than one (*pleious*) idea of equal. For the equal itself is equal to an equal itself. For if it were not equal to something, it would not be equal at all.

IX

Further, by the same argument there will also have to be ideas of unequals. For opposites are alike in that there will be ideas corresponding

83. 30 to both or to neither; and the unequal is also agreed by them to be in more than one thing (*pleiosin*).

X[21]

Again, he made this opinion common ground when he spoke of it as his own, saying 'of which things we say there is no in-itself (*kath' hauto*) genus', speaking of 'genus', instead of 'reality' or 'nature', if a relative is

83. 33 indeed like an appendage, as he said elsewhere.

Third Man Arguments

EUDEMUS' VERSION (83. 34–84. 7)[22]

The argument introducing the third man is the following (*toioutos*):

They say that the things that are predicated in common of ⟨*F*⟩ substances   83. 35
are fully (*kuriōs*) ⟨*F*⟩[23] and are ideas. Further, things that are similar to   84
one another are similar to one another by sharing in some same thing,
which is fully this ⟨i.e. fully *F*⟩; and this is the idea. But if this is so, and
if what is predicated in common of things (*tinōn*), if it is not the same as
any of those things of which it is predicated, is something else besides it[24]   84. 5
(for this is why man-itself is a genus, because it is predicated of the
particulars but is not the same as any of them), then there will be a third
man besides the particular[25] (such as Socrates or (*kai*)[26] Plato) and
besides the idea, which is also one in number.

ARISTOTLE'S VERSION (84. 21–85. 3)[27]

The third man is also proved in this way:

If what is predicated truly of some plurality of things (*pleionōn*)[28] is
also ⟨some⟩ other thing (*allo*) besides (*para*) the things of which it is
predicated, being separated (*kechōrismenon*) from them (for this is what   84. 25
those who posit the ideas think they prove; for this is why, according to
them, there is such a thing as man-itself, because the man is predicated
truly of the particular (*kath' hekasta*) men, these being a plurality, and it
is other (*allo*) than the particular men)—but if this is so, there will be a   85
third man. For if the ⟨man⟩ being predicated is other than the things of
which it is predicated and subsists on its own (*kat' idian huphestōs*), and
⟨if⟩ the man is predicated both of the particulars and of the idea, then
there will be a third man besides the particular[29] and the idea. In the
same way, there will also be a fourth ⟨man⟩ predicated of this ⟨third
man⟩, of the idea, and of the particulars, and similarly also a fifth, and so
on to infinity.

Alexander adds (85. 4–13):
This argument is the same as the first one.[30] For this[31] results for them
because they took similar things to be similar by sharing in some same   85. 5
thing. For men and the ideas ⟨of men⟩ are similar. Now he refuted both
of the arguments that seemed more accurate, the one on the ground that
it established ideas even of relatives, and the other on the ground that it
introduces a third man and then multiplies men to infinity. And a similar
multiplication will be suffered by each of the other things of which they
say there are ideas. While various people used the first exposition of the   85. 10
third man—including Eudemus, who clearly used it in the first book of
On Diction—the last was used by ⟨Aristotle⟩ himself in the first[32] book
of *On Ideas* and a little later in this work.[33]

2

Introduction

1. The interest of the *Peri ideōn*

In *Met.* 1. 9, Aristotle mentions five arguments for the existence of Platonic forms[1] along with some capsule criticisms of them. The arguments and criticisms were set out in detail in book 1 of Aristotle's essay *Peri ideōn* (*On Ideas*), portions of which are preserved by Alexander in his commentary on the *Metaphysics*.[2] My main aim in what follows is to explore these arguments and Aristotle's criticisms of them, in order to see what light they shed on Plato's theory of forms. I shall also say something (more briefly) about what the *Peri ideōn* reveals about Aristotle's understanding of and alternative to Plato.

As is well known, Plato never sets out a theory of forms in systematic detail.[3] Sometimes, to be sure, he offers arguments, or fragments of arguments, whose conclusion is that there are forms; and sometimes he argues that forms (which are assumed to exist) have various features.[4] But he is vague about the precise range and characteristics of forms. For example, it is often thought that in *Rep.* 10 (596a) Plato offers a one over many argument according to which 'there is an Idea answering to every common name'.[5] But elsewhere Plato says that forms 'carve at the natural joints' (*Phdr.* 265e1–2; cf. *Pol.* 262ab), and not every predicate does that. The argument from compresence adverted to in, for example, *Rep.* 7 (523–5) does not even seem to yield forms for every predicate that carves at the natural joints.

The one over many argument is sometimes thought to posit forms as the meanings of general terms. But when forms are said to carve at the natural joints, they seem to be properties conceived in realist fashion. Yet meanings are generally thought to be quite different from properties conceived in realist fashion.

Although forms sometimes seem to be properties conceived in realist fashion, and so a kind of universal, they also seem to be separate, self-predicative paradigms; and it is often thought that if forms have these features, then they are particulars. Yet—or so Aristotle insists—nothing can be both a universal and a particular (see e.g. *Met.* 1086b10–13).[6]

The *Peri ideōn* is of considerable interest for anyone interested in these central issues. For it is the first systematic investigation into Plato's theory of forms;[7] and it provides more precise arguments for their existence and a more precise characterization of their nature than the dialogues do. Asking whether Plato is committed to its arguments and characterizations affords new insights into, and reveals hidden depths in, the dialogues.

Attention to the *Peri ideōn* also illuminates Aristotle's thought. For in recording arguments for the existence of forms, he shows us how he understands Plato; and in criticizing the arguments, he shows us where and why he objects to Plato.

Nor is the *Peri ideōn* of purely historical interest. For a large part of the debate between Plato and Aristotle in the area of metaphysics involves still-current questions about the nature of universals. Can they, for example, exist uninstantiated? Are they perceivable? Everlasting? How are they related to particulars? How many universals are there? How are we to decide about such matters—by a priori speculation, science, or philosophy? Plato is the first to hazard answers to these questions; the *Peri ideōn* is the first reply to his answers. Anyone interested in the problem of universals should be interested in the original controversy.

2. A terminological problem

I noted in the last section that it is disputed whether Platonic forms are particulars or universals, and whether they are properties conceived in realist fashion or the meanings of general terms. These disputes are difficult to resolve. For one thing, Plato never says that forms are universals (*katholou*; *koina*), properties, particulars (*kath' hekasta*), or meanings. Indeed, he has no technical terms for these various sorts of entities. Not even Aristotle has a technical term reserved for 'meaning', although he seems to have coined the words for 'universal' and 'particular'.[8]

Further, the key terms in these disputes are used in different ways. Forms might be universals and/or particulars, properties and/or meanings, on some of these usages but not on others. It will therefore be useful if I begin by saying something about how the key terms are used; about how I use them here and why I so use them; and about Aristotle's understanding of them. What follows is by no means a thorough discussion of these notions; I restrict myself to the main uses involved in some of the central discussions about forms, and even here I shall be brief.

3. Realist and semantic conceptions of universals

Two broad conceptions of universals are relevant for our purposes: a realist and a semantic conception.[9] On the realist conception, universals are properties posited for various explanatory purposes.[10] On this view, not every meaningful predicate denotes a universal, since not every meaningful predicate denotes an explanatory property. ('Grue', for example, does not do so.[11]) On the semantic conception, by contrast, universals are meanings.[12] On this view, universals are discovered, not by explanatory considerations, but by asking what general terms are meaningful. In contrast to the realist view, the semantic view takes every meaningful general term to denote a universal, which is indeed the meaning of that term.[13]

To say that on the semantic conception every meaningful predicate denotes a universal which is the meaning of the term is not to say very much, for there are conflicting accounts of the criteria for determining what predicates are meaningful. Here I shall consider just two criteria: (i) '*F*' is meaningful just in case competent speakers of the language understand it or can easily be brought to understand it;[14] (ii) '*F*' is meaningful just in case there are *F*s (and whether there are *F*s is not determined by our pre-analytic intuitions about what terms an ordinary speaker of a language understands).[15] On (i), which I favour, the semantic conception countenances more universals than the realist conception does. For not all the predicates whose meanings we can easily understand denote explanatory properties. Even on (ii), the semantic conception countenances more universals than the realist conception does. For example, since there are some not-beautiful things, (ii) counts 'not-beautiful' as meaningful, in which case there is a universal, the not-beautiful, even though being not-beautiful is not a genuine property.[16] But (ii) is more parsimonious than (i); (i) but not (ii), for example, presumably takes 'centaur' to be meaningful.

The semantic and realist conceptions therefore countenance different *ranges* of universals. But do they have the same view, or different views, about the *nature* of universals? The answer depends partly on how meanings are conceived.[17] If one favours (i) above, then one is likely to believe that meanings (if they are entities at all) are abstract entities.[18] On this view, meanings and properties are disjoint classes of entities. But on a referential theory of meaning, the meaning of a term just is its extra-linguistic referent. On this view, not all meanings are properties.[19] But a defender of a referential theory of meaning might say that when a predicate denotes a property, that property just is its meaning, in which case some meanings are properties.[20]

We can now see why we need to be careful in assessing the claim that forms are, for example, universals. Is the claim that they are universals conceived in realist fashion? Or is it that they are meanings? And if the latter, precisely how are meanings being conceived?[21]

It will help us on our journey over some rough terminological terrain if we fix the use of some of the key terms. I shall generally follow Aristotle in using 'universal' (which I shall use interchangeably with 'property'[22]) for real, explanatory features of the world that are (or can be) in some sense common or shared.[23] Instead of also calling meanings universals, I shall generally simply call them meanings. Since I believe that any referential theory of meaning that identifies the meaning of a term with its extra-linguistic referent is false, I shall write as though meanings and properties are disjoint classes of entities.[24] So rather than asking whether, if forms are universals, they are properties or meanings or both, I shall generally ask instead whether they are universals (i.e. properties) or meanings or both.[25] But sometimes it will be convenient to use 'universal' not just for properties realistically conceived but also for meanings or in some neutral sense; it should be clear from the context when I use 'universal' in this alternative way.

4. Universals and particulars

So far I have distinguished between two conceptions of universals (the realist and the semantic conception), and two conceptions of the nature of meanings (one on which meanings are abstract entities and one on which they are identical with the extra-linguistic referents of the corresponding terms). I turn now to the question of how universals (that is, explanatory properties) are to be distinguished from particulars.

On one view, universals are abstract entities, whereas particulars are concrete. But as against this, it might be argued that some particulars— e.g. numbers—are abstract; it might also be argued that some universals— e.g. all the world's water—are concrete.[26] On another view, particulars but not universals are perceivable. But redness, for example, might be thought to be a perceivable or observable universal, and quarks or electrons might be thought to be non-perceivable particulars. Anyway, whether or not this criterion for distinguishing between particulars and universals is in fact adequate, it is not a criterion Plato or Aristotle accepts. For they believe that there are perceivable universals and non-perceivable particulars.[27]

In *Int.* 7, Aristotle says that:

Some things (*pragmata*) are universals (*katholou*), others are particulars (*kath' hekaston*). By 'universal', I mean what is naturally predicated of more than one thing; by 'particular', what is not. Man, for instance, is a universal, Callias a particular. (17a38–b1.)

Because Aristotle believes that each universal is naturally predicated of more than one thing,[28] he sometimes says that each universal is 'a one over many': each is some one entity over—predicated of, common to— many particulars.[29] Aristotle also sometimes says that unlike particulars, universals can simultaneously be in more than one place at a time (*Met.* 1040b25–6). In saying this, he does not mean to endorse the position Plato takes to be 'the most impossible of all' (*Phil.* 15b7; cf. *Parm.* 131b1–2), that the whole of a given universal is simultaneously in all of its instances. Rather, he seems to mean that since (e.g.) all the world's water is in more than one place at a time, it is a universal (*Top.* 103a14–23).[30]

None of these ways of differentiating between particulars and universals is entirely satisfactory, and I have no new criterion to offer in their stead. But we have at least obtained some intuitive grip on the sort of distinction that is at issue, and seen how Aristotle views the distinction; and that is enough for our purposes here.

5. Plato's view

Now that terminological matters are somewhat clearer, we may return to Plato and Aristotle. Any discussion of Aristotle's criticism of Plato must take some stand on Plato's views. And although I do not provide a thorough defence of my view of Plato, I try to give some support to the view that forms are not meanings or particulars, but explanatory properties.

One of my main arguments against the view that forms are meanings appeals to arguments for the existence of forms. I shall argue that Plato does not offer semantic arguments for the existence of forms. His arguments are all epistemological, metaphysical, or both.[31] That is, he argues that the possibility of knowledge requires the existence of forms, where the sort of knowledge at issue is not ordinary linguistic understanding, but knowledge as it contrasts with belief; he also argues that we can explain the way the world is only if there are forms in virtue of which things are as they are. These two sorts of arguments are connected, for Plato believes that the possibility of knowledge requires the existence of forms conceived as real properties of things. Of course, even if Plato does not use semantic arguments for the existence of forms, forms might none the less be meanings or be relevant to explaining the meaningfulness of general terms. But the absence of semantic concerns in Plato's discussions of forms casts doubt on the most prominent reasons for supposing that forms play any semantic role.

I noted in sect. 1 that it is often thought that if forms are separate, self-predicative paradigms, then they are particulars. I shall argue, however, that the way in which forms are separate, self-predicative paradigms does not require them to be particulars. The account I provide also challenges the view that forms are ostensive samples, acquaintance with which is necessary for understanding the meanings of the corresponding general terms.

6. Forms and Aristotelian universals

A further reason for favouring the view of Plato just described is that it is suggested by the *Peri ideōn*. For example, we shall see that (with the possible exception of the Object of Thought Argument) its arguments for the existence of forms are not semantic, but epistemological, metaphysical, or both. We shall also see that there is an important sense in which Aristotle takes forms to be not particulars but universals—despite the fact that he sometimes says that forms are not only universals but also particulars (although, interestingly enough, he does not explicitly say this in the *Peri ideōn*). Indeed, as I explain more fully below, Aristotle's primary purpose in *Peri ideōn* 1 is to defend his own conception of universals—which in the *Peri ideōn* he calls 'common things' (*koina*)[32]— against Plato's rival conception of universals as forms.

But precisely how do forms and Aristotelian universals differ? Aristotle thinks they share some features. For example, he is a realist about the existence of universals, and he takes Plato to be one too—that is, he takes both Platonic forms and his own universals to be real entities distinct from such things as particulars, predicates, meanings, concepts, and classes.[33] As attention to the *Peri ideōn* reveals, Aristotle also takes forms to be the basic objects of knowledge, unobservable or nonsensible, everlasting, and (probably) unchangeable.[34] In just the same way, Aristotle takes his own universals to be the basic objects of knowledge; and he takes at least many of them to be everlasting, unobservable, and unchangeable.[35] However, Aristotle takes Platonic forms but not his own universals to be separate, self-predicative, perfect paradigms.[36] So presumably these are the features of forms at which his objections are primarily aimed. Unfortunately, however, Aristotle does not always trouble to say precisely what features of forms he has in mind on a given occasion. Nor does he ever say precisely how he takes these features of forms to go together—whether, for example, if something has one of them it must have the others. However, he tends to treat forms as a 'package-deal', such that if any of their special features are at issue, so too are the rest of them.

7. The structure and moral of *Peri ideōn* 1

Book 1 of the *Peri ideōn* is dense and difficult. It will therefore be useful if, before considering details of particular arguments, I say something about its overall structure. This will also make it clearer that its main goal is to defend an Aristotelian over a Platonist ontology. In *Met.* 1. 9, Aristotle says that:

of the ways in which we prove that there are forms, none appears to succeed. (i) For from some no valid deduction necessarily results, and (ii) from some there are also (*kai*) forms of things of which we do not think there are any forms. (i) For according to the arguments from the sciences, there will be forms of all the things of which there are sciences; and according to the one over many there will also be forms of negations; and according to the ⟨argument⟩ that we think of something when it has perished ⟨there will be forms⟩ of things that have perished, for there is an image of these. (ii) Further, of the more accurate arguments, some produce ideas of relatives, of which things we say there is no in-itself genus (*kath' hauto genos*), and others introduce the third man. (990b9–17 = 13. 4, 1079a4–13.)

Here Aristotle mentions our five arguments: the Arguments from the Sciences, the One over Many Argument, the Object of Thought Argument, the Argument from Relatives, and an argument that introduces the Third Man Argument, which I shall call the Accurate One over Many Argument. In Aristotle's view, the five arguments share two flaws. First, none is a sound argument for the existence of forms ('none appears to succeed'). Indeed for Aristotle there can be no sound argument for the existence of forms. Secondly, if they proved anything at all, they would prove that there are too many forms. The Arguments from the Sciences would prove that there are forms of all the things of which there are sciences (and not, what is wanted, only of some); the One over Many Argument would prove that there are forms of negations; the Object of Thought Argument would prove that there are forms of things that have perished; the Argument from Relatives would prove that there are forms of relatives. The Accurate One over Many Argument would prove that there are too many forms in a different way, by leading to the Third Man Argument, according to which if there is even one form of *F*, there are infinitely many forms of *F*, contrary to Plato's view that there is at most one form for any given predicate.

Although Aristotle links the five arguments in these two ways, he also differentiates among them, by calling the last two 'more accurate'.[37] How do the two more accurate arguments differ from their three 'less accurate' predecessors? In *Met.* 1. 9, Aristotle says that the less accurate arguments are invalid arguments for the existence of forms ('no valid deduction necessarily results').[38] But he significantly does not make the same claim about the more accurate arguments,[39] so perhaps they are more accurate precisely because they are valid arguments for the existence of forms.[40]

This suggestion derives support from the *Peri ideōn*. For there too Aristotle claims that the less accurate arguments are invalid arguments for the existence of forms (79. 15–17; 81. 8–9; 82. 6–7). He also adds a claim not made in *Met.* I. 9: that the less accurate arguments are valid arguments for the existence of his own universals.[41] Further, as there, he conspicuously fails to say that the more accurate arguments are invalid arguments for the existence of forms. Indeed, he says that the Argument from Relatives is more accurate precisely because it is a valid argument for the existence of forms (83. 18–22).[42] Further, although neither Aristotle nor Alexander explicitly says so, the Accurate One over Many Argument is also a valid argument for the existence of forms.

Although both more accurate arguments are valid arguments for the existence of forms, they are so in different ways. The Argument from Relatives is a valid argument for the existence of forms because it is a valid argument for the existence of universals that are also perfect paradigms. The Accurate One over Many Argument is a valid argument for the existence of forms because it is a valid argument for the existence of separate universals. Aristotle therefore believes that there are two ways in which one can show that there are forms—by showing that there are universals that are either perfect paradigms or separate. Since he never suggests any other way in which one could show that there are forms, I shall assume he believes not only that following either of these routes is sufficient, but also that following one of them is necessary, for showing that there are forms.

If the foregoing account is correct, then the structure of *Peri ideōn* I is neatly dilemmatic. The Platonists have two sorts of arguments for the existence of forms, the less and the more accurate arguments. The more accurate arguments are valid arguments for the existence of forms; the less accurate arguments are invalid arguments for their existence.[43] Although the more accurate arguments might seem promising from this point of view, there are other reasons for rejecting them: the Argument from Relatives produces forms of relatives, 'of which we say there is no in-itself class'; the Accurate One over Many Argument leads to the Third Man Argument, a vicious infinite regress. The virtues of validity are outweighed by the vices of the consequences of the arguments. More-over, although the less accurate arguments are not valid arguments for the existence of forms, Aristotle believes that they are valid arguments for the existence of his own universals; that is, we can avoid the vice of invalidity by changing their conclusion from 'And so there are forms' to 'And so there are Aristotelian universals'. Further, minor alterations to the premisses will convert the arguments into sound arguments for the existence of Aristotelian universals.[44] The moral is clear: the Platonists ought to abandon their more accurate arguments for the existence of forms; they also ought modestly to revise the premisses, and alter the conclusion, of their less accurate arguments, thereby embracing Aristotle's alternative conception of universals.

8. Aristotle as a critic of Plato

In assessing Aristotle's criticisms of Plato, we are often asked to choose
between the horns of the following dilemma: either Aristotle interprets
Plato correctly, in which case the theory of forms is inconsistent; or
else he misinterprets Plato, in which case Plato is invulnerable to his
criticisms.[45] Both horns of this dilemma are unattractive: it would be
unattractive to have to conclude that Plato's theory of forms—a central
part of his philosophy, and one of the great metaphysical theories in the
history of philosophy—is inconsistent. It would also be unattractive to
have to conclude that Aristotle simply misunderstood Plato, with whom,
after all, he studied for about twenty years. Of course, sometimes unattractive things happen to be the case. The mere fact that both horns of
the dilemma are unattractive is not sufficient reason to reject them both.
And if the dilemma is exhaustive, then we have no option but to be
impaled on one of its two horns.

Fortunately, however, the dilemma is not exhaustive. For it rests on
the false assumption that Aristotle aims to record and criticize arguments to which Plato is straightforwardly committed. But at least in the
Peri ideōn, this is not Aristotle's strategy.[46] Sometimes he takes an
impressionistic and vague Platonic claim, and provides one literal and
natural reading of it, which he then proceeds to attack. Sometimes he
refuses to give Plato distinctions Plato does not explicitly formulate. Sometimes he completes an incomplete Platonic argument with Aristotelian
claims that Plato may well reject. Sometimes, on the other hand, he
treats part of a Platonic argument as though it were self-contained—not
because he believes that Plato offers only the truncated version, but
because he believes that by focusing on it we can learn something important about Platonism and about the plausibility of Aristotle's alternative. Aristotle thus aims to record, not Plato's clear intentions and
commitments, but a reconstructed version of his arguments, one that aims
to provide philosophical illumination.[47]

Aristotle's criticisms often succeed against these reconstructed arguments. But Plato can reply that he is not committed to them—that he
intends his impressionistic language in some other way, or relies on
distinctions he does not explicitly formulate, or rejects the assumptions
Aristotle saddles him with. In offering Plato this reply, however, we need
not say that Aristotle misunderstands Plato. Rather, he challenges us to
answer the following questions: What does Plato mean if not the literal
reading Aristotle proposes? What justification is there for taking Plato to
rely on distinctions he does not explicitly formulate? Is Platonism worth
holding on to if it is incompatible with the assumptions Aristotle builds
into it? We may in the end decide that the answers to these questions
show that Aristotle's metaphysics is to be preferred. But any such decision

should result from deep reflection, rather than from the misguided thought that Aristotle simply shows that the theory of forms is internally inconsistent. Both Plato and Aristotle deserve better than that.

We shall see as we proceed that this reply to the dilemma solves various problems. But it has a price; for in order to defend it, one needs to attribute to Plato and Aristotle quite subtle and complex positions. Some readers may feel that these positions are *too* subtle and complex. But if we favour a simpler view of their thought, then we face the initial dilemma once again. What level of complexity is it fair to assume in the face of indeterminate texts? (For as we shall see, both the dialogues and the *Peri ideōn* are often indeterminate, in ways that prove illuminating.) What reason is there to expect two such great philosophers as Plato and Aristotle to reason in simple ways, or to be aware of or to intend no more than is explicit in their texts? I hope that the discussion that follows will motivate the reader to consider such questions.

3

Evidence, Provenance, and Chronology

1. Introduction

Many different hypotheses about the *Peri ideōn* have been advanced: that
it is not by Aristotle; that although it is by Aristotle, the arguments
he records for the existence of forms were invented by others in the
Academy; that the criticisms of the arguments are not by Aristotle; that
Alexander records material that is similar to, but not actually from, the
Peri ideōn; that the *Peri ideōn* discusses middle-period Plato; that at some
points it has the late dialogues in mind; that it misunderstands Plato; that
it discusses Platonists other than Plato.

My own view is that Alexander reliably preserves portions of the *Peri
ideōn*; that the *Peri ideōn* is by Aristotle in the sense that he formulated
both its arguments for the existence of forms and its criticisms of them;
that its arguments for the existence of forms aim (perhaps among other
things) to illuminate Plato's arguments for their existence in the middle
dialogues; that although Aristotle's criticisms are often controversial, they
do not misunderstand Plato. The body of this book defends this view on a
case-by-case basis. But it will be useful to begin by considering some
general considerations for and against various hypotheses. Of course,
hypotheses about these large matters cannot be established with certainty.
But it is none the less worth while to consider what can be said for
and against them; and even if none of them is certain, some are more
plausible than others.

2. Evidence that Aristotle wrote the *Peri ideōn*[1]

Both Diogenes Laertius and Hesychius preserve a catalogue of Aristotle's
writings which lists a work called *Peri (tēs) ideas a'*;[2] this is generally
agreed to be Aristotle's essay, *Peri ideōn*.[3] In his commentary on the
Metaphysics, Alexander mentions the *Peri ideōn* three times (79. 4,
85. 11–12, and 98. 21–2), claiming each time to record parts of it.[4]
Two centuries later, Syrianus (d. AD 437), in his commentary on the
Metaphysics, mentions an Aristotelian essay in two books, once calling it
Peri tōn eidōn (120. 33–121. 1, commenting on 1080a9–14), and once
Peri eidōn (195. 22, commenting on 1093b24–5).[5] Unlike Alexander, he

records none of its contents, saying that it simply repeats arguments to be found in the *Metaphysics*. His remarks would be misleading unless he had some sort of access to the *Peri ideōn*; but he does not say enough for it to be clear whether he had independent access to it, or was relying on Alexander's account of it or on some other account now unknown to us.

It is unclear whether anyone after Syrianus had access to the *Peri ideōn*. In commenting on the close of *Met.* 14, 1093b24–5, Pseudo-Alexander[6] says that Aristotle wrote a work in two books, *ta peri tōn eidōn* (836. 34–837. 3); the same claim is made by Pseudo-Philoponus (*in Met.*, f.67B).[7] However, neither Pseudo-Alexander nor Pseudo-Philoponus suggests they had access to the work or any real knowledge of its contents. Finally, a scholiast on Dionysius Thrax says that Aristotle wrote a book, *Peri ideōn*, against Plato's ideas (p. 116. 13–16 Hilgard); once again, no details are provided.

3. Reasons for doubting whether Aristotle wrote the *Peri ideōn*

Although there thus seems to be ample evidence that Aristotle wrote an essay called something like *Peri ideōn*, it has sometimes been doubted whether he did so. Heitz, for example, doubts whether Aristotle wrote a work called *Peri ideōn* on the ground that neither Proclus nor Plutarch mentions one when they discuss Aristotle's criticisms of Plato.[8] But this consideration is without force since, as Moraux notes, neither Proclus' nor Plutarch's enumerations are exhaustive.[9]

Rose argues that the *Peri ideōn* is not by Aristotle on the ground that everything the commentators say can be explained on the hypothesis that they were reflecting on the *Metaphysics*; although the arguments Alexander records are more copious and subtler than those in the *Metaphysics*, their substance can be found there.[10] This consideration is also without force. First, Aristotle's discussion in *Met.* 1. 9 suggests he developed the arguments he alludes to more fully elsewhere; if *Met.* 1. 9 summarizes the *Peri ideōn*, it is not surprising that the two discussions are closely linked.[11] Further, we shall see that *Peri ideōn* 1 meshes so well with Aristotle's understanding of Plato elsewhere that it is reasonable to suppose on this ground too that he wrote the *Peri ideōn*.[12]

4. The *Peri ideōn*'s contents

I shall assume, then, that Aristotle wrote a work called something like *Peri ideōn*; but for a knowledge of its contents, we must depend on Alexander. How much can we learn from him?

According to Rose, we can learn very little. He believes that Alexander records, not material from the *Peri ideōn*, but at best material similar to what was to be found there.[13] He offers two arguments for this claim: (i) the five arguments, and some of the criticisms of them, are introduced with '*toioutos*' (or, in the case of the Arguments from the Sciences, with '*toioutoi*' (79. 5; cf. 79. 17);[14] (ii) Alexander mentions other authors in the context—e.g. Phanias and Eudemus. So how can we be sure that Alexander elsewhere has the *Peri ideōn* in mind—why not Phanias, Eudemus, or other unnamed sources?

Neither (i) nor (ii) is convincing. As against (i), although '*toioutos*' can mean 'similar to', it can also easily have the force of '*houtos*', and that seems the most likely reading here.[15] For Alexander suggests he had access to the work, and there does not seem to be any reason to doubt him. But if he had access to the *Peri ideōn*, why should he cite material that is only similar to it? Further, the fact that *Peri ideōn* 1 is so carefully constructed and so insightful about Plato also makes it likely that this material all belongs together as part of the same work, of which Aristotle is the most likely author;[16] and the most likely work is the one Alexander names, the *Peri ideōn*. As against (ii), we shall see below that Alexander carefully begins and ends his discussion with references to the *Peri ideōn* in a way that suggests that (except when he explicitly mentions another source) he is drawing on it. I shall assume, then, that Alexander in some sense records material from the *Peri ideōn*. But how much of his commentary does so?

Rose excludes from the *Peri ideōn* both the Argument from Relatives and also most of the criticisms of the various arguments. (Of the criticisms, he includes only the first criticism of the Arguments from the Sciences, which says that they are invalid arguments for the existence of forms, and the Third Man Argument.)[17] Unfortunately, he gives no reasons for his parsimony. His exclusion of the Argument from Relatives is curious, given that he includes the Third Man Argument; for as Robin notes,[18] the two arguments are introduced in very similar terms. Further, in *Met.* 1. 9 Aristotle claims that a Platonist argument produces ideas of relatives; as we shall see, the argument Alexander records in explanation of this claim fits well with Aristotle's usual view of Plato and also employs standard Aristotelian distinctions and terminology.

Philippson excludes most of the criticisms for the following reason. In the criticisms, it is claimed that if the Arguments from the Sciences, the One over Many Argument, and the Argument from Relatives proved anything, they would prove that there are forms in cases where the Platonists do not want them. But, according to Philippson, middle-period Plato, against whom he thinks the *Peri ideōn* is aimed, wanted forms in such cases.[19] Hence (unless we are to accuse Aristotle of misinterpretation) these criticisms are not from the *Peri ideōn*. We shall see in due course, however, that even if the criticisms are aimed against middle-period Plato, they do not involve misinterpretation. Philippson and Rose both allow that the first criticism of the Arguments from the Sciences (that they are invalid arguments for the existence of forms) is from the *Peri ideōn*;[20] it seems unreasonable to assume that the second criticism (that the arguments would prove that there are artefact forms if they proved that there are any forms at all) is not also from it. Alexander gives no hint that he is at this point suddenly veering away from the *Peri ideōn*. Further, Aristotle claims that the One over Many Argument is an invalid argument for the existence of forms. It is unclear why Rose excludes this criticism from the *Peri ideōn* but includes the parallel objection to the Arguments from the Sciences.[21]

One might also doubt whether all five arguments and their criticisms are from the *Peri ideōn* on the ground that Alexander does not explicitly say that they are: in discussing book 1, he explicitly mentions the *Peri ideōn* only in connection with the Arguments from the Sciences and the Third Man Argument. But this ground for scepticism is also unwarranted. In *Met.* 990b11–17 Aristotle mentions the arguments and his criticisms all together, in a way that suggests that they were developed more fully, and together, elsewhere. Alexander begins his discussion of this passage from the *Metaphysics* by saying that the Arguments from the Sciences are from the *Peri ideōn*. He then records the next four arguments along with Aristotle's criticisms of them. Each section is introduced in very similar terms; and in Ch. 2.7 we saw that the discussion forms an integrated whole. Then, at the close of the discussion, he again mentions the *Peri ideōn*, this time in connection with the Third Man. So although Alexander does not explicitly mention the *Peri ideōn* in connection with each argument and criticism, his two references to it are carefully placed at the beginning and end of a connected discussion. The natural inference is that he is throughout recording portions of the *Peri ideōn*.

It is true that not all of Alexander's commentary on 990b11–17 is from the *Peri ideōn*. For example, he records two versions of a Third Man Argument; although he assigns the second to the *Peri ideōn*, he assigns the first to Eudemus.[22] But this itself indicates that the five arguments and their criticisms are from the *Peri ideōn*: when Alexander has a different source in mind, he tells us so.[23]

I shall assume, then, that at least our five arguments and their criticisms are from the *Peri ideōn*.[24] But in what sense are they from it? Is Alexander quoting or paraphrasing? And how reliable is he at either task? People can, after all, misquote or give misleading paraphrases.

Unfortunately, since we have virtually no independent access to the *Peri ideōn*, we can never be sure how accurate Alexander is. However, there is no reason for general suspicion. True, since he sometimes uses later, non-Aristotelian, language, he is presumably sometimes paraphrasing rather than quoting.[25] But we need not infer that he paraphrases throughout—although we can never be sure about this, one way or the other. But if, as seems likely, Alexander had access to the work, it is reasonable to suppose that he either quotes it or provides a generally accurate paraphrase. Certainly there are indications that he is generally quite careful in his ·commentary on the *Metaphysics*. We have seen, for example, that when he has a source other than the *Peri ideōn* in mind, he says so. He is accurate in his references to other Aristotelian works elsewhere in the commentary;[26] he mentions variations in different manuscripts of the *Metaphysics*;[27] when he is unsure of Aristotle's meaning, he puzzles over alternative interpretations;[28] he indicates when an argument is his own rather Aristotle's;[29] and so on. Further and more importantly, there is the by now familiar consideration that the material Alexander ascribes to *Peri ideōn* I meshes well both with Aristotle's cryptic account in *Met.* I. 9 and also with his more expansive accounts and criticisms of Plato elsewhere. Surely it is more likely that Alexander accurately records *Peri ideōn* I than that, by being careless, he inadvertently succeeded in capturing Aristotle's thought.

Although one cannot be certain, then, it is reasonable to believe that Alexander is generally accurate in recording portions of *Peri ideōn* I. But those who are unconvinced might still derive something of value from what follows. For even if Alexander invents the material he ascribes to the *Peri ideōn* out of whole cloth, or records material that is a gross misconstrual of what Aristotle actually said, or records material from a work that is not by Aristotle at all, it none the less, I think, sheds enough light on Plato's and Aristotle's thought to be taken seriously on that ground alone.

5. The riddle of the *Peri ideōn*

According to Cherniss, '[t]he riddle of the early Academy is epitomized in the discrepancy between Aristotle's account of Plato's theory of Ideas and the theory as we have it from Plato's writings'.[30] Various solutions have been proposed. Cherniss, for example, argues that Aristotle has the dialogues in mind but misinterprets them.[31] In order to rescue Aristotle from misinterpretation, others suggest that Aristotle correctly records the thought either of Plato's unwritten doctrines or of Platonists other than Plato.

Which solution is right for the *Peri ideōn*? It has not generally been thought that the unwritten doctrines are relevant here, and I shall generally ignore them in what follows.[32] But Isnardi Parente argues that *Peri ideōn* I discusses not Plato but Xenocrates.[33] Cherniss argues that *Peri ideōn* I discusses Plato, but that in at least some cases it misunderstands him. As I have said, I think that *Peri ideōn* I discusses Plato and that it understands him quite well.

The solutions that either accuse Aristotle of misinterpreting Plato or take him to be criticizing a source other than the dialogues rest on an assumption underlying the dilemma sketched in Ch. 2.8, that when Aristotle discusses Plato, he aims to record his views more or less verbatim. But once we see that Aristotle generally aims instead to provide an illuminating rational reconstruction of Plato's thought, we should expect some lack of fit between Aristotle's account and Plato's texts; we should therefore be correspondingly more reluctant either to accuse Aristotle of misinterpreting the dialogues or to search for another source.

Further, Aristotle provides various clues that Plato is his target. True, he does not explicitly ascribe *Peri ideōn* 1's arguments for the existence of forms to anyone; he speaks more vaguely of arguments 'we' or 'they' offer.[34] But in *Met.* 1. 6, he claims to describe *Plato's* reasons for introducing forms—essentially the flux argument.[35] He begins *Met.* 13. 4 by saying that he is going to describe the original motivation for introducing forms, without considering later arguments connecting forms with numbers. He then describes the very same flux argument that, in 1. 6, he ascribes to Plato. To be sure, in 13. 4 he says that 'they' used the flux argument in introducing forms—Plato is not mentioned. But since 1. 6 ascribes the flux argument to Plato, we are entitled to assume that 'they' includes him. (The variation is useful, though, for it shows that Aristotle sometimes uses 'they' when he clearly has Plato—perhaps among others—in mind.) Having described the flux argument, Aristotle almost immediately mentions the material from *Peri ideōn* 1.[36] He then mentions several other arguments about forms; and then, towards the end of his discussion, he mentions the *Phaedo* (13. 5, 1080a1). It is true that at 1079b18–23 he mentions Eudoxus' account of immanent forms. But nowhere else in 13. 4–5 does he suggest that he is suddenly shifting away from Plato's arguments to arguments defended only by others in the Academy. The structure of 13. 4–5 thus suggests that, except when Aristotle names another source (as in the case of Eudoxus), he is considering the initial phases of Plato's theory of forms. If so, then that is also *Peri ideōn* 1's concern.

Of course, perhaps Platonists other than Plato offered the very arguments Aristotle records; perhaps Aristotle simply repeats arguments he found elsewhere—we can never be sure.[37] But the *Peri ideōn* is so illuminating about Plato, especially about his middle dialogues, that I find it difficult to believe that it is not (perhaps among other things) about them.[38]

Alexander believes that Plato is Aristotle's target. For in commenting on Aristotle's claim that 'none of the ways in which we prove that there are forms is convincing' (*Met.* 990b8)—the claim with which Aristotle introduces the *Metaphysics*'s cryptic references to the *Peri ideōn*'s arguments—he says that 'the words "we prove" show that in stating the doctrine of Plato (*legonta ta Platōnos*), he is speaking as if in reference to his own opinions' (78. 1–2).[39] If the foregoing considerations are cogent, then Alexander's view is quite reasonable. We shall find further support for it when we investigate the *Peri ideōn* in the light of Plato's texts. For I argue throughout that the *Peri ideōn* illuminates those texts; and surely it is more reasonable to suppose that Aristotle intends to do so than that he does so quite inadvertently.

But even those who doubt whether the *Peri ideōn* is aimed against Plato might find something of value in what follows. For to justify the doubt one would need to consider the *Peri ideōn*'s arguments in the light of Plato's text and explain the alleged discrepancies. The project I am engaged in is therefore necessary for anyone who even wonders whether the *Peri ideōn* is aimed against Plato.[40]

6. Plato's development

I argued in the last section that it is reasonable to take Plato's middle dialogues to be a central concern of the *Peri ideōn*. Philippson also believes this; but unlike me he believes that the late dialogues revise the theory of forms in its light. Jackson, on the other hand, believes that some of the positions mentioned in the *Peri ideōn* fit the late but not the middle dialogues.[41] In order to adjudicate this dispute, we need to know something about the chronology of Plato's dialogues and about Aristotle's account of Plato's development.

Scholars often divide the dialogues into four main groups: the early Socratic dialogues; the transitional dialogues; the middle dialogues; and the late dialogues.[42] There is disagreement about how, if at all, these groups differ from one another. Some favour a unitarian view, according to which there are no significant differences in doctrine between the different groups; others favour a developmentalist view, according to which there are significant doctrinal differences between them.[43]

On one version of a unitarian account, Plato throughout believes that there are everlasting, non-sensible, separate forms that are also self-predicative paradigms. True, he criticizes some such view in the *Parmenides*. But according to unitarians, the objections either can be rebutted or else deliberately misdescribe Plato's actual theory of forms. In either case, Plato need not revise his theory of forms in their light and does not do so.

On one version of a developmentalist account, the Socratic dialogues adumbrate a theory of forms different from the one in the middle dialogues, which, in turn, differs from the theory found in the late (post-*Parmenides*) dialogues. In the Socratic dialogues, forms are universals, and they are not separate from particulars. In the middle dialogues, forms are either both universals and particulars, or else they are just particulars.

They are also self-predicative paradigms in some more robust sense than that in view in, for example, the *Euthyphro*; they are also separate. In the late dialogues, however, in response to the *Parmenides'* telling criticisms, Plato rejects the existence of such forms. Either he abandons metaphysical realism altogether; or else he reverts to something like the more moderate version of realism favoured in the Socratic dialogues.[44]

Developmentalists and unitarians sometimes agree on one point: that the middle dialogues' theory of forms involves serious mistakes.[45] Indeed, one motive for the developmentalist view is the desire to see Plato improve.

Aristotle is a developmentalist, in so far as he distinguishes between a Socratic and a Platonic theory of forms, and so between the theory of forms in the early and middle dialogues.[46] But in contrast to some developmentalists, he believes that the two theories are importantly continuous, and that such differences as there are are both fewer than and different from those some have believed there were. I discuss this matter in Ch. 4.

Unfortunately, it is far more difficult, perhaps impossible, to know what if any differences Aristotle takes there to be between the forms in the middle and late dialogues, so far as the features discussed in *Peri ideōn* I are concerned. For one thing, although he explicitly says how he believes the Socratic and Platonic theories differ, he never says whether he thinks Plato changed his views about these features of forms; the topic is not broached. None the less, I am inclined to think that on this matter Aristotle is a unitarian.[47]

One consideration in favour of this view is the very fact that Aristotle never says that Plato ceased to believe that forms have the features discussed in *Peri ideōn* I. Nor does he ever indicate that Plato changed his views about the range of forms—about whether, for example, there are or are not forms of artefacts, negations, and relatives. There would be no reason for him to say that Plato had changed his mind here if he thought that Plato had not done so. Throughout the corpus—in, for example, the *Posterior Analytics*, *Physics*, middle books of the *Metaphysics*, and *Nicomachean Ethics*—Aristotle describes Plato's theory of forms in roughly the same terms as in *Peri ideōn* I. Why should he do so if he thought Plato had changed those views?[48]

True, one can criticize views an author no longer holds: not all criticisms of Wittgenstein's *Tractatus* antedate the *Philosophical Investigations*. Still, if Aristotle thought Plato had abandoned the middle dialogues' views on the issues of concern to us here, one might expect him at some stage to indicate this; but he does not. The best explanation of his silence is that he does not think that Plato abandoned these views. Certainly he is not shy about describing differences when he thinks they are there. He tells us how Socrates and other contemporary thinkers differ from Plato. He also indicates other shifts in Plato's views; he suggests, for example, that Plato at some stage associated forms with numbers.[49] Why then would he fail to mention changes in the features of forms he finds most objectionable?

The answer cannot be that he never discusses or draws on the late dialogues. For the *Posterior Analytics* and *Met.* 4 rely on the *Theaetetus*; some passages in *Met.* 4 also seem to be influenced by the *Sophist*; *Met.* 14. 2 (see esp. 1089a20–1) seems to refer to the *Sophist*; the *Nicomachean Ethics* is deeply influenced by the *Philebus*. Aristotle also refers to the *Timaeus* more often than to any other dialogue. Unfortunately, the date of the *Timaeus* is disputed,[50] and Aristotle never indicates when Plato wrote it. (If he had done so, presumably that would settle the dispute.) But the best recent scholarship dates the *Timaeus* after the *Parmenides* and *Theaetetus*. If we assume that that ordering is correct, as I shall do, then it is tempting to say that Aristotle's account of the *Timaeus* shows that in his view at least one post-*Parmenides* dialogue retains the key features he takes to be involved in middle dialogues' theory of forms, since the *Timaeus* describes forms in roughly the same terms as they do.[51]

I suspect that the main reason for resisting my view of Aristotle's account of Plato's development will be the thought that if I am right, then Aristotle misinterprets Plato since he overlooks the differences between the middle and late dialogues. But I am not persuaded that those differences are really there. True, the late dialogues often use different terminology; and (leaving the *Timaeus* to one side) they often sound more moderate. But it not clear that there is a difference in doctrine.

Although I agree with Aristotle's apparent view about Plato's development, I do not always accept his views about Plato's commitments. For example, although I agree with Aristotle that forms remain self-predicative paradigms, and that Plato's views about separation do not clearly change,[52] I sometimes disagree with him about the nature and implications of these features of forms.[53]

Suppose Aristotle accepts the suggested view of Plato's development. Can we then say what phase of Plato's thought is at issue in *Peri ideōn* 1? We can feel safe in supposing that the Socratic dialogues are not one of its targets; for Aristotle often expresses rough agreement with their theory of forms and, as we shall see in more detail in the next chapter, he does not associate with it the features of forms he criticizes in *Peri ideōn* 1. We have already seen evidence that the middle dialogues are of concern, and we shall see further evidence of this as we proceed. But what about the late dialogues? If Aristotle accepts the suggested view of Plato's development, then, so far as their content goes, they could also be a target. But before we could conclude that Aristole might have them in mind, we would need to know that the *Peri ideōn* was written after them. I therefore ask next about its chronology relative to that of Plato's late dialogues.

7. When was the *Peri ideōn* written relative to Plato's dialogues?

One crucial question about the *Peri ideōn* is whether it was written before or after the *Parmenides*, which likewise criticizes a theory of forms. Philippson and Düring favour the view that the *Peri ideōn* antedates the *Parmenides*;[54] most other scholars favour the reverse ordering.[55]

Although there is some dispute about the dating of the *Parmenides*, it seems likely that it was written before the *Theaetetus*.[56] The *Theaetetus*, in turn, was probably written shortly after 369, so probably sometime in the 360s.[57] The *Parmenides* was thus most likely written in the 360s or, possibly, in the 370s.

Now, all our sources agree that Aristotle arrived in Athens in 367 at the age of 17, and left in 347, around the time of Plato's death.[58] So he could have arrived in Athens before the *Parmenides* was written. But it is far from clear that he did; and if he did, he presumably did so not long before the *Parmenides* was written. It is thus just chronologically possible (if not especially likely) that the *Peri ideōn* antedates the *Parmenides*. Are there any positive reasons to think that it does?

One reason that has been offered stems from the fact that the *Parmenides* and *Peri ideōn* criticize a theory of forms in quite similar terms; most strikingly, both record a Third Man Argument. Aristotle never says that he got the Third Man Argument from Plato; yet if the *Parmenides* was written first, surely Aristotle ought to have acknowledged it. In the *Parmenides*, however, Plato refers four times to an Aristotle. So perhaps the *Peri ideōn* was written first, and in the *Parmenides* Plato acknowledges his debt to it?[59]

But this consideration is unconvincing. Even if the Aristotle mentioned in the *Parmenides* is 'our' Aristotle, nothing follows about the relative date of the *Peri ideōn*. Plato might mention an eager new member of the Academy without implying any specific debt. But it is unlikely that Plato is referring to 'our' Aristotle. For he identifies the Aristotle he mentions as a member of the Thirty (127d), a group he was probably not enamoured of; and there is evidence that there was an Aristotle (not 'ours') who was a member of the Thirty. It is more likely that Plato is referring to him than that he acknowledges a debt to our Aristotle by identifying him with, or at any rate naming, some quite different, less admirable, Aristotle. It is also worth noting that Plato does not generally refer to living philosophers by name.[60]

Nor is it surprising, or cause for concern, that Aristotle does not name Plato when he discusses the Third Man Argument, for he generally avoids mentioning Plato by name when he criticizes him.[61] Presumably there were not the same canons then as now for citing the work of others. Further, although there are important similarities between some of the *Parmenides*' and *Peri ideōn*'s arguments, there are also significant differences: each contains arguments the other does not, and even when the shape of the arguments is similar, the details differ. Also, the *Peri ideōn*'s arguments are so much more detailed and precise that it seems more likely that it polishes and refines arguments Plato had already given than that Plato offers cruder, more elliptical, versions of arguments Aristotle formulated first.

Moreover, if the *Peri ideōn* precedes the *Parmenides*, it was written very early in Aristotle's career, perhaps before he was even 20 years old. Though this is possible, it seems unlikely, given the depth of understanding the *Peri ideōn* reveals about the theory of forms. Nor does the *Peri ideōn* only record arguments for the existence of forms; it also criticizes them in ways familiar from other Aristotelian works.[62] On Philippson's and Düring's hypothesis, not only do we have to assume that Aristotle burst on to the scene at the age of 17 and immediately acquired a deeply insightful understanding of the theory of forms, which he then immediately wrote up; but we also have to assume that he had already formulated many of his distinctive philosophical positions.[63]

I believe, then, that the *Peri ideōn* was written after the *Parmenides* and, probably, after the *Theaetetus* as well. But it is harder to say when the *Peri ideōn* was written relative to the *Timaeus, Sophist, Politicus,* and *Philebus* (the post-*Theaetetus* dialogues most important for our purposes). Philippson thinks it was written before them, on the ground that (in his view) these dialogues revise the theory of forms in ways suggesting that Plato accepted the *Peri ideōn*'s criticisms.[64] But as I suggested above, Aristotle does not seem to think the late dialogues differ from the middle dialogues in the relevant ways.[65] So although it is quite possible that the *Peri ideōn* was written before at least some of the late dialogues, we should not be persuaded by Philippson's defence of this chronological hypothesis.

There are some interesting similarities between the *Peri ideōn* and some passages in the late dialogues; indeed, in some cases the similarities are even greater than those that obtain between the *Peri ideōn* and middle dialogues. For example, a crucial notion in the second Argument from the Sciences is that of being indefinite (*apeiron*); '*apeiron*' occurs frequently in the *Philebus*, but not in the middle dialogues. Aristotle says that if the One over Many Argument proved that there are any forms, it would prove that there are forms of negations and of what is not; negations and not-being are discussed more in the *Sophist* than in any of the middle dialogues. Two of the *Peri ideōn*'s arguments consider forms as paradigms; paradigmatism is more prominent in the *Timaeus* than in the middle dialogues. Similarly, the *Timaeus* is more clearly committed to separation than are the middle dialogues; and the *Peri ideōn* criticizes separation. The *Timaeus* also emphasizes the everlasting-ness of forms more clearly than the middle dialogues do; and the ever-lastingness of forms is discussed in the *Peri ideōn*. Given these similarities between the *Peri ideōn* and the late dialogues, I find it difficult to believe that it is entirely independent of them. But I find it impossible to say what the direction of influence is. Perhaps the *Peri ideōn* was written before some of the late dialogues (which ones?), and they (among other things) respond to it. Of course, in my view if Plato responds to them, he does so not by abandoning the middle dialogues' theory of forms, but by reaffirming their commitments, though he might agree that various claims could be better phrased and better defended. Or perhaps the *Peri ideōn* was written after, and draws on, some of the late dialogues (which ones?). In this case, perhaps the *Peri ideōn*, in addition to exploring the middle dialogues, also asks how far the late dialogues differ from them: they use different terminology, and they sound more moderate; but are these superficial or significant changes? It is in many ways attractive to suppose that this is one of the *Peri ideōn*'s aims, but I should hesitate to say that it is correct, partly because the chronological issue is so murky. It is in any case important to be clear that the mere fact that in some few cases the terminology of the *Peri ideōn* matches that of the late rather than of the middle dialogues should not lead us to believe that it has the late rather than the middle dialogues in mind: there is no reason Aristotle should use the language of the middle dialogues in discussing them; he may well have found other language more illuminating or perspicuous. Further, though some themes that are of concern in the *Peri ideōn* are more prominent in the late than in the middle dialogues, we shall see that Aristotle also takes them to be present in the middle dialogues; so neither should this lead us to suppose that the late rather than the middle dialogues are of concern.

8. When in Aristotle's career was the *Peri ideōn* written?

Part of the reason it is difficult to know when the *Peri ideōn* was written relative to the post-*Theaetetus* dialogues is that it is unclear precisely when Aristotle wrote it. We can feel safe, to be sure, in dating the *Peri ideōn* before *Met.* 1. But it is more difficult to say how much earlier it is. It is generally thought to be one of Aristotle's earliest works; most commentators believe it was written while Aristotle was still a member of the Academy.[66]

But some of the reasons for or against any particular dating are tenuous. For example, it is sometimes thought that the *Peri ideōn* was written before most of the late dialogues (and so while Aristotle was still in the Academy) on the ground that the late dialogues revise the theory of forms in its light.[67] But we have seen that the late dialogues do not seem to revise the theory of forms in the relevant ways. On the other hand, some reasons given for a later dating are equally tenuous—for example, the notion that Aristotle would not criticize Plato while he was alive.[68]

I am inclined to think that the *Peri ideōn* was written while Aristotle was a member of the Academy; but I do not think that there are any definitive, or even especially persuasive, arguments in favour of this view. None the less, it is worth mentioning a few considerations that perhaps provide some slight support for a relatively early dating.

There are a few terminological indications in favour of an early dating. For example, the *Peri ideōn* uses '*to koinon*' and '*to koinōs katēgoroumenon*' rather than '*katholou*' for universals; in this respect, it is like various other works (such as the *Categories*, *Topics*, and *Sophistici Elenchi*) that are generally agreed to be early.[69]

Another possible reason for dating the *Peri ideōn* early is that like the *Organon* (which is generally dated early) it does not mention matter, even though it might occasionally have been appropriate to do so.[70] For example, according to the One over Many Argument and the Accurate One over Many Argument, forms are separate from sensibles and from *kath' hekasta*; it would have been natural to say that they are separate from matter, but Aristotle does not say this. Similarly, the second Argument from the Sciences says that *kath' hekasta* are *apeira*; elsewhere '*apeira*' is linked to matter, and it might have been appropriate to indicate the link here as well. In other ways too, the *Peri ideōn*'s terminology is often close to that used in the *Organon*.[71] But since such terminology is also used outside the *Organon*, this is not decisive.

It may also be significant that the *Peri ideōn* seems to be aimed at a smaller audience than, say, the *Metaphysics*' criticisms of Plato.[72] Perhaps it was written for discussion by members of the Academy, in which case it was presumably written while Aristotle was still among them. It is also less full in its criticisms than the *Metaphysics* is; and although Aristotle indicates his own alternative positions, he does not develop them.[73]

One reason for favouring the view that the *Peri ideōn* was written not just early in Aristotle's career but actually while he was still in the Academy is quite mundane: Aristotle was quite prolific. It seems unlikely that there would have been enough time for him to have written all his works after Plato had died; so he presumably wrote some of them in the Academy. Given the similarity between the *Peri ideōn* and the *Organon*, and the fact that the *Organon* is generally agreed to have been written quite early in Aristotle's career, it seems reasonable to suppose that the *Organon* and *Peri ideōn* were all written while Aristotle was in the Academy. (Of course, one could challenge an early dating for the *Organon*.)

I am therefore tempted by the view that the *Peri ideōn* was written while Aristotle was a member of the Academy, and so by the view that it was written before at least some of the late dialogues. But I should not like to hazard a guess about its date relative to the *Timaeus*, *Sophist*, *Politicus*, and *Philebus*; I see no grounds for favouring one relative chronology over another.

Although it would be quite exciting to know the relative (and absolute) date of the *Peri ideōn*, this is in a way not the most important thing to know, so far as assessing the interplay between the *Peri ideōn* and the late dialogues is concerned. For it is not as though Plato could have thought about the *Peri ideōn*'s criticisms only after the work was in its final form, or as though Aristotle could have thought about (say) the *Sophist*'s views only after it was in final form. Presumably Plato and Aristotle spoke with one another as they were developing their views. So even if (e.g.) the *Sophist* was written after the *Peri ideōn*, Aristotle could be thinking of it; at the same time, it could be responding to the *Peri ideōn*. The influence could have been mutual.

Since I see no way of knowing precisely when the *Peri ideōn* was written relative to the post-*Theaetetus* dialogues, I shall take no stand on this matter. But I shall feel free to discuss the late dialogues when they seem especially relevant although, as I have said, my main focus will be the middle dialogues. This focus provides more than enough material for one study.

4

Platonic Questions

1. Introduction

I argued in the last chapter that there are good reasons for supposing that *Peri ideōn* 1 discusses Plato. One central reason for thinking this is that (*a*) it records arguments for the existence of forms that are firmly rooted in the dialogues; another is that (*b*) it meshes well with Aristotle's general understanding of Plato. In order to see whether (*a*) and (*b*) are true, we need to look not only at the *Peri ideōn* but also at the dialogues and at Aristotle's other discussions of Plato. In this chapter I therefore sketch some central aspects of the theory of forms and of Aristotle's account of them outside the *Peri ideōn*. Since Aristotle quite reasonably explains Plato's theory by contrasting it with Socrates', I shall also say something about Socrates' theory of forms and about Aristotle's account of it. I do not pretend that my discussion of these large matters is sufficiently detailed to carry full conviction. I shall be content if I can make a partial account plausible, and show how it fits with the *Peri ideōn*. Even a partial account should help orient the reader to some of the themes and issues that will occupy us later.

2. Aristotle on the origins of the theory of forms

I begin by translating and schematizing three key passages in the *Metaphysics* in which Aristotle describes the origins of Plato's theory of forms and its key differences from the Socratic theory.[1]

In *Met.* 1. 6 Aristotle writes:

The philosophies discussed were succeeded by Plato's work, which followed these in most ways; but it had special features in contrast to the philosophy of the Italians. For in his youth he first became familiar with Cratylus and with the Heracleitean beliefs that all sensibles (*aisthēta*) are always flowing (*rhein*) and that there is no knowledge of them; and he supposed these things later too. But Socrates was concerned with moral questions, and not at all with the whole of nature; he was seeking the universal (*katholou*) in moral things and was the first to turn his thought to definitions. Plato agreed with him; but because of this ⟨Heracleitean view⟩ he supposed that this ⟨defining⟩ applied to different things (*heterōn*) and not to sensibles—for, he thought, it is impossible for the common definition to be of any of the sensibles, since they are always changing (*metaballontōn*). These sorts of beings, then, he called 'ideas'. (987a29–b8.)

Aristotle seems to attribute the following line of thought to Plato:

I

(1) (x) (x is sensible $\rightarrow$ x is always changing).
(2) (x) (x is always changing $\rightarrow$ x is unknowable and indefinable).
(3) Therefore (x) (x is sensible $\rightarrow$ is unknowable and indefinable).
(4) There are definitions and knowledge.
(5) Definitions and knowledge are of something.
(6) Therefore there are objects that are different from (*heterōn*, 987b5) sensibles, and they are the objects of knowledge and definition.
(7) These are forms.[2]
(8) Therefore there are forms.

In *Met.* 13. 4 Aristotle says he will discuss the theory of forms 'as the people who first said that there were ideas understood it at the outset' (1078b11–12). He goes on to say that:

The belief about the forms occurred to those who asserted it because they were convinced of the truth of the Heracleitean arguments that all sensibles are always flowing, so that if knowledge and wisdom are to be about anything, there must be some different (*heteras*) and enduring natures, besides (*para*) the sensible ones, for there is no knowledge of flowing things. Now Socrates was concerned with the moral virtues, and he was the first to seek universal definitions in connection with them . . . It was reasonable for Socrates to try to find what a thing is, because he was seeking to argue deductively, and the starting-point of deductions is what a thing is . . . For there are just two things one might fairly ascribe to Socrates— inductive arguments and universal definitions, both of which are concerned with the starting-point of knowledge. But Socrates did not make universals or definitions (*horismous*) separate (*chōrista*), but they ⟨the Platonists⟩ separated them, and they called these sorts of beings 'ideas'. (1078b12–32.)

Here Aristotle seems to ascribe the following line of thought to Plato:

II

(1) (x) (x is sensible $\rightarrow$ x is always changing).
(2) (x) (x is always changing $\rightarrow$ x is unknowable).
(3) Therefore (x) (x is sensible $\rightarrow$ x is unknowable).
(4) There is knowledge.
(5) Knowledge requires the existence of permanent natures, i.e. of universals.
(6) Therefore there are non-sensible universals.
(7) Non-sensible universals are separate.[3]
(8) Non-sensible universals are forms.
(9) Therefore there are separate forms.

Finally, in *Met.* 13. 9 Aristotle writes:

For they treat ideas both as universals and again, at the same time, as separate (*chōristas*) and as particulars (*tōn kath' hekaston*). But it has been argued before that this is impossible. Those who said that the substances were universals combined these things ⟨universality and particularity⟩ in the same thing because they did not make them ⟨the substances⟩ the same as sensibles. They thought that the particulars in sensibles were flowing and that none of them endured, but that the universal is besides (*para*) these things and is something different (*heteron ti*) from them. Socrates motivated this ⟨view⟩, as we were saying before, through definitions; but he did not separate ⟨universals⟩ from particulars. And he was right not to separate them. This is clear from the results. For it is not possible to acquire knowledge without the universal; but separating is the cause of the difficulties arising about the ideas. But they, on the assumption that any substances besides (*para*) the sensible and flowing ones had to be separate (*chōristas*), had no others, and so they set apart the substances spoken of universally, so that it followed that universal and particular ⟨natures⟩ were virtually the same natures. This in itself, then, would be one difficulty for the view discussed. (1086a32–b13.)

The argument seems to be as follows:[4]

III

(1) Sensibles are always changing. (1086a37–b1)
⟨(2) (*x*) (*x* is always changing → *x* is unknowable and indefinable).⟩
⟨(3) There are definitions and knowledge.⟩
(4) Knowledge and definition require the existence of universals. (1086b5–6)
(5) ⟨Therefore⟩ there are non-sensible universals. (1086b1–2)
(6) Non-sensible universals are forms.
(7) There are non-sensible substances. (1086a36–7, b1–2)
(8) The only candidates for non-sensible substances are non-sensible universals, the forms. (1086b7–10)
(9) Non-sensible substances are separate. (1086b8–9)
(10) Therefore forms are separate.
(11) (*x*) (*x* is separate → *x* is a particular). (1086a33–4, b9–11)
(12) Therefore forms are both universals and particulars. (1086a32–4, b10–11)

3. The 'What is *F*?' question

In the preceding passages, Aristotle tells us that Socrates sought definitions of universals or essences, knowledge of which is necessary for any knowledge at all, and that unlike Plato Socrates neither separated universals nor took them to be non-sensible. Now Socrates does not himself call any entities 'universals' (*katholou*).[5] But in the Socratic dialogues he often asks the 'What is *F*?' question—'What is piety?' in the

Euthyphro; 'What is courage?' in the *Laches*; 'What is temperance?' in the *Charmides*; and so on. Piety and the like—referents of correct answers to 'What is *F*?' questions—are forms (*eidos, Eu.* 6d11; *Meno* 72c7) or ideas (*idea, Eu.* 5d4). In asking the 'What is *F*?' question, Socrates is asking for a definition of *F*; so he takes the objects of definition to be forms. Yet Aristotle tells us that Socrates takes the objects of definition to be universals. Aristotle therefore takes Socratic forms to be universals; and in saying how Socrates viewed universals, he aims to explain the nature of Socratic forms. So in order to assess Aristotle's account of Socrates, we need to understand the nature of Socratic forms.

I begin by asking what sort of answer Socrates wants to his 'What is *F*?' question. Sometimes an answer is rejected because it is too narrow. For example, courage cannot be defined as 'standing firm in battle', since courage can be displayed in other sorts of behaviour (*La.* 191ce). Sometimes an answer is rejected because it is too broad. For example, courage cannot be defined as 'standing firm in battle', since not all cases of standing firm in battle are courageous. Hence the very same answer can be both too narrow, if it fails to capture enough of the relevant instances, and too broad, if it captures some irrelevant ones. Nor can courage be defined as 'endurance of the soul', since some cases of endurance are foolish, and so not good, and so not courageous (*La.* 192cd). Put in the material mode, the form of courage is neither the action-type of standing firm in battle nor the character-trait of endurance.

Another way of putting the point that some answers are too broad is to say that they specify properties or action types that suffer *narrow compresence of opposites.*[6] Something suffers narrow compresence with respect to being *F* if it is *F* and not *F* in virtue of some one and the same aspect of itself. For example, the action type of standing firm in battle, under the description 'standing firm in battle', is both courageous (in so far as it has some courageous tokens) and not courageous (in so far as it has some tokens that are not courageous). Similarly, the character-trait of endurance is both courageous (in so far as it is sometimes courageous to endure) and not courageous (in so far as it is sometimes not courageous to endure). Notice that in these two cases, something universal or general—an action type or character-trait—suffers narrow compresence. Socrates is primarily, perhaps solely, interested in compresence as it attaches to universals.[7]

In addition to being neither too narrow nor too broad, a correct answer to a 'What is *F*?' question must also explain the nature of *F*-ness. In the *Euthyphro* (10–11), for example, Socrates says that although 'piety' and 'being loved by all the gods' are coextensive, 'being loved by all the gods' is none the less an inadequate answer to the question 'What is piety?', since being loved by all the gods is an accidental property (*pathos, Eu.* 11a8) of piety, whereas Socrates wants to know its nature or essence (*ousia*, 11a7; cf. *Meno* 72b1; *Phd.* 65d13). Being loved by all the gods is said to be an accidental property of piety because it does not explain why pious things are pious; rather, the fact that a thing is pious explains why the gods love it. So an adequate account of the essence of *F*-ness will reveal why all *F*s are *F*. For, as Socrates says in the *Euthyphro*, the essence of (e.g.) piety is 'that very form *by which* (*hō(i)*)) all the piouses are pious' (*Eu.* 6d10–11), something that 'is the same in every ⟨pious⟩ action' (5d1).[8]

In Socrates' view, one cannot explain what *F*-ness is, or why *F*s are *F*, by mentioning the many *F*s (*ta polla*—particular *F*s and particular kinds of *F*s); rather, one needs to mention some *one*, non-disjunctive property by which all *F*s are *F*.[9] In the *Laches*, for example, he says that speed is some one thing, the same in running, playing the lyre, speaking, learning, and so on (*La.* 192ab). He tells Euthyphro he wants to know the one thing piety is 'both in the case of murder and in the other cases' (5d1). Similarly, he says, everything (*pan*) that is impious has some one form (*mia tis idea*) (5d3–5). In the *Meno* he argues that although there are different kinds of bees, bees do not differ in so far as they are bees (72b8–9); he makes analogous claims for health, size, and strength (72d4–e8), and for the virtues (72c6–d1).

If Socrates wanted only to articulate ordinary usage, to explain the meaning of '*F*' in the sense of explaining how competent speakers of the language use '*F*', then his rejection of definitions phrased in terms of the many *F*s might seem surprising. But Socrates is not aiming to articulate ordinary usage; he wants to know how things really are. Socratic definitions are real rather than nominal definitions.[10] A real definition of gold, for example, would specify the inner constitution of gold rather than such observable features as that it is heavy, yellow, and shiny. It would specify the features something must have in order to be gold, rather than the features by which ordinary people typically classify something as gold; it would explain what gold really is, rather than what ordinary people mean by 'gold'.[11] Socrates wants to know why, in virtue of what feature, something is *F*. A definition that simply listed the many *F*s would be at best a nominal definition, telling us *that* certain things are *F* or are conventionally classified as *F*s. It would not tell us *why* they are *F*, or whether our conventional classifications are correct. Nor would it enable us to know whether a disputed example belongs on the list. For each of the many *F*s has features that are irrelevant to the nature of *F*-ness as such; inspecting the list will not enable us to know which features further examples must have. In Socrates' view, to know whether a disputed example is *F*—indeed, to know whether anything is *F*—we need to know the one feature all *F*s have in common.

That Socratic definitions are real rather than nominal definitions is suggested not only by the fact that he rejects definitions phrased in terms of the many *F*s but also by the fact that he finds it so difficult to discover adequate definitions. Although articulating ordinary usage is not a simple and straightforward matter, it does not seem to be as difficult a project as Socrates takes the discovery of definitions to be.[12] Or again, he claims that neither he nor his interlocutors know what *F* is.[13] He does not mean that they lack ordinary linguistic understanding of the word '*F*', of how competent speakers of the language use '*F*'. Nor does he mean that they cannot reliably pick out examples of *F*s or that they have no (true) beliefs about *F*s; on the contrary, definitions are generally tested against examples of *F*s and against various beliefs about *F*s.[14] He means that they do not *know* what virtue is, in the sense of knowing its nature or real essence. Further, Socrates is ready to revise ordinary, even widely shared, beliefs in a way that would be inappropriate if his aim were to articulate ordinary usage.[15]

Once we understand the sort of definition Socrates wants, we can also understand why he believes that we need to know the definition of *F* in order to know anything about *F*, including what things instantiate *F*.[16] He does not mean that we need to *know* the definition of *F* in order to have *beliefs* about *F*; on the contrary, he thinks that we have beliefs, even true beliefs, about *F* although we do not know what *F* is. He means that we need to *know* the definition of *F* to *know* anything about *F*. For the definition of *F* explains what it is to be *F*; and in Socrates' view, any knowledge about *F*, including knowledge of what things are *F*, requires such explanations.[17] We can correctly believe that a particular action is just without knowing what justice is; but we cannot *know* whether anything is just without knowing what justice is. Hence, as Aristotle says, Socrates was seeking the essence, or what a thing is, and he believed that such knowledge was necessary for any knowledge whatsoever.

4. Socratic forms

Socrates believes that correct answers to 'What is *F*?' questions specify forms; forms are the objects of definition where, as we have seen, definitions are real definitions. The ontological correlates of real definitions are real essences, non-linguistic universals that explain why things are as they are. Anything that is gold, for example, has the real essence of gold and is gold precisely because it has that real essence. So, as Socrates says, the one thing *by which* all *F*s are *F* is a form (*Eu.* 5d1–5; *Meno* 72c7). Or again, he says that the form of piety is some one thing, the same in (*en*; *Eu.* 5d1–2; cf. *Ch.* 159a1–2, 158e7) everything that is pious; it is that feature of things by which they are pious.

We saw before that Aristotle takes Socratic forms to be universals, and we can now see why he does so. For since the form of piety is in everything that is pious, it is simultaneously in more than one thing at a time, and so it fits one of Aristotle's descriptions of universals.[18] Further, Aristotle says that 'there are two things one might fairly ascribe to Socrates, inductive arguments and universal definitions, both of which are concerned with the starting-point of knowledge (*epistēmē*)' (*Met.* 1078b23–30). In Aristotle's view, real definitions, which specify real essences, are the starting-point of *epistēmē*.[19] So Aristotle takes Socratic forms to be universals not just in the sense that they are or can be in more than one thing at a time but also in the sense that they are real essences, explanatory properties; for these are the sort of universals one needs to know in order to have knowledge.

On the account I have been suggesting, Socrates offers an epistemological argument for the existence of forms: the possibility of knowledge requires explanation, and this, in turn, requires the existence of forms— real properties and kinds. He also offers a metaphysical one over many argument for the existence of forms: the existence of *many F*s requires the existence of some *one* thing, the form of *F*, in virtue of which they are *F*.[20]

David Armstrong has usefully distinguished between *realist* and *semantic* one over many arguments.[21] Realist one over many arguments posit universals to explain sameness of nature; if a group of objects are all *F*, they are *F* in virtue of sharing a genuine property, the property of *F*. (A predicate nominalist, by contrast, would say that they are all *F* because the predicate '*F*' is true of them all; we need not postulate a genuine property that they all share.) Semantic one over many arguments posit universals to explain the meanings of general terms and, indeed, universals just are the meanings of those terms. On the account of Socrates that I have provided, he offers not a semantic but a realist one over many argument. For, as we have seen, he wants to know not the meanings of general terms, but the properties in virtue of which things are as they are.

If forms are properties whose range and nature are determined by explanatory considerations rather than by considerations about meaning, then they are not meanings, if meanings are taken to be something other than properties conceived in realist fashion. But might Socrates view forms as meanings, and take (some) meanings to be properties? He presumably would do so if he accepted a referential theory of meaning. However, it has been cogently argued that Socrates takes the virtue terms to be non-synonymous but co-referential, so he cannot consistently accept a referential theory of meaning.[22] But is Socrates inconsistent? Or does he confusedly view forms not only as properties but also as meanings, where meanings are taken to be something other than properties? It is difficult to be sure, since he does not discuss semantic questions. But so far as I can see, he does not suggest that forms play any semantic role.[23]

If Socrates relies on a realist one over many argument, then he presumably takes every property to be a form.[24] To be sure, he does not explicitly say how many forms there are; as Aristotle says, Socrates is primarily interested in the virtues. But he never suggests a principle that restricts forms to a subclass of properties; and he sometimes explains why each of the virtues is some one thing, and so a form, by appealing to quite heterogeneous sorts of cases.[25]

Although Socrates seems to believe that every *property* is a form, he is not committed to the view that every *predicate* denotes a form. For, again, forms are explanatory properties, and not every predicate denotes an explanatory property.

In addition to suggesting that Socratic forms are universals conceived as explanatory properties, and that on Socrates' view knowledge of them is necessary for having any knowledge at all, Aristotle also claims that Socrates did not take forms to be either non-sensible or separate. I turn now to these claims.

One might argue that Aristotle is wrong to say that Socrates did not take forms to be non-sensible, on the ground that Socrates routinely rejects answers to 'What is *F*?' questions that are phrased in terms of behaviour or action-types. Moreover, at least in the case of the virtues he seems to favour accounts that are phrased in terms of certain states of the soul and these, it might be thought, are not observable. It might then be tempting to infer that Socrates believes that a correct answer to a 'What is *F*?' question must specify a non-observable property, a property not definable in observational terms.

However, although Socrates regularly rejects answers to 'What is *F*?' questions that are phrased in observational terms, he never says that they fail *because* they are so phrased. They fail, as we have seen, because they are too narrow or too broad, or because they are not explanatory; but Socrates does not link these failures to the fact that the answers are phrased in observational terms. He leaves open the possibility that although the proposed accounts fail, some other account phrased in observational terms might be satisfactory.[26] This, however, is enough to vindicate Aristotle if he means only that Socrates does not explicitly say that forms are non-sensible, and so in that sense is not committed to the claim that they are; and that seems to be all Aristotle means.[27]

What, now, about separation? Discussions of separation are difficult, partly because 'separation' is used differently by different people.[28] I shall follow Aristotle's lead and say that A is *separate* from B just in case A can exist without B—that is, just in case A can exist whether or not B exists or, equivalently, just in case A exists independently of B.[29] Separation so defined is a modal notion; if A is separate from B, A *can* exist whether or not B exists.[30] (Hence A can be separate from B even if A never actually exists when B does not.) Separation so defined is also a relational notion: to be separate is always to be separate from something.

In the case of forms, the relevant 'something' is sensible particulars (*Met.* 1086b4, 8).[31] So Socratic forms are separate just in case they can exist whether or not there are any corresponding sensible particulars. If forms are universals, then to say that they are separate is to say that they can exist uninstantiated by the corresponding sensible particulars.[32]

Socrates never explicitly says or denies that forms are separate; nor do his ways of characterizing forms seem to commit him one way or the other. He says, for example, that forms are in things (e.g. *Eu.* 5d1–2). But to say that forms are in things is only to say that various sensibles have them, i.e. have the relevant properties. It does not follow from the fact that sensibles have properties that those properties are not separate, i.e. cannot exist unless some corresponding sensible particulars instantiate them.[33] Other evidence seems equally indeterminate. This, however, is enough to vindicate Aristotle's claim that Socrates did not separate universals, i.e. forms, if, as seems to be the case, he means only that Socrates is not committed to separation.[34]

I close my discussion of Socrates by considering two further claims about forms—that they are self-predicative and that they are paradigms. Although Aristotle does not mention these claims in connection with Socrates, they are important in understanding both Plato and also Aristotle's criticism of him in the *Peri ideōn*; and we can get a better grip on Plato's version of these claims if we look first at Socrates' version.

Socrates believes that the form of F cannot be both F and not F; that is, it cannot suffer narrow compresence with respect to F-ness. It can avoid being both F and not F in one of two ways: by being neither F nor not F, or by being F without also being not F. Although the evidence is meagre, Socrates seems to favour the latter option; he seems to believe, that is, that the form of piety is pious, the form of justice is just, and so on. He thus seems to accept *self-predication* (SP), the thesis that any form of F is itself F.[35]

It no doubt sounds odd to say that the form of justice is just, and it may not be correct to do so. But the claim is more intelligible than it may initially appear to be. We have seen that Socrates says that various action-types and character-traits are F and not F—endurance, for example, is both courageous and not courageous. He does not mean that endurance is courageous or not courageous in the very same way in which a person might be; the property of endurance, for example, does not itself stand firm in battle. Rather, endurance is courageous and not courageous in so far as it explains why some things are courageous and why other things are not.[36] Socrates believes, that is, that if x explains y's being F, then x is itself F, though not necessarily in the very same way in which y is F; rather, x is (or may be) F in a *sui generis* way, simply in virtue of its explanatory role.[37]

We can understand self-predications along the same lines. Forms are properties; the form of justice, for example, is the property of justice. Socrates believes that it is the single feature by which all and only just things are just; it is the ultimate source or explanation of what is just about just things, and it never explains why anything is not just. Socrates does not mean that it is just in the very same way in which Aristides was; he means that it is just simply in virtue of its explanatory role. On this view, Socrates has unusually generous criteria for being included in the class of *F*s; something can be a member of the class of *F*s by being the source or explanation of something's being *F* in the ordinary way. We might well object to these criteria; but they do not commit Socrates to the view that the form of justice, for example, can win moral medals.[38]

On behalf of this account of self-predication, it is worth noting that we readily predicate (e.g.) 'justice' in the 'ordinary' way of categorially different types of things—of, for example, people, acts, institutions, laws, and the like. So perhaps predicating it of the property of justice is not as radical a departure from ordinary usage as it may initially seem to be.[39] Further, we have seen that Socrates is not shy about revising our pre-analytic beliefs;[40] so perhaps one new belief he wants us to acquire is that the form of *F* is itself *F*.

We have seen that Socrates believes that the one thing by which all *F*s are *F* is the form of *F*; he also takes this one thing to be a paradigm (*paradeigma*, *Eu.* 6e4–5), so that by looking to it (*apoblepein eis*; *Eu.* 6e4) one can know of any given thing whether or not it is *F*. Plato and Aristotle use *paradeigma* in a variety of ways. Often, for example, they use it simply to mean 'example'.[41] Aristotle once calls his own forms paradigms (*Phys.* 194b26 = *Met.* 1013a27), by which he seems to mean that they are the formal—structural or functional—properties of things; as such, they are explanatory natures. But as we shall see, he believes that Platonic forms are paradigms in a different, and objectionable, sense.

When Socrates says that forms are paradigms, he seems to mean only that they are standards in the sense that in order to know whether *x* is *F*, one must know, and refer to, the form of *F*. For *x* is *F* if and only if it has the property, i.e. form, of *F*; so in order to know that *x* is *F*, one needs to know what *F* is and use that knowledge in explaining how it is that *x* is *F*. (So paradigmatism and self-predication are closely linked. The form of *F* is *F* because it explains the *F*-ness of things; forms are also paradigms in virtue of their explanatory role.) I shall call this *weak paradigmatism*.

As I interpret Socrates—an interpretation that basically agrees with, but goes beyond Aristotle's—he introduces forms for epistemological and metaphysical, but not for semantic reasons. Further, Socratic forms are universals in the sense that they are explanatory properties. The fact that they are self-predicative paradigms does not jeopardize their status as explanatory properties; on the contrary, they are self-predicative paradigms because they are explantory properties.

Having looked at some key features of Socrates' theory of forms and at Aristotle's and my account of them, I now turn to some questions about Plato's theory of forms, and to Aristotle's and my answers to them. What sorts of considerations led Plato to posit forms? Precisely how do Platonic forms differ from Socratic forms? Is Aristotle's account of Plato, like his account of Socrates, accurate?

5. Plato's Heracleiteanism

Aristotle tells us that Plato agreed with Socrates that since knowledge is possible, there must be definitions of universals; he also says that for Plato these universals are forms. So in Aristotle's view both Socratic forms and Platonic forms are universals that are posited to be the basic objects of knowledge and definition. But Aristotle believes that Plato differed from Socrates in some ways. For he says that Plato accepted the Heracleitean view that since sensibles are always changing, there is no knowledge of them; since knowledge is possible, there must be forms conceived as non-sensible objects of knowledge that are not in flux. Aristotle believes that both Plato's Heracleiteanism and his view that forms are non-sensible distinguish Plato from Socrates. He also claims that unlike Socrates, Plato separated forms or universals from sensible particulars. Aristotle sides with Socrates here, claiming that separation is responsible for the difficulties in Plato's theory of forms (1086b6–7).

What sort of flux or change, in fact and in Aristotle's view, does Plato appeal to in his middle-dialogue arguments for the existence of forms?[42] Typically when we think of change, we think of the succession of opposites. To say that something undergoes succession of opposites is to say that it is F at t_1, but ceases to be F and becomes not F at some later time t_2. For example, I was fat before I went on a diet, and then I became thin. Commentators have discussed various sorts of succession in connection with Plato. For example, there is *moderate Heracleiteanism* (MH), according to which objects at every moment undergo succession of opposites in some respect or other. There is also *extreme Heracleiteanism* (EH), according to which objects at every moment undergo succession of opposites in every respect. In addition, things can come into or go out of existence. I shall call this GCH, for the Heracleiteanism that, as Aristotle might put it, involves the generation and corruption of things.[43]

In addition to succession, there is a phenomenon that interests Socrates, the compresence of opposites. Standing firm in battle is both courageous (in some circumstances) and not courageous (in others); returning what one owes is both just (in some circumstances) and not just (in others) (*Rep.* 331c).

One might think that we need not consider compresence here; for our concern is the sort of change that Plato, both in fact and in Aristotle's view, appeals to in the middle dialogues in arguing that there are forms. And surely compresence is not a type of change? However, we can certainly speak of compresence in temporal terms, whether or not in doing so we mean to count it as a type of change. For example, bright colour changes from being beautiful in, say, this painting to being ugly in this different one (where it is merely gaudy); I change from being tall (in relation to one person) to being short (in relation to another). Hence if Plato or Aristotle speaks in temporal terms, we should not automatically infer that they have succession rather than compresence in mind.

In any case, the crucial question here is not whether compresence is in fact a type of change, but whether Plato or Aristotle thinks it is; and there is some evidence that they do. In the *Theaetetus* (152d2–e9), for example, Plato counts cases of compresence, along with cases of succession, as all alike illustrating the thesis that 'nothing ever is, but things are always coming to be (*gignetai*)' (152e1); both compresence and succession are types of 'flux and change' (152e8). Aristotle also sometimes uses the language of change for compresence. In the *Nicomachean Ethics* (1134b24–1135a5), for example, he contrasts what is naturally just and what is just by convention. What is naturally just is 'unchangeable (*akinēton*) and the same everywhere' (1134b25–6); what is conventionally just changes (*kinoumena*; 1134b27) from city to city. He seems to mean that certain action-types have tokens, some of which are just (in one city, in virtue of its laws) and others unjust (in another city, in virtue of its different laws). For example, it is just for the Callatian Indians to eat their dead fathers, but it is not just for the Greeks to do so.[44]

To say that Plato and Aristotle use the language of change in discussing compresence is not to say that they take compresence to be a type of succession, nor is it to say that they are confused about the nature of change. It is only to say that they use 'change' in a broad sense that includes both compresence and succession. Given this broad use of 'change', we cannot tell from the mere use of the language of change whether compresence or succession is at issue.[45]

Let us assume, then, that when Plato argues from the flux of sensibles to the existence of forms, and when Aristotle says that Plato so argues, it is possible that they have compresence in mind. For all we have said so far, however, it is also possible that they have some sort of succession in mind. Can we choose between these options? Three main answers have been proposed: (i) both Plato and Aristotle have succession in mind (the usual view is that they have EH in mind); (ii) both Plato and Aristotle have compresence in mind; (iii) Plato has compresence in mind, but Aristotle mistakenly believes that he has succession in mind.[46]

I myself doubt that Plato ever accepted EH, and I shall simply assume here that he did not.[47] If he never accepted EH, then if we can avoid saying that Aristotle ascribes EH to him, that is surely desirable. I think we can avoid this;[48] and so I shall from now on generally ignore EH. However, that still leaves us with (i)–(iii); all we have ruled out so far are versions of (i) and (iii) that appeal to EH.

One might argue that Aristotle has some other sort of succession (MH or GCH) in mind, on the ground that this is required by the correct interpretation of Plato. However, several commentators have recently argued—and I concur—that in the middle dialogues Plato argues that there are forms by appealing not to the succession but to the compresence of opposites.[49] Thus in, for example, *Phaedo* 74bc (a passage sometimes thought to inaugurate the middle dialogues' theory of forms) Plato argues that since sensible equals are 'equal to one, unequal to another', there must be a non-sensible form of equal which is not at all unequal. The interpretation of this passage is controversial; but on the interpretation I favour it claims that because sensibles suffer compresence, there must be non-sensible forms that escape compresence.[50] In *Rep.* 5 (479ad) Plato says that each of the many beautifuls (*ta polla kala*, 479a3)—sensible properties like bright colour—is both beautiful and ugly; beauty therefore cannot be defined in sensible terms, and so there must be a non-sensible form of beauty that escapes compresence. In *Rep.* 7 (523–5) he argues from the claim that any sensible length makes some things large and others small to the conclusion that there is a form of largeness and one of smallness. In all these crucial passages, and there are others as well,[51] Plato argues that there are forms by appealing to facts not about succession but about compresence. This seems to be his view of what he does too; for when in the *Parmenides* he looks back on the origins of the theory of forms, he mentions compresence, but not succession, as the motivating factor (127d–130a).[52]

In all these passages, the sort of compresence at issue is what I earlier called narrow compresence. Bright colour, so described, is both beautiful and ugly; three inches, in so far as it is three inches, makes some things long and others short. Further, like Socrates, Plato focuses on compresence in sensible properties.[53]

It is true that Plato sometimes, even soon after passages that focus on compresence, speaks in more temporal-sounding language. Consider, for example, the following passage from the *Phaedo*:[54]

But what about the many beautifuls—e.g. men or horses or cloaks or anything else at all of that kind—or equals or any other things that bear the same name as those? Are they always in the same state, or are they altogether opposite to those others, and virtually never in any way in the same state, either in relation to themselves or to one another? (78d10–e4)

Although this passage is sometimes taken as evidence of EH or MH,[55] it more probably says that classes of sensible objects suffer compresence when they are described in terms of sensible properties. 'The many beautiful men', that is, refers not to each particular beautiful man, but to classes of beautiful men (e.g. the class of tall, thin men, and the class of tall, dark men); each such class changes from being beautiful to being ugly, in so far as some tall, thin men are handsome, others ugly, and so on.[56] The same interpretation explains Plato's claim in, for example, *Rep.* 6 (485b2–3), that sensibles belong to the realm of *genesis* and forms to the realm of *ousia*: sensibles come to be *F* and not *F* in that they suffer compresence, whereas forms are always and only *F*. On this view, '*genesis*' and '*ousia*' are used without a grammatical complement, for coming to be *F* and not *F*, on the one hand, and for being always and only *F*, on the other.[57] There is a clear advantage to this interpretation of *Phd.* 78de and *Rep.* 6 (485b2–3). For just before these passages, Plato argues that since sensibles suffer compresence, there must be non-sensible forms that escape compresence. If the later passages advert only to compresence, then he is entitled to say what he says; but he would not be justified in suddenly shifting to a claim about succession.[58]

Now in the three *Metaphysics* passages with which we began, Aristotle says that Plato takes the fact that sensibles are always changing to require the existence of forms. Aristotle does not say what sort of change he has in mind, and the immediate context does not decide the issue. But Plato and Aristotle both count compresence as a type of change, and in the middle dialogues Plato takes compresence but not succession to require the existence of forms. Since Aristotle can be read as saying that Plato takes compresence to require the existence of forms, and since it is only if he is so read that he interprets Plato correctly, it is reasonable to read him in this way. I thus provisionally conclude that in the three *Metaphysics* passages Aristotle correctly claims that Plato posited forms because of compresence in sensibles, and so I favour option (ii) of the three options mentioned above. As we go through the *Peri ideōn*, we shall ask whether it provides evidence for, or against, this view.

6. Compresence, knowledge, and separation

Why does Plato take the compresence of opposites to require the existence of non-sensible forms that escape compresence? Aristotle rightly says that the reasons are metaphysical and epistemological. The metaphysical reason is especially prominent in the famous *aitia*-passage in the

Phaedo (96a ff.), where Plato lays out criteria for adequate explanations.[59] In his view, if x is F and not F, it cannot explain why anything is F; it cannot, in other words, be that in virtue of which anything is F. Since some sensible properties of F suffer compresence, reference to them does not explain why anything is F, and so they cannot be what F-ness is. Since explanation is possible, in these cases things are F in virtue of a non-sensible property, the form of F. So Plato concludes that 'if anything else is beautiful besides the beautiful itself, it is so for no other reason than that it participates in the beautiful' (*Phd.* 100c4–6). Or again, it is not because of 'bright colour or shape or anything else of that sort' (100d1–2) that anything is beautiful; rather 'it is because of the beautiful that all beautiful things are beautiful' (100d7–8). For sensible properties suffer compresence in so far as bright colour, for example, is sometimes beautiful, sometimes ugly. In Plato, the Socratic view that the form of F is the one thing by which all Fs are F becomes the view that forms are *aitiai*, causal or explanatory factors—at least in certain cases, things are as they are because they participate in non-sensible forms that escape compresence.

This metaphysical reason for positing forms has epistemological repercussions. For like Socrates, Plato thinks that knowledge requires explanation;[60] since he believes that in at least some cases explanation requires reference to forms, he also believes that in these cases one can have knowledge only if one knows the relevant forms. Since knowledge in these cases is possible, there must be forms.

This epistemological reason for positing forms is especially prominent in *Rep.* 5–7, where Plato asks the 'What is F?' question and assumes that one needs to know what F is in order to know anything about F—where, as with Socrates, the knowledge at issue is knowledge as it contrasts with belief, and where definitions are real definitions.[61] The sight-lovers believe that we can answer the question 'What is beauty?' by simply mentioning the many beautifuls (*ta polla kala*, 479d3)—sensible properties like bright colour. For in their view each such sensible property explains some range of cases. Bright colour, for example, explains what makes this Klee painting beautiful; sombre colour explains what makes this Rembrandt painting beautiful; and so on.

Against the sight-lovers, Plato points out that each such property suffers compresence since (e.g.) some brightly coloured things are beautiful, others are ugly. In his view, if x is F and not F, it cannot explain why *anything* is F; so no such property can explain why anything is beautiful. Further, in his view as in Socrates', we can explain why Fs are F only if F-ness is some *one* thing (479d3), the same in all cases; so F-ness cannot be a disjunction of properties. It is therefore a single non-sensible property, the form of F. This is required, in Plato's view, by the possibility of knowledge.

Like Socrates, then, Plato posits forms as universals whose existence is necessary for explanation and so for the possibility of knowledge. He also agrees with Socrates that *F*-ness itself cannot be not *F*. Unlike Socrates, however, Plato insists that forms are non-sensible. A related difference is that Socrates countenances a form for every property. But as Plato points out in, for example, *Rep.* 7 (523–5), only some predicates have sensible instances that suffer narrow compresence—'thick' and 'thin' are such predicates, but 'finger' is not.[62]

Like Socrates' arguments for the existence of forms, Plato's argument from compresence posits forms to explain, not the meaningfulness of general terms or linguistic understanding or even belief, but the possibility of explanation and knowledge. Indeed, the sight-lovers in *Rep.* 5 have rather sophisticated beliefs even though they do not countenance forms. Similarly, in *Rep.* 7 (523–5) sight can identify examples of thick and thin things, of hard and soft things; what it cannot do is define thickness and thinness, hardness and softness. For it is confined, naturally enough, to sensible properties, but in Plato's view one cannot define thickness and thinness and so on in such terms.[63]

Nor does the argument from compresence take forms to be particulars. Like Socrates, Plato assumes that a correct answer to a 'What is *F*?' question will specify the property of *F*. His interlocutors generally seem to agree; at least, their answers are typically phrased in terms of properties (e.g. bright colour). The dispute between Plato and his interlocutors is about the nature of various properties: the sight-lovers take them to be sensible; Plato takes them to be non-sensible forms.[64]

The argument from compresence takes forms to be the *basic* objects of knowledge—one must know them in order to have any knowledge at all. It does not follow that forms are the *only* objects of knowledge. Nor is it clear why the fact that something suffers compresence should make it unknowable. Since bright colour is both beautiful and ugly, it cannot be what beauty is; but it does not follow that we cannot know that bright colour is both beautiful and ugly, or that something is brightly coloured. Yet it is often thought that Plato takes sensibles to be unknowable, and it is often thought that Aristotle interprets Plato in this way.

I have argued elsewhere, however, that Plato is committed only to the claim that forms are the basic objects of knowledge, in the sense that in order to know anything at all one must know them; he leaves open the possibility that if one knows them one can use that knowledge in such a way as to acquire knowledge of other things.[65] It is tempting to suppose that Aristotle agrees. To be sure, *Met.* 1. 6 and 13. 4 can be read as saying that Plato takes whatever changes to be unknowable. But perhaps Aristotle means only that Plato takes whatever changes to be unknowable in itself, independently of its relation to forms, so that whatever changes cannot be the basic object of definition or knowledge. *Met.* 13. 9 seems congenial to this interpretation. For Aristotle says there that 'it is not possible to acquire knowledge without the universal'—a claim that plainly leaves open the possibility of knowing more than universals. Further, although he repeats the claim that Plato thinks that sensibles are always changing, he does not say that in Plato's view that makes them unknowable. So perhaps Aristotle means to commit Plato only to the claim that forms are the basic objects of knowledge.

The argument from compresence shows that forms are *different* from both sensible particulars and sensible properties. But it does not show that forms are *separate*, i.e. that they can exist whether or not the corresponding sensible particulars exist. Difference does not imply separation. Yet it is sometimes thought that Plato, both in fact and in Aristotle's view, argues in this invalid way.[66]

The *Metaphysics* passages, however, do not saddle Plato with this invalid argument. *Met.* 1. 6 says only that flux (i.e. on my interpretation, compresence) shows that forms are different (*hetera*; cf. *Phd.* 74a11, c7) from sensibles; separation is not mentioned. In 13. 4, Aristotle says that Plato separated forms; but he does not say why Plato did so. He mentions separation not as the conclusion of an argument, but simply as a distinguishing feature of the Platonic theory. In 13. 9, however, Aristotle explains (III (1–6); see sect. 2) that Plato inferred from the flux of sensibles that there must be forms conceived as non-sensible universals that are the basic objects of knowledge and definition. He adds (III (8–10)) that Plato took forms to be substances, i.e. basic beings;[67] since substances must be separate, forms are separate. Aristotle seems to believe, then, that the 'flux argument' shows only that forms are non-sensible universals that are the basic objects of knowledge and definition; that forms are separate follows only with the aid of further premisses. These further premisses give Plato a valid argument for separation.

I think Aristotle is right not to claim that Plato argues from the flux of sensibles to the separation of forms; at least, Plato never does so explicitly.[68] But is Aristotle right to say that Plato takes forms to be separate, if for other reasons? It is difficult to be sure. For one thing, Plato never *says* that forms are separate; he never, that is, uses any form or cognate of '*chōrizein*' of forms, at least not in the relevant sense.[69] Nor do any of his explicit arguments imply that forms are separate.

In the *Timaeus*, however, Plato seems to be committed to separation. For he says there that forms are everlasting and that the cosmos is not everlasting; there has always been a form of man, but there have not always been particular men. It follows that the form of man existed before the cosmos came into being, and so it existed when there were no sensible particular men; hence it can exist whether or not they do, and so it is separate. Now in the middle dialogues Plato sometimes says that forms are everlasting. But he does not say that the cosmos is not everlasting, so the *Timaeus'* route to separation is not mentioned.[70] Indeed, nothing said in the middle dialogues seems to me to involve clear commitment to separation.[71] None the less, separation fits well with the tenor of the middle dialogues, and the casual way in which separation emerges in the *Timaeus* perhaps suggests that Plato takes it for granted. So I shall assume that Aristotle is right to say that Plato separated forms, though it is important to be clear that Plato never argues, or even says, that forms are separate.

Aristotle argues that since forms are separate, they are particulars (13. 9). Since he also takes forms to be universals, he concludes that forms are both universals and particulars. But as I (following Aristotle) understand separation, the claim that forms—universals—are separate is simply the claim that they can exist whether or not any corresponding sensible particulars exist. Why does Aristotle take this to show that forms are particulars? The answer is that he believes that universals exist when and only when they are instantiated;[72] in his view, only substance particulars are separate (see e.g. *Met.* 1028a33–4). So he claims that if forms are separate they are (substance) particulars because *he* accepts the controversial view that universals cannot exist uninstantiated. He is therefore not convicting Plato of internal inconsistency: he means that Plato's views do not square with the truth. He sees that Plato introduces forms simply to be universals; that they are particulars results only if we accept the controversial Aristotelian assumption, which Aristotle takes Plato to reject, that universals cannot exist uninstantiated. Aristotle's complaints about separation therefore rely on one of the argumentative strategies described in Ch. 2.8: he intrudes into Platonism assumptions he accepts but that he thinks Plato rejects. Once we see that this is what Aristotle is doing, we can see that although he claims that forms are particulars, there is a sense in which he agrees with me that they are, or are intended to be, only universals.

7. Self-predication and paradigmatism

I conclude my discussion of Plato by considering two further claims about forms whose counterparts we looked at in concluding our discussion of Socrates: that they are self-predicative and that they are paradigms. Though Aristotle does not discuss these claims in the *Metaphysics* passages, they are relevant to the interpretation of the *Peri ideōn*.

We have seen that in Plato's view, if something is *F* and not *F*, it cannot be the form of *F*. Like Socrates, Plato seems to assume that the form of *F* escapes compresence not by being neither *F* nor not *F*, but by being *F* without also being not *F*; the form of equal is itself equal, the form of beauty is itself beautiful, and so on.[73] Plato thus seems to accept self-predication (SP). But what is his version of it? Here I shall discuss just two accounts, *narrow self-predication* (NSP) and *broad self-predication* (BSP).[74] On both accounts, to say that the form of F is F is to assert a predication claim rather than, for example, an identity claim.[75] But NSP and BSP differ over how, in what way, the form of F is F.

(i) *Narrow self-predication* (NSP):[76] On this view the form of F is F in roughly the way in which sensible particulars are F; so, for example, the form of dog, if there is one, can wag its tail; the form of white, if there is one, is coloured white. Of course, there must be some differences in the ways in which sensible particulars and the form of F are F, since (according to Plato) the form of F is perfectly F whereas sensible Fs are imperfectly F. But on NSP the differences consist only in such facts as that the form of large, for example, is the largest thing there could be, the form of small is the smallest thing there could be, and so on. NSP seems to lead to absurdity; how, for example, could the incorporeal form of large be the largest thing there is?[77] But even if NSP is absurd, Plato might none the less be committed to it.

(ii) *Broad self-predication* (BSP):[78] On this view, as on NSP, the form of F is predicatively F; the form of F is a member of the class of Fs. But BSP countenances more ways of being F, of being included in the class of Fs, than NSP does. In particular, on BSP the form of F is F in quite a different way from the way in which sensible particulars are F.[79] For example, any particular sensible object that is equal is equal in virtue of having the same measures as something. But when Plato suggests that the form of equal is equal, he does not mean that it has the same measures as something. He means that it is equal because it explains why particular sensible things are equal to one another; it does this because it is the non-sensible determinable property of equality. For Plato as for Socrates, that is, if x explains y's being F, x is itself F, simply in virtue of its explanatory role. Since the property (form) of F explains the F-ness of F things, it is predicatively F, though in a *sui generis* way, simply in virtue of its explanatory role.[80]

Now we saw before that when Socrates says that endurance is both courageous and not courageous, he means that the character-trait of endurance explains not only what is courageous about some actions but also what is foolish, and so not courageous, about other actions.[81] He presupposes that courage itself (the character-trait) must be courageous without also being not courageous. But all he means is that the form of courage must explain the courage of all the courageous things there are, and it must never explain why anything is not courageous. For Socrates, then, the form of F is F and not also not F because it explains why all F things are F and it never explains why anything is not F. So Socrates' version of SP is BSP.

I think Plato's version of self-predication is also best interpreted as BSP.[82] We have seen that like Socrates, Plato readily speaks of properties as being both F and not F—he says, for example, that sensible properties of beauty (e.g. bright colour) are both beautiful and ugly. I think he means what Socrates means, that bright colour no more explains why some things are beautiful than it explains why other things are ugly. If Socrates and Plato mean the same thing in saying that various properties are F and not F, why should we take them to mean something different in saying that the form of F is F?

The main reason, of course, is that it has been thought that Platonic forms are so different from Socratic forms; in particular, it has been thought that whereas Socratic forms are properties, Platonic forms are perfect particulars. However, on the account of Platonic forms that I have been developing, they are properties and not particulars. If this account is right, and if my account of Socrates on self-predication is also right, then BSP is a natural interpretation of Plato's self-predication assumption. There is of course a two-way street here. Platonic forms are sometimes thought to be particulars partly because SP is true of them. But if I can provide an account of SP that allows Platonic forms to be properties, then that removes one main reason for supposing that they are particulars.

Like Socrates, Plato occasionally claims that forms are paradigms.[83] In doing so, I think he once again means basically what Socrates means— that forms are paradigms in so far as they are standards, in the sense that one can know what it is to be F only if one knows, and refers to, the form of F.[84] For the form of F is the property of F; it is therefore the ultimate explanation of why Fs are F. Since knowledge requires explanation, one can know that something is F only if one knows the form of F in virtue of which Fs are F. (So for Plato, as for Socrates, forms are self-predicative paradigms in virtue of their explanatory role.) To be sure, Plato goes beyond Socrates in so far as he offers a more detailed explanation of what entitles forms to be paradigms. For he seems to think that forms are paradigms because they are perfect whereas sensibles are imperfect, and because sensible Fs are F derivatively from the form of F, whereas the form of F is not derivatively F.[85] Socrates does not make these claims. So let us say that whereas Socrates accepts only weak paradigmatism, Plato accepts *perfect paradigmatism*. However, although the language of perfection and imperfection is new, the claim it is intended to capture is in a way not new. For in Plato's view, the form of F is perfectly F only because it enjoys the sorts of features that Socrates ascribes to forms[86]— because it is F and not also not F (that is to say, because it explains why all Fs are F and it never explains why anything is not F), and so on. On this account, just as the fact that forms are self-predicative does not jeopardize their status as universals, so the fact that they are perfect paradigms does not jeopardize their status as universals. On the contrary, the fact that forms are universals—and so are explanatory—explains the sense in which they are self-predicative, perfect paradigms.

8. Conclusion

Socrates and Plato are often thought to be at loggerheads on a variety of topics. But if the argument of this chapter has been correct, they share some important views. Both Socratic and Platonic forms are universals or properties, introduced for metaphysical and epistemological reasons; they are not perfect particulars or meanings.[87] Both Socrates and Plato accept SP, but their version of it is best construed as BSP. Neither Socrates nor Plato denies that sensibles are knowable. Neither takes the sensible world to be in EH. Nor do they argue that there are forms by appealing to any sort of succession,[88] although they both appeal to compresence.

There are, however, some differences between Socrates and Plato. For example, Socrates does not say that forms are non-sensible; Plato repeatedly emphasizes that they are. Socrates is not committed to separation; but at least in the *Timaeus*, Plato is committed to it. Plato, but not Socrates, insists that forms are perfect and that sensibles are imperfect. But even here, it would be wrong to see a sharp break. For example, although Plato but not Socrates is committed to separation, Plato is like Socrates in so far as he does not argue, or even say, that forms are separate; commitment to separation emerges more indirectly. Similarly, in claiming that forms are non-sensible and perfect, Plato is not veering off in a radically new direction. Rather, he is offering what he takes to be the most plausible defence of Socrates, or developing Socrates' views in what he takes to be the most plausible way. In particular, Platonic forms are not different entities from Socratic forms. Rather, Plato is attempting to offer what he views as a better account of the same entities.

One might argue that there must be something wrong with my account, on the ground that Aristotle thinks that Socrates and Plato differ more radically than I have suggested. For example, in *Met.* 13. 9 he says that Platonic forms are not only universals but also particulars; he never suggests that Socratic forms are particulars. Or again, elsewhere he seems to commit Plato to NSP and to a more objectionable version of paradigmatism than I have described; he does not suggest that Socrates is committed to NSP or to an objectionable version of paradigmatism. Surely he would know?

But matters here are less straightforward than one might take them to be. For as I suggested in Ch. 2.8, Aristotle's accounts and criticisms of Plato's arguments involve a variety of complex strategies. Once we see how this is so, we shall see that in some ways the differences between Aristotle and me are more apparent than real. I have already provided one example of this in describing Aristotle's claim that separation implies particularity; other examples will emerge as we proceed.

In this chapter, I hope to have introduced some of the central issues that inevitably face anyone thinking about the theory of forms, and to have provided a partial and tentative account of my own and Aristotle's views about some of them. In subsequent chapters, we shall see to what extent the *Peri ideōn* confirms this account.

5

The Arguments from the Sciences: Forms and Knowledge

1. Introduction

The first arguments in the *Peri ideōn* are the so-called Arguments from the Sciences. According to these three arguments (I–III), the existence of sciences or branches of knowledge (*epistēmai*)[1] requires the existence of forms. Aristotle levels the same two objections against each of these arguments. In IV he argues that they are all invalid arguments for the existence of forms (but valid arguments for the existence of his own *koina*).[2] In V he argues that if they proved that there are any forms at all, they would prove that there are artefact forms—a result he claims the Platonists would not welcome.

The Arguments from the Sciences are the only arguments in the *Peri ideōn* that attempt to prove that there are forms by explicitly appealing to considerations specifically about knowledge. In the last chapter we saw that, in the three key *Metaphysics* passages, Aristotle says that Plato introduced forms because of considerations about knowledge. So perhaps attention to the Arguments from the Sciences will help us to understand what view Aristotle attributes to Plato in those passages: whether, for example, Aristotle takes the relevant sort of change to be compresence or succession, and whether he thinks that in Plato's view forms are the basic, or the only, objects of knowledge.

The Arguments from the Sciences are often thought to argue that since (*a*) sensibles are always changing (GCH, MH, EH), (*b*) they are unknowable.[3] If they argue in this way, they pose a challenge to a tentative conclusion reached in the last chapter, that in Aristotle's view (at least in the three *Metaphysics* passages), Plato argues instead that since (*a'*) some sensibles exhibit compresence of opposites, (*b'*) they cannot be the basic objects of knowledge (although they might none the less be knowable).

How exactly do I–III argue for the existence of forms? Are Aristotle's objections to I–III reasonable? Is Plato is committed to any of I–III? In this chapter I discuss the first question and Aristotle's first objection, about validity. In the next chapter I consider Aristotle's second objection, about artefact forms; in Ch. 7 I ask about Plato's commitments.

2. The first Argument from the Sciences

The first Argument from the Sciences (AS I) may be formulated as follows:

I

(1) Every science works by referring to some one and the same thing (*hen ti kai to auto*).

(2) No science works by referring to particulars (*kath' hekasta*).

(3) Therefore for every science there is something other than (*allo*), besides (*para*), sensibles (*aisthēta*), which is everlasting (*aidion*)[4] and a paradigm (*paradeigma*) of the things that come to be within that science (*tōn kath' hekastēn epistēmēn ginomenōn*).

(4) Therefore, there are forms.

AS I(1) says that every science works by referring to some one and the same thing in its domain.[5] Plato and Aristotle sometimes use 'refers to' in connection with something basic or primary, such that one explains the less basic by referring it to, explaining it in terms of, the more basic.[6] This is the usage at issue here; the point is that in order to know anything, one must be able to explain it in terms of something suitably basic.[7] So let us say that I(1) claims that the function of every science is to explain everything in its domain in terms of some one and the same *basic object*.

On this reading, I(1) does not restrict knowledge to basic objects; it claims only that in order to know anything, one must be able to explain it in terms of the relevant basic objects. So even though forms turn out to be the only basic objects of the sciences, it does not follow that they are the only objects of knowledge; it follows only that in order to know anything besides forms, one must be able to explain it in terms of the appropriate forms. AS I thus does not restrict knowledge to forms.[8]

The claim that every science works by referring to some *one and the same* basic object involves the claim that, in order to know anything about *F*s, one needs to know the one thing it is to be *F*, in virtue of which all *F*s are *F*.[9] I(1) presumably takes each basic object to be (in Aristotle's terms) one in genus or definition; for these are the sorts of oneness that are relevant to knowledge, which is what is at issue here.[10] If something is one in genus or definition, then it is a genuine property. Science or knowledge aims to understand the nature of the world, how things are; hence it aims to discover properties that are one in so far as they 'carve at the natural joints', by being the real kinds (species and genera, objects of real definitions) that there are. There is a science of health, but none of grue; for grue is not a genuine unity, but an arbitrarily defined notion that fails to pick out an explanatory feature of the world. So like the three *Metaphysics* passages explored in Ch. 4, AS I takes forms to be explanatory properties, since it takes them to be genuine unities, a knowledge of which is necessary for any knowledge at all.[11]

On the account I have provided, the 'one and the same' requirement does not say or imply that the basic objects of knowledge must be everlasting or unchanging. 'One and the same' indicates only that some *one* property is to be invoked in explaining a variety of objects.[12]

I(2) claims that *kath' hekasta* cannot be the basic objects of any science. Aristotle uses '*kath' hekasta*' in two ways, both for particulars in contrast to all universals (Callias, as opposed to man or animal) and for low-level types or properties, which may be said to be particular in relation to something more universal (man in contrast to animal).[13] Are the *kath' hekasta* at issue here particulars (as they contrast with all universals), particular types, or both?[14] Since Aristotle takes AS I to be a valid argument for his own universals, *kath' hekasta* should include all particulars. For otherwise, in saying that the sciences work by referring to something other than *kath' hekasta*, it would be left open that they work by referring to some sort of particular. The crucial question is thus whether *kath' hekasta* are only particulars or also particular types.[15]

One might suppose that *kath' hekasta* are only particulars on the ground that Aristotle identifies *kath' hekasta* with sensibles (*aisthēta*),[16] and one might think that all sensibles are particulars. However, Aristotle recognizes not only sensible particulars (e.g. Callias) but also sensible properties (e.g. red as opposed to virtue).[17]

Aristotle seems to identify *kath' hekasta* not only with *aisthēta* but also with *ginomena* (things that come to be). '*Ginomena*' can be used to indicate both coming into existence and also change in the sense of succession; and we have seen that Plato sometimes uses it without a grammatical complement to indicate compresence. If '*ginomena*' were used in any of these ways here, it might provide a clue about the scope and defect of *kath' hekasta*.[18] But in the present context '*ginomena*' is used with a preposition (*kata*)—the things that come to be according to, or within, each science (79. 8). This suggests that it means something like 'the things that are, or are considered to be, the objects of the sciences' or 'the things grouped together as being the objects of the sciences'.[19] So understood, '*ginomena*' provides no clues about the scope or defect of *kath' hekasta*; *ginomena* are simply the non-basic objects of the sciences, whatever they turn out to be.

They turn out to be something other than *kath' hekasta*. But why is this? Unfortunately, AS I does not tell us; it says *that* no science works by referring to *kath' hekasta*, but it does not say *why* this is so. But presumably the implicit reason is that they are not one and the same. *Kath' hekasta*, that is, whether considered individually or collectively, are not the one thing in virtue of which all *F*s are *F*; and so reference to *kath' hekasta* cannot explain what *F*-ness as such is since *F*-ness is the one thing in virtue of which all *F*s are *F*. Nor do *kath' hekasta*, considered in themselves, have the sort of unity that basic objects must have. AS II provides further insight into this implicit line of reasoning.

If AS I disqualifies *kath' hekasta* from being the basic objects of knowledge on the ground that they are not one and the same, then it does not disqualify them on the ground that they change (MH, EH) or are not everlasting. For as we have seen, the 'one and the same' requirement indicates not unchangeability or everlastingness, but that some one property is to be invoked in explaining a variety of cases. Further, if this is the reason for disqualifying them, then low-level universals easily fall within their scope.

I(3) infers from (1) and (2) that the basic objects of the sciences are everlasting, non-sensible paradigms. Since *kath' hekasta* and sensibles are the same, it is legitimate to infer, as in (3), that the basic objects of knowledge are non-sensible. But it is not legitimate to infer, as in (3), that the basic objects of knowledge are everlasting. At least, we have seen that the 'one and the same' requirement does not imply this; nor is it clear what else in the context might do so.[20]

What about the inference to paradigmatism? We saw in Ch. 4.4 that Socrates takes forms to be *weak paradigms*: forms are standards in that one can know whether or not something is *F* only if one knows, and refers to, the form of *F*; for the form of *F* is the property of *F*, and things are *F* by having the property of *F*. In the middle dialogues, however, Plato takes forms to be *perfect paradigms*. That is, he claims that the form of *F* can function as a standard in the Socratic sense because it is perfectly *F* and other *F* things are *F* derivatively from it.

Aristotle would take an inference to weak paradigmatism to be valid, for in his view sciences refer to weak paradigms; if one wants to know anything about (e.g.) health, one needs to know what health is. And the paradigms in (3) seem to be weak paradigms, since the language of perfection and imperfection is not used. But Aristotle would take an inference to perfect paradigmatism to be invalid, on the ground that AS I does not provide an account of perfection or say anything to explain why its paradigms should be taken to be perfect.

Whether or not the inference to paradigmatism is justified, it is clear why Aristotle says that AS I is invalid. For there is no reading of the argument on which he would believe that both (3) and (4) are validly inferred. For example, even if we allow that (3) is validly inferred, Aristotle would say that it does not imply (4) since, in his view, the existence of non-sensible, everlasting weak paradigms is not sufficient for the existence of Platonic forms.[21] If, on the other hand, (3) says that there are non-sensible, everlasting perfect paradigms, then Aristotle would say that it implies (4).[22] But we have seen that if (3) is so read, then he would take it to be invalidly inferred.

Aristotle may also have another invalidity in mind. For in the *Posterior Analytics* (cf. *APo.* 77a5–9), he says:

Further, if there is some one account (*heis logos*) and the universal is not homonymous, it will exist not less than some of the particulars (*eniōn tōn kata meros*) do, but actually more, in so far as imperishable things (*aphtharta*) are found among universals, whereas particulars are perishable (*phtharta*). And further, it is not necessary to believe that this is a thing besides (*para*) these on the ground that it reveals one thing. (85b15–19.)

Aristotle means that although the existence of a single account implies that there are universals, it does not imply their separation. Similarly, then, perhaps Aristotle believes that although the 'one and the same' requirement implies that there are universals, it does not imply their separation.[23]

Although Aristotle takes AS I to be an invalid argument for the existence of Platonic forms, he claims that its premisses imply that there are universals. This claim is justified if (as in *DI* 17a38–b1) he takes particulars and universals to be exhaustive and if in AS I *kath' hekasta* include all particulars. The idea would then be that since the sciences do not work by referring to *kath' hekasta* but must work by referring to something, they work by referring to universals; hence there are universals.[24] If Aristotle reasons in this way, then there is a second reason to suppose that AS I takes forms to be universals;[25] for otherwise Aristotle's claim that AS I is a valid argument for the existence of universals is not justified. Aristotle's point is that although Plato sees that the possibility of knowledge requires the existence of universals, he misconceives their nature.

3. The second Argument from the Sciences

The contrast between 'determinately and indeterminately . . .' has no meaning at all when it is simply set down without any further explanation, as it is here. (Descartes, *Reply to Seventh Objections*, AT vii. 520/CSM ii. 354.)

The second Argument from the Sciences (AS II) may be formulated as follows:

II

(1) The objects of the sciences are (*esti*).
(2) Particulars (*kath' hekasta*) are indefinite (*apeira*) and indeterminate (*ahorista*).
(3) The objects of the sciences are determinate (*hōrismena*).
(4) Therefore, there are objects besides (*para*) particulars (*kath' hekasta*).
(5) Therefore there are forms.

AS II(1) claims that the basic objects of every science are (*esti*).[26] '*Esti*' can be used existentially, predicatively, and veridically. (It can also be used for identity, but that use need not concern us here.) Hence II(1) might mean that (1*a*) the basic objects of the sciences exist,[27] that (1*b*) the basic objects of the sciences are *F* (for some property *F* to be specified in the context), or that (1*c*) the basic objects of the sciences are true.[28] (1*c*) is the familiar claim, accepted by both Plato and Aristotle, that knowledge implies truth;[29] it therefore specifies what we might call the *content* of knowledge (namely, true propositions). (1*a*) and (1*b*), by contrast, are about the nonpropositional basic *objects* of knowledge. Since the only candidates considered for being basic objects of knowlege are particulars and forms, AS II presumably intends (1*a*) or (1*b*) rather than (1*c*). Of the two, I am inclined to favour (1*a*), for otherwise the inference to (4) is unwarranted. (2)–(3) tell us that *kath' hekasta* do not meet the conditions (basic)[30] objects of knowledge must satisfy. Without the assumption that there are objects of knowledge, it does not follow that there are any objects besides *kath' hekasta*: perhaps there are only *kath' hekasta* and so no objects of knowledge.[31] Further, (2) and (3) plainly make predicative claims; (3), for example, specifies a property any (basic) object of knowledge must have. If (1) is read as (1*b*), it is simply elliptical for (3); if it is read as (1*a*), it is a distinctively different premiss and so makes more of a contribution to the argument. I shall assume, then, that (1) is to be read as (1*a*). So read, it expresses realism about the objects of knowledge; the point is that knowledge requires the existence of certain sorts of objects.

The basic objects of every science exist, then (1); and they also have certain properties (3). But what are the relevant objects and properties? Like AS I, AS II rules out sensible *kath' hekasta*.[32] But unlike AS I, AS II explicitly says why it does so: because sensible particulars are *apeira* and *ahorista*, whereas the (basic) objects of the sciences must be *hōrismena*.

'*Ahoriston*' means 'indeterminate', 'indefinite', or 'indefinable'; the indeterminacy can be quantitative or qualitative. That is, it can be indeterminate how many of something we are dealing with—for example, how many particulars instantiate a given universal, or how many properties a given thing has. (This second sort of quantitative indeterminacy shows that a single thing can be quantitatively indeterminate.) Or there can be some indeterminacy in the nature of, or in a given description of, some or all of a thing's properties. If, for example, we say only that something is hot, or hotter than something else, it is indeterminate what degree of heat it has; similarly, reference to a given property *F* might leave it indeterminate, and so unexplained, what something else, *G*, is. '*Ahoriston*' more often and more naturally indicates qualitative than quantitative indeterminacy, but some contexts seem to refer to quantitative indeterminacy.[33]

'*Apeiron*' means, literally, 'without limits' where, again, the limits can be qualitative or quantitative.[34] Unlike '*ahoriston*', '*apeiron*' does not naturally mean 'indefinable'. But if something is *apeiron* in the sense of being qualitatively unlimited or indeterminate, then it is indefinable.

'*Apeiron*' and '*ahoriston*', then, can be used more or less interchangeably; but they can also convey different things.[35] It is unclear whether they are used more or less interchangeably here. Fortunately, however, this is unimportant. For Aristotle contrasts both notions with being *hōrismena*; so whether '*apeira*' and '*ahorista*' have the same force or different forces here, their total conjunctive force simply contrasts with '*hōrismena*'. But this does not tell us what their total conjunctive force is, since '*hōrismena*' can convey different things: both qualitative and quantitative determinacy, or definability in a sense stronger than mere qualitative determinacy.

There is, then, some initial difficulty in knowing precisely what determinacy and indeterminacy consist in. Aristotle, however, frequently uses some of the relevant terms in epistemological contexts. Perhaps a look at some of these contexts will help us decide what is meant here.[36]

(i) In *Met.* 999a25–b16, Aristotle presents his eighth *aporia*, the 'greatest' difficulty concerning principles: either (*a*) there is something besides (*para*) *kath' hekasta* or (*b*) there is not. If (*b*), no knowledge of *kath' hekasta* is possible; for they are *apeira* but 'everything we know (*gnōrizomen*), we know in so far as some one and the same thing, i.e. in so far as some universal, belongs to it' (999a28–9). If (*a*), various other difficulties arise. Aristotle resolves the puzzle by agreeing with (*a*) that there is something besides *kath' hekasta*, and by arguing that we can resolve the difficulties raised for (*a*) by adopting an Aristotelian rather than a Platonic ontology. He also suggests that since there is something besides *kath' hekasta*, they are knowable after all, so long as one applies universals to them.

Aristotle means that *kath' hekasta* (which are here only particulars and not also low-level types) are not knowable in themselves in that if only they existed—if there were no universals—they would be bare particulars, and so they would be indefinite, inaccessible, unidentifiable (*apeira*). In order to know something, one must be able to identify and recognize it as being something or other; and this, in turn, requires attributing properties to it. (The indeterminacy at issue here is therefore qualitative; the point concerns not how many of something there are, but what something is like.) The existence of universals or properties is therefore a necessary condition for knowing particulars.[37]

This passage probably captures part of AS II, for it is surely a necessary condition for knowing something that one be able to identify and recognize it as being something or other. Further, Aristotle's central point here, as in criticizing AS II, is that knowledge requires the existence of something determinate; and this, in turn, shows that there are Aristotelian universals but not that there are Platonic forms. However, the Arguments from the Sciences concern knowledge as it contrasts with belief, whereas (i) concerns recognition, which is just as necessary for belief as for knowledge. Hence (i)'s notion of determinacy—as exemplifying a universal in such a way as to be identifiable—is too weak to capture everything AS II intends.[38]

(ii) In *Met.* 7. 15, Aristotle argues that knowledge requires demonstration and definition (*horismos*), which are restricted to what is necessary and to universals. Hence sensible *kath' hekasta* cannot be known; for they come and cease to be, and they have matter which is capable of being and not being.[39]

Like (i), (ii) restricts *kath' hekasta* to particulars; and the determinacy at issue (which this time is strict definability) is again qualitative. But unlike (i), (ii) precludes the possibility of knowing particulars under any conditions. Moreover, the knowledge at issue is much more demanding than in (i). For example, (i) allows the crafts to be sciences; but (ii) does not, since the crafts are not demonstrative.

Just as Aristotle believes that determinacy, in (i) and AS II, requires the existence of Aristotelian universals but not of forms, so he believes that demonstration and definition require the existence of Aristotelian universals but not of forms. As he says in the *Posterior Analytics*:[40]

It is not necessary, in order for there to be demonstration, that there be forms or a one besides (*para*) the many; but it is necessary for it to be true to say that one holds (*kata*) of many. For otherwise there will be no universal; and if there is no universal, there will be no middle term, and so no demonstration either. So it is necessary that there be some one and the same nonhomonymous thing in addition to (*epi*) many. (77a5–9.)

Although (ii) sounds like AS II in some ways, they probably make different points. First, although (ii) uses '*horismos*', it does not use '*apeira*', a key term in AS II. Secondly, just as (i) conceives of knowledge in too low-level a way, so (ii) conceives of it in too high-level a way. For example, (ii) does not count medicine as a science, since it is not demonstrative; but the Arguments from the Sciences count medicine as a science. (AS III explicitly counts medicine as a science, so presmably I and II also take it to be a science.) Thirdly, if (ii) were correct, it would vitiate Aristotle's objection in V, according to which if the Platonists believe that the possibility of *epistēmē* requires the existence of forms, they are committed to the existence of artefact forms, a result he claims they would not welcome. For if *epistēmē* involves demonstration, crafts do not count as *epistēmai* and so, contrary to Aristotle, the Platonists could use the Arguments from the Sciences without being committed to the existence of artefact forms.[41] Although we need not assume that Aristotle's objections to the Arguments from the Sciences ultimately succeed, we should attempt to interpret the arguments in such a way that his objections do not so immediately and obviously fail.

(iii) In the *Rhetoric* Aristotle says:[42]

None of the crafts (*technai*) considers (*skopei*) the particular (*kath' hekaston*). Medicine, for example, does not consider what makes Socrates or Callias healthy, but what makes anyone of this sort healthy, for this is its concern. But the particular is indefinite (*apeiron*) and ⟨so⟩ unknowable (*ouk epistēton*). (1356b30–3.)

Aristotle's point, I take it, is that medicine functions at a certain level of generality: it states its explanations not in terms of particulars such as Callias but in more general terms. An explanation of the flu, for instance, will not mention anything peculiar to Socrates' manifestation of it, but something true of a variety of people; for it aims to help doctors project to new cases. Since each particular case has features peculiar to it, mentioning them will not be explanatory in further cases. For medical understanding of the sort at issue here, then, one needs to abstract from particular peculiarities to a statement of more general truths. If this is right, then particulars are *apeiron* in the sense that each has irrelevant features, that is, features that are not explanatory for the particular purpose at hand.

In the *Rhetoric* passage, Aristotle's examples of *kath' hekasta* are all particulars; but a parallel passage in *Met.* I. I (980b25–981b9) makes it clear that his point applies to low-level types.[43] Here Aristotle explains how craft (*technē*) and knowledge (*epistēmē*) go beyond experience (*empeiria*). A merely experienced person might be aware (*gnōsis*, 981a16) *that* a certain medicine cured Socrates and Callias. But to have craft or scientific knowledge, one must know a universal (*katholou*, 981a6) that explains *why* the medicine worked, and that and why it would work in relevantly similar circumstances. Not every universal will do here. An experienced person might be aware that a group of people who exhibited certain symptoms—say, spots—were cured by a given medicine. Although she grasps a universal, she none the less lacks craft or scientific knowledge, for she does not know in virtue of what physiological features the medicine worked.

Craft and scientific knowledge, then, require not just a *grasp* of *any old* universal, but *knowledge* of the universals that are *explanatory* in the circumstances. The *kath' hekasta* that are precluded from being the basic objects of knowledge (as opposed to experience) are thus not only particulars but also particular types—we cannot explain the nature of health either in terms of Callias' health or in terms of particular sorts of health. The low-level types, moreover, will often be sensible properties—observable surface symptoms of a disease, for example, rather than underlying, unobservable, physiological features.[44]

The indeterminacy at issue here is both quantitative and qualitative. It is quantitative in so far as there are an indeterminate number of people with any given disease and an indeterminate number of ways of exhibiting any given disease. But qualitative indeterminacy is more important. For even if there were a determinate number of people with the flu, or a determinate number of types of flu, we still could not explain what the flu as such is by reference to them. For each of them is qualitatively indeterminate in so far as each has properties that are not essential to, and so are not explanatory of, the nature of the flu. We need to know the underlying explanatory properties in virtue of which something counts as a case or type of the flu; simply listing people who have the flu, or particular types of flu, will not allow us to know this. In contrast to the many *kath' hekasta*, these underlying explanatory properties are qualitatively determinate, in virtue of marking off a genuine class in the appropriate way, ignoring irrelevant features; that is why reference to them confers genuine understanding.

Aristotle adverts to the same notion of determinacy in a difficult but important passage in *Met.* 4. 4.[45] He argues that in order to say something (*legein ti*, 1006a22), one must signify some one thing; for not to signify some one thing is to signify nothing, that is, not to signify at all (1006b7). What one signifies, moreover, must be definite (*hōrismenon*, a25), indeed, definite in number (b4), not indefinite (*apeira*, b6).[46] Aristotle goes on to argue (1007a25) that the one thing one signifies is something's essence (*ousia*). For, he explains, coincidents are indefinite (1007a14–15)—that is, each thing has an indefinite number of coincidental properties, and reference to them is not explanatory. The essential properties of a thing, by contrast, are both qualitatively and quantitatively determinate: each thing has a finite, indeed small, number of essential properties; and they are qualitatively determinate in so far as reference to them is explanatory.

Like (i) and AS I and II, (iii) does not preclude knowledge of *kath' hekasta*. It claims that they cannot be basic objects of knowledge, since they are indeterminate in themselves. But if one knows the relevant basic objects, then one can understand *kath' hekasta* in their light; and when they are so viewed, they become determinate. Although we cannot understand what health is simply by inspecting Callias' exemplification of it, once we know what health is we can know that and why Callias is healthy.

(iii) is quite a promising parallel to AS II. First, it explains Aristotle's claim that AS II is an invalid argument for the existence of Platonic forms but a valid argument for the existence of his own *koina*. For he believes that explanations of the sort at issue here require the existence of *koina* but not of Platonic forms.[47] Secondly, (iii) conceives of knowledge in an appropriate way. For unlike (i), it concerns knowledge as it contrasts with belief; but unlike (ii), it counts geometry and medicine as sciences, which, in view of III, it should do. At the same time, it is appropriately unclear whether crafts fall within its scope. Its notion of determinacy also seems appropriate. I shall therefore assume that (iii) captures AS II's central point.[48]

If indeterminacy is so interpreted, then like AS I, AS II does not disqualify *kath' hekasta* from being the basic objects of knowledge on the ground that they change (GCH, MH, EH). For to be indeterminate is not to change, but to have features that are explanatorily irrelevant in a given context.[49] Further, on this interpretation, AS II, like AS I, allows us to know particulars, so long as they are viewed in the light of the appropriate explanatory theory.

If indeterminacy is interpreted in this way, then AS II fills in a gap in AS I. AS I implicitly disqualifies *kath' hekasta* from being the basic objects of knowledge on the ground that they are not suitably one and the same; but it does not say why *kath' hekasta* are not one and the same. AS II allows us to speculate that they are not one and the same because they are (considered in themselves) indeterminate—that is, because they have features that are irrelevant to, and so are not explanatory of, the nature of *F*-ness. Hence they cannot be the one thing in virtue of which the many *F*s are *F*. That Aristotle has this connection between AS I and II in mind is suggested by the fact that elsewhere he connects being one (AS I) and being determinate (AS II). In *Met.* 4. 4, for instance, he says that in order to signify something, one must signify some one thing which is determinate (1006a20–b11)—the relevant sort of oneness, that is, implies determinacy. So perhaps in AS I, *kath' hekasta* fail to be one precisely because they are indeterminate.[50]

Like AS I, AS II takes forms to be universals. For Aristotle says that AS II is a valid argument for the existence of universals. His reasoning is that there are basic objects of knowledge; since they cannot be *kath' hekasta*, they must be universals. This inference is valid if the distinction between universals and *kath' hekasta* is exhaustive.[51] Since forms are said to be different from *kath' hekasta*, they must be universals. As in AS I, Aristotle's point is that although Plato sees that knowledge requires the existence of universals, he misconceives their nature.

4. The third Argument from the Sciences

The third Argument from the Sciences (AS III) may be formulated as follows:

III

(1) Medicine is the science not of this (*tode*) health but of health without qualification (*haplōs*); geometry is the science not of this equal and this commensurate but of equal and commensurate without qualification.

(2) Therefore, there is such a thing as health itself (health *auto*), equal itself, and commensurate itself.

(3) Therefore, there are forms.

AS III(1) contrasts being this (*tode*) *F* (elsewhere, Aristotle tends to say being some (*ti*) *F*) and being *F* without qualification, or *F* as such (*F haplōs*). This is the distinction between being *F* with, and without, some qualification or other; what the relevant qualification is varies from context to context.[52] In *Met.* 7. 1, for instance, Aristotle says that 'it is because of substance that each of the other things is also a being, so that the primary sort of being, what is not something ⟨else⟩ (*ti*), but is without qualification (*haplōs*), is substance' (1028a29–31). He means that the sitting thing (for instance) is something else, a man, whereas no substance is anything else in this same way; *x* is some *F* if it is *F* partly by being or belonging to something else, and *x* is unqualifiedly *F* if it is not *F* by being or belonging to something else (at least, not in just the same way).[53] Similarly, a genus is unqualifiedly *F* whereas each of its species is some *F*; for the species is the genus with the addition of a differentia, whereas the genus in itself does not have the differentia added. So in the *Topics* (123b34–5), for example, Aristotle contrasts health and disease *haplōs* with health and disease *ti*—health and disease as such (the genera), as opposed to particular sorts of health or disease (e.g. a cold or the flu).

Like Aristotle, Plato also uses '*haplōs*' and '*ti*' to contrast genera with their species. In the *Meno* (73), for example, he says that justice is virtue *tis*, not virtue *haplōs*—it is a particular kind of virtue, not virtue as such. In *Rep.* 4 (438d11–e8), he contrasts knowledge *haplōs* with knowledge *ti*—knowledge as such, as opposed to particular sorts of knowledge. But sometimes Plato (like Aristotle) uses '*ti*', not for a kind of *F*, but for a particular *F*. In *Rep.* 10, for example, he says that god made the form of bed, what bed is (*ho esti klinē*), whereas an ordinary craftsman makes a particular bed (*klinē tis*) (597a1–d3).

'*Haplōs*' and '*ti*', then, are used to contrast both universals with particulars and the more with the less universal (e.g. a genus with its species). Unfortunately, AS III does not provide any examples that allow us to know which use is at issue here. Nor does it say why, if something is this *F*, it cannot be a basic object of knowledge. However, given AS II, it seems reasonable to suppose that AS III disqualifies things that are this *F* from being basic objects of knowledge on the ground that they contain additional, hence irrelevant, features. (So just as AS II fills in a gap in AS I, so it fills in a gap in AS III.) Both Callias' health and any type of health, for example, are this health, and so they are health only with addition; these additions are irrelevant to the nature of health as such. In order to understand what health as such is, one needs to abstract from these additions and find what is common to them all. For only this will explain why all the particular cases are manifestations of the same thing. If this is AS III's point, then both particulars and low-level types easily count as 'this *F*'.

Met. 1007a8–20 supports this suggestion about how AS II explains AS III. For Aristotle says there that if one is asked what man is *haplōs*, one ought not to say that he is pale and tall. For such coincidents are *apeira*, and so one cannot mention them all; but it would be inappropriate to mention just some of them. Rather, one should just state the one determinate thing that man signifies. The one determinate thing that man signifies is what man is *haplōs*—that is, as the ensuing discussion makes clear, its essence. To specify something *haplōs*, then, is to specify something determinate, that is, the relevant essential properties, which are the explanatory ones. AS II's claim that *kath' hekasta* are not determinate thus explains AS III's claim that we cannot specify what *F* is *haplōs* by mentioning *kath' hekasta*.

In claiming that medicine should be defined in terms of health as such, AS III means, not that one can know only health as such, but that knowledge of health is necessary for knowledge of healthy things. So like AS I and II, AS III leaves open the possibility that sensibles can be known, so long as they are understood in terms of the appropriate explanatory theory. Further, like AS I and II, AS III does not disqualify *kath' hekasta* from being the basic objects of knowledge on the ground that they change (GCH, MH, EH). Rather, it disqualifies them on the ground that they are only this *F*; they therefore have features that are additional to those constitutive of what it is to be *F*, and so we cannot explain what it is to be *F* in terms of them. Given II's claim that the basic objects of the sciences exist, and given that medicine is a science, it follows that there is such a thing as health. Does it also follow that there is such a thing as health itself (health *auto*), and so a Platonic form of health?

In order to answer this question, we need to know what it is to be *F auto*. '*Auto*' is a reflexive adjective meaning 'itself'; as such, it is frequently used in non-technical contexts. But in the relevant Aristotelian contexts, it is generally used to refer either to a universal or property in a neutral sense, or to a Platonic form (since Plato takes universals to be forms).[54] If 'itself' is used in the second way here, then Aristotle would say that the inference from (1) to (2) is invalid. For in his view it does not follow from the fact that there is such a thing as health that there is a Platonic form of health; health might be an Aristotelian universal instead. If (2) in effect asserts that there is a Platonic form of health, then it implies (3); but since in Aristotle's view the inference to (2) is then invalid, he would still take AS III to be invalid. If, on the other hand, 'itself' is used for a universal in a neutral sense, then Aristotle would take the inference from (1) to (2) to be valid.[55] But he would then take the move from (2) to (3) to be invalid; for he does not take the fact that there is a universal, health, to imply that there is a Platonic form of health.

Although both readings of '*auto*' allow us to explain Aristotle's claim that AS III is an invalid argument for the existence of forms, (2) seems to use '*auto*' to refer to universals in a neutral sense. For AS III is then more of an argument, and it is also clearer what Aristotle accepts and rejects in it. From (1), it is inferred in (2)—correctly, in Aristotle's view—that there are universals. But then in (3) it is inferred—fallaciously, in Aristotle's view—that universals are forms. So like AS I and II, AS III takes forms to be universals; once again, Aristotle's point is that although Plato sees that knowledge requires the existence of universals, he misconceives their nature.[56]

5. Conclusion

I noted in sect. 1 that the Arguments from the Sciences are often taken to argue that since (*a*) sensibles are always changing (GCH, MH, EH), (*b*) they are unknowable. But on the interpretation defended here, they argue neither (*a*) nor (*b*). They argue instead that we cannot explain the nature of *F*-ness by appealing to sensible *kath' hekasta*—to particular *F*s or to particular types of *F*s—on the ground that they are not one and the same (AS I), or determinately *F* (AS II), or unqualifiedly *F* (AS III). None of these failures adverts to change (GCH, MH, EH); even if squareness, for example, is everlasting and unchanging, it still (for the purpose of explaining the nature of shape) possesses the defects the Arguments from the Sciences call attention to, and so we still cannot define shape in terms of it. Further, although the Arguments from the Sciences conclude that Platonic forms are the basic objects of knowledge, they do not argue that they are the only objects of knowledge.

In addition to taking forms to be the basic objects of knowledge, the Arguments from the Sciences also take them to be non-sensible universals.[57] Indeed, the Arguments from the Sciences are valid arguments for the existence of non-sensible universals. Aristotle claims, however, that they are invalid arguments for the existence of forms, since they do not show that universals are separate perfect paradigms, yet in his view Platonic forms are separate perfect paradigms.

We have therefore already explained Aristotle's first objection to the Arguments from the Sciences—that they are invalid arguments for the existence of forms. But we still need to consider his second objection—that if they produced any forms at all, they would produce artefact forms, which in his view the Platonists do not want. We also need to ask whether Plato is committed to the Arguments from the Sciences. Another matter should also be addressed. Even if the Arguments from the Sciences do not concern change (GCH, MH, EH), it does not follow that they concern compresence. Perhaps they concern neither succession nor compresence. I address this matter in Ch. 7.

6

Forms of Artefacts

Aristotle's second objection to the Arguments from the Sciences is that (*a*) if they show that there are any forms at all, they show that there are forms corresponding to the products of each of the crafts (*technai*);[1] but (*b*) 'they' do not want forms corresponding to the products of each of the crafts. Commentators have generally believed that (*a*) is justified. But (*b*) has seemed puzzling on the ground that (it is thought) Plato obviously countenances artefact forms. Indeed, the very passages in which he seems to do so—in the *Gorgias*, *Cratylus*, and *Rep.* 10—are among the passages that are most reminiscent of the Arguments from the Sciences. I begin by considering (*a*). I then consider various explanations of (*b*).

I′ claims that just as every science works by referring to some one and the same thing, so every craft 'refers the things that come to be by its agency to some one thing'. II′ claims that just as the basic objects of the sciences are, so too the basic objects of the crafts are; and that just as particulars cannot be the basic objects of the sciences, so they cannot be the basic objects of the crafts. III′ claims that just as the sciences are not of things that are this *F* but of things that are unqualifiedly *F*, so too are the crafts.[2] Hence if I–III show that forms are the basic objects of the sciences, they also show that forms are the basic objects of the crafts. How reasonable are I′–III′?

I′ seems reasonable. Indeed, Plato himself mentions artefact forms in connection with claims that sound like AS I's premisses. In the *Cratylus*, for example, he says that in making a shuttle, the craftsman looks to something so constituted by nature as to shuttle (*toiouton ti ho epephukei kerkizein*, 389a7–8)—that is, to something the nature of which is to shuttle. This sounds like AS I's claim that every science works by referring to one and the same thing. What is so constituted by nature as to shuttle is then identified as a form just as, in AS I, what a science refers to in its work is identified as a form. In the *Gorgias* (503e) Plato says that craftsmen look to something in their work, so that their products will embody the appropriate forms; the same claim is made in *Rep.* 10 (596b). The real puzzle is not that Aristotle levels I′, but that he claims that 'they' deny that there are artefact forms. I address this puzzle below.

AS II's key point is that every branch of knowledge (every *epistēmē*) involves an explanatory theory; and this, in turn, requires the existence of universals at a certain level of generality—according to the Arguments from the Sciences, these are forms. If, as *Met*. 1. 1 and the *Rhetoric* assume, the crafts involve the same sort of explanatory theory as the sciences do, then presumably they require the existence of the same sort of universals; so if the sciences require the existence of forms, so too do the crafts. Once again, Plato may seem to agree. For in the *Gorgias* (465a and 501a), which *Met*. 1. 1 clearly echoes, Plato claims that crafts involve a *logos* (account) and an *aitia* (explanation).

III′ also seems reasonable, and Plato again seems to agree. For in *Rep*. 10 he distinguishes between being *klinē tis*, a particular bed, and being *ho esti klinē* (what bed is), the form of bed. So he believes that at least some crafts are of something that is not merely some *F*, and so they are of forms. The language is very close to that used in AS III.

I′–III′ thus seem reasonable.[3] Indeed, not only does Aristotle seem justified in *committing* 'them' to the existence of artefact forms, but also Plato seems to countenance such forms *explicitly* and on the basis of premisses at least very like those involved in the Arguments from the Sciences. So let us turn to the more puzzling question of why Aristotle claims that 'they' do not want artefact forms. I consider six possibilities.[4]

(i) Aristotle does not claim that they do not want forms of artefacts; V is an Alexandrian interpolation based on a misunderstanding of Aristotle.[5]

On behalf of this suggestion, one might argue as follows. With the possible exception of V, Aristotle nowhere says that the Arguments from the Sciences produce artefact forms if they produce any forms at all. In *Met*. 1. 9, for example, he says instead that if the Arguments from the Sciences succeeded, they would prove that there are forms for 'all the things of which there are sciences' (990b12–13). Of course, Aristotle could be subsuming the crafts under the sciences, as both Plato and he sometimes do;[6] but the fact remains that the crafts are not explicitly mentioned. Moreover, a few lines later Aristotle says that 'there are sciences not only of substances but also of other things' (990b26–7); the 'other things' seem to be not artefacts, but items in non-substance categories (e.g. qualities and quantities). And Aristotle proceeds to explain why such forms are, or at any rate should be, unwanted.[7] If one looked only at this passage in *Met*. 1. 9, one would have no hint that an alleged defect of the Arguments from the Sciences is that they produce artefact forms if they produce any forms at all; nor would one have any hint that in Aristotle's view the Platonists do not want such forms.

One might then argue that when Alexander represents Aristotle as claiming that the Arguments from the Sciences prove that there are artefact forms if they prove that there are any forms at all, he mis-interprets him. Aristotle's complaint in *Met*. 1. 9 is that the Arguments from the Sciences would prove that there are forms of non-substances (e.g. of qualities); Alexander misinterprets the substance/non-substance contrast as that between the natural and the non-natural (artificial).[8]

However, I do not think we should accuse Alexander of misinterpretation on this score.[9] First, we have seen that it is reasonable to suppose that the Arguments from the Sciences produce artefact forms if they produce any forms at all. Secondly, the more troubling claim is that 'they' did not want such forms; and Aristotle makes that claim elsewhere (though not in connection with the Arguments from the Sciences).[10] For example, in *Met.* 12. 3 he says: 'and so Plato was not far wrong when he said that there are as many forms as there are ⟨kinds of⟩ natural objects' (1070a18–19). Aristotle is most naturally read as claiming that Plato[11] countenanced forms *only* for kinds of natural objects, and so not for the crafts. For he is contrasting the way in which natural objects come into being with the way in which artefacts come into being; and he argues that it is more reasonable to posit forms in the former than in the latter case.[12] If Plato recognized forms in both cases, Aristotle would not commend him as he does. His point seems to be that in limiting forms to natural things, Plato anticipated his view that natural and artificial things come into being in different ways.[13] Similarly, in *Met.* 1. 9, 991b6–7 (= 13. 5, 1080a5–6), Aristotle says that 'we' (in 1080, 'they') do not want forms of house or ring. Since the remark occurs in his discussion of the *Phaedo*, it seems likely that he has Plato in mind.[14]

There thus does not seem to be adequate reason to accuse Alexander of misinterpretation. Even if we do, the basic problem will still arise from the text of the *Metaphysics*.

(ii) Aristotle's criticism is directed not against Plato but against other Platonists who, unlike Plato, denied that there are artefact forms.[15]

The main alternative candidate is Xenocrates, who apparently defines forms as 'the paradigmatic cause of whatever is always constituted according to nature (*aitia paradeigmatikē tōn kata phusin aei sunestōtōn*)'.[16] It is sometimes thought that as Xenocrates uses 'nature' it excludes artefacts, in which case he rejects the existence of artefact forms. However, Proclus says that Xenocrates 'propounded this definition of an idea as being in accord with the view of his master' (tr. Morrow and Dillon); and at least sometimes his master Plato uses '*phusis*' for genuine properties and kinds and takes artefacts to be genuine kinds.[17] So if Xenocrates is indeed following Plato, then it is far from clear that he uses '*phusis*' so as to exclude artefacts.[18]

It is true that some later Platonists denied that there were artefact forms.[19] Indeed, Alcinous says that *most* of the Platonists denied that there were artefact forms.[20] But he unfortunately names no names, nor does he say whether any such Platonists lived early enough for Aristotle to be able to have them in mind.

So although there seems to be ample evidence that some Platonists denied that there were artefact forms, it is not clear that any Platonists in Aristotle's time did so. But even if they did, I am reluctant to believe that

Aristotle's objection is directed only against them, and not also or instead against Plato. For as we saw in (i), this would be at best a stopgap measure, since Aristotle elsewhere associates the denial with Plato in particular.

(iii) Aristotle's criticism is directed not against the early or middle dialogues (which countenance artefact forms) but against the late dialogues (which reject their existence).[21]

In favour of this interpretation, it can be said that the late dialogues do not explicitly mention artefact forms[22]—although, equally, neither do they say anything incompatible with their existence.[23] None the less, I am inclined to reject (iii). For we saw that in *Met.* 1. 9 (13. 5) Aristotle says that the Platonists deny that there are forms of house or ring, and he seems to associate the denial with the *Phaedo*, a middle dialogue. Nor does Aristotle ever explicitly say that the middle and late dialogues differ as to whether there are artefact forms, though he is not usually shy about indicating changes in Plato's views.[24] Finally, in (vi) I argue that a better explanation of Aristotle's criticism is available.

Whereas (i) seeks to absolve Aristotle from misinterpretation by accusing Alexander instead, (ii) and (iii) seek to absolve him by choosing a different target from the middle dialogues for him to be aiming at. On a fourth interpretation, his target includes the middle dialogues, which, however, he unfortunately misinterprets:

(iv) Robin suggests that Plato countenances forms corresponding to the productive but not to the imitative crafts; there is a form of bed, but not of painted bed. Aristotle mistakenly believes that Plato rejects forms for all the crafts.[25]

Plato does distinguish between the productive and imitative crafts; and he sometimes says that productive but not imitative craftsmen look to forms. In *Rep.* 10, for instance, he says that in making a bed, a craftsman looks to the form of bed. But although he also counts painting as a craft (601d1-2), he says that painters do not look to forms in fashioning their creations: they look only to the sensible particulars they wish to imitate. (Presumably he believes not only that painters do not look to any forms but also that there is no form of e.g. painted bed.) However, in the *Gorgias* (503e) Plato seems to say that *all* craftsmen look to forms in fashioning their creations; and here he counts painting as a craft. But even if Plato's considered view is that productive but not imitative craftsmen look to forms, I am reluctant to suppose that Aristotle's criticism involves generalizing from imitative to all craftsmen. For it seems so clear that the *Cratylus* and *Rep.* 10 posit artefact forms in productive cases (forms of shuttle, bed, and table are mentioned) that it is hard to believe that Aristotle simply fails to see that he does so.

(v) Frank defends a modified version of (iv).[26] He agrees with Robin that Plato rejects forms for the imitative crafts and accepts them for the productive crafts. But he argues that Aristotle does not misinterpret Plato. For Aristotle claims only that Plato denies that *all* artefacts have forms corresponding to them, which leaves open the possibility that he takes Plato to admit forms corresponding to *some* of them. Aristotle's criticism is that the Arguments from the Sciences commit Plato even to forms for the imitative crafts, a result he would not welcome.

Frank is right about the linguistic point; in V (80. 6) Aristotle says that Plato does not want forms corresponding to the products of each of the crafts, which leaves open the possibility that in his view Plato acknowledges forms corresponding to the products of some of the crafts. But I do not think this linguistic point bears the weight Frank wants to rest on it. First, since Aristotle elsewhere suggests that Plato does not want forms in productive cases, it seems reasonable to assume that the productive crafts fall within the scope of his present objection.[27] Secondly, if Frank were right, Aristotle's list of examples would be odd. He first lists carpentry, then sculpture, painting, and building: he begins and ends with productive examples, sandwiching two imitative examples in between. There is no hint that Plato would welcome forms for the first and fourth cases, but not for the second and third.[28]

So although Plato distinguishes between productive and imitative crafts, and even denies (in *Rep.* 10 if not in the *Gorgias*) that imitative craftsmen look to forms, that does not provide us with a satisfactory explanation of Aristotle's puzzling remark. What we need is an interpretation that (unlike (iv) and (v)) covers both productive and imitative crafts, and (unlike (ii) and (iii)) allows Aristotle's target to include the middle dialogues. I suggest the following:

(vi) Aristotle distinguishes between various sorts of forms (*eidē*) both in discussing Socrates and Plato, and also within his own ontology. For example, he believes that Plato but not Socrates takes forms to be separated and non-sensible. Within his own ontology, he uses '*eidos*' to refer to species, to particular or individual forms, to the form without matter that a perceiver receives, and to the form in the soul of a craftsman.[29] Aristotle believes that different contexts involve different sorts of forms. For example, he believes that natural production involves an extra-mental form of some sort, but not a Platonic form. By contrast, he believes that in building a house, a builder consults only a form of house in his soul—a mental representation of a house.[30]

Now Aristotle believes that the Arguments from the Sciences aim to prove that there are forms of the distinctively Platonic sort—forms that are, in Aristotle's view, everlasting, non-sensible, separated, perfect paradigms. His objection is that if the Arguments from the Sciences show that there any such forms, they show that there are such forms of artefacts. Perhaps Aristotle believes this would be unwelcome to Plato, not because Plato denies that there are artefact forms of some sort, but because he denies that artefact forms have all the features that Aristotle associates with (other) Platonic forms.

On behalf of this suggestion, it can be said that when Aristotle suggests, outside the *Peri ideōn*, that Plato rejects artefact forms, he seems to have in mind Platonic forms rather than, say, hygienic Socratic forms.[31] Further, since Aristotle himself believes that artificial and natural production involve different sorts of forms, he would presumably be sensitive to any such differences that might be hinted at in the dialogues. Moreover, as I shall now argue, there are remarks in the dialogues which can be taken to suggest (though they certainly do not show) that Plato is sometimes tempted not to ascribe to artefact forms all the features that Aristotle, at any rate, associates with the distinctively Platonic forms.

The *Gorgias* and the *Cratylus* both posit artefact forms. But the *Gorgias* is a Socratic dialogue, and so in Aristotle's view it does not countenance distinctively Platonic forms. Nor is Aristotle likely to believe that the *Cratylus* has such forms.[32] For example, its forms are not said to be perfect or non-sensible, key features that distinguish Platonic from Socratic forms.[33] So although the *Gorgias* and *Cratylus* show that Plato at some stage countenanced artefact forms of some sort, they do not show that he ever countenanced artefact forms of the distinctively Platonic sort, and so they do not threaten interpretation (vi).

Nor does Plato's central argument for the existence of forms in the middle dialogues—the argument from narrow compresence—commit him to the existence of artefact forms of *any* sort; for nothing is, in the narrow sense, both (say) a shuttle and not a shuttle. Further, with one exception to be discussed below, Plato never mentions artefact forms of the distinctive sort. Perhaps this indicates that he does not (generally) countenance them. In this connection, it is striking that when, in the *Parmenides* (130bd), he asks whether various cases require the existence of forms, he does not mention artefacts; nor is it clear that they fit into any of the groups he discusses.[34] Of course, *ex silentio* arguments can never be conclusive; but they can sometimes give one pause.

It is also noteworthy that although Socrates takes the crafts to be paradigmatic examples of sciences, Plato demotes them.[35] This is especially evident in the *Philebus* (55 ff.), where Plato distinguishes between three main types of knowledge, ranked in order of increased accuracy:[36] empirical disciplines (such as music, medicine, and building); the pure mathematical sciences; and dialectic. Although various crafts count as types of knowledge, they are the least exalted type; so perhaps they do not require their own forms. On behalf of this suggestion is the fact that the lowest sort of knowledge (which includes the crafts) is said to rely on the senses more than the other sorts of knowledge do; so perhaps it does not require the existence of non-sensible forms.[37]

The *Philebus* passage suggests a way in which Plato might reply to Aristotle's claim that the Arguments from the Sciences produce artefact forms if they produce any forms at all: he might say that knowledge of *F*s does not always require the existence of a form of *F*. Rather, only the more exalted sorts of knowledge require the existence of the corresponding forms, and craft knowledge is not sufficiently exalted. Aristotle's objection in V, Plato might say, assumes too low an epistemic level. One might then say that although I'–III' are *prima facie* reasonable, they are not reasonable in the end. (However, this reply shows at most that Plato can use the Arguments from the Sciences without being committed to the existence of artefact forms. It does not show that Plato is not committed to their existence for other reasons; nor does it explain why Aristotle says that Plato does not want artefact forms, which is the central puzzle here.) To this Aristotle might reply that, at least in the middle dialogues, Plato does not make this point clear, and he is under no obligation to give Plato distinctions that Plato does not clearly draw.[38] This is a familiar Aristotelian ploy, and one we shall meet again.

So far we have uncovered some evidence in favour of the suggestion that Plato does not take artefact forms to have all the features that Aristotle, at any rate, associates with (other) distinctively Platonic forms: for sometimes Plato countenances only Socratic artefact forms; sometimes he focuses on arguments that do not establish that there are any sort of artefact forms; sometimes he demotes the crafts in a way that suggests that at least craft knowledge does not require the existence of distinctively Platonic forms. However, other evidence might seem less favourable to interpretation (vi). I consider two ways of challenging it.

First, we have seen that in *Rep.* 10 Plato posits a form of bed and one of table; and, as we shall see in Ch. 8.7 its forms, both in fact and in Aristotle's view, are distinctively Platonic rather than Socratic, at least in so far as they are taken to be perfect and non-sensible.

But perhaps this first challenge can be met. For one might argue that although *Rep.* 10's forms are distinctively Platonic rather than Socratic, they do not have *all* the features that Aristotle associates with Platonic forms.[39] For example, nothing in the passage implies that its forms are everlasting or separate.[40] But whatever is in fact true of *Rep.* 10, we shall see in Ch. 8.7 that Aristotle probably takes its forms to be everlasting and separate. Still, *Rep.* 10 is in many ways quite odd, so perhaps we could say that in his criticism in V Aristotle has in mind, not this aberrant passage, but what he takes to be a different strand of Plato's thought.

Secondly, although with the possible exception of *Rep.* 10 Plato never mentions artefact forms of the distinctively Platonic sort, and although the argument from narrow compresence does not show that there are artefact forms of any sort, perhaps he has other arguments that commit him to the existence of distinctively Platonic artefact forms. I consider this matter in Ch. 7.6.

While I do not think that interpretation (vi) is free from difficulties, it has something to be said in its favour: it avoids the objections the other interpretations we have considered are vulnerable to; it meshes well with the way in which Aristotle discriminates between artificial and natural production, and between different sorts of forms; and it has some basis in the dialogues. If we add that Plato's dialogues are often indeterminate, and that different lines of thought tell in different directions, then perhaps we can say that interpretation (vi) gives Aristotle a reasonable criticism of one tendency in Plato's thought.

7

Plato and the Arguments from the Sciences

We have seen so far that Aristotle is right to say that the Arguments from the Sciences are invalid arguments for the existence of forms, if forms are taken to be non-sensible, everlasting, separate, perfect paradigms. He is also right to say that if the Arguments from the Sciences produced any such forms at all, they would produce artefact forms of this sort—a result Plato may not welcome. But does Plato accept the premisses of the Arguments from the Sciences? If so, does he draw an invalid conclusion from them? Does he use the premisses of the Arguments from the Sciences, or something like them, in a way that commits him to the existence of artefact forms of a sort he does not want? If so, Aristotle has good criticisms not just of the Arguments from the Sciences but also of Plato. If not, Plato is not vulnerable to Aristotle's objections; but Aristotle then seems to misinterpret him. Here, then, we face an instance of the dilemma sketched in Ch. 2.8: Aristotle either refutes or misinterprets Plato. Is there a way out of this dilemma in this particular case?

1. Socrates and the Arguments from the Sciences

An argument that sounds very like the first Argument from the Sciences can easily be extracted from the Socratic dialogues. In both the *Euthyphro* (5d1–5; 6d9–e6) and *Meno* (72ab),[1] for example, Socrates insists that adequate accounts must specify some *one* thing; he also assumes that in order to know anything about *F*, including what instantiates *F*, one needs to know the one thing it is to be *F* (*Meno* 71b). Socrates therefore seems to accept AS I(1).[2] Socrates also argues that adequate answers to 'What is *F*?' questions cannot be phrased in terms of the many *F*s (particular *F*s and particular kinds of *F*s), in which case the many *F*s cannot be the basic objects of knowledge; so Socrates also accepts I(2).[3]

Although Socrates accepts (1) and (2), he is not committed to (3); for as we saw in Ch. 4.4, he is not committed to the claim that forms are non-sensible. So far as I can see, neither is he committed to the claim that forms are everlasting. But in the *Euthyphro* he says that he wants to know the one thing it is to be *F*, and he then describes this one thing as a paradigm (6e3–6). Aristotle believes that Socratic paradigms are weak paradigms,[4] and he believes that (1) and (2) imply that there are weak paradigms. Since (3) involves weak paradigmatism, Socrates accepts *part* of (3), and it is arguable that he infers that part of (3) from (1) and (2).

Socrates also accepts a claim that sounds like (4) in so far as he says that there are forms (*Eu.* 5d4, 6d11, e3; *Meno* 72c7, e5). Moreover, he sometimes seems to infer the claim that sounds like (4) from (1), (2), and (possibly) the part of (3) that he accepts. At least, all these claims are mentioned in the same context, and it is reasonable to assume that (1), (2), and perhaps the accepted part of (3) are meant to support (4), even though Socrates does not say so explicitly.[5]

Despite these verbal, and some substantive, similarities between some Socratic contexts and AS I, we should not conclude that AS I aims to capture a Socratic argument. First, Socrates accepts only part of (3). Secondly, although he accepts a claim that sounds like (4), he is not committed to (4). For although he believes that there are entities called 'forms', (4) uses 'forms' to refer to Platonic forms as Aristotle conceives them—non-sensible, everlasting, separated, perfect paradigms. If (4) is so read, then in Aristotle's view Socrates is not committed to it.

An argument that sounds like the second Argument from the Sciences can also be found in the Socratic dialogues. According to AS II(1), knowledge requires the existence of certain sorts of objects. Although Socrates does not assert this in so many words, he seems to assume it. He assumes, for example, that correct answers to 'What is *F*?' questions (the understanding of which confers knowledge) specify forms—objective, mind-independent universals. According to AS II(2) and (3), the basic objects of the sciences must be something other than *kath' hekasta*, since *kath' hekasta* are *apeira* and *ahorista* whereas the objects of the sciences must be *hōrismena*. Socrates certainly agrees that the basic objects of knowledge must be *hōrismena*, in so far as he believes that they are the objects of definition. And although he does not say that *kath' hekasta* are *apeira*, we have seen (in Ch. 4.3) that he disqualifies them from being the objects of definition on the ground that they contain features that are inessential to the nature of *F*-ness, in which case they are indeterminate. Not only does Socrates accept AS II's premisses: he also uses them to argue that there are forms, and so he asserts a claim that sounds like AS II's conclusion. But, again, in Aristotle's view Socrates does not accept AS II's conclusion, since it asserts that there are Platonic forms.

The same story can be told about Socrates and the third Argument from the Sciences. In the *Meno* (73e1–74a10), for example, Socrates asks Meno to say what virtue as such (*haplōs*) is, not merely to specify different sorts (*ti*) of virtue, such as justice and temperance. So the *Meno* seems to accept AS II(1). Unlike AS III, the *Meno* does not explicitly infer, or even claim, that there is something properly designated '*auto*'.

But AS III(2) seems to mean only that there are universals, and so (since the *Meno*'s forms are universals) the *Meno* accepts it and may indeed think that (1) implies it.[6] The *Meno* also assumes that correct answers to 'What is *F*?' questions specify forms (*eidos*, 72c7, e5), and so it may seem to assert AS III's conclusion. But it does not clearly do so. For AS III asserts that there are Platonic forms, but the *Meno* seems to countenance only Socratic forms.

The premisses of the Arguments from the Sciences are therefore recognizably Socratic. But Socrates does not draw an invalid inference from these premisses, nor is Aristotle likely to think that he does. On the contrary, since he says that the premisses of the Arguments from the Sciences imply that there are *koina*, he presumably thinks that they imply that there are Socratic forms, for he takes his own universals to be essentially the same as Socrates' forms.

It is worth remarking that Socrates seems to use the premisses of the Arguments from the Sciences in a way that commits him to the existence of artefact forms. (But he does not use them in a way that commits him to the existence of Platonic-style artefact forms, for, as Aristotle insists, the premisses of the Arguments from the Sciences do not imply that there are any such forms; nor does Socrates take their premisses to imply that there are any such forms.) For, as we saw in the last chapter, Socrates takes the crafts to be paradigmatic examples of the sciences; so, since he takes the sciences to require the existence of forms, he presumably takes the crafts to require the existence of the corresponding forms. And so it is not surprising that, as we also saw in the last chapter, the *Gorgias* and *Cratylus* explicitly countenance artefact forms.[7]

We have seen so far that the Socratic dialogues have the premisses but not the conclusion of the Arguments from the Sciences. In Aristotle's view, however, the middle dialogues have the conclusion of the Arguments from the Sciences—that is, in his view they are committed to the existence of distinctively Platonic forms. So let us turn to the middle dialogues, to see whether they argue for this conclusion with the premisses of the Arguments from the Sciences. If they do, then Plato argues invalidly and is committed to the existence of artefact forms of a sort he may not want.

2. Plato and the premisses of the Arguments from the Sciences

The argument at the end of *Rep.* 5 is the most extended, systematic discussion of knowledge in the middle dialogues, so I shall focus on it. Ross thinks this argument is basically the same as the Arguments from the Sciences.[8] But his reason is that he thinks that it, allegedly like the Arguments from the Sciences, argues that there are forms by appealing to succession. In Ch. 4.5–6, however, I suggested that *Rep.* 5 argues that there are forms by appealing not to succession but to compresence.[9] Frank agrees with this claim. But he thinks it shows that *Rep.* 5 is not the source for the Arguments from the Sciences; for, he argues, unlike the Arguments from the Sciences, the argument from compresence does not show that there are artefact forms.[10]

I agree that *Rep.* 5 is in this respect narrower than the Arguments from the Sciences, and in a way that leaves Plato invulnerable to Aristotle's second objection, about artefact forms. But in the rest of the present section, I argue that *Rep.* 5 accepts instances of the premisses of the Arguments from the Sciences in a way that makes it relevant to wonder whether Plato is vulnerable to Aristotle's first objection, about invalidity. Moreover, the gap between *Rep.* 5's focus on compresence and the Arguments from the Sciences' broader focus is not as great as it may appear to be. Once we see how this is so, the question about Plato's commitment to the existence of artefact forms of a sort he may not want resurfaces. I discuss this matter in sect. 6.

In *Rep.* 5 Plato says that beauty is not many but one (479a4); like Socrates, he means that everything that is beautiful is beautiful in virtue of some one thing. *Rep.* 5 also assumes that knowledge requires explanation.[11] For Plato assumes (479de) that since the sight-lovers do not know the definition of beauty, they do not know anything at all about beauty. Since knowing the definition of beauty involves knowing its explanation, this is to assume that knowledge requires explanation. So Plato seems to believe that at least some sciences work by referring to some one and the same thing, in which case he accepts some instances of AS I(1).[12] Plato also seems to accept at least some instances of AS I(2), for he argues that, in cases where the instances of a predicate '*F*' suffer narrow compresence, *F*-ness cannot be defined in terms of the many *F*s, in which case they cannot be the basic objects of knowledge.[13]

The first premiss of AS II says that 'the objects of the sciences are', by which it means that basic objects of knowledge exist. The *Rep.* 5 argument begins with a suspiciously similar-sounding premiss, that 'knowledge is of what is' (477a).[14] I have argued elsewhere, however, that Plato means only that knowledge is truth-entailing;[15] he uses 'is' veridically, whereas AS II uses it existentially. But we need not conclude that Aristotle misunderstands Plato. For although no occurrence of 'is' in the *Rep.* 5 argument is best translated as 'exists', an existential claim is tacit. For having argued that if there were only sensibles there would be no knowledge, Plato infers that there must be non-sensible objects of knowledge, the forms (479e–480a13). This inference is valid only if it is being assumed that the possibility of knowledge requires the existence of suitable objects of knowledge. So although AS II(1) does not state the central, explicit premiss in *Rep.* 5 (that knowledge is truth-entailing), it usefully highlights a crucial tacit premiss (that knowledge requires the existence of suitable objects). So here Aristotle does not record Plato's claims verbatim; rather, he uncovers important tacit premisses. This strategy, so far from involving distortion or misinterpretation, is philosophically illuminating.

Unlike AS II(2), *Rep.* 5 does not say that *kath' hekasta* are *apeira* and *ahorista*. But it does say that the many *F*s are *F* and not *F*; and if something is *F* and not *F*, it obviously has features inessential to the nature of *F*-ness and so it is indeterminate with respect to *F*-ness. *Rep.* 5 therefore accepts instances of AS II(2). So compresence and indeterminacy are connected at least in so far as suffering compresence is a way of being indeterminate.[16] Further, like AS II(3), *Rep.* 5 assumes that the basic objects of knowledge must be *horismena*, in so far as it assumes that the basic objects of knowledge are what we define in answering the 'What is *F*?' question.

Unlike AS III(1), *Rep.* 5 does not explicitly say that knowledge must be of something that is unqualifiedly *F* rather than of something that is this *F*. But presumably it accepts at least instances of this claim. For III(1) means that every science is defined in terms of something at a certain level of generality; medicine, for example, is defined in terms of health as such rather than in terms of particular sorts of health. AS III insists on this because things at a lower level of generality are only this *F*; they therefore have features that are additional to the nature of *F*-ness, and so they have features that are irrelevant to explaining the nature of *F*-ness. This matches Plato's reasons for ruling out definitions phrased in terms of the many *F*s; for the many *F*s, like the *kath' hekasta* corresponding to '*F*', are simply *F* particulars and low-level types, i.e. entities that are not at the appropriate level of generality and so have features that are irrelevant for the explanatory task at hand.

In AS III(2) it is inferred that the basic objects of knowledge must be *auto F*—that they must be universals. *Rep.* 5 seems to agree that the possibility of knowledge, in the cases it considers, requires the existence of universals, and so it assumes instances of AS III(2) (whether or not as an inference from (1)). The dispute between Plato and the sight-lovers is not about the existence of universals, but about whether universals are sensible properties or non-sensible forms.[17]

I conclude that a reasonable case can be made for the claim that Plato accepts (instances of) the premisses of the Arguments from the Sciences. To this extent, they are not just Socratic claims. Moreover, the way in which Plato accepts these premisses shows that compresence is relevant to the Arguments from the Sciences at least in so far as suffering compresence is a way of being indeterminate, and (since AS II mentions indeterminacy, and explains AS I and III) indeterminacy is the root problem in all AS I–III.

However, although a reasonable case can be made for the claim that *Rep.* 5 accepts instances of the premisses of the Arguments from the Sciences, it is important to see that these are not its only premisses. First, *Rep.* 5 emphasizes a premiss not mentioned in the Arguments from the Sciences, that knowledge but not belief implies truth. (Perhaps Aristotle takes this premiss to be too obvious to require special mention?) Secondly, unlike the Arguments from the Sciences, it focuses on narrow compresence rather than on the broader phenomenon of indeterminacy. (But being in compresence is a way of being indeterminate; and in the next section we shall see that there are interesting reasons for focusing on the broader phenomenon.) Thirdly and most importantly, *Rep.* 5 seems to take sensibles to be imperfect and so inadequate as the basic objects of knowledge. In *Rep.* 476, for example, the person who does not acknowledge forms is said to be dreaming rather than awake; in Plato's view, dream images are less perfect than the physical objects (trees, etc.) one encounters while awake. Similarly, in 478, belief is said to be darker and less clear than knowledge, partly because the objects on which it tends to focus (sensibles) are less clear, and so presumably less perfect, than basic objects of knowledge (which turn out to be forms) must be. The Arguments from the Sciences, by contrast, do not suggest that sensibles are imperfect.

Rep. 5's premisses therefore say both more and less than the Arguments from the Sciences' premisses. They say less in so far as they are less general; for they focus on narrow compresence, and so on a way of being indeterminate, rather than on indeterminacy as such. They say more in so far as they contain additional premisses—for example, the claim that sensibles are imperfect and so are not adequate as the basic objects of knowledge.

3. Plato and the conclusion of the Arguments from the Sciences

Each of the Arguments from the Sciences concludes that the basic objects of knowledge are Platonic forms—that is, in Aristotle's view, non-sensible, everlasting, separated, perfect paradigms. Does Plato infer either from (instances of) the premisses of the Arguments from the Sciences or from the fuller argument contained in *Rep.* 5 that there are such entities?

Rep. 5 certainly concludes that the basic (though not the only) objects of knowledge are forms.[18] Since the Arguments from the Sciences likewise conclude that forms are the basic (but not the only) objects of knowledge, they get Plato right on a fundamental point on which he has often been misunderstood. Further, like the Arguments from the Sciences but unlike Socrates, Plato takes forms to be non-sensible; so in this respect too the Arguments from the Sciences correctly capture a key Platonic claim.

But does *Rep.* 5 take forms to be perfect paradigms, and if so does Plato reason invalidly? Unlike AS I, *Rep.* 5 does not call forms paradigms. But in book 6 (500e) Plato mentions the 'heavenly paradigm' the guardians will look to in attempting to mould better people and practices. These are probably forms; and Aristotle would take any paradigms mentioned in this context to be perfect paradigms. Let us agree with Aristotle about this. Since there is no intervening argument for the existence of forms between the *Rep.* 5 argument and the suggestion that forms are perfect paradigms, presumably the *Rep.* 5 argument is meant to justify the suggestion (if anything is meant to justify it); so let us ask whether it does so.

We saw in Ch. 4.7 that in saying that forms are perfect paradigms Plato means that they are paradigms of the Socratic sort[19]—standards we must refer to in order to know what properties things have—because they are perfect, in so far as they are basic objects of knowledge that escape compresence and so on. So Plato would probably say that if he has a valid argument for the claim that forms escape compresence and so on, then he has a valid argument for the claim that they are perfect paradigms; for no more is really involved in being a perfect paradigm than escaping compresence and so on. Since his argument for the claim that forms enjoy these latter features is valid,[20] he takes himself to have a valid argument for the claim that they are perfect paradigms. Moreover, we saw in the last section that, unlike the Arguments from the Sciences, *Rep.* 5 seems to disqualify sensibles from being the basic objects of knowledge on the ground that they are imperfect; this assumes that the basic objects of knowledge must be perfect.

But we need not say that Aristotle misunderstands Plato, if he takes the Arguments from the Sciences both to capture *Rep.* 5 and to be an invalid argument for the existence of perfect paradigms. For even if I am right to say that Plato takes the fact that forms escape compresence and so on to show that they are perfect paradigms, he certainly does not offer a full or precise account of what perfection and paradigmatism consist in. Indeed, in *Rep.* 5, at any rate, he does not even *explicitly* say that they are perfect or paradigms, although such claims are not far below the surface.[21] So perhaps Aristotle does not mention perfection in the Arguments from the Sciences because he feels no obligation to give Plato premisses Plato assumes but does not trouble to articulate clearly. Aristotle probably also believes that if perfect paradigmatism involves no more than I have suggested, then Plato should have described his view in some other way; for his grandiose descriptions of forms most naturally suggest a more robust reading.[22] So perhaps Aristotle formulates the Arguments from the Sciences as he does in order to emphasize the point that Plato speaks misleadingly and tells us too little. In this case, he is following his familiar strategy of not giving his opponents claims they are not careful to formulate precisely. This strategy may not be especially charitable. But it does not involve any misunderstanding, and it is useful in calling our attention to argumentative gaps.

Does *Rep.* 5 (like the first Argument from the Sciences) take forms to be everlasting? At the end of *Rep.* 5, Plato says that forms are always in the same condition (*aei kata tauta hōsaustōs onta*, 479e7–8); and at the beginning of book 6 he contrasts forms that are always (*aei*) with sensibles that 'wander between becoming (*genesis*) and ceasing to be (*phthora*)' (485b2–3). One might take Plato to be contrasting everlasting and unchanging forms with sensibles that change and are not everlasting. But as we saw in Ch. 4.5, the claim that forms are always and that sensibles 'wander between *genesis* and *phthora*' might indicate instead that forms are always and only *F*, in contrast to sensibles, which are *F* and not *F*. This contrast—unlike a contrast between everlasting, unchanging forms and changing, perishable sensibles—is justified by the preceding context, which gives us one reason to assume that that is the contrast Plato intends to draw.

AS I, however, uses '*aidion*' rather than '*aei*'; and '*aidion*' probably indicates everlastingness.[23] Perhaps Aristotle thinks that passages like *Rep.* 6 (485b2–3) advert to everlastingness? An alternative is that he agrees that such passages are not concerned with everlastingness, in which case they do not argue invalidly for it. But perhaps he wants to point out that Plato none the less believes that forms are everlasting, in which case it is worth while asking whether any of his arguments justify the belief, and worth while pointing out that at least arguments like those contained in *Rep.* 5 do not justify it. (This Aristotelian criticism is unaffected by the fact that *Rep.* 5 contains premisses beyond those contained in the Arguments from the Sciences, since adding those premisses does not validate an inference to everlastingness.)

What, finally, about separation? Aristotle is right to say that the Arguments from the Sciences do not imply that forms are separate. Nor does the fuller argument in *Rep.* 5 imply that they are. But perhaps Plato would agree. Certainly he never explicitly argues, in *Rep.* 5 or elsewhere, that forms are separate; indeed, he never even claims without argument that forms are separate. But it does not follow that Aristotle is mistaken if he suggests that Plato takes the Arguments from the Sciences (or the fuller argument contained in *Rep.* 5) to establish separation. For Aristotle might be arguing as follows: Plato never argues that forms are separate; he seems simply to assume that they are, perhaps because he believes it is in the nature of universals to be separate. But in Aristotle's view, so far from its being in the nature of universals to be separate, they cannot be separate, and so Plato's controversial—indeed, in Aristotle's view, false—assumption requires argument. Aristotle then asks whether the Arguments from the Sciences imply separation, not because he thinks that Plato takes them (or his fuller argument) to show this, but as part of a whittling-away process, in his effort to show that Plato has no arguments that imply separation.[24]

4. The Imperfection Argument

So far in discussing Plato's commitment to the Arguments from the Sciences, I have focused on *Rep*. 5, arguing that although it is narrower in scope than the Arguments from the Sciences, it is none the less relevant to them in so far as it contains instances of their premisses. But it is worth asking why Aristotle suggests that Plato offers an argument of broader scope.

One possibility is that he is combining premisses of the Socratic dialogues with conclusions he finds in the middle dialogues; for we have seen that the premisses of the Arguments from the Sciences are recognizably Socratic. But another possibility is worth considering.

Although *Rep*. 5's scope is narrower than the Arguments from the Sciences, there are passages in the middle dialogues that are of broader scope. For example, in *Rep*. 6 Plato mentions a form of the square and one of the diagonal (510de), but their existence is not established by narrow compresence. In *Rep*. 10 (596b1), Plato mentions a form of bed and one of table; their existence is not sanctioned by narrow compresence either. Perhaps Plato uses the Arguments from the Sciences on their behalf? I defer discussion of *Rep*. 10 until Ch. 8.7; here I ask why *Rep*. 6–7 posit geometrical forms.

Unfortunately, Plato does not explicitly provide an argument on their behalf. But one reasonable and attractive possibility is that the *Rep*. 5 argument—the only argument for the existence of forms in the preceding context—is meant to be extended or generalized so as to establish the existence of geometrical forms. What might this more general argument be?

Here is one possibility. We have seen that in Plato's view, if something is F and not F in the narrow sense, it is imperfectly F in the sense that we cannot understand what it is to be F, or why things are F, by reference to it; so (since knowledge of Fs is possible), there must be a perfect form of F. The form of F is perfect in that it explains the F-ness of all the F things there are and in that, by referring to it, one can understand what it is to be F. For it to be able to play this role, it must escape narrow compresence—it must be F and not also not F. It does this because, being the determinable property of F, it explains why all F things are F, and it never explains why anything is not *F*. Let us then say that Plato accepts the *Imperfection Argument* for the existence of forms, which we may abbreviate into the following conditional:

If a group of things are all of them imperfectly *F*, they are *F* in virtue of a perfect form of *F*.

Now, particular squares and the like are not, in the narrow sense, also not squares. But perhaps Plato believes that they are none the less imperfectly square in a way that requires the existence of a perfect form of square. And it is not too difficult to see what the relevant imperfection might be; for every particular square, and every type of square, has features that are inessential to the nature of squareness as such, and so we cannot explain what it is to be square, or why all squares are square, by reference to particular squares or particular types of squares.

If this is right, then perhaps Plato focuses on narrow compresence, not because he thinks that there are forms only in such cases, but because he takes it to be a salient instance of the sort of imperfection that requires the existence of perfect forms. Perhaps he is sure that narrow compresence is a sort of imperfection that requires the existence of perfect forms and that there are perfect forms in further cases as well, but unsure how many further forms there are and unsure about precisely why they are required; so he focuses on what he views as the clearest case, without meaning to suggest that it is the only sort of case that requires the existence of perfect forms. If so, his failure to mention an argument, besides the one from narrow compresence, for the existence of geo-metrical forms, is not so troubling after all. We just need to see that we are meant to generalize from his focus on narrow compresence.

How far is the generalization meant to go—that is, how many forms does the Imperfection Argument posit? Plato is not explicit about this. But he sometimes seems to think that (like Socrates' realist one over many argument) it posits forms for every property. At least, the reason Plato seems to have in mind for counting particular squares and types of squares as imperfect (for the purpose of understanding what squareness as such is, and why squares are squares) seems to apply to all particular *F*s and particular types of *F*; for each of them has features that are inessential to the nature of *F*-ness so that, to understand what *F*-ness is we need to go beyond particular *F*s and types of *F*s to a perfect form of *F*.

Precisely what features does Plato take perfection to involve? Once again, he is not explicit. But forms seem to be perfect because they are explanatory, in that we can understand what *F*-ness is, and why things are *F*, only if we know the form of *F*. This, in turn, requires forms to escape compresence; it also requires them to be non-sensible. For at least by the time of the *Theaetetus* and *Timaeus*, Plato seems to believe that no property can be defined in sensible or observational terms; reference to sensibles is therefore not explanatory, in which case all sensibles are imperfect.[25] Plato no doubt believes that forms have further features. But their perfection seems to consist chiefly in the facts that they escape compresence and are non-sensible and explanatory; at least, these are the key features emphasized in argumentative passages that focus on the perfection of forms, and these arguments do not require forms to have any further features, such as being separate or everlasting.

If Plato uses the Imperfection Argument in the broad way I have suggested, then we can answer a question posed in Ch. 2.1. I noted there that Plato sometimes countenances forms whose existence is not justified by the argument from (narrow) compresence; and I wondered how Plato argues that they exist, and whether they are like or unlike the forms whose existence is justified by (narrow) compresence. We have just seen that Plato sometimes seems to use the Imperfection Argument as an argument for the existence of these further forms. These further forms are like the forms posited by the argument from narrow compresence in so far as they are all perfect, and so they all escape compresence and are explanatory and non-sensible.[26]

I also noted in Chs. 2 and 4 that people sometimes take forms to be meanings on the ground that, they think, Plato posits forms for every predicate. Now, the Imperfection Argument does not posit forms for every predicate; but Plato sometimes seems to take it to posit forms for every property. It therefore allows us to see how Plato can posit a broad range of forms without conceiving forms as meanings. For the Imperfection Argument is a metaphysical and epistemological, rather than a semantic, argument for the existence of forms: it takes the possibility of knowledge to require the existence of explanatory forms, conceived as non-sensible properties. So the mere fact that Plato countenances a broad range of forms should not encourage us to suppose that he takes forms to be meanings.

I began this section by asking why, when Plato focuses on narrow compresence, Aristotle formulates the Arguments from the Sciences in broader terms. The account I have given of Plato's Imperfection Argument suggests an answer. For I have suggested that Plato focuses on narrow compresence at least partly because it is a salient instance of a more general sort of imperfection that he takes to require the existence of forms. Something is imperfectly *F*, in the more general way, just in case it has features that are inessential to, and so not explanatory of, the nature of *F*-ness as such. But this sort of imperfection is just indeterminacy of the sort at issue in AS II. So perhaps Aristotle focuses on indeterminacy as such because he sees that Plato sometimes does so implicitly.

5. Broad compresence

A more speculative suggestion is also worth mentioning. I have suggested
so far that narrow compresence is a salient instance of a more general sort
of imperfection that Plato takes to require the existence of perfect forms;
this more general sort of imperfection is indeterminacy of the sort mentioned in the Arguments from the Sciences. But this more general sort of
imperfection—i.e. indeterminacy—may itself be a type of compresence,
which we may call *broad compresence*.

So far the only sort of compresence I have discussed is narrow compresence, which requires something to be F and not F in virtue of some
one and the same aspect of itself. Bright colour, for example, makes some
things beautiful and other things ugly; the action type of standing firm in
battle has some courageous and some not courageous tokens. But in the
Timaeus, for example, Plato says that every sensible sample of fire is both
fire and not fire. No sensible sample of fire is both fire and not fire in the
narrow sense. Plato means instead that although each is fire, each is also
not fire in so far as each has features that are not essential to the nature
of fire, since each has bits of earth and the other elements mixed in
(49c–51d); no sensible sample of fire is pure fire. Let us then say that
sensible samples of fire are fire and not fire in the sense of broad compresence. Something is F and not F in the broad sense just in case, in
addition to being F, it is also not F in virtue of having features that are
not essential to being F as such. If something is in narrow compresence it
is also in broad compresence, but the converse is not true. Although
square, for instance, is not both shape and not shape in the narrow sense,
it is both shape and not shape in the broad sense. For it is shape and,
since it has features that are not essential to the nature of shape as such,
it is also not shape. Every F thing other than the property of F is F and
not F in the broad sense.[27]

Broad compresence is the same phenomenon as the indeterminacy at
issue in AS II. To be indeterminately F is to be F, and to have properties
that are inessential to the nature of F-ness. But to be F, and to be not F
in virtue of having properties that are inessential to the nature of F-ness,
is to be in broad compresence with respect to F-ness.

Plato and Aristotle themselves connect indeterminacy and compresence.
In the *Philebus*,[28] Plato says that a mark or sign (*sēmeion*, 24e5) of the
nature of the indeterminate is that it admits 'the more and the less',
'the strongly and the weakly' (24e); he also says that the indeterminate
involves a 'struggle of opposites' (25e). In music, for example, any given
note is higher than some notes and lower than others; so if we describe
a given note indeterminately—as being e.g. high or low—we cannot
identify what note it is. To do that, we need to describe it determinately
—we need to explain its precise location on the musical scale. Plato thus

explains indeterminacy not in terms of succession, but in terms of compresence.[29] Similarly, Plato says that impure pleasures—pleasures whose essence involves pain—are indeterminate (52c2 ff.). A pure pleasure is a pleasure unmixed with any pain, just as pure white is whiteness without any other colour mixed in (52d6–53b6). Once again, compresence and indeterminacy go hand in hand. And Plato's point is familiar: we cannot understand what whiteness is by focusing on mixed colours, just as (in the middle dialogues) we cannot understand what *F*-ness is by appealing to something that is *F* and not *F*. In order to know what *F*-ness is, we must appeal to something that escapes compresence; for anything that suffers compresence is for that very reason indeterminate, and so it cannot be a basic object of knowledge.

In *Met.* 4. 4, Aristotle says that 'the same thing is a thousand times a man and not a man' (1007a16–17), for Socrates, who is a man, is also pale and tall. But then, in attempting to signify one thing (*hen*, 1007a13; cf. 1007a5: *to auto kai hen*), one ought not to go through the coincidents, since they are *apeira* (1007a14). Socrates is a man and not a man, not in the narrow, but only in the broad, sense. So like Plato, Aristotle adverts to broad compresence, which he explains in terms of indeterminacy.[30]

There is, then, some evidence that both Plato and Aristotle sometimes take indeterminacy to be the same phenomenon as broad compresence. If this is right, then in focusing on indeterminacy, the Arguments from the Sciences focus on compresence after all—not merely in the sense that narrow compresence is an instance of indeterminacy, but also in the sense that broad compresence and indeterminacy are the same phenomenon. But whether or not this speculative suggestion is correct, it is reasonable to suppose that Aristotle formulates the Arguments from the Sciences as he does because he believes that indeterminacy captures the broader sort of imperfection on which Plato sometimes relies and of which narrow compresence is a salient instance.[31]

6. Artefact forms again

We may now seem to face a problem. In the previous chapter, I suggested that when Aristotle says that 'they' do not want artefact forms, he can be taken to mean that Plato does not take artefact forms to have all the features he takes other forms countenanced in the middle dialogues to have. But I also said that it would be a stumbling-block for this suggestion if Plato has (or if Aristotle believes he has) an argument that commits him to the existence of distinctively Platonic artefact forms no less than to distinctively Platonic geometrical forms. It might seem that we have now found such an argument. For the broad version of the Imperfection Argument seems to commit Plato to the existence of perfect artefact forms no less than to the existence of perfect moral forms. At least, it seems reasonable to suppose that just as we cannot explain what it is to be shape in terms of particular shapes, so we cannot explain what it is to be, say, a bed in terms of particular beds.[32] (I return to this point in the next chapter.) So is Plato committed to the existence of artefact forms that have all the features that Aristotle associates with the distinctively Platonic forms? No, for as we have seen the Imperfection Argument does not seem to imply that forms are separate or everlasting—the features that, we speculated in the last chapter, Plato may deny to artefact forms. At least, as he understands the relevant notion of perfection, it does not seem to require forms to be everlasting or separate.[33] If there is a fault in Aristotle's reasoning, it is in his suggestion that Plato takes the premisses of the Arguments from the Sciences to imply that *any* forms are everlasting or separate. But in sect. 3 we saw that we need not convict Aristotle of misinterpretation on this score either. So here as elsewhere, once we understand Aristotle's interpretative strategies, we can avoid saying that Aristotle either misinterprets or refutes Plato.

8

The One over Many Argument: Forms and Predication

1. Introduction

According to the One over Many Argument, there are separated, ever-lasting forms corresponding to every general term true of groups of things. Aristotle levels two objections against the argument. His first objection is that if it proved that there are any forms, it would prove that there are too many; in particular, it would prove that there are forms of 'negations and of things that are not' (IIA). Yet, he explains, it would be absurd for there to be such forms (IIB). Aristotle assumes the Platonists would agree, for he says that 'of such things they did not want genera or ideas' (81. 7–8). Aristotle's second criticism (III) rescues them from the absurdity. For according to it, the One over Many Argument is not a valid argument for the existence of forms, and so it does not prove that there are forms of negations or of anything else. But Aristotle believes that its premisses imply that 'what is predicated in common is some other thing than the particulars of which it is predicated' (81. 9–10). That is, the premisses of the One over Many Argument imply that there are *koina*, but not that there are forms.[1]

It is widely believed that Plato uses a one over many argument to establish the existence of forms corresponding to every general term. It is also often believed that Plato's one over many argument is a semantic argument according to which forms are the meanings of general terms.[2] Does Plato offer a semantic one over many argument for the existence of forms? Is he committed to the existence of forms corresponding to every general term? If so, why does Aristotle say that Plato did not want forms of negations? Does Plato use any version of a one over many argument to establish the existence of separated, everlasting forms?

I begin by examining the One over Many Argument (sects. 2 and 3). I then explore Aristotle's first objection to it (sect. 4). Subsequent sections ask about the argument's Platonic credentials, and whether Plato is committed to the existence of forms of negations.

2. The One over Many Argument

The One over Many Argument may be formulated as follows:

(1) Whenever many *F*s (*polla*) are *F*, they are *F* in virtue of having some one thing, the *F*, predicated of them.[3]
(2) No *F* particular (*kath' hekaston*) is *F* in virtue of itself.
(3) The *F* is in every case (*aei*) predicated in the same way of all the numerically successive *F*s (*tōn kat' arithmon allassomenōn*).
(4) Therefore the *F* is something besides (*para*) particular *F*s.
(5) Therefore the *F* is separated from (*kechōrismenon*)[4] particular *F*s and is everlasting (*aidion*).
(6) Whatever is a one over many, separated, and everlasting is a form.
(7) Therefore the *F* is a form.

(1) talks about something's being predicated of each of the *many F*s (*polla*, 80. 9). In 80. 12, Aristotle uses '*kath' hekasta*' instead; at 80. 13 he uses '*ta kat' arithmon allassomena*'. As we have seen, *kath' hekasta* can be particulars, low-level types, or both. In the Arguments from the Sciences they seem to include low-level types. In the One over Many Argument, however, they are probably only particulars. For in Aristotle's view, only particulars are numerically one (*hen arithmō(i)*); universals are one only in various other ways.[5] The particulars at issue again seem to be sensible or observable.[6]

The phrase 'numerically successive particulars' sometimes indicates change in the sense of succession.[7] But '*allassomena*' is also often used to mean 'taken in exchange for one another' or 'taken in turn',[8] and that seems to be how it is used here: the argument is concerned not with the fact that the many *F*s change, but only with the fact that they are many, with their plurality.[9] If this is right, then succession is irrelevant not only to the Arguments from the Sciences but also to the One over Many Argument.

(1) and (3) tell us that the *F* is in each case (*aei*) predicated of the many *F*s in just the same way and in virtue of some one thing.[10] (4) infers that what is predicated of the many *F*s is different from each and all of them. This inference is valid. For according to (1) and (3), each of the many *F*s there (timelessly) is is *F* in just the same way and in virtue of some one thing. Suppose that the *F*s in question are men, and that the one thing is Callias. According to (2), none of the many *F*s is *F* in virtue of itself; hence Callias cannot be a man in virtue of himself. But if Socrates is none the less a man because Callias is predicated of him, then contrary to (1) Socrates and Callias are not men in virtue of some one thing. Analogous reasoning shows that the *F* in virtue of which particular *F*s are *F* cannot be one of the many *F*s.[11]

(5) infers that the *F* is both separated and everlasting. Neither conjunct follows. To say, as (5) does, that what is predicated is separated from what it is predicated of is to say that it can exist whether or not any corresponding sensible particulars exist. But the fact that what is predicated is *different* from what it is predicated of does not imply that it is *separated* from what it is predicated of: difference does not imply separation. (So although the three *Metaphysics* passages explored in Ch. 4 do not attribute an invalid argument for separation to Plato, the One over Many Argument is such an argument.) Similarly, (1)–(4) imply that the *F* exists so long as there are *F* particulars; but in order to infer that the *F* is everlasting, we need the additional assumption, not mentioned in the One over Many Argument, that there always are some *F* particulars.[12]

(6) claims that if something is a one over many, separated, and everlasting, it is a form.[13] Aristotle uses 'one over many' (*hen para ta polla*) to refer to universals.[14] So like the *Metaphysics* passages and the Arguments from the Sciences, the One over Many takes forms to be universals. But Aristotle uses 'one over many' for two different sorts of universals. In the *Posterior Analytics* (77a5–9), for example, he criticizes the Platonists for positing a *hen para ta polla*, although he insists that demonstration requires the existence of a *hen kata pollōn* and a *hen epi pleionōn*. Here '*para*' indicates separation; Aristotle's point is that although demonstration requires the existence of universals, it does not require the existence of *separated* universals. Elsewhere in the *Posterior Analytics* (100a7), however, he says that each of his own universals is a *hen para ta polla*. Here '*para*' indicates not separation but difference; Aristotle's point is that each universal is some one thing that is different from the many particulars of which it is predicated.[15] This is inconsistency in terminology, not in doctrine; Aristotle uses '*para*' both for separation and difference.

(6) seems to use '*para*' for difference.[16] For otherwise it would be redundant, saying twice over that forms are separate. But Aristotle's point seems to be that although the Platonists rightly countenance the one over many—i.e. universals—they wrongly take the one over many to be separate. (1)–(4), that is, imply that there are universals that are different from particulars; but they do not imply that universals are separate from particulars.

Aristotle would take the inference from (6) to (7) to be valid. But since the inference in (5) is invalid, Aristotle is right to say that the One over Many Argument is an invalid argument for the existence of forms. For as I indicated in Ch. 2.7, Aristotle seems to think that for an argument to be a valid argument for the existence of forms, it must be a valid argument for the existence of universals that are either separate or perfect paradigms. Since paradigmatism is not in the offing here, presumably Aristotle believes that the One over Many Argument does not show that there are forms because it does not show that universals are separate. The key fault in the argument is therefore in the inference to separation in (5).[17] But if we resist this inference and rest content with an argument for the claim that the one over many exists and is different from what it is over, then, Aristotle claims in III, we have a valid argument for the existence of *koina*. Aristotle's point here, then, as in commenting on the Arguments from the Sciences, is that although Plato sees that there are universals, he misconceives their nature.

We have thus already vindicated Aristotle's second objection to the One over Many Argument (III), that it is an invalid argument for the existence of forms, and so I shall not consider it further here. But we still need to assess his first and longer objection, that the One over Many Argument yields forms of negations and of things that are not (II). We also need to ask whether Plato is committed to the One over Many Argument. Before turning to these matters, however, I shall consider the first premiss of the One over Many Argument in more detail; for it is a crucial premiss whose precise content we need to understand in order to assess Aristotle's first criticism and Plato's commitments.

3. What is predicated?

According to (1), whenever particular *F*s are *F*, they are *F* in virtue of having some one thing, the *F*, predicated of them. What is the *F* in virtue of which particular *F*s are *F*? One possibility is that it is a linguistic predicate:

(1a) Whenever a group of particulars are *F*, they are *F* in virtue of having some one predicate, '*F*', predicated of them.

(1a) might seem to be a natural and plausible reading of (1). But it is not the correct reading. First, Aristotle's talk of 'predication' certainly does not speak in its favour. It is as natural in Aristotle's Greek to say that man—a secondary substance, on his view of the matter in the *Categories*—is predicated as it is to say that 'man' is; predication, for Aristotle, need not be a linguistic affair.[18] Secondly, even if (1a) seems plausible on its own, what it would be used to prove would not be: that linguistic predicates, since these are what are predicated, are forms. But forms are not linguistic predicates; the form of man is not the predicate 'man'. Thirdly, Aristotle takes the One over Many Argument to be a valid argument for the existence of *koina*; but *koina* are not linguistic predicates any more than forms are.[19] Fourthly, Aristotle's criticisms of the One over Many Argument in II would immediately fail if (1) were read as (1a). Although his objections need not ultimately succeed, we should if possible avoid interpreting the One over Many Argument so that they obviously and immediately fail; and, as we shall see, we can avoid this.

One might argue that a closely related reading of (1) is correct:

(1*b*) Whenever a group of particulars are *F*, they are *F* in virtue of having some one meaning, the meaning of '*F*', predicated of them.

According to (1*b*), the meanings of predicates, rather than the predicates themselves, are predicated. Like (1*a*), (1*b*) might seem to be a natural and plausible reading of (1). It would make the One over Many Argument a semantic one over many argument for the existence of forms, positing forms as the meanings of general terms. Moreover, as we have seen, Plato is often thought to offer a semantic one over many argument for the existence of forms. None the less, I do not think (1) should be read as (1*b*). For, again, Aristotle takes the One over Many Argument to be a valid argument for the existence of *koina*; but *koina* are not meanings.[20] Further, with (1*b*) Aristotle's objections to the One over Many Argument in II would so obviously fail that we should avoid this interpretation if we can—and, as we shall see, we can avoid it. It might also be a further count against (1*b*) that the One over Many Argument seems to posit forms only when a predicate is true of a group of things. For if forms were meanings, whether or not the corresponding predicate was true of a group of things would seem to be irrelevant.[21]

If (1) is not read as (1*b*), then the One over Many Argument does not conceive forms as meanings. I ask below whether Plato offers a semantic one over many argument for the existence of forms. The point for now is only that the One over Many is not such an argument.

Yet another reading of (1) is:

(1*c*) Whenever a group of particulars are *F*, they are *F* in virtue of having some one thing, the property of *F*, predicated of them.

According to (1*c*), whenever a group of particulars are *F*, for any '*F*', they are *F*, not because '*F*' or the meaning of '*F*' is predicated of them, but because they share the property of being *F*. Every term true of a group of things denotes a property. If 'grue' is true of a group of things, then grue is a property. On both (1*b*) and (1*c*), it turns out (according to the One over Many Argument) that there are forms for every general term true of groups of things; but (1*b*) and (1*c*) are none the less different claims. According to (1*b*), meanings are predicated; according to (1*c*), properties are. If (1) is read as (1*b*), then the One over Many Argument takes forms to be meanings; if it is read as (1*c*), it takes them to be properties. But meanings and properties are disjoint classes of entities.[22]

(1*c*) avoids the objections we raised to (1*a*) and (1*b*). For, again, Aristotle claims that the One over Many Argument is a valid argument for the existence of his own *koina*; but his own *koina* are, not predicates or meanings, but properties conceived in realist fashion. And unlike (1*a*) and (1*b*), (1*c*) allows us to make sense of his criticisms of the One over Many Argument. I thus believe that (1) ought to be read as (1*c*).[23] If so, then whatever is true of Plato, Aristotle does not suggest here that forms are meanings. He suggests instead that the Platonists believe (or are committed to believing) that there are properties (and so, it turns out, forms) corresponding to every general term true of groups of things— where properties (forms) are conceived in realist fashion. Aristotle then argues, quite correctly, that one ought not to countenance so wide a range of properties.[24] Notice, though, that the One over Many Argument posits fewer forms than is sometimes thought. For it posits forms only when a predicate is true of some group of things. If a predicate is not true of anything, then the One over Many Argument does not posit a corresponding form.

I now turn to Aristotle's first criticism of the One over Many Argument, and then to the One over Many Argument's Platonic credentials; in so doing, we shall find further support for (1c).

4. Negations

Aristotle's first and longer objection to the One over Many Argument is that if it proved that there were any forms, it would prove that there are forms of 'negations and of things that are not'. For one and the same negation, such as not-man, may be predicated of a plurality of particulars (of all those particulars that are not men), in which case premiss (1) is satisfied; not-man is not the same as any of the things of which it is predicated (2); and it is predicated in the same way of the similar particulars of which it is predicated (3). It follows that not-man is a one over many, separated, and everlasting, and so it is a form. But, Aristotle protests, this is absurd (*atopon*).

What are 'negations and things that are not'? Cherniss suggests that 'things that are not' are non-existent things—fictional entities such as the Chimaera and centaurs.[25] But none of Aristotle's examples is of fictional entities; they are all of negations—not-man, not-musical, and the like. Further, having said that it would be absurd for there to be forms of negations, Aristotle immediately asks: 'For how could there be an idea of not-being?' (81. 2). He then goes on to explain what is wrong with forms of negations. On Cherniss's reading, the question is inserted inappropriately between two discussions of negations. Nor does it receive a separate answer; Aristotle explains only why it would be absurd to countenance forms of negations. Moreover, the One over Many Argument posits forms only for general terms true of groups of things. This may require us to posit forms of negations on the reasonable assumption that groups of things are not-beautiful and so on. But it does not require us to posit forms of, for example, centaurs, since nothing is a centaur. Examples of non-existent things would thus actually be inappropriate here.[26]

An alternative to Cherniss's reading is ready to hand. The '*kai*' that links '*apophaseis*' and '*ta mē onta*' is epexegetic, not conjunctive. '*Ta mē onta*' is a gloss on or explanation of '*apophaseis*': it introduces no new set of examples. Aristotle thus discusses only the absurdity of countenancing forms of negations; fictional entities are irrelevant here.[27]

Still, what are negations? We can best answer this question by asking another one: why does Aristotle think it would be absurd to countenance forms of negations? If forms were being conceived as predicates or meanings—if (1a) or (1b) were in play—it would be difficult to penetrate his reasons. For surely whatever else may be wrong with 'not-man', it is a single predicate, and it may be assigned a perfectly determinate meaning. If Aristotle took forms to be predicates or meanings, it is not clear why he should think that the Platonists would welcome a form of man but not of not-man, for 'not-man' is as much a general term as, and is just as definable as, 'man' is.[28]

Aristotle's reason for supposing that forms of negations are absurd is not that they are not predicates or that their names are meaningless, but that they would 'group together things different in genus', 'things different in every way'.[29] The idea is that forms are supposed to be real properties, explaining genuine resemblances. But, Aristotle protests, the fact that a group of things are all not men does not show that they share a property; that a group of things fail to share a property is not a genuine unifying feature of them.[30] The Platonists therefore ought not to countenance forms of negations; yet the One over Many Argument commits them to their existence.

Aristotle makes the same point about negations in a different way in the *De Interpretatione*, when he says that 'not-man' is not a name (16a30); it is only an 'indefinite name' (16a32), for what 'not-man' 'signifies is in a way one thing, but indefinite' (19b9). As Ackrill explains, Aristotle 'probably thinks of ["not-man"] as a single word but thinks that it fails to name anything in the way in which an ordinary name does: it stands for no definite kind of thing and can be applied to a wildly various range of objects'.[31]

If this is right, then the criterion for negations is not syntactic; not every negative word denotes a negation, nor does every non-negative word fail to do so. We can always coin positive and negative words as we like (say 'schman' for 'not-man'), but we do not thereby dispose of or create negations. Rather, not-*P* is a negation just in case *P* is a property; negations are the complements of properties or kinds. Hence we can know what negations there are only when we know what properties there are, and this is not a matter to be determined by syntax or, for that matter, semantics.

If this is Aristotle's account of negations, then it supports a claim made in the previous section, that (1) should be read not as (1a) or as (1b), but as (1c). Hence like the *Metaphysics* passages and the Arguments from the Sciences, the One over Many Argument conceives forms not as predicates or meanings, but as properties. Though various philosophers believe that Plato offers a semantic one over many argument for the existence of forms, Aristotle is not among them.

Aristotle's criticisms of the One over Many Argument are cogent. For it is not a valid argument for separation; and it is reasonable to deny that negations are genuine properties. But we do not yet know whether Aristotle has criticized anything Plato professes; for we do not yet know whether Plato is committed to the One over Many Argument. Here three chief questions will concern us: first, is Plato committed to (1c)? Secondly, does he countenance forms of negations? Thirdly, does he use a one over many argument to establish the existence of separated forms?

5. Plato's One over Many Argument

In Ch. 4.4, I suggested that Socrates accepts a realist one over many argument according to which there are forms corresponding not to every predicate but to every property. Since not every term true of a group of things is a genuine property, Socrates is not committed to (1c). If he is not committed to (1c), he is not committed to the One over Many Argument that Aristotle records. Even if Socrates were committed to (1c), Aristotle would not take him to be committed to the One over Many Argument. For it argues that there are *separated* forms; but in Aristotle's view, Socrates is not committed to the existence of such forms. So although Socrates accepts a one over many argument for the existence of forms, it is not the one over many argument Aristotle records; nor is Aristotle likely to think that it is.[32] Let us then consider other contexts.

Cherniss suggests that the 'closest approach to a formal statement' of a one over many that aims to establish forms for every predicate occurs in the *Parmenides*:[33]

I suppose it is because of the following sort of thing that you think that each form is one. Whenever many things seem large to you, there perhaps seems to you to be, when you have looked at them all, some one and the same idea. Hence you think the large is one. (132a1–4.)

Socrates agrees without demur and is thereby subjected to the Third Man Argument.[34] But what has he agreed to? Certainly to (among other things) something appropriately called a 'one over many argument', some version of which plays a crucial role in the Third Man Argument. But the relevant one over many argument does not demand a form for every predicate. Socrates says that when a group of things are large, they are large in virtue of a form of large. We have no licence to infer that he believes that if a group of things are *F*, for *any* '*F*', they are *F* in virtue of a form of *F*. 'Large' denotes a property, and Socrates' acceptance of a corresponding form does not commit him to the existence of a form corresponding to every general term.[35] Certainly we shall see later that the Third Man Argument does not require a one over many argument according to which there are forms for every predicate.

The surrounding context might be thought to show that Plato is not just uncommitted to, but positively rejects, the existence of forms corresponding to every predicate. For just before the Third Man Argument, he claims that there are no forms of hair, mud, or dirt (*Parm.* 130c5–d5). Either the two passages are flatly inconsistent, or else the one over many thesis mentioned in 132a1–4 does not require the existence of a form for every predicate.[36] But perhaps we should not appeal to the *Parmenides* on behalf of any view. For it might well describe a theory of forms *not* previously adumbrated, in an effort to warn us against possible misreadings of Plato's actual views.

But we need not rely on the *Parmenides* for evidence that Plato at some stage rejected the existence of forms corresponding to every predicate. For in the *Politicus* (262ae) he considers someone who divides human beings into just two classes, Greeks and *barbaroi* (= non-Greeks). Plato says that this division is not an explanatory one to choose in the circumstances, since the class of *barbaroi* is indeterminate (*apeirois*, 262d3).[37] Yet someone might none the less choose this division on the ground that there is a name, '*barbaros*', and so a corresponding form. Plato objects that the mere fact that there is a name, '*barbaros*', does not show that there is a form of *barbaros*. To know what forms there are, we need to know not what words our language contains, but what the genuine divisions in nature are.[38] At least in the *Politicus*, then, Plato denies that there are forms corresponding to every general term. He does so, moreover, for the reason Aristotle mentions in criticizing the One over Many Argument: forms are supposed to carve at the natural joints, yet not every predicate does so. The *Politicus*, however, is a late dialogue, and our main concern is with the middle dialogues. Perhaps they espouse a different view?

One might think that the middle dialogues are if anything more parsimonious about the range of forms. For their main argument for the existence of forms is narrow compresence, which produces forms only in a limited range of cases. However, the argument from narrow compresence does not preclude the existence of further forms. And it is often thought that, whatever is true elsewhere, at least in *Rep.* 10 (596a6–7) Plato uses a one over many argument—some would say, a semantic one over many argument—according to which there are forms corresponding to every general term.[39] For 596a6–7 is commonly translated as follows: 'We are, I suppose, in the habit of positing some one form for each group of many things to which we apply the same name.'[40]

But what should we infer? Noting that the *Politicus* is a late dialogue, following the *Parmenides'* criticisms of the theory of forms, we might infer that Plato has retrenched: early on, he believed that there were forms corresponding to every general term; he then came to see that that view leads to the difficulties the *Politicus* describes, and so he abandoned it.[41] If this were right, then Aristotle's criticism would be one that Plato levelled against himself.[42]

While this suggestion cannot be decisively rejected, I should like to suggest an alternative. The wording of *Rep.* 596a does not commit Plato to the existence of a form for every predicate. For Plato may well use 'name' (*onoma*) not for every predicate, but for every name that denotes a property or, as we might say, for every *property-name*.[43] To be sure, Plato sometimes, as in the *Politicus* passage, uses 'name' quite broadly. But in the *Cratylus*, the only dialogue in which he discusses the nature of names in any detail, he seems to use 'name' in a more restricted way that is also in play in the *De Interpretatione*. According to the *Cratylus*, 'n' counts as a name only if it denotes a real property or kind and reveals the outlines of its essence.[44] If, like the *Cratylus*, *Rep.* 596a restricts names to property-names, then it is committed to the existence of forms corresponding only to every property-name. *Rep.* 596a6–7, so far from disagreeing with *Politicus* 262ae, would then agree with it.

But ought we to interpret 'name' in this way in *Rep.* 596a? After all, the passage does not explain its use of 'name', and Plato sometimes uses 'name' more widely. Nor does it provide any examples of names that might resolve the issue; it mentions only names that Plato takes to be property-names. This reveals nothing about whether he admits forms for further predicates.

One reason to suppose that *Rep.* 596a has the *Cratylus'* restricted use of 'name' in mind, however, is that the two contexts are very similar.[45] It would then not be surprising if they also used 'name' in the same way. Further, 596a says it is a *habit* to posit forms when we apply the same name. We should therefore not read the passage in isolation; we have to ask what Plato's habit is. On the account I have been developing, his habit is to posit forms at most for every property-name.[46] If so, then that is also all 596a6–7 does.

Now even if *Rep.* 596a6–7 posits forms only for every property-name, it could posit them for semantic reasons, on some accounts of meaning. But the passage does not require such a reading. For one thing, it does not say *why* forms are needed for every (property-)name; it only says *that* they are needed in this range of cases.[47] To this extent, it is not even clear that *Rep.* 596a6–7 states a one over many argument of any sort.[48] It says something about the range of forms, but it says nothing about reasons for positing them. However, it is reasonable to suppose that, although the passage does not unambiguously say so, something properly called a one over many argument is in the offing, so I shall not press this point. But is its one over many argument semantic? Plato says that 596a6–7 expresses a familiar view; but the one over many argument that is familiar is the Socratic one, which is realist rather than semantic.[49] Nor does anything in the context of *Rep.* 10 require a semantic reading; nor have we yet found Plato offering a semantic argument for the existence of forms.[50] It thus seems reasonable to assume that if *Rep.* 10 has a one over many argument, it is realist rather than semantic. Aristotle is thus quite right not to suggest that Plato defends a semantic one over many argument.

But why does Aristotle ascribe (1c) to Plato? One possibility is that he does not think that Plato ever uses 'name' in the *Cratylus*' restricted way. But this seems implausible. For Aristotle himself uses 'name' in the same restricted way in the *De Interpretatione*, and there are clear echoes of the *Cratylus* throughout the *De Interpretatione*.[51]

A better explanation is that Aristotle sees that although Plato sometimes uses 'name' in a restricted way, he also sometimes (as in the *Politicus*) uses it more broadly. *Rep.* 596a6–7 does not say which use it has in mind; it simply speaks of correlating names and forms, without telling us how many names are correlated with forms. Perhaps Aristotle sees that Plato wants forms at most for every property-name. But he might believe that Plato does not make this sufficiently clear since he does not say which use of 'name' he has in mind. Aristotle then points out some of the difficulties that arise if we assume a broader use of 'name' than the one Plato, without giving us fair warning, intends. If this is Aristotle's criticism, then once again he is relying on his familiar strategy of not giving his opponent distinctions he does not explicitly formulate and properly emphasize. So interpreted, Aristotle does not misunderstand Plato nor is he unfair to him;[52] none the less, we need not say that Plato is vulnerable to his objection.

6. Forms of negations?

I have argued so far that Plato, at least in the contexts we have explored, posits forms corresponding at most to every property-name. If he posits forms only in such cases, one might expect him to deny that there are forms of negations.[53] For negations are the complements of properties and, as Aristotle says, the complements of properties do not seem to be properties. Yet many believe that in the *Sophist* Plato explicitly countenances forms of negations. For the *Sophist* has a form of not-being; and it is also often thought to have forms of not-beautiful, not-large, and the like.

If Plato countenances forms of negations, then we need to ask why Aristotle says that 'they' do not want forms of negations—just as, in considering the Arguments from the Sciences, we faced the question of why Aristotle says that 'they' do not want forms of artefacts, when Plato seems to admit them. Further, one might well wonder what his reason for positing forms of negations could be other than something like (1c) or—the more usual alternative—(1b).[54] I turn, then, to the *Sophist*, to see whether it acknowledges forms of negations and, if it does, why it does so and why Aristotle might none the less claim that the Platonists do not want such forms.

Plato argues in the *Sophist* that the different (*thateron*) is a form no less than being and same are; indeed, it is one of the 'greatest kinds' (*megista genē*, 254d4), pervading everything that is. But, it turns out, the form of the different is the form of not-being; and so there is a form of not-being.[55]

But although not-being is a form, it is not a negation. 'Not-being' is, to be sure, syntactically negative; but the criterion for negations is not syntactic. In any case, Plato emphasizes that statements about not-being can be rewritten positively and more perspicuously in terms of difference, and 'difference' is not syntactically negative.

For not-being to be a negation, it would have to be the complement of being, but it is not.[56] Something *is* just in case it is the same as itself, or is something or other; something *is not* just in case it is different from something or other, or is not *F*, for some property *F*. Nor does not-being apply to all and only those things that being fails to apply to, since both being and not-being apply to everything that is; indeed, something can not-be only if it is.[57]

But even if not-being is not a negation, does it not (like same and being, for that matter) group together things that 'are different in genus' —indeed, 'different in every way'—and is it not objectionable on that count? As Aristotle objects, being (and so presumably also not-being) is not a genus (*APo.* 92b14; *Met.* 998b22–7). Is not Plato then wrong to suppose that we should countenance forms (and so properties) here—and for just the reasons that Aristotle and the *Politicus* describe?

It is true that if we group together all the things that are, or all the things that are not, we collect a heterogeneous group of things. Indeed, as Plato well recognizes, we collect everything that is, since everything that is both is (the same as itself, and something or other) and is not (the same as anything else, and something or other); being and not-being are all-pervasive.

None the less, Plato's reasons for countenancing a form (and so a property) of not-being are intelligible if controversial. He wants to know what the fundamental features of reality are, how to describe the nature of what is. In his view, a full understanding of any entity requires us to know not only what it is but also what it is not, what it excludes no less than what it includes. Moreover, in so far as things are beings and are different, there are interesting truths about them. This view flows naturally from Plato's holism, his belief that knowledge of any entity is indissolubly linked to knowledge of other entities.[58]

These reasons for countenancing forms of being and not-being do not involve (1c); for they rely on special facts about being and not-being that cannot be assumed to carry over to every property. Nor do his reasons suggest (1b). To be sure, Plato is at pains to argue that 'not-being' and so on are meaningful. Nor does he distinguish between difference, being, same, and so on extensionally, since they have just the same extensions. But to say that properties are not conceived of purely extensionally is not to say that they are meanings.[59] Nor does Plato argue that the fact that 'not-being' is meaningful requires the existence of a form of not-being. He is asking about beings in so far as they are beings, i.e. what properties something must have to be a being. Here as elsewhere, then, forms are genuine features of reality, in which case they are not meanings if meanings are taken to be e.g. abstract entities. But neither is a referential theory of meaning in the offing. For Plato takes difference, being, and so on to be coextensive but non-synonymous.

Whatever fault we may find with the form of not-being, then, at least its existence is not defended by a simple-minded appeal to the fact that, after all, our language happens to contain the corresponding name. That is the procedure correctly criticized in the *Politicus*; but Plato does not follow it here or elsewhere. In this connection, it is worth noting that the *Politicus* looks back favourably on the *Sophist*'s treatment of not-being (284b7–9), even though it denies that every term has a corresponding form.[60] It is also worth noting that Aristotle, in *Met.* 4, insists that there is a science of being *qua* being—even though he denies that being is a genus.

What, now, of such parts of not-being as the not-beautiful, the not-large, and the like? Surely these are negations, signifying, as Plato himself insists, only that the things of which they are true are other than what follows the 'not' (257b9–c3)? Hence, if the not-beautiful and so on are forms, Plato recognizes forms of negations after all.

But the not-beautiful and so on are not forms.[61] Certainly Plato never explicitly calls them forms, although he does not hesitate to say that not-being is a form (*eidos*); he says instead that the not-beautiful and so on are parts (*merē*) of the form of not-being. Now in the *Politicus* (263ab) he distinguishes between the parts and the forms of a genus or class. Every way of dividing a class succeeds in dividing it into parts, but only parts that 'carve at the natural joints' (*Phdr.* 265e1–2) are forms. So every form is a part, but not every part is a form. To be sure, Plato says that such parts as the not-beautiful are no less than the beautiful is (258b8–c4); but not everything that is is a form. Nor does Plato say, as he does of not-being, that the not-beautiful 'has a nature of its own' (258b10).[62]

If Plato does not recognize forms of negations even in the *Sophist*, then Aristotle may well be right to say that Plato does not want forms of negations—at least, he never explicitly mentions them. Aristotle would be wrong, however, to say that Plato is committed to their existence, for not only does he not explicitly mention them but neither do any of his arguments imply that they exist.[63] But we need not convict Aristotle of misinterpretation. For presumably he raises his objection in order to emphasize the fact that in passages like *Rep.* 596a Plato is not careful to tell us that he means to restrict 'name' to 'property-name'; and if 'name' is not so restricted, then he is committed to the existence of forms of negations, which he does not want. Here as elsewhere, Aristotle criticizes Plato's failure to spell out his views in sufficient detail and with sufficient clarity, and he points out difficulties Plato faces if he is read in ways he leaves open but does not intend.[64]

We have now answered two of the three questions raised at the end of sect. 4: Plato never explicitly mentions forms of negations, nor is he committed to their existence. Hence neither is he committed to (1c). (Nor have we yet seen anything to commit him to (1b).) We now need to address our third question: does Plato use a one over many argument on behalf of *separated* forms? Of course, we have seen that he does not use the One over Many, since he does not use (1c). But perhaps he thinks that his alternative one over many argument shows that forms are separate?

7. Separation

It is surprising that Aristotle suggests that Plato uses a one over many argument to show that there are *separated* forms. For although a one over many argument is common enough in the Socratic dialogues, it is not at all common in the middle dialogues. Yet in Aristotle's view, separation does not enter the scene until the middle dialogues. One's first thought might then be that Aristotle illegitimately combines premisses from the Socratic dialogues with what he takes to be a conclusion from the middle dialogues. However, we have seen that it is reasonable (though not uncontroversial) to suppose that Plato mentions a one over many argument in *Rep.* 10;[65] so let us now consider it in more detail.

One might argue that Plato does not take *Rep.* 10 to show that there are separated forms, on the ground that it does not even mention separation. However, *Rep.* 10 is in this respect no different from any other dialogue; for Plato never says that forms exist separately (*chōris*). Still, Aristotle believes that Plato takes forms to be separate; so it is reasonable for him to wonder whether Plato has an argument that implies that they are.

In *Rep.* 10, as we have seen, Plato says that 'we are, I suppose, in the habit of assuming some one form for each group of many things to which we apply the same name' (596a6–7). It is reasonable to suppose that this is the Socratic procedure of positing a single form of *F* to explain the common feature in virtue of which the many *F*s are *F*. This one over many argument is, as Plato says, familiar; but it is familiar from Socratic contexts, which in Aristotle's view have only non-separated forms. Plato might agree; for he says nothing—at least, not just yet—to suggest that the forms sanctioned by 596a6–7 are separate. He says that we assume one form for every group of things to which we assign the same (property-)name; but he says nothing—yet—about the nature of such forms. Perhaps, as in Aristotle's view of the Socratic dialogues, only non-separated forms are so far in the offing.

Plato says next that in every case in which there is even one form of *F*, there is just one (596b). This is the uniqueness assumption (U):[66]

(U) There is exactly one form corresponding to every predicate that has a form.

But to say that there is exactly one form of *F* if any at all does not imply that forms can exist uninstantiated by the corresponding sensible particulars. So we have still not been given any reason to suppose that *Rep.* 10's forms are separate.

Plato next suggests that a craftsman makes an actual physical bed or table; in doing so, he consults the form of bed or table (596b6–9).[67] The craftsman does not create forms (apparently a god does that: 597b); but he is guided by forms in constructing actual beds and tables. This makes it clear that forms are *different* from sensible particulars. But it does not follow that they are *separated* from them. Perhaps Plato does not see this point and invalidly infers separation from difference—as the One over Many itself does. But it seems uncharitable to assume this; for Plato has not yet said anything about the form of bed that suggests that it is separate.

At 597a ff., Plato distinguishes between three (sorts of) beds, ordered in increasing degrees of excellence or perfection: pictured beds (which are apparently beds in a way: 596e10; 597b5–15),[68] actual beds for sleeping on, and the form of bed, which is the most complete or perfect bed (*teleōs on*, 597a5). Now Plato never says that perfection involves separation. Nor do his reasons for thinking that there must be perfect forms require forms to be separate.[69] On the other hand, he never denies that perfection involves separation; he never spells out precisely what perfection involves. So perhaps Aristotle thinks that, since both separation and perfection are distinctive of Platonic (as opposed to Socratic) forms, separation is built into perfection; alternatively, perhaps he assumes that even if Plato does not take perfection to involve separation, still, if a given context takes forms to be perfect, it also takes them to be separate.

So Aristotle probably believes that the form of bed in *Rep.* 10 is separate;[70] and since Plato arguably begins this section by mentioning a one over many argument, Aristotle might well assume that it is supposed to ground the (alleged) separation claim. Even if Aristotle does not think that it is intended to ground separation, he thinks separation needs grounding; and so he probably feels justified in asking whether the one over many argument—which seems to be mentioned in the context— grounds it.

However, it is not until some time after 596a6–7 that Plato claims that the form of bed is more perfect than the corresponding sensibles are. Perhaps he justifies this claim, and so possibly separation, by appealing to something other than the one over many argument mentioned in 596a6–7?

Unfortunately, Plato does not say why the form of bed is the most perfect bed. But Glaucon suggests that the claim will be familiar to 'those versed in this sort of reasoning' (597a8–9); so in order to understand the claim, we need to look elsewhere. Elsewhere in the middle dialogues, when Plato claims that forms are more perfect than the corresponding sensibles, he generally does so by arguing that, unlike the corresponding sensibles, forms escape narrow compresence. But Plato obviously cannot have this point in mind here, since sensible beds are not both beds and not beds in the sense of narrow compresence. Indeed, Plato makes this point explicitly, saying that although a bed *appears* differently from different angles, it is not really different (598a10)—that is, it is not both a bed and not a bed.

But we saw in Ch. 7.4, that narrow compresence seems to be just one sort of imperfection that Plato takes to require the existence of perfect forms. So perhaps Plato thinks that the Imperfection Argument (rather than any version of a one over many argument) requires the existence of perfect artefact forms, though in their case the relevant sort of imperfection is not narrow compresence.

This suggestion is supported by the fact that *Rep.* 10 makes it clear that there are other sorts of imperfection than narrow compresence. For example, Plato says that pictured beds are imperfectly beds because they capture how things appear rather than how they are, because they capture only a small portion of the object—for instance, how it appears from a given angle (598bc)—and because they depict only superficial observable features of things (601a) rather than their inner function, what they are for. These deficiencies of pictured beds provide a clue about the imperfection of ordinary beds. For just as we cannot tell from inspection of pictured beds what it is to be a bed, so inspection of actual beds will not confer such understanding, and for similar reasons. For what features of an actual bed should a craftsman seek to embody? Its shape or size or material? But beds come in various shapes, sizes, and materials. In order to know what a bed is, one needs to know not the shape and size of actual beds, but what beds are for. As Aristotle points out in, for example, *Ph.* 2. 7, what something is for, at least in such cases, is also what it is; to specify a thing's functional properties is to specify its form. So to know how to create an actual bed, a craftsman must know (or be guided by someone who knows) the form of bed and this, as we have just seen, cannot be captured in sensible terms.

I suggest, then, that when Plato says that the form of bed is the most perfect bed, he means to justify this claim, not by a one over many argument, but by his familiar Imperfection Argument. If this is right, then Plato is justified in claiming, as he does, that the forms in *Rep.* 10 are unobservable and perfect. But Plato does not suggest that the relevant sort of perfection involves separation; the form of bed seems to be perfect only because it is explanatory in a way in which sensible beds and pictured beds are not, where the relevant sort of explanation does not require separation. At least, this is all that is required by his argument. So just as Plato does not suggest that his one over many argument implies separation, so he does not suggest that the Imperfection Argument implies separation.

The answer to our third question—does Plato use a one over many argument to show that forms are separate?—thus parallels our answer to our first two questions. Plato never infers separation from a one over many argument, not even in *Rep.* 10. But *Rep.* 10 describes forms in a way that would lead Aristotle to think that they are separate; and it probably mentions a one over many argument. So it is reasonable for Aristotle to ask whether Plato has a one over many argument that implies separation, and he is right to say that he does not.

9

The Object of Thought Argument:
Forms and Thought

1. Introduction

According to the Object of Thought Argument, forms must exist to explain the possibility of thought. Aristotle raises two by now familiar objections. The first is that if the Object of Thought Argument proved that there are any forms at all, it would prove that there are forms in cases where the Platonists do not want them—this time, for perishable particulars and fictional entities (II, III). The second objection rescues the Platonists from the first: it claims that the Object of Thought Argument does not prove that there any forms at all (IV). LF 82. 7–9 adds a claim not made in OAC: that although the Object of Thought Argument does not prove that there are forms, it does prove that there are universals.[1]

Are Aristotle's criticisms of the Object of Thought Argument cogent? Is Plato committed to the argument? If not, does Aristotle misinterpret Plato? And if not, does Plato argue in some other way that the possibility of thought requires the existence of forms? If so, is this argument valid or invalid? In sect. 2 I schematize the Object of Thought Argument and the objections Aristotle raises to it in II and III; I also explore the Object of Thought Argument. In sects. 3 and 4 I discuss Aristotle's objections to the argument. In sects. 5 and 6 I ask whether Plato takes the possibility of thought to require the existence of forms.

2. The Object of Thought Argument

We may schematize the Object of Thought Argument and Aristotle's criticisms as follows:

I

(1) Whenever we think of (e.g.) man, we think of something that is.
(2) We have the same thought even when particular men have perished.[2]
(3) Therefore, whenever we think of man, we think of something other than any particular man.
(4) Therefore, whenever we think of man, we think of the form of man.
(5) Therefore there is a form of man.

II

(1) Whenever we think of (e.g.) Socrates, we think of something that is.
(2) We think of, and have an appearance of, Socrates whether or not Socrates is.
(3) Therefore, whenever we think of Socrates, we think of something other than Socrates.
(4) Therefore, whenever we think of Socrates, we think of the form of Socrates.
(5) Therefore there is a form of Socrates.

III

(1) Whenever we think of (e.g.) centaur, we think of something that is.
(2) Centaurs are not at all.
(3) Therefore, whenever we think of centaur, we think of something other than any particular centaur.
(4) Therefore, whenever we think of centaur, we think of the form of centaur.
(5) Therefore there is a form of centaur.

(1) says that whenever we think of (*noein*) of (e.g.) man, we think of something that is. This premiss can be read in a variety of ways. The differences matter in assessing the plausibility of the argument and of Aristotle's criticisms of it, and in assessing whether Plato is committed to it.

Both Plato and Aristotle use '*nous*' in two ways. Sometimes they use it for any sort of thought, including the most mundane; let us call this *broad thought* (BT). Sometimes, however, they reserve '*nous*' for the most exalted sort of thought: in Plato, for knowledge as such or, sometimes, for the best sort of knowledge (*epistēmē*); in Aristotle, for a cognitive condition more exalted than knowledge.[3] Let us call this *high-level thought* (HLT). The Object of Thought Argument thus argues that we can have either certain BTs or certain HLTs only if there are forms to serve as the objects of those thoughts.

Now according to the Arguments from the Sciences, the possibility of knowledge (*epistēmē*) requires the existence of forms. Since the Object of Thought Argument is separated off from them, it is reasonable to suppose that it considers a different cognitive condition.[4] Moreover, as we shall see in sect. 3, Aristotle's criticisms of the Object of Thought Argument assume that it concerns BT. I shall therefore generally assume that the argument concerns BT, but I shall occasionally ask what difference it makes if it concerns HLT instead.

(1) also says that whenever one thinks of (e.g.) man, one thinks of something that *is* (*esti*). As we have seen, '*esti*' can be used existentially, predicatively, and veridically.[5] So (1) says that whenever one thinks of

(e.g.) man, one thinks either of (*a*) something that exists, or of (*b*) something that is something or other, or of (*c*) something that is true.

It is plausible to suppose that every thought about man—indeed that every thought—involves propositional content. But (*c*) makes the stronger claim that every thought about man involves (only) true propositional content.[6] Plausible or not, however, it seems relatively clear that (*c*) is not intended. For the only candidates mentioned as objects of thought are particulars and forms—propositions are not mentioned. This leaves (*a*) and (*b*). If the predicative reading were intended, we might expect the context to provide the relevant complement; but it does not. Moreover, it turns out that particulars and fictional entities are inadequate as objects of thought because they do not always exist. The existential reading therefore seems to be intended, and so I shall assume from now on.[7]

(1) tells us, then, that whenever one thinks of some range of entities, one thinks of something that exists. But what is the relevant range of entities? Plato and Aristotle would both classify (1)'s examples—man, footed, animal—as real properties or kinds;[8] so perhaps (1) should be read as:

(1*d*) Whenever one thinks of a real property or kind, one thinks of something that exists.

But there are other possibilities. Thoughts about man, footed, and animal are also general thoughts; so perhaps (1) should be read as:

(1*e*) Whenever one has a general thought, one thinks of something that exists.

More broadly still, the claim might be:

(1*f*) Whenever one has a thought, one thinks of something that exists.

Although (1), considered on its own, can be read as any of (1*d*)–(1*f*), Aristotle's criticisms assume (1*f*). I shall therefore generally assume that the Object of Thought Argument involves (1*f*), although I shall occasionally ask what difference it makes if it involves (1*d*) or (1*e*) instead.

(1) is indeterminate in yet a further way. It might assert either that:

(1*g*) Whenever one thinks of x (for some range of substituends for 'x'), x exists;

or that:

(1*h*) Whenever one thinks of x (for some range of substituends for 'x'), one thinks of something, y, that exists.

(1*g*) claims that one can think *only* of what exists; (1*h*) allows one to think of things that do not exist, so long as one does so by thinking of something that exists. With (1*g*), forms turn out to be the only objects of thought; with (1*h*), they turn out to be the *basic* objects of thought, in so far as they enable us to think of other things if only indirectly. The distinction between ($1g$) and ($1h$) parallels a distinction drawn in Ch. 5, between forms being the only, and the basic, objects of knowledge.

If we assume ($1d$), the choice between ($1g$) and ($1h$) is unimportant. At least, since Plato and Aristotle believe that there are real properties and kinds, they would accept the conjunction of ($1d$) and ($1g$).[9] But if we assume ($1e$) or ($1f$), the choice between ($1g$) and ($1h$) becomes important. The conjunction of ($1e$) and ($1g$) implies that one can think of centaurs only if they exist. But then either one cannot think of them at all (since they do not in fact exist); or else the fact that (as it seems) we can think of them means that (contrary to fact) they do exist. Both options are unattractive.[10] Similarly, the conjunction of ($1f$) and ($1g$) implies that one can think of Socrates only when he exists. But then either we cannot think of him now (since he no longer exists); or else, if we can think of him now, then he (contrary to fact) exists precisely because we can think of him. Once again, both options are unattractive.

The difficulties just described do not arise if we couple ($1e$) or ($1f$) with ($1h$). For we then need not say that one can think of centaurs only if centaurs exist, or that one can think of Socrates only when he exists. We need to say only that if one can think of centaurs or of Socrates, one does so partly by thinking of something that exists when one thinks of them; but the something need not be a centaur or Socrates. Just as on a representative causal theory of perception one perceives physical objects through the intermediary of ideas or sense-data of them, so with ($1h$) one can think of non-existent things by thinking of existing things.

But what must these existing things be like? As phrased, ($1h$) leaves open the possibility that I can think of Socrates by thinking of anything whatsoever (say, a rock or a tree) so long as it exists; ($1h$) imposes no restrictions on substituends for 'y' other than that they must exist. Call this *unrestricted* ($1h$).

Now on a representative causal theory of perception, I indirectly or mediately perceive Socrates by directly or immediately perceiving something else. But the something else cannot be just any old thing. It must be suitably *of* Socrates—an idea or sense-datum of him, something that bears the appropriate causal relation to him and so explains why I am perceiving him in particular. This suggests a more restricted reading of ($1h$); call it *restricted* ($1h$). On restricted ($1h$), if I think of x, I do so by thinking of something, y, that exists *and that is suitably of x*—something proprietary to x, such that my thinking of y explains how my thought is also of x.

Although (1), considered on its own, can be read with ($1g$), restricted ($1h$), or unrestricted ($1h$), the overall context suggests that either ($1g$) or restricted ($1h$) is intended. At least, the argument comes closer to yielding its intended conclusion with ($1g$) or restricted ($1h$) than it does with unrestricted ($1h$). Moreover, Aristotle's criticisms of the argument assume that (1) involves ($1g$) or restricted ($1h$). I shall therefore assume that the Object of Thought Argument involves ($1g$) or restricted ($1h$), between which I see no way to choose.

(2) claims that whenever anyone thinks of man, the thought is the same.[11] This plainly cannot mean that the thought-*tokens* are the same: if you and I think of man, or if I do so on two different occasions, the thought-tokens are numerically distinct. The point of (2) is presumably that the *content* of the thoughts is the same.[12]

Now if, as (2) says, every thought of man has the same content, and if, as (1) says, every thought is of something that exists, then—so (3) infers—I can never think of man by thinking (solely) of a particular man, not even if he exists at the time of my thought. The intuition here seems to be that two thoughts can have the same content only if they are about the same object—an object that, given (1), must exist at the time of the thought. So if I think of man by thinking of George Bush, and Plato does so by thinking of Socrates, the content of our thoughts cannot be the same since our thoughts focus on different objects. Since all particulars are perishable, it follows that one can think of man only by thinking of something other than a particular, something everlasting.[13] This can only be a form; and so (4) concludes that everyone who thinks of man does so by thinking of the same form. It is not explicitly said what form is involved in every thought of man, and with unrestricted ($1h$) any form would do. But presumably the relevant form is the form of man, in which case the Object of Thought Argument assumes ($1g$) or restricted ($1h$).

According to the Object of Thought Argument, then, if one can think of x, either x is a form ($1g$) or else x has its own unique form (restricted ($1h$)). With ($1g$), it follows that man just is the form of man. With restricted ($1h$), one could say that although one thinks of man by thinking of the form of man, man is not identical with the form of man; but this seems ontologically excessive. So in this case (whatever might be true in other cases), ($1h$) collapses into ($1g$).

Like the other arguments we have explored, the Object of Thought Argument implies that forms are not particulars: they must therefore be universals.[14] Further, again like these other arguments, the Object of Thought Argument ignores succession (MH, EH). However, in the Object of Thought Argument the defect of *kath' hekasta* seems to be that they are not everlasting; so in this respect, GCH is relevant to the Object of Thought Argument in a way in which it is not relevant to the Arguments from the Sciences or to the One over Many Argument.[15]

The Object of Thought Argument is unsound.[16] (At least, this is so if it is read with ($1g$) or restricted ($1h$); and we have seen that it ought to be so read.) To be sure, the conjunction of ($1g$) or restricted ($1h$) with ($1d$) simply asserts realism about properties and kinds; so read, (1) is controversial, though both Plato and Aristotle accept it. But the conjunction of ($1g$) or restricted ($1h$) with ($1e$) or ($1f$) is far more problematical. When (1) is so read, it is still true in so far as thought must have *content*; I cannot think, and think (of) nothing. However, what my thought is about need not exist. For example, I can think about centaurs or have a centaur-thought even if there are no centaurs, so long as I think that (e.g.) centaurs have horns or are fictional entities. My thought has content (I consider the proposition that centaurs have horns), but it is not about any existing entity, since there are no centaurs. We might then say that the conjunction of ($1g$) or restricted ($1h$) with ($1e$) or ($1f$) is true on a *contents*, but not on an *objects*, reading. But we have seen that (1) intends an objects reading: particulars and forms are the only candidates mentioned as possible objects of thought. The conjunction of ($1g$) or restricted ($1h$) with either ($1e$) or ($1f$) is therefore false, and it seems reasonable to suppose that it confuses the content and object of thought.

(2) claims that every thought of (e.g.) man is the same—that is, every thought of man has the same content. Now if we take the content of a thought to be a proposition, then this claim, considered on its own, is controversial but not outrageous. But the Object of Thought Argument assumes that two thoughts can have the same content only if they are about the same extra-mental, extra-linguistic object, an object that, it turns out, must be everlasting. This assumption also seems to confuse the content and object of thought.[17]

Now on a referential theory of meaning, the meaning of a term just is its referent; the meaning of 'man', for example, is man.[18] It is easy to see how, if one believes that the meaning of a term is its referent, one might also believe that a thought can have content only if it is about an existing object, and that two thoughts can have the same content only if they are about the same really existing object. For suppose that the content of my thought is a proposition. If there is real content here, the proposition must be meaningful: a string of meaningless noises will not secure a genuine thought. But a proposition can be meaningful only if its terms are; and on a referential theory of meaning, the meaning of a term is its extra-linguistic referent. So for a thought to have content, it must have extra-linguistic referents, since such referents just are the content of the thought.

Although the referential theory of meaning has been discredited, it is a theory that has tempted some—Parmenides, for one, and, so many think, Plato.[19] Now Aristotle does not explicitly say that the Object of Thought Argument rests on a referential theory of meaning; he does not explicitly say anything about meaning at all. So it would go too far to say that in ascribing the Object of Thought Argument to Plato he attributes to him a referential theory of meaning. The referential theory of meaning is at best a theory *we* can introduce to explain why the Object of Thought

Argument might seem tempting. In this sense the Object of Thought Argument is not explicitly semantic. Still, although Aristotle does not present it as a semantic argument, it is reasonable for us to wonder whether, if Plato accepts the Object of Thought Argument, he does so because he accepts, or tacitly relies on, a referential theory of meaning.

3. Aristotle's first objection to the Object of Thought Argument

In II and III Aristotle argues that if the Object of Thought Argument showed that there are any forms at all, it would show that there are more forms than the Platonists would welcome. In particular, it would show that there are forms of 'perishable particulars' (82. 2) such as Socrates and Plato (II), and of fictional entities (III).

II is an objection because Aristotle assumes that although Plato wants forms corresponding to at least many general terms, he does not want them corresponding to the particulars falling under the term: there may be a form of man, but there is not also one of Socrates and another of Plato. Yet it is clear how the Object of Thought Argument seems to produce the unwanted forms. For—so Aristotle assumes—just as we can think of man, so we can think of Socrates, even when he has perished. Assuming (1*f*), this thought, like the thought of man, must be of something that exists. So if we think of Socrates when he is not, we must be thinking of something that then exists, and so of something other than Socrates. If, as (2) says, every thought of Socrates is the same—has the same content and so is of the same existing object—then even when Socrates exists, we must, when we think of him, think of something other than Socrates (indeed, of something other than any particular, since all particulars are perishable), and so of his form.

Aristotle's objection fails if the Object of Thought Argument is read with unrestricted (1*h*). For with unrestricted (1*h*), the most we can conclude is that whenever I think of Socrates, I think of some form or other which need not, however, be the form of Socrates; it could e.g. be the form of man. But his objection succeeds if the argument is read with (1*g*) or restricted (1*h*); so presumably that is how Aristotle reads it. We have also seen that it is most naturally so read in any case, since it aims to show that the form of man is the form involved in thoughts about man.

Aristotle seems right to say that if we can think of Socrates (even when he has perished) no less than of man, and if the same conditions govern thoughts about Socrates as govern thoughts about man, then if thinking about man requires a form of man, thinking about Socrates requires a form of Socrates. But why would it be undesirable to admit one?

With (1*g*), the difficulty is that whenever we attempt to think of Socrates, the sole object of our thought is his form. But then either

Socrates is identical with his form, or else we cannot think of Socrates at all. The first option is unavailable, however. For Socrates is a particular and forms are universals; and, as Aristotle insists, nothing can be both a particular and a universal. Nor would Plato favour the first option; at least, although he likens souls to forms in various ways, he does not take souls to be forms.[20] The only alternative is that we cannot think of Socrates at all—a clearly counter-intuitive line to take, at least with BT.[21] Aristotle has an easy way out of this dilemma. He would embrace its first horn, saying that Socrates is identical with his form. But this does not mean that Socrates is identical with a universal; rather, Socrates is identical with his particular or individual form, his soul.[22]

With (1*h*), the first horn of the foregoing dilemma does not arise, since (1*h*) does not restrict objects of thought to forms. Still, how can thinking of the form of Socrates enable us to think of Socrates? For the form is a universal, and every universal can be predicated of more than one thing. Suppose two things instantiate the form of Socrates—'our' Socrates and one in Sparta. How could the form help us to discriminate between them? Which one are we really thinking of? The form seems insufficient to ground our thought.[23] These problems might be avoided if the form of Socrates were a particular. But then, since all forms are universals, the form of Socrates would be both a universal and a particular. But nothing can be both a universal and a particular.

Aristotle does not develop III in the same detail as II (nor shall I focus on it in my account of Plato): it gets just one brief sentence.[24] But its point is not difficult to discern. We can—so Aristotle assumes—think of things that never exist, that 'in no way are', in contrast to Socrates who is in some way in so far as he at some point exists. But then there must be forms corresponding to all such thoughts as well, and so there are forms of fictional individuals (Chimaera) and fictional kinds (e.g. hippocentaur).

Aristotle again seems to assume that the Object of Thought Argument concerns BT. At least, he himself denies that one can know fictional entities, although he allows BT about them.[25] Since III assumes that one can think about fictional entities, it most likely concerns BT. III also assumes that the same conditions govern thoughts about fictional entities as govern thoughts about real properties and kinds, and so III assumes (1*f*). In assuming that the Object of Thought Argument implies that there are forms proprietary to each object of thought, it also assumes (1*g*) or restricted (1*h*).

Plato will clearly wish to resist forms corresponding to fictional particulars if he wishes to resist forms corresponding to particulars in general. But why should he be unhappy with forms corresponding to fictional kinds? Anyone who believes that Plato wants forms corresponding to every general term should find Aristotle's objection puzzling.[26]

Now those who think that Plato wants forms corresponding to every general term generally do so because they take forms to be the meanings of general terms. In so far as Aristotle's criticisms of the Object of Thought Argument assume that Plato does not want forms corresponding to every general term, it challenges this version of the view that forms are meanings.

On the other hand, the Object of Thought Argument seems at some level to rest on a referential theory of meaning. And if Plato accepts a referential theory of meaning, it is clear how he could both take forms to be meanings and also limit their range. All he has to do is to say that there are fewer meaningful general terms than one might have supposed. Since there are no centaurs, for example, 'centaur' is not meaningful, and one cannot think about centaurs even if it seems to one that one can; one therefore need not countenance a form of centaur.

But III blocks this reply. For here Aristotle simply insists that we obviously can think about such things as centaurs. Since according to the Object of Thought Argument, one can think of *x* only if *x* is a form or has its own unique form, such thoughts can be explained only by introducing the corresponding forms. Yet that conflicts with Plato's view that forms are supposed to be real properties that carve at the natural joints.

Aristotle thus in effect presents Plato with a dilemma. On the one hand, forms are real properties, and so there are forms only for a limited range of predicates, since not every predicate denotes a property. On the other hand, it is reasonable to suppose that we can think of all sorts of things besides real properties. Given the Object of Thought Argument's conditions on the possibility of thought, Plato can explain such thoughts only by positing the corresponding forms, in which case there are forms for more than real properties. This is a good objection. In sects. 5 and 6, I ask how Plato might respond to it.

4. Aristotle's second objection to the Object of Thought Argument

I turn now to Aristotle's second objection (IV), that the Object of Thought Argument is an invalid argument for the existence of forms, and to LF's claim that it is a valid argument for the existence of Aristotelian universals.

We have already seen that the Object of Thought Argument is unsound. But Aristotle seems to believe that it is also invalid. Here as elsewhere, whether this further claim is justified depends partly on how much is required of forms.

If forms must be everlasting, then the Object of Thought Argument is invalid, since it implies only that objects of thought must exist so long as there are beings capable of thought. In order to infer that objects of thought are everlasting, we need the additional assumption that there always are such beings; but the Object of Thought Argument does not make this claim.[27] Aristotle also presumably means, as he seems to mean in making the analogous objections to the Arguments from the Sciences and the One over Many Argument, that it does not imply that universals are separate perfect paradigms; and he is certainly right about that.[28]

However, the Object of Thought Argument is a valid argument for the existence of universals. For it says that in thinking of say, man, one thinks of something that exists and that is not a particular; it must therefore be a universal, and so there are universals.[29] Since the *Peri ideōn* takes *kath' hekasta* and *aisthēta* to be coextensive, the Object of Thought Argument is a valid argument for the existence not just of universals but of *non-sensible* universals. If the existence of non-sensible universals is sufficient for the existence of forms, then the Object of Thought Argument is a valid argument for the existence of forms. Since Aristotle does not take the existence of non-sensible universals to be sufficient for the existence of forms, he takes the Object of Thought Argument to be an invalid argument for the existence of forms; others who are less demanding might reach a different verdict.

Since the Object of Thought Argument is a valid argument for the existence of universals, LF's claim that it is is warranted.[30] Hence each of the less accurate arguments—the Arguments from the Sciences, the One over Many Argument, and the Object of Thought Argument—is an invalid argument for the existence of Platonic forms but a valid argument for the existence of Aristotelian universals. By contrast, we shall see that the more accurate arguments—the Accurate One over Many Argument and the Argument from Relatives—are valid arguments for the existence of Platonic forms, as Aristotle conceives of them.

Even if Aristotle takes the Object of Thought Argument to be a valid argument for the existence of universals, he presumably does not think that it is a sound argument for their existence, since he does not believe, for example, that there are universals corresponding to fictional entities.[31] But I shall not explore here Aristotle's own account of the possibility of thought—a large task that would require, among other things, a full discussion of his account of thinking in *De An.* 3. 4–8 and his motivation for introducing individual forms. I focus instead on the question of whether Plato is committed to the Object of Thought Argument.

5. Plato and the Object of Thought Argument

Is Plato committed to the Object of Thought Argument as Aristotle reads it—with BT, (1*f*), and (1*g*) or restricted (1*h*)? If not, is he committed to it on one of its other possible readings? If not, does he argue in some other way that the possibility of some or all thought requires the existence of, and perhaps also thinking about, forms? If so, is this because he accepts or tacitly relies on a referential theory of meaning? Do his views

about the possibility of thought commit him to as wide a range of forms
as Aristotle claims the Object of Thought Argument is committed to? In
this section, I consider a variety of passages that might seem to mandate
'yes' answers to at least some of these questions. In the next section, I
draw together the results of my survey of a variety of passages.

At the end of *Rep.* 5 (476d8–480a13), Plato argues from the claim that
knowledge is of what is to the conclusion that knowledge is in some sense
of forms.[32] Like the Object of Thought Argument, *Rep.* 5 correlates a
cognitive condition with what is. But there are at least four important
differences between the two arguments. First, *Rep.* 5 concerns knowledge
in particular, whereas the Object of Thought Argument (as Aristotle
reads it) concerns BT. Even if we read the Object of Thought Argument
with HLT, the two arguments differ. For, secondly, when the Object of
Thought Argument says that thought is of what is, it means that if one
thinks of *x*, one thinks of something that exists. But when *Rep.* 5 says that
knowledge is of what is, it means that knowledge entails truth.[33] Thirdly,
Rep. 5 involves premisses—e.g. that knowledge entails truth, and that it
requires adequate explanations which, in turn, must refer to forms—that
are not present in the Object of Thought Argument. Fourthly, the conclusions of the arguments differ if the Object of Thought Argument has
BT, and (1g) or restricted (1h). For the Object of Thought Argument
then concludes that if one thinks of *x*, either *x* is a form or one thinks of a
form proprietary to *x*. But *Rep.* 5 concludes only that if one knows *x*,
then either *x* is a form or else one can suitably relate *x* to a relevant form;
but the relevant form need not be a form of *x* in particular. I might, for
example, know that a variety of actions are just by (among other things)
relating them to the form of justice.[34] Otherwise put, *Rep.* 5 involves only
unrestricted (1h), whereas the Object of Thought Argument involves (1g)
or restricted (1h).

In the *Theaetetus*, Plato argues as follows:[35]

soc. Well, now, does this sort of thing happen in any other case?
тнт. What sort of thing?
soc. That someone sees something, but sees nothing.
тнт. Of course not.
soc. But if someone sees some one thing, then he sees something that is. Or do
     you think the one ⟨thing⟩ can be found among the things which are not?
тнт. No.
soc. So if someone sees some one thing, he sees something that is.
тнт. Evidently.
soc. And if someone hears something, he hears some one thing, and a thing that
     is.
тнт. Yes.
soc. And if someone touches something, he touches some one thing, and a thing
     that is, since it's one?

THT. Yes, that's right too.

SOC. Well now, if someone believes, doesn't he believe some one thing?

THT. Necessarily.

SOC. And if he believes some one thing, doesn't he believe something that is?

THT. I grant that.

SOC. So if someone believes what is not, he believes nothing.

THT. Evidently.

SOC. But if one believes nothing, one doesn't believe at all.

THT. That seems clear.

SOC. So it's impossible to believe what is not, either about the things that are or just by itself.

THT. Evidently. (*Tht.* 188e3–189b3.)

If one sees or hears or touches something, one sees or hears or touches some one thing, something that is. Similarly, if one has a belief, it must be (of) some one thing, (of) something that is. So if I allegedly have a belief that is not (of) something that is, I really have a belief about nothing, and so have no belief at all. Just as one cannot see but see nothing, so one cannot have a belief about nothing.

Unlike *Rep.* 5, this argument concerns belief as such rather than knowledge in particular. It also uses 'is' existentially rather than veridically, and it has (1*f*) and (1*g*). And the argument evidently trades on just the sort of confusion between content and object that, I suggested, most likely motivates the Object of Thought Argument (if it is read as Aristotle reads it).

None the less, this passage does not show that Plato is committed to the Object of Thought Argument (as Aristotle reads it), as attention to the wider context reveals. At 187b, Theaetetus proposes that knowledge is true belief. Plato embarks on a long discussion of false belief in order to show that if one identifies knowledge with true belief, one cannot accommodate false belief. The passage just quoted is part of that discussion. It is intended as a *reductio* of the identification of knowledge with true belief. Since Plato does not accept the identification, he is not committed to the conclusion of the argument.

Even leaving this point to one side, the argument in *Tht.* 188e–189b differs from the Object of Thought Argument. For although it has (1*f*) and (1*g*), it does not require any objects of thought to be everlasting. Nor does it introduce forms as objects of thought; it allows one to have beliefs directly about perishable particulars, at least when they exist.

In the *Parmenides*, Plato suggests that 'each of these forms is a thought that can exist only in souls' (132b4–5). Plato proceeds to rebut this conceptualist suggestion as follows:[36]

PARM. Then is each of these thoughts (*noēmatōn*) one, and yet a thought (*noēma*) of nothing?

soc. Impossible.

parm. So is it a thought of something?

soc. Yes.

parm. Of something that is, or of something that is not?

soc. Of something that is.

parm. Won't it be of some one thing which, being over all the cases, that thought thinks, i.e. some one idea (*idean*)?

soc. Yes.

parm. Then won't this thing which is thought to be one [*or*: this one object of thought], which is always the same over all the cases, be a form (*eidos*)?

soc. That again seems necessary. (*Parm*. 132b7–c8.)

Here, in contrast to *Rep*. 5 and *Tht*. 188e–189b, Plato uses *noēsis* and its cognates, thereby providing a more direct link with the Object of Thought Argument. Further, 'is'—as in the Object of Thought Argument and in *Tht*. 188e–189b but in contrast to *Rep*. 5—seems to be used existentially, not veridically; and—as in *Rep*. 5 but in contrast to *Tht*. 188e–189b—Plato seems to be speaking in his own voice. Moreover, in contrast to *Tht*. 188e–189b, he seems to argue that since thought must be of what exists, there must be forms to serve as objects of thought. So should we conclude that the *Parmenides* passage is committed to the Object of Thought Argument? To answer this question, we need to place the passage in its context.

Socrates had earlier proposed that if a number of things are large, they are large by participating in a single form of largeness (132a2–4); or, in general, if a group of things are *F* (for some range of substituends for '*F*'), they are *F* by participating in a single form of *F*. The reasoning underlying this suggestion was subjected to the Third Man Argument, according to which if there is even one form of *F*, there are infinitely many.[37] To avoid this result, it is suggested that forms are thoughts rather than items existing in extra-mental reality. 132bc is part of the argument against this suggestion.

Plato argues that if we identify forms with thoughts, we run the risk (not of an infinite regress, as in the Third Man Argument, but) of a mini-regress.[38] For the form-thought must be of something, of something that exists, indeed of an extra-mental form; and so there will be two forms if any at all—the form-thought and the extra-mental form that the form-thought is of. In order to avoid this mini-regress, we should take forms to be, not thoughts, but extra-mental objects of thought.

But why do we need to introduce the second, extra-mental form? The reason seems to be as follows. Forms are supposed to explain shared natures. So if forms are thoughts, then *F* things (for some substituends of '*F*') are *F* by being suitably related to a form of *F* which is a thought in minds. Plato then argues that thoughts cannot adequately explain shared natures: if a group of things are *F*, they must be *F* in virtue of a shared, extra-mental feature of them. David Armstrong advances a similar argument:[39]

it seems clear that the whiteness of a white thing is independent of the existence of a concept of whiteness in men's minds. There is something about a white thing which makes the concept of whiteness applicable to it. Concept Nominalism gives no account of this something.

Similarly, according to this passage in the *Parmenides*, since forms are supposed to explain what groups of things have in common, they cannot be concepts or thoughts but must be features of mind-independent reality.

This line of argument involves (1*d*): whenever we think of a real property or kind, we think of something that exists—in fact, as it turns out, of a form. The argument, that is, expresses realism about properties and kinds, and it takes them to be forms. But the argument does not suggest that every thought, or even that every general thought, involves thinking of something extra-mental, let alone of forms; so neither (1*e*) nor (1*f*) is in play. Nor is (1*g*) or restricted (1*h*) in play. For Plato makes it plain that forms are 'over all the cases', i.e. they are general or shared, not proprietary to a given object. Finally, Plato's claim is that we can adequately explain shared natures only by postulating a shared property and so a shared form. To say that realism about properties and kinds is more explanatory than any rival theory is not (like the Object of Thought Argument, on Aristotle's reading of it) to confuse the content and object of thought.

Later in the *Parmenides* Plato writes that:

If in view of all these difficulties and others like them, one does not admit that there are forms of things or does not distinguish a form in every case, one will have nothing on which to fix one's thought (*dianoia*), so long as one does not allow that each thing has an idea (*idean*) which is always the same; and in so doing one will completely destroy the significance of all dialectic (*dialegesthai*). (135b5–c3.)

Cornford suggests that Plato here 'acknowledges that to deny the existence of the Forms is to destroy the possibility not only of philosophy, but of all significant discourse'.[40] But it is not clear that the passage concerns the possibility of significant discourse. For although '*dialegesthai*' can mean 'discourse', it can also mean 'dialectic'.[41] Dialectic is not discourse as such, but a method of philosophical reasoning that enables one to move from belief to knowledge. So far as I can see, the passage neither requires nor precludes either discourse or dialectic.

Even if the passage concerns discourse rather than dialectic, it is not committed to the Object of Thought Argument. First, it does not clearly say that any thoughts involve *thinking* of forms; it may instead say only that if one is to be able to think, forms must *exist*. This is considerably weaker than the Object of Thought Argument on any of its possible readings. Secondly, even if it says that every thought involves thinking of forms, the passage still differs from the Object of Thought Argument ((1g) or restricted (1h)) in that it does not suggest that one can think of x only if x either is a form or has its own proprietary form. To be sure, Plato says that 'each thing has a form which is always the same'; but he does not say that the form of each thing is unique to that thing. For all Plato says here, the form of man, for example, could be the form that each man has. Hence the passage endorses at most unrestricted (1h).

In *Tht*. 181–3 Plato offers his final refutation of the Heracleitean thesis that all things change in all ways (182a1, e4–5). According to Cornford:[42]

> Plato's point is that, if 'all things' without exception are always changing, language can have no fixed meaning . . . The conclusion Plato means us to draw is this: unless we recognize some class of knowable entities exempt from the Heracleitean flux and so capable of standing as the fixed meanings of words, no definition of knowledge can be any more true than its contradictory. Plato is determined to make us feel the need of his Forms without mentioning them. Without the Forms, as his Parmenides said, there can be no discourse.

But this is not Plato's point. He may argue—although here I am unsure[43] —that language would be impossible if every object in the world changed in every way. But he does not suggest that the possibility of language requires the existence of forms, whether they are conceived as fixed meanings or as anything else. He at most argues that the possibility of language requires the existence of objects that are minimally stable; but he takes ordinary physical objects to be such objects. He says, for example, that if something moves but does not alter, there is no difficulty in describing it (182c9–11). Just as forms and fixed meanings are irrelevant to *Tht*. 188e–189b, so they are irrelevant to 181–3.[44]

In *Tht*. 184–6 Plato argues that knowledge is not perception because to know something requires attaining truth, which, in turn, requires grasping the *koinon* of being, which perception cannot do. Once again, Plato links a cognitive condition with being; so perhaps the Object of Thought Argument is in the offing? But let us look at the argument more closely.[45]

At 151e, Theaetetus proposes that knowledge is perception. Knowledge implies truth. So if knowledge is perception, perception must be able to attain the truth about its objects. In order to attain the truth about what one perceives, one must be able to identify it as being something or other; this involves applying the *koinon* of being to it. For the *koinon* of being is the incomplete being—being something or other. (So in contrast to *Rep*. 5, being is not veridical; in contrast to the Object of Thought Argument, neither is it existential. Once again, apparently similar claims are importantly different.) Whenever x is F, for any F, the *koinon* of being applies to x in so far as x is something, has some properties or other. But *koina* are not perceivable, as perception is understood here.

Hence perception cannot identify what it perceives as being anything; hence it cannot attain the truth about what it perceives, and so it cannot be knowledge.

Now some (by no means all) would argue that *koina* are forms.[46] But even if they are, 184–6 does not commit Plato to the Object of Thought Argument if it is read with (1g) or restricted (1h). For 184–6 does not suggest that one can have a belief about *x* only if *x* is a form or has its own unique form; it at most says that one can have a belief about *x* only if one applies the *koinon* of being (and perhaps also other *koina*, such as same and difference) to it. But the *koinon* of being (like all *koina*) is shared among a variety of objects: it is not proprietary to any given object. Nor do Plato's reasons for requiring the application of the *koinon* of being match the Object of Thought's reasons for introducing forms. Plato's point is not that every thought must be of something that exists or is everlasting. It is that in order to have any beliefs about what one perceives (or, perhaps, about any existing object), one must be able to identify it as being something or other. His thought is similar to one we saw Aristotle advancing in *Met.* 3: that to recognize or identify a thing is to recognize or identify it *as* something or other, which involves applying various properties to it.[47]

In the *Sophist* (249b5–6, c3–4), Plato says that *nous* requires the existence of stable objects—objects that are plausibly, though not uncontroversially, identified as forms.[48] But since he gives no reason for the claim, the premisses of the Object of Thought Argument are not in the offing. Nor is it clear that its conclusion is. First, it is not clear whether *nous* is HLT or BT.[49] Secondly, there is no suggestion that one can think of or know *x* only if *x* is a form or has its own form; so neither (1g) nor restricted (1h) is in play. Thirdly, not even unrestricted (1h) is in play. For the passage does not say that *nous* involves *thinking* of forms; it says at most that the possibility of thought requires the *existence* of forms. This is weaker than the Object of Thought Argument, no matter how it is read.

At *So.* 259e5–6 Plato says that 'it is because of the interweaving of forms with one another that we come to have *logos*'. He is generally thought to mean that the possibility of language or thought requires the interweaving —and hence the existence—of forms. However, it has recently been argued that he rather means only that *truth* requires the interweaving of forms, from which it does not follow that language or thought requires the interweaving of forms.[50] Even if the first, more usual, interpretation is correct, there is no commitment to the Object of Thought Argument, no matter how it is read. For there is no commitment even to unrestricted (1h), let alone to (1g) or restricted (1h). Plato does not argue that any thought requires one to think of forms, let alone that one can think of *x* only if *x* exists or one thinks of a form of *x*. He argues at most that the possibility of language or thought requires forms to be interrelated in various ways.[51]

But is the passage at least evidence that forms are meanings? So Ackrill, among others, believes.[52] In his view, the passage suggests that language requires forms, meanings, to be connected in various relations of compatibility and the like. But so far as I can see, the passage can equally well be understood—indeed, I think that it is better understood —on the assumption that forms are properties. Plato's point is then that the possibility of thought requires the *world* to be a certain way in that forms, properties, must be connected in various ways. The idea in this case is close to one I suggested Plato makes in *Tht.* 181–3 and 184–6, and that Aristotle takes up in various places:[53] we can have thoughts—at least, thoughts about objects in the world—only if the world is minimally stable and has repeatable properties.

The end of the *Cratylus* (439c–440d) is sometimes taken to be relevant to the Object of Thought Argument.[54] Plato begins (439d) by setting aside the question of whether sensibles are in flux, in order to ask whether forms are in flux.[55] He argues that if the form of beauty ceased to be beautiful, it would cease to exist. Indeed, any change in a form would be an existence change. So if forms change, they cannot be 'things' (*ti*); for an object to exist, it must be minimally stable and endure for more than an instant. Nor could such things be known (439e7–440a4). Moreover, Plato continues, if everything (not, now, just forms) were in constant flux, there could be no knowledge—not because knowledge or thought can only be of what is (or even requires knowing or thinking of something that is), but because knowledge itself, the nature of knowledge, must be stable. If the nature of knowledge changed from one moment to the next, there could be no such thing as knowledge (440a6–b4). Plato also says that 'if what knows and what is known always exist, and the beautiful and the good and each one of ⟨such⟩ things exist, then I do not think they can resemble flux or change' (440b4–c1). But neither does this restrict knowledge, let alone thought, to forms; nor does it say that all knowledge or thought involves knowing or thinking about forms. It says only that if knowledge and forms exist, they cannot change. This neither restricts knowledge to forms nor even says that all knowledge involves knowledge of forms.

In the *Timaeus* (51d3–e2) Plato argues that since *nous* differs from true belief, there must be non-sensible forms.[56] The fact that Plato contrasts *nous* with true belief makes it clear that *nous* is HLT; so if the Object of Thought Argument concerns BT, the two arguments are quite different. They are different even if the Object of Thought Argument involves

HLT. For as in *Rep.* 5 but in contrast to the Object of Thought Argument (if it is read with (1g) or restricted (1h)), the *Timaeus* does not claim that one can know x only if x is a form or one knows the form of x; it claims that one can know x only if x is a form or one can suitably relate x to a relevant form, which need not, however, be a form proprietary to x. Like *Rep.* 5, that is, the *Timaeus* may have HLT and unrestricted (1h); but it does not have (1g) or restricted (1h).

Further, Plato's reasons for the claim that knowledge requires knowledge of forms differ from the Object of Thought Argument's reasons for positing forms. Plato argues that knowledge and true belief differ in various ways that require the existence of forms. One difference is that knowledge, but not true belief, is always accompanied by a true *logos* (account or explanation) (51e3): as in *Rep.* 5, knowledge requires adequate explanations which, in turn, require the existence of forms. Admittedly, Plato does not spell the argument out in any detail; but then, he explicitly excuses himself from doing so (51c5–d2). When he does so elsewhere, as in *Rep.* 5, he does not use the Object of Thought Argument.

One final passage requires our attention: the famous recollection argument in the *Phaedo* (72e3–78b3). According to it, at least some of my thoughts can be explained only on the hypothesis that I recollect forms, which I knew in a prior life. But which thoughts are to be so explained? On one interpretation, the theory of recollection aims to explain concept acquisition: I can acquire the concept of F, for every F, only by recollecting the form of F; on some versions of this view, the form of F just is the concept of F.[57] If this interpretation were correct, Plato might seem to be committed to the existence of forms of fictional kinds. For, as Aristotle points out, we have a concept of hippocentaur no less than of man.[58] Further, on this view, presumably every thought involves thinking of forms, since all thought is conceptual. Plato might then seem to be committed to the Object of Thought Argument if it is read with BT, (1f), and unrestricted (1h).

However, this interpretation is not correct. For the theory of recollection does not claim that I can acquire the concept of F only by recollecting the form of F. It claims at most that recollection is needed to explain the acquisition of those concepts that cannot be explained in terms of perception and other forms. On this view, I may need to recollect the form of equality to acquire the concept of equality; but I do not need to recollect the form of hippocentaur to acquire the concept of hippocentaur. For it can be explained in terms of perception plus recollection of other forms.[59]

Indeed, I would go further and argue that the theory of recollection does not aim to explain the acquisition of any concepts. Rather, it aims to explain a higher-level cognitive process, one we engage in only after concepts are to hand.[60] In the *Meno* (81a–86b), for example, the slave begins recollecting only once Socrates begins questioning him—only, that is, after he has various concepts. Recollection enables him to advance from his confused to a clearer cognitive condition; it does not explain how he acquired any concepts. Similarly, in the cave allegory in *Rep.* 7 the prisoners have *eikasia* before practising dialectic (that is, before recollecting): they begin recollecting only when, as in the *Meno*, they are questioned in various ways, and so begin the journey from *eikasia* to *pistis*. But clearly *eikasia* involves concepts; the concepts may be somewhat confused, but they are there. Or, in the context to hand, Plato suggests that recollection begins when one asks oneself such questions as whether sensible equals fall short of what equal is. Plainly this is not an ordinary thought: it is a question one can ask oneself only once one has the concept of equality. Once again, recollection of forms occurs only after concepts have been acquired, and only in connection with certain sorts of thoughts about them.[61] Indeed, most of us never recollect at all, since in Plato's view most of us never make the initial move from *eikasia* to *pistis*.[62]

It is true that the theory of recollection aims to explain more than the critical inquiry some people are privileged to partake in. For Plato believes that everyone has the innate capacity to recollect (even if most of us never actualize this capacity); and in his view, this capacity can be explained only by positing pre-natal knowledge of forms. Plato believes, however, that such knowledge is, at birth, entirely forgotten; so the theory of recollection is not a theory of innate knowledge. Nor is it a theory of innate concepts or beliefs.[63]

The theory of recollection, then, does not aim to explain concept acquisition. It aims to explain certain innate capacities and our ability to reason in various ways once concepts are at hand. There is much to object to in all this—for example, capacities need not be grounded in any sort of knowledge, innate or prior. But for us, the crucial point is that if the theory of recollection does not concern concept acquisition, or thought as such, then it does not concern BT, and so it does not commit Plato to the Object of Thought Argument if that argument is read with BT. More generally, it does not commit him to the view that we need to grasp forms in order to understand the meanings of terms. It does not even commit him to the view that forms must exist to confer meaning on general terms. Here as elsewhere Plato ignores questions of meaning and linguistic understanding; his concern is how we move from belief to knowledge.[64]

6. Conclusion

I have examined a number of Platonic passages that sound similar to one another and to the Object of Thought Argument. But despite their apparent similarity, many of them are in fact quite different from one another. They are all alike, however, in that none of them is committed to the Object of Thought Argument. It may help, in concluding, to review precisely why this is so, and what alternative connection Plato thinks there is between forms and the possibility of thought.

We saw that the Object of Thought Argument, considered on its own, can be read in a variety of ways. Aristotle takes it to involve BT, (1*f*), and (1*g*) or restricted (1*h*). On any reading, it involves (1*g*) or restricted (1*h*); at least, although (1) on its own can be read with unrestricted (1*h*), in context that does not seem to be how it ought to be read. We have seen, however, that Plato is not committed either to (1*g*) or restricted (1*h*). If he is not committed to either of them, then he is not committed to the Object of Thought Argument.

Nor is he committed to the Object of Thought Argument's claim that one can think only of what exists. To be sure, this claim is made in *Tht.* 188e–189b.[65] But it occurs in a passage that is part of a *reductio* of a view Plato does not accept, and so we cannot assume that Plato accepts the claim. If he is not committed to the view that we cannot think of what does not exist, then he is not committed to the most familiar version of a referential theory of meaning. To be sure, Plato does not provide a systematic explanation of how we can think about non-existent things. Like Aristotle, he does not seem to have been much exercised by the problem. But he does not say anything that precludes the possibility of thinking about them; nor does he say anything that commits him to the view that if we can think about them then the corresponding forms must exist.

Although Plato is not committed to the Object of Thought Argument, he accepts some of its claims (on some of their possible readings), as well as some related claims. For example, if it is read with HLT and unrestricted (1*h*), then its conclusion can be taken to say that knowledge requires knowledge of forms;[66] and Plato accepts this claim. However, he accepts this claim for a reason not mentioned in the Object of Thought Argument: that knowledge requires adequate explanations, which, in turn, require the existence of certain sorts of objects. This is a controversial claim about the nature of adequate explanations; and it also involves realism about properties and kinds. But it does not involve a content–object confusion, nor does it yield forms in unwanted cases.

Plato also accepts parts of the Object of Thought Argument (on some of its readings) even if it is read with BT. For example, he accepts (1*d*) even if it is conjoined with (1*g*); for this only asserts realism about properties and kinds. He may also accept (1*e*) and (1*f*), so long as we assume unrestricted (1*h*) rather than (1*g*) or restricted (1*h*). That is, he may think that whenever I have a thought, I think of something that is—in fact, of some form or other. Thinking of Socrates, for example, may involve thinking of a form of man. However, Plato does not very often suggest that the possibility of thought requires *thinking* of some form or other. He more often seems to suggest that it requires the *existence* of forms; but even this claim is not often pressed.

When Plato seems to suggest that the possibility of thought requires the existence of, or thinking of, forms, no referential theory of meaning is in the offing; nor do such contexts assume in some other way that forms are meanings or that they must exist if the corresponding terms are to be meaningful. Plato argues instead that the possibility of thought requires that the world be a certain way, in that it must be reasonably stable and exhibit certain sorts of regularities. This in turn requires the existence of properties persisting through time. Sometimes Plato may also suggest that we must be able to identify some of these properties if we are to have certain beliefs. But this line of argument, like the other arguments we have explored, takes forms to be properties, not meanings.

It is interesting and important to note that the passages that connect forms to the possibility of thought are all from the late dialogues. The middle dialogues take it for granted that we have beliefs and understand the terms we use; and they do not ask how this is possible. They posit forms only for metaphysical reasons (e.g. to explain shared natures) and to explain the possibility of knowledge or, in the case of the theory of recollection, the possibility of progressing from belief to knowledge.

It is also interesting and important to note that the passages in the late dialogues that seem to posit forms to explain the possibility of thought do not describe forms in the ways familiar from the middle dialogues. In such contexts, for instance, forms are not said to be perfect or non-sensible.

If Plato is not committed to the Object of Thought Argument, why does Aristotle ascribe it to him? The general sort of reason is by now familiar. Plato often correlates some sort of cognitive condition with something that is; and sometimes forms are on the scene as well. For example, *Rep.* 5 argues that there are forms by appealing to the claim that knowledge is of what is. *Tht.* 188e–189b says that belief is of what is. Now I argued that *Rep.* 5 means that knowledge is truth-entailing, whereas *Tht.* 188e–189b means that one can have beliefs only about existing objects. But Plato does not explicitly tell us that he uses 'is' in these different ways; nor does he explicitly tell us that he uses '*nous*' both for BT and for HLT. If we are not careful to draw these distinctions, then the Object of Thought Argument may seem to result. Here as elsewhere Aristotle is perhaps pointing out unwelcome consequences Plato faces if he is not clear about various distinctions.

But although Plato does not explicitly say that he is using various terms in different ways, it does not follow that he is confused about the differences between them; one can observe distinctions without drawing them explicitly. And as I have interpreted the relevant passages, they do not trade on confusing them. But we need not conclude that Aristotle misinterprets Plato. At least, this is so if we take him to be saying, not that Plato explicitly offered the Object of Thought Argument, but only that it is fair to commit him to it in so far as he does not explicitly draw the distinctions necessary for avoiding commitment to it. Once again, the key to avoiding the dilemma sketched in Ch. 2.8 lies in understanding Aristotle's style of philosophical criticism.

The Argument from Relatives

1. Introduction

Having looked at the less accurate arguments, I turn now to the more accurate arguments, beginning with the Argument from Relatives.[1] One difference between the less accurate arguments and the Argument from Relatives is immediately evident: each of the less accurate arguments posits forms for a broad range of predicates, but the Argument from Relatives contrasts predicates like 'man' with those like 'equal', and it posits forms only for the latter.[2] In doing so, it obviously recalls contexts like *Rep.* 7 (523–5), which likewise distinguish between such predicates and posit forms only for the latter sort. Similarly, although *Phd.* 73–4 does not explicitly distinguish between these different sorts of predicates, it focuses on the predicate 'equal', and the argument it gives posits forms only for such predicates. Another difference between the Argument from Relatives and the less accurate arguments is that only the Argument from Relatives describes forms as perfect self-predicative paradigms.[3] We have seen that Plato also describes forms in this way.

Now in Ch. 4.5 I argued that Plato takes the distinction between predicates like 'man' and those like 'equal' to be that unlike the former, the latter have sensible instances that exhibit narrow compresence—no sensible man is also, in the narrow sense, both a man and not a man, but sensible equals are both equal and unequal. I also argued in Ch. 4.5 that when Aristotle, in the three *Metaphysics* passages, says that Plato introduced forms because of change, we should, if possible, take him to mean that Plato introduced forms because of compresence. For both Plato and Aristotle use the language of change to describe cases of compresence; and it is only if Aristotle so uses it in the *Metaphysics* passages that he interprets Plato correctly. I also argued that Plato's flux argument, both in fact and in Aristotle's view, is a metaphysical and epistemological, not a semantic, argument. I also argued that the fact that Plato takes forms to be self-predicative perfect paradigms does not turn forms into particulars; on the contrary, the fact that they are explanatory properties explains the sense in which they are self-predicative perfect paradigms.

The Argument from Relatives is a crucial piece of evidence for assessing these views. For it is the only argument in the *Peri ideōn* that follows Plato in distinguishing between predicates like 'equal' and those like 'man'; and it is the only argument, other than the flux argument recorded in the three *Metaphysics* passages, that Aristotle ascribes to the Platonists that mentions some sort of change.[4] Yet the Argument from Relatives is generally thought to advert, not to compresence, but to succession.[5] It is also often thought to be a semantic argument for the existence of forms.[6] And it is also often thought to conceive forms not as properties but as perfect particulars. As Owen puts it, according to the Argument from Relatives (and, in his view, according to Plato) each form is 'a Standard Case, exhibiting rather than being the character it represents'.[7]

In this chapter, however, I shall argue that the Argument from Relatives, like its Platonic sources, posits forms not because of succession but because of compresence,[8] and that it does so, not for semantic, but for metaphysical and epistemological reasons. I shall also argue that the Argument from Relatives can be taken to conceive forms as properties and not as particulars.

2. An overview of the argument

The Argument from Relatives states three, presumably exhaustive, ways in which something can be predicated of a group of things (*pleiō*) not homonymously but so as to reveal (*dēloun*) or signify (*sēmainein*) some one nature. If F is predicated non-homonymously of x, y, and z, then either (*a*) x, y, and z are fully (*kuriōs*) F, as when we call Socrates and Plato man; or (*b*) x, y, and z are likenesses (*eikones*) of something that is truly (i.e. fully) F, as when we predicate man of pictured men; or (*c*) of x, y, and z, one is the paradigm (*paradeigma*) and the rest are likenesses of it, as if one were to call both Socrates and likenesses of him man.[9]

So if F is predicated non-homonymously, something is fully F. (In case (*c*), the paradigm is fully a man, although this is not explicitly said.) What is fully F, however, need not be in the group under consideration. In case (*b*), for example, the group under consideration consists solely of likenesses of Socrates, none of whom is fully a man. Man is none the less predicated of them non-homonymously, since something else of which they are likenesses—Socrates—is fully a man. Further, if F is predicated non-homonymously of x, and x is not fully F, then it is a likeness of something that is fully F.

Part I of the Argument from Relatives tells us that man is predicated non-homonymously and that particular men are fully men. Subsequent parts tell us that like man, equal is predicated non-homonymously, in which case something must be fully equal. However, although sensible men are fully men, sensible equals are not fully equal. There must therefore be something non-sensible that is both fully equal and a paradigm of which sensible equals are likenesses and in virtue of which they are equal. The Platonic form of equal is a non-sensible paradigm that is fully equal, and sensible equals are equal by being likenesses of it; hence there is a form of equal. More generally, there are forms for whatever non-homonymous properties or universals lack full sensible instances—that is, for properties or universals that function like equal rather than man.

3. Homonymy, synonymy, and focal connection

The notion of homonymy is clearly crucial to the argument, so I begin with it. 'Homonymy' means, literally, 'having the same name'; x and y are homonymously F just in case both are named 'F'. For example, Bill and Ben are homonymously men, since both are named 'man'. Similarly, river banks and financial banks are homonymously banks, since both are named 'bank'. Plato uses 'homonymy' in this simple, literal sense.[10] Aristotle, however, uses the word in a different, technical sense. I shall take it as established by Owen that the Argument from Relatives uses 'homonymy' in its Aristotelian sense, so I turn now to it.[11]

Aristotle defines homonymy, along with the correlative notion of synonymy (which, like homonymy, literally means 'having the same name') in *Cat.* 1:

When things have only a name in common and the account of the essence (*logos tēs ousias*) which corresponds to the name is different, they are called homonymous . . . When things have a name in common and the account of the essence which corresponds to the name is the same, they are called synonymous. (1a1–2, 6–7; Ackrill trans. revised.)

On this account, x and y are homonymously F just in case (i) they share the name 'F', but (ii) the accounts of the essence which correspond to 'F' are different; x and y are synonymously F just in case (i) they share the name 'F', and (ii) the accounts of the essence which correspond to 'F' are the same.

What does Aristotle mean when he says that in homonymy, the 'account of the essence which corresponds to the name is different', whereas in synonymy it is the same? On one view, Aristotle has in mind lexical or nominal definitions or essences: x and y are homonymously F just in case 'F', as applied to them, is ambiguous or has multiple meanings; x and y are synonymously F just in case 'F', as applied to them, has a single meaning. Let us call this the *meaning* interpretation of homonymy and synonymy.[12] On a second view, Aristotle has in mind real definitions or essences: x and y are homonymously F just in case they have different real natures of F; they are synonymously F just in case they have the same real nature of F. On this view, 'account of the essence' indicates not nominal or lexical definition, but real definition, which specifies a real essence. Let us call this the *real-essence* interpretation of homonymy and synonymy.[13]

If the meaning view were correct, then the Argument from Relatives might be a semantic argument; at least, in discussing homonymy and non-homonymy, it would be discussing questions about meaning. However, Irwin and MacDonald have cogently argued that the real-essence view is correct.[14] If so, the Argument from Relatives is not a semantic argument. For example, in asking in Parts II and following whether equality is predicated homonymously or non-homonymously, it is asking about the real definition of equality, and so about the nature of the property of equality. The Argument from Relatives is therefore metaphysical and (since one needs to know a real definition to have knowledge) epistemological. We shall see how this works in detail later on.

A related question about homonymy is whether the *extreme* or *moderate* view is correct:[15]

(*a*) *the extreme view*: if *x* and *y* are homonymously *F*, they have the name '*F*' in common; but the definitions corresponding to '*F*' have nothing in common, do not overlap.

(*b*) *the moderate view*: if *x* and *y* are homonymously *F*, they have the name '*F*' in common; but the definitions corresponding to '*F*' are different. (They may, though they need not, overlap.)

On the moderate view, homonymy and synonymy are exhaustive options; on the extreme view, they are not. Now Aristotle often discusses cases where definitions differ but are connected in some way or other. He countenances a variety of sorts of connected definitions, but one especially important sort—and a sort sometimes thought to be important in the Argument from Relatives—is *focal connection*.[16] In *Met.* 4. 2, for example, Aristotle says that one will supply different definitions of the healthy depending on whether one considers a healthy person (one who enjoys good health), a healthy diet (one conducive to someone or something's health), or a healthy complexion (one indicative that someone or something is healthy). Although there are different definitions of health, they are all related to one central focus, that of health. Or again, Aristotle also says in *Met.* 4. 2 that being exhibits focal connection: in the focal case, to be is to be a substance; what it is to be a non-substance— e.g. a quality or quantity—must be explained by reference to substance.[17] If *F*s are focally connected, the focus F_1 has the definition *G*, and subordinate cases have the definition $G + H$, $G + J$, and so on. F_1 is the focal case, because all other *F*s include its name or definition in theirs, but not conversely.[18] Focally connected *F*s are also all genuine *F*s.

Other cases of connected definitions collect what Aristotle takes to be both genuine and non-genuine *F*s. For example—and it is an example we shall return to—a man and a pictured man presumably have connected definitions. But since, in Aristotle's view, a pictured man is not genuinely

a man, there is no focal connection here. Or again, Aristotle believes that
a severed hand is not genuinely a hand, since it can no longer perform its
function; its definition is connected with that of a genuine hand, but the
connection is not focal connection.[19]

On the moderate view, all cases of connected definitions are cases of
homonymy; for although the definitions of (e.g.) a substance and a
quality differ, their definitions overlap (both include a reference to substance). On the extreme view, no cases of connected definitions are cases
of homonymy. For on the extreme view, homonymous definitions do not
overlap: they have nothing in common. Plainly cases of connected
definitions are not synonyms either; for the definitions differ, but for
synonymy the definitions must be the same. On the extreme view, then,
all cases of connected definitions count as a *tertium quid* between
homonymy and synonymy—something for which the extreme but not the
moderate view leaves room.

I shall take it as established by Irwin that Aristotle favours the
moderate view.[20] The division between homonymy and synonymy is then
exhaustive; and connected definitions, including focally connected ones,
are cases of homonymy.

4. A puzzle

Part I lists three, presumably exhaustive, types of non-homonymous predication, each of which 'reveals some one nature'. On the real-essence
view, the 'nature' that is revealed is the real nature. Further, on the
moderate view, Part I lists three types of synonymy, the only alternative
to homonymy; focal connections, and connected definitions generally, are
therefore so far irrelevant.

In I*a*, man is predicated of several flesh-and-bone men, each of whom
is said to be fully (*kuriōs*) a man. In I*b*, man is predicated of a group of
pictured men, none of whom is fully a man. In I*c*, man is predicated of a
group consisting of flesh-and-bone men and of pictured men. In this case,
flesh-and-bone men are said to be paradigms (in which case they are fully
men) of which the pictured men are likenesses.

Part I raises a puzzle. I*a* is a straightforward case of non-homonymy,
indeed (as even a defender of the extreme view would agree) of
synonymy. I*b* is also (as a defender of the extreme view would again
agree) a straightforward case of synonymy. One might be tempted to add,
however, that man has different definitions in I*a* and I*b*: rational animal
in I*a*; likeness of a rational animal in I*b*. As Owen puts it, 'we are
inclined to add that now we are not using the predicate in the same sense
as in the first case; otherwise we should be mistaking paint and canvas for
flesh and blood'.[21] I*c*, on the other hand, seems to involve two natures—

that of man and that of pictured man. Yet Aristotle says that every case of non-homonymy reveals some *one* nature. I*c* thus does not seem to fit Aristotle's claim that non-homonymy always reveals some one nature; nor, in contrast to I*a* and I*b*, does it seem to involve synonymy.[22]

Various resolutions of the puzzle have been proposed.[23] LF, for example, supplies a different reading, classifying I*c* as a case of homonymy (83. 5). Owen follows OAC and argues that 'the problem is fictitious'.[24] But he resolves the puzzle in two incompatible ways.

Owen's first solution is to say that although I*c* involves two natures— that of man and that of pictured man—this is compatible with the claim that every case of non-homonymy reveals some one nature. For the two natures reveal some one nature in so far as they 'have a common factor', man; it is just that one of them also involves a second nature (likeness of a man). This solution invokes focal connection, for the crucial claim is that the two natures 'have a common factor'; it therefore presupposes the extreme view. For Part I claims to describe cases of *non-homonymy*; if focal connection is a type of non-homonymy, then the moderate view cannot be in play.

Owen's second solution is to say that the puzzle rests on two mistaken assumptions: that (i) I*b* is meant to reveal a different nature from that revealed in I*a*, and that (ii) I*c* is meant to reveal two natures. In fact, each of I*a*–*c* involves only one, and the same, nature, that of man; each of I*a*–*c* therefore involves synonymy. To be sure, men and pictured men may not in fact, or in Aristotle's view, be synonymously men, but that is beside the point. The crucial point is that the Argument from Relatives purports to elucidate Plato's views; and in Plato's view, each of I*a*–*c* is a case of synonymy. As Owen puts it, 'the analysis in I would mis-represent its Platonic sources if I(*c*) were *not* a type of unequivocal [i.e. synonymous] predication'.[25] Moreover, Owen adds, Aristotle regularly assumes that Plato takes forms and sensibles to be synonyms.[26] Owen's second solution presupposes the moderate view. For, again, Part I purports to elucidate three exhaustive types of non-homonymy. On Owen's second solution, every type of non-homonymy turns out to be a type of synonymy, which is just what the moderate but not the extreme view claims.

Owen's two solutions are incompatible. The first invokes focal connection, the second invokes synonymy; the first rejects the moderate view, the second assumes it. But focal connection and synonymy are exclusive options; in focal connection the definitions differ, but in synonymy they are the same. Accepting and rejecting the moderate view are also exclusive options.[27]

Owen's second solution is entirely adequate. First, if the moderate view of homonymy is correct, then in claiming to discuss non-homonymy, Part I should discuss only synonymy. Secondly, I agree with Owen that

Plato—both in fact and also as Aristotle interprets him—takes pictured
Fs and Fs to be synonymously F. In the *Republic*, for example, he calls a
pictured bed, a bed, and the form of bed three beds (*trittai tines klinai*,
597b5), ordered in increasing degrees of perfection.[28] Or again, in the
Symposium (210a–211b), he describes a series of beautiful things,
ranging from beautiful bodies to beautiful souls, to beautiful laws and
institutions, to beautiful knowledge and, finally, to the most beautiful
thing of all, the form of beauty. Yet as Aristotle reasonably says, if x is
more F than y, x and y are synonymously F.[29] Hence Part I should discuss
synonymy if it intends to capture Plato's view. Thirdly, not only does
focal connection not capture Plato's view of how pictured Fs and Fs
are related, but neither does it capture Aristotle's view. For as we have
seen (and as Owen agrees), Aristotle takes pictured Fs and Fs to be
homonyms, though not of the focal connection sort since, in his view,
pictured men are not genuinely men. If focal connection captures neither
Plato's nor Aristotle's explanation of the cases described in Part I, then it
is irrelevant to the argument so far.[30]

Our first puzzle is thus resolved: each of the cases described in Ia–c
involves synonymy because the Argument from Relatives aims to record
Plato's views, and that is how Plato describes these cases. The real puzzle
is not that Ia–c are all said to involve synonymy, but that Plato takes
them to.

Now it is indeed puzzling that Plato takes men and pictured men to be
synonymously men—that is, to be members of the class of men.[31] But
this puzzle too can be at least partly resolved if we look more closely
at what *ho gegrammenos* is supposed to be. There seem to be three
possibilities: (*a*) a picture of Socrates; (*b*) the man the picture is of; (*c*)
the man in the picture. Suppose the picture is of Socrates. Then on (*a*),
ho gegrammenos is a piece of canvas and oil that depicts or represents
Socrates; on (*b*), it is Socrates. On (*c*), it is neither of these; for like
Socrates and unlike the piece of canvas and oil, the man in the picture
(let us suppose) is short, poorly clad, and has a pug nose; but unlike
Socrates, he is not continually inquiring into virtue, married, and the like
(assume the picture depicts none of these things).[32]

With (*b*), the first puzzle is easily dissolved. For on (*b*) it is straightforwardly true that *ho gegrammenos* is a man, since on (*b*) *ho gegrammenos*
is Socrates, and he is a man. But when Aristotle discusses pictured Fs in
his own right, he typically seems to have (*a*) in mind.[33] And on (*a*), the
first puzzle arises, since it is puzzling, indeed false, to say that a piece of
canvas and oil is a man.

I speculate, however, that Plato favours (*c*). With (*c*), one's first
inclination is to say that the man in the picture is not really a man; for
there could not be a man with all and only the features the man in the
picture has—at least, not given our normal criteria for being a man.

However, we have seen that Plato does not accept the normal criteria for belonging within the extension of a predicate. In his view, for example, the form of F is F because, being the property of F, it explains why things are F. The form of F is F in a different way from the way in which 'ordinary' Fs are F; but it is none the less, in Plato's view, F in the same sense of 'F' as that in which 'ordinary' Fs are F. So perhaps he also believes that pictured Fs are F in the same sense of 'F', though they are F in a different way from the way in which ordinary Fs are F. Of course, pictured Fs will not be F for the same reason that the form of F is, since pictured Fs do not explain why Fs are F; but perhaps Plato takes them to be genuine Fs because he thinks they share a certain number of features with 'ordinary' Fs or are related in a certain way to 'ordinary' Fs by being likenesses of them.[34] So although (c) is puzzling, it is less puzzling than (a); and puzzling or not, we have seen why Plato might accept it.

5. A second puzzle

Parts II–III, when considered in conjunction with Parts IV–V, raise a second puzzle. II turns from man—a property for which there are sensible paradigms—to equal. It is sometimes thought that Parts II–III claim that, unlike man, equal is homonymous; it is also sometimes thought that Parts IV–V claim that equal is non-homonymous in way I*b*. Parts II–III thus appear to conflict with Parts IV–V.

Once again, various resolutions have been proposed. LF, for example, again supplies a different reading. Instead of saying, as Part II does, that we predicate the equal itself homonymously of things here, it says that we predicate it of them either homonymously or synonymously. It then goes on to say that it is not predicated of them either synonymously and fully (*sunōnumōs men kai kuriōs autoisa ouk an rhētheien*, 83. 9) (i.e. in way I*a*) or homonymously (83. 11). Since, in LF, Part II does not say that the equal itself is predicated homonymously of things here, the alleged incompatibility between Part II, on the one hand, and Parts IV–V, on the other, disappears.[35] However, it is undesirable to alter OAC; and we shall see that there is no need to do so.[36]

The most interesting recent account is that proposed by Owen.[37] He rightly notes that Part II does not say that we predicate *equal* homonymously of things here, i.e. of sensibles; it says that we predicate *the equal itself* (*to ison auto*; Owen translates instead 'absolutely equal') homonymously of things here.[38] Owen then suggests that to predicate 'the equal itself' of things here is not to predicate 'equal' of them, but to predicate 'fully equal' of them. For, Owen believes, the sense of 'itself' ('absolutely', in his translation) is the same as the sense of 'fully' (Owen translates '*kuriōs*' as 'strictly').[39] 'Thus', according to Owen, 'the question broached by II is just whether *ison* can be used *kuriōs* of things in this world, i.e. as a case of the non-derivative predication illustrated in I(*a*); and the answer is that, except by a sheer ambiguity, it cannot be so used'.[40] That is, in his view, Part II says only that nothing in this world is fully equal, from which it follows only that nothing in this world is non-homonymously equal in way I*a*. Part III, Owen believes, precludes non-homonymy only of type I*c*. Parts II–III thus rule out non-homonymy only of sorts I*a* and I*c*; they leave open non-homonymy of sort I*b*. But I*b* is just the option seized upon in Parts IV–V. Since there is no conflict between denying non-homonymy of sorts I*a* and I*c*, and affirming non-homonymy of sort I*b*, the alleged conflict disappears.

Owen's interpretation of the claim that *to ison auto* is predicated homonymously of things here faces two difficulties. First, I shall argue later that, contrary to Owen, '*auto*' and '*kuriōs*' do not mean the same. Secondly, II*a* claims quite generally that when we predicate the equal itself of things here, we do so homonymously. But if homonymy is involved, then *none* of I*a*–*c* can be left open; for each of them is a case of *non*-homonymy.[41]

To resolve the second puzzle, we need to see how Parts II–III can rule out *all* of I*a*–*c*, compatibly with Parts IV–V's affirming non-homonymy of sort I*b*. This may seem to be an impossible task; but I believe it can be done. The key lies in understanding two salient differences between Part I, on the one hand, and Parts II ff., on the other. First, Part I considers predications of *man*, whereas Parts II ff. consider predications not of equal, but of *the equal itself*. Second, Part I considers predicating man of *various things* (*pleiō*), whereas Parts II–III consider predicating the equal itself *of things here* (*ta entautha*). I take up these two differences in turn.

In explaining how man can be non-homonymously predicated of a number of things, Part I explains the various ways in which something can have the property of being a man non-homonymously. If Parts II ff. were engaged in the same project for equal, then they should ask about conditions for predicating *equal* non-homonymously of various things. But they ask instead about predicating *the equal itself* non-homonymously. We saw that in the third Argument from the Sciences, Aristotle seems to use '*auto*' to refer neutrally to a property. I suggest that that is also how it is being used here. Parts II ff., that is, are not asking what things have the property of *being equal*; they are asking what has the property of *being the equal itself*, i.e. what has the property of being the property of equality. Another way of putting the concern of Parts II ff. would be to say that they want to know what the property of equality is, or how it is to be defined.[42] If this is right, then contrary to Owen the sense of '*auto*' is not the same as the sense of '*kuriōs*'. To ask what *auto to* F is is to ask what the property of *F* is; to ask what is *kuriōs* F is to ask what bears the property fully.[43]

The shift from the ontologically neutral 'of various things' to the narrower 'of things here' indicates a restriction to sensibles.[44] The question is what happens if we identify equality with, or define it in terms of, something sensible. The answer is that equality would then be homonymous.

6. Why equality is homonymous if it is defined in sensible terms

That this is the correct resolution of the second puzzle gains support from Parts II–III's reasons for claiming that equality is homonymous if it is defined in terms of, identified with, something sensible.

II*a*–*c* offer a three-pronged explanation of the homonymy that then results. II*a* says that the equal itself is predicated homonymously of things here, since the same account or definition (*logos*) does not fit them all. Since different definitions are involved, so too is homonymy.[45]

Why are different accounts involved if equality is defined in sensible terms? The reason is familiar. Suppose that *a* and *b* are each three inches long; we might then infer that to be equal is to be three inches long. But three inches does not explain why *c* is equal to *d* (suppose they are each five inches long); to explain their equality, we need to mention (given that at this stage we are restricted to sensibles) a different sensible length, five inches. The different *logoi*, that is, are the specifications of the different measurements of sensible objects. If we restrict our accounts to sensibles we need different definitions (measurements), since no one definition (measurement) phrased in sensible terms can explain why all equal things are equal. On this account, sensible equals are not individual equal objects, but sensible properties: three inches, not this stick. This is just what we would expect on the real-essence view of homonymy; for if homonymy is involved, then so too are different properties or natures.

The claim that defining various properties in sensible terms leads to homonymy has clear Platonic roots.[46] The sight-lovers in *Rep.* 5, for example, believe that beauty should be defined in sensible terms. But no single sensible property can explain the beauty of all the beautiful things there are, so the sight-lovers conclude that beauty is to be identified with many sensible properties, in which case beauty is not one, but many (478e7–479a5). But if beauty is not one—if it is identified with many sensible properties—then it is homonymous. As in Parts II–III, so in *Rep.* 5, the attempt to define properties (at least, properties like beauty or equality) in sensible terms leads to homonymy.

II*b* says that 'nor do we signify the true equals; for quantity in sensibles changes and constantly fluctuates and is not determinate'. As Owen notes, II*b* 'can be read to imply (what it certainly does not say) that phenomenal things are continually changing in all respects and so not *kuriōs* the subjects of any predicates. But such an interpretation would be the death of' the argument[47]—because Part I assumes that some sensibles are *kuriōs*, fully, men. Owen suggests instead that II*b* 'seems to add the rider that, since the dimensions of sensible things are constantly fluctuating, even to say "having the same size as A" is to use a description without fixed meaning'.[48] That is, although sensibles are not constantly changing in every respect, they are constantly changing their dimensions.

This interpretation of II*b* is unsatisfactory. First, as Owen agrees, change in the sense of succession is irrelevant to the rest of the argument; if we interpret II*b* as Owen does, it does not fit its context.[49] This is especially true if, as I have suggested, the sensible equals at issue here are sensible properties, for they do not undergo succession. If II*b* none the less adverts to succession, then it ascribes to sensible properties a sort of change they cannot undergo.

Secondly, if the Argument from Relatives did have succession in mind, it would misrepresent its sources. For in distinguishing between predicates like 'man' and 'equal', the Argument from Relatives plainly recalls contexts like *Rep.* 523–5, which likewise distinguish between such predicates; the same contrast is implicit in *Phd.* 74, which, like Parts II ff., uses 'equal' as its sample predicate.[50] Yet we have seen that in arguing that there are forms, such contexts appeal not to succession but to narrow compresence.[51]

Fortunately, there is an alternative interpretation of II*b* that avoids these difficulties. For like its Platonic sources, II*b* can be read in terms of narrow compresence. On this interpretation, II*b*'s point is not that (e.g.) this stick is not stably three inches long. Rather, its point is that the property of being (e.g.) three inches changes from being equal to being unequal, in that although three inches is equal in this context (where this three-inch thing is equal to another), it is unequal in another context (where this three-inch thing is unequal to a five-inch thing).[52] As we saw in Ch. 4.5, Aristotle elsewhere uses the language of change for compresence, so there is no presumption against supposing that he so uses it here as well. And if we interpret II*b* in this way, then it both fits well with the rest of the Argument from Relatives and correctly captures its Platonic sources. These are good reasons to read II*b* in terms of compresence. I suggest, then, that II*b* debars sensible equals from being fully or truly equal on the ground that they suffer narrow compresence.[53]

If we read II*b* in terms of compresence, then, like the other *Peri ideōn* arguments, the Argument from Relatives does not advert to succession. But the Argument from Relatives differs from these arguments in that they do not explicitly advert to compresence either, whereas compresence is one of the Argument from Relatives's central concerns.[54] Indeed, the Argument from Relatives is the only argument for the existence of forms recorded by Aristotle, other than the flux argument described in the three *Metaphysics* passages explored in Ch. 4, in which change of any sort is mentioned as a reason for introducing forms. Since the relevant sort of change in the Argument from Relatives seems to be compresence rather than succession, the suggestion made in Ch. 4.5, that that is also the sort of change that Aristotle has in mind in the *Metaphysics* passages, is reinforced.[55]

A further point about II*b* should be noticed. II*b* is part of the explanation of the claim that if we predicate the equal itself of anything sensible, then it is homonymous. II*b*'s reason for this claim is that sensible properties of equality are not true equals (i.e. they are not fully equal), since they are both equal and unequal. So according to II*b*, if sensible equals are not fully equal, they have not the property of being the equal itself—that is, they are not the equal itself. The Argument from Relatives therefore assumes that the equal itself, the property of equality, must be a true equal or, in other words, must be fully equal, in which case it must be equal without also being unequal. The Argument from Relatives, in other words, assumes that the property of F is itself F.[56] But how could the property of equality be equal? We have already been given a clue. Sensible equals are equal and unequal because each of them explains why some things are equal and why other things are unequal—since some three-inch things, for example, are equal, whereas others are unequal.[57] In assuming that the equal itself must be fully equal, and so must escape compresence, the Argument from Relatives assumes the familiar Platonic view that the F itself is F and not also not F, in the sense that it is the one thing that explains why all Fs are F and it never explains why anything fails to be F. So to say that the equal itself, the property of equality, is equal and not also unequal is simply to say that it explains why all equal things are equal and that nothing is ever unequal in virtue of it. I return to this point later.

II*c* claims that nothing in this world receives the definition of the equal accurately (*akribōs*).[58] This seems simply to put in the formal mode what II*b* puts in the material mode, namely, that sensible equals are not fully equal; for, as II*b* explains, they are both equal and unequal.

Part III adds, what is implicit in Part II, that no sensible equal is a paradigm of others. For a paradigm of F things must be fully F yet, as Part II explains, sensible equals are not fully equal. Like Part II, Part III is part of the explanation of the claim that the equal itself cannot be sensible. Part III claims that sensible equals are not paradigms in virtue of which equal things are equal. The Argument from Relatives thus assumes not only that the equal itself is fully equal but also that it is a paradigm in virtue of which equal things are equal. One might wonder how equality could be a paradigm. But Ch. 4.7 suggests an answer: equality is a paradigm because every equal thing is equal in virtue of it, and so one needs to know and refer to it in explaining why something is equal; it is a paradigm in virtue of its explanatory role.

If my detailed account of Parts II–III is correct, then it is clear why equality is homonymous if it is defined in sensible terms. Since, as II*b* explains, sensible equals are not fully equal, I*a* cannot apply. If sensible equals are not fully equal, then neither are they paradigms, and so I*c* is also ruled out. And I*b* is a non-starter; for Parts II–III assume that we are restricted to sensibles. There is, then, no non-sensible paradigm—no entity outside the group of sensibles—that we can appeal to.

7. How to avoid homonymy

Parts II–III argue that if equality is defined in sensible terms, it is homonymous. So either equality just is homonymous, or else it is not to be defined in sensible terms. Parts IV–V choose the latter option. No explanation of the choice is given, but since Plato and Aristotle take homonymy to be problematical for epistemological and metaphysical reasons, it is reasonable to assume that the Argument from Relatives also does so—as we should expect, given the real-essence view of homonymy. We have seen that Plato, for example, believes that knowledge requires explanation; and this, in turn, requires the existence of certain sorts of properties. In his view, we can explain the *F*-ness of things only if *F*-ness is some one thing, the same in all cases. The possibility of knowledge of *F*s therefore requires that *F*-ness be non-homomymous. In the *Posterior Analytics* (77a5–9), Aristotle agrees with Plato, saying that demonstration—which in his view confers knowledge (*epistēmē*)—requires the existence of non-homonymous properties.[59] Parts IV–V therefore conclude, not that equality is homonymous, but that it is non-sensible, because the possibility of knowledge, and so of explanation, requires this. If this is right, then the Argument from Relatives is not asking how we possess ordinary linguistic understanding or what it is for a predicate to be meaningful. Even if 'equal' is homonymous, it can be meaningful and we can understand it; but we should lack genuine knowledge.

Part IV reminds us of a point made clear in I: that paradigms and their likenesses are not homonymously related.[60] This suggests a way of preserving the non-homonymy of equality that was not available in Parts II–III: perhaps, although sensible equals are not paradigms or fully equal (and so are not the equal itself), there is a non-sensible paradigm that is fully equal and in virtue of which all sensible equals are equal (and which is therefore the equal itself). If so, we can preserve the non-homonymy of equality by lifting Parts II–III's restriction to sensibles and introducing a non-sensible paradigm that is fully equal; this non-sensible paradigm will also be the equal itself. Equality is therefore non-homonymous in way I*c*;

it is just that the paradigm that is fully equal is non-sensible rather than sensible.

Notice that the paradigmatism at issue in the Argument from Relatives is perfect paradigmatism. For paradigms are fully F, and this is, or contributes to, their perfection. By contrast, the first Argument from the Sciences does not say that paradigms are fully or perfectly F. Further, unlike the first Argument from the Sciences, the Argument from Relatives says that the corresponding sensibles are likenesses of paradigmatic forms and that they fail to be fully F and so are deficiently F; this too is part of what is involved in perfect paradigmatism.

Part V infers that the non-sensible paradigm that is fully equal is the form of equal; and so there is a form of equal. More generally, there is a form corresponding to every non-homonymous predicate that lacks full sensible instances—for all predicates that are relevantly like 'equal', in contrast to 'man'.[61]

Like Parts II–III, Parts IV–V also have clear Platonic roots. The sight-lovers seek to define e.g. beauty in sensible terms. They see that beauty cannot be identified with any single sensible property, so they invoke many sensible properties. This commits them to the view that beauty is homonymous. Like Socrates, however, Plato assumes that each of the predicates that concerns him denotes a single property—this is required, in his view as in Socrates', by the possibility of knowledge. He sees that nothing sensible will do; so he concludes that the properties that concern him are non-sensible forms. Thus, for example, at the end of *Rep.* 5, he argues against the sight-lovers that beauty is not many, but one; he then infers that it is non-sensible, and then that it is a form. Similarly, in the *Phaedo* he argues that *auto to ison*—the equal itself, the property of equality—cannot be identified with anything sensible, and so it must be a non-sensible form (74a9–c5).[62]

8. How the Argument from Relatives conceives forms

The Argument from Relatives takes the form of F to be a non-sensible paradigm that is fully F, and it takes sensible Fs to be F by being likenesses of it. If the form of F is a paradigm that is fully F, then it is F, and so it is self-predicative. In Owen's view, it follows that each form 'is a Standard Case, exhibiting rather than being the character it represents'[63] —that is, in his view the Argument from Relatives takes forms to be particulars rather than properties. It is partly because Owen takes forms to be so conceived that he advocates a semantic interpretation of the Argument from Relatives, according to which forms are posited to serve as ostensive samples, acquaintance with which confers understanding of the corresponding general terms.[64]

If Owen were right, forms would be conceived quite differently in the Argument from Relatives, on the one hand, and in the other *Peri ideōn* arguments, on the other; for we have seen that elsewhere in the *Peri ideōn* forms are conceived as universals.[65] Of course, this by itself is not troubling. Outside the *Peri ideōn*, Aristotle sometimes claims that forms are particulars.[66] Perhaps the other arguments in the *Peri ideōn* explore the role of forms as universals, and the Argument from Relatives explores their role as particulars.

However, that the Argument from Relatives conceives forms as properties is indicated by two facts. First, we have seen that sensible equals in the Argument from Relatives are sensible properties; the form of equal should therefore also be a property. The Argument from Relatives first points out difficulties that arise if equality is taken to be a sensible property or properties; it resolves these difficulties by taking equality to be a non-sensible property. Secondly, in 83. 6–7 Aristotle speaks of predicating *to ison auto*; he uses '*auto*' to indicate that the project now to hand is to discover what the property of equality is. The Argument from Relatives first rules out the possibility that *to ison auto*—the property of equality—is a sensible property or properties. Then, at 83. 15, it is inferred that there is *ti autoison kai kuriōs*, which is clearly the form of equal. '*Auto*' seems to have the same force in both places—in which case it designates a property in both places.[67] If this is right, then the Argument from Relatives, like the other arguments in the *Peri ideōn*, takes forms to be properties. In each case, the strategy is to argue that at least some properties must be forms. That this is correct is also suggested by the fact that, as we noted above, in the *Posterior Analytics* Aristotle takes himself to agree with Plato in saying that knowledge requires the existence of non-homonymous properties. Of course, Aristotle goes on to make the familiar point that universals should not be conceived as forms; but the crucial point is that in his view, when Plato posits forms to explain non-homonymy, they are universals.

But does the Argument from Relatives then take forms to be both universals and particulars? We need not say so. For in Ch. 4.7 we saw how forms could be self-predicative perfect paradigms without being particulars. For Plato's version of self-predication is best understood as BSP, which does not import particularity; neither does perfect paradigmatism, as I interpreted it in Ch. 4.7, import particularity. And I have in effect interpreted the Argument from Relatives in terms of BSP and my account of perfect paradigmatism. For I suggested that in saying that the form of equal is fully equal, it means that it explains why all equal things are equal and never explains why anything fails to be equal; it does this because it is the determinable, non-sensible property of equality. Similarly, the form of equal is a paradigm because, being the property of equality, it is that in virtue of which all equal things are equal, and so we need to know and refer to it if we are to know that anything is equal. Hence we need not say that the Argument from Relatives takes forms to be particulars.

9. Why the Argument from Relatives is a more accurate argument

Aristotle classifies the Argument from Relatives as a 'more accurate argument' than the Arguments from the Sciences, the One over Many Argument, and the Object of Thought Argument. In Ch. 2.7 I suggested that by this he means that it is a valid argument for the existence of forms. By contrast, the Arguments from the Sciences, the One over Many Argument, and the Object of Thought Argument are less accurate arguments because they are invalid arguments for the existence of forms. Although the Argument from Relatives has the advantage, from the Platonists' point of view, of being a valid argument for the existence of forms, Aristotle argues that it is vulnerable elsewhere. I explore his objections in the next chapter.[68] Here, however, I need to justify my claim that Aristotle takes the Argument from Relatives to be a valid argument for the existence of forms; and whether or not my claim is correct, we should ask whether it is in fact a valid argument for the existence of forms.

Aristotle says that the Argument from Relatives:[69]

seems (*dokei*) more carefully and more accurately and more directly to aim at the proof of the ideas. For this argument does not, like the ones before it, seem to prove simply that there is some common thing besides the particulars, but rather ⟨it seems to prove⟩ that there is some paradigm of the things here which is fully. For this seems to be especially characteristic of the ideas. (83. 18–22.)

And later he says that:

The idea's being an idea lies in (*en*) its being a paradigm. (86. 15.)

In the first passage, Aristotle says that the premisses of the preceding arguments in the *Peri ideōn*—i.e. of the less accurate arguments—prove only 'that the common thing is something besides the particulars'. That is, they prove that there are universals, but not that universals are Platonic forms. By contrast, the Argument from Relatives proves that there are paradigms that exist fully and in virtue of which the corresponding sensibles have their properties; and being a paradigm of this sort is 'especially characteristic' of forms. There are two readings of this claim. On the first reading, Aristotle claims only that being a perfect paradigm is essential to being a form. The second passage can also be read as saying no more than this. On this reading, the first passage does not unambiguously say that the Argument from Relatives is a valid argument for the existence of forms; for perhaps the existence of a perfect paradigm is only necessary and not also sufficient for the existence of a form. However, even on this reading I think the first passage still means to suggest that the Argument from Relatives is a valid argument for the existence of forms. For we have seen that the Argument from Relatives takes forms to be universals; and even if Aristotle does not believe that being a perfect paradigm is sufficient for being a form, he surely believes that if something is both a perfect paradigm and a universal, then it is a form. So on the first reading, the passage is elliptical; it means that given that the Argument from Relatives takes forms to be universals, the fact that it is a valid argument for the existence of perfect paradigms (that are also universals) shows that it is a valid argument for the existence of forms.[70]

But the two passages can also be read in a second way, as saying that being a perfect paradigm is 'especially characteristic' of being a form, and that the being of forms 'lies in' their being paradigms, not just in the sense that this is an essential feature of forms, a feature perhaps shared by other entities as well, but in the sense that only forms are such entities, so that if the Argument from Relatives is a valid argument for the existence of such entities, it follows that there are forms. On this reading too, the first passage means to say that the Argument from Relatives is a valid argument for the existence of forms.

On both readings of the passages, then, Aristotle claims that the Argument from Relatives is a valid argument for the existence of forms (and not just for the existence of entities that have an essential feature of forms).

That Aristotle takes the Argument from Relatives to be a valid argument for the existence of forms is also suggested by further facts. For example, he never says that the Argument from Relatives is an invalid argument for the existence of forms, although he does not hesitate to fault it elsewhere. Nor is he shy about alleging invalidity: he faults all the less accurate arguments on just this ground. It should be quite surprising if he thought the Argument from Relatives was also an invalid argument for the existence of forms but did not say so. Moreover, in *Met.* i. 9, he seems to contrast the less and the more accurate arguments by saying that the former but not the latter are invalid arguments for the existence of forms; at least, if this is not what he means, then the difference between the less and the more accurate arguments is left totally unexplained.

It is further support for this suggestion that the Argument from Relatives is in fact a valid argument for the existence of forms. It is certainly valid through Part IV. For it is evidently valid to infer the existence of a non-sensible paradigm that is fully equal—given the assumption that equal is non-homonymous, given the account of non-homonymy in Part I, and given Parts II–III's insistence that sensible equals are not fully equal. Further, it is also assumed that this non-sensible paradigm is a property or universal. Since (as Aristotle agrees) it is valid to infer from the existence of a non-sensible property of F that is also a paradigm that is fully F to the existence of a form of F, the Argument from Relatives is a valid argument for the existence of forms.

It is true that the first Argument from the Sciences also takes forms to be both paradigms and properties; yet I agreed with Aristotle that it is an invalid argument for the existence of forms (if forms are conceived as Aristotle conceives them). But the reason for the different verdicts about validity, despite the seeming similarities in language, is clear. For in the first Argument from the Sciences, the only sort of paradigmatism that can be validly argued for is weak paradigmatism, whereas the Argument from Relatives argues validly for the existence of perfect paradigms. In Aristotle's view, the existence of non-sensible universals that are weak paradigms is not sufficient for the existence of Platonic forms, but the existence of non-sensible universals that are perfect paradigms is sufficient for their existence.[71]

10. Conclusion

In Ch. 4.5 we saw that it is often thought both that Plato introduced forms because sensibles undergo change in the sense of succession, and that Aristotle interprets Plato in this way. At various stages, we have seen that it is also often thought both that Plato introduced forms for semantic reasons and that, since forms are self-predicative paradigms, they are particulars. The Argument from Relatives has been taken to support all these views; but on the account I have given it does not involve any of them. For I have argued that the only sort of change it adverts to is compresence; that it takes various properties to be non-homonymous not for semantic, but for epistemological and metaphysical reasons; and that although it takes forms to be self-predicative paradigms, this does not jeopardize their status as universals. The Argument from Relatives therefore fits well with, indeed supports, the views I have been defending throughout.

Completeness and Compresence: Owen on the Argument from Relatives

1. Introduction

The account I have provided of the Argument from Relatives is quite different from Owen's account in 'A Proof in the *Peri ideōn*'. In view of the difficulty and influence of his account, I should now like to explore it in more detail.[1]

Two central, and connected, differences between Owen's account and mine have already been mentioned. First, Owen thinks the Argument from Relatives is a semantic argument for the existence of forms, whereas I think it is epistemological and metaphysical. Secondly, Owen thinks the Argument from Relatives conceives forms as perfect particulars, whereas I think it conceives them as universals. These differences are connected in the following way. On my account, the Argument from Relatives assumes that the possibility of knowledge requires the existence of non-homonymous properties. For like Plato, it assumes that we can explain the F-ness of things only if F-ness is some one thing, the same in all cases; since in a certain range of cases, no sensible property of F can explain the F-ness of all the F things there are, there must be non-sensible properties, the forms, that can play this explanatory role. On Owen's account, the Argument from Relatives assumes that we can understand the meanings of general terms only if we are acquainted with a perfect sample or example of the predicate in question; since in a certain range of cases the sensible world lacks such samples, there must be forms, conceived as non-sensible perfect samples.

There are also further differences between Owen and me, many of which were mentioned in the previous chapter, at least in passing. A third difference, for example, is that Owen thinks that focal connection is relevant to the Argument from Relatives, whereas I argued that it is not. This difference between us is related to a fourth difference: Owen favours the extreme view of homonymy, whereas I favour the moderate view. Fifth, Owen favours the meaning view of homonymy, whereas I favour the real-essence view. (This difference obviously partly explains the first difference.) Sixth, Owen believes that Parts II–III rule out only I*a* and *c*, leaving I*b* open; I argued that Parts II–III preclude each of I*a*–*c*, and I explained how this could be so compatibly with Parts IV–V endorsing non-homonymy of type I*b* (as both Owen and I believe it does). This difference is related to a seventh difference: Owen believes that '*auto*' and '*kuriōs*' are synonymous or in some way have the same force, whereas I argued that this is not the case. Eighth, Owen believes that in the Argument from Relatives sensible equals are individual objects considered singly (e.g. a given stick) (see p. 174; pp. 177–9); I argued that they are sensible properties (e.g. being three inches). (This difference is obviously related to the second difference.) Ninth, Owen thinks that II*b* claims that particular sensible objects are constantly changing their dimensions; I argued that II*b* claims only that sensible equal properties exhibit narrow comprescence. (The eighth and ninth differences are also connected.)

2. Completeness

I return to some of these differences below. But first I want to look at a tenth difference that has not yet been mentioned: Owen and I offer quite different accounts of what it is to be *kuriōs*—fully or, in Owen's translation, strictly—*F*. This difference underlies and explains some of our other differences, including the two crucial differences mentioned at the outset.

I argued that, according to the Argument from Relatives, sensible equals are not fully equal because they suffer comprescence of opposites, and the form of equal is fully equal partly because it does not suffer comprescence of opposites (for, being the determinable property of equality, it explains the equality of all the equal things there are and never explains why anything is unequal, and so it is equal without also being unequal). In Owen's view, by contrast, the Argument from Relatives is not concerned with comprescence. In his view, when the Argument from Relatives says that sensible equals are not fully equal, it means that they are *incompletely* equal; and when it says that the form of equal is fully equal, it means that it is *completely* equal.

Before looking at Owen's account of completeness and incompleteness, I need to make some terminological points. We have seen that Owen takes '*auto*' and '*kuriōs*' to be synonymous or to have the same force. He also believes that *x* is *kuriōs F* just in case it receives the definition of *F* accurately (*akribōs*; Owen translates this as 'without qualification'). He also believes that to be *F* accurately is to be *F haplōs* (e.g. p. 176 nn. 39 and 40) and *kath' hauto*. Further, if *x* is not fully (accurately, etc.) *F*, then it is *F* only *pros ti*; there is an exclusive and exhaustive dichotomy between being fully *F* (etc.), on the one hand, and being *F pros ti*, on the other. This dichotomy, Owen believes, is the dichotomy between being completely and incompletely *F*.[2]

Of these various terms, the Argument from Relatives uses only '*auto*', '*kuriōs*', and '*akribōs*'.[3] In his criticisms of the Argument from Relatives (but not in the Argument from Relatives itself), Aristotle uses '*kath' hauto*' and '*pros ti*' (though none of the other terms on Owen's list).[4] Neither the Argument from Relatives nor Aristotle's criticisms use '*haplōs*'. These facts will prove important later.

In Owen's view, then, to be fully (accurately, etc.) *F* is to be completely *F*, and to be *F pros ti* is to be incompletely *F*. But what is it to be completely or incompletely *F*? Unfortunately, Owen does not give a precise account.[5] But in 'Dialectic and Eristic', he cites approvingly Strang's account of incomplete predicates as 'predicates which require completion if they are to be applied unambiguously to things in this world'.[6] On this account, '*F*' is used incompletely if it *requires* a complement. As Owen puts it, 'we *have* to ask what X is larger *than*, what it is a certain number *of*, what it is equal *to*' (p. 175; first emphasis added). Let us call this *semantic incompleteness*. That Owen has some sort of semantic incompleteness in mind is also suggested by the fact that he favours the meaning view of homonymy; so he takes the Argument from Relative's concern with homonymy and non-homonymy to be a concern with the meanings of terms—hence with semantic completeness and incompleteness.

What then is it for '*F*' to be used completely? There are two possibilities: (*a*) '*F*' is used completely if it does *not require* (although it may admit) a complement; or (*b*) '*F*' is used completely if it does *not admit* a complement. Since Owen claims that completeness and incompleteness are exhaustive, one might expect him to favour (*a*); for on (*a*), but not on (*b*), the division between completeness and incompleteness is exhaustive. And Owen does sometimes suggest (*a*).[7] However, Lesley Brown has convincingly argued that as Owen understands completeness in 'Plato on Not-Being', he requires (*b*).[8] The same generally seems true in our context. For example, we will see that it is crucial to his account of the form of equal that it *cannot* be equal to anything—'equal', as applied to it, cannot admit a complement. I shall therefore generally write as though (*b*) captures the relevant notion of completeness.[9]

Owen uses the general contrast between the complete and the incomplete in at least three ways. First, he speaks of complete and incomplete uses of a given predicate. Secondly, he speaks of complete and incomplete predicates, counting 'man', for example, as a complete predicate, and 'equal' (at least 'as we ordinarily apply it to things': p. 174) as an incomplete predicate. He means that a predicate is complete if it in fact has only complete uses, and that a predicate is incomplete if it in fact has only incomplete uses (or if it is always used incompletely in its 'ordinary applications', i.e. in its applications to particular sensible objects).[10] Thirdly, Owen speaks of complete uses of incomplete predicates.[11] Here the point is that although some predicates are in fact incomplete (have only incomplete uses), Plato mistakenly believed that they must apply completely to something—if not to something in the sensible world, then to a form. In addition to these three contrasts, we may also speak of an *object*'s being completely or incompletely *F*: *x* is incompletely *F* if '*F*' applies to it incompletely; *x* is completely *F* if '*F*' applies to it completely (pp. 177–8).[12]

3. Owen's account of the Argument from Relatives

II*c* claims that sensible equals fail to receive the definition of the equal accurately (*akribōs*). Owen takes this to mean that 'equal' applies to sensibles only incompletely, in the sense that any sentence of the form '*x* is equal', where '*x*' denotes an individual sensible object, is semantically incomplete; we need to add 'to *y*', specifying what *x* is equal to. As Owen puts it, 'to explain why one thing is called equal (and here again we have to note that equality is treated as an attribute of the individual thing) is to specify another with whose dimensions those of the first tally' (p. 176). Since no sensible equal object is equal without being equal to something, none receives the definition of the equal accurately.

II*a*, Owen believes, 'seems only the other face of this coin, for different cases of equality will require the *logos* to be completed in different ways' (p. 176): when I say '*x* is equal', I need to complete what I say by adding 'to *y*'; when I say '*z* is equal', I need to complete what I say by adding 'to *w*'. 'To *y*' and 'to *w*' are the different additions required to complete the explanation (*logos*) of why one thing is equal to another.

We have already looked briefly at Owen's account of II*b*. He thinks it says that sensibles are constantly changing not in every respect, but in their dimensions (p. 176).

On Owen's account, then, Part II denies that sensible equals are fully equal, on the ground that each is equal only by being equal to something. (II*b* irrelevantly adds that particular sensible objects are constantly changing their dimensions.) But we know from Part I that if a predicate is non-homonymous, something must bear it fully. The Argument from Relatives assumes that 'equal' is non-homonymous. So there must be something that is fully equal—that is, on Owen's view, some *x* such that *x* is equal all on its own, without being equal to anything. On Owen's view, Parts IV–V deduce the existence of a form of equal which is equal without being equal to anything—to which 'equal' applies completely. As he puts it, '[w]here a Paradigm is required for a predicate that is incomplete in its ordinary use it must indeed be . . . a Standard Case, exhibiting rather than being the character it represents. But more: it seems that the Form, and the Form alone, must carry its predicate *kath' hauto* in the sense given by the dichotomy [i.e. completely]. *auto to ison* is indeed equal, but how can we without absurdity ask to what it is equal?' (p. 177)—a rhetorical question meant to explain why 'equal' applies to the form completely. (Notice that here Owen seems to say that '*F*' applies to *x* completely only if '*F*' does not admit a complement. For if the form of equal could be equal to something, if 'equal' admitted a complement as applied to it, then there would be no absurdity in asking what the form of equal is equal to.)

Now it seems absurd to suppose that something can be equal without being equal to anything. As Owen puts it, 'if "equal" does not behave as tractably as "man" in this world, that does not entail that there is another world in which it does: the use of "equal" is *irreducibly* different from that of "man"' (p. 178). He concludes that the Argument from Relatives rests on a mistake about the logic of incomplete predicates, a mistake that Owen thinks Aristotle uncovers in his criticisms. For in VII Aristotle says that the Argument from Relatives produces 'an in-itself (*kath' hauto*) class of relatives (*pros ti*)'; and in X he says that 'we' do not admit such a class. Owen takes Aristotle to mean that the Argument from Relatives conceives forms as complete (*kath' hauto*) instances of incomplete (*pros ti*) predicates, though there are none such.

In Owen's view, then, the Argument from Relatives misunderstands the logic of incomplete predicates or, as he sometimes also calls them, relative predicates. This mistake turns some forms into 'logically impossible' entities.[13] Unfortunately, however, we cannot simply dismiss the Argument from Relatives as an argument unfairly foisted on Plato. For, Owen believes, it is 'substantially faithful' (p. 167) to its Platonic sources.

4. Three criticisms

Owen's account is deep and ingenious, but it is subject to some difficulties. I consider three of them.

(*a*) Owen does not provide a satisfactory explanation of II*a*'s claim that when we predicate the equal itself of things here, we do so homonymously.

Owen takes II*a* to say that if we were to predicate 'equal' of sensibles *kuriōs*, on its own, we would predicate it of them homonymously. Thus, consider the following four sentences:

(1) *x* is equal.
(2) *z* is equal.
(3) *x* is equal to *y*.
(4) *z* is equal to *w*.

Owen believes that in (1) and (2), 'equal' is predicated *akribōs*, without addition, and therefore homonymously; whereas in (3) and (4), it is predicated with addition ('to *y*' and 'to *w*') and so non-homonymously. 'Equal', he believes, can be predicated non-homonymously of things here only if it is predicated with addition. But exactly why does omitting the additions yield homonymy, whereas including them avoids it? Owen's answer seems to be that in (1) I need to substitute, as the definition (*logos*) of 'equal', 'of the same measures as *y*'; in (2) I need to substitute 'of the same measures as *w*'. By contrast, in (3) and (4) all that needs to be substituted is 'of the same measures as'. If we omit the relevant additions, as in (1) and (2), then equality requires different definitions, and so it is homonymous; if the relevant additions are provided, as in (3) and (4), then equality receives the same definition, and so it is not homonymous.

But contrary to Owen, 'equal' is not predicated homonymously in (1) and (2). The definition of 'equal' in (1) and (2), as in (3) and (4), is 'of the same measures as'. 'To *y*' and so on indicate different *cases* of equality, but they are not part of the *definition* of 'equality'.[14] If they are not, then Owen has not explained how homonymy arises if 'equal' is predicated fully, in his view, without addition. This should make us suspicious about the adequacy of his account of what the Argument from Relatives means by '*kuriōs*' and '*akribōs*'.

(*b*) On Owen's account of the Argument from Relatives, its Platonic credentials are not as firm as he takes them to be.

We have already seen one way in which this is so: Owen thinks that II*b* says that sensibles are constantly changing their dimensions. But he thinks that the sources that the Argument from Relatives have in mind argue for the existence of forms by appealing to compresence rather than to succession (see e.g. p. 175).[15] Here, then, is one place where Owen avoids an opportunity to import compresence into the Argument from Relatives, when doing so would have helped him to secure that argument's Platonic credentials.

There are further difficulties too. For example, in VII Aristotle says that forms exist *kath' hauta*. Owen takes this to mean that '*F*' applies completely to the form of *F*. Now according to Owen, Plato also says that forms exist *kath' hauta*. So does not Plato, like Aristotle in VII, claim that '*F*' applies completely to the form of *F*? But here there are two difficulties. First, although Plato often says that forms exist *auta kath' hauta*, he does not, contrary to Owen, say that forms exist *kath' hauta*;[16] and it is unclear that these two phrases are interchangeable.[17] Secondly and more importantly, when Plato says that forms exist *auta kath' hauta*, he does not mean that their predicates apply to them completely—as Owen agrees. As he puts it, 'in characterizing a case of X as *kath' hauto* he evidently means rather to exclude the opposite of X than to exclude the relativity which gives rise to an opposite' (p. 178). That is, Plato uses *'auta kath' hauta'* of forms not to indicate their completeness, but to indicate their freedom from compresence.[18] So although Plato and Aristotle describe forms in similar terms, they do so, on Owen's view, to make different points—Aristotle refers to completeness, Plato to freedom from compresence.

There are more serious difficulties than this terminological discrepancy. For example, Owen says that it was 'the compresence of opposites that the Form was invented to avoid' (p. 175).[19] Yet in Owen's view, the Argument from Relatives does not even mention compresence;[20] rather, its 'main point' (p. 178) is that every non-homonymous predicate must apply completely to something. At least in this respect, the Argument from Relatives, as Owen interprets it, fails to capture Plato's main reason for positing forms.[21]

One might argue that this is not a serious difficulty, on the ground that incompleteness and compresence inevitably go together. But they do not inevitably go together. True, Owen says that '[i]n this world what is large or equal, beautiful or good, right or pious, is so in some respect or relation and will always show a contradictory face in some other' (p. 174)—by which he seems to mean that in this world, incompleteness always gives rise to compresence.[22] However, as he notes, even if incompleteness always gives rise to compresence in this world, it does not always do so in the world of forms; some forms of *F* can escape compresence even if they are incompletely *F*.[23] The form of the good, for example, is better than anything else but it is not also bad. Similarly, the form of beauty is more beautiful than anything else but it is not also ugly. So the mere fact that *x* is *F* in some context or comparison, that '*F*' applies to it incompletely, does not ensure that it will be not *F* in some other context or comparison. Here, then, is one way in which incompleteness and compresence pull apart.

There is also another divergence: not every predicate whose instances exhibit compresence is an incomplete predicate. For example, the action-type of returning what one owes is both just and not just. But 'just' is not an incomplete predicate; when I say that returning my sword is on this occasion just, what I say does not demand completion. Owen himself notes that 'beautiful' has to be 'forced into this mould' (p. 174)—that is, it is not in fact an incomplete predicate.

Incompleteness and compresence thus do not inevitably go together. Some forms of *F* escape compresence even if they are incompletely *F*; and some predicates that are not incomplete have instances that exhibit compresence. So if, as Owen says, Plato invented forms to avoid compresence, but the Argument from Relatives claims that all forms are complete instances of incomplete predicates, then the Argument from Relatives misrepresents its Platonic sources.[24]

However, although Owen agrees that *some* forms of *F* can escape compresence even if they are incompletely *F*, he does not think that *all* forms can do so. He believes, for example, that if the form of equal were equal to anything, it would be unequal to something else (p. 177); so the form of equal can escape compresence only if it is completely equal, equal without being equal to anything. So even if the Argument from Relatives, as Owen interprets it, captures neither Plato's main, explicit argument for forms (which has to do with compresence) nor a consequence of that argument that affects all forms (since not all forms need to be complete instances of their predicates to escape compresence), still, he thinks, at least it focuses on a consequence of Plato's argument that affects some forms.

Moreover, Owen believes, it is a consequence Plato himself explicitly calls attention to in the *Phaedo*: 'This is the natural sense of Socrates' warning that the "equal" he is to discuss is not "stick equal to stick or stone equal to stone but just *equal*" (*Phd.* 74a)'.[25] But all Plato means here is that he wants to know not about sensible instances of equality but what equality itself, that property, is. To say that he wants to focus on the property in and of itself is not to say that he takes it to be a complete instance of its predicate. Indeed, at this stage Plato has not said anything about the nature of the property in question.

Owen thinks that Plato also points to the incompleteness of 'equal' as applied to sensible things, and to its completeness as applied to the form, when he says that sensible equals 'appear equal to one but not to another' (*Phd.* 74b8–9), whereas the equal itself, i.e. the form of equal, never 'appeared unequal to you' (74c1). Owen takes Plato to mean that any given stick, for example, is equal to one thing but unequal to another, whereas the form of equal is, simply, equal—that is, it is equal without being equal to anything.[26]

I doubt, however, whether this interpretation is correct. On the alternative I favour, Plato says only that sensible equals are equal and unequal, whereas the form of equal is not unequal, i.e. they suffer compresence but it does not. But he does not say *how* the form of equal escapes compresence; in particular, he does not say that it is equal without being equal to anything, or independently of any relation. The most Owen can argue, I think, is that the form can *in fact* avoid compresence only if 'equal' applies to it completely; but he goes too far if he thinks that Plato *claims* this. Plato explicitly makes only the familiar point that forms escape compresence. To be sure, if one agrees with Owen that forms are 'Standard Cases' rather than properties, then his explanation of how Plato takes the form of equal to be equal without also being unequal might seem reasonable.[27] But on the account of forms that I have been defending, according to which they are only properties, an alternative explanation is available: the form of equal escapes compresence because it is the determinable property of equality and, as such, it explains the equality of all the equal things there are and it never explains why anything is unequal. The form of equal can escape compresence in this way without being completely equal in Owen's sense.[28] If this is right, then not only does *Phd.* 74 not explicitly say that the form of equal escapes compresence by being completely equal but neither does that view underlie or explain the claim that the form escapes compresence.

If importing completeness into the argument fails to explain the homonymy claim and makes the argument less faithful to its Platonic sources than Owen claims, we should be suspicious of the attempt to import it. This leads to my third criticism:

(*c*) Contrary to Owen, the key terms in the Argument from Relatives and in Aristotle's criticisms of it do not indicate semantic completeness or incompleteness.

Owen believes that when IIc says that sensible equals do not receive the definition of the equal *akribōs*, it means that if we predicate 'equal' of them on its own, it applies to them incompletely; for since each is equal only by being equal to something, the relevant something needs to be specified. More generally, he believes that for *x* to receive the definition of '*F*' *akribōs* is for '*F*' to be predicated of *x* completely, in which case *x* is *F* but not in relation to anything. Further, if the definition of '*F*' applies to *x akribōs*, then it applies *haplōs* and *kath' hauto*, and *x* is *kath' hauto* *F*, as opposed to being *F pros ti*; if *x* is *F pros ti*, it is *F* only in relation to something, and '*F*' applies to it only incompletely.

Owen's argument for these claims has several strands. He claims, for example, that in his criticisms of the Argument from Relatives, Aristotle uses '*kath' hauto*' and '*pros ti*' as the Academy does, and that they use the terms for completeness and incompleteness. Notice first that even if this is so, it does not necessarily help Owen's case; for neither '*kath' hauto*' nor (a relevant occurrence of) '*pros ti*' occurs in the Argument from Relatives.[29] So even if Aristotle's criticisms invoke some sort of distinction between the complete and the incomplete, it does not follow that the Argument from Relatives, which uses different terms, also does so.[30]

Secondly and more importantly, I argue in the next chapter that even if VII and X use the terms in a special Academic way, they do not indicate completeness and incompleteness; for contrary to Owen, the Academy does not use '*kath' hauto*' and '*pros ti*' to distinguish between the complete and the incomplete.[31] Thirdly, I also argue in the next chapter that Aristotle's criticisms most likely use '*kath' hauto*' and '*pros ti*' not as the Academy does, but in order to distinguish between the Aristotelian categories of substance and relative. This distinction is neither the same as nor even coextensive with the distinction between the complete and the incomplete.[32]

Not all Owen's arguments rely on an alleged Academic use of our key terms. He also cites Aristotelian passages that contrast being *F haplōs* or *akribōs* with being *F kata prosthesin* or *pros ti* or *ti*; and he argues that these passages contrast being *F* without any qualification (i.e. completely) and being *F* with some qualification (i.e. incompletely). I shall now argue that this is not the contrast in these (or other similar) passages.[33]

Owen initially cites four passages: *APo.* 87a34–7, *Met.* 982a25–8 and 1078a9–13, and *EN* 1148a11.[34] The first three passages, however, simply say that a science A is more accurate than a science B if it involves fewer principles. Arithmetic, for example, is more accurate (*akribesteron*) than geometry, because geometry involves principles additional (*kata prosthesin*) to those involved in arithmetic. But, plainly, both arithmetic and geometry involve some principles or other; there is a difference of degree, not of kind. In the *Nicomachean Ethics* passage, a person is said to be incontinent *haplōs* if he is incontinent with respect to the appetites characteristic of incontinence (e.g. those having to do with food and sex); a person is incontinent *kata prosthesin* if he is incontinent with respect to other appetites, e.g. anger. In all these contexts, being *F haplōs* or *akribōs*, as opposed to being *F kata prosthesin*, indicates being *F* without *certain* additions or qualifications—*not* being *F* without *any* additions or qualifications.[35]

Nor do the relevant additions or qualifications have anything to do with *semantic* incompleteness. To say that Jones is incontinent *kata prosthesin* whereas Smith is incontinent *haplōs* is not to say that the first but not the second attribution is ambiguous. Although the passages Owen cites discuss something that might be called incompleteness, they do not discuss the sort of incompleteness Owen has in mind. Once again, semantic concerns are far less prominent than they have often been taken to be.

Nor do other Aristotelian occurrences of '*haplōs*' or '*akribōs*' support Owen. Sometimes, for example, Aristotle contrasts *einai haplōs* with *einai ti*. But as Owen himself notes, for Aristotle to be is always to be something or other.[36] For something to be *haplōs* is for it to be a substance; for something to be *ti* is for it to be a non-substance. Here again, both *haplōs* and *ti* involve a complement. Or again, in the *Eudemian Ethics* (7. 2) discussion of friendship (a passage on which Owen crucially relies; cf. p. 176 n. 40), Aristotle contrasts *kuriōs* friendship with derivative sorts of friendship. In the *kuriōs* kind of friendship, one chooses and loves a thing because it is good and pleasant *haplōs*, whereas in the derivative sorts of friendship, one chooses and loves a thing because it is good and pleasant *pros ti* or *tini*. To say that something is good and pleasant *haplōs*, rather than *pros ti* or *tini*, is not to say that it is completely good in Owen's sense, good without being good to anything, or independently of any context or relation; it is rather to say that it is good *to a good person*. Once again, *haplōs* is as incomplete as *ti* is.[37] Nor is the relevant sort of incompleteness semantic; in so far as there is any incompleteness here, it is metaphysical.[38] For example, the claim that *x* is *ti* (is a non-substance) is not ambiguous; it indicates that *x* is ontologically dependent on a substance.

In general, then, the contrast between being *F haplōs* or *akribōs*, on the one hand, and being *F ti* or *pros ti* or *kata prosthesin*, on the other hand, is not the contrast between being completely and incompletely *F*. Rather, it is the contrast between being *F* without some given qualification and being *F* only with that qualification, where the relevant qualification is made clear in the context. Further, the qualifications at issue are metaphysical rather than semantic. So when the Argument from Relatives claims that sensible equals are not *kuriōs* equal, and do not receive the definition of the equal accurately (*akribōs*), it does not mean that, unfortunately, they can be equal only by being equal to something; that is not the defect of sensibles to which the Argument from Relatives calls our attention.

I conclude that the Argument from Relatives does not advert to semantic incompleteness; and that is just as well, since neither do its Platonic sources.[39] My conclusion in this chapter therefore reinforces my conclusion in the last chapter, that in arguing that there are forms neither Plato nor the Argument from Relatives appeals to semantic considerations.

12

Kath' hauto and *pros ti*

1. Introduction

Aristotle levels three objections against the Argument from Relatives; I explore them in the next chapter. In this chapter I undertake some preliminary work relevant to his first objection (VII) and a related remark made in X. In both places, Aristotle objects that the Argument from Relatives produces forms of relatives (*pros ti*), yet there can be no such forms. For since forms are substances (*ousiai*), they exist in themselves (*kath' hauto*). But since relatives 'have their being in their relation to one another', forms of relatives could not exist in themselves.

In order to assess these remarks, we need to understand their key terms, '*kath' hauto*' and '*pros ti*'. Alexander believes Aristotle uses '*kath' hauto*' for a feature special to substances, and '*pros ti*' for his category of relatives. Owen criticizes Alexander's interpretation and suggests an alternative: that Aristotle uses '*kath' hauto*' and '*pros ti*' to mark an allegedly Academic dichotomy 'inherited from Plato' between complete and incomplete (uses of) predicates.[1]

In sect. 2 I argue that Plato uses '*kath' hauto*', '*pros ti*', and related phrases in a variety of different ways, none of which marks the distinction between the complete and the incomplete. In sect. 3 I defend Alexander's interpretation against Owen's criticisms. In sect. 4 I challenge Owen's reading of the passages he cites as evidence of an Academic distinction between the complete and the incomplete. I conclude that just as completeness and incompleteness are irrelevant to the Argument from Relatives, so they are irrelevant to VII and X.

2. Plato on *kath' hauto* and *pros ti*

As relevant Platonic uses of '*kath' hauto*' and '*pros ti*', Owen cites *So.* 255cd, *Phil.* 51c, *Rep.* 438bd, *Charm.* 168bc, and *Tht.* 160b.[2]

In *So.* 255c12–13, as part of an argument distinguishing being from difference, Plato writes:[3]

But I think you agree that some of the things that are are said to be themselves by themselves (*auta kath' hauta*), while some are said to be in relation to other things (*pros alla*).

This passage is often thought to distinguish either between complete and incomplete predicates, or between a complete and an incomplete use of 'be'.[4] However, I agree with those who think that it distinguishes instead between two incomplete uses of 'be', identity and predication. To say that *x* is 'itself by itself' is to say that *x* is self-identical; to say that *x* is 'in relation to something else' is to predicate of *x* something that is different from *x*. Indeed, Owen himself came to favour this view, and so he retracted his earlier view that *So.* 255c distinguishes between the complete and the incomplete.[5]

In the *Charmides*, Plato asks whether something can be *F* in relation to itself (*pros heauto*, 168d1),[6] or only in relation to something else (*tinos*). He asks, for example, whether what is greater is always greater than something else, or whether something can be greater than itself. He seems to have in mind the distinction between reflexive and irreflexive relations—but this is a distinction *within* the category of relations, not a distinction between the complete and the incomplete. Hence this passage too fails to draw the distinction Owen claims to find in VII and X.[7]

In *Rep.* 4 (438bd), Plato mentions the different sorts of correlates one needs to specify for things that are somehow of something; the greater, for example, is always greater than the less, the much greater than the much less. He then distinguishes between knowledge itself (*autē*) and knowledge *tis*—that is, between the genus knowledge and its various species.[8] He says that knowledge itself (the genus) is of whatever knowledge as such is of, whereas each species of knowledge is of some particular sort of knowledge. According to the *Republic*, knowledge as such is set over truth (477a9; cf. *Parm.* 134). Medicine (a particular sort of knowledge) is of (the truths about) health. Here Plato draws a distinction *within* the class of things that are somehow *pros* something—between the sorts of correlates one specifies for a genus, and the sorts one specifies for the species. Once again, there is no distinction between the complete and the incomplete. This is so for two reasons. First, knowledge itself and particular sorts of knowledge are both of something.[9] Secondly, the way in which they are of something does not involve semantic incompleteness. 'Some people study medicine' for example, is semantically complete, even though the sentence does not say what medicine is of; 'medicine' is not ambiguous, even though no complement is provided.

In the *Theaetetus*, Plato says on Protagoras' behalf that nothing is anything itself by itself (*auto eph' hautou*, 160b10), but only 'for someone or of something or in relation to something' (*tini . . . ē tinos ē pros ti*, 160b9). Protagoras' point is that an object is *F* if and only if it is *F* 'for someone'—that is, if and only if someone perceives it as being *F*. Further, someone perceives only if she perceives something.[10] Hence, as Plato explains, 'whenever I come to be perceiving, I come to be perceiving something; because it is impossible to come to be perceiving, but not perceiving anything. And whenever it comes to be sweet, bitter, or anything of that kind, it necessarily comes to be so for someone; because it is impossible to come to be sweet, but not sweet for anyone' (160a8–b3).

The first point to make here is that Plato is describing Protagoras' view, not his own. Indeed, it is a view he proceeds to criticize.[11] So even if the passage draws a relevant complete/incomplete distinction, it provides no evidence that *Plato* accepts such a distinction. Still, it is worth asking what distinction the passage draws.

Protagoras certainly does not use '*auto eph' hautou*' for entities like man, and 'for someone' and so on for entities like equal; for he argues that *nothing* is *auto eph' hautou*. Nor does '*auto eph' hautou*' indicate completeness in the sense of not admitting or not requiring a comple-ment; it indicates only being *F* independently of a perceptual encounter. If there could be an *x* that was equal independently of perception, then so far as the present passage goes Protagoras would count it as being *auto eph' hautou* equal—even if it were equal only by being equal to some-thing. Protagoras is not concerned to stress, as he should be on Owen's view, that objects can be, for example, large or equal or beautiful only compared *with one another*; his point is that they can have properties if and only if they are perceived to have them.

Similarly, in saying that nothing is *auto eph' hautou*, Protagoras does not mean that predicates apply to objects only incompletely—at least, this is so if incompleteness is semantic incompleteness. Protagoras does not seem concerned to say that 'Socrates is a man', for example, is *semantically* incomplete. We can say, if we like, that he believes that it is *metaphysically* incomplete, in so far as it does not express the fact that Socrates is a man if and only if he is perceived to be one. In this sense, he believes that objects have their properties only relationally. But to say that objects have all and only the properties they are perceived to have is not to say that all predicates are semantically incomplete.

In the *Philebus* (51cd), Plato distinguishes between things that are beautiful *kath' hauta* and those that are beautiful *pros ti*—certain simple shapes and colours, for example, are beautiful *kath' hauta*, but most things are beautiful only *pros ti*.[12] The point seems to be related to one made in the *Republic* (420cd), where Plato says that for a statue to be as beautiful as possible, one might have to paint its eyes a colour that is not the most beautiful colour there is. Even if purple is the most beautiful colour, a given statue might be more beautiful if its eyes are painted black.

Once again, Plato is obviously not distinguishing between complete and incomplete predicates; for he distinguishes between two ways of exemplifying a single predicate, 'beautiful'. Further, as Gosling notes, Plato's dichotomy does not seem to be exclusive;[13] a given token of purple, for example, might be beautiful both intrinsically and also when it is considered in a given context. Yet Owen takes the relevant Academic distinction to be exclusive. Nor does Plato suggest that if *x* is *kath' hauto* F, 'F' does not admit a complement; yet Owen at least sometimes so understands completeness. Conversely, to say that something is beautiful *pros ti* is not to say that 'beauty' applies to it incompletely, in the sense that it demands completion. Plato does not suggest that 'This statue is beautiful' is semantically incomplete, though he does say that the statue is beautiful only *pros ti*—presumably because its beauty is a function of its various parts. As in the *Theaetetus*, if this is any sort of incompleteness, it is metaphysical rather than semantic—though the relevant metaphysical distinction here is different from the one Protagoras emphasizes.

I conclude that none of the Platonic passages that Owen cites uses '*kath' hauto*' and '*pros ti*' to distinguish between complete and incomplete predicates, or between complete and incomplete uses of a given predicate. Nor do any two of them draw the same distinction as one another—there is no single, fixed Platonic usage of the phrases. If some members of the Academy use '*kath' hauto*' and '*pros ti*' to distinguish between complete and incomplete predicates, or between complete and incomplete uses of a given predicate, they are more innovative than Owen suggests.

3. Alexander on *kath' hauto* and *pros ti*

Alexander believes that Aristotle uses '*kath' hauto*' for a feature special to substances, and '*pros ti*' for the category of relatives. Owen raises two objections to Alexander's interpretation.[14] First, the Argument from Relatives is said to establish forms *from* (*ek*) relatives (82. 11). Owen takes this to mean that it establishes forms for all and only relatives. But, Owen believes, the Argument from Relatives is meant to show that there are forms not only for Aristotelian relatives but also for predicates like 'beautiful' and 'good'. So he concludes that 'relative' extends beyond the Aristotelian category of relatives. Secondly, later in the *Peri ideōn* (86. 5–6) Aristotle classifies number not, as one might expect, as a quantity but as a relative.[15] Owen thinks this also shows that Aristotle is using '*pros ti*' not to name his category of relatives, but in a broader sense.

I agree with Owen that the Argument from Relatives is meant to show that there is a form not only of, for example, equal, but also of, for example, good. So if the Argument from Relatives is supposed to prove that there are forms for all and only relatives, and if 'relative' names the Aristotelian category of relatives, then it proves that there are too few forms since good, for example, is not an Aristotelian relative. (It would also prove that there are too many forms, for the Argument from Relatives is not meant to show that there is a form of, for example, slave; yet slave is an Aristotelian relative.)

But contrary to Owen, the label 'Argument from Relatives' does not imply that the argument is meant to show that there are forms for all and only relatives. It indicates only that the argument proceeds from a relative (a point that is true on both Alexander's and Owen's account of 'relative'), not that all and only relative predicates can be substituted for 'equal'. And it is not surprising that Aristotle should name the argument by focusing on one special case for which it produces forms; for he finds it an especially striking and problematical case.[16] Owen's first objection can therefore be answered.

I have two replies to his second objection. First, even if 86. 5–6 uses 'relative' in an unusually broad sense, it does not follow that VII and X also do so. And in fact, it is not clear that 86. 5–6 uses 'relative' as VII and X do, for it gives a different explanation of 'relative': 86. 5–6 says that number is a relative because every number is *of something*, whereas VII says that relatives *have their being in their relation to one another*. Whatever we want to say about 86. 5–6, VII's description of *pros ti* fits Aristotle's usual way of describing his category of relatives.

Secondly, although 86. 5–6 seems to give a broader account of relatives than VII does, it may none the less describe Aristotle's category of relatives. For the account is very close to Aristotle's first account of relatives in the *Categories* (6a36–7). If that account is intended here, then 86. 5–6, like VII and X, has only the Aristotelian category of relatives in mind. If number turns out to be a relative on this account, that is a difficulty not for Alexander's interpretation, but for Aristotle.[17] Owen's second objection to Alexander's interpretation can therefore also be answered.

There are also more positive reasons to accept Alexander's interpretation. First, we will see in the next chapter that on Alexander's interpretation Aristotle's criticisms are relevant both to the Argument from Relatives and to his own concerns. Secondly, outside the *Peri ideōn*, Aristotle at least once uses '*kath' hauto*' and '*pros ti*' to contrast substances and relatives. For in X Alexander quotes *Met.* 990b16–17 and alludes to *EN* 1096a17–22,[18] where Aristotle says:

Those who introduced this view did not mean to produce an Idea for any [genus] in which they spoke of prior and posterior [members]; for that was why they did not mean to establish an Idea [of number] for [the series of] numbers. But the good is spoken of both in the [category of] what-it-is [i.e. substance] (*tō(i) ti esti*), and in the [categories of] quality and relative; and what is in itself (*kath' hauto*), i.e. (*kai*) substance (*ousia*), is by nature prior to what is relative, since a relative would seem to be an appendage and coincident of being (*paraphuadi gar tout' eoike kai sumbebēkoti tou ontos*). (Irwin's translation.)

Here (as on Alexander's interpretation of Aristotle's objection) Aristotle uses '*kath' hauto*' for substance and '*pros ti*' for the category of relatives. That this is so is supported by two facts. First, in 1096a20 Aristotle mentions the what-it-is (*tō(i) ti esti*), quality, and *pros ti*—that is, three of his ten categories: substance, quality, and relative. Then, in continuing the sentence in 1096a20–1, he contrasts *kath' hauto* and *pros ti*. He explains that by '*kath' hauto*' he means '*ousia*' (I take it that '*kai*' is epexegetic). Now, '*ousia*' is a familiar label for the category of substance, and so the explanation suggests that he is using '*kath' hauto*' for the category of substance. This is especially so given that 1096a20 has just mentioned substance; we ought to expect that in the continuation of the sentence in 1096a20–1 '*kath' hauto*' and '*ousia*' also indicate substance. Similarly, since 1096a20 uses '*pros ti*' for the category of relatives, presumably 1096a21 does so as well.[19] Secondly, his explanation of the second occurrence of '*pros ti*' is close to a point made more fully at *Met.* 1088a22–5, where he says that 'the relative is least of all the categories a nature or substance, and is posterior to quality and quantity; and the relative is an affection (*pathos*) of quantity, as was said'.[20] He means that every relative is what it is by also being something else in another category, whereas no non-relative is what it is by being something else in another category. A slave, for example, is what he is by also being a man, a substance; what is equal is what it is by also being a quantity; and so on. By contrast, although quantities, for example, are both ontologically and definitionally dependent on substances—for every quantity belongs to some substance, and the definition of quantity refers to substance—they are not quantities by also being something in another category.[21]

Outside the *Peri ideōn*, then, Aristotle uses '*kath' hauto*' and '*pros ti*' in the way Alexander takes him to use them here, to indicate the categories of substance and relative. We have seen that the Argument from Relatives uses Aristotelian terminology even though it records a Platonic argument. It is reasonable to assume that in his criticisms he also uses his own terminology. Certainly it is unclear why he should suddenly switch to Academic terminology used neither by Plato nor elsewhere by himself. I thus favour Alexander's interpretation of VII and X.

None the less, since it is sometimes thought that VII and X advert not to Aristotle's categorial scheme but to a different Academic one, it will be interesting and worth while to see how the Academics use '*kath' hauto*' and '*pros ti*'.

4. The Academy on *kath' hauto* and *pros ti*

Owen thinks VII and X use '*kath' hauto*' and '*pros ti*' as the Academy allegedly does, to indicate an exclusive and exhaustive dichotomy between the complete and the incomplete.[22] As relevant sources for this view, he cites four passages:[23] one from Simplicius about Xenocrates (*in Cat.* 63. 21–64. 12; 63. 21–3 = Xenocrates, fr. 12 Heinze); a passage in which Simplicius claims to record material from Hermodorus (*in Phys.*

247. 30–248. 15); a passage in Diogenes from the so-called *Divisiones Aristoteleae* (DL 3. 108–9); and a passage in which Sextus purports to elucidate the views of some unnamed Pythagoreans (*Adv. Math.* 10. 263–6). It is unclear how reliable this evidence is for uncovering an Academic distinction on which Aristotle might be relying.

Xenocrates is an Academic from the right period—he was a contemporary of Aristotle's, and head of the Academy after Speusippus. Moreover, Simplicius is generally reliable, and there does not seem to be any reason to be suspicious about this particular passage; so I count it as good evidence for relevant Academic views. But the other passages raise more qualms. To be sure, Hermodorus is an Academic from the right period—he was a fourth-century-BC pupil of Plato's who apparently wrote a work *On Plato*. But all that survives of this work is the Simplicius fragment; and Simplicius says he took the passage from Porphyry (3rd c. AD) who, in turn, took it from a book by Dercyllides (1st c. AD). It is unclear how reliable this complex chain of transmission is.

Although Diogenes says he is recording Aristotle's account of ways in which Plato divided things, the *Divisiones Aristoteleae* is not by Aristotle; nor is it clear that the work was written in Aristotle's lifetime. Moraux remarks on the generally low quality of the work; he suggests not only that it is not by Plato or Aristotle but also that it is not even by one of their especially gifted pupils.[24] Given the inferior quality of the work and the uncertainty about when it was written, we should be reluctant to rely on it as evidence for any distinction Aristotle might appeal to. Perhaps it could confirm an interpretation for which there is some independent evidence, but it should not be used as the sole evidence in support of an interpretation.

Sextus does not say what Pythagoreans he has in mind. We are not entitled to assume that they are Academics on whom Aristotle might be relying.[25]

So even if the passages Owen cites distinguish between the complete and the incomplete, the last three passages, especially the last two, are not good evidence that there was an Academic distinction between them on which Aristotle might have drawn. But even if it is risky to rely on all these passages for evidence of Academic views, they are worth exploring.

Simplicius records Hermodorus as saying that Plato[26]

says that of the things that are, some are in their own right (*kath' hauta*), like men and horses, others are in relation to other things (*pros hetera*); and of the latter, some are in relation to contraries (*pros enantia*)—like good and bad—and others are in relation to something (*pros ti*); and of the latter, some are determinate, others indeterminate. (*in Phys.*, 248. 2–5.)

Hermodorus draws an exclusive and exhaustive dichtomy not between *kath' hauto* and *pros ti* but between *kath' hauto* and *pros heteron*; *pros ti* is a subdivision within the *pros heteron* category. Good is said to belong in the category of *pros enantia*—it is a *pros heteron* item, but not of the *pros ti* variety. So Hermodorus does not draw an exclusive and exhaustive dichotomy between *kath' hauto* and *pros ti*; nor does he classify all the relevant predicates as *pros ti*, since he does not so classify 'good'.

Perhaps the terminological variation is insignificant?[27] But this suggestion will not do. For just as Hermodorus' category of *pros ti* is too narrow for Owen's purposes (since it does not include e.g. 'good'),[28] so his category of *pros heteron* is too broad for Owen's purposes (since unlike me he believes that the Argument from Relatives is supposed to produce forms for all and only relatives). At least, this seems to be the case if we reflect on the possible basis of Hermodorus' division. Although he does not provide a clear account, one attractive and plausible (though by no means certain) suggestion is that *kath' hauto* items are definitionally or ontologically independent, whereas *pros heteron* items are definitionally or ontologically dependent—either their definitions, unlike the definitions of *kath' hauto* items, need to mention other entities; or else their existence, allegedly unlike the existence of *kath' hauto* items, depends on the existence of some other entity or entities. If this is right, then Hermodorus' distinction seems to correspond to Aristotle's distinction between substances and non-substances.[29] Certainly all Hermodorus' examples of *kath' hauto* items are substances, and all his examples of *pros heteron* items fall into one or another Aristotelian non-substance category; further, all the latter items are of something, just as all Aristotelian non-substances are of substance.[30] If Hermodorus' distinction is between substance and non-substance, then his category of *pros heteron* is too broad for Owen's purposes. For it would then include, for example, 'sitting' and 'in the Lyceum', yet the Argument from Relatives is presumably not meant to generate forms for them.

Nor is the distinction between substance and non-substance the same as, or even coextensive with, the distinction between complete and incomplete predicates. 'White' and 'slave', for example, are non-substance predicates; but they are not incomplete predicates.

In his commentary on the *Categories* (*in Cat.* 63. 21–64. 12), Simplicius says that Xenocrates and Andronicus[31] oppose *kath' hauto* and *pros ti*; he adds that others (whom he unfortunately does not name) draw the same distinction in different terms, using '*ousia*' and '*sumbebēkota*' instead. Simplicius says that Xenocrates and Andronicus favour their terminology on the ground that all *sumbebēkota* are of something, i.e. depend on substance. He also says that Xenocrates and Andronicus preferred their simpler categorial scheme to Aristotle's more complex one because it brought out a feature common to all non-substances, that they are all somehow of or dependent on substance.

Unlike Hermodorus, Xenocrates and Andronicus use '*kath' hauto*' and '*pros ti*' to form an exclusive and exhaustive dichotomy. And it seems clear that Simplicius takes their distinction to be that between substance and non-substance—which, as we have seen, may also be what Hermodorus has in mind in distinguishing between *kath' hauto* and *pros heteron*. But if Xenocrates and Andronicus use the terms to distinguish between substance and non-substance, then they do not use them to distinguish between complete and incomplete predicates; for, again, the two contrasts differ.[32]

Although Simplicius believes that Xenocrates and Andronicus distinguish between substance and non-substance, Elias says that Andronicus uses '*pros ti*' for the Aristotelian category of relatives, and '*kath' hauto*' to name all the other nine categories.[33] If Elias is right, then '*pros ti*' names the Aristotelian category of relatives rather than a broader category that might be thought to include all and only incomplete predicates. In this case, '*pros ti*' is used as Aristotle standardly uses it and as Alexander thinks he uses it here—and so not to cover all and only incomplete predicates.

According to Diogenes Laertius (3. 108–9), Aristotle says that Plato says that:

Of things that are, some are in themselves (*kath' heauta*) and some are relative (*pros ti*). Things are said to be in themselves when they need nothing added in their interpretation (*hermēneia*), e.g. man, animal, horse, and the other animals. For none of these things gains by interpretation. Things are said to be relatives when they need something added in their interpretation, e.g. greater than something, quicker than something, more beautiful, and such things. For the greater is greater than a lesser, and the quicker is quicker than something. So of things that are, some are themselves in themselves (*auta kath' hauta*) and others are relative. And in this way, according to Aristotle, Plato also used to divide the primary things (*ta prōta*).

The *kath' heauto/pros ti* (or, as it is also called, the *auto kath' hauto/ pros ti*) division that Diogenes records seems to be exclusive and exhaustive: something is *kath' heauto* (or *auto kath' hauto*) 'if it needs nothing added in its interpretation'; something is *pros ti* if it needs something added. This account of *pros ti* items sounds like Owen's main notion of incompleteness, in so far as it says that *pros ti* items *need* something added. Moreover, 'interpretation' is often used for linguistic expression in particular; so unlike Hermodorus and Xenocrates, Diogenes may record a syntactic or semantic division, and in that way too his division is closer to Owen's notion of completeness and incompleteness than are the divisions favoured by Hermodorus and Xenocrates. But some further features of the passage might give us pause.

First, it is not clear that *kath' hauto* items do not admit a complement. Yet we have seen that at least sometimes Owen takes complete predicates to be those that do not admit a complement.

Secondly, although Diogenes may intend to record a division between complete and incomplete predicates, various other interpretations seem equally plausible. All his examples of *kath' hauto* items are Aristotelian substances (man and the other animals); and all his examples of *pros ti* items are Aristotelian relatives. The *pros ti* items, moreover, are all relatives of a particular sort—explicit comparatives (e.g. greater than and more beautiful than).[34] Now the distinction between Aristotelian substances and relatives is not exhaustive; yet the passage seems to have in mind an exhaustive distinction. So where do the other non-substances go? If they go in the *kath' hauto* side of the divide, then the distinction may be between relatives and all the other categories; this is the distinction Elias ascribes to Andronicus. In this case, the *Div. Ar.* does not distinguish between complete and incomplete predicates, since the distinction between non-relatives and relatives is not the distinction between complete and incomplete predicates. Suppose instead, then, that the *Div. Ar.* classifies all non-substances as *pros ti* items. In this case, it still does not distinguish between complete and incomplete predicates, since the distinction between substance and non-substance is not the same as the distinction between complete and incomplete predicates.

The Diogenes passage certainly does not preclude Owen's interpetation. But it does not support his interpretation more than it supports the alternative interpretations I have suggested. And I am inclined to think that the passage distinguishes between substances and non-substances; for we have independent evidence that that distinction was of central concern in the Academy, but not that a distinction between complete and incomplete predicates was of concern. In any case, the very indeterminacy of the passage provides yet another reason, beyond those cited at the beginning of this section, for being wary about using it as the sole evidence of an Academic distinction on which Aristotle might have relied.

Sextus Empiricus ascribes the following view to some unnamed Pythagoreans:

Of things that are, they say, some are thought of according to a difference (*noeitai kata diaphoran*), some according to a contrariety, some in relation to something (*pros ti*). Those ⟨thought of⟩ according to a difference are in themselves (*kath' heauta*) and are subjects according to their own special separation, e.g. animal, horse, plant, earth, water, air, fire. For each of these is thought of independently, and not according to its relation to something else. Those ⟨thought of⟩ according to contraries are those thought of in their opposition to one another, e.g. good and bad, just and unjust, advantageous and disadvantageous, holy and unholy, pious and impious, in motion and at rest, and all other things similar to these. Those ⟨thought of⟩ in relation to something are the things thought of in relation to something else, e.g. right and left, above and below, double and half. For right is thought of as standing in relation to left, and left as standing in relation to something right; and below as related to something above, and above as related to something below; and similarly in the other cases.   (*Adv. Math.* 10. 263–6.)

Sextus goes on to explain how these Pythagoreans distinguished between things thought of according to a contrary and things thought of in relation to something.[35] He says that the destruction of one contrary gives rise to the other, whereas relatives coexist and are co-destroyed. Further, there is no intermediate state between contraries, but there is an intermediate state between relatives. He also says that the genus for all things thought of according to a contrary is equal, whereas the genus for all things thought of in relation to something is excess and defect.

Unlike our other sources, the Pythagoreans operate with a threefold, rather than with a twofold, division. But their threefold division sounds like Hermodorus' twofold division between *kath' heauto* and *pros heteron*, the latter being divided into two classes, contraries and relatives. There is, however, an important dissimilarity: Hermodorus classifies equal as a determinate relative, whereas the Pythagoreans classify it as the genus of things thought of according to a contrary (271). If, as seems reasonable, that means that they take equal to be one of the things thought of according to a contrary, rather than one of the things thought of in relation to something, then their use of '*pros ti*' is clearly inadequate for Owen's purposes since it does not even pick out equal.

Nor do their two classes of things thought of according to a contrary and things thought of in relation to something *taken together* seem to pick out all and only incomplete predicates. For they classify pain, for example, as something thought of according to a contrary (266); but 'pain' does not seem to be an incomplete predicate. They also so classify 'life' and 'death', which do not seem to be incomplete predicates either (although Plato may believe there are forms here, so perhaps Owen would wish to classify them as incomplete predicates). But even if we concede that these two classes taken together are coextensive with incomplete predicates, still, that does not seem to be the feature of them that interests the Pythagoreans. Their division seems to concern the way we think of things. Annas and Barnes speak here of epistemological relativity, which they distinguish from both semantic and ontological relativity. The Pythagoreans' point, they suggest, is that one thing is relative to another (i.e. is thought of either according to a contrary or in relation to something) when 'one thing cannot be *known* or *recognized* without the other being known or recognized'.[36] This interpretation seems right. But if so, then the Pythagoreans have in mind a different distinction from any we have yet explored.[37]

Our survey of the evidence has produced a complicated story. For it has emerged that there is no single Academic theory of categories, demarcated in fixed terms. Further, with the possible but by no means certain exception of Diogenes, none of the passages we have explored distinguishes either between complete and incomplete predicates or between complete and incomplete uses of a given predicate. We therefore have no clear evidence that there was an Academic distinction between complete and incomplete predicates, or between complete and incomplete uses of a given predicate, on which Aristotle might have relied.

But we need not be troubled by this result. For even if such an Academic distinction were available to Aristotle, we might doubt its relevance in VII and X. For we have seen that Plato does not use the relevant terms to distinguish between the complete and the incomplete; nor does Aristotle (elsewhere) do so in his own right; nor does the Argument from Relatives do so. All this makes it unlikely that VII and X distinguish between the complete and the incomplete—which is just as well, when the quarry has proved so elusive.[38] In the next chapter, I shall therefore explain Aristotle's objections to the Argument from Relatives on the assumption that Alexander's interpretation of '*kath' hauto*' and '*pros ti*' is correct. As we will see, this assumption allows us to make good sense of Aristotle's objections.

13

Aristotle's Objections to the Argument from Relatives

Aristotle levels three objections against the Argument from Relatives; I explore them in turn (sects. 1–3). I then turn to a related objection that he raises later in the *Peri ideōn* (sect. 4).

1. Aristotle's first objection: No substance is a relative

Alexander says that Aristotle objected to the Argument from Relatives as follows:[1]

VII. He says, then, that this argument establishes ideas even of relatives (*kai tōn pros ti*). At least (*goun*), the present proof has been advanced on the basis of the equal, which is a relative. But they used to say that there are no ideas of relatives. For in their view the ideas subsist in themselves (*huphestanai kath' hauta*), being, in their view, kinds of substances (*ousiai*), whereas relatives have their being in their relation to one another. (83. 22–6.)

Alexander adverts to the same objection a bit later on, when he says:

X. Further, he made this opinion common ground when he spoke of it as his own, saying 'of which things we say there is no in-itself (*kath' hauto*) genus', speaking of 'genus' instead of 'reality' or 'nature', if a relative is indeed like an appendage, as he said elsewhere. (83. 30–3.)

The argument may be schematized as follows:

(1) Forms are substances (*ousiai*).
(2) If *x* is a substance, *x* subsists in itself (*x* is *kath' hauto*).
(3) Therefore forms subsist in themselves.
(4) If *x* is a relative (*pros ti*), *x* has its being in relation to another relative.
(5) If *x* has its being in relation to another relative, then *x* does not subsist in itself.
(6) Therefore no form is a relative.
(7) The form of equal is a relative.
(8) Not both: (6) and (7).

Aristotle thus believes that, like the other arguments we have explored, the Argument from Relatives produces forms in unwanted cases; this time the unwanted forms are forms of relatives. However, the way in which the Argument from Relatives produces too many forms differs from the way in which the earlier arguments do so. The earlier arguments allegedly produce forms for predicates for which the Platonists do not want forms (for the crafts, for negations, and for perishable particulars and fictional entities respectively). But Aristotle cannot mean that here; for the Argument from Relatives uses 'equal' (a relative predicate) as a key example of a predicate demanding a form. Aristotle is rather objecting that the Platonists' explicit acknowledgement of forms of relatives is incompatible with the view that all forms are substances and so exist in themselves.[2] Aristotle thinks these two views are incompatible because in his view no relative can exist in itself, since relatives 'have their being in their relation to one another' (83. 25–6).

I begin by asking why Aristotle believes that the form of equal is both a relative and a substance. I then ask why, and with what justification, he claims that no relative can be a substance.

In the *Metaphysics* (1. 6, 13. 4, and 13. 9), Aristotle says that Plato takes forms to be substances, i.e. basic beings, because they satisfy such important criteria for substantiality as being fundamental for knowledge and definition.[3] So all forms are substances simply *qua* forms, irrespective of the particular forms they are.

Although the form of equal is a substance that exists in itself simply *qua* form, it is a relative *qua* the particular form it is, *qua* the form corresponding to the predicate 'equal'. It seems plain that the form of equal is viewed not only as corresponding to the predicate 'equal' but also as itself being equal. This is no doubt because Aristotle believes that Plato is committed to SP (any form of *F* is itself *F*), so that if there is a form of equal, it is equal.

The form of equal is thus a substance that exists in itself *qua* form; but it is equal, and so a relative, *qua* the particular form it is. Call properties that forms have in virtue of their being forms 'A-level properties'; and call properties that forms have in virtue of their being the forms they are 'B-level properties'.[4] We can then say that Aristotle is offering a 'two-level paradox', one that alleges contradiction between an A- and a B-level property.

Now some two-level paradoxes may initially seem troubling, though they are not in fact troubling. For example, one might think that nothing can be both one and many; so if one could argue that a given form is both one and many, it might seem that one has raised a serious difficulty. But if it turns out that the form is one in so far as it is one form, and many in so far as it is the form corresponding to the predicate 'many', then the seeming difficulty disappears. However, some two-level paradoxes are genuinely troubling. To illustrate with an example not about forms: if I say that all policemen have to be over 5 foot 6 inches, and that Jones is only 5 foot 4 inches, then Jones cannot be a policeman—even though it is not *qua* policeman that he fails to be over 5 foot 6 inches.

What about the present two-level paradox? Would there be a genuine difficulty if it could be shown that the form of equal is a substance *qua* form, and a relative *qua* the form corresponding to the predicate 'equal'? I think there would be—given Aristotle's belief that nothing can be both a substance and a relative.[5] For in saying that all forms are supposed to be substances, Aristotle is imposing criteria that anything that counts as a form must satisfy—this is like saying that all policemen must be over 5 foot 6 inches. In Aristotle's view, if something is a relative it cannot satisfy those criteria—this is like saying that if Jones is only 5 foot 6 inches, he cannot be a policeman. This paradox cannot be disarmed simply by noting that it is a two-level paradox.

If the present two-level paradox is not suspect simply in virtue of being a two-level paradox, then VII is valid.[6] The only questions to be raised, then, are whether it correctly captures Plato's views and whether it is sound.

Aristotle seems right to say that Plato views all forms as substances and (assuming SP) that the form of equal is a relative. He also seems right to suggest that of the two allegedly conflicting claims—that all forms are substances and that some forms are relatives—Plato would prefer to jettison the second. Aristotle gives no explanation of that claim here, but he presumably believes that it is more important to Plato to safeguard the status of forms as substances, as basic beings, than to countenance any particular form.

But why does Aristotle believe that nothing can be both a substance and a relative? His reason is that every substance exists in itself, whereas relatives 'have their being in their relation to one another'. But what is it for something 'to exist in itself' or for relatives to 'have their being in their relation to one another'? Unfortunately, it is not at all easy to understand Aristotle's views on these matters.[7]

For something to exist in itself (in its own right, *kath' hauto*) is for it to enjoy some sort of independence; the independence could be existential or definitional. I am inclined to think that Aristotle has definitional independence in mind here.[8] At least, when he wants to say that Platonic forms are existentially independent, he typically uses a form or cognate of '*chōrizein*' instead.[9] Moreover, the different varieties of being *kath' hauto* described in the *Posterior Analytics* (1. 4)—in passages that are quite similar to our context—seem to involve definitional rather than existential claims. I shall therefore begin by assuming that '*kath' hauto*' indicates definitional independence; but later I shall briefly consider the force of Aristotle's argument if it is interpreted in terms of existential independence.

What sort of definitional independence might be at issue? One possibility is that Aristotle means that substances exist in themselves because each can be defined without mentioning anything distinct from it, whereas no relative can be defined without mentioning something distinct from it.

Now it is sometimes held that at least in the middle dialogues Plato denies that anything can be said of the form of F other than that it is F.[10] If this view were correct, then Plato would not want to allow that in defining one form one needs to mention something else. So perhaps Aristotle has in mind the first possibility and urges it as an *ad hominem* argument against Plato?

If so, his argument fails; for Plato does not deny that in defining a given form, one needs to refer to other forms, and so to something distinct from the form—substance—being defined. In the *Parmenides* (133b–134e), for example, he admits, indeed insists, that at least relational forms are defined in terms of one another; the form of master, for example, is defined in terms of the form of slave. Nor is this a late development.[11] Even in the middle dialogues Plato insists that in defining any given form one needs to refer to others. In the *Phaedo*, for example, he says that whatever is odd is odd in virtue of participating in the form of odd; so the form of three is odd in virtue of participating in the form of odd.[12] In the *Republic* (e.g. 505ab, 506a, 508d–509b) he insists that a full account of a thing requires relating it to the form of the good. In Plato's view, every form (not just relational forms) is essentially related to the form of the good, and that fact must be reflected in a full account of any form. So Aristotle can hardly urge, as an *ad hominem* argument against Plato, that some forms have definitions that refer to other things; for that is a point on which Plato himself insists.

Might Aristotle then mean that although Plato allows that in defining forms one needs to refer to other things, he ought not to do so? In this case, Aristotle's objection would not be the *ad hominem* one that Plato is, but would not want to be, committed to mentioning something besides the form of equal in defining it. Rather, his objection would be that although Plato believes that in defining the form of equal one needs to mention something else, he ought not to believe that, given his view that forms are substances.

But Aristotle is not well placed to urge this argument, since his own substances do not exist in themselves in this sense. Socrates, for example, can only be defined[13] by reference to his species, which is distinct from him (e.g. it survives his loss and is predicated of more than one thing).[14] Similarly, the species man can only be defined by reference to its genus, animal, which is distinct from it.

The first possibility thus seems wrong; it works neither as an *ad hominem* objection nor as an objection Aristotle is well placed to voice in his own right. So let us consider a second possibility. Perhaps the thought is that substances exist in themselves because each can be defined, not independently of everything, but without reference to any non-substance. Perhaps Aristotle believes that the form of equal is not a substance because it fails this condition? He seems to believe, at any rate, that definitions of substances need not refer to non-substances (cf. e.g. *Met.* 7. 1), and he may be able to defend this claim better than he can defend the claim that a substance can be defined without reference to anything distinct from it.[15]

But why does the form of equal fail this condition? We might again first try interpreting the argument as an *ad hominem* one: perhaps the thought is that the definition of the form of equal must refer to something *Plato* regards as a non-substance? If Aristotle could argue that, for example, the equality of the form of equal can only be explained by reference to sensible equals (or to anything sensible) that would disturb Plato (on the assumption that he does not count sensibles as substances). But Plato is committed to no such thing.[16] If the form of equal must be equal to something, then, as Aristotle points out in VIII, it could be equal to another form of equal.[17] But in Plato's view, that is only to refer to another substance; and we have seen that Aristotle too must allow that in defining one substance, one needs to refer to others. Once again, then, Aristotle's argument fails if it is taken to be *ad hominem*.

However, I doubt whether the argument is *ad hominem*. Aristotle no doubt sees that Plato believes that any form of equal is a substance; his objection is that Plato ought not to believe that. For any form of equal is a relative and—so Aristotle believes—no relative can be a substance. So if one needs to refer to another form of equal in explaining any given form of equal, then one needs to refer to a relative and so to something Aristotle takes to be a non-substance.

If this is right, then we have here, as so often in the debate between Plato and Aristotle, a confrontation between two opposed metaphysical outlooks. Plato and Aristotle agree that substances must be definitionally basic. But Plato believes, whereas Aristotle denies, that some relatives enjoy the requisite definitional basicness. It is Aristotle's disagreement with Plato on this fundamental issue that motivates his present argument.[18]

So far I have explicated the notion of being in itself in terms of definitional independence. If it is interpreted in terms of existential independence, my account still holds, *mutatis mutandis*. Neither Aristotelian nor Platonic substances exist independently of everything else. Socrates (an Aristotelian substance) cannot exist unless the species man exists. For Plato, forms cannot exist unless the form of the good exists. Aristotle would say that shows that all forms depend on a non-substance (since in his view 'good' is a non-substance predicate and so, given SP, the form of the good is a non-substance); Plato would say that it shows only that forms depend on another substance, since in his view the form of the good is a substance.[19] But if Platonic forms are separate, they can exist whether or not the corresponding sensibles (i.e. Platonic non-substances) exist. It is not clear, however, that Aristotelian substances can exist without Aristotelian non-substances; Socrates, for example, cannot exist unless he has some height and weight, although he does not need to have any determinate height or weight in order to exist. If we turn to the existential reading, Platonic substances (assuming separation, and allowing that all forms are substances) satisfy the 'in itself' require-ment *better* than Aristotle's own substances do.

At least, Plato is *internally* better off than Aristotle is. But Aristotle would no doubt object that my defence of Plato requires the false assump-tion that forms are separate. If we deprive Plato of this view, then he is not internally better off than Aristotle is. Once again, then, the debate between Plato and Aristotle turns on their conflicting intuitions—this time (as often), about whether universals can exist uninstantiated.

VII is a good illustration of an Aristotelian strategy mentioned in Ch. 2.8: Aristotle neither misinterprets Plato nor shows that he is guilty of internal inconsistency. He objects that a Platonic argument fails once an Aristotelian assumption that Plato rejects is intruded into it. The dispute involves hard philosophical questions about the nature of substances and universals.

As I interpret VII, it is quite a natural criticism for Aristotle to make of the Argument from Relatives. The Argument from Relatives posits a form of equal; given SP, this form is a relative. In VII Aristotle argues that since forms are substances, there cannot be relative forms. It is true that this criticizes a consequence of the Argument from Relatives rather than its main concern (to avoid homonymy by finding entities that escape compresence); but it is obviously legitimate to criticize consequences of arguments. Moreover, the consequence violates one of Aristotle's most deeply held metaphysical views—that substances must exist in them-selves, that they must enjoy a degree of definitional (and existential) independence that, he believes, no relative enjoys. It is not surprising that Aristotle faults the Argument from Relatives for (as he thinks) violating this view.[20] Further, I concluded Ch. 12 by saying that if VII's key terms are interpreted as Alexander interprets them, we can make good sense of the argument; we need not turn to an allegedly Academic understanding of them. I hope to have vindicated this claim as well.

2. Aristotle's second objection: Self-predication and Uniqueness conflict

Aristotle's second objection to the Argument from Relatives runs as follows:

VIII. Further, if the equal is equal to an equal, there will be more than one idea of equal. For the equal itself is equal to an equal itself. For if it were not equal to something, it would not be equal at all.   (83. 26–8.)

The argument may be schematized as follows:

(1) Whatever is equal is equal to something.
(2) The form of equal is equal.
(3) Therefore, the form of equal is equal to something.
(4) The form of equal can be equal only to another form of equal.
(5) Therefore, if there is even one form of equal, there are at least two forms of equal.
(6) There is exactly one form of F if any at all (= Uniqueness).
(7) Therefore, if there is even one form of equal, there is just one form of equal.
(8) Not both: (5) and (7).

Aristotle's strategy is again clear. On the one hand, Plato accepts SP; so the form of equal must be equal. Anything that is equal must be equal to something; so the form of equal must be equal to something. It can be equal only to another form of equal; so if there is even one form of equal, there are at least two forms of equal. But this violates the uniqueness assumption (U), according to which if there are any forms corresponding to 'F', there is just one. SP and U thus conflict at least in the case of the form of equal.[21]

Later in the *Peri ideōn*, Aristotle argues that the forms generated by the Accurate One over Many Argument are vulnerable to an infinite regress: if there is even one form of F, there are infinitely many forms of F, again in conflict with U. This is the famous Third Man Argument. One premiss of the Third Man Argument is SP. As we shall see in Ch. 16.5, Aristotle seems to believe that the forms generated by the Argument from Relatives are immune to the Third Man Argument. But his present objection shows that he also believes that at least one of the forms it countenances falls prey to a 'mini-regress', in so far as he argues that if there is even one form of equal, there are two forms of equal. So even if the forms generated by the Argument from Relatives escape the Third Man Argument, at least one of them violates U, and this is partly because of SP.[22]

Like VII, VIII is valid. But we can again raise questions about its soundness and about its effectiveness as an *ad hominem* objection to Plato.

I begin by considering (2). Since I think Plato accepts SP, I think he accepts (2). However, I think his self-predication assumption is best interpreted as BSP. On BSP, the form of equal is equal, not because it is equal to something, but because, being the non-sensible, determinable property of equality, it explains why all equal things are equal and it never explains why anything is unequal. If Plato's self-predication assumption is best interpreted as BSP, then he is not committed to (1) or (3). If he is not committed to (1) or (3), the rest of the argument cannot go through.[23]

Aristotle, however, commits Plato not only to (2) but also to (1) and (3). In doing so, he seems to assume that Plato is committed to NSP. At least, it seems more reasonable to commit Plato to (1) and (3) if he is committed to NSP than it does if he is committed only to BSP.[24] Does Aristotle then misinterpret Plato? We need not say so. For Aristotle can reply as follows: 'Plato uses self-predicational language; NSP is the most straightforward, intuitive reading of such language. If Plato is so read, my argument succeeds. Of course, one might protest that Plato should be read in some other, less straightforward, way. But then he should not speak as he does; and he certainly never spells out what alternative he has in mind. Further, if the form of equal is not equal to something, it cannot be equal at all; it violates ordinary beliefs too far to suppose that something can be equal without being equal to something. Not only, then, is BSP not spelled out in anything like the necessary detail; but it also revises ordinary beliefs too far to be credible.'[25]

Read in this way, Aristotle's criticism rests on another familiar strategy mentioned in Ch. 2.8: he interprets what he views as vague language in what he takes to be the most natural way, and he criticizes Plato so read. His criticism may well succeed if Plato is so read.[26] But Plato can protest that he ought not to be so read. Once again, Aristotle does not misinterpet Plato, but neither does he level a fatal blow. He raises a reasonable question: what does Plato mean, if not the natural interpretation Aristotle assumes?

3. Aristotle's third objection: The Argument from Relatives establishes two forms of unequal

IX. Further, by the same argument there will also have to be ideas of unequals. For opposites are alike in that there will be ideas corresponding to both or to neither; and the unequal is also agreed by them to be in more than one thing (*en pleiosin*). (83. 28–30.)

Aristotle argues here that if Plato is committed to the existence of a form of equal, then he is committed to the existence of a form of unequal; more generally, Plato is committed to the existence of forms of opposites. He then argues that the same argument that shows that Plato is committed to the existence of two forms of equal shows that he is committed to the existence of two forms of unequal. So there is again a reduplication of a form, and so another violation of U.

One might argue that this objection fails, since Plato is not committed to the existence of forms of opposites, at least not on the basis of the Argument from Relatives. The Argument from Relatives basically generates a form of equal on the ground that sensible equals are imperfectly equal. But if they are imperfectly equal, are they not perfectly unequal? And if they are perfectly unequal, then we do not need a form of unequal.[27]

But this argument fails. For sensible equals are imperfectly unequal in just the way in which they are imperfectly equal. Every sensible object that is equal is imperfectly equal, because each is both equal (to some things) and unequal (to others); and every sensible property of equality (e.g. being three inches) is imperfectly equal, because each no more explains why things are equal than why they are unequal. But these facts about sensible equal objects and properties also show that they are imperfectly unequal: every sensible equal object is imperfectly unequal, for example, because each is equal (to some things) and unequal (to others). So if the imperfect equality of sensible equals requires a perfect form of equal, then the imperfect inequality of sensible equals requires a perfect form of unequal.

Aristotle is thus correct to say that the Argument from Relatives commits Plato to the existence not only of a form of equal but also to a form of unequal. But Plato would not be upset at being so committed; he seems happy to acknowledge not only a form of equal but also one of unequal; indeed, he seems to acknowledge forms of opposites quite generally.[28]

But Aristotle does not misinterpret Plato; for his objection concerns not the initial postulation of a form of unequal but its reduplication. His objection is not that Plato is, contrary to his desires, committed to the existence of a form of unequal. His objection is that Plato is, contrary to his desires, committed to the existence of two forms of unequal, for the same reason that he is committed to the existence of two forms of equal. But we have already seen how Plato could respond to this objection. If his self-predication thesis is best interpreted as BSP, then we do not need a second form of unequal in order to explain the inequality of the form of unequal.[29] Of course, we have also already seen how Aristotle would continue the debate.

4. A fourth objection: All forms are relatives[30]

Further, it follows that they must say that what is relative (*pros ti*) is a principle of and is prior to what exists in itself (*kath' hauto*), in so far as for them the idea is a principle of substances (*ousiai*). Yet what it is for an idea to be an idea lies in its being a paradigm, and a paradigm is a relative; for a paradigm is a paradigm of something. Again, if being for ideas lies in their being paradigms, then things that come into being relative to them and of which they are ideas will be likenesses of them; and so someone might say that according to them all naturally constituted things turn out to be relatives; for all things are likenesses and paradigms. Again, if being for ideas lies in their being paradigms, and a paradigm exists for the sake of what comes into being relative to it, and what exists on account of something else is less worthy than that thing, then the ideas will be less worthy than what comes into being relative to them.   (86. 13–23.)

The passage may be schematized as follows:

(1) Forms are principles of, and so are prior to, substances.
(2) Forms are essentially paradigms.
(3) If *x* is a paradigm, *x* is a relative.
(4) Therefore, forms are relatives.
(5) Relatives are posterior to substances.
(6) Hence forms are posterior to substances.
(7) Not both: (1) and (6).
(8) Things that come into being in relation to paradigmatic forms are likenesses of them.
(9) Likenesses are relatives.
(10) Forms and things that come into being in relation to forms are the only naturally constituted things.
(11) Therefore all naturally constituted things are relatives.
(12) Paradigms exist ⟨only⟩ for the sake of what comes into being in relation to them.
(13) If *x* exists ⟨only⟩ for the sake of *y*, *x* is inferior to *y*.
(14) Therefore forms are inferior to sensibles.

I begin by considering (1)–(7). They are interestingly related to the first objection (VII), where Aristotle argues that since the form of equal is a relative, it cannot be a substance. VII involves a two-level paradox, alleging contradiction between a property the form of equal has *qua* form (namely, being a substance) and a property the form of equal has *qua* the particular form it is (namely, being a relative). In (1)–(7), by contrast, Aristotle presents a one-level paradox, alleging contradiction between two properties every form has simply *qua* form. (In the terminology introduced before, the one-level paradox is between two A-level properties.) For every form, simply *qua* form, is a principle of substance; but if *x* is a principle of *y*, *x* must be prior to *y*. Forms must thus be prior to substances. However, every form, simply *qua* form, is also a paradigm; and paradigms are relatives. But if forms are relatives, they cannot be prior to substances since (in Aristotle's view) relatives are the least basic beings there are, whereas substances are the most basic. Forms therefore cannot be both principles and paradigms.

Like the other arguments we have explored, this argument is valid. But we can again raise questions about its soundness and about its effectiveness against Plato.

(1) claims that forms are the principles of, and so are prior to, substances. I shall assume this means that forms are supposed to be the principles of the entities *Aristotle* takes to be substances—that is, of such entities as an individual man or horse or tree. Plato clearly believes (1) if it is so read.[31]

As to (2), Plato certainly claims that forms are paradigms.[32] Indeed, he also seems to believe that they are *essentially* paradigms. At least, he certainly believes that forms are essentially perfect (because they escape compresence, and so on); and he seems to think that the fact that they are perfect explains why they are paradigms.

The suggestion in (3) is that if x is a paradigm, it is a paradigm *of* something; but if x is of something, then it is a relative. Let us agree about this too.[33] Later stages of the argument make it clear that Aristotle takes forms to be paradigms of sensibles; the form of beauty, for example, is a paradigm for or of sensible beautiful things. I assume that Plato believes this in some sense too. At least, in the *Phaedo* (100d) he says that if anything other than the form of beauty is beautiful, it is beautiful by being suitably related to the form of beauty; and he sometimes explains the relevant relation by saying that sensibles are copies or likenesses of paradigmatic forms (although he does not say this in the *Phaedo*). None the less, as we shall see, there are questions to be raised about precisely how forms are relative to sensibles, and about the implications of their being relative to them.

(6) concludes that forms are not, as (1) claims, prior to substances, but posterior to them. As I suggested above, presumably Aristotle means that since relatives are the least basic beings, they cannot be the principles of, and so cannot be prior to, anything whatsoever. Still less, then, can they be the principles of, and so be prior to, substances, basic beings.[34]

Aristotle is here following the same strategy as in VII. He believes that relatives are the least basic beings there are, and that (his) substances are the most basic. He then uses these beliefs in order to argue that relatives cannot be principles of (his) substances. Plato has a ready reply, however, analogous to his reply to VII. For in his view, just as the fact that something is a relative does not preclude it from being a substance, so it does not preclude it from being a principle of substance. Further, he of course denies that Aristotle's candidates for substancehood are the right ones. Just as Plato and Aristotle disagree about the candidates and some of the criteria for substantiality, so they disagree about the candidates and some of the criteria for being principles. Once again, then, Aristotle's argument fails if it is taken to be *ad hominem*; but it may succeed from his alternative metaphysical perspective.[35]

So far we have explored Aristotle's objection at quite an abstract level;

but it is worth probing more deeply. In saying that forms are paradigms of, and so are relative to, sensibles, Aristotle seems to be suggesting that forms depend either definitionally or ontologically on sensibles. In exploring VII we saw that Plato would not mind if it could be shown that forms must be defined in terms of one another, or depend ontologically on one another; on the contrary, he seems to insist on both claims. But if he accepts separation, then he does not believe that forms are ontologically dependent on sensibles. And he presumably believes that forms are in some sense definitionally more basic than sensibles. Aristotle's present objection thus seems more threatening than VII. But how good an argument can he mount for the claim that forms depend either definitionally or ontologically on sensibles? As before, I consider definitional dependence first.

Plato could insist, first of all, that even if definitions of forms need to mention sensibles, still, it is equally true that definitions of sensibles need to mention forms; so sensibles are at least not definitionally prior to forms.

But does Aristotle's objection not at least show that forms and sensibles are on a par, and would not that trouble Plato? In fact, it is not clear that Aristotle's objection shows that forms and sensibles are on a par. Plato might argue that forms are definitionally more basic than sensibles even if their definitions refer to sensibles. Here we can take a leaf out of Aristotle's *Categories*, where he says that 'in cases where two things reciprocate in implication of being, still, if one is in some way the explanation of the being of the other, it would reasonably be said to be naturally prior' (14b11–13).[36] And Plato plainly believes that forms are prior in explanation to sensibles. Forms are the entities we define in asking the 'What is F?' question; we can know that x is F, for any x, only if we know the form of F. Forms explain the beings of things, why things are as they are and come to be as they do, in a way that (so far as I can see) is not compromised by admitting that fully to understand how forms can play this explanatory role, one must mention the entities they are invoked to explain.[37] If this is right, then Aristotle once again fails to level a successful *ad hominem* objection.

Nor is it clear that his argument succeeds from his alternative metaphysical perspective. To be sure, we have seen that he sometimes claims (in e.g. *Met.* 7. 1) that substances—which, in the *Metaphysics*, I take to be individual forms—are definitionally basic in so far as their definitions do not need to mention any non-substances, whereas the definitions of non-substances do need to mention substances. However, he also sometimes claims that universals are the basic, perhaps the only, objects of knowledge and definition (see esp. 7. 15); yet in the *Metaphysics* no universal is a substance (see esp. 7. 13, at e.g. 1038b8–16). It is unclear, then, that Aristotle can consistently maintain that his substances (certain particulars) are definitionally prior to universals (his correlate, for present purposes, to Platonic forms)—though perhaps the way in which he sometimes takes them to be definitionally prior is not compromised by the (different?) way in which he sometimes seems to favour universals.

What, now, about ontological dependence? Can Aristotle mount a good argument for the claim that if forms are essentially paradigms and so relatives, their existence depends on the existence of sensibles, in violation of separation? The answer perhaps depends on what sort of relatives forms are (if we concede that they are relatives). Aristotle reasonably believes that some relatives cannot exist at t_1 unless their correlatives also exist at t_1. For example, nothing can be a father at t_1 if he has not a child at t_1; nothing can be a master at t_1 if he has not a slave at t_1. If forms were relative to sensibles in this way, then they could not be separate from them, that is able to exist whether or not sensibles exist. But Aristotle believes that there are also some relatives that can exist even if their correlatives never exist (*Cat.* 7b15 ff.; *Met.* 5. 15; cf. *DA* 425b25–426a1, 426a15–25).[38] He says, for example, that the knowable can exist even if knowledge never does (*Cat.* 7b22–33). As he explains in the *Metaphysics*, the knowable is none the less a relative because knowledge is so called from it (1021a29–30). If we concede to Aristotle that forms are essentially paradigms in a way that makes them essentially relative to sensibles, then I think we should say that they are relatives in much the way in which Aristotle says that the knowable is a relative. For sensibles are so called from forms, just as knowledge is so called from the knowable. On this view, forms could be essentially relatives quite compatibly with their also being separate in the sense that they can exist even if sensibles never do.[39] As with the first objection, so here: turning to existential independence does not help Aristotle's case.

(1)–(7) are the most important stretch of the argument, but it is none the less worth looking briefly at the rest of the argument. (8)–(9) imply that sensibles are relatives. This result would trouble *Aristotle*. For in his view, sensibles like Socrates are primary substances, and so in his view they cannot be relatives. But it is far from clear that *Plato* would be reluctant to admit that sensibles are relatives, in that they are what they are by being related to forms. Indeed, that simply seems to be his view.[40] Nor does this even conflict with Aristotle's claim that no substance is a relative, since for Plato sensibles are not (primary) substances.

(12)–(13) imply (14); and Plato does not accept (14). (13) seems true if we take it to say that if x exists *only* for the sake of y, and if y does not at all exist for the sake of x, then x is (at least to that extent and in that respect) inferior to y. If (12)–(13) imply (14), and (13) is true, then Plato can avoid (14) only by denying (12). And he would surely do so. No doubt *some* paradigms—e.g. blueprints and designs—exist only for the sake of what they are paradigms of. But not all paradigms are like this.[41]

For example, we have seen that forms are paradigms in so far as they are standards; to know whether or not anything is F, one needs to refer to the form of F. If forms are paradigms in this way, they do not exist only for the sake of their likenesses.

Here, however, Aristotle might protest that if this is all that is involved in paradigmatism, then it is a hopeless metaphor and so best dispensed with. If forms are literally paradigms, then someone must be guided by them in their work. As he puts it in the *Metaphysics*, 'to say that ⟨forms⟩ are paradigms and that other things participate in them is to use empty words and poetical metaphors. For what is it that works by looking towards ideas?' (991a20–23).[42] Aristotle in effect poses a dilemma: if forms are literally paradigms, someone must use them in their work; but no one does. The only alternative is that paradigmatism is a useless metaphor.[43]

I think Plato would reject both horns of this dilemma. First, he would probably say that even if no one produces things by consulting forms, paradigmatism is not a hopeless metaphor. Here history is on Plato's side; at least, if there is a metaphor here, it is one that survived for some time, so at least some other philosophers presumably did not find it too misleading. Locke, for example, takes real essences to be paradigms in much the way in which Plato takes forms to be paradigms.[44] Secondly, Plato would probably also say that there *are* workers who look to forms. The guardians in the *Republic*, for example, strive to instantiate the form of the good as widely as possible (500c–501c); since the demiurge in the *Timaeus* wanted the world to be as good as possible, he referred to forms in fashioning his creation (28a–30a). In such contexts, paradigmatism, in Plato's view, is not metaphorical but literally true.

Aristotle no doubt knows that Plato believes this; but he thinks that Plato ought not to believe it. For example, in Aristotle's view, no demiurge, or any sort of creator, caused the world to come into being; in his view, the cosmos has always existed (see e.g. *DC* 2. 1).

There are several further moves involved in this particular debate between Plato and Aristotle.[45] But perhaps enough has been said to make it clear that, once again, what might initially seem to be an *ad hominem* objection is in fact part of a complex philosophical debate—this time about, among other things, the origin of the world and the proper explanation of various events in it.

14

The Accurate One over Many Argument

In *Met.* 1. 9 (990b15–17) Aristotle says that 'of the more accurate arguments, some produce ideas of relatives, of which we say there is no in-itself genus, and others introduce (*legousi*) the third man'. In Ch. 10 we explored the first more accurate argument; we now need to explore the second more accurate argument.[1]

Robin and Cherniss believe that the second more accurate argument is simply the One over Many Argument that we have already explored.[2] There are good reasons for hoping that they are wrong. First, the *Peri ideōn* would be quite awkwardly arranged if they were right: Aristotle would first set out and criticize the One over Many Argument; he would then mention a couple of further arguments; and he would then return to the One over Many Argument, levelling a new objection against it. Why, if Robin and Cherniss are right, does Aristotle not level all his objections against the One over Many Argument at once? Secondly, in *Met.* 1. 9 Aristotle classifies the One over Many Argument as a *less* accurate argument for the existence of forms; but he classifies the argument that leads to the Third Man Argument as a *more* accurate argument for the existence of forms. On Robin's and Cherniss's view, Aristotle classifies the One over Many Argument as both a less, and a more, accurate argument for the existence of forms; surely this is quite awkward. Thirdly, we have seen that a 'more accurate' argument for the existence of forms is a valid argument for their existence.[3] But as Aristotle notes (81. 8–10), the One over Many Argument is not a valid argument for the existence of forms. Fourthly, Aristotle says that the second more accurate argument involves the Third Man Argument—that is, its premisses give rise to the Third Man regress.[4] But we will see in the next chapter that the One over Many Argument does not lead to the Third Man Argument. If the One over Many Argument is none the less the second more accurate argument, then Aristotle misunderstands either it or the Third Man Argument.

There are thus good reasons for wanting to reject Robin's and Cherniss's view. And we shall see that we should reject it, for although the second more accurate argument is *a* one over many argument, it is not the One over Many Argument already explored. Rather, it is a distinct one over many argument, which I have been calling the Accurate One over Many Argument.[5] Unlike the One over Many Argument, the Accurate One over Many Argument is a valid argument for the existence of forms, and it leads to the Third Man Argument.

I turn now to a consideration of the Accurate One over Many Argument and of how it differs from the One over Many Argument. Aristotle writes that[6]

If (AOM) what is predicated truly of some plurality of things (*pleionōn*) is also (NI) ⟨some⟩ other thing (*allo*) besides (*para*) the things of which it is predicated, (G-Sep) being separated from them (*kechōrismenon autōn*) (for this is what those who posit the ideas think they prove; for this is why, according to them, there is such a thing as man-itself, because (OM) the man is predicated truly of the particular men (*tōn kath' hekasta anthrōpōn*), (AOM) these being a plurality (*pleionōn ontōn*), and it is other (*allo*) than the particular men)—but if this is so, there will be a third man.   (84. 22–7.)

The long parenthesis recalls the One over Many Argument; indeed, the verbal parallels are quite exact. As before, Aristotle speaks of predications of particulars (*kath' hekasta*; 84. 25, 26–7); and he says that what is predicated of them is something other (*allos*, 84. 26) than they. This recalls premisses (1) and (4) of the One over Many Argument:

(1) Whenever many Fs (*polla*) are F, they are F in virtue of having some one thing, the F, predicated of them.

(4) The F is different from the F particulars (*kath' hekasta*) of which it is predicated.[7]

However, the long '*gar*'-clause that introduces the parenthesis suggests that what stands outside it (84. 21–3) is not the One over Many Argument, but its underlying motivation. Aristotle suggests that the Platonists accept the One over Many Argument because (*gar*, 84. 24; *dia touto gar*, 84. 24; *hoti*, 84. 25) they tacitly rely on claims that are not explicit in the One over Many Argument itself. Aristotle mentions these tacit assumptions both before the parenthesis and at appropriate places within it. They may be formulated as follows:

(AOM) Whenever a plurality of things (*pleiō*) are F, they are F in virtue of having some one thing, the F, predicated of them (84. 21–2).

(NI) Any F that is predicated is different (*allo*) from the F things of which it is predicated (84. 23).

(G-Sep) Any F that is predicated is separated from (*kechōrismenon*)— i.e. exists independently of—the F things of which it is predicated (84. 23–4).

AOM (= accurate one over many) is a one over many assumption, but it differs from the one over many assumption involved in the One over Many Argument (= premiss (1) of the One over Many Argument), which I shall from now on call 'OM'. It is important to be clear about the differences between AOM and OM; for otherwise we will not be able to understand either the logic of the Third Man Argument or how the Accurate One over Many Argument differs from the One over Many Argument.

According to OM, whenever many *particulars* (*polla*; *kath' hekasta*) are *F*, they are *F* in virtue of having some one thing, the *F*, predicated of them—where, as we have seen, particulars are *sensible particulars*. According to AOM, whenever a plurality of *things* (*pleiō*) are *F*, they are *F* in virtue of having some one thing, the *F*, predicated of them.[8] OM posits some one thing, the *F*, only over groups of *F* sensible particulars. By contrast, AOM posits some one thing, the *F*, over groups of *F* things, where 'things' are not restricted to sensible particulars. AOM implies OM, but not conversely; AOM is a generalized version of OM. If there is a group of *F* sensible particulars, both one over many assumptions tell us that they are *F* in virtue of having some one thing, the *F*, predicated of them. If there is a group of *F* things not all of which are *F* sensible particulars, AOM tells us that they too are all *F* in virtue of having one thing, the *F*, predicated of them. But OM does not tell us this; for the group contains more than *F* sensible particulars, and OM says nothing about such groups. In the next chapter, we will see that this difference between OM and AOM is important to the logic of the Third Man Argument.

NI (= non-identity) corresponds to, but differs from, premiss (4) of the One over Many Argument. According to premiss (4) of the One over Many Argument, the *F* that is predicated is different from the *F sensible particulars* of which it is predicated; so like OM, premiss (4) of the One over Many Argument considers predications only of groups of *F* sensible particulars. But NI (like AOM) ranges more widely; it claims that any *F* that is predicated is different from the *F things* of which it is predicated, where *F* things are not restricted to *F* sensible particulars. In the next chapter, we shall see that this difference between NI and premiss (4) of the One over Many Argument is also important to the logic of the Third Man Argument.

G-Sep (= generalized separation) corresponds to, but differs from, one clause in premiss (5) of the One over Many Argument, which says, in full:

(5) The *F* is separated from particular *F*s and is everlasting.

(5) involves the separation assumption we have heretofore been discussing:[9]

(Sep) Any form of *F* exists independently of *F* sensible particulars.

Just as AOM is a generalization of OM, and just as NI is a generalization of OMA (4), so G-Sep is a generalization of Sep. For G-Sep says that the *F* exists independently not just of the *F* sensible particulars of which it is predicated but of *everything* of which it is predicated, where again predications are not restricted to *F* sensible particulars. If a group of sensible particulars are all *F* in virtue of having a form of *F* predicated of its members, both Sep and G-Sep tell us that that form exists independently of the members of that group. If a group of things that includes not only *F* sensible particulars are all *F* in virtue of having a form of *F* predicated of its members, then G-Sep tells us that that form exists independently of *all* the members of that group. Sep tells us only that the form exists independently of the *F* sensible particulars in the group; it says nothing about whether the form exists independently of the other members of the group. Just as AOM implies OM but not conversely, so G-Sep implies Sep but not conversely.

In the Accurate One over Many Argument, NI is validly inferred from G-Sep.[10] So whereas the Accurate One over Many Argument validly infers a difference claim (NI) from a separation claim (G-Sep), the One over Many Argument invalidly infers a separation claim (Sep) from a difference claim.[11] Further, in the One over Many Argument, Sep is argued for (though invalidly), whereas in the Accurate One over Many Argument, G-Sep is assumed rather than argued for.

G-Sep implies not only NI but also Sep. Of course, this inference is not very exciting; but since the two separation assumptions differ, the inference is at least not from *p* to *p*. And the fact that the inference is valid is important, for it shows that in contrast to the One over Many Argument, the Accurate One over Many Argument is a valid argument for the existence of Separated forms.[12] For suppose there is a group of *F* sensible particulars. AOM tells us that they are *F* in virtue of having some one thing, the *F*, predicated of them. G-Sep tells us that the *F* is separated from, exists independently of, the members of that group. The *F* is therefore Separate, and so it has been validly argued that the *F* that is predicated of *F* sensible particulars is both Separate and (since it is a one over many) a universal. Since in Aristotle's view the existence of Separated universals is sufficient for the existence of forms, he takes the Accurate One over Many Argument to be a valid argument for the existence of forms.

Note that like the other arguments in the *Peri ideōn*, the Accurate One over Many Argument also conceives forms as universals. For Aristotle says that they are predicated of many things, which is just how he defines universals (*DI* 17a39–40).

I suggest, then, that the second more accurate argument is not the One over Many Argument, but a distinct argument, the Accurate One over Many Argument. Unlike the One over Many Argument, the Accurate One over Many is a valid argument for the existence of forms; as we shall see in the next chapter, it also leads to the Third Man Argument. So unlike the One over Many Argument, it satisfies our two criteria for being a more accurate argument of the second sort.

Why does Aristotle record two one over many arguments? The answer seems to be contained in the long and complicated parenthesis, whose point seems to be that the Platonists find the One over Many Argument compelling because they tacitly rely on the Accurate One over Many Argument. Perhaps Aristotle records the One over Many Argument because he thinks it is closer than the Accurate One over Many Argument is to Plato's explicit one over many argument. But he also records the Accurate One over Many Argument because he thinks it captures Plato's tacit reasoning. In suggesting this, Aristotle in a way mitigates one of his earlier criticisms. For he criticizes the One over Many Argument on the ground that it is an invalid argument for the existence of forms. But if Plato also uses or relies on the Accurate One over Many Argument, then he has a valid one over many argument for the existence of Separate forms, and one that in some sense underlies or explains his (alleged) use of the One over Many Argument. On the other hand, Aristotle never suggests that Plato argues for G-Sep. So although he gives Plato a valid one over many argument for the existence of Separate forms, he is likely to feel that at a deeper level Plato simply assumes some sort of separation.[13] But it would not be inappropriate for Aristotle to suggest this, for we have seen that Plato never argues for Sep, though he is at various stages committed to it and probably assumes it throughout.

Why does Aristotle believe that Plato finds the One over Many Argument tempting because he tacitly relies on the Accurate One over Many Argument? Perhaps for the following two reasons. First, the One over Many Argument discusses predications of *sensible particulars*. Perhaps Aristotle thinks that it is not the fact that some things are sensible particulars that leads Plato to think that something must be predicated of them; rather, it is the fact that they are all alike in being *F*. In Aristotle's view, that is, Plato uses a one over many argument not to explain *particularity*, but to explain *similarity*. The Accurate One over Many Argument brings this out by focusing on the *F*-ness of *F* things, without restricting the relevant things to sensible particulars. Given Plato's belief that the form of *F* is also an *F* thing, though not an *F* sensible particular, this will turn out to be important. Aristotle may well be right to say that, in Plato's view, there is an explanation of why every *F* thing, whether or not it is an *F* particular, is *F*. But whether the Accurate One over Many Argument captures Plato's explanation is another question, which I address in Ch. 16.4–5.

Secondly, perhaps Aristotle believes that Plato takes forms to be Separate from sensible particulars because he believes that Plato accepts the more general view that, if A is predicated of B, then, no matter what A and B are, A exists independently of B. Perhaps Aristotle thinks, that is, that Plato accepts Sep because of a more general belief, just as, in Aristotle's view, Plato accepts OM because of a more general belief. In Ch. 16.4 I ask whether Plato accepts, or is committed to, G-Sep.

I suggested in Ch. 2.7 that Aristotle organizes *Peri ideōn* 1 so as to convey the following moral. The Platonists have two sorts of arguments for the existence of forms, the less and the more accurate arguments. The more accurate arguments are valid arguments for the existence of forms, but they cannot be sound since they have intolerable consequences: the Argument from Relatives produces forms of relatives, and the Accurate One over Many Argument leads to the Third Man Argument. The less accurate arguments avoid these consequences; but they are invalid arguments for the existence of forms. However, invalidity is easily avoided if we change the conclusion of the less accurate arguments from 'And so there are forms' to 'And so there are *koina*'. The moral is clear: we should abandon Platonism in favour of an Aristotelian ontology. If I have correctly described the differences between the Accurate One over Many Argument and the One over Many Argument, then these two arguments mirror on a smaller scale the overall structure and moral of *Peri ideōn* 1. For the Accurate One over Many Argument is a valid argument for the existence of forms, but this virtue is outweighed by the vice of the Third Man Argument. The Platonists might seek to avoid this vice by retreating to the One over Many Argument, but it is an invalid argument for the existence of forms. To avoid this new vice, they should change the conclusion of the One over Many Argument from 'And so there are forms' to 'And so there are *koina*', thereby embracing Aristotle's ontology. The fact that, on my interpretation, the One over Many Argument and Accurate One over Many Argument mirror on a small scale the overall structure and moral of *Peri ideōn* 1 gives us yet another reason to distinguish between them in the way I have suggested.

So far I have explained why the Accurate One over Many Argument (unlike the One over Many Argument) is a valid argument for the existence of forms; and I have claimed that its premisses (unlike those of the One over Many Argument) lead to the Third Man Argument. In order to substantiate this latter claim, we need to look at the Third Man Argument.

15

Third Man Arguments

1. Introduction

Aristotle says that the premisses of the Accurate One over Many Argument give rise to the Third Man Argument. The Third Man Argument (TMA) purports to show that if there is even one form of F, there are infinitely many forms of F; if, for example, there is even one form of man, there are infinitely many forms of man.

The TMA has received a great deal of scholarly attention, and it is easy to see why; for it is often thought to be a devastating objection to Plato's theory of forms, and Aristotle is sometimes thought to have worked out his own theory of predication and the categories by reflecting on it.[1] If the TMA undermines Plato's theory of forms, and if reflection on it inspired Aristotle's metaphysical alternative to Plato, it deserves careful attention.

Here we are somewhat hampered, however, by the fact that the name 'Third Man Argument' does not clearly have a unique referent. In the *Parmenides*, Plato describes two regress arguments, each of which has been called a Third Man Argument, although Plato himself never so calls them. Plato's regress arguments are so called because Aristotle in various places mentions an argument that he calls the Third Man (*in Met.* 84. 23–85. 3; cf. 93. 1–7; cf. also *Met.* 990b17 = 1079a13, *SE* 178b36 ff., and *Met.* 1039a2) and that commentators generally believe is identical with (one of) Plato's regress arguments. In addition to Plato's two regress arguments and Aristotle's various accounts of a Third Man Argument, Eudemus describes a Third Man Argument that, according to Alexander (85. 4–6), is the same as Aristotle's.[2]

There are at least four 'Third Man Arguments', then: two recorded by Plato in the *Parmenides*, one recorded by Aristotle,[3] and one recorded by Eudemus. What is the relation between them? Their explicit, surface formulations certainly differ. But are they none the less logically equivalent, involving just the same premisses and just the same inferences? Is Plato vulnerable to any or all of them? In this chapter I explore the logic of and interconnections between the four regress arguments; in the next chapter I ask whether Plato is vulnerable to any of them.

But before exploring the details of the various Third Man Arguments, we should ask why a regress of forms would be troubling; after all, not all infinite regresses are vicious. The TMA might be troubling for more than one reason. But Plato gives the following explanation. He accepts the uniqueness assumption (U), according to which there is exactly one form of F if any at all. According to the TMA, however, so far from there being exactly one form of F if any at all, there are infinitely many forms of F if any at all. Indeed, Plato's version of the TMA argues that the very premisses that he once took to imply that there is exactly one form of F if any at all actually imply that there are infinitely many forms of F if there are any at all. So one reason the regress is troubling is that it conflicts with Plato's uniqueness assumption.

The regress is also troubling for another reason. Plato believes that knowledge is possible and that knowledge (in the sorts of cases at issue here) requires explanation.[4] Plato believes that one can know that something is F only if one knows the form of F, which involves explaining its nature.[5] Since, by SP, any form of F is F, explaining the nature of a form of F involves explaining why it is F. Suppose that it is F in virtue of a further form of F, and so on *ad infinitum*. Plato seems to think that in that case, we could never know that anything is F; in order to know that something is F, there must, in his view, be something that is self-explanatorily F, F in virtue of itself. But if the TMA is sound, nothing is F in virtue of itself. The TMA thus challenges not only U but also the possibility of knowledge.[6]

2. Plato's Third Man Argument (P-TMA): *Parmenides* 132a1–b2

Since most of the recent literature on Third Man Arguments focuses on the first regress argument in the *Parmenides*, I begin with it.[7] The argument runs as follows (I insert numbers for ease of reference):

I suppose it is because of the following sort of thing that you think that (1) each form is one (*hen hekaston eidos*):[8] (2) Whenever many things (*poll' atta*) seem large to you, there perhaps seems to you to be, when you have looked at them all, some one and the same idea (*mia tis idea hē autē*). Hence you think (3) the large is one.
True, he said.
(4) What, then, if in the same way you look in your soul at all these—at the large itself and the other large things? (5) Will not some one large appear again, by which all these will appear large?
It seems so.
So another form (*eidos*) of largeness will appear besides (*para*) the large itself and its participants. (6) And in addition to all these, yet another, by which all these will be large. (7) And so each of the forms will no longer be one for you, but infinitely many (*apeira to plēthos*).

(1) states the uniqueness assumption:

(U) There is exactly one form corresponding to every predicate that has a form.[9]

P-TMA explores Plato's reasons for accepting U; it argues that, so far from supporting U, those reasons undermine U. In fact, they lead to a very strong denial of U: if there is even one form of F, there are infinitely many (7).[10]

(2)–(6) play a double role: they both give Plato's reasons for believing U and explain why those reasons undermine U. (2)–(6) play this double role by focusing on a particular case, that of large. Hence P-TMA might more accurately be called 'The Third Large Argument': Plato generates a regress of forms of large; the predicate 'man' plays no role in his argument. In the next chapter, I ask whether the difference in predicates is significant.

Since most contemporary discussion of P-TMA has been influenced by Vlastos' seminal paper, 'The "Third Man" Argument in the *Parmenides*' (= 'TMA I'), I begin by considering it. Vlastos notes that the only explicit premiss offered on behalf of (an instance of) U, on the one hand, and as generating a regress, on the other, is (2), which he generalizes as follows:

(A1) If a number of things a, b, c are all F, there must be a single form F-ness in virtue of which we apprehend a, b, c as all F.

From (2), Plato eventually infers (5), which Vlastos generalizes as follows:

(A2) If a, b, c and F-ness are all F, there must be another form, F-ness$_1$, in virtue of which we apprehend a, b, c and F-ness as all F.

(A1) obviously does not imply (A2). We can either conclude that the argument is invalid or else attempt to uncover the assumptions on which Plato tacitly relies. Vlastos favours the second option, asking: 'What are the simplest premisses, not given in the present Argument, which would have to be added to its first step, to make (A2) a legitimate conclusion?'[11] He replies that we 'need'[12] to supply the following self-predication and non-identity assumptions:

(SPV) Any form can be predicated of itself. Largeness is itself large. F-ness is itself F.

(NIV) If anything has a certain character, it cannot be identical with the form in virtue of which we apprehend that character. If x is F, x cannot be identical with F-ness.

Although (A1) does not engender a regress by itself, it does so in conjunction with SPV and NIV. For suppose that a, b, and c are all F. According to (A1), there is then a single form, call it F-ness$_1$, in virtue of which a, b, and c are F.[13] Given SPV, F-ness$_1$ is F. According to (A1), there must then be a single form in virtue of which a, b, c, and F-ness$_1$ are all F—call it F-ness$_2$. According to NIV, F-ness$_2$ cannot be identical with F-ness$_1$. Hence there are two forms corresponding to 'F'—F-ness$_1$ and F-ness$_2$. By SPV, F-ness$_2$ is F. Now consider the set of F things that consists of a, b, c, F-ness$_1$, and F-ness$_2$. Given (A1), the members of this set are all F in virtue of a single Form—call it F-ness$_3$. Given NIV, F-ness$_3$ cannot be identical with F-ness$_1$ or with F-ness$_2$. Hence there are three forms corresponding to 'F'—F-ness$_1$, F-ness$_2$, and F-ness$_3$. Obviously the same reasoning can be repeated *ad infinitum*.

Although the premisses Vlastos supplies validly generate a regress, they do so at a price. For, as Vlastos notes, SPV and NIV are jointly inconsistent.[14] NIV says that if x is F, x is not identical with F-ness. SPV says that F-ness is F. But then F-ness is not identical with F-ness. But everything is identical with itself. Since SPV and NIV are inconsistent, it is trivially true that their conjunction engenders a regress: from a contradiction, one can derive any conclusion one likes.

One might think it unlikely that Plato would formulate an argument with inconsistent premisses. Vlastos replies that all that is unlikely is that Plato would *knowingly* offer such an argument. So Vlastos concludes, not that we ought to reconstruct the argument in some other way, but that the TMA is 'a record of honest perplexity';[15] had Plato been aware that its premisses were inconsistent, he would never have propounded it. Worse still, Vlastos argues, Plato's theory of forms involves SPV and NIV; so not only is that theory vulnerable to the TMA but it is also internally inconsistent.

Vlastos claims that SPV and NIV are 'needed' as premisses of the argument, that they 'have to be added' to (A1) to validate the inference to (A2). But, as Cohen points out, since the conclusion of P-TMA—that there are infinitely many forms of F if there are any at all—is not itself contradictory, inconsistent premisses, though sufficient for the conclusion, are not necessary.[16] It is then worth asking how to generate the regress from a consistent premiss set, while still remaining faithful to the text.

Most commentators agree that P-TMA involves a self-predication and a non-identity assumption, and that seems right. (4), for example, invites us to look at the form of large[17] and the *other* large things. This assumes that the form of large is large, and so some sort of self-predication assumption is involved. (5)–(6) assume that the form of large in virtue of which the members of some set of large things are large is not a member of that set; this is the basic intuition underlying non-identity assumptions.

Although P-TMA thus assumes a self-predication and a non-identity assumption, these assumptions need not be formulated as Vlastos formulates them. I suggest the following alternative formulations:

(SP) Any form of F is itself F.
(NI) Nothing is F in virtue of itself.

Unlike SPV, SP does not say *how*, or in virtue of what, any form of F is F; it says only *that* any form of F is itself F.[18] Of course, if the relevant self-predication assumption is SP, then the *label* 'self-predication' is something of a misnomer, since SP does not involve the claim that any form is predicated of itself.[19] None the less, since the label is so well entrenched, I shall retain it.

NI says that nothing is F in virtue of itself, which is the claim Vlastos intends NIV to capture. If I am right about why Plato finds the regress troubling, then he should reject NI. For NI precludes the possibility that anything is F in virtue of itself; but if nothing is F in virtue of itself, then knowledge is impossible. But to say that Plato should reject NI is not to say that he is not (perhaps, as Vlastos believes, unwittingly) committed to it.

Unlike SPV and NI, SP and NI are consistent; and they seem faithful to the text. But unlike SPV and NI, SP and NI are not sufficient for the regress. Before asking what else is involved, however, let us look more closely at SP and NI.

Like Vlastos, I assume that SP uses 'is' in the class-membership sense; it says that any form of F is a member of the class of F things. Both NSP and BSP involve the claim that any form of F is a member of the class of F things. In this sense, both NSP and BSP are adequate as self-predication assumptions for the TMA, though neither is required.[20]

As Vlastos noted long ago, it is important to distinguish between *weak* and *strong* non-identity.[21] According to weak non-identity, *sensibles* are not F in virtue of themselves (they are F by being suitably related to a form of F).[22] According to strong non-identity, *nothing* is F in virtue of itself; not even a form of F can be F in virtue of itself. Strong non-identity implies weak non-identity, but not conversely. NI expresses strong non-identity, and P-TMA requires strong non-identity.

NI must be distinguished not only from weak non-identity but also from Separation. Separation is the claim that any form of F can exist whether or not there are any F sensible particulars. Separation implies weak but not strong non-identity. Strong non-identity does not imply Separation. Hence commitment to one of Separation or NI does not require commitment to the other. Separation, so far as I can see, is irrelevant to P-TMA. Plato does not mention it, nor does the logic of his argument require it.[23]

I have now provided formulations of the relevant self-predication and non-identity assumptions that are jointly consistent; and I have described several of their features. But SP and NI are not sufficient for the regress. What else is involved?

As I noted before, (2) is the only premiss that is actually explicit in the text, so let us now consider it.[24] (2) says that whenever many things (*poll' atta*) are large, they are large in virtue of (or, as Plato also puts it, by participating in) some one form.[25] In 'Plato's "Third Man" Argument' (= 'TMA II'), Vlastos makes it clear that he believes (2) should be read as[26]

(2a) If there is a set of large things, then there is exactly one form of large, and the members of the set are large in virtue of it.

(2a) is an instance of U.[27] It might initially seem attractive to read (2) as (2a). For (3), which is an instance of U, is represented as an inference from (2); and (2a) implies (3). But there are two serious objections to (2a).

First, as I noted above, (2) plays a double role in the argument. It is both a premiss from which (3) is inferred and also a premiss of an argument whose conclusion is that if there is even one form of large, there are infinitely many. If we read (2) as (2a), and assume SP and NI, then the argument for this conclusion has inconsistent premisses: this time, there is an inconsistent triad, rather than, as on Vlastos' original account in 'TMA I', an inconsistent pair.[28] This can be seen as follows. Suppose there is a set of large things. By (2a), the members of this set are large in virtue of the one and only form of large, call it the form$_1$ of large. Given SP, the form$_1$ of large is large. Now consider a new set of large things, one that consists of the members of the initial set of large things and the form$_1$ of large. By (2a), they must all be large in virtue of the one and only form of large. But the one and only form of large is the form$_1$ of large, which is in the set now under consideration. So the form$_1$ of large must be large in virtue of itself. But that is inconsistent with NI. We have already seen, however, that it is both unnecessary and undesirable for the TMA's premisses to be inconsistent.[29]

Secondly, it is actually a *defect*, rather than an advantage, of (2a) that it implies (3). For the whole point of P-TMA is to show that Plato's (alleged) reasons for U *do not imply* U. (2) is the reason he gives on behalf of (an instance of) U. What he wants us to see is that (2) does not imply (3). Of course, the move from (2) to (3) should be tempting, since Plato claims that it tempted him. But it should be a resistible temptation.

(2) should thus not be read as (2a). (2) is an instance not of U but of a one over many assumption. Plato's point is that he used to believe that some sort of one over many assumption implies U; he now argues that that earlier belief is false. In fact, not only does the relevant one over many assumption not imply U; but it also (when combined with SP and NI) engenders a regress. (So for Plato as for Aristotle, some version of a one over many argument leads to the Third Man.)

To say that (2) is an instance of a one over many assumption does not get us very far; for there are a variety of one over many assumptions. It is sometimes thought that (2) should be read as:[30]

(2b) If there is a set of large things, then there is at least one form of large in virtue of which the members of the set are large.

(2*b*), SP, and NI (and the assumption that there are some large things) generate a regress. For suppose there is a set of large things. By (2*b*), the members of this set are large in virtue of at least one form of large, call it the form$_1$ of large. By SP, the form$_1$ of large is large. Now consider a different set of large things, one that consists of the members of the initial set of large things and the form$_1$ of large. By (2*b*), the members of this set are all large in virtue of at least one form of large—say, in virtue of the form$_2$ of large. By NI, the form$_1$ of large is not identical with the form$_2$ of large. Hence there are two forms of large—and so on *ad infinitum*. Not only can we generate a regress from (2*b*), SP, and NI (and the assumption that there are some large things); but the suggested premisses are also jointly consistent.

Vlastos in effect raises three objections to (2*b*).[31] His first objection is that since every occurrence of 'one' in P-TMA (with the possible exception of its occurrence in (2)) means 'exactly one', and since in a number of other Platonic passages 'one form' means 'exactly one form', rather than 'at least one form', in (2) 'one' should also mean 'exactly one', not 'at least one'. His second objection is that if 'one' means 'at least one' in (2), but 'exactly one' in (1) and (3), then Plato equivocates. His third objection is that it would be a 'transparent fallacy' to infer from the claim that there is at least one form corresponding to 'large' that there is just one form corresponding to 'large'.[32]

Vlastos's first objection is not compelling. From the fact that Plato often, even in our context, uses 'one' to mean 'exactly one', it does not follow that it means 'exactly one' in (2). Certainly Plato often uses 'one' without meaning 'exactly one'.[33] Nor is the second objection compelling on its own. At least, the mere fact that an argument involves more than one use of a term need not be problematical; perhaps there is an illuminating link between the different uses.[34] But Vlastos's third consideration—that the move from 'at least one' to 'exactly one' is such a transparent fallacy that Plato would never have been tempted by it— seems reasonable. However, Vlastos goes too far in the other direction when he reads (2) as (2*a*), so that it implies (3). What we want is a reading of (2) on which it is a fallacy, but not a transparent fallacy, to infer (3) from (2)—a reading that might have tempted Plato to infer uniqueness from a one over many assumption, even though the inference fails.

There is also a fourth problem with (2*b*). Suppose that, as (2*b*) allows, there is more than one form of *F*; and suppose that there is a set of *F* things. (2*b*) tells us only that the members of this set are *F* in virtue of at least one form of *F*. But, intuitively, not just any old form of *F* will do. Presumably (if there is more than one form of *F*) some one form of *F* bears a special relation to the members of the set whose *F*-ness we want to explain. (2*b*) does not capture this fact.

A reading of (2) that avoids some of the defects of (2*a*) and (2*b*) is:[35]

(2*c*) There is exactly one form of large in virtue of which all and only the members of the set of large sensibles are large.

(2*c*) takes '*poll' atta megala*' to refer to all and only large sensibles; and it posits exactly one form of large in virtue of which all and only they are large. Like (2*a*) but unlike (2*b*), (2*c*) takes 'one' to mean 'exactly one'. But whereas (2*a*) says that there is exactly one form of large *tout court*, (2*c*) says only that there is exactly one form of large in virtue of which all and only large sensibles are large. (2*c*) thus leaves open the possibility, which (2*a*) forecloses, that there is more than one form of *F*. None the less, (2*c*) might tempt one to believe (3).

Despite these virtues of (2*c*), it is not the right one over many assumption either. For (2*c*), SP, and NI (and the assumption that there are some sensible large things) do not generate the regress. For the regress to arise, sets that contain both *F* sensibles and at least one form of *F* must be *F* in virtue of exactly one form of *F* that is not a member of the set. But (2*c*) does not posit new forms for sets that contain forms. '*Poll' atta megala*' should thus not be restricted to groups that contain *only* large sensibles.[36]

What we need, then, is a one over many assumption that is more generous than (2*c*)—a one over many assumption that posits exactly one form for (and only for) *every* set relevantly like the set that consists of all and only large sensibles.[37] Let us try to formulate such an assumption.

Plato plainly distinguishes between different levels of reality; in his view, forms, for example, are 'more real' or have 'more being' than sensibles do. Let us follow his lead and say that all and only sensibles are at level 0. Let us also say that all sensible *F*s at level 0 are a *maximal set* of *F*s. Let us also say that all and only the members of this maximal set are *F* in virtue of (i.e. by participating in) the unique form of *F* at level 1.[38] Further, any set that consists solely of all the *F* entities at a given level and all the *F* entities at every lower level is also a maximal set; and every maximal set is at the level of its highest-level member.[39] So, for example, the set that consists of the members of the maximal set of *F*s at level 0 plus the form of *F* at level 1 is a maximal set at level 1. Let us say that all and only the members of this set are *F* in virtue of (i.e. by participating in) the unique form of *F* at level 2. We can now formulate the following one over many assumption:[40]

(OM-TMA) For any maximal set of *F*s at level *n*, there is exactly one form of *F* at level $n + 1$ over it (where 'over' means 'participated in by all and only the members of').

OM-TMA is an adequate one over many assumption for P-TMA.[41] First, OM-TMA, SP, and NI are consistent.[42] Secondly, together with the assumption that there are some *F* things, they generate the regress. For consider the maximal set of large sensibles. This set is at level 0. By OM-

TMA, there is exactly one form of large over this set. By NI, this form is not a member of the set.[43] By SP, it is large. Now consider a second maximal set, one that consists of the initial form of large and the members of the maximal set of large sensibles. This set is at level 1. OM-TMA says there is exactly one form of large over it. By NI, this form is not a member of the set; by SP it is large. Now consider a third maximal set of large things, one that consists of the members of the second maximal set and the form of large at level 2—and so on *ad infinitum*.

Thirdly, OM-TMA is an exactly one, rather than an at least one, assumption; and so it might make U seem tempting, although it does not imply U.[44] Fourthly, OM-TMA captures an intuitive point missing from (2*b*), that we cannot appeal to just any old form of *F* to explain the *F*-ness of a group of *F* things; for on OM-TMA, there is some one form that bears a special relation to each maximal set of *F* things—the unique form over that set.

One further aspect of OM-TMA calls for comment. It is often thought that the TMA's one over many assumption posits a form for every predicate.[45] OM-TMA certainly can be so read; but it need not be so read. At least, we can restrict it to property-names without affecting the logic of P-TMA. And it is desirable to restrict OM-TMA to property-names, for it is then closer to being a claim Plato accepts, in which case P-TMA is an argument more worth reckoning with.[46]

I suggest, then, that P-TMA involves OM-TMA, SP, and NI; these three premisses are mutually consistent;[47] and, given the assumption that there are some *F* things, they validly generate a regress. If Plato is committed to OM-TMA, SP, and NI, he is vulnerable to the regress. Before deciding about Plato's commitments, however, let us consider a regress argument that Plato describes later in the *Parmenides*.

3. The Resemblance Regress: *Parmenides* 132d1–133a3

In order to forestall P-TMA, Socrates suggests that 'each of these forms is a thought (*noēma*) that cannot properly exist anywhere except in minds' (132b3–5). It is not clear how this is meant to block P-TMA; but the suggestion is in any case rejected. Forms are real, mind-independent objects of thought, not thoughts themselves.[48]

Socrates next suggests that 'forms are set in nature like paradigms. The other things are likenesses of them and are similar to them; and this participation they have in forms is nothing but their being made like them' (132d1–4). Earlier in the *Parmenides* (131a4–e7), Plato had suggested two ways of explicating the participation relation: either the whole or a part of each form is in each of its participants. These accounts of participation were apparently rejected. But although Plato initially spoke as though they were exhaustive, he now introduces an allegedly third account of participation: if x participates in y, then y is a paradigmatic form of which x is a likeness or copy.[49]

Plato then argues that if we explain the participation relation in this way, a regress arises—let us call it the Resemblance Regress. It goes as follows:

> Forms are set in nature like paradigms, and the other things are like them and are similar to them (*ta de alla toutois eoikenai kai einai homoiōmata*); and this participation they have in forms is nothing but their being made like them.
>
> If, then, he said, a thing is like (*eoiken*) a form, is it possible for the form not to be similar (*homoion*) to what has been made like it, in so far as it has been made similar to it? If something is similar, must it not be similar to something that is similar to it?
>
> It must be.
>
> And must not the thing which is similar and the thing it is similar to participate in one and the same form?[50]
>
> That is necessary.
>
> And will not that in which the similar things participate, so as to be similar, be the form itself (*auto to eidos*)?
>
> Certainly.
>
> If so, then nothing can be similar to the form, nor can the form be similar to anything else. For otherwise, another (*allo*) form will always make its appearance in addition (*para*) to the ⟨previous⟩ form, and if that one is similar to something, then another ⟨form⟩, and there will be no end to the generation of a new form, if indeed the form is to be similar to the thing participating in it.

The following steps seem explicit in the text:

(1) If a is F, a is F by participating in a form of F, form$_1$ of F, which is a paradigm of which a is a likeness.

(2) Paradigms and their likenesses are similar to one another.

(3) Therefore, if a participates in form$_1$ of F, a is similar to it.

(4) If any two things are similar to one another, they are similar by participating in some one form.

(5) Therefore, if a and form$_1$ of F are similar to one another, there is some one form in which they both participate, in virtue of which they are similar.

(6) Therefore there is another form of F, form$_2$ of F, in which a and form$_1$ of F both participate, in virtue of which they are similar.

The argument is clearly valid through (5). Let a be some sensible large thing.[51] By (1), a participates in a form of large—call it the form$_1$ of large—which is a paradigm of which a is a likeness. Since paradigms and their likenesses are similar to one another (2), a and the form$_1$ of large are similar to one another—presumably, by both being large (3).[52] If a and the form$_1$ of large are similar to one another by both being large, then, like P-TMA, the Resemblance Regress involves a self-predication assumption. As in P-TMA, the relevant self-predication assumption is only SP, that any form of F is F. In this sense, and also because it contributes to a consistent premiss set, BSP is adequate as the self-predication assumption of the Resemblance Regress, just as it is adequate as the self-predication assumption of P-TMA.[53]

We know so far that a and the form$_1$ of large are alike in being large. (4) tells us that they are both large by participating in some one form. This involves a one over many assumption, which I return to in a moment.

(5) validly infers that a and the form$_1$ are both large by participating in a form, call it the form$_2$ of large.[54] (6) infers that the form$_1$ of large is different from the form$_2$ of large. (1)–(5) do not license this inference. But it is licensed if we assume NI. Hence the Resemblance Regress (on pain of invalidity) assumes NI.[55]

We have seen so far, then, that the Resemblance Regress involves SP, NI, and some sort of one over many assumption. But what is the operative one over many assumption? It has some features in common with OM-TMA. First, as in P-TMA, we can again restrict the relevant similarities to *genuine* similarities. We may need a form of dog to explain what the members of a set of dogs have in common; but we do not need a form of grue to explain what the members of a set of grue things have in common. The Resemblance Regress's one over many assumption, that is, can be restricted to property-names.[56] Secondly and more importantly, the groups that require forms contain forms; the relevant groups are not restricted to sensibles. Thirdly (since the Resemblance Regress assumes NI), RR assumes that the form in virtue of which the members of a set of Fs are F is not a member of that set.

It does not yet follow, however, that the Resemblance Regress assumes, or is best interpreted with, OM-TMA. For we have not yet seen anything that suggests that all and only the members of each maximal set of Fs are F in virtue of the only form of F at the next-highest level. But further features of the argument—or, where the text is indeterminate, considerations about what Plato is likely to intend—suggest that it assumes this or, at least, that it is best so read. First, we have seen that any one over many assumption that would tempt Plato would be an exactly one assumption; and the Resemblance Regress merits more serious consideration to the extent that it contains claims that are (close to) ones Plato accepts. Further, if we are going to admit that there is more than one form of F (though only one at any given level) and if, as the Resemblance Regress assumes, nothing is F in virtue of itself, then (as in P-TMA) it seems intuitively reasonable to assume that each maximal set of Fs will be specially related to just one form of F—presumably to the one form of F over that set. Plato's repeated use of the definite article with 'form' suggests this; it seems to indicate that exactly one form bears a special relation to the entities it is over, and that at each stage just one new form arises.

So of the one over many assumptions that are consistent with the text, OM-TMA seems to be the most desirable one. For it allows us to generate the regress from a consistent premiss set, it gives the regress some intuitive plausibility, and it comes closest to being a one over many assumption that might have tempted Plato.

The Resemblance Regress thus involves the same crucial premisses as P-TMA: OM-TMA, SP, and NI. It also draws the same conclusion from them: that if there is even one form of F, there are infinitely many forms of F. Since the Resemblance Regress and P-TMA have exactly the same premisses and inferences, they are logically the same argument.[57]

The Resemblance Regress and P-TMA none the less differ, not in their logic, but in various other ways. One difference,[58] not in P-TMA and the Resemblance Regress themselves but in the larger context in which they are embedded, is that in presenting P-TMA, Plato emphasizes that a one over many assumption had led him to believe U when it in fact (in combination with other premisses) leads to a strong denial of U; in presenting the Resemblance Regress, by contrast, Plato emphasizes that if we take forms and sensibles to be alike, then (given further premisses) a regress arises. So in his presentation of P-TMA Plato highlights OM-TMA, whereas in his presentation of the Resemblance Regress he highlights SP. But since both arguments contain both premisses, this is not a difference in their logic; it simply gets us to see that there are different premisses one could reject in order to avoid the regress.

Another difference is that P-TMA does not say what participation consists in, whereas the Resemblance Regress explains participation in terms of paradigmatism; it says that if a is F, it is F by being a likeness of a paradigmatic form of F. Owen seems to believe that this difference shows that P-TMA takes forms to be both universals and particulars, whereas the Resemblance Regress takes them to be just particulars (and not also universals).[59] But his sole reason for thinking that P-TMA takes forms to be (not only universals but also) particulars seems to be that it takes them to be self-predicative. And his sole reason for thinking that the Resemblance Regress takes forms to be particulars (and not also universals) seems to be that it takes them to be self-predicative paradigms.[60] We have seen, however, that BSP is an adequate self-predication assumption for both regresses; since BSP does not imply that forms are particulars, the self-predication assumption of the regresses does not imply that forms are particulars. Nor does conceiving forms as paradigms require them to be particulars; if, for example, they are paradigms of the sort I have been taking them to be, the regress still goes through.[61]

I conclude so far, then, that P-TMA and the Resemblance Regress are logically the same argument. That is, they involve the same crucial premisses (OM-TMA, SP, and NI), and they draw the same inference from those premisses—that if there is even one form of *F*, there are infinitely many forms of *F*. Further, in both arguments forms can be viewed as universals; they need not be viewed as particulars. In the next chapter I ask why Plato adduces what is in effect the same argument twice over and whether he is vulnerable to it. But first we need to look at Aristotle's and Eudemus' regress arguments.

4. Aristotle's *Peri ideōn* formulation of the Third Man Argument (A-TMA) (84. 21–85. 3)

Alexander says that Aristotle describes the following version of a Third Man Argument:

If what is predicated truly of some plurality of things (*pleionōn*) is also ⟨some⟩ other thing (*allo*) besides (*para*) the things of which it is predicated, being separated (*kechōrismenon*) from them (for this is what those who posit the ideas think they prove; for this is why, according to them, there is such a thing as man-itself, because the man is predicated truly of the particular (*kath' hekasta*) men, these being a plurality, and it is other (*allo*) than the particular men)—but if this is so, there will be a third man. For if the ⟨man⟩ being predicated is other than the things of which it is predicated and subsists on its own (*kat' idian huphestōs*), and ⟨if⟩ the man is predicated both of the particulars and of the idea, then there will be a third man besides the particular and the idea. In the same way, there will also be a fourth ⟨man⟩ predicated of this ⟨third man⟩, of the idea, and of the particulars, and similarly also a fifth, and so on to infinity.

In the last chapter, we saw that Aristotle says that the premisses of the Accurate One over Many Argument give rise to the TMA. Just as Plato argues that a one over many thesis (when combined with other claims about forms) does not prove U but leads to a regress, so Aristotle argues that the premisses of a one over many argument for the existence of forms lead to a regress.[62] Is Aristotle's Third Man Argument the same as, or different from, Plato's regress?[63]

As we have seen, the Accurate One over Many Argument involves two initial premisses:[64]

(AOM) Whenever a plurality of things (*pleiō*) are *F*, they are *F* in virtue of having some one thing, the *F*, predicated of them (84. 22–3).

(G-Sep) Whatever is predicated of a plurality of things is separate from—i.e. exists independently of—the things of which it is predicated (84. 23–4).

From G-Sep, Aristotle infers:

(NI) Whatever is predicated of a plurality of things is something besides (*para*) the things of which it is predicated (84. 23–4).

Aristotle then says that it follows that 'there will be a third man' (84. 27)—that is, as 85. 1 makes clear, a third man 'besides the particulars and the idea'.[65] To see why this is so, we need to explore the premisses of the Accurate One over Many Argument.

NI in the Accurate One over Many Argument says that what is predicated of a plurality of things is different from the things of which it is predicated and, as we have seen, in the Accurate One over Many Argument predications extend beyond sensibles. NI is therefore the claim that nothing is F by being predicated of, i.e. in virtue of, itself.[66] A-TMA thus involves the same non-identity assumption as P-TMA and the Resemblance Regress.

In the last chapter, we saw that AOM states a one over many assumption. But precisely what one over many assumption is it? It has some features in common with OM-TMA. For example, it imposes no explicit restriction on the predicates that have corresponding forms (on permissible substituends for 'F') although we can again, without threat to the logic of the argument, restrict the predicates that have corresponding forms to property-names. Further and more importantly, the sets of things that require forms include more than sensibles. As we saw in Ch. 14, that is why Aristotle uses the ontologically neutral '*pleiō*' rather than the more restrictive '*kath' hekasta*'. (This partly explains why the Accurate One over Many Argument, but not the One over Many Argument, gives rise to the TMA. For unlike the One over Many Argument, the Accurate One over Many Argument posits forms for groups that contain forms.) Moreover, Aristotle's formulation of the regress (like Plato's) seems to assume that there is just one form of man at each level greater than 0. This is perhaps indicated by the fact that he uses 'the first man' to refer to sensibles, 'the second man' to refer to the first form of man, and so on—that is, 'first', 'second', and so on pick out entities at different levels. So just as the first and second men are at different levels, so too are the second and third; so presumably the second and third men are the only forms of man at their levels. (Would the fourth man be a level lower than the third man?) Aristotle's use of '*ho anthrōpos*' (with the definite article) also suggests that there is just one form of man at every level greater than 0.[67]

It is true that, unlike OM-TMA, AOM does not imply NI; indeed, as I go on to say, in Aristotle's formulation NI is inferred not from AOM but from G-Sep.[68] But the conjunction of AOM and NI is equivalent in force to OM-TMA, and so A-TMA is in that sense involved in OM-TMA.[69]

It is interesting to note that Plato's and Aristotle's formulations of the relevant one over many assumption differ in that whereas Plato says that

F things are *F* by participating in, or in virtue of, a form of *F*, Aristotle says that they are *F* because the *F* (e.g. the man, *ho anthrōpos*) is predicated of them. I think Aristotle uses 'is predicated of' to highlight the fact that forms are universals or properties; for as we have seen, in his view universals but not particulars can be predicated of many things (*DI* 17a38–b1).

AOM and NI are not sufficient for a regress. This can be seen as follows. By AOM, all and only sensible men are men in virtue of having some one thing, a property of being a man (*ho anthrōpos*, 84. 25), predicated of them, a property the Platonists take to be a form at level 1.[70] The Platonists, that is, take *ho anthrōpos* (a property of being a man) to be a form of man—what at 84. 25 Aristotle calls *autoanthrōpos* and what we may call man-itself$_1$, since it is the first form of man, the form at the next highest level after sensible men. By NI, *autoanthrōpos*, man-itself$_1$, is not a member of this group. But this does not yet allow us to infer that there is another form of man. In order to be able to infer this, there has to be a maximal set at level 1, all of whose members are men. That is to say, we can infer that there is another form of man only if man-itself$_1$ is a man. But neither AOM nor NI assures us that it is. For the regress to proceed, SP thus again needs to be assumed.[71] With SP, we can form a second maximal set, one that consists of the members of the initial maximal set plus man-itself$_1$. 84. 29–85. 1 says that there is *another* property of being a man (another *ho anthrōpos*) in virtue of which all and only the members of this second maximal set are men. If the first property of being a man is a form of man, then the second property of being a man is also a form of man; call it man-itself$_2$. There is thus a third man (84. 27)—i.e. a man besides the sensible men and man-itself$_1$—and so on *ad infinitum*.

Although Aristotle does not state SP at the outset, and although he says that there is a third man before he states SP, he goes on to make it clear that the regress requires SP. For at 84. 29–85. 1 he says that 'the man is predicated both of the particulars and of the idea'—that is, a property of being a man is predicated of both sensible men and the form of man. Since the property of being a man is predicated of sensible men in the class-membership sense, it is presumably predicated of the form of man in that sense too. For otherwise, not only would there be no regress but also one and the same occurrence of 'is predicated of' in 84. 29 would be being used in two different senses—for class membership as applied to sensibles, and in some other sense as applied to the form. It is surely preferable (and possible) to assume that the property of being a man is predicated of both the form of man and sensible men in the same class-membership sense. Hence like P-TMA and the Resemblance Regress, A-TMA involves SP.[72] Further, like P-TMA and the Resemblance Regress, A-TMA does not require NSP; for, again, SP says only that any form of *F* is predicatively F, is a member of the class of F things. If the form of F is BSP F, then it is predicatively F, and so it satisfies SP. In this sense, and also because it contributes to a consistent premiss set, BSP is adequate as A-TMA's self-predication assumption.

AOM, NI, SP, plus the assumption that there are some F things, generate the regress. For if SP obtains, there is a maximal set of men that consists of all sensible men and man-itself$_1$. By AOM, the members of this set are all men in virtue of exactly one form of F, the only form of F at its level. By NI, this form cannot be man-itself$_1$, since man-itself$_1$ is a member of the set. Hence we need a second form, man-itself$_2$—a form of man at the next highest level. The same procedure can obviously be repeated *ad infinitum*, and so if there is even one form of man, there are infinitely many forms of man.

If, however, we substitute OM for AOM, the regress does not arise. For OM posits forms only for sets that contain only sensibles; the TMA requires us to posit forms over sets that contain forms. Hence the One over Many Argument avoids the TMA.[73] Hence it cannot be the second more accurate argument, since the second more accurate argument gives rise to the TMA.

A-TMA thus involves the same premisses as P-TMA and the Resemblance Regress: OM-TMA, NI, and SP. (Hence, like P-TMA and the Resemblance Regress, it has a consistent premiss set.[74]) Moreover, A-TMA draws the same conclusion from these premisses: that if there is even one form of F, there are infinitely many forms of F. As in P-TMA and the Resemblance Regress, this inference is valid. If A-TMA has the same premisses and inferences as P-TMA and the Resemblance Regress, then they are all logically the same argument.[75]

Although A-TMA is logically the same argument as P-TMA and the Resemblance Regress, its mode of expression is distinctive. One difference is that whereas P-TMA uses 'large' as its sample predicate (and the Resemblance Regress uses no sample predicate at all), A-TMA uses 'man'—it generates a regress of forms of man rather than of forms of large.[76] A second difference is that whereas P-TMA and the Resemblance Regress *can* be taken to conceive forms as universals, in A-TMA forms not only *can* be but also *are* so conceived. For *ho anthrōpos* is a property of being a man, which is then promoted into a form. Perhaps Aristotle formulates A-TMA as he does in order to bring out more clearly than P-TMA and the Resemblance Regress do that forms are universals. If so, then here, as often, Aristotle takes a clear stand where Plato is indeterminate.

A third difference is that Plato does not mention any separation assumption in connection with P-TMA or the Resemblance Regress, but Aristotle mentions a separation assumption in connection with A-TMA. We know that Aristotle believes that Plato separated forms and that separation is responsible for many of the difficulties with the theory of forms; he now tells us that some sort of separation assumption is somehow relevant to the TMA. We saw in the last chapter that the Accurate One over Many Argument's separation assumption is not Separation (the assumption Aristotle elsewhere has in mind when he discusses Plato on separation), but G-Sep:[77]

(G-Sep) Any *F* that is predicated is separate from—i.e. exists independently of—the *F* things of which it is predicated.

How if at all is G-Sep relevant to the TMA?[78] We should hope that Aristotle does not take it to be necessary for the regress; for SP, OM-TMA, NI (plus the assumption that there are some *F* things) are sufficient. Nor does Plato mention a separation assumption in P-TMA or the Resemblance Regress. Nor does Aristotle elsewhere explicitly mention a separation assumption in connection with the TMA. (Indeed, so far as I know, Aristotle nowhere else mentions G-Sep in any connection.) But although G-Sep is not necessary for the regress, Aristotle indicates (84. 22–3) that it implies NI, which is a premiss of the TMA. So perhaps he thinks that Plato is committed to NI because he is committed to G-Sep.

Aristotle may also mention G-Sep for the following reason. When he discusses the TMA outside the *Peri ideōn* (at *SE* 178b36–179a10 and *Met.* 1038b35–1039a3), he says that the Platonists are vulnerable to it because they treat a such (*toionde*) as a this (*tode ti*), i.e. they treat universals as particulars.[79] His thought seems to be that since Plato treats universals (i.e. forms) as particulars, he must lump them together with sensible particulars in such a way that, if there is exactly one form over each maximal set of sensible particulars, then there is also exactly one form over maximal sets that contain forms; Plato does not differentiate between sensible particulars and forms in a way that allows him to stop with the forms at level 1. This may be connected to a point about SP. For Aristotle may think that if forms are particulars, they enjoy NSP (given that SP is true of them anyway). For if the form of man is a particular, and if SP is true of it, then surely it is a particular man, in which case surely NSP is true of it. If the form of man is just another particular man, surely it must be lumped together with sensible men in a way that requires a further form of man.[80]

Now the *Peri ideōn* formulation of the TMA does not explicitly say that forms are both universals and particulars—indeed, it is striking and important that Aristotle does not explicitly say this anywhere in the *Peri ideōn*. But he may mention G-Sep to hint at the point. For if forms are separate, then in Aristotle's view they are particulars.[81] A-TMA also takes forms to be universals. So it in effect takes forms to be both universals and particulars, though this is hinted at rather than, as elsewhere, stated outright.

I do not mean to suggest that Aristotle takes a separation premiss to be necessary for the regress; I think he sees that OM-TMA, SP, and NI (plus the assumption that there are some *F* things) are sufficient. His view rather seems to be that because Plato accepts some sort of separation assumption, he is committed to some of the TMA's premisses.[82] I assess this view in Ch. 16. Here the crucial point is that the regress Aristotle records is the same as Plato's, despite the fact that he mentions a separation assumption in connection with it (though not as a premiss of it).

5. Eudemus' version of the Third Man Argument (E-TMA) (83. 34–84. 7)

Alexander says that Eudemus offered the following version of a Third Man Argument:

They say that the things that are predicated in common of ⟨*F*⟩ substances both are fully (*kuriōs*) ⟨*F*⟩ and are ideas. Further, things that are similar to one another are similar to one another by sharing in some same thing, which is fully this ⟨i.e. fully *F*⟩; and this is the idea. But if this is so, and if what is predicated in common of things (*tinōn*), if it is not the same as any one of those things of which it is predicated, is something else besides it (for this is why man-itself is a genus, because it is predicated of the particulars but is not the same as any of them), then there will be a third man besides the particular (such as Socrates or Plato) and besides the idea; and this is also one in number.

Alexander claims that Eudemus' Third Man Argument (E-TMA) is the same as A-TMA (85. 4). If he is right, and if I was right to say that A-TMA is logically the same as P-TMA and the Resemblance Regress, then all four arguments are logically the same, even though their modes of expression and general setting differ.

Eudemus begins with the following two premisses:

(1) What is predicated in common of *F* substances is fully (*kuriōs*) *F* and is a form of *F*.

(2) If *a* and *b* are similar to one another in being *F*, they are similar to one another by participating in some one thing that is a form that is fully *F*.

(1)–(2) involve SP. For (1) says that what is predicated of a group of *F* things—a form of *F*—is 'such as' (*toiauta*) the things of which it is predicated (83. 35); that is, it is like them in being *F*. (1)–(2) also say that the form of *F* is this (*touto*, 84. 2; cf. 83. 35)—i.e. *F*—fully (*kuriōs*). As the Argument from Relatives explains, if something is fully *F*, it is *F*; so if the form of *F* is fully *F*, it is *F* and so enjoys SP. Alexander takes E-TMA (and A-TMA) to involve SP. For he says that according to both A-TMA and E-TMA, 'similar things are similar by sharing in some same thing. For men and the ideas ⟨of men⟩ are similar' (85. 4–5).

Notice that E-TMA's self-predication assumption is again only SP. For it says only that any form of F is F; it does not say how that comes about—whether it is because the form of F is F in virtue of itself, or in some other way. (So as in the other regress arguments, BSP is adequate as E-TMA's self-predication assumption.) Thus, so far as SP goes, forms can be conceived in E-TMA as universals. As we saw in Ch. 10, the claim that any form of F is fully F is also compatible with treating forms as universals. Further, E-TMA takes forms to be what is 'predicated in common' of various things—a phrase that, at least in Aristotle, imports universality.

(1)–(2) also involve a one over many assumption. (1) seems more restricted than OM-TMA, for it licenses forms only for groups of *substances*. Eudemus seems to use 'substance' in roughly the way in which Aristotle uses 'primary substance' in the *Categories*—for such entities as an individual man or horse or tree. If so, substituends for 'F' in (1) are narrower than in any of the other one over many assumptions we have canvassed, for they all posit forms for e.g. large things no less than for sensible men.[83]

Although (1) seems narrower than OM-TMA, (2) is more general.[84] For (2) claims that whenever a group of *things* (*tina*) are F, they are F by participating in some one form of F.[85] This seems to include two features of OM-TMA. First, like OM-TMA, (2) involves no restriction on suitable substituends for 'F' (although restricting them to property-names does not affect the logic of the argument). Secondly and more importantly, (2) does not restrict the sets that require forms to sets that contain only sensibles. But these two points of similarity do not show that (2) involves OM-TMA; nor does (2) by itself suggest OM-TMA. For one thing, it leaves open the possibility that if a and b are both F (and if at least one of them is a form of F), they are F in virtue of one of either a or b. But OM-TMA rules this out.[86]

We of course do not need OM-TMA in order to rule this out; for NI rules it out. And in fact Eudemus supplies another premiss that is tantamount to NI:

(3) What is predicated in common of things (*tina*) is not the same as any of the things of which it is predicated (84. 3–4).

(3) says that if x is predicated of something, then it is different from that thing.[87] It follows that nothing is predicated of itself, and so nothing is F in virtue of itself. Hence (3) involves NI.

But even if E-TMA involves NI and posits forms for groups of things quite generally, it need not involve OM-TMA. And we have seen nothing yet to suggest that (as OM-TMA says) for every maximal set of Fs there is exactly one form of F over it—for we have seen nothing yet that says anything about levels. But the appropriate claim about levels is suggested by a further feature of the argument. For like A-TMA, E-TMA seems to view all sensible men collectively as the first man, the first form as the second man, and the second form as the third man. This suggests that sensible men and each of the forms are all at different levels. This in turn suggests that the first form is over the maximal set of sensible men, that the second form is over the maximal set that contains sensible men and the first form of man, and so on. OM-TMA thus seems to be the best one over many assumption for E-TMA, as it is for the other versions of the regress.[88]

E-TMA thus involves the same premisses as the other regress arguments we have explored—OM-TMA, SP, and NI. It also draws the same inference from them—that there will be a third man.[89] Since E-TMA involves the same premisses and draws the same inference as P-TMA, the Resemblance Regress, and A-TMA, they are all logically the same argument. (Hence I shall from now on speak indifferently of the TMA, unless a specific version is relevant.)

None the less, like the other versions of the TMA, E-TMA is in some ways distinctive. One distinctive feature is that only E-TMA says that any form of *F* is *fully* (*kuriōs*) *F*. However, although this further claim is not explicit in the other versions of the TMA, it may be implicit in the Resemblance Regress. For it says that forms are paradigms of which sensibles are likenesses; and according to the Argument from Relatives, if something is paradigmatically *F*, it is fully *F*. But even if the Resemblance Regress and E-TMA agree that forms are fully *F*, there may be a related difference between them. For the Resemblance Regress claims that sensibles are likenesses of forms, which suggests that sensibles are imperfectly rather than fully *F*. E-TMA, by contrast, does not suggest that sensibles are imperfectly, or not fully, *F*. For example, although it says that participants in forms are *similar* to those forms, it conspicuously does not say that they are *made to be similar* to them.[90] Indeed, in calling at least some of them substances, it may implicitly deny that they are imperfectly *F*. I return to this possible difference between E-TMA and the Resemblance Regress in the next chapter.

Another verbal difference between E-TMA and the other versions of the regress is that only E-TMA says that each form is 'one in number' (84. 7). But although this phrase occurs only in E-TMA, perhaps it is used to make a familiar point. For we have seen that for Aristotle, if something is one in number, it is a particular.[91] We have also seen that outside the *Peri ideōn*, Aristotle says that Plato is vulnerable to the TMA because he treats universals as particulars; although Aristotle does not explicitly say this in the *Peri ideōn*, he may mention G-Sep to hint at it. If Eudemus uses 'one in number' as Aristotle does, and if, like Aristotle, he believes that if something is predicated of many things it is a universal, then perhaps he too means to suggest that Plato is vulnerable to the TMA because he treats universal forms as though they were particulars. But like Aristotle, Eudemus does not suggest that this is part of the logic of the argument. One can, unfortunately, be vulnerable to the TMA even if one does not treat universals as particulars, so long as one is none the less committed to SP, NI, and OM-TMA.

6. Conclusion

We have now explored four versions of the Third Man Argument. They all involve the same crucial premisses: SP (which does not say how it is any form of F is F), OM-TMA (which can be restricted to property-names), and NI. They also all draw the same inference from these premisses—that if there is even one form of F, there are infinitely many forms of F. Hence they are logically the same argument.[92] Further, each argument can be taken to conceive of forms as properties; more strongly, A-TMA and (probably) E-TMA do so conceive of forms.

None the less, each argument differs in its mode of expression and in its general setting. For example, in presenting P-TMA, Plato suggests that the regress is troubling because it challenges U; this point is not explicitly made in connection with any of the other versions of the regress. Or again, in presenting the Resemblance Regress, Plato suggests that the troubling premiss is that sensible Fs and the form of F are similar in being F; this suggestion is not so explicit in the other versions of the regress. But these are differences in the setting of each regress, not in their logic. Further, only Aristotle mentions G-Sep and only Eudemus says that forms are one in number. But these claims are not premisses of the regress; rather, they are mentioned to hint at what gets Plato into the regress.

Further, only the Resemblance Regress characterizes forms as paradigms and participants as likenesses of them; only E-TMA says that forms are predicated of substances, which might suggest that sensibles are fully F (a claim the Resemblance Regress seems to deny). Only E-TMA describes forms as being fully F (thereby using language that is prominent in the Argument from Relatives). E-TMA emphasizes SP at the outset, delaying the introduction of NI;[93] A-TMA emphasizes NI at the outset, delaying the introduction of SP. P-TMA uses the predicate 'large'; A-TMA and E-TMA use 'man'; the Resemblance Regress does not use a sample predicate.

Although these differences between the various versions of the TMA do not affect its logic, they may involve different conceptions of forms (are they paradigms? are they particulars, universals, or both?), of sensibles (are they imperfect?), and of the relation between forms and sensibles (is participation to be explicated in terms of paradigmatism?). One possible moral is that whether or not we view forms as paradigms, as particulars or as universals or both, whether or not we view sensibles as being fully F, no matter what form is at issue (the form of man, or of large), Plato is still vulnerable to the TMA. But ought we to draw this moral? I attempt to answer this question in the next chapter.

16

Is Plato Vulnerable to the Third Man Argument?

1. Some preliminaries

Having looked at the logic of the TMA, we are now in a position to ask whether Plato is vulnerable to it.[1] He is vulnerable to it just in case he is committed to OM-TMA, NI, and SP. I have argued that Plato accepts SP, and that his version of it is best understood as BSP; he is not committed to NSP. It is sometimes thought that NSP is necessary as the self-predication assumption of the TMA. If this were right, then Plato would not be vulnerable to the TMA, since he is not committed to NSP. But we have seen that BSP is adequate as the TMA's self-predication assumption; so Plato accepts a self-predication assumption that is adequate as the self-predication assumption of the regress.[2] If he is not vulnerable to the TMA, it must be because he is not committed to at least one of NI and OM-TMA. I begin by considering various Platonic views that are sometimes thought to commit him to NI or to OM-TMA, although they do not in fact do do. (Neither, however, are they incompatible with them.)

In the last chapter I distinguished between *weak* and *strong non-identity*. According to weak non-identity, *sensible Fs* are F in virtue of something distinct from themselves; according to strong non-identity (= NI), *nothing* is F in virtue of itself. Now, in some phases of his career, Plato seems to believe that there is a form for every property-name; so he is sometimes committed to weak non-identity. For if there is a form of F, then sensible Fs are F by being suitably related to it, and so in virtue of something distinct from themselves.[3] Plato could, however, accept weak non-identity without being committed to strong non-identity. Yet strong non-identity—NI—is the non-identity assumption needed for the regress.[4]

Plato seems to believe that forms are not only different but also Separate from sensibles—that is, he seems to believe that the form of F can exist whether or not there are any F sensible particulars. But Separation does not imply NI any more than weak non-identity does.[5] Not only does Separation not imply NI, but neither does it imply any of the other premisses of the TMA; nor do any of its premisses imply Separation. Plato can therefore accept Separation without being committed to any of the TMA's premisses. On the other hand, if he is vulnerable to the TMA, rejecting Separation would not provide him with an escape-route from it.[6]

Cohen argues that Plato accepts OM-TMA in the middle dialogues but rejects it in the late dialogues. He suggests that Plato rejects OM-TMA in the late dialogues by rejecting the view, which Cohen believes he held in the middle dialogues, that every predicate has a corresponding form.[7] If rejecting the view that every predicate has a corresponding form were sufficient for rejecting OM-TMA, then Plato would indeed reject OM-TMA, and so be invulnerable to the TMA, in the late dialogues; for in, for example, the *Politicus* he rejects the view that every predicate has a corresponding form.[8] However, if rejecting the view that every predicate has a corresponding form were sufficient for rejecting OM-TMA, then Plato would not be committed to OM-TMA in the middle dialogues either. For the middle dialogues are not committed to the existence of forms corresponding to every predicate.

I have argued, however, that OM-TMA can be restricted to property-names. If this is right, then denying that there is a form corresponding to every predicate is not sufficient for rejecting OM-TMA. Of course, if (as the *Politicus* says) there is no form of barbarian, then there is no regress of forms of barbarian, since there is not even an initial form. But rejecting a form of barbarian does nothing, by itself, to avoid a regress in those cases where there is an initial form.

The relevant aspect of OM-TMA, for the purposes of the TMA, is not so much the number of *predicates* that have corresponding forms as the sorts of *groups* within any given predicate that have corresponding forms. The crucial question is whether the members of a set of F things that contains a form of F are F in virtue of a form of F that is not a member of the set.[9] We have not yet asked what Plato thinks about this; so we do not yet know whether he is committed to OM-TMA. We know only that the fact that he is not committed to the existence of a form corresponding to every predicate does not show that he is not committed to OM-TMA.

I have suggested so far that Plato is committed to SP (which is best understood as BSP), to weak non-identity, and to Separation; in at least some phases of his career, he also seems to accept a one over many assumption. But Plato's commitment to these claims, at least as they have so far been discussed, does not commit him to NI or to OM-TMA; nor do they say anything incompatible with them. Hence we do not yet know whether Plato is vulnerable to the TMA.

2. A partial escape-route

There is, however, one central strand of thought in the middle dialogues that avoids the TMA, since it is not committed to NI or to OM-TMA.[10]

We have seen that in, for example, *Rep.* 523–5, Plato distinguishes between predicates like 'large', on the one hand, and predicates like 'finger', on the other, on the ground that sensible properties corresponding to the former but not to the latter suffer narrow compresence of opposites. Plato believes that if something suffers narrow compresence with respect to *F*-ness, it is imperfectly *F*; and he argues that if something is imperfectly *F*, it is *F* by participating in a non-sensible form that is perfectly *F*. As we have seen, Plato therefore accepts the *Imperfection Argument* for the existence of forms:[11]

If a group of things are all of them imperfectly *F*, they are *F* in virtue of a perfect form of *F*.

Consider a group of sensible large things, each of which is (in the narrow sense) also small; they are therefore imperfectly large. The Imperfection Argument tells us that they are all large in virtue of a perfect form of large, call it the form$_1$ of large. Now consider a second group of large things, one that consists of the members of the first group and the form$_1$ of large. The Imperfection Argument does not tell us that all the members of this group are large in virtue of yet another perfect form of large, the form$_2$ of large; for not all the members of this group are imperfectly large. Now consider a third group, one that consists of sensible men. According to *Rep.* 523–5, they are not both men and not men. It may then seem that they are not imperfectly men, in which case the Imperfection Argument does not posit even an initial form of man.[12]

We can now see how the Imperfection Argument avoids commitment to NI and OM-TMA. The Imperfection Argument tells us that all *imperfectly F* things are *F* in virtue of something distinct from themselves (in virtue of a perfect form of *F*). But it does not tell us that *nothing* is *F* in virtue of itself, and so it is not committed to NI.

The Imperfection Argument avoids OM-TMA in two ways. First, as described in *Rep.* 523–5, it does not posit a form even for every property-name; it posits a form of large but not a form of man. Hence, as the Imperfection Argument is used in *Rep.* 523–5, there is no regress of forms of man or of forms relevantly like the form of man. Secondly and more importantly, we can infer that there is a form of *F* only when we have a group that consists only of imperfectly *F* things. Thus, the Imperfection Argument (in its *Rep.* 523–5 version) posits forms both for a restricted range of *predicates* and also for a restricted range of *groups*. No group of *F* things that contains a form of *F* requires a second form of *F*, since the form in the group is not imperfectly *F*. Hence the Imperfection Argument avoids OM-TMA not only in the case of man but also in the case of large. If the Imperfection Argument does not involve NI and OM-TMA, then it avoids the TMA—even if Plato accepts SP, weak non-identity, and separation.

To say that the Imperfection Argument is not committed to NI or to OM-TMA is not to say that it is incompatible with them; and it is not. But reflection on it might naturally lead one to reject them. For one might come to think that only imperfectly F things need to be explained in terms of something distinct from themselves; by contrast, if something is perfectly F, it is F in virtue of itself.[13]

3. A problem and a possible resolution

In the last section, we avoided the TMA for predicates like 'man' by appealing to *Rep.* 523–5's version of the Imperfection Argument, which does not posit even an initial form of man. But Plato cannot avoid the TMA for such predicates in this way in every phase of his career. For at least in *Rep.* 10, the *Timaeus*, and the *Philebus*, he is committed to the existence of a form of man.[14] The argument on its behalf plainly cannot be *Rep.* 523–5's version of the Imperfection Argument; so we cannot avoid the TMA for the form of man, once granted its existence, by appealing to *Rep.* 523–5's version of the Imperfection Argument. Perhaps Aristotle and Eudemus formulate the regress with 'man' rather than with 'large' because they believe that the Imperfection Argument is not available for the form of man, which therefore falls prey to the regress.

However, we have seen that Plato sometimes seems to rely on a broader version of the Imperfection Argument than the one described in *Rep.* 523–5. On this broader version, something is imperfectly F if it is not only F but also has features that are inessential to the nature of F-ness. This version of the Imperfection Argument generates a form of man; for every sensible man is not only a man but also has features (e.g. being snub-nosed) that are inessential to what it is to be a man. Sensible men are therefore imperfectly men, and so they are men by participating in a perfect form of man.

Although the Imperfection Argument, when it is used in this broader way, posits an initial form of man, it avoids a second form of man in just the way in which it avoids a second form of large. For it posits a form of F only over groups that consist only of imperfectly F things.[15] If sensible men are imperfectly men, and the form of man is perfectly a man, the Imperfection Argument does not posit a second form of man. Plato can thus use the Imperfection Argument to avoid a regress of forms of man, even when he acknowledges the existence of a form of man, so long as he at the same time views sensible men as being imperfectly men.

Instead of saying that the TMA is avoided because the form of F is perfectly F whereas sensible Fs are imperfectly F, we could say that it is avoided because sensibles are deficient copies of paradigmatic forms;

for in Plato's view, forms are paradigms of which sensibles are deficient likenesses precisely because forms are perfect and sensibles are imperfect.[16] Yet the Resemblance Regress suggests that if forms are paradigms of which their participants are deficient likenesses, then a regress arises. Owen, for one, agrees; and he then suggests that Plato responds to the TMA by dropping paradigmatism.[17] Indeed, one reason Owen dates the *Timaeus* before the *Parmenides* is that the *Timaeus* emphasizes the paradigmatic nature of forms; if it was none the less written after the *Parmenides*, then, Owen believes, Plato would not have seen the force of the TMA.[18]

But on my view, paradigmatism actually suggests an escape-route from the TMA.[19] This can be seen more clearly if we return for a moment to the Resemblance Regress. We saw that the Resemblance Regress is valid through (5), but that the inference to (6) is fallacious; to justify it, NI has to be assumed.[20] But if forms are paradigms, we can see how to avoid NI, and so how to avoid the move from (5) to (6). For perhaps not every group of *F* things is *F* in virtue of a form of *F* distinct from any member of the group. Rather, only imperfectly *F* things are *F* in virtue of something distinct from themselves—in virtue of a perfect, paradigmatic form of *F*, from which they are derivative, by being likenesses of it. (In just the same way, the Imperfection Argument does not say that every group of *F* things is *F* in virtue of a form distinct from every member of the group; and we have seen how reflecting on the Imperfection Argument might lead one to think that not every group of *F* things is *F* in virtue of a form distinct from every member of the group.) So perhaps Plato does not explicitly state NI in his account of the Resemblance Regress in order to hint that that is where he would jib. And perhaps he mentions paradigmatism in order to explain precisely how he would jib: by arguing that not every group of *F* things is *F* in virtue of a form of *F* that is not a member of the group. Although we need to explain why deficient likenesses are *F* by reference to something distinct from them (by reference to the paradigm they are likenesses of), we do not need to explain the nature of the paradigm by reference to something distinct from it. For unlike its imperfect likenesses, it is intrinsically *F*, *F* in virtue of itself.[21] If forms are paradigms, Plato has good reason to reject NI and OM-TMA.[22] Paradigmatism thus allows us to avoid the TMA, and so we need not date the *Timaeus* before the *Parmenides* on the ground that since it has paradigmatism, it is vulnerable to the TMA. On the contrary, perhaps the *Timaeus* newly emphasizes paradigmatism, after the criticisms of the *Parmenides*, to make it clear how to avoid the TMA.

We noticed in the last chapter that although E-TMA says that the form of *F* is fully *F*, it does not say that it is a paradigm. Nor does it say that sensible *F*s are imperfectly *F*; indeed, in calling them substances, it may suggest that they are not imperfectly *F*. Perhaps Eudemus sees that the

TMA can be avoided if forms are paradigms of which their participants are imperfect copies. And perhaps he wants to suggest that this escape-route is not always available to Plato. For although Plato consistently takes the form of F to be perfectly F, he sometimes, as in *Rep.* 523–5, seems to view (e.g.) sensible men as being perfectly men; they are not, at any rate, men and not men in the narrow sense. Eudemus may conclude that Plato therefore cannot escape the TMA by invoking the distinction between the perfect and the imperfect, or between paradigms and their likenesses.

However, *Rep.* 523–5 is not committed to the existence of a form of man; and even though Plato says there that sensible fingers are not both fingers and not fingers in the narrow sense, it does not follow that he takes them to be perfect. Although suffering narrow compresence is sufficient for being imperfect, it may not be necessary. Whenever Plato countenances a form of F, he seems to take the corresponding sensibles to be imperfectly F. The suggestion that in some cases Plato is committed to a form of F even when the corresponding sensibles are perfectly F seems to weave strands of his thought into the wrong pattern—though, to be sure, he is not always careful to tell us what pattern he prefers.

I have argued that the broad version of the Imperfection Argument allows all forms to escape the TMA. For it posits a form of F only over groups of imperfectly F things; since no form of F is imperfectly F, the Imperfection Argument never posits a form of F over a group that contains a form of F. Vlastos argues that if the form of F is perfectly F and sensible Fs are imperfectly F (or if forms are paradigms of which sensibles are deficient likenesses), then the form of F and sensible Fs must be F in different senses of 'F'. He writes, for example, that 'if the Form, Largeness, is superlatively large, while large mountains, oaks, etc., are only deficiently large, it must follow that the single word, *large*, stands for two distinct predicates'.[23] Yet in Ch. 10 I argued that Plato and Aristotle take the form of F and sensible Fs to be F in the same sense of 'F'.[24] Does my escape-route from the TMA then conflict with that claim? No; for, contrary to Vlastos, the perfectly (paradigmatically) F and the imperfectly (derivatively) F are not F in different senses of 'F'. To be sure, they are F in different ways and to different degrees. But as Aristotle insists, if x is more F than y, x and y are F in the same sense of 'F'.[25]

It is sometimes argued that if the form of F and sensible Fs are F in the same sense of 'F', then the TMA arises. Owen, for example, says that if forms and sensibles are synonymously F, then 'they can be treated as a single class whose existence entails that of a further Form'.[26] Was I then wrong to say that the Imperfection Argument and paradigmatism afford an escape-route from the TMA? No; for although they take the form of F

and sensible Fs to be synonymously F, F in the same sense of 'F', they also take them to be F in different ways, and a difference in ways is sufficient for avoiding the TMA.[27]

4. The Third Bed Argument (TBA) (*Rep.* 597c1–d3)[28]

In the previous section I argued that a central strand of Plato's thought—the Imperfection Argument—provides him with an escape-route from the TMA for all forms, for the form of man no less than for the form of large, even if forms are paradigms, and even if forms and sensibles are synonymous. But to say that a central strand of Plato's thought provides an escape-route from the TMA is not to say that there are no passages that might give one pause. And at least one passage has been thought to show that Plato is vulnerable to the TMA. For in *Rep.* 10 (597c1–d4) Plato sets out the so-called Third Bed Argument (TBA). One premiss of the TBA is a one over many assumption. Cohen thinks that its one over many assumption is OM-TMA.[29] Vlastos believes that NI is a premiss of the TBA.[30] If Cohen and Vlastos are right, and if the TBA also involves SP, then the premisses of the TBA give rise to the TMA. And so it is not surprising that Strang suggests that the TBA 'is itself ripe for the TMA treatment'.[31]

On the other hand, Cherniss and others have argued that the TBA rejects SP.[32] If they are right, then the TBA, so far from giving rise to the TMA, actually rejects one of its premisses. However, if Plato avoids the TMA by rejecting SP, then perhaps I was wrong to say that Plato (elsewhere) accepts SP and that we should therefore focus on OM-TMA and NI in asking whether he is vulnerable to the TMA.

The TBA is interesting for a further reason as well. For it is an argument for Uniqueness (U), the claim that there is exactly one form of F for every predicate 'F' that has a corresponding form.[33] In setting out the TMA, Plato argues not only that some premisses that he allegedly accepted give rise to a regress but also that those very premisses explain why he believed U. So far we have focused on the regress, asking whether Plato is committed to its premisses. But we should also ask how, if at all, he argues for U.

So let us turn to the TBA, asking how it defends U and whether the argument gives rise to the TMA. Plato argues as follows:[34]

Now god, whether because he did not want to or because there was some necessity for him not to make more than one bed in nature, made only that one itself ⟨to be⟩ what bed is (*ho esti klinē*). (4) But two or more such beds were never brought into being by god, nor will they ever be.

Why is that?, he said.

Because, I said, (1) if he were to make only two, (2) then another one would appear whose form (*eidos*) they both in their turn would have, and (3) it, not the two, would be what bed is.

Right, he said.

(5) I think, then, that god, knowing these things and wanting to be the real maker of the bed that has real being (and not just any bedmaker of some particular bed) brought it into being as one by nature.

So it seems.

Schematically, the argument goes as follows:

(1) Suppose there are two forms of bed at a given level.[35]
(2) Therefore there is a third form of bed, whose form the initial two forms of bed have.
(3) Therefore the third form, but neither of the initial two, is a form of bed.
(4) Therefore there cannot be more than one form of bed at any given level.
(5) Therefore there is exactly one form of bed (= U).

The move from (1) to (2) involves a one over many assumption: if there are *many* forms of bed at a given level, then there is *one* form of bed *over* them.[36] What is the relevant one over many assumption this time? As elsewhere, it need not apply to more than property-names. But we have seen that restricting a one over many assumption to property-names does not provide a general response to the TMA. A more important point is that the TBA's one over many assumption posits forms for groups that contain (purported) forms. For according to the TBA, the existence of two forms of bed at a given level would require the existence of a third form of bed. This shows that we cannot say that Plato avoids the TMA by accepting, not OM-TMA, but only OM. For the TBA requires a one over many assumption that (like OM-TMA and unlike OM) posits forms for groups that contain forms.[37] But although the TBA's one over many assumption is stronger than OM, it need not be as strong as OM-TMA. There is an alternative one over many assumption that is adequate for the TBA:

(OM-TBA) All the F objects at level n (if there is more than one F object at that level) are F in virtue of exactly one form of F at level $n + 1$.

OM-TBA is importantly different from OM-TMA. OM-TMA says that for every maximal set of Fs, there is *exactly* one form of F over it, even if the set's members are at different levels.[38] OM-TBA posits exactly one form of F only for sets of Fs all of whose members are at the same level. OM-TMA and OM-TBA both posit exactly one form of F in virtue of which the members of the maximal set of sensible Fs are F;[39] and they would both posit exactly one form of F for two forms of bed at the same level. But OM-TMA also posits exactly one form of F over the maximal set that consists of F sensibles and the form of F at level 1. OM-TBA does not posit a form over this set, since not all its members are at the same level.[40]

Just as OM-TMA involves a non-identity assumption, so too does OM-TBA. Moreover, just as the TBA's one over many assumption cannot be as weak as OM, so its non-identity assumption cannot be as weak as weak non-identity. For the TBA argues that neither of the two forms of bed is a bed in virtue of itself, and so it extends the range of things that are not F in virtue of themselves beyond sensible Fs. Hence we cannot say that Plato avoids the TMA because his non-identity assumption is only weak non-identity. But just as the TBA does not require OM-TMA, so it does not require NI. An alternative that is adequate for the TBA is:[41]

(NI-TBA) All the F objects at level n (if there is more than one F object at that level) are F in virtue of a form of F that is at a different level.

Unlike NI, NI-TBA does not say that *nothing* is F in virtue of itself; it says only that if there is more than one F at a given level, they cannot be F in virtue of themselves (or in virtue of one another). Although NI-TBA is weaker than NI, it is strong enough to explain why the initial two forms of bed cannot be beds either in virtue of themselves or in virtue of one another. For NI-TBA tells us that, since they are at the same level, they must be beds in virtue of something at a different level.[42]

Although OM-TBA and NI-TBA are adequate as the TBA's one over many and non-identity assumptions, respectively (in which case the TBA requires neither OM-TMA nor NI), they do not by themselves license the move from (1) to (2). If, however, we also assume that the two forms of bed are beds, then the move from (1) to (2) is licensed. For we then know that there are two beds at the same level and so, given OM-TBA, there must be exactly one form of bed at the next highest level in virtue of which they are beds. There is, then, a third form of bed.

If the move from (1) to (2) assumes that the initial two forms of bed are beds, then at least at this stage the TBA assumes self-predication. As in the TMA, the relevant self-predication assumption, so far as the move from (1) to (2) goes, requires no more than SP (the claim that any form of F is F). So at least at this stage we do not need a self-predication assumption that says how, in virtue of what, any form of F is F. So far, then, the TBA does not require NSP; BSP is again adequate as the relevant self-predication assumption.

So far we have seen that although the inference from (1) to (2) requires SP, it does not require OM-TMA or NI. Let us now consider the inference from (2) to (3). Strang thinks that this inference depends upon

denying SP. For in his view, the only reason Plato offers for denying that
the first two alleged forms are really forms is that they both have the
eidos of the third form. But, Strang thinks, '[t]he assumption behind this
must be that anything which has the *eidos* of A cannot itself be the Form
of A; and it follows from this that F(A) cannot itself be A. So it appears
that one of the premisses of the TBA is the denial of Self-Predication'.[43]
If Strang is right, then the TBA rejects one of the premisses of the TMA,
in which case it is not vulnerable to the TMA.

But although it is desirable for Plato not to be vulnerable to the TMA,
it is not desirable for the TBA to reject SP. For as we have seen, and as
Strang himself insists, the surrounding context assumes SP.[44] Indeed, we
have seen that the TBA itself assumes SP in the move from (1) to (2).
Nor need we convict Plato of both assuming and rejecting SP in some one
context. For contrary to Strang, Plato assumes that the third form of bed
is a bed. For he says that the first two forms of bed are beds, not because
they have the third form of bed, but because they have the *form of* the
third form of bed. This implies that the third form of bed has the form of
bed; if it has the form of bed, it is a bed. The TBA thus consistently
assumes SP.

In saying that the first two alleged forms of bed are not really forms
because they have the form of the third form of bed, Plato seems to be,
not denying SP, but assuming that:[45]

(SE) Any form of *F* is *F* in virtue of itself.

(I call this assumption 'SE' since it says, in effect, that any form of *F* is
self-explanatory.) SE implies that if there are two forms of bed, each is a
bed in virtue of itself. But given OM-TBA and NI-TBA, two 'forms' of
bed at the same level would be beds in virtue of something different from
themselves, and so they would not be forms after all.

We have now seen how Plato argues that the first two forms of bed are
not really forms. The same argument shows that there can be at most one
form of *F* at any given level.[46] For if there were more than one 'form' of
F at level *n*, then by OM-TBA they would all be *F* in virtue of a form at
level *n* + 1. But then the alleged forms of *F* at level *n* would not be *F* in
virtue of themselves, and so they would not really be forms.

To say that there can be at most one form of *F* at any given level is not
to say that there actually are any forms. So although Plato has justified
(3)'s claim that the first two alleged forms of bed are not forms, he has
not justified its claim that the third form of bed is genuinely a form.
Perhaps, for example, there are further (purported) forms of bed at its
level, in which case it would not genuinely be a form.

But perhaps in assuming that the third form of bed is genuinely a form,
and so the only form of bed at its level, Plato reasons as follows. Knowledge is possible, and it requires justification, which, in the sorts of

cases at issue here, requires explanation. Explanation must therefore be possible. We can explain why sensible Fs are F only if we know, and refer to, a form of F at level 1;[47] given SP, this form is itself F. Since knowledge must be based on knowledge,[48] we must know this form in order to know the sensibles it is invoked to explain. To know this form, we must be able to explain why it is F. Suppose that the explanation involves a form of F at level 2, and so on *ad infinitum*. But then, Plato believes, we could never explain why anything is F; for in his view, we can explain the F-ness of things only if something accessible to us is self-explanatorily F, F in virtue of itself. But only forms are F in virtue of themselves.[49] So, since knowledge is possible, there must be forms accessible to us. Let us assume that the forms accessible to us are at the level of the third form of bed; so (assuming that knowledge of beds is possible) the third form of bed is genuinely a form, in which case it is the only form of bed at its level. The inference to (3) has therefore now been justified.[50]

Since, as has just been argued, the third form of bed is the only form of bed at its level, OM-TBA does not require a further form over it.[51] So the TBA does not imply that there is more than one form of bed, and so it does not lead to the TMA regress. Indeed, not only does the TBA not give rise to the TMA, but it also rejects one of its key premises. For since the third form of bed is genuinely a form, it is a bed in virtue of itself. But this conflicts with NI, according to which nothing is F in virtue of itself. The TBA thus seems to depend, not on the denial of SP, but on the denial of NI.[52] I return to this point below, after the rest of the TBA has been discussed.

We have seen so far why the first two purported forms of bed are not forms after all and why the third form of bed is genuinely a form. Since the third form of bed is the first real form of bed we have encountered, let us from now on call it the first form of bed. It is then the one form in virtue of which sensible beds are beds.[53]

In (4) it is inferred that there is at most one form of bed. This inference is not yet licensed. All that has been argued so far is that there is at most one form of bed at any given level, and that there must be some level accessible to us at which there is exactly one form of bed. But this leaves open the possibility that there is more than one form of bed, for there might be exactly one form of bed at each of several different levels.[54] Unless Plato can rule out this possibility, he cannot establish U.

But perhaps Plato would argue as follows. We know that the first form of bed is a bed in virtue of itself. For it is genuinely a form, and every form of F is F in virtue of itself. If, however, there is also exactly one form of bed at the next-highest level, there would be nothing besides itself for it to explain. For the only other possibilities are that it would explain why either the first form of bed or sensible beds are beds. But the first form of bed explains these things.[55] Yet it is definitionally true that forms are the sorts of things that can explain some range of phenomena besides themselves.[56] There can therefore be at most one form of bed. The inference to (4) is then licensed.

(5) infers that there is exactly one form of bed. This does not follow from (4) alone; for to say that there can be at most one form of bed does not imply that there is exactly one form of bed. Perhaps there are no forms of bed at all. But we have seen that in order to justify the inference to (3), we had to supply a sub-argument whose conclusion is that there is at least one form of bed. From (4) plus the claim that there is at least one form of bed we can validly infer (5).[57]

Having explored the TBA in some detail, I can now provide a fuller formulation of it than the brief one with which I began:

TBA (final version):
(1) There are two forms of bed at a given level.   (Assumption)
(2) Any form of F is F.   (SP)
(3) Therefore the two forms of bed are both beds.
(4) All the F objects at level n (if there is more than one F object at that level) are F in virtue of exactly one form of F at level $n + 1$.
                                                                     (OM-TBA)
(5) Therefore all the F objects at level n (if there is more than one F object at that level) are F in virtue of a form of F that is at a different level.   (NI-TBA)
(6) Therefore the two forms of bed are beds in virtue of exactly one form of bed at the next-highest level; call it the third form of bed.
(7) Therefore neither of the first two forms of bed is a bed in virtue of itself.
(8) Any form of F is F in virtue of itself.   (SE)
(9) Not both: (6) and (8).
(10) Therefore not (1).
(11) Therefore there is at most one form of F at any given level.
(12) Knowledge is possible.
(13) Knowledge requires justification, and justification (in the sorts of cases at issue here) requires explanation.
(14) Therefore explanation is possible.
(15) We can explain the F-ness of things only if there is something accessible to us that is F in virtue of itself.
(16) Only a form of F is F in virtue of itself.
(17) Therefore for every F such that knowledge of Fs is possible, there is at least one form of F accessible to us.
(18) Knowledge of beds is possible.
(19) Therefore there is a level accessible to us at which there is exactly one form of bed.
(20) Assume that this is the level of the third form of bed.
(21) Therefore the third form of bed is genuinely a form, and so it is the only form of bed at its level.

(22) Any form of *F* must be such that it can explain some range of phenomena besides itself.

(23) If there were a form of bed in addition to the third form of bed, there would be nothing besides itself for it to explain.

(24) Therefore there is at most one form of bed.

(25) Therefore there is exactly one form of bed. (= U; from 19 and 23)

As I have reconstructed the TBA, it is a valid argument for U. But it includes the claims that any form of *F* is *F* in virtue of itself and that there are forms; hence it is inconsistent with the TMA's claim that nothing is *F* in virtue of itself (= NI). So far from the TBA's leading to the TMA, it shows us how to avoid the TMA. The TBA also shows us that Plato is not committed to the Accurate One over Many Argument. For G-Sep is a premiss of the Accurate One over Many Argument. But G-Sep implies NI. Since Plato rejects NI, he rejects G-Sep, in which case he is not committed to the Accurate One over Many Argument.

But perhaps I have made matters too easy for myself? Perhaps, although the TBA rejects NI, other passages are committed to it?[58] But the TBA's rejection of NI is not an isolated aberration. The whole thrust of the theory of forms counts against NI. For example, the Imperfection Argument—Plato's central argument for the existence of forms—is at least not committed to NI; and we have seen how reflection on it might naturally lead one to reject it. Further, I have been arguing that forms are properties and that Plato's version of SP is best interpreted as BSP; if I am right, then it would be natural for Plato to reject NI. For presumably anything that is *F* is *F* in virtue of having the (or a) property of *F*. Since Plato takes the property, form, of *F* to be *F* (in virtue of its explanatory role), it is *F* in virtue of having the (or a) property of *F*. But (as the TBA argues) there cannot be two forms—properties—of *F*. So if the property—form—of *F* is itself *F*, it must be *F* in virtue of itself. Perhaps the point of the TBA is to justify Plato's more or less unselfconscious assumption that there is at most one form per predicate. The assumption is eminently reasonable if forms are properties; the TBA none the less provides an argument on its behalf.[59] Further, we have seen that Socrates and Plato both assume that everything that is *F* is *F* in virtue of a (or, as they tend to say, in virtue of the) form of *F*. True, in saying this, they seem to have primarily sensibles, or non-forms, in mind.[60] But on the account I have given, it would be natural to include forms in the scope of 'everything'; it is just that, unlike sensibles, any form of *F* is *F* in virtue of itself. I conclude that we have more reason to suppose that Plato consistently rejects NI than that he was ever committed to G-Sep.[61]

If I am right to say that Plato avoids the TMA—indeed, that he rejects two of its premisses[62]—then perhaps Plato does not offer the TMA either as a record of honest perplexity or as a fatal objection to his theory. Perhaps he offers it in order to force us to clarify what sort of self-predication, non-identity, and one over many assumptions he actually

accepts. Once we are clear about this, we can see that he is not committed to the versions that are required for the TMA, and that the
versions to which he is committed do not compromise his view that
knowledge is possible.

5. Aristotle on Plato and the Third Man Argument

I have argued that Plato is not vulnerable to the TMA. But Aristotle
seems to think that Plato is vulnerable to it. In this section I explore the
sources of our seeming disagreement. We will see that, here as elsewhere,
the differences between us are in some ways not as great as they may at
first appear to be.

For a start, Aristotle seems to agree that the forms posited by the *Rep.*
523–5 version of the Imperfection Argument escape the TMA. For
he says that 'of the more accurate arguments, some produce ideas of
relatives, of which we say there is no in-itself class, and others introduce
the third man' (*Met.* 990b15–17). This suggests that Aristotle does
not think that the forms posited by the Argument from Relatives are
vulnerable to the TMA. For he says that *another* more accurate argument
—the Accurate One over Many Argument—gives rise to the TMA.
Further, although Aristotle raises various objections to the Argument
from Relatives, he never suggests that it gives rise to the TMA.[63] Nor is
this surprising. For the Argument from Relatives matches the restricted
Imperfection Argument: they both posit forms only in cases of narrow
compresence, and they do so on the ground that if something is *F* and not
F in the sense of narrow compresence, then it is imperfectly (not fully) *F*,
and so it must be *F* in virtue of a perfect (paradigmatic) form of *F*. Since
sensible equals are both equal and unequal, there is a form of equal; since
sensible men are not both men and not men (in the narrow sense),
neither the Argument from Relatives nor the restricted Imperfection
Argument posits a form of man. Perhaps Aristotle avoids formulating the
regress with 'large' because he sees that when Plato uses the Imperfection
Argument to argue that there is a form of large, he avoids the TMA.

But I suggested that Plato can avoid the TMA not only for large
but also for man. For he sometimes uses a broader version of the Imperfection Argument to argue that there is a form of man. When he argues
in this way, the form of man escapes the TMA in just the way in which
the form of large does. Aristotle, however, formulates the regress using
'man'. This suggests that although he agrees with me that the form of
large (at least sometimes) escapes the regress, he believes that the form
of man falls prey to it. Why might Aristotle believe this? I consider four
possibilities.

Owen suggests the following answer: Aristotle believes that (i) according to the Argument from Relatives, forms and sensibles are focally connected; (ii) Plato takes sensible men and the form of man to be synonymously men; and (iii) synonymy gives rise to the TMA.[64] But we have seen that although (ii) is true, (i) and (iii) are false. Aristotle seems to agree, for the Argument from Relatives takes sensibles and forms to be synonymous, yet Aristotle does not think that its forms are vulnerable to the TMA.

A second possibility is that although Aristotle agrees that synonymy does not give rise to the TMA, and that the forms posited by the Argument from Relatives escape the TMA, he does not think that Plato ever uses the Imperfection Argument as an argument for the existence of a form of man.[65] But Aristotle must surely know that Plato sometimes uses the Imperfection Argument quite broadly. For the Argument from Relatives says that paradigms and their likenesses are synonyms; and surely Aristotle knows that at least in the *Timaeus* Plato says that the contents of this world are copies of paradigmatic forms—where the contents include not just large things but also men and so on.[66] But perhaps Aristotle would reply in a by now familiar way: Plato says this, but it is an implausible view. For if the contents of this world are copies of paradigmatic forms, then something must have consulted forms in producing those contents, but nothing does. Of course, Plato disagrees; in his view, the demiurge consults forms in producing portions of the world. But Aristotle believes that this view is quite mistaken: in his view, Socrates' existence is not to be explained by invoking a designer; a man produces a man.[67] So perhaps Aristotle sees that Plato sometimes uses the Imperfection Argument quite generally; but perhaps he thinks that doing so involves Plato in such grave mistakes that he is entitled to discount this strand of Plato's thought.

Plato might reply that we need not rely on the demiurge in order to show that sensible men are imperfectly men; for they are imperfectly men in virtue of having features that are not essential to what it is to be a man. Here Aristotle might object that this fact is not enough to show that sensible men are imperfectly men; on the contrary, in Aristotle's view sensible men are primary substances, and this gives us at least one sense in which they are not imperfectly men. We can therefore not block the TMA by saying that sensible men and the form of man are men in different ways, in so far as the former are imperfectly men, the latter perfectly a man. If this is Aristotle's reasoning, then he once again disallows Plato one of his (Plato's) beliefs on the ground that he (Aristotle) thinks that it is false.

Here is a third possibility. Perhaps Aristotle agrees that the forms posited by the Imperfection Argument escape the TMA; and perhaps he even agrees that Plato sometimes uses the Imperfection Argument for all forms, including the form of man. None the less, he might argue, Plato has other arguments for the existence of forms, some of which give rise to the TMA. This would not be an entirely unreasonable suggestion. For we have seen that Plato sometimes—as in *Rep.* 523–5—might be taken to suggest that sensible men are perfectly men; at least, they are not both men and not men in the narrow sense. If at the same time Plato countenances a form of man, then we cannot block a second form of man by saying that sensible men and the form of man are men in significantly different ways since only the former are imperfectly men. In sect. 3 I wondered whether this was Eudemus' reason for suggesting that Plato is vulnerable to the TMA. The same response I made to him there is appropriate here as well. But Aristotle can say in reply that Plato is not careful to disentangle the different strands of his thought (sometimes he uses the Imperfection Argument in a way that produces a form of man, but sometimes he uses it in a way that does not do so; sometimes he takes sensible men to be perfectly men, sometimes he does not do so), in which case it is fair to combine these different strands to see what results.

We have also seen that the TBA uses a one over many assumption, a self-predication assumption, and a non-identity assumption. Although I argued that the TBA is incompatible with the TMA, it takes some work to see that this is so; and certainly Plato does not explicitly tell us how his actual one over many and non-identity assumptions differ from those involved in the TMA. Perhaps Aristotle would once again say that Plato does not do enough to explain the differences, and that he is under no obligation to give Plato distinctions he does not trouble to draw himself; and so it is fair to say that he is vulnerable to the TMA.

One final possibility. We have seen that outside the *Peri ideōn*, Aristotle says that Plato is vulnerable to the TMA because he treats a such as a this, universals as particulars. Forms are universals, Aristotle believes, because each is a one over many; and they are particulars because they are separate. Further, if forms are particulars then, given that Plato accepts SP, he is committed to NSP. If forms enjoy NSP, then they can be grouped together with sensibles in such a way as to require a further form.

But this line of argument involves at least two quite controversial claims. First, it is quite controversial to claim that separation implies particularity; the claim would be rejected by anyone who believes that there can be uninstantiated universals. Secondly, even if forms are particulars, and even if NSP is true of them, Plato could still avoid the TMA by saying that the form of *F* and sensible *F*s are *F* in fundamentally different ways—the form of *F* is perfectly *F*, whereas sensible *F*s are imperfectly *F*. If forms are particulars and enjoy NSP, then forms and sensibles are more on a par in *some* ways, in ways that might *seem* to require further forms. But it does not make the TMA impossible to avoid, for forms and sensibles can still differ in *other* ways that are sufficient for avoiding the TMA. Aristotle sometimes seems to agree, in so far as he seems to think that the Argument from Relatives is committed to NSP but avoids the TMA.

I conclude that here as elsewhere Aristotle neither misinterprets Plato nor offers a decisive objection to him; we can see this once we understand how complicated his argumentative strategy is. Part of his argument depends on intruding into Platonism claims Plato probably rejects but that Aristotle takes to be true (such as the claim that universals cannot exist uninstantiated). Part of it depends on disallowing Plato claims he accepts but that Aristotle takes to be false (for example, the claim that sensible men are imperfectly men). Part of it depends on disallowing Plato arguments he hints at but does not defend in sufficient detail (such as the version of the Imperfection Argument that applies to man no less than to large). Part of it depends on seeing what happens if one commits Plato to claims he does too little to rule out, even if he does not intend them (this might be Aristotle's strategy in interpreting *Rep.* 523–5 and the TBA). Aristotle presents his criticisms of Plato briefly, and one might think they are straightforward and simple. But, like Plato's arguments, they are highly compressed and presuppose a variety of complex and controversial moves. Once we uncover Plato's and Aristotle's background assumptions, we can see that once again it is not easy to decide how successful Aristotle's criticism is.

NOTES

NOTES TO CHAPTER 1

1. D. Harlfinger, 'Edizione critica del testo del "De Ideis" di Aristotele', in W. Leszl, *Il 'De Ideis' di Aristotele e la teoria platonica delle idee* (Florence, 1975), 15–39. Harlfinger excludes at least one passage that I take to be from the *Peri ideōn* (sect. VI in the Argument from Relatives; see below); see also sect. X in the Argument from Relatives, with n. 21.

2. In 1987 Gigon published a new collection of Aristotle's fragments, including the *Peri ideōn* fragments. But he simply reproduces Hayduck (though he omits Hayduck's critical apparatus) and takes no account of Harlfinger's text. Gigon also introduces his own new pagination, but I throughout use Hayduck's pagination, which is also used by Harlfinger and in all the translations known to me.

3. For discussion of the two recensions, see Harlfinger. The MSS are: O = Florence, Laur. 85. 1; A = Paris gr. 1876; C = Paris, Coislin 161; L = Florence, Laur. 87. 12; F = Milan, Ambros. F. 113.

4. In *Met.* 990b11–13.

5. '*toioutos*' often means 'such'. But Alexander often uses '*toioutos*' to mean '*houtos*' ('this'), which seems to be how he uses it here. Cf. LF 79. 2, '*houtoi*'; cf. Ch. 3.4.

6. Here '*toioutos*' perhaps indicates that the features just mentioned are characteristic of ideas. But LF 79. 7 has '*touto*', and the parallel passages at 79. 11 and 79. 15 have '*tauta*'; so another possibility is that '*toioutos*' again means 'this' (see n. 5).

7. That is, there will be such a thing as health itself.

8. Here Alexander refers back to the three Arguments from the Sciences just given: '*toioutos*', as often, refers to what immediately precedes. Cf. LF 79. 15, '*toutōn*'.

9. For this sense of '*ou pantōs*', see H. Bonitz, *Index Aristotelicus* (Berlin, 1870), 561a46.

10. If '*kai*' is translated as 'also', then Aristotle seems to say that the sciences are of *koina* as well as of forms. But he does not think that the sciences are of forms, since he denies that there are any forms. '*kai*' therefore seems to be emphatic.

11. '*husteros*' refers to the third Argument from the Sciences (79. 11–15) (and not, as *ROT* assumes, to the second one). Cf. LF 79. 21, '*ho tritos logos*'; Leszl, *Il 'De Ideis*', 120–1; and D. H. Frank, *The Arguments 'From the Sciences' in Aristotle's Peri Ideon* (New York, 1984), 26, n. *p*.

12. OAC has '*ti toutōn*', but it is difficult to see how to translate this. '*toutōn*' should have a back-reference, but the only possible back-reference is to the many *F*s. But the text then seems to say that what is predicated is among, i.e. is one of, the many *F*s. The point being made here, however, is that what

is predicated is *not* one of the many *Fs*. W. E. Dooley, *Alexander of Aphrodisias: On Aristotle, Metaphysics I* (London, 1989), 117, translates 'there must be something belonging to [all of] them'. (Cf. T. Penner, *The Ascent from Nominalism* (Dordrecht, 1987), 248: 'some being [belonging to all] of them'.) Dooley says in defence of his translation that '*toutôn* must be accounted for, and that the *ti kekhôrismenon* (something separated) "belongs to" the particulars is a valid statement, since, as Alexander has just pointed out, it is properly predicated of them. Cf. 88. 17–18 below: "the fact that one thing is predicated in reference to many, a thing that, [being] the same, belongs (*huparkhei*) to all of them", etc.' (n. 250). But that Dooley's translation yields 'a valid statement' does not mean that it is a possible translation of the Greek, and I am not sure that the simple genitive can indicate belonging to, in the sense of being predicated of. Perhaps the text should therefore be emended to follow Asclepius' close paraphrase: in place of '*ti toutôn*' he has '*touto*' (*in Met.* 74. 17). At any rate, my translation follows Asclepius.

13. *ROT* has 'the changing particulars'; Penner, *Ascent*, 248, has 'of the varying numerically different cases'. I explain and defend my translation in Ch. 8.2.

14. I follow Asclepius, *in Met.* 75. 5, in reading '*esti ti*'.

15. This is the only occurrence of '*eidos*' in *Peri ideōn* 1 (though cf. 87. 15); elsewhere, '*idea*' is used for Platonic forms.

16. I follow AC in omitting '*phantasma . . . ontōn*' in 82. 4–5.

17. Here (as elsewhere) LF differs from OAC in using '*katholou*' for universals. On Aristotle's ways of referring to universals, see esp. Ch. 2.2 n. 8.

18. I follow G. E. L. Owen, 'A Proof in the *Peri Ideōn*', in id., *Logic, Science, and Dialectic*, ed. M. Nussbaum (Ithaca, 1986; cited hereafter as *LSD*), 165–79 at 166, in reversing the main clause and the participial clause. Although this alters the syntax of the sentence, I do not think it alters its sense. Owen's translation is criticized by R. Barford, 'A Proof from the *Peri Ideon* Revisited', *Phronesis*, (1976), 198–219, and by C. J. Rowe, 'The Proof from Relatives in the *Peri Ideon*: Further Reconsideration', *Phronesis*, 24 (1979), 270–81. Although their translations (as well as Dooley's, 119) follow the syntax of the Greek more closely than mine does, they do not seem to capture its sense. I discuss the point of the sentence in Ch. 10.5.

19. Harlfinger deletes '*kai eikōn*' (83. 16). However, Terry Irwin has plausibly suggested that '*kai eikōn*' might be a corruption of '*kai ekei on*', in which case the phrase should be flanked by daggers rather than by braces. On this reading, the phrase indicates that whereas sensibles are here (*entautha*), forms are there (*ekei*). Cf. *Rep.* 500d4.

20. Harlfinger omits this passage, but, as I explain in Ch. 10 n. 69, the reasons that have been given for doubting whether it is from the *Peri ideōn* do not seem to me to be persuasive.

21. Harlfinger omits this passage. The passage might be Alexander reflecting on and recording *Met.* 990b16–17. But perhaps in *Met.* 990b16–17 Aristotle is repeating a claim he made in the *Peri ideōn*, in which case at least part of X is from the *Peri ideōn*.

22. As Alexander explains below, this passage is not from the *Peri ideōn* but from Eudemus' *Peri lexeōs*.

23. '*Toiauta*' at 83. 35 seems to indicate that what is predicated is 'such as' the things of which it is predicated in that they are all *F*.

24. OAC at this point reads '*par' ekeino*'; but a second hand in A reads '*par' ekeina*', which is printed by Hayduck. '*Ekeina*' is presumably motivated by the thought that what is predicated is different from all the things of which it is predicated, not merely from one of the things of which it is predicated. But '*ekeino*' presumably picks up '*tini*' in the previous line. And we can make sense of the singular as follows: what is predicated is different from any one of the things of which it is predicated. That is, consider any given thing of which the *F* is predicated: the *F* is different from that thing. It follows that the *F* is different from each of the things of which it is predicated.

25. One might have expected the plural rather than the singular (Dooley, 121, translates as though there were a plural). But the singular allows us to explain why there is a *third* man: the first man is the particular (i.e. any particular man; the passage takes particular men to be collectively the first man, or men at the first level, so to speak); the second man is the first form of man; and the third man is the second form of man. See Ch. 15 n. 65.

26. Since 84. 6 has the singular (*ton kath' hekasta*), presumably '*kai*' means 'or' rather than 'and'. Cf. J. D. Denniston, *The Greek Particles* (2nd edn., Oxford, 1954), 292, I(8).

27. Here Alexander resumes his account of the *Peri ideōn*. In between Eudemus' and Aristotle's versions of the Third Man, OAC records two other versions of the Third Man. They do not seem to be due to Alexander, nor are they relevant to us here; see Ch. 3 n. 22.

28. *ROT* unfortunately translates both '*pleiō*' and '*kath' hekasta*' as 'particulars'. But, as I explain in Ch. 14 n. 8 and in Ch. 15.4, the two phrases need to be distinguished or else the points of the Accurate One over Many Argument and of the Third Man Argument are obscured.

29. Like Harlfinger, I follow O in reading *ton* at 85. 1. AC, which is followed by Hayduck, has *tous*. Note the parallel singular at 84. 6; for its force both there and here, see n. 25.

30. That is, Alexander takes Aristotle's version of the Third Man to be the same as Eudemus'.

31. That is, the Third Man regress.

32. In OAC, 85. 11 has '*tetartō(i)*' (i.e. Δ); and 'fourth' is printed by Brandis, Bonitz, and Hayduck. However, V. Rose (*Aristotelis Pseudepigraphus* (Leipzig, 1863; cited hereafter as *Ar. Ps.*), 187 and 191; *Ar. Fr.*, fr. 188, p. 151) proposed substituting '*protō(i)*' (i.e. A). He is followed by E. Heitz, *Fragmenta Aristotelis* (Paris, 1869); P. Wilpert, *Zwei aristotelische Frühschriften über die Ideenlehre* (Refensburg, 1949) (cited hereafter as *ZaF*); W. D. Ross, *Aristotelis Fragmenta Selecta* (Oxford, 1951) (cited hereafter as *Ar. Fr.*); and Harlfinger.

33. That is, later in *Met*.

NOTES TO CHAPTER 2

1. It is conventional for those writing in English to use an initial upper-case letter in 'Form' (or, sometimes, 'form of (e.g.) Equality or form of the Equal')

in discussing Plato's allegedly distinctive forms, and an initial lower-case in discussing Socratic and Aristotelian forms and forms whose status is unclear. This was not, however, a convention in ancient Greek or in Latin, nor, for that matter, is it a convention in German (which always uses an initial upper-case for nouns). Nor shall I follow the convention. For it is motivated by the thought, which I reject, that Socratic and Platonic forms are different entities (rather than the same entities differently described). Further, even those who favour the convention sometimes disagree about when an initial lower- or upper-case is called for; rejecting the convention allows us to avoid making some awkward and controversial decisions.

2. It is disputed whether the *Peri ideōn* is by Aristotle, whether Alexander preserves portions of it, and whether it discusses Plato. I discuss these and related disputes in Ch. 3. Many other claims made in the present chapter are also controversial; they are defended in due course.

3. Indeed, it is sometimes argued that he has no theory of forms at all; see e.g. J. Annas, *An Introduction to Plato's Republic* (Oxford, 1981), 217, 233–40. G. Vlastos, *Socrates: Ironist and Moral Philosopher* (Ithaca, NY, 1991), Ch. 2, denies that Socrates has one. It is certainly true that Socrates and Plato do not systematically reflect on forms or integrate their various remarks about them. But they do say various things about forms, and it is these remarks I have in mind when I speak of their theories of forms.

4. This is sometimes disputed. For example, D. Gallop, *Plato's Phaedo* (Oxford, 1975), 95, while not disputing that Plato has something properly called a theory of forms, claims that the theory is 'everywhere assumed rather than proved'; see also R. Hackforth, *Plato's Phaedo* (Cambridge, 1955), 50.

5. W. D. Ross, *Plato's Theory of Ideas* (Oxford, 1951), 24; cf. 36, 225.

6. On the other hand, it is sometimes thought that forms are only particulars, in which case Plato would be a nominalist about the existence of universals; see D. Brownstein, *Aspects of the Problems of Universals* (Lawrence, Kans., 1973), Ch. 4. (I take nominalism to be the view that there are only particulars; there are no universals.) G. Vlastos, 'The "Third Man" Argument in the *Parmenides*', in R. E. Allen (ed.), *Studies in Plato's Metaphysics* (London, 1965), 231–63 (cited hereafter as 'TMA I'), at 252–3, believes that although forms are intended to be universals, Plato 'blurs' the distinction between universals and particulars; he thinks that separation partly explains Plato's confusion.

7. At least, it is the first such investigation by someone other than Plato. In the first part of *Parm.*, however, Plato explores various reasons for positing forms and various ways of characterizing forms. There are interesting connections between *Parm.* and the *Peri ideōn*; I explore some of them in what follows.

8. Plato and Aristotle use various words (e.g. *sēmainein*) that came to be used technically for 'meaning'; and they sometimes use such words to indicate linguistic meaning. But they do not use such words technically, nor do they use them only for meaning.

Although Plato does not have a word for universals, he does use the adverbial phrase *kata holou*, according to the whole (*Meno* 77a6). To examine virtue as a whole—*kata holou* or *katholou*—is to examine the characteristics common to all virtues. By contrast, to examine virtue part by part (*kata meros* or *kath' hekaston*) is to examine particular species of virtue (e.g. justice, courage) or particular virtuous people or actions (e.g. Socrates, this token action of standing firm in battle). Aristotle moves from such adverbial uses of '*katholou*' to substantival uses, so that what we examine as a whole (e.g. virtue) comes to be called a *katholou*, a universal, and what we examine part by part (e.g. particular species of virtue, and particular virtuous people and actions) comes to be called a *kath' hekaston*, a particular. (For more on *kath' hekasta*, see Ch. 5 n. 13.) For lucid discussion of this Aristotelian terminology, see J. Whiting, 'Aristotelian Individuals' (unpublished MS). Plato does not use '*kath' hekasta*' (although *So.* 259b almost has it; cf. also *Tht.* 188a). He instead uses '*ta polla*' or '*polla hekasta*' (for the latter, cf. *Rep.* 494a1, 507b2).

Although Aristotle's standard word for universals is '*katholou*', this word is not used in the OAC version of the *Peri ideōn*. Instead, Aristotle uses '*koina*' (79. 19; 83. 19 (omitted in Harlfinger); cf. 85. 21). LF, however, has '*katholou*' (cf. 79. 17 with 19; 82. 8; cf. also LF 83. 17–20 (printed in Hayduck but not in Harlfinger)). But in e.g. *EN* 1180b15, Aristotle uses '*koina*' and '*katholou*' interchangeably, so I assume that *koina* and *katholou* are the same. The *Peri ideōn* also speaks of what is predicated in common of particulars (*to koinōs katēgoroumenon tōn kath' hekasta*; 81. 9–10; cf. 84. 22–3); and in *DI* 17a39–40 (which I discuss further below) Aristotle defines *katholou* in very similar terms, as 'what is naturally predicated of more than one thing'. So I assume that 'what is predicated in common of particulars' also denotes universals. In *SE* 22 (179a8–9) Aristotle uses '*to para tous pollous hen ti*' for what is predicated in common, hence presumably for a universal. Cf. also *APo.* 77a1, *hen ti para ta polla*; 100a7, *hen para ta polla*; in *Met.*, 80. 14, *hen epi pollois*. (I use 'one over many' for these and related locutions—such as '*hen kata pollōn*' and '*hen epi pleionōn*' (*APo.* 77a5–9)— since the phrase is so well entrenched and since Aristotle does not seem to have any systematic distinction in mind in using the various locutions.) For more on Aristotle's use of the phrase 'one over many', see Ch. 5.2 and Ch. 8.2. For more on ways of referring to universals, see Ch. 3 n. 69.

9. For the distinction between these two conceptions of universals, see D. M. Armstrong, *Universals and Scientific Realism* (Cambridge, 1978), i, pp. xiii–xiv; Pears. (According to D. Pears, 'Universals', *Philosophical Quarterly*, 1 (1950), 218–27 at 219, '[t]hough Plato and Aristotle sometimes distinguished these two [conceptions of universals], it was characteristic of Greek thought to confuse' them. But in n. 5 he suggests that Aristotle's criticisms of Plato's theory of forms primarily assume the realist view.) Of course, some semantic conceptions are also realist; but so long as my terminology is understood it should do no harm, and my reasons for favouring it should become clear.

10. For contemporary realist accounts of universals, see Armstrong; S. Shoemaker, *Identity, Cause, and Mind* (Cambridge, 1984), Chs. 10–11; and M. Tooley, *Causation: A Realist Approach* (Oxford, 1987). Armstrong and Tooley believe that universals are discovered by science; Shoemaker believes they are discovered by philosophical reflection. Within this broad conception of universals, there is room for dispute both about which predicates denote universals, and also about what universals are like in more detail. For example, although the realist conception takes universals to be explanatory

properties, it need not (though it may) claim that universals must be instantiated. But even if it countenances uninstantiated universals, it none the less claims that every universal (whether or not it is instantiated) is explanatory by being, for example, the sort of thing that is referred to in a law of nature. Aristotle believes that a universal exists when and only when it is instantiated; see e.g. *Cat.* 14a7–10. By contrast, Armstrong believes that a universal can exist at a time *t* only if it is instantiated at some time or other (ii. 76). One of Tooley's main themes is that an adequate account of scientific laws requires the existence of universals that are never instantiated; see also P. Butchvarov, *Resemblance and Identity* (Bloomington, Ind., 1966), 183–197.

Properties are sometimes distinguished from species and types. I use 'property' more broadly, so that it includes all these types of entities. (Hence I sometimes say that e.g. man, and not just being a man, is a property.) Although it is often important to distinguish between them, the differences will not matter to us here since, among other things, neither Plato nor Aristotle distinguishes between them. The crucial point for our purposes is that on the realist conception universals are explanatory entities of roughly the sort that properties conceived in realist fashion have been taken to be. I shall use 'property', 'explanatory property', and 'genuine property' interchangeably. See also n. 22.

11. 'Grue' 'applies to all things examined before *t* just in case they are green but to other things just in case they are blue' (N. Goodman, *Fact, Fiction, and Forecast* (Indianapolis, 1965), 74). In saying that on the realist conception not every meaningful predicate denotes a universal, I assume that a predicate can be meaningful even if it does not denote a genuine property of things. That is, of the two criteria that I go on to discuss for determining what predicates are meaningful, I favour (i) over (ii).

12. Gallop, for instance, writes that the form of *F* is 'the one thing common to each of the many *F*s, the single feature *F*-ness shared by its many instances, the meaning of their common name. In this capacity, it functions as what later came to be called a "universal"'' (p. 96). (Actually, in this passage he takes forms to be both properties and meanings.)

13. Another possible view is that every meaningful general term denotes a universal, but universals are not the meanings of general terms. If one held this view, one might argue either that (*a*) universals must none the less exist if the corresponding general terms are to be meaningful, or that (*b*) universals need not exist for the corresponding terms to be meaningful. N. P. White, *Plato on Knowledge and Reality* (Indianapolis, 1976), 7, may suggest (*a*); for (*b*), see Ch. 8.

14. Here I have in mind ordinary linguistic understanding; and I am assuming that we can have ordinary linguistic understanding of '*F*' even if there are no *F*s. For this account of meaning, see H. Putnam, 'How Not to Talk about Meaning', in id., *Philosophical Papers* (Cambridge, 1975), ii. 117–30, esp. 126–30. Those who think that Plato takes forms to be the meanings of every general term generally have this notion of meaning in mind; see e.g. Gallop (above, n. 12). M. Frede, *Prädikation Und Existenzaussage* (Göttingen, 1967), esp. 92–4, thinks that Plato holds this view in *Rep.* 596a.

15. Frede (see n. 14) believes that Plato holds this view in *So*. Anyone who accepts a referential theory of meaning presumably accepts (ii), although the converse is not true. Among many who ascribe a referential theory of meaning, and so (ii), to Plato, see Owen, 'Notes on Ryle's Plato', in id., *LSD* 85–103, and 'Plato on Not-Being', ibid. 104–37 (who speaks, not of Plato's referential theory of meaning, but of his semantic atomism).

16. However, if one accepts a referential theory of meaning, one might deny that 'not-beautiful' is meaningful; at least, some referential theories of meaning have trouble accommodating meaningful negative predications. Further, perhaps anyone who infers from the fact that there are some not-beautiful things that there is a universal or form of not-beautiful would also believe that 'not-beautiful' denotes a genuine explanatory property of things.

17. Above, I discussed criteria for determining what predicates are meaningful. My present concern is the ontological status of meanings.

18. 'Abstract entity' is used in different ways; see D. Lewis, *On the Plurality of Worlds* (Oxford, 1986), 81–6. I use it here simply as a convenient label for the sort of entity meanings are taken to be by those who take them to be entities distinct from properties.

19. I assume that (e.g.) 'not-beautiful' is meaningful but does not denote a genuine property; but see n. 16.

20. S. M. Cohen, 'Plato's Method of Division', in J. M. E. Moravcsik (ed.), *Patterns in Plato's Thought* (Dordrecht, 1973), 181–91 at 187, may attribute this view to Plato.

21. To see that this is not merely an abstract difficulty that we need not worry about, consider the following seeming dispute about whether Socratic forms are universals. Aristotle says that Socratic forms are universals (see Ch. 4.3). But T. Penner, in 'The Unity of Virtue', *Philosophical Review*, 82 (1973), 35–68, and T. Irwin, in *Plato's Moral Theory* (Oxford, 1977) (cited hereafter as *PMT*), 306 n. 6 and 318 n. 24, argue that Socratic forms are not universals. Despite appearances, Penner and Irwin do not disagree with Aristotle about the nature of Socratic forms; rather, they disagree with him about the nature of universals. When Penner and Irwin say that forms are not universals, they mean that forms are, not meanings conceived as abstract entities, but such things as conditions of persons; the form of bravery, for example, is the feature of a person in virtue of which she is brave. But when Aristotle says that forms are universals, he does not mean that they are meanings conceived as abstract entities; he means that they are real, explanatory properties of things. Aristotle, that is, has a realist conception of universals (see n. 33). He therefore agrees with Penner and Irwin about the nature of Socratic forms; he disagrees with their account of universals. In *PMT* Irwin takes universals to be abstract entities existing outside space and time, and he assumes that what some have called scattered particulars—e.g. all the world's water—are not universals. But in *Aristotle's First Principles* (Oxford, 1988) (cited hereafter as *AFP*), he argues that Aristotle has a realist conception of universals, according to which universals are something like what others have called scattered particulars; see sect. 41 and p. 512 n. 11. The issue is even more complicated. For G. Vlastos, in e.g. 'The Unity of the Virtues in the *Protagoras*', in id., *Platonic Studies* (2nd edn., Princeton, 1981; cited here-

after as *PS*), 221–69 at 252, uses 'universal' as Penner and Irwin do; but he argues that Socratic forms are universals so conceived. So although he and Aristotle both *say* that forms are universals, whereas Penner and Irwin deny that they are, Penner and Irwin agree with Aristotle about the nature of forms, whereas Vlastos disagrees with them.

22. Although properties are sometimes viewed as a subclass of universals (the monadic ones), along with relations or polyadic universals, I shall speak interchangeably of properties and of universals. For the distinction between monadic and polyadic universals is not of central concern here; it is often more natural to use 'property' than 'universal'; and my proposed terminology corresponds to Aristotle's way of speaking. (Here I mean, not that Aristotle does not countenance both monadic and polyadic universals, but that he does not tend to say that universals fall into just two classes, monadic and polyadic. He tends to distinguish between substance and non-substance universals, or between universals in each of the ten categories; relational universals are universals in just one of the ten categories.) See also n. 10.

23. I intend this account of universals to correspond roughly to Aristotle's account of universals, which I discuss briefly in the next section. I do not, however, take it to be definitionally true that universals must be instantiated. Aristotle certainly believes that universals exist when and only when they are instantiated (see n. 10); but it is unclear whether he builds this into his definition of 'universal'; see n. 28.

24. Although there are more sophisticated versions of a referential theory of meaning than the one I consider here, they have not usually been associated with Plato, and so I shall for convenience generally speak of 'the referential theory of meaning' as though there were only one version. For the classic refutation of the referential theory of meaning so understood, see G. Frege, 'On Sense and References', in id., *Philosophical Writings*, trans. and ed. P. T. Geach and M. Black (Oxford, 1952). As he points out, the referential theory of meaning cannot accommodate the fact that there are co-referential but non-synonymous terms (such as 'The Evening Star' and 'The Morning Star'). To say that the referential theory of meaning is false is not to deny that what exists in the world is relevant to determining the meanings of terms; it is only to deny that the meaning of a term simply is its extra-linguistic bearer.

25. Of course if, as I believe, the referential theory of meaning is false, then nothing can in fact be both a property and a meaning. None the less, Plato might falsely believe that forms are both, or Aristotle might argue that Plato is committed to treating them as both.

26. Further, 'abstract entity' is used in different ways (see n. 18). As I explain below, not everyone views all the world's water as a universal.

27. Plato, for example, views souls as non-perceivable particulars; for Aristotle, the prime mover is a non-perceivable particular. In *Rep.* 5 the many beautifuls (*ta polla kala*, 479a3) are perceivable universals (e.g. bright colour, rather than e.g. the Parthenon). For places where Aristotle connects perception and universality, see e.g. *APo.* 100a17–b1; *DA* 424a21–4. For perception as directed to particulars rather than to universals, see e.g. *APo.* 72a; 81b6; 87b29–30 (though here Aristotle emphasizes that to perceive a particular is to perceive it as being of a certain kind—i.e. as exemplifying

some universal—rather than as being a particular as such); 100a17 (though here Aristotle also in some way connects perception to universals). See also J. M. Cooper, *Reason and Human Good in Aristotle* (Cambridge, Mass., 1975), 43; J. Barnes, *Aristotle's Posterior Analytics* (Oxford, 1975), 184–5. (Rather than saying that Plato and Aristotle believe that there are perceivable universals, it might be better to say that they believe that some properties are definable in observational terms or have instances that are accessible to sense-perception.)

Interestingly enough, however, although Aristotle countenances non-perceivable particulars outside the *Peri ideōn*, in the *Peri ideōn* he seems to assume that all particulars are perceivable. Since he takes particulars and universals to be exhaustive (see *DI* 17a38–b1, cited and discussed below), it follows that if something is not perceivable it is a universal. Although the *Peri ideōn* does not seem to countenance non-perceivable particulars, it seems to countenance observable universals, so, given our purposes here, we should still not take the distinction between particulars and universals to be that between the perceivable and unperceivable.

28. Aristotle's claim that universals are naturally predicated of more than one thing might mean either that (i) for something to be a universal, it must *actually* be predicated of more than one thing; or that (ii) for something to be a universal, it must be such that it *can* be predicated of more than one thing. If he means (i), then a given universal exists when and only when it is multiply instantiated. (So if just one man exists, the universal, man, does not exist; it exists when and only when more than one man exists.) Even if he means (ii), he clearly believes that (iii) for something to be a universal, it must actually be predicated (not necessarily of more than one thing, but) of something (see n. 10); but on (ii), he does not make it definitionally true that universals must be instantiated in order to exist. For some discussion, see Irwin, *AFP*, sects. 41 and 143; ch. 12 n. 44.

29. See n. 8.

30. Aristotle says here that water taken from the same spring is specifically but not numerically one. In his view, something is numerically one if and only if it is a particular (*Cat.* 4a11–17; *Top.* 103a8 ff.; *Met.* 1033b31). So if water taken from the same spring is only specifically one, it is a universal. (He might be taken to mean only that a given bucketful of water is not numerically one with another. But he seems to mean instead that all the water from the spring, taken together, is specifically but not numerically one.) By contrast, W. V. O. Quine, *Word and Object* (Cambridge, Mass., 1960), 98–9, says that all the world's water is not a universal but a scattered particular. Armstrong would also deny that all the world's water is a universal, since in his view if something is a universal, *all* of it must be in each of its instances (i. 111–13); he therefore accepts the position Plato takes to be 'the most impossible of all'. That Aristotle takes (at least some) universals to be something like what others take to be scattered particulars is suggested by Irwin, *AFP*, ch. 4 n. 11 (p. 512); see also G. E. M. Anscombe and P. T. Geach, *Three Philosophers* (Ithaca, NY, 1961), 31–2. On this account, Aristotle's distinction between universals and particulars resembles Strawson's distinction between general and particular; see P. T. Strawson, 'Particular and General', *Proceedings of the Aristotelian Society*, 14 (1953–4), 233–60.

31. In Ch. 9.5 and 6 I modify this claim, but not in a way that suggests that forms are meanings. For the contrast between semantic, metaphysical, and epistemological arguments for the existence of forms, see e.g. White, *Plato on Knowledge and Reality*, esp. pp. 6–10.

32. See n. 8.

33. For a defence of the claim that this is Aristotle's view of universals, see my 'The One over Many', *Philosophical Review*, 89 (1980), 197–240, sect. 3, and Irwin, *AFP*, sect. 41. For the view that Aristotle is a nominalist, see e.g. D. Sachs, 'Does Aristotle have a Doctrine of Secondary Substances?', *Mind*, 57 (1948), 221–5; B. Jones, 'Introduction to the First Five Chapters of Aristotle's *Categories*', *Phronesis*, 20 (1975), 146–72 at 167; and E. Hartman, *Substance, Body, and Soul* (Princeton, NJ, 1977), 17. A. C. Lloyd, *Form and Universal in Aristotle* (Liverpool, 1981), 259–60, takes Aristotelian universals to be classes. In subsequent chapters, I defend the view that Aristotle takes forms to be universals realistically conceived.

34. *Peri ideōn* 1 does not clearly claim that forms cannot change. But 98. 21 (in book 2's discussion of Eudoxus) may say that forms cannot change. (Whether it says this depends on the force of *akinētoi*; as I explain in Ch. 4.5, such words need not refer to unchangeability in the sense of succession of opposites).

35. Aristotle frequently insists that the possibility of knowledge requires the existence of universals; see e.g. *Met.* 1086b5–6, cited and discussed in Ch. 4. *Cat.* 14a7–10 says that if at any given time everyone were healthy, at that time health but not sickness would exist; so at least some Aristotelian universals can come into and go out of existence. But in e.g. *APo.* 73a29 (cf. 85b5–10), Aristotle claims that (many) universals are everlasting. *Met.* 1087a19–20 allows that some universals are perceivable *kata sumbebēkos*, but some universals are not perceivable at all. *Phys.* 224b5–16 says that *eidē kai pathē* do not move or change *kath hauto*, but Aristotle allows that they can change *kata sumbebēkos*, in so far as the things they are in change; cf. *Phys.* 211a17–23.

36. Aristotle criticizes the Platonists for separating forms in e.g. *Met.* 13. 9 (discussed in Ch. 4.6); see also *APo.* 77a5–9. He criticizes their view that forms are paradigms in e.g. *Met.* 991a20–b1; I discuss this criticism esp. in Ch. 13.4. He criticizes self-predication, at least indirectly, in criticizing the Argument from Relatives (see Ch. 13.2). His repeated insistence (see e.g. *Met.* 1038b8–11) that no universal can be a substance is aimed against Plato's view that forms (universals) are the basic, and so the most perfect, beings; I discuss Aristotle's view that universals cannot be substances esp. in Ch. 13.

37. Aristotle writes as though there are more than two more accurate arguments, but I shall throughout write as though the Argument from Relatives and the Accurate One over Many Argument are the only two more accurate arguments, since they are the only ones he mentions.

38. An argument is valid just in case its premises imply its conclusion. An argument is sound just in case it is valid and has all true premises. Aristotle's phrasing here is somewhat odd (*ex eniōn men gar ouk anagkē gignesthai sullogismon*). One might have expected him to say simply there *there is* no valid deduction rather than that no valid deduction *necessarily* results. But I take him to mean that the premises do not imply the stated conclusion.

39. In saying this, I assume that the less accurate arguments illustrate (i) and that the more accurate arguments illustrate (ii). (For (i) and (ii), see the passage cited above from *Met.* 1. 9.) I also assume a particular interpretation of the '*kai*' at 990b11. It can be understood in at least three ways, giving us three readings of (ii): (*a*) some arguments are not only invalid but also produce forms in undesirable cases; (*b*) some arguments produce forms not only in desirable cases but also in undersirable cases; (*c*) some arguments (although they are not, like the arguments in (i), invalid) also (like the arguments in (i)) produce forms in undesirable cases. I follow Alexander (see his illuminating discussion at 78. 1–25) in favouring (*c*)—though admittedly on (*c*) Aristotle is quite elliptical. (*b*) seems preferable to (*a*). For if (*a*) were correct, then Aristotle would not illustrate (i) in 1. 9 at all. (Alexander speculates that if, contrary to his own view, Aristotle does not illustrate (i) in 1. 9, the explanation might be that, since Aristotle believes that even the Platonists' better arguments fail, there is no need to spend time criticizing their less good arguments. Alexander also provides some suggestions about what arguments Aristotle might have in mind if (*a*) were correct; it is disputed whether the arguments he mentions were part of the *Peri ideōn*. Harlfinger prints 78. 13–18 as *dubia*.) Moreover, (*a*) in effect classifies 'the more accurate arguments' as invalid arguments for the existence of forms; but (as we shall see) Aristotle seems to believe that they are valid arguments for their existence. In 'Aristotle and the More Accurate Arguments', in Nussbaum and Schofield (eds.), *Language and Logos*, 155–77 at 157 n. 4, I unaccountably favour (*a*), which is exactly wrong for the interpretation of the structure of *Peri ideōn* 1 that I defended there, and also favour here.

40. If Aristotle takes the more accurate arguments to be valid but unsound arguments for the existence of forms, then he must reject at least one premiss of each argument. For the rejected premisses of the Argument from Relatives, see Ch. 10 nn. 36 and 51; for the rejected premiss of the Accurate One over Many Argument, see Ch. 14 n. 12.

41. Aristotle can instead be read as saying that the less accurate arguments are unsound arguments for the existence of forms but would become sound arguments if their conclusion were changed from 'And so there are forms' to 'And so there are Aristotelian universals'. But see Ch. 5 n. 2. Although Aristotle claims that the Arguments from the Sciences and the One over Many Argument are valid arguments for the existence of his own universals, in OAC no parallel claim is made on behalf of the Object of Thought Argument; but the claim is made in LF (82. 7–9). I argue in Ch. 9 that the Object of Thought Argument is a valid argument for the existence of Aristotelian universals, in which case the LF claim is warranted.

42. I discuss this passage in Ch. 10.9; its interpretation is controversial.

43. The structure is even more intricate than this. For example, one less accurate argument (the first Argument from the Sciences) and one more accurate argument (the Argument from Relatives) describe forms as paradigms; one less accurate argument (the One over Many Argument) and one more accurate argument (the Accurate One over Many Argument) describe forms as separate. Two different traits of forms are therefore considered from two different points of view.

44. Of course, any unsound argument with a true conclusion can be converted into a sound argument by changing its premisses. Aristotle's point is that in the case of the less accurate arguments the necessary revisions are quite minor. (In the case of the Arguments from the Sciences, perhaps no revision is necessary; see Ch. 5 n. 2.)

45. Owen generally accepts the first horn; see e.g. 'The Platonism of Aristotle' in id., *LSD* 200–20, 'Proof', and 'Dialectic and Eristic in the Treatment of Forms', in id., *LSD* 221–38. H. F. Cherniss, in e.g. *Aristotle's Criticism of Plato and the Academy* (Baltimore, 1944), generally accepts the second horn.

46. I do not think it is generally his strategy elsewhere either; but here I focus mainly on the *Peri ideōn*.

47. I therefore reject the view favoured by e.g. H. Karpp, 'Die Schrift des Aristotles Περὶ ἰδεῶν', *Hermes*, 68 (1933), 384–91 at 390; S. Mansion, 'La Critique de la Théorie des idées dans le ΠΕΡΙ ΙΔΕΩΝ d'Aristote', *Revue Philosophique de Louvain*, 47 (1949), 169–202 at 199; and P. Moraux, *Les Listes anciennes des ouvrages d'Aristote* (Louvain, 1951), 329, that Aristotle's objections in the *Peri ideōn* are purely 'immanent'.

NOTES TO CHAPTER 3

1. Some of the issues discussed in this and the following two sections are also discussed by Owen in his unpublished MS on the *Peri ideōn*, and my discussion is heavily indebted to his.

2. For lists of Aristotle's works, see Moraux, and I. Düring, *Aristotle in the Ancient Biographical Tradition* (Göteborg, 1957). Diogenes and Hesychius both rely on a catalogue that is generally ascribed to Hermippus. It is sometimes doubted whether Hesychius is the author of the catalogue generally ascribed to him; hence Moraux, for example, calls it 'le catalogue anonyme'. So instead of saying that the catalogue is to be found in the *Vita Hesychii*, it is sometimes (as by Moraux) said to be found in the *Vita Menagiana*, so called because it was first edited by Gilles Ménage as an appendix to his 1663 edition of Diogenes. Unlike Diogenes and Hesychius, Ptolemy *al-Gharīb* (see n. 3) seems to rely on Andronicus' catalogue.

3. Moraux, 24, no. 54; Düring, *Tradition*, 44, no. 54. (They also list a work called *Peri eidōn kai genōn*, but this is now thought to be *Topics*, book 4; see Düring, 43, n. on no. 31.) Düring, 44, in a note on no. 54, says that 'num idem sit atque liber *Peri ideōn* ab Alexandro aliisque citatus, valde dubium est'. Unfortunately, he gives no reasons for his doubt. But Moraux mentions and adequately rebuts two possible reasons for doubt: first, the titles cited in the lists that derive from Hermippus refer to a work in one volume, whereas Alexander and other commentators refer to a work in two volumes (though cf. the next note, on '*tetartō(i)*'); secondly, the titles cited in these lists use the singular, *Peri (tēs) ideas*, whereas the commentators use the plural, *Peri tōn ideōn* or *Peri tōn eidōn*.

   Against the first of these reasons, Moraux notes that different editors could easily have divided the work in different ways; this would not be an anomaly for the Aristotelian corpus. This reply gains supports if the three-volume work listed by Ptolemy *al-Gharīb* ('the Unknown'), *On the Forms, whether they exist or not* (Moraux, 295; Düring, 223, no. 15), is the same as that recorded by Diogenes and Hesychius. But the Arabic title *'Fārī 'aydūln'* indicates that the Greek text probably read *'Peri eidōlōn'*—though if it did, perhaps that was a misreading of *'Peri eidōn'*. (So Düring, 243, n. on no. 15, assumes; he does not ask whether the work is the same as the *Peri ideōn.* Moraux does not comment on the work.) Since there is no other evidence of an Aristotelian work *Peri eidōlōn*, or of a second work by Aristotle entitled *'Peri eidōn'*, considerations of economy favour the identification.

As to the second reason, not even the commentators give precisely the same title. Syrianus (see below) calls it *Peri (tōn) eidōn*, yet he makes it clear that he has in mind the same work that Alexander calls *Peri ideōn*. (This is doubted by F. Ravaisson, *Essai sur la métaphysique d'Aristote*, i (Paris, 1837), 74–5, on the ground that Syrianus says that the *Peri ideōn* was a two-volume work, whereas Alexander mentions four volumes. But see n. 4.) Nor is the use of the singular cause for concern. Aristotle, for example, uses both the singular and the plural in referring to the realm of ideas; indeed, in e.g. *Met.* 1078b9–10 he does so in the space of a single sentence (*peri tōn ideōn*; *tēn kata tēn idean doxan*; cf. Simplicius, *in Cat.* 105. 8–9: *peri tēs ideas*).

Moraux's own view is that the work listed in the catalogues can 'probablement' be identified with the *Peri ideōn* referred to by the commentators (p. 88).

4. *In Met.* 79. 4 refers to arguments from the first book of the *Peri ideōn*; *in Met.* 98. 21–2 to arguments from its second book. *In Met.* 85. 11 mentions arguments from its fourth book; but see Ch. 1 n. 32.
5. Interestingly, he calls his discussion of *Met.* 13. 4 '*ho peri tōn ideōn logos*' (103. 13). '*Peri ideōn*' is also the subtitle of Plato's *Parm.*: see Diogenes Laertius (3. 58). (The subtitles are not of Plato's own devising, but they seem to be at least as old as the tetralogical edition of Plato.)
6. Ps.-Alexander is now generally agreed to be the 12th-c. commentator Michael of Ephesus; see e.g. K. Praechter's review of *CAG* in R. Sorabji (ed.), *Aristotle Transformed: The Ancient Commentators and their Influence* (Ithaca, NY, 1990), 31–54.
7. *Apud* Ravaisson, i. 75 n. 1.
8. Heitz, 87; Proclus *apud* Philoponus, *De aeternitate mundi* 2. 2 (p. 31. 7 Rabe); Plutarch, *adv. Colotem* 14, 1115b. The Proclus passage is cited in Düring, *Tradition*, 329.
9. Moraux, 91.
10. *De Aristotelis Librorum ordine et auctoritate commentatio* (Berlin, 1854), 83.
11. There are, to be sure, some differences between the *Peri ideōn* and *Met.* 1. 9, but not ones that should lead us to doubt that Aristotle wrote the *Peri ideōn*. I discuss some of the relevant differences later.
12. Rose would presumably not like this way of putting my objection, since he denies that most of the criticisms are from the *Peri ideōn*; see Rose, *Ar. Fr.*, frr. 187–8, pp. 149–51. I take up this point below.
13. *Ar. Ps.* 186. I say 'at best' because (see below) he thinks that some of the arguments and criticisms recorded by Alexander are not from the *Peri ideōn*

even in the attenuated sense of being similar to its material. In what follows, I largely restrict my attention to Rose's arguments about *Peri ideōn* 1, though some of my points are more general. Against Rose's arguments, see also L. Robin, *La Théorie platonicienne des idées et des nombres d'après Aristote* (Paris, 1908), 604–5.

14. 80. 8, 81. 25, 82. 11, 83. 34. Karpp, 390, thinks the '*toioutoi*' introducing the Arguments from the Sciences indicates that we cannot be sure Alexander's versions of them are from the *Peri ideōn*; but although he cites Rose in his behalf, he differs from Rose in that he does not make a parallel claim about the other uses of '*toioutos*'. Perhaps he thinks the plural can more naturally be taken as Rose suggests. But the most natural explanation of the plural is that Alexander is recording several arguments from the *Peri ideōn*, not just one. Further, if, as Karpp seems to agree, the ensuing uses of '*toioutos*' have the force of '*houtos*', it seems reasonable to suppose that so too has '*toioutoi*'. Karpp also bases his claim on an implausible reading of '*toioutos*' at 83. 34.

15. LF apparently agrees: at 79. 2 it has '*houtoi*', and at 79. 15 it has '*toutōn*'. (Elsewhere, however, LF retains OAC's '*toioutos*'.) At 25. 14–15, Alexander uses '*dia toioutou*' where he clearly means the argument he goes on to record, not one similar to it. Cf. also 103. 5–6. (I owe these last two references to Owen, MS on the *Peri ideōn*.)

16. On the structure of *Peri ideōn* 1, see Ch. 2. 7. In subsequent chapters I argue that the *Peri ideōn* is insightful about Plato and fits well with Aristotle's view of Plato elsewhere.

17. *Ar. Fr.*, frr. 187–8, pp. 149–51. As we have seen, Rose says that none of the arguments or criticisms are directly from the *Peri ideōn*; they are only like arguments and criticisms to be found there. Perhaps his two claims are consistent in the following way: when he claims that none of the arguments or criticisms are from the *Peri ideōn*, he means that Alexander neither quotes nor paraphrases the *Peri ideōn*. When he claims that some of the arguments and their criticisms are from the *Peri ideōn*, he means that Alexander records material similar to that in the *Peri ideōn*.

18. Robin, 604–5.

19. R. Philippson, 'Il Περὶ ἰδεῶν di Aristotele', *Rivista di filologia e d'istruzione classica*, NS 14 (1936), 113–25 at 123. Part of his argument is based on his views about the date of the *Peri ideōn* and about Plato's development; I discuss this in sects. 6 and 7. Others take Plato's alleged desire for forms in cases where Aristotle claims that 'they' did not want them to support the view that the *Peri ideōn* is aimed against someone other than Plato; see sect. 5.

20. Philippson, 121; Rose, *Ar. Fr.*, fr. 187.

21. For further criticism of Philippson, see Cherniss, *Aristotle's Criticism*, 241 n. 145.

22. He ascribes the first version to Eudemus' *Peri lexeōs* (85. 13). Sandwiched in between his account of Eudemus' and Aristotle's versions of the Third Man Argument are two further versions: one is ascribed to some unnamed sophists, the other to the sophist Polyxenus in a version said to be recorded in Phanias' *Pros Diodōron* (84. 16). Cherniss, *Aristotle's Criticism*, 500–1, notes that these versions seem not to have been recorded by Alexander but to have been inserted later. As Cherniss notes, LF, Syrianus, and Asclepius disregard

them (although they were present in the text read by the Ps.-Alexander who wrote a commentary on the *SE*). Ross excludes 84. 16–21; Harlfinger includes it. It is unclear what grounds there are for including 84. 8–16 but excluding 84. 16–21. If Alexander did not include these versions, then presumably he recorded Aristotle's version directly after Eudemus'.

23. See Cherniss, *Aristotle's Criticism*, 226–7. n. 135.

24. The view that this material is in some sense from the *Peri ideōn* is also defended by P. Wilpert, 'Reste Verlorener Aristotelesschriften bei Alexander von Aphrodisias', *Hermes*, 75 (1940), 369–96, esp. 385–7. Ross's and Harlfinger's texts include this material. But there has been more dispute about two further passages, 85. 15–88. 2 and 97. 27–98. 21. The first concerns *Met.* 1. 9, 990b17–22, where Aristotle says that some arguments for the existence of forms are incompatible with the existence of principles; the second concerns 991a14–19, where he says that one could raise numerous objections to a theory of immanent forms, such as was held by Eudoxus. Alexander claims that the objections to immanent forms were also set out in the *Peri ideōn*, and he again claims to record some of them for us. (He does not explicitly assign the arguments about principles to the *Peri ideōn*, but that by itself is not grounds for suspicion.)

Karpp and Philippson deny that the arguments about principles are from the *Peri ideōn*. Cherniss, *Aristotle's Criticism*, 300–1 and n. 199, App. 6, allows that 86. 13–23 may be from the *Peri ideōn*, but he does not assign the rest of the passage to it. The main grounds for doubting a *Peri ideōn* source have been: (i) Alexander introduces his discussion by referring not to the *Peri ideōn* but to the *Peri tagathou*; if the discussion were from the *Peri ideōn*, presumably he would have said so. (ii) The arguments seem to involve views that are quite different from those discussed elsewhere in the *Peri ideōn*.

These arguments are countered, in my view fairly persuasively, by J. Annas, in 'Forms and First Principles', *Phronesis*, 19 (1974), 257–83. She argues, in brief, that (i′) the reference to the *Peri tagathou* shows only that Alexander (in her view, mistakenly) believes that the arguments he is now recording from the *Peri ideōn* are similar to those in the *Peri tagathou*; and that (ii′) the arguments do not in fact differ from materials discussed elsewhere in the *Peri ideōn*. (Even if they do, it is not clear why the *Peri ideōn* could not be thus wide-ranging.) Wilpert was the first to argue for the inclusion of these arguments ('Reste', 378–85; *ZaF* 97–118; in his review of *ZaF*, *Mind*, 61 (1952), 102–13, J. L. Ackrill criticizes Wilpert for including them); see also Mansion, 'Critique', esp. 196–8; E. Berti, *La filosofia del primo Aristotele* (Padua, 1962), 225–32.

For a discussion of the source of the arguments against Eudoxus, see Cherniss, *Aristotle's Criticism*, App. 7; he argues for a *Peri ideōn* source (though he says that Alexander gives 'the arguments only in the incomplete and compressed form of an abstract', p. 531; cf. 530). I agree with Cherniss's verdict; for given that Alexander seems to have had access to the *Peri ideōn*, and that he seems to be generally accurate in his account of the five arguments and their criticisms, it is unclear what grounds there could be for assuming that when he turns to the criticisms of Eudoxus, he suddenly veers away from the *Peri ideōn* despite his claim to be discussing it; it is also unclear why he should be inaccurate just in this particular case. For a more sceptical verdict, see R. Dancy, *Two Studies in the Early Academy* (Albany, NY, 1991), 28–35. For a reply, see my 'Ancient Metaphysics: A Critical Notice of R. M. Dancy's *Two Studies in the Early Academy*' *Canadian Journal of Philosophy*, 22 (1992), 393–410.

Although there is dispute about Alexander's sources and accuracy in these two cases, most of this material is now generally assigned to the *Peri ideōn*. (I say 'most' because a few passages are sometimes thought to be Alexandrian interpolations, though I am not convinced that all are.) Rose, Ross, and Harlfinger assign the arguments against Eudoxus to the *Peri ideōn*; Ross and Harlfinger, but not Rose, also assign the arguments about principles to it.

Since these arguments are now generally assigned to the *Peri ideōn*—and since even those who are sceptical about a *Peri ideōn* source generally think that Alexander is in any case recording Aristotelian material—I shall feel free to draw on them when it is appropriate to do so. Since I am inclined to believe that they are from the *Peri ideōn*, I shall generally write as though they are, but I shall not defend that assumption here.

25. See e.g. '*charaktēristikon*' and '*huphestanai*' in the discussion of the Argument from Relatives. Further, the arguments against Eudoxus may be only an abstract, presumably of Alexander's own devising (see n. 24).

26. See e.g. *in Met.* 7, for references to the *EN* and *APo*.

27. See e.g. 58. 31–59. 8; 91. 5–6.

28. See e.g. his discussion of homonymy, *in Met.* 51; see also 76. 10, 91. 12, 96. 35. Also, his whole discussion of the beginnning of 1. 9 is quite tentative, in a way that contrasts with the confidence he displays when he claims to be discussing the *Peri ideōn*.

29. See 103. 9: *hōs deixō*.

30. *The Riddle of the Early Academy* (Berkeley and Los Angeles, 1945), 31.

31. His solution to the riddle therefore matches his solution to the dilemma sketched in Ch. 2.8; see Ch. 2 n. 45.

32. Some key words and phrases, however, are sometimes associated with the unwritten doctrines: e.g. '*apeira*' in the second Argument from the Sciences, and the contrast between '*kath' hauto*' and '*pros ti*' in the criticisms of the Argument from Relatives.

33. I discuss some of her reasons in Chs. 6 and 10. Others, while not favouring any particular Platonist other than Plato, think that Aristotle did not himself devise the arguments for the existence of forms recorded in *Peri ideōn* 1; he simply records arguments that were formulated by others in the Academy. See e.g. Rose, *Ar. Ps.* 186; Wilpert, *ZaF* 27; J. Barnes, 'Editor's Notes', *Phronesis*, 30 (1985), 103. If they were right, then Aristotle's own original contribution would be limited to his brief criticisms of the arguments. (And we have seen that it has been doubted whether all those are his.) But I doubt that even this more nuanced view is right. Wilpert seems to have two reasons for his claim, neither of which is convincing: (i) he appeals to the use of 'we' in *Met.* 1. 9; and (ii) he suggests that if Aristotle had invented the arguments, he would not mention them so briefly in *Met.* 1. 9, as though they were generally familiar. As against (i), Aristotle often uses 'we' (and 'they') to

describe arguments he elsewhere ascribes to Plato in particular (see below, n. 34). As against (ii), if the *Peri ideōn* were generally known, it would not be surprising if Aristotle took its arguments to be familiar.

That the arguments Alexander records are so cleverly put together and that the overall structure of the *Peri ideōn* is so intricate also counts against Rose's and Wilpert's view; it makes more sense to suppose that Aristotle put together the arguments as he does in order to convey the moral described in Ch. 2.7. Further, the arguments are very schematic; they are the sort of thing a philosopher might well formulate in attempting to explain what he takes his target to be committed to. This is a pretty familiar way of evaluating what someone says, to say, 'Look, this is the real force of his argument', and then to present a schematic argument that brings out the real content of a more informal or less clear presentation.

Cherniss, *Aristotle's Criticism*, 234, writes, more moderately than Rose or Wilpert: 'None of these arguments to establish the existence of the ideas occurs in the Platonic dialogues in the form in which they are here reported by Alexander . . . It is possible, however, to find in Plato's own writings arguments which could easily have been developed into these demonstrations, whether such developments were the work of Plato himself or of one or another of his students in the Academy.' I am suggesting that Aristotle himself developed the arguments in the form in which they occur in the *Peri ideōn*, in an effort to (perhaps among other things) illuminate Plato's thought.

34. The only person Aristotle names in what remains of the *Peri ideōn* is Eudoxus. But in citing the first version of the Third Man Argument, Alexander names Eudemus; 84. 16–21 mention Phanias and Polyxenus, but these lines do not seem to be due to Alexander (see n. 22). As we shall see, Alexander, if not Aristotle, mentions Plato. W. Jaeger, *Aristotle: Fundamentals of the History of his Development*, trans. R. Robinson (2nd edn., Oxford, 1948), 197, argues that when Aristotle describes Platonist arguments using 'we', he views himself as a member of the Academy; when he uses 'they', he does not so view himself. Against this view, see Cherniss, *Aristotle's Criticism*, esp. App. 2; and J. Annas, *Aristotle's Metaphysics, Books M and N* (Oxford, 1976), 83–4. (But Cherniss's own explanation of Aristotle's use of 'we' in 1. 9 is weak; see p. 491.)

35. I discuss Aristotle's account of the flux argument in Ch. 4.5.

36. A brief paragraph (1078b32–1079a4) separates the discussion of the flux argument from our five arguments, but it seems simply to draw out an inference of the flux argument (or perhaps to record an argument similar to the flux argument—cf. '*hōste*', 1078b32; but also '*schedon*', 1078b32–3). We have no way of knowing whether this passage had a counterpart in the *Peri ideōn*. Although in 13. 4 Aristotle records the *Peri ideōn* material just after his account of the flux argument, he does not do so in *Met.* 1. He records the flux argument in 1. 6; but he does not get to the *Peri ideōn* material until 1. 9.

37. But see n. 33.

38. That Aristotle has Plato in particular in mind is perhaps also supported by the fact that he never (elsewhere) displays as deep an interest in other Platonists as in Plato, at least not when discussing forms. Further, Aristotle was referred

to as 'the Reader' (see Düring, *Tradition*, 108–9, 368–72). One reason for this may be that he read texts carefully, wondering precisely what they meant; see e.g. his discussion in *Pol.* 2 of what Plato means in various passages in *Rep.* This perhaps makes it more likely that the *Peri ideōn* aims to understand a written source (in my view, Plato's dialogues) than that it simply records arguments floating about in the Academy. It is also worth remarking that there was no fixed theory of forms; Speusippus, for example, appears to have rejected any theory of forms, and Eudoxus' theory of forms is quite different from Plato's. So it is not clear that there is a source other than Plato who might have formulated precisely the arguments that Aristotle records in the *Peri ideōn*—unless he did so in order to understand Plato; but then, why suppose that Aristotle simply writes up someone else's account of Plato's real commitments?

39. As I mentioned in sect. 2, one scholiast on Dionysius Thrax also claims that the *Peri ideōn* is aimed against Plato in particular.

40. I owe this point to Alan Code. See also the last paragraph of sect. 4.

41. H. Jackson, 'Plato's Later Theory of Ideas', *Journal of Philology*: I, 10 (1882), 253–78; II, 11 (1882), 287–331; III, 13 (1885), 1–40; IV, ibid. 242–72; V, 14 (1885), 172–230; VI, 15 (1886), 289–305. He suggests e.g. that *Pol.* is the source of the Arguments from the Sciences; see I, 279–80 n. 1. He also argues that although *Phd.* and *Rep.* countenance forms corresponding to every general term, the late dialogues reject forms of artefacts, negations, and relatives—the very cases for which Aristotle says that 'they' do not want forms. See e.g. IV, 242. (Philippson agrees about this; but he does not take the claim that they deny that there are such forms to be from the *Peri ideōn*.)

42. The early dialogues are generally thought to be *Ap.*, *Cri.*, *Eu.*, *Ch.*, *La.*, *Lys.*, *HMi.*, *Eud.*, *Ion*, *Prot.* The transitional dialogues are *Gorg.*, *Meno*, *HMa.*, *Crat.* The middle dialogues are *Phd.*, *Symp.*, *Rep.*, *Phdr.* The late dialogues are *Parm.*, *Tht.*, *Tm.*, *Crit.*, *So.*, *Pol.*, *Phil.*, and *Laws*. Some scholars favour a tripartite division into early, middle, and late. The dates of some dialogues are disputed; in particular, some place *Tm.* in the middle group rather than, as I have done, in the last group. I discuss this matter briefly in 'Owen's Progress: A Review of *Logic, Science and Dialectic*', *Philosophical Review*, 97 (1988), 373–99; see also Ch. 16.3. For the best discussion of the dating of the dialogues (though based only on stylometrics), see L. Brandwood, 'The Dating of Plato's Works by the Stylistic Method: A Historical and Critical Survey', Ph.D. thesis (University of London, 1958); see also his *Word Index to Plato* (Leeds, 1976) and, most recently, *The Chronology of Plato's Dialogues* (Cambridge, 1990).

43. In what follows, I restrict my attention to developmentalist and unitarian accounts of the features of forms relevant to *Peri ideōn* 1. It is of course possible that a particular developmentalist or unitarian view of these features of forms is correct, but that the corresponding view of e.g. ethical theory or of other features of forms is incorrect. Although there are different developmentalist and unitarian accounts, for the sake of simplicity I shall generally use 'developmentalist' and 'unitarian' for the particular versions of the accounts that I go on to consider.

44. It is difficult to find pure advocates of the unitarian and developmentalist accounts just described. But for something like the developmentalist account see Ross, *Plato's Theory of Ideas*, 11–21, 228–31; G. E. L. Owen, 'The Place of the *Timaeus* in Plato's Dialogues', in id., *LSD* 65–84; 'Proof', 'Platonism', and 'Notes'; Ackrill, 'Συμπλοκὴ εἰδῶν', in G. Vlastos (ed.), *Plato: A Collection of Critical Essays*, i: *Metaphysics and Epistemology* (New York, 1971; cited hereafter as *Plato I*), 208 (though Owen and Ackrill do not discuss the Socratic dialogues); C. Strang, 'Plato and the Third Man', in Vlastos (ed.), *Plato I*, 198; and H. Teloh, *The Development of Plato's Metaphysics* (University Park, Pa., and London, 1981). W. J. Prior, *Unity and Development in Plato's Metaphysics* (London and Sydney, 1985), defends a more moderate version of developmentalism.

    In 'TMA I', Vlastos seems to think that Plato did not revise his theory of forms in response to the *Parmenides'* criticisms; to this extent, he is (in this article) a unitarian about the middle and late dialogues. But he believes there are significant differences between the Socratic and middle dialogues; see 'Socrates', *Proceedings of the British Academy*, 74 (1988), 89–111, and *Socrates*, ch. 2. In 'The Relation of the *Timaeus* to Plato's Later Dialogues', in Allen (ed.), *Studies in Plato's Metaphysics*, 363, Cherniss argues that the late dialogues do not abandon paradigmatism. P. Shorey, *The Unity of Plato's Thought* (Chicago, 1903), 32, and R. E. Allen, *Plato's Euthyphro, and the Earlier Theory of Forms* (London, 1970), 136, believe that the forms in both the early and middle dialogues are separate.

45. Vlastos and Owen believe this; but Cherniss does not. The different verdicts are partly explained by the fact that Vlastos and Owen interpret the middle dialogues differently from Cherniss. If Vlastos's and Owen's interpretation were correct, it would be reasonable to conclude that the theory of forms involves serious error.

46. For a defence of the claim that the views Aristotle ascribes to Socrates are the views he finds in the Socratic dialogues, see Vlastos, 'Socrates'; W. D. Ross, 'The Socratic Problem', *Proceedings of the Classical Association*, 30 (1933), 7–24.

47. W. D. Ross, *Aristotle's Metaphysics* (Oxford, 1924), i, introd., sect. ii, seems to agree.

48. Another small piece of evidence in favour of the view that Aristotle does not take the late dialogues to have a different theory of forms from the middle dialogues, so far as the features relevant to *Peri ideōn* 1 go, might be that in *Met.* 1. 6 Aristotle says that Plato first became acquainted with Heracleitus' views in his youth, views he continued to accept 'later' (987a33–b1). Perhaps 'later' indicates that Aristotle believes that Plato, from the *Phd.* on, held essentially the same theory of forms. However, it is not clear how much later Aristotle means; and anyway, the remark applies only to Plato's Heracleiteanism, not necessarily to other features of the theory of forms.

49. It is disputed whether Plato did actually ever identify forms with numbers and, if he did, where and when he did so. (In the *Phil.*? In the so-called unwritten doctrines? In 'Platonism and Mathematics: A Prelude to Discussion', in A. Graeser (ed.), *Mathematics and Metaphysics in Aristotle* (Berne, 1987), 213–40, M. F. Burnyeat argues that the identification occurs

as early as *Rep.*) I make no claims about Aristotle's accuracy in saying that Plato, or some Platonists, identified forms with numbers; my point is only that when he believes that Plato changes his views, he does not hesitate to say so.

50. See n. 42.

51. There are some important differences between *Tm.* and middle dialogues (see e.g. the discussion of separation in Ch. 4.6), but they are not ones that give comfort to developmentalists.

52. For a qualification to the claim about separation, see Ch. 4.6.

53. I explain later why, despite saying this, I do not think Aristotle is guilty of misinterpretation.

54. This is a main thesis of Philippson's article. I. Düring advocates this view in *Aristoteles: Darstellung und Interpretation Seines Denkens* (Heidelberg, 1966), 49, although he gives no reasons in its favour. In his edition of the *Protrepticus* (Göteborg, 1961), 287, he favours the reverse dating, although he suggests that the other dating is possible; again, he gives no reasons for his dating. His fullest discussion of the relative dating of the *Peri ideōn* is in 'Aristotle and Plato in the Mid-Fourth Century', *Eranos*, 54 (1956), 109–20, where he seems to think that the *Peri ideōn* was probably but not certainly written after *Parm.*

55. See e.g. Moraux, esp. 328–33 (he also criticizes Philippson's arguments, as does Cherniss, *Aristotle's Criticism*, 538–9); D. J. Allan, 'Aristotle and the *Parmenides*', in I. Düring and G. E. L. Owen (eds.), *Aristotle and Plato in the Mid-Fourth Century* (Göteborg, 1960), 143. Leszl, *Il 'De Ideis'*, 352, says that Aristotle wrote the *Peri ideōn* at about the age of 30; this would date it at about 354, and so after *Parm.* but before some of the late dialogues. Owen seems to believe that the *Peri ideōn* was written while Aristotle was still a member of the Academy (see e.g. 'Logic and Metaphysics in Some Early Works of Aristotle', in id., *LSD* 188–99 at 199); but so far as I can tell, he does not commit himself to any view about the dating of the *Peri ideōn* relative to that of *Parm.* or other late dialogues. He believes that the late dialogues significantly revise the theory of forms in ways that reflect sensitivity to *Parm.*'s criticisms; but he does not explicitly say whether he believes that the alleged revisions were partly inspired by the *Peri ideōn*.

56. Jaeger, *Aristotle*, 16, dates *Parm.* after *Tht.*, but he gives no reasons for doing so. J. McDowell, *Plato: Theaetetus* (Oxford, 1973), is also inclined to that dating; see his notes to 142a–143c, 176b7–177a8, 183e7–184a1, 203e2–205c3. His main reason seems to be that he takes *Tht.* to be incorrect on an issue about which he takes *Parm.* to be correct. But since *Tht.*'s error occurs in a dialectical context, the error need not be Plato's own; it might be required by the position he is criticizing. The main reason for dating *Parm.* before *Tht.* is that at 183e *Tht.* alludes to a meeting between Socrates and Parmenides; the most reasonable explanation is that this is a back-reference to *Parm.*, which records a dialogue between Socrates and Parmenides. (The main alternatives are that (i) *Tht.* alludes to an historical meeting between Socrates and Parmenides, not to the fictional one recorded in *Parm.*; but although this is just about historically possible, it does not seem very likely; (ii) *Tht.* refers ahead to *Parm.* (so Jaeger, 16; see also McDowell); the

reference was added after *Parm.* was written. Neither (i) nor (ii) seems as plausible as supposing that *Parm.* was written before *Tht.*) Brandwood dates *Tht.* after *Parm.*

57. This date for *Tht.* seems firm, since *Tht.* begins by saying that Theaetetus has just recently died; and we know he died in 369. However, we do not know how 'recently' Plato means, so although we can be confident that *Tht.* was written later than 369, we do not know how much later.

58. There is dispute, however, about whether he left just before or just after Plato's death, and about the reasons for his departure. For some discussion, see Owen, 'Philosophical Invective', in id., *LSD* 347–64.

59. See Philippson, 121. Düring, 'Aristotle and Plato in the Mid-Fourth Century', 112, writes that '[n]o reasonable explanation has hitherto been offered of the fact that Aristotle in his *Peri ideōn* criticizes the theory of Ideas almost exactly along the same lines as Plato in the Parmenides without even men-tioning that dialogue or Plato's name or the fact that Plato dismissed these objections as not valid. Why did Plato, who always sets his scene and chooses his actors and speakers with artistic art and a certain purpose, introduce a young man called Aristotle as interlocutor?' In this article, however, Düring does not conclude that the *Peri ideōn* was written before the *Parmenides*; and indeed (in this article, though not always elsewhere) he if anything seems to favour the reverse dating (see n. 54). G. Ryle, *Plato's Progress* (Cambridge, 1966), 290, suggests that Plato's reference to an Aristotle is to his 'new hero', our Aristotle. Against the identification, see Moraux, 332; F. M. Cornford, *Plato and Parmenides* (London, 1939), 109 n. 1. Cherniss, *Aristotle's Criticism*, 292–3, canvasses various explanations of the fact that Aristotle does not cite Plato as the author of the Third Man.

60. See Moraux, 334. As David Sedley has pointed out to me, however, there is at least one exception: the *Phaedo* mentions Phaedo.

61. See Ross, *Aristotle's Metaphysics*, introd., sect. ii, p. xxxix.

62. This is sometimes denied; see the references cited in Ch. 2 n. 47.

63. Philippson would protest that most of the criticisms do not come from the *Peri ideōn*; I criticize that view above.

64. We have seen that Philippson favours the view that the *Peri ideōn* was written even before *Parm.*

65. In *Peri ideōn* 2, Aristotle criticizes Eudoxus for countenancing immanent forms on the ground that, unlike the forms in the middle dialogues, immanent forms can move and change. Philippson argues that in *So.*, Plato takes forms to be immanent; but unlike the forms in the middle dialogues, these forms are mobile and capable of change. Philippson concludes that *So.* revises the theory of forms to take account of the *Peri ideōn*'s criticism. But contrary to Philippson, *So.* does not claim that forms can move or change. (See Vlastos, App. I to 'An Ambiguity in the *Sophist*', in id., *PS* 270–322; contrast Owen, 'Plato and Parmenides on the Timeless Present', in id., *LSD* 27–44.) Or again, the *Peri ideōn* says that Eudoxan forms must be capable of mixing with one another. In Philippson's view, the middle dialogues deny that forms can mix with one another, whereas the late dialogues admit various sorts of mixture. Unlike Philippson, however, I think the middle dialogues allow that forms can mix with one another. In other cases, too, I should argue that

either the late dialogues do not contain the views Philippson believes they do, or else they do not differ from the middle dialogues in the ways he supposes they do.

66. This seems to be Owen's view; see e.g. 'Logic and Metaphysics', 199. Unfortunately, he gives no reasons for his view. W. Jaeger, in his review of Wilpert's *ZaF*, *Gnomon*, 23 (1951), 246–52, allows that the *Peri ideōn* may have been written while Aristotle was in the Academy. This is quite interesting. For in *Aristotle*, Jaeger defends the view that Aristotle began as a loyal Platonist, and only developed anti-Platonic views after he left the Academy. The *Peri ideōn* is anti-Platonic; so if Jaeger allows that it was written while Aristotle was still in the Academy, he concedes that his account of Aristotle's development requires significant qualification. (Jaeger's view of Aristotle's development is criticized by Owen in 'Platonism'.) Leszl, *Il 'De Ideis'*, 352, says that the *Peri ideōn* was written when Aristotle was around 30—so around 354. Moraux, 334, thinks the *Peri ideōn* was written 'dans les dernières années de Platon', and after 355/4. (Eudoxus is supposed to have died in 355/4; he is the only philosopher Aristotle names in the *Peri ideōn*. Moraux speculates that Aristotle would hesitate to criticize Plato by name while he was still alive.) This would presumably place it after *So.* and *Pol.*, and perhaps after *Phil.* as well. C. J. de Vogel, 'The Legend of the Platonizing Aristotle', in Düring and Owen (eds.), *Aristotle and Plato in the Mid-Fourth Century*, 248–56 at 254, thinks the *Peri ideōn* was written 'shortly after 347—perhaps a few years earlier'. Wilpert, *ZaF* 10, thinks it 'might well' (*dürfte*) have been written in the first years after Plato's death. Mansion, 'Critique', 169, accepts Jaeger's view (in *Aristotle*) that Aristotle began as a loyal Platonist, and so she places the *Peri ideōn* at the beginning of his anti-Platonic phase, and so presumably (although she does not say so explicitly) after Plato's death. So all these authors date the *Peri ideōn* relatively early in Aristotle's career, and most but not all date it before the *Laws*; but they disagree about a more precise dating.

67. We have seen that this is Philippson's view. Relatedly, Karpp, 391, favours an early dating on the ground that the *Peri ideōn* does not refer to the view that forms are numbers. However, if 85. 15–88. 2 is from the *Peri ideōn* (see n. 24), then this consideration loses some of its force. Even if the *Peri ideōn* does not mention the view that forms are numbers, it does not follow that it is an early work; for even if Aristotle knew about a later phase of Plato's thought, he might wish to focus on an earlier phase.

68. For this ground for a late dating, see Mansion, 'Critique', 169; and n. 66 above.

69. For Aristotle's various ways of referring to universals, see Ch. 2 n. 8. Although *Cat.* discusses universals, it does not call them '*katholou*'. *Top.* uses '*katholou*' only adverbially and not as a noun. *APo.* uses '*koina*' not for universals as such but for principles that are common (by analogy) to several sciences, as opposed to *idia*, principles restricted to a single science: see e.g. 76a37–b2; 77a26–31. (Similarly, in *Tht.* 184–6, Plato contrasts *koina*, properties common to the objects of more than one sense, with *idia*, properties special to a given sense.) In *SE* 22, Aristotle says that to avoid the Third Man, one should deny that what is predicated in common (*to koinē(i)*

katēgoroumenon is a this (*tode ti*) (179a8–11; cf. 178b38); in a parallel passage in the later *Met.* (7. 13, 1038b35–1039a3), he uses '*katholou*' interchangeably with 'what is predicated in common'. (The claim about *Met.* 7. 13 has been challenged.)

70. *Cat.* counts heads and hands (3a29–32, 8a13–28), bodies (2b1–2), logs (8a23), and honey (9a33) as substances; in later works, some of these count as matter, and so not as (the best) substances. For some discussion, see Irwin, *AFP*, sect. 40. Nor does *APo.* 2. 11 mention matter when it discusses the four causes. (But Barnes argues that *APo.*'s account is 'a sophisticated and not a naïve version of the notion of material explanation' (*Posterior Analytics*, 216). If this were correct, then one might argue that the failure to mention matter is not—at least, not in this case—evidence of an early dating, though Barnes does not himself argue this.)

71. For example, the Argument from Relatives contrasts homonymy and non-homonymy (i.e. synonymy); *Cat.* opens with that contrast. It is interesting to note that the *Peri ideōn* uses terminology and distinctions not to be found in Plato. For example, unlike Plato, it uses '*kath' hekasta*'. In his criticisms of the Argument from Relatives, Aristotle adverts to a theory of categories not to be found in the dialogues. (Some ancient commentators think the ten categories can be found in Plato. Alcinous, *Didaskalikos* 6. 10, for example, tells us that they may be found 'in the *Parmenides* and elsewhere' in Plato.) The *Peri ideōn* uses '*koina*' as a general term for universals; although Plato uses '*koina*', he does not use it as a general term for universals. All this might suggest that the *Peri ideōn* is later than Plato's late dialogues, on the ground that the terminology became current only after Plato's death. But there is no reason to suppose that every member of the Academy used just the same terminology; perhaps Aristotle invented the terminology while Plato was using other terminology, or perhaps he took over Academic distinctions that Plato, for whatever reasons, did not care to use.

   J. M. Cooper assumes an early dating for the *Peri ideōn* and appeals to the similarity between it and *MM* in defending an early dating for the latter; see 'The *Magna Moralia* and Aristotle's Moral Philosophy', *American Journal of Philology*, 94 (1973), 327–49 at 339–42. One might reverse his strategy and argue that since *MM* is early (as can be argued on other grounds), its similarity to the *Peri ideōn* suggests that the *Peri ideōn* is also early.

72. This consideration presupposes that Alexander reliably preserves the style of the *Peri ideōn*. Further, since some of the criticisms in *Met.* 1. 9 rely on the *Peri ideōn*, this consideration is not very telling.

73. This assumes that Alexander faithfully preserves most of the *Peri ideōn*.

NOTES TO CHAPTER 4

1. I discuss these passages in more detail in 'Separation', *Oxford Studies in Ancient Philosophy*, 2 (1984), 31–87, which also defends many of the points I make about Socrates, and about separation in sect. 6, in more detail.

2. In the corresponding part of the text, Aristotle uses 'ideas' rather than 'forms'. But he uses 'idea' and 'form' interchangeably in speaking about

Platonic forms (the next passage I discuss, for example, begins with 'forms' and ends with 'ideas'), and I shall generally use 'form' rather than 'idea'.

3. Aristotle also claims that Plato separated definitions, but I take him to mean that Plato separated the *objects* of definition. In just the same way, Aristotle sometimes uses *logos* to refer to the thing or property defined rather than to the defining formula itself; see e.g. *Phys.* 193a31, *GC* 335b7, *Met.* 1042a28.

4. I take the material enclosed in square brackets to be implicit in the argument.

5. See Ch. 2. n. 8.

6. In Ch. 7.5 I distinguish between narrow and broad compresence.

7. For a defence of the view that Socrates focuses on compresence in universals rather than in particulars, see A. Nehamas, 'Confusing Universals and Particulars in Plato's Early Dialogues', *Review of Metaphysics*, 29 (1975), 287–306. It is arguable that in the moral sphere (to which Socrates largely restricts himself) not all the corresponding action tokens or character instances exhibit narrow compresence. A given token action of standing firm in battle, for example, might be only courageous and not also not courageous; a given token action of returning what one owes might be just and not also not just, even if the action-type of returning what one owes has both just and unjust tokens.

8. Cf. also *Prot.* 332b4–7, 360c1–7 (the former uses the dative case; the latter uses *dia*); *Meno* 72c8 (*di' ho*), 72e4–6 (dative); *HMa.* 294a8–b4 (*hō(i)*)).

9. Socrates seems to believe that *everything* that is *F* is *F* in virtue of just one property of *F*. By contrast, Aristotle argues that although healthy people are healthy in virtue of one property of health, healthy diets are healthy in virtue of another. Healthy things are therefore healthy in virtue of different properties of health. But he believes that these different properties are systematically related to one central focus, that of health. He agrees with Socrates that adequate definitions cannot simply list examples; but he does not agree that this shows that everything that is *F* is *F* in virtue of some one property. He offers focal connection as an alternative both to Socrates' insistence on one property and to definitions phrased in terms of examples. For the focal connection of health, see *Met.* 1003a34–6. In e.g. *EN* 1.6 (see also *EE* 1236a22–30), Aristotle criticizes Plato for ignoring focal connection. I discuss Aristotle on focal connection in Ch. 10.3; see also my 'Owen's Progress', and T. Irwin, 'Homonymy in Aristotle', *Review of Metaphysics*, 34 (1981), 523–44.

Socrates' view is also criticized by Wittgenstein; see e.g. *The Blue and Brown Books* (Oxford, 1958), 20; *Philosophical Grammar*, trans. A. Kenny (Oxford, 1974), sect. 76. In the first passage, he criticizes Socrates for not even considering examples in attempting to formulate adequate definitions; he may also mean to criticize Socrates for not believing that correct definitions consist simply in listing examples. (The first criticism misinterprets Socrates; the second criticism interprets him correctly, though it does not follow that we should favour Wittgenstein's alternative view of the nature of correct definitions.) For a useful discussion of Wittgenstein's and Plato's views about the role of examples in definitions, see M. F. Burnyeat, 'Examples in Epistemology: Socrates, Theatetus, and G. E. Moore', *Philosophy*, 52 (1977), 381–98.

10. For the classic distinction between real and nominal definitions, see J. Locke,

An Essay Concerning Human Understanding, ed. P. Nidditch (Oxford, 1975), III. iii, vi, x, IV. vi. 4–9, xii. 9. The realist view of Socratic definitions is defended by Penner, 'The Unity of Virtue', and by Irwin, *PMT*, ch. 3; and my discussion is indebted to theirs. (But Penner defends a causal view, according to which Socratic forms are causally efficacious. I prefer to speak of the realist view. For as Vlastos points out in 'What did Socrates Understand by His "What is *F*?" Question?', in id., *PS*, 410–17, Socrates recognizes forms in non-causal contexts, e.g. in mathematics. However, Vlastos then fallaciously infers that forms are 'purely logical' entities (p. 413) that are never even causally relevant. What seems true to me is that (i) forms are real essences, i.e. explanatory properties that are real features of things; and that (ii) in some (but not all) contexts, forms, real essences, are causally relevant. I defend these views in more detail in 'Forms as Causes: Plato and Aristotle', in Graeser (ed.), *Mathematics and Metaphysics*, 69–112.) The meaning view is defended by e.g. Vlastos, in 'The Unity of the Virtues', 252 ff., and in 'What did Socrates Understand?'.

11. Of course, what ordinary people mean by '*F*' might capture what *F* really is. But the two can pull apart. In Socrates' and Locke's view, the two quite frequently pull apart, since on their view many of our ordinary conceptions are inadequate.

12. D. Bostock, *Plato's Phaedo* (Oxford, 1986), 69–72, may disagree.

13. For denials of knowledge, see, among many such passages, *Ap.* 21b2–5; *Ch.* 165b5–c2; *La.* 186b8–c5; *Gorg.* 509a4–6; *Meno* 71a1–7.

14. See e.g. *Ch.* 159c1, 160e6; *La.* 192c5–7; *Prot.* 349e3–5, 359e4–7. In all these places Socrates tests various accounts of a virtue against the belief that virtue is admirable (*kalon*), good (*agathon*), and beneficial (*ōphelimon*). See also *Meno* 87e1–3.

15. In the *Laches* (197ac), for example, he is ready to jettison the widely shared belief that lions are courageous, on the ground that lions do not know what courage is; for in Socrates' view, such knowledge is necessary for being courageous.

16. That Socrates believes this emerges most clearly in the *Meno* (71b3–4). It is disputed whether he believes this in all the earlier dialogues. For a defence of the view that he does, see Irwin, *PMT*, ch. 3. For a defence of the view that he does not, see R. Kraut, *Socrates and the State* (Princeton, NJ, 1984), ch. 8. I discuss the *Meno* on this matter in 'Inquiry in the *Meno*', in R. Kraut (ed.), *Cambridge Companion to Plato* (Cambridge, 1992), 200–226.

17. Socrates' view that knowledge requires some sort of account emerges most clearly in the *Meno* (98a); see my 'Inquiry in the *Meno*'. There is dispute about whether he means that all knowledge requires *justification* or *explanation*. My own view, which I shall not defend here, is that he takes all knowledge to require justification, but also believes that in many (though not clearly in all) cases justification requires explanation. (He believes, e.g. that in order to know that a particular action is just, one must know the nature of justice. But he does not so clearly believe that in order to know, say, what my name is, I need to know an explanation of, say, what a person is. Here perhaps knowledge requires only justification of a less demanding sort.) However, since only cases in which knowledge requires explanation are

relevant here, I shall often write as though Plato takes all knowledge to require explanation.

18. See Ch. 2.4.

19. Aristotle describes his conception of *epistēmē* in e.g. *APo.* 1. 2. He distinguishes between real and nominal definitions in e.g. *APo.* 93b29–94a10, a passage which also makes it clear that the starting-point of demonstration, and so of *epistēmē*, is real definition, since only real definitions explain why things are as they are and, as *APo.* 1. 2 insists, knowledge involves understanding why things are as they are. For some discussion, see T. Irwin, 'Aristotle's Concept of Signification', in Nussbaum and Schofield (eds.), *Language and Logos*, 241–66.

20. Plato never uses the phrase 'one over many' (*hen epi pollōn*; *hen para polla*). But he contrasts the one and the many, and he sometimes says that forms are *para* various things. (*Parm.* 132a11–12 has *epi toutois au pasin heteron*; 132c3 has some one thing which is *epi pasin.*) The phrase 'one over many' is Aristotelian (see e.g. *APo.* 77a5–7, 100a7). As Aristotle uses the phrase, 'one' denotes a universal and 'many' denotes particulars. (By contrast, we have seen that as Socrates uses 'many', it includes both particulars and lower-level universals (e.g. this particular square object and also square as such, which is a lower-level universal than shape). Plato also uses 'many' in this broader way.)

In Aristotle's view, not every argument for the existence of a one over many—i.e. for the existence of universals—is a one over many argument. For example, although each of the arguments in *Peri ideōn* 1 is an argument for the existence of a one over many, Aristotle does not call each of them a 'one over many argument'. An argument is a one over many argument just in case it argues that the fact that many things are *F* (or share the predicate 'F') requires the existence of some one thing, the *F*, in virtue of which they are *F*. By contrast, the Arguments from the Sciences, for example, posit the existence of universals by appealing not to the mere fact that many things are *F* but to epistemological considerations.

In distinguishing between Socrates' epistemological and one over many arguments for the existence of forms, I follow Aristotle, who likewise distinguishes between them. But the two arguments are obviously closely linked.

21. Vol. i, pp. xiii–xiv. In Ch. 2.3 I discussed the two conceptions of universals involved in these two arguments; but I did not distinguish between two versions of a one over many argument, which is my present concern.

22. See Penner, 'The Unity of Virtue', and Irwin, *PMT*, ch. 3. See also C. C. W. Taylor, *Plato: Protagoras* (Oxford, 1976), 103–8 (though Taylor is less sure than Penner and Irwin are that Socrates is clear about the difference between sense and reference; see pp. 106–7). In 'Plato on Naming', *Philosophical Quarterly*, 27 (1977), 289–301, I in effect argue that *Crat.*—which contains an extended discussion of names, and of language more generally—does not involve a referential theory of meaning, or confuse sense and reference. If *Crat.* articulates Socrates' views, then it provides further evidence that he is not committed to a referential theory of meaning and does not confuse sense and reference. By contrast, Vlastos, 'The Unity of the Virtues', 227, claims that neither Socrates nor Plato ever distinguishes between sense and reference.

But even if they do not draw the distinction explicitly, they might rely on it; and Socrates seems to do so if, as I believe, he takes the virtue terms to be co-referential but non-synonymous. (For Vlastos' reply to Penner, Irwin, and Taylor, see his 'What did Socrates Understand?'.)

23. White, *Plato on Knowledge and Reality*, 9, agrees that semantic considerations are not 'wholly explicit' in the Socratic dialogues, but he believes that *Meno* 72–4 and *Eu.* 5c8–d5 suggest such considerations 'less openly'. On the account of these passages that I have defended, however, they are not semantic. For both passages concern the 'What is *F*?' question, which asks not for the meaning of '*F*', but for a real definition of *F*. Perhaps in mentioning the *Meno* passage, White has in mind 74d5–6, where Socrates tells Meno that since he calls various things by the name 'shape', Meno should be able to tell him what shape is. But Socrates seems to mean only that since Meno thinks that there are various shapes, he should be able to tell Socrates what shape is—it is the fact that the name applies to something, rather than the fact that there is such a name, that suggests that shape is something. To say that if a name, '*F*', applies to something, there is such a thing as *F*-ness does not imply that every general term denotes a property or form, or that forms are the meanings of the terms to which they correspond, or even that forms are relevant to explaining the meanings of general terms.

24. See n. 20 on the scope of one over many arguments. Recall that I use 'property' for *genuine* properties.

25. In *La.* 192ab, for example, Socrates argues that just as speed is some one thing, so too is courage. In *Meno* 72a–74a, he argues that just as being a bee is some one thing, so too is virtue.

26. Contrast Vlastos, *Socrates*, 66, who holds that Socratic forms are non-sensible.

27. Allen, by contrast, thinks that *Met.* 1. 6 'implies that Socrates identified the objects of definition with sensibles, which is another way of saying that he did not distinguish Forms from their instances' (*Plato's Euthyphro*, 134; cf. 136). But *Met.* 1. 6 says only that Socrates did not take them to be non-sensible, which leaves open the possibility that Socrates did not take them to be sensible either—he was uncommitted either way.

Even if Aristotle means that Socrates took the objects of definition to be sensible, it would not follow that he thought that Socrates did not distinguish them from sensible particulars (which is what Allen seems to mean by 'instances'). For Aristotle believes that there are not only sensible particulars but also sensible or observable properties or universals (see Ch. 2.4). And in *Met.* 13. 9, he commends Socrates for acknowledging the existence of universals as entities distinct from particulars, since 'it is not possible to acquire knowledge without the universal' (1086b5–6). If Aristotle claims both that Socrates recognized the existence of universals and also that he took them to be sensible, then the sensibles at issue here should be sensible universals rather than sensible particulars.

28. Indeed, Aristotle himself recognizes different sorts of separation; in *Met.* 1042a26–31, for example, he distinguishes between unqualified separation (*chōriston haplōs*) and separation in account (*chōriston logō(i)*). Unless otherwise noted, I restrict myself here to unqualified separation, since when he discusses separation in connection with Socratic and Platonic forms, this is

generally what he has in mind, as, for example, in the second and third of the *Met.* passages (the first passage does not mention any sort of separation). (In Ch. 13 I discuss definitional independence; but in the passage under consideration, Aristotle uses, not any form or cognate of '*chōriston*', but '*kath' hauto*'.) Aristotle speaks of forms existing separately (*chōris*), of their being *chōrista*, and of their being separated *(kechōrismena)*. '*-tos*' endings can either express a settled state or have a modal sense; so to say that forms are *chōrista* could be to say that they are separate or that they are separable. When Aristotle says that forms are *chōrista*, I take him to mean that they are separate, although, as I go on to say, I think that in his view A is *chōriston haplōs* from B just in case A can exist whether or not B exists—actual separation, that is, is modal. Since in the contexts that concern us '*chōriston*' means 'separate', I take it to be interchangeable with '*kechōrismenon*'.

D. Morrison, 'Χωριστός in Aristotle', *Harvard Studies in Classical Philology*, 89 (1985), 89–105 at 92–3, speculates that Aristotle coined the word '*chōriston*', probably some time after *Cat.* and *Top.*, which do not use the word. But '*chōriston*' occurs in the *Peri ideōn* (85. 22; cf. 80. 12; 84. 23) and so, possibly, earlier than the *Cat.* and *Top.* (Morrison suggests that perhaps it 'crept in where it was not originally written' (p. 92) or that perhaps the *Peri ideōn* is not so early after all.) It seems unlikely that Aristotle coined the word. For although it seems to occur first in Aristotle, Vlastos, *Socrates*, 263, points out that in *Parm.* Plato repeatedly uses '*chōris*'; he also uses '*achōristos*' (*Rep.* 524c1), '*chōrizein*' (*Phd.* 67c6), and other forms and cognates of the word. So it seems reasonable to suppose that '*chōriston*' was in general circulation.

29. I take 'A exists independently of B' to be equivalent to 'A can exist whether or not B exists'. To say that A is separate from B is compatible with saying that B is separate from A. If A is separate from B but B is not separate from A, then A is not only separate from but also ontologically prior to B. Ontological priority implies separation, but separation does not imply ontological priority.

30. This can be interpreted in more than one way. For example, it might mean that (*a*) if a form of *F* is separate, then, for all *t*, it can exist whether or not there are any *F* sensible particulars at *t*; or that (*b*) if a form of *F* is separate, then there is a *t* such that it can exist at *t* whether or not there are any *F* sensible particulars at *t*. On (*a*), if forms are separate they can exist whether or not they are ever instantiated by the corresponding sensible particulars. On (*b*), if they are separate they can exist without always being instantiated by the corresponding sensible particulars. Aristotle probably believes that Platonic forms can exist whether or not they are ever instantiated by the corresponding sensible particulars; but even (*b*) distinguishes forms from his own universals since in his view universals exist when and only when they are instantiated.

31. In these two passages, '*kath' hekasta*' and '*aisthēta*' denote only particulars.

32. Hence the claim that forms are separate is weaker than the claim that they can exist uninstantiated *tout court*. If forms can exist uninstantiated, they are separate, but the converse is not true.

33. If Socrates believes that a form can exist *only* if it is in something, then he

rejects separation; for the view that he believes this, see Vlastos, *Socrates*, 74; cf. pp. 55–66, 72–80. (By contrast, in 'The Unity of the Virtues', 252, Vlastos says that Socratic forms or universals are not 'ontological dependencies of persons'; this seems to say that they exist independently of sensible particulars, in which case they are separate.) But although Socrates assumes that forms are in things, I do not see that he commits himself to the view that they would not exist unless they were in things.

34. By contrast, Allen, *Plato's Euthyphro*, 136, argues that Socrates separated forms.

35. See e.g. *Prot.* (330c3–e2, where justice is said to be just, and piety pious); *HMa.* 291d1–3 (beauty 'will never appear ugly to anyone anywhere'—though even if it never appears ugly, it does not follow that it appears beautiful); *Eu.* 6e3–6 (the *eidos* of piety is pious) and, possibly, *Eu.* 5d1–5 (but cf. Vlastos, *Socrates*, 57 n. 48); *Lys.* 217ce. As I go on to suggest, commitment to self-predication also seems to be tacit or assumed elsewhere.

    As I use 'self-predication', only those sentences of the form 'the *F* is *F*' that express class membership are self-predications. Further, on my usage self-predication does not say how it is that the form of *F* is *F*—whether by being predicated of itself or in some other way. As Vlastos notes, this makes the label 'self-predication' misleading; but since it is so well entrenched, I shall retain it. See Vlastos, Addendum to 'TMA I', 263; and 'Plato's "Third Man" Argument (*Parm.* 132a–b2): Text and Logic', in id., *PS* 342–65 at n. 36 (hereafter cited as 'TMA II').

    Even if SP does not say how the form of *F* is *F*, one might think that we have already seen that Socrates is committed to the view that it is *F* in virtue of itself. For he says that *everything* that is *F* is *F* in virtue of some one thing, the form of *F*. So, since the form of *F* is *F*, it must be *F* in virtue of itself. Call the claim that any form of *F* is *F* in virtue of itself *self-explanation* (SE). But when Socrates says that everything that is *F* is *F* in virtue of some one thing, 'everything' seems to indicate the many *F*s. This is not to say that Socrates rejects SE; he probably did not consider it. I shall ignore it here as well until Ch. 16.

36. More precisely, Socrates believes that endurance no more explains why one thing is courageous than why another thing is not. For in his view the only real—or, at least, the ultimate—explanation of anything's being *F* is the one thing by which all *F*s are *F*. But it will be convenient to speak as I do in the text.

37. To say that if *x* explains *y*'s being *F*, it is itself *F*, though perhaps in a different way from the way in which *y* is *F*, is not to say that *x* and *y* are *F* in different *senses* of '*F*'. To illustrate the difference between different ways of being *F* and different senses of '*F*': horses and cows are animals in different ways, but 'animal' means the same in 'Horses are animals' and in 'Cows are animals'. 'Seal', however, means something different as applied to the seals in a zoo and the Great Seal of the United States; see S. Peterson, 'A Reasonable Self-Predication Premise for the Third Man Argument', *Philosophical Review*, 82 (1973), 451–70 at 464. I elaborate on this point below in discussing Plato on *SP*; see also Chs. 10, 15, and 16.

    If *x*'s explaining *y*'s being *F* is a *sui generis* way of being *F*, then Socrates' view of self-predication is not refuted by the fact that e.g. saccharine tastes bitter but makes other things taste sweet. Nor does saccharine therefore suffer narrow compresence of opposites, since it is not both sweet and bitter in virtue of some one and the same aspect of itself. It is sweet because it makes other things taste sweet; it is bitter because of its own taste.

38. C. C. W. Taylor interprets Socrates' notion of self-predication in a somewhat similar way, saying that 'if justice is seen as a force in a man causing him to act justly, it is by no means *obviously nonsensical* to describe it . . . as just' (pp. 119–20; contrast pp. 112–13). See also Irwin, *PMT* 306 n. 6. However, they seem to think that Socrates takes the form of justice, for example, to be just in the very same way in which a person is just.

39. For this point, see Peterson, 466.

40. That Socrates revises ordinary beliefs was one count in favour of the view that Socratic definitions are real rather than nominal definitions; see above, sect. 3. The way in which Socrates revises beliefs supports the suggestion that although he takes the form of *F* and sensible *F*s to be *F* in different ways, he does not take them to be *F* in different senses of 'F'. For when he revises beliefs about the nature of *F*-ness, he does not take himself to be giving a new sense to the predicate 'F'. Rather, he is uncovering what he thinks we in some sense meant all along. For this point, see my 'Immanence', *Oxford Studies in Ancient Philosophy*, supplementary volume (1986), 71–97 at 85.

41. In Plato, see e.g. *Ap.* 23b1; *Gorg.* 525c6–7; *So.* 251a7; *Phdr.* 262c9; *Pol.* 277d1; *Laws* 663e9. In Aristotle, see e.g. *Top.* 151b21, 157a14, 15.

42. In discussing Plato in this chapter I largely restrict myself to the middle dialogues, since (like Aristotle in *Met.*) I am focusing on the origins of the theory of forms. Note that I am asking, not what sorts of change Plato mentions in the middle dialogues, but only what sorts of change he takes to require the existence of forms.

43. Except when I explicitly contrast GCH with succession, I count it as a type of succession.

44. For this example, see Herodotus, *History*, 3. 38. Aristotle might not agree about this particular example, but it is the *sort* of example he has in mind. It is also significant that Aristotle speaks of Plato's *Heracleiteanism*; and both Plato and Aristotle take compresence of opposites to be a Heracleitean concern. In Plato, see e.g. *HMa.* 289a, *So.* 242e2–3; in Aristotle, see e.g. *EN* 1155b4–6 and 1176a5–8; *Top.* 159b31, *Phys.* 185b20. This by itself is not decisive, however, since Plato and Aristotle need not think that Heracleitus' interest in compresence is an interest in change. But Plutarch (DK, B91) seems to interpret the river fragment—which many interpret in terms of succession—in terms of compresence: 'or rather, neither again nor later, but *at the same time* it comes together and ebbs away'. Plato may interpret the river fragment in this way in *So.* 242e2–3.

45. For a modern parallel, consider P. T. Geach's use of the phrase 'Cambridge change', defined as follows: 'The thing called "*x*" has changed if we have "F(*x*) at time *t*" true and "F(*x*) at time *t*¹" false, for some interpretations of "F", "*t*", and "*t*¹"' (*God and the Soul* (London, 1969), 71). Geach points out that this criterion yields the result that I change when I come to be shorter than you in virtue of your growth. Perhaps in the same way, Plato and

Aristotle use '*gignetai*' and so on in a broad way, sometimes to indicate what we would view as genuine change through time, sometimes to indicate compresence. (Unlike compresence, Cambridge change occurs only over time. But compresence can be described as occurring over time. In any case, the crucial parallel is that 'change' can be used to cover cases that do not pick out what we should intuitively count as genuine changes.)

46. For (i) (read with EH), see F. M. Cornford, *Plato's Theory of Knowledge* (London, 1935), 99–101; Cherniss, *Aristotle's Criticism*, 211–18 (cf. 'The Relation of the *Timaeus*', 349–60); R. Bolton, 'Plato's Distinction between Being and Becoming', *Review of Metaphysics*, 29 (1975), 76–7; for (ii), see Irwin, *PMT*, ch. 6, and 'Plato's Heracliteanism', *Philosophical Quarterly*, 27 (1977), 1–13; for (iii), see Annas, *Aristotle's Metaphysics M and N*, 154–5.

47. The strongest evidence for EH in the middle dialogues is *Phd.* 78d10–e4, translated and discussed below. For arguments against the view that Plato ever took sensibles to be in EH, see Irwin, 'Plato's Heracleiteanism'.

48. For arguments against supposing that Aristotle takes Plato to rely on EH in arguing that there are forms, see Irwin, 'Plato's Heracleiteanism', esp. 11–13.

49. See e.g. Owen, 'Proof'; Irwin, *PMT*, ch. 6, and 'Plato's Heracleiteanism'.

50. I discuss *Phd.* 74bc further in Ch. 11 n. 26.

51. See e.g. *HMa.* 289a2–c6, 293b5–e5; *Phd.* 102bd.

52. Proclus, *in Parm.* 4. 852–5, also takes the motivation for the theory of forms to be compresence rather than succession.

53. Plato may sometimes have particulars in mind. *Phd.* 74bc, for example, seems to say that a given stick is both equal (to some things) and unequal (to others). *HMa.* 289a2–c6 may say that a beautiful girl is also ugly. (For an alternative interpretation according to which only sensible properties are at issue, see Nehamas, 'Confusing Universals and Particulars', 297–303.) But even if Plato occasionally mentions compresence in particulars, it is only compresence in properties, and not compresence in particulars, that he takes to require the existence of forms. For further discussion of this claim, see Irwin, *PMT*, ch. 6, and 'Plato's Heracleiteanism'; and my 'The One over Many' and 'Owen's Progress'.

54. I follow Gallop and Burnet in bracketing '*kalōn*' in 78e1 rather than in 78d10. For parallel passages, see *Rep.* 485a1–b4, 508d4–9; *Symp.* 210e6–211a1.

55. For an interpretation of the passage in terms of EH, see Bolton, 82–4. Plato does say that the many *F*s are 'altogether (*pan*) opposite' to unchanging forms. But if forms are always unchanging in every way, then the many *F*s can be altogether opposite to them by not always being unchanging in every way, which does not require EH. (The contradictory opposite of *p* is not-*p*; and 'altogether opposite' is quite naturally taken to refer to the contradictory opposite.) 'Virtually' (*hōs epos eipein*) at 78e4 suggests that Plato does not mean to assert EH, for the phrase probably indicates a self-conscious exaggeration (contrast Bolton, 82 and n. 29). Further, if EH were at issue in 78de, then it would contradict 80c, which says that corpses last 'a fairly long time' and that some parts of the body last so long that they are practically immortal. Since we need not interpret the passage in terms of EH, and since so interpreting it makes the *Phd.* internally inconsistent, we ought not to

interpret it in terms of EH. For cogent criticism of the view that this passage adverts to EH, see Vlastos, *Socrates*, 69–71. He interprets the passage in terms of MH.

56. For this interpretation, see Irwin, 'Plato's Heracliteanism', 10.

57. Forms and cognates of '*gignesthai*' and '*einai*' are often used in this way. For Plato's focus on incomplete uses of 'is', see e.g. Owen, 'Plato on Not-Being'. In *Phys.* 1. 7 and elsewhere, Aristotle distinguishes between qualified and unqualified coming to be; the first is coming to be *F*, the second is coming into existence.

58. I do not deny that Plato sometimes contrasts unchanging forms with changeable particulars; he seems to do so in e.g. *Symp.* 211ab; see also *Tm.* 27d5–28a4, 29a2, 5, and, perhaps, 51d–52a (although it is tempting to interpret this passage in terms of compresence instead). Further, even when Plato is not contrasting forms and sensibles, he often enough mentions the obvious fact that sensible particulars undergo one or another sort of succession. But although this fact distinguishes sensible particulars (though not sensible properties) from forms, it is not a fact that Plato, in the middle dialogues, takes to require the existence of forms.

59. I discuss this passage in more detail in 'Forms as Causes', sects. 6 ff.

60. For Plato's insistence that knowledge requires an account, see *Phd.* 76b4–6, *Rep.* 531e4–5, 534b3–6, *Tm.* 51e3. Passages in which Plato asks the 'What is *F*?' question also assume that knowledge requires an account; for he believes that one needs to know what *F* is in order to know anything about *F*, and knowing what *F* is involves knowing an account of it. For references to places where Plato asks the 'What is *F*?' question, see below and the next note. (In all these passages, the relevant sort of account involves explaining the natures of the relevant entities; but see n. 17.)

61. For references to the 'What is *F*?' question, see e.g. *Rep.* 523d4–5, 524c11, e6. In *Rep.* 5 Plato infers from the fact that the sight-lovers do not know what beauty is that they know nothing about beauty; this assumes that one needs to know what *F* is in order to know anything about *F*. I discuss *Rep.* 5 further in Ch. 7. For a more detailed discussion, see my 'Knowledge and Belief in *Republic* V', *Archiv für Geschichte der Philosophic* 60 (1978), 121–39, and 'Knowledge and Belief in *Republic* V–VII', in S. Everson (ed.), *Companions to Ancient Thought*, i: *Epistemology* (Cambridge, 1990), 85–115.

62. This is not to say that Plato posits forms only for predicates whose instances suffer narrow compresence. It is only to say that although the argument from narrow compresence is continuous with Socrates' reasons for positing forms, it posits fewer forms than Socrates does; at least, this is so if we focus on contexts like *Rep.* 523–5. I ask about the range of Platonic forms in Ch. 7.4–6, and in Ch. 8.5–6.

63. *Rep.* 523–5 is sometimes thought to concern not definitions of properties but identification of examples. For some discussion, see Irwin, *PMT*, ch. 6, esp. 318 n. 26, and 320–1 n. 39. I discuss this matter further, though still briefly, in 'The One over Many' and in 'Plato on Perception', *Oxford Studies in Ancient Philosophy*, supplementary volume (1988), 15–28.

64. Contrast e.g. Penner, *Ascent*, who takes the dispute between Plato and the

sight-lovers to be a dispute between realism and nominalism respectively (see e.g. pp. 60, 90–1, 102 ff., 236–7). For some discussion of Penner's view, see my review in *Nous*, 25 (1991), 126–32.

Of course, even if the argument from compresence does not suggest that forms are particulars or play any semantic role, other arguments or claims might do so: (i) It is sometimes thought that in *Rep.* 10 Plato uses a semantic one over many argument according to which forms are meanings. (ii) It is also sometimes thought that the theory of recollection discussed especially in *Phd.* takes forms to be relevant to the meaningfulness of general terms. (iii) It is also sometimes thought that Plato takes facts about compresence to be relevant not only to the possibility of knowledge but also to the possibility of linguistic understanding, in a way that makes forms seem more like perfect particulars than like properties. I discuss (i) in Ch. 8; (ii) in Ch. 9.5–6; and (iii) in Ch. 9.5–6, and in Chs. 10 and 11.

The dispute about whether Plato believes that an apprehension of forms is necessary not just for knowledge but also for ordinary linguistic understanding goes back to antiquity. Epictetus, for example, writes: 'What deceives most people is the same as what deceived Theopompus the orator, who somewhere actually attacks Plato for wanting to define each sort of thing. What does he say? "Did none of us before you ever speak of good or just? Or did it happen that because we did not grasp what each of these is, we were uttering the sounds emptily and without signifying anything?" And who tells you, Theopompus, that we did not have natural conceptions (*ennoiai*) and preconceptions (*prolēpseis*) of each of these things?' (Epictetus 2. 17. 5–7). Theopompus seems to assume that Plato believes that we need to grasp definitions of forms (the good or just) before we can understand the meanings of terms; Epictetus (in my view rightly) objects that this is not Plato's view. (I owe the reference to Epictetus to T. Irwin.)

65. See the articles cited in n. 61.
66. See e.g. Irwin, *PMT*, ch. 6, and 'Plato's Heracleiteanism'. Although, as I go on to argue, the *Met.* passages do not suggest that Plato infers invalidly from difference to separation, the One over Many Argument, to be explored in Ch. 8, involves this invalid inference.
67. Presumably Aristotle thinks Plato took forms to be substances at least partly because they are the basic objects of knowledge and definition; see Ch. 13. I discuss Plato's and Aristotle's criteria for substantiality further in 'Plato and Aristotle on Form and Substance', *Proceedings of the Cambridge Philological Society*, 209 (1983), 23–47.
68. In *Phd.* 74a9–c5, for example, he infers from the fact that sensible equals are equal and unequal that there must be a form of equal that is different from, non-identical with, sensible equals. Separation is not mentioned.
69. Neither *Tm.* nor the middle dialogues use any form or cognate of '*chōrizein*' of forms. In *Parm.*, Plato says that 'similarity itself exists separately (*chōris*) from the similarity we ourselves have' (130b4); Vlastos, *Socrates*, 259–61, takes him to mean that forms exist independently of sensibles, i.e. can exist whether or not they do. However, in the just preceding lines Plato asks: 'Have you yourself, as you say, distinguished in this way, on the one hand, separately certain forms themselves, on the other, separately, in turn, the

things which participate in them?' (130b1–3). Here he suggests, not that forms *exist* independently of sensibles, but that they can be *distinguished* separately from them, just as sensibles can in their turn be distinguished separately from forms. 130b4 seems to illustrate this general point by way of a particular example; it does not make a new point about existential independence. (The illustration is elliptical, however, since 'distinguished' is not repeated, and only one half of the contrast is given. That he gives only half the contrast is not surprising, since it is the half that he is going to focus on.) That existential independence is not in view is supported by the fact that nothing Plato goes on to say requires it: in general, '*chōris*' can be used in more than one way; we can tell how it is used only by attention to the context. If nothing in the context requires it to mean existential independence, then it is not clear what grounds there are for so interpreting it. Plato also uses '*chōris*' of forms in *So.* 248, where, however, it seems to indicate only difference; certainly the context requires no more than that. Plato frequently says that forms exist *auta kath' hauta*, which Vlastos takes as evidence of separation (see his ' "Separation" in Plato', *Oxford Studies in Ancient Philosophy*, 5 (1987), 187–96, and *Socrates*, 256–62); but one of his main reasons is that Plato uses *auto kath' hauto* interchangeably with *chōris* in *Parm.* Nor does Plato's use of the phrase *auto kath' hauto* in the middle dialogues seems to me to require it to indicate separation; in Ch. 11 I suggest that he uses it to indicate freedom from compresence. (It perhaps indicates more than this; but so far as I can see it need not indicate separation.) I discuss these and related matters further in 'Separation'.

70. Actual uninstantiation is sufficient but not necessary for separation. My point is that unlike *Tm.*, the middle dialogues are not clearly committed to this particular sufficient condition. *Rep.* 10 has a form of bed. If it is everlasting, presumably it has not always been instantiated, since presumably there have not always been sensible beds, in which case it is separate. But see Ch. 6, interpretation (vi).

71. In Ch. 3. 6 I agreed with Aristotle that Plato's views about separation do not change as between the middle and late dialogues. This claim requires modification if *Tm.* is committed to separation but the middle dialogues are not clearly committed to it. But for two reasons I should not want to make too much of this difference. (i) As I say in the text, even if the middle dialogues are not clearly committed to separation, it fits in well with their general tenor. (ii) Even if *Tm.* and the middle dialogues differ in this way, the difference does not support the developmentalist view, according to which the middle but not the late dialogues are committed to separation.

72. See Ch. 2 n. 10. If Aristotle believes that universals cannot exist uninstantiated, then he accepts a stronger claim than that they are not separate; see n. 32.

73. See e.g. *Phd.* 74bc, 100b–105e; *Symp.* 210e–212a; *Rep.* 597; *Parm.* 129b and 132ab. Moreover, like Socrates, Plato rejects answers to 'What is *F*?' questions that are phrased in terms of something that is *F* and not *F*; the way in which he does so suggests he assumes that the *F* itself must be *F*. Further, again like Socrates, Plato says that various action-types and character-traits are *F* and not *F*; this also suggests that he takes the form of *F* to be *F*.

74. I focus on NSP and BSP, out of several available options, because (i) NSP has dominated contemporary discussion of self-predication, and it is the account of SP to which Aristotle seems to think Plato is committed; and (ii) I think Plato's version of self-predication is best interpreted as BSP, in the sense that BSP seems to me to be the most innocuous interpretation of self-predication that is consistent with the text (which is not to say that BSP is innocuous or that Plato explicitly formulated or clearly intended it). It is worth noting that although NSP has dominated contemporary discussion, it did not find favour with all ancient Platonists and in that sense it is not 'traditional'. Proclus, for example, sometimes seems to ascribe to Plato something that sounds rather like BSP; see e.g. *in Parm.* 4. 855.

75. Since on my usage 'the form of *F* is *F*' is a self-predication only if it is a genuine predication (see n. 35), the identity view is not a version of but an alternative to self-predication. For the identity view, see e.g. Cherniss, *Aristotle's Criticism*, 298; R. E. Allen, 'Participation and Predication in Plato's Middle Dialogues', in id. (ed.), *Studies in Plato's Metaphysics* (London, 1965), 143–64 at 46. For criticism of the identity view, see Peterson, 460 n. 16; A. Nehamas, 'Self-Predication and Plato's Theory of Forms', *American Philosophical Quarterly*, 16 (1979), 93–103 at 96 n. 14; Vlastos, 'The Unity of the Virtues', 263 n. 111; R. E. Heinaman, 'Self-Predication in Plato's Middle Dialogues', *Phronesis*, 34 (1989), 56–79 at 65–7.

76. In e.g. 'TMA I', Vlastos assumes that Plato accepts NSP. But in various later articles he rejects it in favour of 'Pauline predication'; see e.g. 'A Note on "Pauline Predications" in Plato', *Phronesis*, 19 (1974), 95–101, and n. 80 below.

77. For a defence of the view that NSP is not obviously absurd, see J. Malcolm, 'Vlastos on Pauline Predication', *Phronesis*, 30 (1985), 79–91.

78. I provide a brief sketch of BSP in 'Immanence'. Peterson provides a similar account of Plato's self-predication assumption. More precisely, she describes a general strategy called reinterpretation, which comes in two versions, conservative and expansive. She favours the conservative version; BSP corresponds to the expansive version.

79. On the other hand, sensible properties of *F* and the form of *F* are *F* in rather similar ways. To say that sensible *F* particulars and the form of *F* are *F* in different *ways* is not to say that they are *F* in different *senses* of '*F*'. In Ch. 10 I argue that Plato takes sensible *F* particulars and the form of *F* to be *F* in different ways but in the same sense of '*F*' (for more on different ways and different senses, see n. 37). We shall also see there that Aristotle and Alexander agree with this view. (For Alexander's agreement, see *in Met.* 50. 19–51. 25, discussed in Ch. 10 nn. 10 and 30.)

80. To say that the form of *F* is *F* in virtue of its explanatory role (for it is the property of *F* and, as such, explains the *F*-ness of *F* things) is not to say that 'the form of *F* is *F*' is an identity statement. On BSP, 'the form of *F* is *F*' is a predication; the form of *F* has the property of being *F* because (being the property of *F*) it explains the *F*-ness of *F* things. Nor is BSP the same as Pauline predication (see n. 76). On Pauline predication, to say that the form of *F* is *F* is only to say that necessarily, whatever is *F* is *F*. (The phrase

'Pauline predication' is meant to recall St Paul's remark that 'charity suffereth long and is kind', by which he meant not that the property of charity is patient or kind, but that whoever is charitable is patient and kind. For some criticism of the Pauline interpretation, see Malcolm; and Heinaman, 'Self-Predication in Plato's Middle Dialogues', 67–8.) BSP incorporates an explanatory claim absent in Pauline predication; unlike Pauline predication, BSP is not reductive.

It is hardly new to claim that Plato believes that if x explains y's being F it is itself F. But the claim is usually offered in support of the view that he is committed to NSP. I am suggesting that he believes that if x explains y's being F, it is F in a *sui generis* way that does not commit him to NSP.

Is it reasonable to believe that if x explains y's being F, it is F in a *sui generis* way, but in the same sense of 'F' as that in which y is F? Intuitions may well differ here. But I am trying to provide the most reasonable account of SP that retains Plato's view that sensible Fs and the form of F are F in the same sense of 'F'; even if we disagree with his view, we should try to explain it as sympathetically as possible. BSP is my effort to do this. We can also say on his behalf that the boundary between different senses and different ways is far from clear. (In n. 37 I gave an example to indicate the difference between different senses and different ways, and there are some clear cases; but not every case is clear.) Further, as remarked above in connection with Socrates on self-predication, 'just', for example, is generally thought to be univocal even though it is applied to categorially different things (e.g. to people, acts, institutions, and laws); perhaps taking the property of justice to be a member of the class of just things is not so great an expansion of the extension of the predicate as it may initially appear to be. And like Socrates, Plato is willing to revise our views about what counts as being within the extension of a given predicate. For helpful remarks on the difference between different senses and different ways, and a plausible defence of the claim that BSP requires only different ways, see Peterson, 464–70.

81. See n. 36.
82. For what I mean by 'best', see n. 74.
83. At e.g. *Rep.* 500e3 (though I do not think there is a form of the ideal city) and 540a; *Parm.* 132d2 and (by implication) *Tm.* 28–9. It is worth noting that Plato calls forms 'paradigms' far less frequently than is sometimes supposed. He does not, for example, so call them anywhere in *Phd.*, where one might expect him to. The claim is more prominent in *Tm.* than the middle dialogues.
84. Forms are also paradigms in so far as they are ideals aimed at. They are also relevant in productive contexts, as when a craftsman looks to a form in fashioning his creations. But these aspects of paradigmatism are derivative from the fact that forms are standards in the sense I have specified. At least, these further aspects of paradigmatism do not require forms to have any further intrinsic features; rather, forms are ideals aimed at and are relevant in productive contexts because of how they are viewed or used, and they can be so viewed or used because they are standards of the sort described.
85. Thus in e.g. *Phd.* 74d4–75a4 he says that sensible equals fall short of the equal itself, that is, of the form of equal; in *Rep.* 597a5 he says that the form

of bed is *teleōs on*, completely or perfectly (a) being. Although in one sense, forms are paradigms because they are perfect, in another sense, they are perfect at least partly because they are paradigms, i.e. because they are standards of the sort described.

The way in which Plato speaks of forms as paradigms of which sensibles are but imperfect copies or likenesses is similar to the way in which Locke, in *An Essay Concerning Human Understanding*, speaks of the real essences of things as standards, models, and archetypes that other things partake in. See e.g. II. xxxi. 6 (the mind refers 'to real essences, as to archetypes which are unknown'); III. vi. 15 ('nature, in the production of things, always designs them to partake of certain regulated established essences, which are to be the models of all things to be produced'). Locke sometimes uses such terminology in describing a scholastic account he rejects; but he sometimes seems to endorse it, if it is properly understood. For both Plato and Locke, the root claim is that in order to know whether or not *x* is *F*, one needs to know what *F* is, i.e. the real essence of *F*, which, in the cases that centrally interest Plato and Locke, are non-sensible properties that are generally unknown. The form or real essence is a model or paradigm in that it is a standard for determining whether or not other things are genuinely *F*. Sensibles are imperfect at least partly because they are not standards for determining when something is *F*.

86. There are obviously some differences; for example, Plato but not Socrates insists that forms are non-sensible.

87. At least, I argued that Socratic forms are not particulars or meanings and that Plato's central argument for forms in the middle dialogues—the argument from compresence—views forms not as particulars or meanings but as properties. But we have yet to consider whether other aspects of the theory of forms suggest that forms are particulars or meanings. See n. 64.

88. At least, Plato does not appeal to succession in the middle dialogues' arguments for the existence of forms. I have not asked whether he does so in the late dialogues.

NOTES TO CHAPTER 5

1. '*Epistēmē*' is variously translated as 'knowledge', 'science', 'scientific knowledge', and 'understanding'. Like 'knowledge' but unlike 'science', '*epistēmē*' can refer either to the cognitive state of a knowing person or to a body of known or knowable propositions (in this latter sense, mathematics, for instance, is an *epistēmē*). (See M. F. Burnyeat, 'Aristotle on Understanding', in E. Berti (ed.), *Aristotle on Science: The Posterior Analytics* (Padua, 1981), 97–139 at 97.) In the Arguments from the Sciences, '*epistēmē*' is always used in the latter way. Like 'science' but unlike 'knowledge', '*epistēmē*' readily takes a plural. In the Arguments from the Sciences, the plural is to the fore: they are about branches of knowledge, or sciences. (Aristotle speaks both of *kath' hekastēn epistēmēn* (e.g. 79. 8) and of *pasa epistēmē* (e.g. 79. 5). The former clearly refers to a branch of

knowledge, or a science. The latter is ambiguous as between 'all knowledge' and 'every ⟨sort of⟩ knowledge'. If it is taken the first way, it could refer to the state of knowledge; but the context makes it plain that it should be taken the second way.) As '*epistēmai*' is used here, it can be translated equally well as 'sciences' or as 'branches of knowledge'; but if it is translated in the former way, it should be understood in the sense of '*scientia*' or in the sense it has in the phrase 'the moral sciences', where it conveys the notion of a general, systematic discipline, the proper study of which confers understanding on a person. Although '*epistēmai*' can equally well be translated in these two ways, I shall retain the probably more familiar label, 'The Arguments from the Sciences', since 'science' more readily takes a plural; but I shall feel free to use 'knowledge' rather than 'science' when it is convenient or appropriate to do so.

2. Alexander records Aristotle as saying that the Arguments from the Sciences '*ou deiknuousin*' (79. 17) that there are forms, but *deiknuousi* that there are *koina*. This might mean either that (*a*) the Arguments from the Sciences are invalid arguments for the existence of forms but valid arguments for the existence of *koina*; or that (*b*) the Arguments from the Sciences are unsound arguments for the existence of forms but sound arguments for the existence of *koina*. In favour of (*b*) is the fact that Aristotle generally uses '*deiknunai*' and its cognates to mean 'succeeds in showing', and so to indicate soundness. However, (*a*) on the whole seems preferable here: (i) On (*b*), Aristotle would be committed to the existence of artefact *koina*; but I am not sure he would want to be so committed. (Perhaps in his early works he would not mind being so committed; *Cat.* and *Phys.*, for example, seem to view artefacts as substances. But by the time of *Met.*, they do not count as (the best) substances. See Ch. 6.8.) But even if Aristotle thinks that the Arguments from the Sciences are sound arguments for the existence of *koina*, he does not think that the One over Many or Object of Thought Arguments are sound arguments for their existence; for he believes that if they proved that there are any *koina* at all, they would prove that there are *koina* of negations, and of particulars and fictional entities, respectively; yet he never seems to countenance *koina* in these cases. He seems to think that the less accurate arguments are all on a par, so far as their cogency in proving that there are *koina* or forms is concerned; this suggests that he means to claim only that the Arguments from the Sciences are valid arguments for the existence of *koina*. Contrast 'The One over Many', 212 n. 24, and 'Aristotle and the More Accurate Arguments', 155 and *passim*. (ii) In *Met.* 990b9, he speaks of the ways in which we *deiknumen* that there are forms (in 13. 4, 1079a5, he uses '*deiknutai*'); he plainly does not mean that the Platonists succeed in proving that there are forms in these ways, for in his view there cannot be a sound argument for the existence of forms. (iii) Each of the Arguments from the Sciences is in fact an invalid argument for the existence of forms, as Aristotle conceives of forms. (iv) Aristotle's contrast between the less and the more accurate arguments also suggests that he takes the less accurate arguments to be invalid arguments for the existence of forms; see Ch. 2.7.

3. See e.g. Ross, *Aristotle's Metaphysics*, i. 193; Wilpert, *ZaF*, 32; Cherniss, *Aristotle's Criticism*, 235–6. n. 141; Ackrill, 'Review of *ZaF*', 105; Leszl, *Il*

'*De Ideis*', 95–7. (These authors do not all clearly have the same sort of succession in mind.) Frank, *The Arguments 'From the Sciences'*, 33, defends (*b*) but rejects (*a*).

4. I use 'everlasting' to mean not only unending but also beginningless existence (some would use 'sempiternity' here instead). '*Aidion*' most naturally indicates being everlasting (in the sense just specified) or eternal (but the dispute as to whether forms are everlasting or eternal will not concern us here). In this respect, '*aidion*' contrasts with '*aei*' (always), which, although it is often used temporally, is also often and naturally used non-temporally, to mean 'in every case'; '*aei*' can also be used incompletely, as in 'John is always reliable', which does not suggest that he always exists. It is perhaps just possible to read '*aidion*' incompletely, to mean 'everlastingly *F*' (sc. and not also not *F*), but this is not the most natural way to read it.

5. 'Works' (literally, 'does its work', *poiei to hautēs ergon*) and related phrases are common in connection with productive crafts; but they can also be used more generally, in connection with anything that has a function. In *Rep.* 477d1–5, for example, Plato uses '*apergazetai*' in saying that the function or work of knowledge is to know truths, or to be truth-entailing. For two reasons, I think the more general sense is involved here: (i) AS III counts geometry as a science, but it is not a productive craft. (If III counts geometry as a science, then presumably so too does I. LF agrees; it amplifies I by giving a geometrical example (79. 4–5).) (ii) In V, Aristotle objects that if the Arguments from the Sciences showed that there are any forms, they would show that there are artefact forms, which he claims the Platonists do not want. If AS I *explicitly* argues that considerations about productive crafts require the existence of forms, it would be odd were Aristotle to claim that the Platonists do not want artefact forms. (On the other hand, the Argument from Relatives explicitly takes its start from a relative predicate, yet Aristotle objects that the Platonists do not want relative forms. See Chs. 10 and 13.)

Like 'does its work', 'refers to' (*anapherein*) is familiar in productive contexts, as when a craftsman refers to, and attempts to embody or imitate, a paradigm in his work. See e.g. *Crat.* 389a5–8, where Plato says that in making a shuttle, a craftsman looks to something so constituted by nature as to shuttle. But, again, the productive sense is too restrictive here. Plato sometimes uses a related word, '*apoblepein*' (to look to), both in productive contexts and for understanding in general. In *Rep.* 477c6–d5, for example, he says that in attempting to decide what knowledge is, and whether it is the same as or different from belief, he looks to (477d1) the function of knowledge (and to what knowledge is 'set over', *epi*). Here the phrase indicates a concern not with production in particular but with understanding in general. (It is tempting to say that Aristotle uses '*anapherein*' rather than '*apoblepein*' in order to avoid the irrelevant and misleading visual connotations of the latter word.)

6. Aristotle says e.g. that one refers the non-substance categories to the most basic category, that of substance (cf. *Met.* 1045b28; 1004a25–6). In *Crat.* 422b4 Plato uses '*anapherein*' in speaking of resolving complex words into their primary elements. In *Phdr.* 237d1–2 he says that one needs to refer to a definition of love in order to know whether love is beneficial or injurious; in

Rep. 484c9 he says that the guardians should refer to a paradigm of justice to help them establish just laws in the state.

7. This is not to say that Plato or Aristotle believes that all knowledge requires explanation rather than justification in some less demanding sense. But in the sorts of cases at issue in the Arguments from the Sciences, the relevant justification requires explanation. I shall therefore speak interchangeably of justification and explanation. See Ch. 4 n. 17.

8. (1) is not the only premiss in AS I; but it is the only premiss relevant to the issue of whether or not knowledge is restricted to basic objects. Nor is there an invalid inference from I(1) to the conclusion that knowledge is so restricted.

9. It is important to see that in saying this, I(1) does not restrict the scope of any science to just one basic object: it leaves open the possibility that a given science has, say, both *F* and *G* as basic objects. But in that case, just as everything that is *F* is *F* in virtue of some one and the same thing, so everything that is *G* is *G* in virtue of some one and the same thing. I(1) also seems to say that if a given science involves more than a single basic object, they must be suitably unified with one another. There may be a science that studies both equality and commensurability, but no science studies both equality and redness, since they are not a genuine unity. (If I(1) restricted the scope of each science to a single basic object, then it would conflict with III, which counts both equality and commensurability as basic objects within geometry. On the account I am suggesting, this conflict is avoided.) I(1) may also mean to claim that even though a given science can involve more than a single basic object, none can involve indefinitely many basic objects; as Aristotle puts it in *Met.* 4. 4 (1006a31–b4), their number must be limited or definite. I return to questions about definiteness or determinacy in the next section.

There is, of course, room for dispute about what constitutes a genuine unity and about how many basic objects can fall within the scope of a given science. In *APo.* 1. 7, for example, Aristotle restricts the scope of each science to a single genus, and in *EN* 1. 6 he criticizes Plato for having too generous a conception of what falls within the scope of a given science. But he does not air those objections here.

The claim that I(1) allows certain sorts of pluralities to count as collectively being one is certainly left open by Aristotle's use of '*hen*'; for he uses the word to indicate having a certain sort of unity, not all of which involve numerical oneness (see e.g. *Met.* 5. 6; 10. 1–3).

10. In the terms used in *Met.* 5. 6, I(1) therefore requires each basic object of science to be intrinsically one, or one in its own right (*kath' hauto*), rather than coincidentally one. Being one in genus and definition are the relevant sorts of intrinsic oneness or unity in connection with knowledge, because knowledge (in the sorts of cases at issue here: see n. 7) requires explanation, which, in turn, involves definition. In Plato see e.g. *Meno* 98a; *Rep.* 534b3–6. In Aristotle see e.g. *APo.* 1. 2.

11. That AS I (like the other Arguments from the Sciences) takes forms to be properties receives further support below.

12. It also indicates the intrinsic unity of each basic object and the unity of the

conjunction of the basic objects of any given science (see n. 9); but the feature just mentioned in the text is the crucial one for present purposes. For uses of 'one and the same' where neither everlastingness nor unchangeability is implied, see *Met.* 1061b36 and *Pol.* 1280b35. At *Cat.* 4a10 the phrase implies persistence through (a finite stretch of) time, but not everlastingness or unchangeability. In his second objection to AS I Aristotle repeats '*hen*' but not '*auto*' (79. 20), which reinforces the suggestion that I(1) says, not that basic objects must be everlasting or unchangeable, but only that each must be one in all the cases it is invoked to explain. (LF, 79. 19, interestingly adds '*kai koinon*' to '*hen*', presumably to make the phrasing of Aristotle's objection parallel the phrasing of AS I. This addition also reinforces the suggestion that (1) is concerned with their being the identical property in a variety of cases, rather than with everlastingness or unchangeability.) Cherniss, *Aristotle's Criticism*, 235–6 n. 141, however, believes that 'one and the same' indicates that basic objects must be 'unalterable' and 'unchanging', and that they must exist 'at all times', be 'ever one and the same'.

13. For *kath' hekasta* as particulars, see e.g. *Met.* 999b33, 1039b28–31, 1086a32–4; *Cat.* 2b3; *DI* 18a33; *APr.* 43a27; *GA* 768a1–2; *EN* 1112b33–1113a2. For *kath' hekasta* as low-level types, see e.g. *Cat.* 15b1–2; *HA* 539b15; *GA* 763b15; *APo.* 79a4–6, 97b28–31. For some discussion, see Cooper, *Reason and Human Good*, 28–9; D. Devereux, 'Particular and Universal in Aristotle's Conception of Practical Knowledge', *Review of Metaphysics*, 39 (1986), 483–504. '*Kath' hekasta*' seems to mean something like 'taking (considering) each singly (one by one, individually, on its own)'. (The phrase is thus similar in sense to '*allassamenōn*' as it is used in 80. 13–14; see Ch. 8.2. See also the discussion below of '*tōn kath' hekastēn epistēmēn ginomenōn*'.) Note that since Plato does not use *kath' hekasta* (see Ch. 2 n. 8), the *Peri ideōn* at this point (as elsewhere) uses Aristotelian terminology even when it aims to elucidate a Platonic argument. I throughout translate '*kath' hekasta*' as 'particulars'; but I sometimes use 'particulars' for particulars as they contrast with all universals, sometimes for particulars which include low-level types. The context should make it clear which extension is in view.

14. Frank, *The Arguments 'From the Sciences'*, argues that they are primarily low-level universals. Barnes, 'Editor's Notes', 103, thinks that they are only sensible particulars.

15. If *kath' hekasta* include low-level types, the point is not that there is no knowledge of them, but that we cannot explain what it is to be some higher-order universal by referring only to them. We cannot explain what it is to be e.g. an animal as such by referring only to specific sorts of animals. But what counts as a *kath' hekaston* in one context might count as a basic object in another. Thus dog is a *kath' hekaston* if the inquiry is into what it is to be an animal, but not if the inquiry is into what it is to be a dog.

16. (2) mentions only *kath' hekasta*; (3) mentions only *aisthēta*. Unless the two are equivalent, there is an obvious gap in the argument. 79. 17 makes it clear that *kath' hekasta* and *aisthēta* are identified throughout the Arguments from the Sciences. (I assume '*kai*' is epexegetic.) Aristotle also seems to identify *kath' hekasta* and *aisthēta* elsewhere in the *Peri ideōn*: see 81. 11–19; 81. 28. One might think that if *kath' hekasta* and *aisthēta* are identified, then *kath'*

hekasta are only a subclass of particulars; for elsewhere Aristotle acknowledges the existence of non-sensible particulars (see Ch. 2 n. 27). However, if Aristotle leaves open the possibility that there are non-sensible particulars, then he would not be justified in his claim that the Arguments from the Sciences are valid arguments for the existence of universals; he could say only that they are valid arguments for the existence of something besides sensible *kath' hekasta*, which would leave open the possibility that they show only that there are non-sensible particulars.

17. See Ch. 2 n. 17; Ch. 4 n. 27.

18. Leszl, *Il 'De Ideis'*, 95, thinks that '*ginomena*' indicates coming into existence. One might defend this view by noting that the basic objects are said to be everlasting (*aidion*). However, although being everlasting is necessary for being a basic object, it is not sufficient, and so we need not assume that no *kath' hekasta* are everlasting. Even if AS I assumes that *kath' hekasta* are not everlasting, '*ginomena*' does not express that claim (as I shall shortly argue). Although the Arguments from the Sciences are often thought to advert to succession (MH, EH), I know of no one who explicitly appeals to '*ginomena*' in defence of that suggestion, so I shall not try to say how the argument goes if '*ginomena*' is so interpreted. Nor do I know of anyone who suggests that '*ginomena*' here indicates compresence.

19. LSJ cites *kata xustaseis g.*, to be formed into groups (Thucydides, 2. 21); this illustrates what I take to be the relevant usage. Robin's translation, p. 16, suggests that he may understand '*ginomena*' as I do.

20. If we assume that the sciences always exist, then it would follow that their basic objects are everlasting. But the Arguments from the Sciences do not say that the sciences always exist. Whether it is plausible to assume that they always exist depends on how *epistēmai* are conceived (see n. 1). If they are taken to be actual sciences, then presumably not all sciences always exist; there has not always been a science of medicine or of mathematics. If, however, they are taken to be knowable propositions, then presumably they have always existed. Whether or not it is legitimate to infer that the basic objects of knowledge are everlasting, the passage cited below from *APo.* 85b suggests that Aristotle may take the inference to be legitimate.

21. Further, (3) seems to be invalidly inferred, since the inference to everlastingness does not seem to be warranted. But Aristotle may disagree about this; see n. 20.

22. See Ch. 2.7; Ch. 10.9. At least, Aristotle would say that the existence of universals that are also non-sensible everlasting perfect paradigms is sufficient for the existence of Platonic forms; and we have seen that AS I takes forms to be universals.

23. In the *APo.* passage, Aristotle seems to think that the oneness requirement implies that universals are everlasting, so perhaps he thinks that AS I validly implies that basic objects are everlasting, in which case his objection to it lies elsewhere. *APo.* 85b15–19 denies that there are universals *para* particulars, whereas in commenting on the Arguments from the Sciences, Aristotle allows that there are universals *para* particulars (79. 15–19; cf. *APo.* 100a7). This is inconsistency in terminology, not in doctrine. Sometimes Aristotle uses '*para*' hygienically, to indicate a claim about difference that he accepts; sometimes

he uses it to indicate the Platonic separation that he rejects. *APo.* 85b15–19 and 77a5–9 use '*para*' in the second way; in *APo.* 100a7 and in commenting on the Arguments from the Sciences, he uses it in the first way (see Cherniss, *Aristotle's Criticism*, 77 n. 56; and N. P. White, 'A Note on Ἔκθεσις', *Phronesis*, 16 (1971), 164–8 at 165). In both passages, he therefore means to suggest that there are universals that are different but not separate from particulars. R. Dancy, *Sense and Contradiction* (Dordrecht, 1975), 86, 124–5, by contrast, infers from Aristotle's use of *para* at 79. 15–19 that he at one stage accepted separation. Barnes, *Posterior Analytics*, 139–40, 177, seems to believe that at *APo.* 77a5–9 and 85b15–19, Aristotle means only that there must be universal propositions.

24. If, as I have allowed, *kath' hekasta* include low-level types, then the claim, again, is that we cannot understand what it is to be *F* in terms of particular *F*s or low-level types of *F*s. See n. 15.

25. The first reason is that basic objects must be one in definition or genus, which, in Aristotle's view, implies that they are universals.

26. I assume that Aristotle is again speaking of the basic objects of knowledge rather than of every knowable object. Certainly the genitive (*hōn epistēmai eisi*) can be used in this way.

27. (*1a*) can itself be interpreted in at least three ways: (i) the basic objects of knowledge always exist; (ii) the basic objects of knowledge exist at some time; (iii) the basic objects of knowledge are knowable at t_1 only if they exist at t_1. (i) seems the least likely option here, since AS II does not mention everlastingness. I see no way to choose between (ii) and (iii); but fortunately for our purposes it makes no difference which we assume.

28. So far I have been using 'basic object' primarily non-propositionally for e.g. the essence of health. (*1c*) uses 'basic object' for propositions instead. As I go on to say, it would be more appropriate to speak here of the *content* of knowledge.

29. In Plato, see e.g. *Rep.* 477a; *Gorg.* 454d; *Meno* 98a. In Aristotle see e.g. *APo.* 1. 2; 2. 19.

30. Here and elsewhere I enclose 'basic' in parentheses when a given claim applies not only to basic objects of knowledge but also to every knowable object.

31. Of course, Aristotle takes AS II to be an invalid argument for the existence of forms; but he seems to locate the invalidity in the inference from (4) to (5) rather than in the inference to (4). For since he thinks that the premisses of AS I imply that there are *koina*, they should imply that there is something besides *kath' hekasta*. If (1) is read as (*1a*), then it parallels the first premiss of the Object of Thought Argument; see Ch. 9. It is interesting that existential claims at various stages seem prominent in the *Peri ideōn*; for the *Peri ideōn* aims to articulate Platonic arguments, yet it is often said that Plato never explicitly isolates an existential use of '*einai*'. While I agree that Plato does not explicitly do so, it does not follow that he never relies on or uses existential claims; I explore this matter in Chs. 7 and 9.

32. II does not explicitly mention sensibles, but see 79. 17 and n. 16.

33. See e.g. *Met.* 1006b4: *hōrismenoi de ton arithmon.* Cf. Alexander, *in Met.* 89. 5.

34. '*Apeiron*', however, indicates quantitative limitlessness more naturally than '*ahoriston*' does (though it is itself used equally naturally for both qualitative and quantitative indeterminacy). Hence Aristotle, in discussing the infinite in *Phys.* 3. 4–8, uses '*apeiron*' rather than '*ahoriston*'. '*Apeiron*' can mean not just 'limitless' but also 'infinite'. It has the latter meaning in the Third Man Argument (see Ch. 15) and often in *Phys.* 3. In this chapter, however, I shall not treat quantitative limitlessness and infinity separately.

35. Thus Anaximander calls his basic principle 'the *apeiron*' because of its qualitative indeterminacy: it does not possess in any clearly articulated fashion the determinate elements familiar in our world; it is not definitely hot, or cold, or wet, or dry, and so on (DK 12 A 9). (The *apeiron* is also spatially and temporally limitless, but that is not why he calls it 'the *apeiron*'.) Anaximenes, by contrast, says that his 'underlying nature', air, is *apeiron* but not *ahoriston*. Air is *apeiron* because it is spatially (and perhaps also temporally) limitless; but it is not *ahoriston*, because it has a definite nature, that of, air (DK 13 A 5).

36. Aristotle also uses '*apeira*' in non-epistemological contexts (see e.g. *Phys.* 3. 4–8), but since such contexts are irrelevant here I shall pass them by. I focus on Aristotle rather than on Plato since (with the exception of *Phil.*) Plato does not use any of the relevant terms systematically; indeed, he never uses '*hōrismena*' or '*ahorista*' at all, although in the *Laws* (643d6, 916e2, e4) he occasionally uses other forms of these words. Various forms of '*horos*' and '*horizein*' are standard throughout Plato, but they generally occur in non-technical contexts. *Pol.* 262d seems to use '*apeiron*' in a relevant way; see Ch. 8 n. 29. See Ch. 7.5 for a brief discussion of *Phil.*'s use of some of the key terms.

37. For a similar interpretation, see Barnes, *Posterior Analytics*, 178.

38. In Ch. 9 I ask whether Plato, in fact or according to Aristotle, believes that the existence of forms is necessary not just for knowledge but also for belief. Against my suggestion that (i) does not concern knowledge in particular is the fact that 999a28 uses '*epistēmē*'. But the point Aristotle goes on to make concerns only identification and recognition; so even if knowledge is at issue, (i) considers only a necessary condition for knowledge that does not distinguish it from belief. That the Arguments from the Sciences are concerned with knowledge as it contrasts with belief is suggested by the fact that AS I, for example, mentions the 'one and the same requirement': both Plato and Aristotle impose this requirement not on belief but on knowledge. Thus we have seen that in *Rep.* 5 Plato imposes this requirement (or something like it) on adequate definitions. Similarly, Aristotle believes that non-homonymous properties, and so something that is suitably one, are necessary for demonstration and so for *epistēmē*; see *APo.* 77a5–9 (cited below), and Ch. 10.7.

39. Unlike the *Peri ideōn*, *Met.* 7. 15 discusses non-sensible particulars. Further, unlike the Arguments from the Sciences, which take forms to be universals, 7. 15 takes forms to be particulars (see esp. 1040a8–9).

40. Cf. also *APo.* 85b, discussed in sect. 2; and *EN* 6. 3–4. I discuss homonymy in Ch. 10.3.

41. In *EN* 6. 4–5, Aristotle says that although science is concerned with what is necessary and everlasting, crafts are concerned with what comes to be and

with what can be otherwise (see e.g. 1140a1–2, 14–15, 22–3, 31–b5). So *epistēmē* is used more narrowly here than in the Arguments from the Sciences.

42. For a helpful discussion of the passages from *Rhet.* and *Met.* I. I, see Devereux, 'Particular and Universal'. Some of the relevant issues are also well discussed in M. Frede, 'An Empiricist View of Knowledge: Memorism', in Everson (ed.), *Companions to Ancient Thought*, i: *Epistemology*, 225–50.

43. One verbal difference between the two passages is that unlike *Met.* I. I, *Rhet.* uses '*apeira*'. But *Met.* I. I says that knowledge requires knowledge of something that is one (*mia katholou*, 981a6; *eidos hen*, 981a10); a grasp of many particulars (*kath' hekaston, polla*, 981a9) will not do. In saying that *kath' hekasta* are *polla*, Aristotle means to make the same point that he makes in *Rhet.* when he says that they are *apeira*. The contrast between *hen eidos*, on the one hand, and *polla* and *kath' hekasta*, on the other, also obviously recalls AS I.

44. Plato also contrasts empirical medicine with genuinely scientific medical knowledge in e.g. *Laws* 720ac; 857cd. For the same sort of point applied more widely, see *Phil.* 55 ff., on which see Ch. 6, interpretation (vi).

45. This passage raises many questions that I cannot discuss here; for some discussion, see Irwin, 'Aristotle's Concept of Signification', and *AFP* 179–88. One important difference between *Met.* 4. 4 and the *Rhet.* passage is that whereas the *Rhet.* says that *kath' hekasta* are *apeira*, *Met.* 4. 4 says that coincidents are *apeira*; and *kath' hekasta* and coincidents are different. For example, some very generic properties are coincidents; but low-level types are the only universals that count as *kath' hekasta*. But in *Rhet.*, as we have seen, *kath' hekasta* are *apeira* primarily because they have coincidental properties, i.e. properties irrelevant for a given explanatory purpose. Moreover, as we shall see, '*apeira*' has the same force in both contexts, even if it is applied to different entities (coincidents and *kath' hekasta*).

   Met. 6. 2 is yet another relevant context (though as in *Met.* 4. 4, Aristotle discusses the indeterminacy of coincidents rather than of *kath' hekasta*). Here Aristotle says that no *epistēmē*—practical, productive, or theoretical—deals with the coincidental, since coincidents are *apeira*. A house-builder, *qua* house-builder, for example, aims to build, simply, a house, not a house pleasing to A, displeasing to B, and so on (1026b2 ff.). But a science should be defined in terms of what is always or usually the case (in its domain), or else teaching and learning would be impossible (1027a19–25). One will never succeed in training someone to be a house-builder if one says only such things as 'This house is pleasing to A, displeasing to B.' A suitable explanation must be phrased in terms of the essential, not the non-essential, properties of a thing. The essential properties of a thing are both qualitatively and quantitatively determinate: they are qualitatively determinate in so far as they are explanatory; and they are quantitatively determinate in so far as the essential properties of any given thing are few in number. For further discussion, see C. Kirwan, *Aristotle's Metaphysics, Books* Γ, Δ, *and* E (Oxford 1971), nn. *ad loc.*

46. Determinacy is required here, then, not for craft and scientific knowledge,

but for signification, which is weaker. (Aristotle also says that signifying one thing is necessary if one is to *noein ti*, 1006b10. '*Noein*' can indicate knowledge, but it does not seem to do so here. I discuss '*noein*' in Ch. 9.) None the less, the notion of determinacy is the same, even if it is invoked for a different purpose.

47. (i) and (ii) would also explain why Aristotle believes that AS II is an invalid argument for the existence of Platonic forms but a valid argument for the existence of his own universals; but they do not possess all the virtues of (iii).

48. The main reason I can see for rejecting this suggestion would be the belief that *Phil.* uses '*apeira*' in some quite different way that, moreover, seems especially appropriate in connection with AS II. In Ch. 7.5, however, I suggest that *Phil.* uses '*apeira*' in a way that is quite close to the way it is used in (iii). (I assume that *Phil.* is the main relevant Platonic context, since it is the only Platonic context that uses '*apeira*' at all systematically; see n. 36.) Elsewhere too, Plato uses '*apeira*' in a way close to the way in which it is used in AS II; see e.g. *Pol.* 262d with Ch. 8 n. 29.

49. If (ii) captured the correct interpretation, then GCH would be relevant; but on independent grounds we have seen that (ii) is not the correct interpretation. It is true that succession (GCH, MH, EH) is sufficient for indeterminacy, in that if something undergoes succession it presumably has inessential properties and so is indeterminate. But it is indeterminate not because it undergoes succession, but because it has inessential features. Nor is succession necessary for indeterminacy. Squareness, for example, is unchanging and everlasting, but it is none the less indeterminate for the purposes of explaining what shape is.

50. In the next section we shall see that *Met.* 4. 4 also explains the connection between AS II and III.

51. If *kath' hekasta* include low-level types, however, then the distinction is not exclusive.

52. By contrast, Leszl, *Il 'De Ideis'*, 98–101 (cf. 308–10), seems to think that to be unqualifiedly *F* is to be *F* and nothing else, and that to be this (or some) *F* is to be *F* and to have other properties as well. For some cogent criticism of Leszl on this score, see the reviews by C. J. Rowe, *Classical Review*, NS 29 (1979), 77–9 and by A. R. Lacey, *Mind*, 87 (1978), 281–3. Leszl's interpretation of the distinction is close to Owen's in 'Proof' (although Owen does not discuss the Arguments from the Sciences). In Ch. 11 I discuss Owen's account and provide a further defence of my own interpretation of the distinction between being this (or some) *F* and unqualifiedly *F*.

53. Similarly, in *Met.* 8. 1 (1042a29–31) Aristotle says that only substance as compound is always separate *haplōs*; for substance as form sometimes requires (additional or a different sort of) matter for its existence, whereas substance as compound already includes the requisite matter. He means, not that substance as compound does not need matter (it does, since it includes it), but that it does not need matter in the way in which substance as form does. Or again, in *Phys.* 190a31–4, Aristotle contrasts unqualified (*haplōs*) coming to be with coming to be something (*ti*). When some material is carved into a statue, a new substance comes into being; this is unqualified coming to

be. By contrast, when Socrates becomes musical, a substance undergoes an alteration (it comes to be something), but no new substance comes into existence.

54. See Owen, 'Dialectic and Eristic', 237–8. In *Met.* 997b5–12 and 1040b32–4, for example, Aristotle seems to use '*auto*' to refer to Platonic forms. But in *Met.* 1036b13–17 and 1050b34–1051a2 (with which compare 1087a10–25), he seems to use it to refer to a universal in a neutral sense (or, at any rate, to something other than Platonic forms). As we shall see in Ch. 10, the Argument from Relatives uses '*auto*' in both ways. At 83. 7 it denotes a universal; at 83. 15 it also seems to refer to a Platonic form.

55. A nominalist, however, would presumably dispute the inference to (2) even when (2) is so read.

56. Aristotle makes this point on both readings of '*auto*'. But the point emerges more clearly if '*auto*' refers to universals in a neutral sense.

57. AS I also takes the basic objects to be everlasting; but neither II nor III says that they are everlasting.

NOTES TO CHAPTER 6

1. Aristotle's objection concerns not who consults forms but the range of forms. That is, he claims not that (i) builders do not consult forms in practising their craft, but that (ii) there is no form of e.g. house. Neither (i) nor (ii) implies the other: there might be a form of house even if builders do not consult it; and even if there is no form of house, builders might consult other forms— e.g. of certain shapes—in practising their craft. In what follows, I speak interchangeably of artefact forms, of forms corresponding to the crafts, and of forms corresponding to the products of the crafts.

2. I′ and II′ are presumably meant to parallel I and II, but they fail to state some of the relevant premisses. For example, whereas I says that every science is of some one and *the same* thing, I′ says only that each of the crafts is of some one thing (LF, 79. 19, supplies '*kai koinon*'); and unlike I, I′ does not mention everlasting paradigms. II′ says that the basic objects of the crafts are (*esti*). It also says that they are not particulars. But unlike II, it does not disqualify particulars from being basic objects on the ground that they are *apeira kai ahorista* whereas basic objects must be *hōrismena*. The parallel between III and III′ is more exact. III′ says not only that every craft is of something that is unqualifiedly (*haplōs*) F but also that therefore every craft is of something that is F itself (*auto*) (80. 1); like III (and unlike I, II, I′, and II′), it also provides an example, which is spelt out in some detail. (LF provides examples in explaining I and III, but not in explaining II.) I shall assume that the omissions are insignificant.

3. To say that they seem reasonable is not to say that they succeed. In interpretation (vi) I consider a way in which Plato might be able to argue that they do not succeed.

4. For detailed discussion of various possibilities, see Robin, 173 ff., and

Cherniss, *Aristotle's Criticism*, 235–60. A possibility that I shall not consider here is that Aristotle's claim that Plato did not want artefact forms is really only 'a somewhat esoteric joke ... playfully ascribed' to Plato. For this view, see Ackrill, 'Review of *ZaF*', 105–6.

5. Although Philippson, 123, and Rose doubt that V is from the *Peri ideōn* (see Ch. 3.4), they do not suggest that it is Alexander's interpolation; so a variation on (i) is that V is at any rate not due to Aristotle. Rose gives no reasons for his doubts. Philippson's reason is that (in his view) Plato rejected the existence of artefact forms only 'in his last years and in his lectures', yet (in his view) the *Peri ideōn* was written before then; so unless we are to convict Aristotle of misinterpretation, V cannot be from the *Peri ideōn*. I ask below whether there is any evidence that Plato changed his views about the existence of artefact forms.

6. In Plato, see e.g. *Phil.* 55 ff. In Aristotle, see e.g. *Met.* I. 1; *EN* 1094a28; 1180b16–23.

7. For his argument, see 990b27–991a1 (= 1079a19–33). For some discussion, see Alexander, *in Met.* 88. 5–90. 3; Owen, 'Dialectic and Eristic'; G. Vlastos, 'The "Two-Level Paradoxes" in Aristotle', in id., *PS* 323–34; J. Annas, 'Aristotle on Substance, Accident and Plato's Forms', *Phronesis*, 22 (1977), 146–60. As Alexander in effect points out, each of the *Peri ideōn*'s arguments would prove that there are forms of some non-substances if they proved that there are any forms at all (*in Met.* 88. 5–89. 7).

8. Aristotle himself vacillates as to whether artefacts are substances. They seem to count as substances in the early *Cat.* and *Phys.* The wide range of examples of substances mentioned in *Cat.* (see Ch. 3 n. 70) suggests that artefacts count among their ranks. Although *Phys.* 2. 1 distinguishes between natural organisms and artefacts, it seems to count them both as substances. But in the central books of *Met.* artefacts do not count as (the best sort of) substances (see e.g. 1041b28–31, 1043b21–3), precisely because they are not natural and so are not suitably one, i.e. they are not genuine unities. So, as I remark in Ch. 5 n. 2, it is not clear whether Aristotle recognizes *koina* of artefacts. For in his view, there are universals corresponding only to entities that fall within a single category; but artefacts are either substances or else do not fall into any category. So at least when Aristotle denies that artefacts are substances, he presumably also denies that there are universals corresponding to them. (D. Wiggins, *Sameness and Substance* (Oxford, 1980), 94–5, raises questions about the identity and essences of artefacts that are interestingly similar to Aristotle's reasons for doubting whether artefacts are substances.)

9. Cherniss agrees. He suggests (*Aristotle's Criticism*, 258–60) that the discrepancy between the *Peri ideōn* and *Met.* I. 9 indicates, not that Alexander misinterprets the latter, but that Aristotle became dissatisfied with the *Peri ideōn* account and so substituted a vaguer criticism in I. 9. Cherniss also suggests that the dissatisfaction is due to a dispute among Platonists who used the Arguments from the Sciences as to whether there were forms of artefacts; hence the blanket assertion that they did not want such forms came to seem too sweeping.

10. So too does Alexander; see *in Met.* 77. 6–10.

11. Averroës reports that Alexander read *hoi ta eidē tithemenoi ephasan*;

apparently Themistius read this as well. But all the manuscripts of Aristotle have *Platōn* (or *ho Platōn*) *ephē*. Even if both the Greek commentators read *hoi ta eidē tithemenoi ephasan*, it seems reasonable to suppose that the phrase includes Plato within its scope. But for a defence of the manuscript reading, see Cherniss, *Aristotle's Criticism*, 244 n. 149.

12. Aristotle takes it to be more reasonable to countenance forms in natural cases than in artificial cases because he thinks that in the former case we at least need to posit some sort of extra-mental form, whereas in the latter case we need to posit only a form in the soul of the artist, i.e. a mental representation of e.g. a house. This is connected to his worries about whether artefacts are substances; see n. 8.

13. Robin, 177; Cherniss, *Aristotle's Criticism*, 243–4; and Ross, *Plato's Theory of Ideas*, 171, all agree that in 1070a18 Aristotle implies that Plato rejected forms of artefacts. Contrast R. S. Bluck, 'Aristotle, Plato, and Ideas of Artefacta', *Classical Review*, 61 (1947), 75–6.

14. Ross, *Plato's Theory of Ideas*, 175, however, believes that Aristotle has only other Platonists in mind.

15. See e.g. M. Isnardi Parente, 'Le *Peri ideōn* d'Aristote: Platon ou Xénocrate?', *Phronesis*, 26 (1981), 135–52 at 136 and 139. She suggests Xenocrates as a possible alternative target. Cherniss, *Aristotle's Criticism*, 241, thinks it is unclear whether Aristotle associates the denial of artefact forms with 'all Platonists, Plato included, or [with] one party of the Academy only'.

16. The definition is preserved by Proclus, *in Parm.* 888. 18–19 Cousin = Xenocrates, fr. 30 Heinze. For some discussion of Proclus' text, along with that of Alcinous (or, as Cherniss believes, Albinus) and Diogenes (mentioned below), see Cherniss, *Aristotle's Criticism*, 257 n. 167. Proclus takes '*aei*' to show that Xenocrates also excluded forms of particulars on the ground that they are not everlasting. However, perhaps Xenocrates intended '*aei*' non-temporally. On forms of particulars, see Ch. 9.

17. *Crat.* 386d ff., for instance, uses the example of shuttling in order to illustrate the thesis that things have an essence that is in accord with nature: shuttling is taken to be in some sense natural and objective; cf. 389c3–7.

18. Proclus believes that neither Plato nor Xenocrates countenances artefact forms. But that still counts against (ii), in so far as (ii) assumes that Plato and Xenocrates differ as to whether there are artefact forms. Diogenes Laertius says that Plato takes forms to be 'causes and principles by which the things that are constituted by nature are such as they are' (*aitias tinas kai archas tou toiauta einai ta phusei sunestōta hoiaper estin auta*; DL 3 77). But, again, since as Plato uses '*phusis*' it at least sometimes includes artefacts, Diogenes' report does not by itself show that Plato rejects artefact forms.

19. See e.g. Proclus, *in Parm.* 827–9; 947–9; Syrianus, *in Met.* 107. 6–108. 7.

20. *Didaskalikos* 9. 2.

21. For this view, see Wilpert, *ZaF*, 56, 59, 63–6; and Heinze, 53–4. Jackson, 'Plato's Later Theory of Ideas', esp. I, 10, pp. 255–8; II, 11, p. 323 n. 1, also argues that Plato rejected artefact forms in the late dialogues. For criticism of Wilpert's version of this view, see Ackrill's review, 105–7.

22. Contrast Ross, *Plato's Theory of Ideas*, 172, who believes that *Tm.* 28a6–b1

and *Laws* 965b7–c8 countenance artefact forms. (He also cites the *Seventh Letter*, since at 342d3–e2 it countenances forms of *ta skeuasta*. I doubt whether the *Seventh Letter* is genuine; certainly I should not want to rely on it alone for committing Plato to anything. On the other hand, Ross says of the suggestion that perhaps Plato changed his mind as to whether there were artefact forms, that '[t]his view cannot be definitely rejected; but we can at least say that there is no evidence, in Plato or in what we read about him elsewhere, of such a change' (p. 173). This leaves (iii) open, though as a remote possibility; cf. also p. 175.) The *Tm.* passage, however, claims only that the demiurge looked to various forms in creating the *cosmos*; it does not suggest that human craftsmen also look to forms. Indeed, the passage if anything implies that in at least some cases they do not do so. For the demiurge needed to look to forms because he wanted to create something as good as possible, and so needed to be guided by the best possible paradigms—perfect forms. But in e.g. *Gorg.* 462c ff. and *Rep.* 10 (602), Plato suggests that at least some craftsmen—e.g. painters—do not aim to embody the good; so presumably in *Tm.* Plato believes that such craftsmen look not to forms but only to the sensible, created paradigms mentioned in *Tm.* 28e–29c. In *Laws* 965b7–10 Plato writes that 'a consummate craftsman or guardian in any sphere must not only be able to look at (*blepein*) the many, but must also go on to know (*gnōnai*) the one, and the organization of all other detail in the light of that knowledge'. The 'one' is identified as 'one form' (965bc2, *idea*). But this passage does not commit Plato to the existence of artefact forms. For his claim is not about every craftsman, but only about 'the consummate craftsman or guardian' where the 'or', I take it, as often in Plato, is epexegetic.

The passages Ross cites from *Tm.* and *Laws* thus do not commit Plato to the existence of artefact forms. Nor do other passages in the late dialogues seem to be committed to their existence—at least, not in passages in which the nature of the crafts is at issue. For example, *So.* 265a ff. distinguishes between divine and human craftsmanship, but nothing is said about forms of any sort. *Phil.* 55 ff. distinguishes between different types of knowledge, and it counts at least some crafts as types of knowledge, although as less exalted types than dialectic and pure mathematics. But it is unclear that artefact forms are thereby in the offing. Crafts count as types of knowledge in so far as they admit precise measurement; although this might require the existence of forms of e.g. geometrical shapes, it does not seem to require the existence of artefact forms. I discuss *Phil.* further in interpretation (vi).

Aristotle might be taken to argue that since Plato requires forms for divine craftsmanship, he also requires them for human craftsmanship. But this argument would be justified only if there were no relevant disanalogies between the two cases, yet Plato thinks there are. As we have seen, for example, the divine craftsman is guided by considerations of goodness in a way not all human craftsmen are (at least, this is so when painting, for instance, is counted as a craft rather than as a knack). It is true, though, that Plato does not trouble to spell out the relevant differences in any detail or with any sort of care.

23. One might then defend a weaker version of (iii), according to which Aristotle

has only the late dialogues in mind and correctly says that they are not committed to the existence of artefact forms. But the considerations adduced next in the text count against even this weaker version of (iii).

24. See Ch. 3.6. Cherniss, *Aristotle's Criticism*, 245, says that 'it is certain that [Plato] posited ideas of artefacts; and there is no suggestion in these writings nor any *direct* evidence in Aristotle's that he ever *altered* his opinion on this subject'. Note that (iii), as well as the weaker version of it mentioned in the previous note, assume that the *Peri ideōn* was written before the relevant late dialogues. If, as I speculated in Ch. 3.7, the *Peri ideōn* was written before the *Laws*, then no matter what its view of artefact forms is, Aristotle would presumably not have it in mind. If, as I am inclined to think, *Phil.* is quite late, then it is not clear that Aristotle could have it in mind either. However, we have seen that the chronological issue is murky; and even if *Phil.* and *Laws* were written after the *Peri ideōn*, perhaps Plato discussed their views with Aristotle.

25. Robin, 178 n. 175. See also Ross, *Plato's Theory of Ideas*, 173 ff., and *Aristotle's Metaphysics*, note *ad loc.*; Cherniss, *Aristotle's Criticism*, 247 ff.

26. D. H. Frank, *The Arguments 'From the Sciences'*, 91–2. His suggestion is endorsed by Barnes, 'Editor's Notes', 102–3.

27. In *Met.* 1. 9, Aristotle says that 'we' do not want forms of house or ring; these are productive examples. Similarly, just before he commends Plato, in *Met.* 12. 3, 1070a, for denying that there are artefact forms, he gives the example of building. So even if we accept Frank's explanation of Aristotle's claim in the *Peri ideōn*, the same puzzle arises elsewhere; it would be preferable to find an explanation that fits what he says not only in the *Peri ideōn* but also in these other contexts.

28. Frank's only reply to this objection is that it 'does not constitute proof that [productive and imitative crafts] are not to be so distinguished for the purposes of this argument' ('A Disproof in the "*Peri Ideon*"', *Southern Journal of Philosophy*, 22 (1984), 49–59 at 59 n. 15.)

29. See e.g. *Cat.* 2a14 for *eidos* as species; *Met.* 1071a28 for *eidos* as individual form; *DA* 424a17–21 for the form without matter that a perceiver receives; *Met.* 1032b1 for the form in the soul of a craftsman.

30. For a brief account of why he believes this, see n. 12.

31. *Met.* 1. 9, for example, is discussing *Phd.*, which in Aristotle's view has the distinctively Platonic forms; *Met.* 12. 3, 1070a also seems to have the distinctively Platonic forms in view. (I follow Ross in reading *eiper estin eidē alla toutōn* at 1070a19 (rather than, with Jaeger, *all' ou toutōn*), and in interpreting the phrase to indicate separation rather than merely difference; cf. Ross, n. *ad loc.* Cf. *para* at 1070a14.)

32. The date of *Crat.* and the status of its forms are disputed. J. V. Luce, 'The Date of the *Cratylus*', *American Journal of Philology*, 85 (1964), 136–54, and 'The Theory of Ideas in the *Cratylus*', *Phronesis*, 10 (1965), 21–36, argues that *Crat.* antedates *Phd.* and *Rep.*, and that its forms are non-separated. B. Calvert, 'Forms and Flux in Plato's *Cratylus*', *Phronesis*, 15 (1970), 26–47, agrees about the dating, but thinks the *Crat.*'s forms may be separated; he is followed by C. H. Kahn, 'Language and Ontology in the *Cratylus*', in E. N. Lee *et al.* (eds.), *Exegesis and Argument* (Assen, 1973), 152–76. Brandwood

places *Crat.* even before the *Meno.* Owen, on the other hand, dates *Crat.* after *Parm.*; see 'Place', 72 n. 39. I shall assume that Brandwood's dating is roughly correct.

33. It is also interesting to note that in *Crat.* 389b1–3 Plato says that the craftsman looks, not to *broken* shuttles, but to the form of shuttle. He conspicuously neglects to say whether looking to a non-defective actual shuttle would do.

34. He discusses four cases: (i) likeness, one, and many; (ii) beautiful, just, and good; (iii) man, fire, and water; and (iv) hair, mud, and dirt. He unhesitatingly accepts forms in cases (i) and (ii), and it is clear why he does so, since the relevant sensible properties suffer narrow compresence. He is unsure about (iii), and he is tempted to reject the existence of forms for (iv). Sensible examples of (iii) and (iv) are not in narrow compresence (no piece or sort of mud, for example, is both mud and not mud in the narrow sense). Artefacts plainly do not belong in (i) or (ii). Do they belong in (iii) or (iv)? One might favour (iv), on the ground that, like mud and so on, artefacts are 'trivial and undignified', and are 'just what we see them to be', i.e. they are definable in observational terms. But it is not clear that Plato believes this; and certainly, as I shall suggest more fully later, one might argue that artefacts are not definable in observational terms. Further, the examples mentioned in (iv) might be viewed as mass terms, but artefact terms are sortals. So it is not clear that artefacts belong in (iv). The examples mentioned in (iii) are sortals. But fire and water are two of the traditional four elements, and man is a natural kind, perhaps a privileged natural kind. It is not clear whether artefacts are exalted enough to belong on this list. So it is not clear that artefacts belong in (iii) either. Whether or not they do, Plato's failure to mention them is striking.

35. That Socrates takes the crafts to be paradigmatic examples of sciences is indicated by e.g. *Cri.* 47a2–48a7; *La.* 184e11–185e6, 195b2–196a3; *Eu.* 13a2–e11, 14c3–e7; *Ch.* 165c4–166c3 (this last passage shows that Socrates uses '*technē*' and '*epistēmē*' interchangeably). See Irwin, *PMT*, esp. ch. 3, for discussion of Socrates' view of the crafts. By contrast, in *Rep.* 6–7 the best sort of knowledge is dialectic, not craft knowledge. The crafts are presumably either at the second stage of the line (*pistis*), since manufactured objects are placed there (510a1–3), or else at the third stage of the line (*dianoia*), since *technai* belong there (511c6) (though they do not seem to fit the description Plato gives of the third stage of the line). Even if both geometry and the crafts belong at the third stage of the line, *Rep.* 7 ranks the latter as a lower form of knowledge on the ground that it is not concerned with pure being. As I go on to say, *Phil.* also demotes the crafts. (But since the middle dialogues also demote them, I am not now endorsing even the modified version of (iii).) We have seen that Aristotle takes craft knowledge to be less exalted than demonstrative knowledge; see Ch. 5.3.

36. For a helpful discussion of this passage, see J. M. Cooper, 'Plato's Theory of the Human Good in the *Philebus*', *Journal of Philosophy*, 74 (1977), 714–30 at 719–24.

37. In n. 22 I suggested that the crafts might require the existence of e.g. *geometrical* forms; it does not follow that they require the existence of *artefact* forms.

38. See n. 22.

39. If Aristotle were thinking along these lines, then he would not always view forms as a 'package-deal', such that if any of their special features are in the offing, all of them are. See Ch. 2.6.

40. Annas, *Aristotle's Metaphysics, Books M and N*, 161, suggests that *Rep.* 10's forms are not separate. Proclus, *in Parm.* 827–8, says that 'the products of the arts do not have a pre-existing form or an intelligible paradigm of their existence' (tr. Morrow and Dillon). But he believes, not that *Rep.* 10 takes artefact forms to differ in some ways from other Platonic forms, but that it does not countenance artefact forms at all.

   On behalf of the suggestion that *Rep.* 10's artefact forms are not everlasting, one might note that Plato says that the form of bed was created by a god. However, the remark applies to *all* forms, not just to artefact forms, so if it shows that, in Plato's view, artefact forms are not everlasting, it equally shows that, in his view, no forms are everlasting. But perhaps Plato means to suggest just this, in which case this is simply one respect in which *Rep.* 10 is aberrant. On the other hand, even if a god created forms, there are some theories of creation on which it would not follow that forms are not everlasting. I am not sure whether Plato means to suggest in *Rep.* 10 that forms are not everlasting; but he says nothing that implies that they are everlasting.

   If Plato believes that artefact forms are not everlasting, perhaps his reason is that he thinks that the form of shuttle (e.g.) came into existence only when someone had the idea of shuttling. (Frank, *The Arguments 'From the Sciences'*, 89–90, suggests this possibility.) In a somewhat similar vein, Proclus, *in Parm.* 947, says that 'it is only our needs that produced ⟨artefacts⟩ in our world'. But, again, he takes this to show, not that artefact forms differ in some ways from other forms, but that there are no artefact forms. It is true that Plato believes that there must be pre-existing forms of natural kinds to guide the demiurge's activity. But it does not follow that there must be everlasting artefact forms to guide human craftsmen.

   If artefact forms come into existence only when someone has the idea of the corresponding sort of artefact, then artefact forms are not separate, in the sense that they would not exist whether or not anyone ever thought of them, whereas perhaps the moral forms, either in Plato's view or in Aristotle's view of Plato, would exist whether or not anyone ever thought of them.

   In 'Separation', sect. 9, I assumed that artefact forms are everlasting, and I used that assumption to argue that artefact forms are separate, on the ground that if they are everlasting, then they existed before there were any sensible artefacts (since there was presumably a time when there were e.g. no sensible shuttles) and so they existed uninstantiated. Indeed, I even argued— paradoxically, given the Arguments from the Sciences—that artefact forms in some ways provide the clearest evidence that Plato separated forms. (Artefact forms are presumably separate if they are everlasting; but if they are not everlasting it does not follow that they are not separate.)

NOTES TO CHAPTER 7

1. Although the *Meno* is a transitional rather than a Socratic dialogue, it is reasonable to discuss it in connection with Socrates on this point, since the forms it countenances seem to be Socratic (they are not, for example, said to be perfect).

2. AS I(1) also involves further claims (see Ch. 5.2 and n. 9), which Socrates does not so clearly address; but I shall none the less write as though he accepts I(1) as such, both because the further aspects of I(1) are irrelevant to anything I shall argue here and also because I believe that Socrates accepts them.

3. Although he disqualifies both particular *F*s and particular kinds of *F*s from being the basic objects of knowledge, he focuses on the defects of low-level types; so if '*kath' hekasta*' captures his main concern, it should include low-level types.

4. At least, he never claims that Socrates takes forms to be paradigms in an objectionable sense. Further, since he contrasts Socratic and Platonic forms, and takes the latter to be paradigms of an objectionable sort, the natural inference is that he does not take Socratic forms to be paradigms of an objectionable sort.

5. Although *Eu.* has (1), (2), and paradigmatism, referents of correct answers to 'What is *F*?' questions are called 'forms' and 'ideas' before they are called paradigms. Although the *Meno* has (1) and (2), paradigmatism is not explicitly mentioned. (But *Meno* 72c8 uses '*apoblepein eis*', which might suggest paradigmatism.) So it is not clear that Socrates appeals to the existence of paradigms in arguing that there are forms (hence my parentheses in the text).

6. In *Meno* 77a, Plato says that he wants to know what virtue is *kata holou*. See Ch. 2 n. 8.

7. *Gorg.* is generally agreed to be a Socratic dialogue. On the date of *Crat.*, see Ch. 6 n. 32. In Ch. 6, interpretation (vi), we saw that the *Crat.* does not say that artefact forms are e.g. perfect. That Socrates is happy to countenance artefact forms is also suggested by the fact that, as we saw in Ch. 4.4, he believes that there are forms for every property (although one might deny that the names of artefacts denote genuine properties; see Ch. 6 n. 8.)

8. Ross, *Aristotle's Metaphysics*, i. 193. He also cites *Tm.* 51–2. Although *Tm.* undoubtedly discusses change in the sense of succession, *Tm.* 51–2 does not argue from the fact that sensibles change to the existence of forms. Rather, it argues as follows:

(1) If knowledge and true belief are different, then there are non-sensible forms that exist *auta kath' hauta*.

(2) Knowledge is conveyed by instruction, true belief by persuasion; knowledge, but not true belief, is always accompanied by an account (*logos*); true belief, but not knowledge, can be overcome by persuasion; everyone has true belief but only the gods and a few men have knowledge.

(3) Therefore, knowledge and true belief are different.

(4) Therefore, there are forms.

This argument does not mention the changeability of sensibles. It is true that Plato goes on to describe the differences between sensibles and forms in terms that suggest that sensibles but not forms change in various ways. But we have seen that in the middle dialogues, Plato sometimes uses the language of change even when he has compresence in mind, and perhaps the same is true in *Tm*; this is in some ways a tempting interpretation of the passage. But even if Plato goes on to distinguish between forms and sensible particulars by saying that the latter but not the former change, it does not follow, and is not true, that he uses that fact as a premiss in the preceding argument for the existence of forms.

9. I have also provided reasons, independent of the interpretation of Plato, for supposing that the Arguments from the Sciences do not argue from succession to the existence of forms.

10. Frank, *The Arguments 'from the Sciences'*, 81–2. He also suggests another reason for doubting whether *Rep.* 5 is the source for the Arguments from the Sciences: it focuses on knowledge as such, whereas they focus on branches of knowledge (p. 32). But at *Rep.* 438cd Plato says that knowledge itself is of whatever knowledge itself is of; branches of knowledge are of branches of whatever knowledge itself is of. According to *Rep.* 475–80, knowledge itself is of truth (i.e. it is truth-entailing); so particular branches of knowledge are of the truths about the objects in their respective domains. Hence at *Parm.* 134ab Plato says that just as knowledge itself is of truth (*alētheia*, 134a4), so each branch of knowledge is (of certain truths) about the beings (*onta*, 134a7) in its domain. Platonic contexts dealing with knowledge as such are therefore relevant to the question of whether Plato is committed to the Arguments from the Sciences, even though the Arguments from the Sciences focus on particular branches of knowledge.

11. Interestingly enough, however, Plato leaves this assumption tacit in *Rep.* 5, although he highlights it elsewhere (see Ch. 4 n. 60).

12. There are further features of AS I(1) that are less clearly in play here, but see n. 2.

13. In *Rep.* 5, as generally elsewhere in the middle dialogues, the many *F*s are low-level types (see Ch. 4.5). So if the Arguments from the Sciences aim to capture Plato's main concern, *kath' hekasta* should include low-level types.

14. Similar-sounding claims occur elsewhere in Plato too; see Ch. 9.5.

15. See my 'Knowledge and Belief in *Republic* V' and 'Knowledge and Belief in *Republic* V–VII'.

16. In sect. 5 I speculate about a closer connection between compresence and indeterminacy. By contrast, undergoing change in the sense of succession is not a type of indeterminacy, although it is sufficient for indeterminacy; see Ch. 5 n. 49.

17. Contrast Penner, *Ascent*, 60, 90–1, 102ff., 236–7, who takes the dispute between Plato and the sight-lovers to be a dispute between realism and nominalism; for a brief criticism of his view, see my review of *Ascent*. Unlike AS III(2), *Rep.* 5 seems to use '*auto*' only to refer specifically to forms, not to universals more neutrally. See e.g. 479a1–5, where *auto kalon* is the form (*idea*) of beauty, and opposed to the many *F*s, which are properties (e.g. bright colour). I discuss '*auto*' further in Ch. 10.

18. For a defence of the claim that *Rep.* 5 does not restrict knowledge to forms, see the articles cited in n. 15.

19. See Ch. 4 n. 86.

20. For a defence of this claim, see the articles cited in n. 15.

21. In the last section, I said that *Rep.* 5 seems to take sensibles to be imperfect in so far as it compares them to dream-images and in so far as it says that belief is less clear than knowledge partly because the objects on which it tends to focus (sensibles) are less clear than basic objects of knowledge must be. But he does not explicitly say that forms are e.g. *teleōs onta*.

22. I take up this line of argument in Ch. 13.4.

23. On '*aidion*', see Ch. 5 n. 4. Plato typically uses '*aei*' rather than '*aidion*' in characterizing forms, and '*aei*' can be used incompletely more naturally than '*aidion*' can be. '*Aidion*' is indeed surprisingly rare in Plato's descriptions of forms. The middle dialogues never explicitly say that forms are *aidia*, although they implicitly do so once (*Phd.* 106d3). The word is used more frequently, though still not often, in *Tm.* (29a3, 5, 37c6, 37d1, 37e5) and *Phil.* (66a8), and *Tm.* is more clearly concerned with the contrast between everlasting forms and sensible particulars, which are not everlasting, than are the middle dialogues. (I am not sure to what extent *Phil.* has this concern.) The word is more common in Aristotle than in Plato. Perhaps Aristotle uses it in AS I in order to resolve the ambiguity in '*aei*', or to indicate that whatever Plato means in saying that forms are *aei*, he at any rate believes that they are everlasting.

24. We saw in Ch. 4.6, that in *Met.* 13. 9 Aristotle gives Plato a valid argument for separation; in Ch. 14 we shall uncover another one. But presumably Aristotle does not mean that Plato explicitly offered these arguments. Further, both arguments ultimately rest on undefended premisses in a way that fits well with my present claim. For example, in describing the argument recorded in *Met.* 13. 9, Aristotle says that the Platonists assumed that substances must be separate, and could not think of any other candidates for substancehood than non-sensible universals. This suggests that, in Aristotle's view, there is a sense in which Plato assumes without argument that forms are separate. As we shall see in Ch. 14, the same is true of the other valid argument for separation that Aristotle gives to Plato.

25. I discuss this point in 'The One over Many', sects. 6 and 7 (though I now reject several of the claims made there), and in 'Plato on Perception'. Plato seems to agree with Descartes that perception has access only to e.g. particular instances of colours and determinate colours; since he does not think one can understand colour as such by reference to its particular instances or lower-level types, he infers that such understanding requires one to go beyond perception. That Descartes holds this view of perception seems presupposed in e.g. the wax passage in Meditation 2; for some discussion, see M. Wilson, *Descartes* (London, 1978), 78–8.

26. We saw in Ch. 6, however, that Plato might take artefact forms to differ in some ways from (other) distinctively Platonic forms; e.g. perhaps they are not separate or everlasting. I return to this point in sect. 6.

27. Everything is in broad compresence with respect to *some* of its properties. For example, the property of being square is, in the broad sense, both shape

and not shape; for it is shape, and it has features that are inessential to the nature of shape, since not every shape is square. But no property is in broad compresence with respect to the property it is. The property of being square, for instance, has no features that are inessential to the nature of square as such. (Has it not the inessential property of—say—being known by Socrates? No; for that is not a genuine property, and only genuine properties are relevant here.)

28. At 230 ff., Plato divides *ta onta* into four classes: indeterminates, determinants, combined things, and causes. It is disputed whether he means that *each* of the things that is has both an indeterminate and a determinate element or aspect, or whether he means that *some* of the things that are are indeterminate whereas other things that are are determinate. Like many commentators, I favour the first interpretation. (For a defence of this interpretation, see Cooper, 'Plato's Theory of Human Good in the *Philebus*'.) Frank, *The Arguments 'From the Sciences'*, 58–61, argues that on this interpretation, *Phil.* is irrelevant to AS II. For on it, *Phil.* then claims that *everything* is *apeiron*; but AS II takes *kath' hekasta*, but not forms or universals, to be *apeira*. However, Frank's argument at most shows that the *extensions* of '*apeira*' differ in the two contexts; it does not show that their *senses* differ. Nor do I think that Frank's argument even shows that the extensions differ. AS II claims that *kath' hekasta* are indeterminate when they are considered independently of forms; and it conceives of forms described in determinate fashion. That is perfectly compatible with *Phil.*'s claim that one can describe forms in an indeterminate fashion, and sensibles in a determinate fashion. The form of square, for example, is indeterminate for the purposes of explaining what shape as such is; but it is none the less appropriate to call it a determinant, since it is the only thing that is in the relevant way determinately square. Every form of *F* is determinately *F*, although it is indeterminately various other things; see n. 28. Frank also argues that if sensibles can be described determinately, then they are knowable, a possibility that, in his view, AS II precludes. Since in my view AS II does not preclude this possibility, neither is this a stumbling-block to assimilating *Phil.* to AS II. So I think that *Phil.* uses '*apeiron*' in a way that is close to the way in which it is used in AS II, as I interpreted it in Ch. 5.

29. For a similar interpretation, see Cooper, 'Plato's Theory of Human Good in the *Philebus*', 716. Notice that although Plato does not have succession in mind in explaining indeterminacy, he none the less (as in the middle dialogues) sometimes speaks in temporal-sounding language. He says, for example, that the higher 'keeps on advancing and does not stand still' (24d4). He means, not that a given high note is continually getting higher (a claim about succession), but that for any high note, there is always a higher one, so that what is higher than one note is lower than another; this involves compresence.

30. Aristotle also links indeterminacy and compresence in the Argument from Relatives. But here the compresence is narrow rather than broad; see Ch. 10.6.

31. This is not to say that the Imperfection Argument and the Arguments from the Sciences are just the same: we have seen various ways in which they

differ. For example, I said before that the Arguments from the Sciences do not explicitly say that *kath' hekasta* are imperfect, whereas according to the Imperfection Argument a certain range of sensibles are imperfect. But AS II claims that *kath' hekasta* are indeterminate; and my present suggestion is that Plato, in using the Imperfection Argument, takes indeterminacy to be a kind of imperfection. So both the Imperfection Argument and the Arguments from the Sciences advert to the same phenomenon, of indeterminacy, but only the Imperfection Argument takes indeterminacy to be a kind of imperfection.

32. In the last chapter, I said that *Phil.* 55 ff. may suggest that craft knowledge is not exalted enough to require the existence of artefact forms. Does that not conflict with my present suggestion that the Imperfection Argument seems to require the existence of artefact forms? No, for even if craft knowledge does not require the existence of artefact forms, other sorts of knowledge might require their existence. And perhaps *Phil.* 55 ff. means only that the crafts do not require forms with certain features, which leaves open the possibility that they require forms with other features.

33. This is not to say that Plato denies that (most) forms are everlasting or separate. It is only to say that he does not seem to take the Imperfection Argument to imply that forms are everlasting or separate.

NOTES TO CHAPTER 8

1. Aristotle's objections to the One over Many Argument thus parallel his objections to the Arguments from the Sciences.

2. See e.g. Frede, *Prädikation*, 92–4, and Gallop, *Plato's Phaedo*, 96–7. Ross, *Plato's Theory of Ideas*, 24, 36, 225, and Annas, *An Introduction to Plato's Republic*, 227, and 'Forms and First Principles', 277, believe that Plato's one over many argument posits forms for every general term, but they do not say that it takes forms to be meanings. According to G. Matthews and S. Marc Cohen, 'The One and the Many', *Review of Metaphysics*, 21 (1968), 630–55, a linguistic concern 'especially gives life to' the One over Many Argument (p. 631).

3. The text at this point says that *something* (*ti*) is predicated, not that some *one* (*hen*) thing is. (By contrast, in AS I '*hen*' is explicit.) But *ti* is clearly taken to be one thing; for otherwise, the inference to there being a *one* over many would be invalid and Aristotle would not claim, as he does, that the One over Many Argument is a valid argument for the existence of *koina*. Nor does the text explicitly say at this point that what is predicated of the many *F*s is the *F*. But the One over Many Argument clearly argues that what is predicated of the many *F*s is the form of *F*. Hence what is predicated of the many *F*s is the *F*, and the question is what the *F* is: a Platonic form, a *koinon*, or something else. I formulate (1) so as to make clear these tacit assumptions of the corresponding part of the text.

4. On '*kechōrismenon*', see Ch. 4 n. 28.

5. For references to places where Aristotle connects '*hen arithmō(i)*' with particularity, see Ch. 2 n. 30. On various ways of being one, see e.g. *Met.* 5. 6; 10. 1–3.

6. This is not explicit in the One over Many Argument proper, but cf. 81. 19.

7. See e.g. *Rep.* 380d3; *Parm.* 139a1. Penner, *Ascent*, 248 with 401–2 n. 20, thinks that '*allassomenōn*' is so used in the One over Many Argument.

8. See e.g. *Laws* 733b2; Euripides, *Phoenissae* 74. LSJ, sv. III and IV, cites several further references. When '*allassamena*' is so used, it is connected to '*kath' hekasta*' (see Ch. 5 n. 13), and the phrase 'numerically successive particulars' is then similar in force to *ta kath' hekastēn epistēmēn ginomena* in AS I.

9. That this is the correct interpretation is supported by the fact that in the parallel passage at 80. 21 Aristotle substitutes *kata tōn homoiōn*, making it clear that what is at issue is simply the fact that there are many things that are alike in being *F*; change is not relevant. Nor does the parallel argument at 81. 10–22, which appeals to negation rather than to affirmation, mention change.

10. This recalls AS I's claim that every science works with reference to some one and the same thing (though cf. n. 3). But in AS I some one and the same thing is needed for every *science* or body of knowledge, whereas in the One over Many Argument some one thing is needed for every *predication*; depending on how many predications there are, the One over Many Argument and the Arguments from the Sciences might generate different ranges of forms. (In sect. 3 I ask what counts as a predication.) I take '*aei*' to mean 'in every case', in which case just as everlastingness is not involved in AS I's 'one and the same' requirement, so it is not involved in premiss (3) of the One over Many Argument.

11. The One over Many Argument thus assumes *weak non-identity*, the view that no sensible *F* is *F* in virtue of itself. For as we will see, it argues that every property is a form. So for any property *F* that a sensible *x* has, *x* is *F* in virtue of the form of *F* and so in virtue of something distinct from itself. I discuss weak non-identity in more detail in chs. 15 and 16.

12. The same mistaken inference occurs in AS I. But we have seen (Ch. 5.2 and n. 20) that Aristotle may take the inference to be valid.

13. See n. 17 for two different ways of reading (6).

14. Aristotle uses various phrases that I generally translate indifferently as 'one over many', since he does not seem to intend any difference in sense in his various locutions. In the One over Many Argument, for example, he uses '*epi*' both with the dative and with the genitive, although he does not seem to intend any difference in sense. Unlike me, Leszl, *Il 'De Ideis'*, 108–15, does not believe that Aristotle always uses 'one over many' for universals; for, he argues, Aristotle says that each form is a one over many yet, in Leszl's view, forms are not universals. For further discussion of Aristotle's use of the phrase 'one over many', see Ch. 2 n. 8; and the end of Ch. 5.2. For the point I go on to make about the two different uses of 'one over many', see also Ch. 5 n. 23.

15. Cf. *Met.* 1040b26–30, where Aristotle says that the Platonists are right to separate forms, since forms are substances, but wrong to take *to hen epi pollōn* to be a form. Aristotle means that the Platonists are right to separate

forms, given that they take forms to be substances, for all substances are separate. Their mistake is to take forms to be substances; for forms are universals but, in Aristotle's view, universals cannot be separate since, in his view, they cannot exist uninstantiated.

16. Contrast my 'The One over Many', n. 6.
17. We have seen that the inference to everlastingness is also invalid. But it is not clear that Aristotle would agree; at least, we have seen that he may take the inference to everlastingness in AS I to be valid (see n. 12). Further, as we shall see in Ch. 14, Aristotle seems to take the Accurate One over Many Argument to be a valid argument for the existence of forms because it is a valid argument for the existence of separate universals; everlastingness is not mentioned. Whatever Aristotle thinks about the inference to everlastingness here, I assume that he is mainly concerned with separation, and so I shall focus on it.

(6) can be read in two ways: (i) being a separated, everlasting, one over many is sufficient for being a form; (ii) being a form consists in being a separated, everlasting, one over many. ((ii) implies (i), but not conversely.) On (ii), being separated and everlasting is necessary for being a form. If (ii) is right, then, since the inference to separation and everlastingness is not valid, the One over Many Argument does not imply that there are forms. But (i) leaves open the possibility that forms need not be separated or everlasting, in which case the fact that the One over Many Argument does not imply separation or everlastingness does not by itself mean that it does not imply that there are forms. I am inclined to think that (6) should be read as (i). But the explanation given in the text makes it reasonable to suppose that Aristotle none the less takes the One over Many Argument to be invalid primarily because it does not imply that universals are separate.

18. For man as a secondary substance, see e.g. *Cat.* 2a14–19. For man—not 'man'—as what is predicated, see e.g. *Cat.* 1b10–15. Of course, 'man' can also be predicated: see e.g. 2a19–33. The point is only that things no less than words can be predicated. I generally use 'predicable' for non-linguistic entities that are predicated, and 'predicate' for linguistic entities. The species man, for example, is a predicable; the term 'man' is a predicate.
19. For a brief discussion of *koina*, see Ch. 2, esp. sects. 4 and 6.
20. See n. 19.
21. It would be irrelevant if, as I believe, a predicate is meaningful just in case a competent speaker of the language understands or can easily be brought to understand it. However, the One over Many Argument might be a semantic argument on some other account of meaning. For more on meaning, see Ch. 2.3.

How can the One over Many Argument both posit forms only for predicates true of groups of things and also take forms to be separate? One possible answer is that its inference to separation is, after all, invalid. Another possible answer is that it posits a form of F just in case there are F sensible particulars at some time, which leaves open the possibility that the form of F can exist at t_1 even if there are no F sensible particulars at t_1.
22. That is, meanings and properties are in fact disjoint classes of entities (see Ch. 2.3). Whether Plato and Aristotle realize this is a further question. The

considerations I go on to adduce suggest that Aristotle realizes this. I consider Plato below.

23. In ascribing (1c) to Plato, Aristotle seems to ascribe to him the view that every meaningful term denotes a real property, though properties are not identified with meanings nor is their existence taken to be necessary for the corresponding terms to be meaningful. This position was mentioned in Ch. 2 n. 13.

24. But does Aristotle then countenance *koina* corresponding to every predicate true of groups of things? No, which is why he believes that the One over Many Argument is not a sound argument for the existence of *koina*: although it correctly generates *koina* as properties, it generates too many of them. If (1) took what is predicated to be a linguistic predicate or a meaning, it would not even be a valid argument for the existence of *koina*. See Ch. 5 n. 2.

25. Cherniss, *Aristotle's Criticism*, 261; cf. 254, 256. *ROT* seems to agree, for it translates '*ta mē onta*' as 'things that do not exist'.

26. At least, examples of things that never exist (e.g. fictional entities) would be inappropriate, although examples of things that do not exist now though they exist at some other time would not be. See n. 21.

27. Further support (for some of which I am indebted to Owen, in class notes): the *Met.* passages that mention the One over Many Argument (990b13–14, 1079a9–10) mention only *apophaseis* and not also *ta mē onta*, suggesting that the latter are not a separate class from the former. (Did Alexander add '*ta mē onta*', perhaps for the sake of parallelism with The Object of Thought Argument?) In place of *ta mē onta*, the Object of Thought Argument has *ta mēd' holōs onta* (which I assume are non-existent things), and it provides appropriate examples (*hippokentauron*, *chimairan*) (but see Ch. 9 n. 24). Syrianus (*in Met.* 110. 18–29) and Asclepius (*in Met.* 74. 12–28) mention only negations, and not also things that do not exist.

28. Here I use 'definition' for lexical rather than real definition. There is no real definition of not-man, since not-man is not a genuine property. One might argue that on a referential theory of meaning, 'not-man' cannot be defined; for since it denotes nothing, it is meaningless. Whatever the merits of this argument, either in fact or as something Plato believes, it is clearly not the reason Aristotle goes on to give for finding fault with negations.

29. Aristotle says there cannot be an idea of not-being, i.e. I take it, of negations; and he then goes on to explain why: (i) there would then be forms 'of things different in genus'; (ii) there would then be forms of things that are *ahorista* and *apeira*; and (iii) there would then be a single form for things that are primary and secondary, e.g. of man and animal. (The syntax suggests that man is taken to be prior to animal. This is true on some, but not all, of the sorts of priority that Aristotle recognizes. See e.g. *Cat.*, chs. 12–13, *Met.* 5. 11.) I take it that (ii) and (iii) illustrate (i), rather than providing further examples, and so I shall not discuss them separately in the text; but a few brief remarks are in order.

(ii) is odd in so far as, in one sense, there obviously are forms of things that are *ahorista* and *apeira*. For as AS II explains, sensibles, considered in themselves, are *apeira* and *ahorista*; yet there are certainly forms corresponding to some sensibles. Presumably, then, Aristotle uses the same phrase differently here. LF not surprisingly omits the phrase altogether; Bonitz and Hayduck omit '*kai tōn ahoristōn te*'. I assume Aristotle means that there would be forms of negations for kinds of things that are indeterminate, in so far as they do not constitute a genuine kind or share any genuine property; cf. *Pol.* 262d, and also the *DI* passages I go on to cite.

(iii) is also odd in so far as there seem to be forms of some things that are primary and secondary. For example, in *Rep.* 6–7 Plato countenances a form of the good; but some goods are prior to others. Perhaps Aristotle means that although Plato acknowledges a form of the good and believes that some goods are prior to others, he *ought* not to countenance a form of the good, since he wants to restrict forms to genuine properties, yet goods do not as such constitute a natural kind, and goodness is not a single property. Aristotle's objection would then be not that Plato explicitly denied the existence of forms for every series containing prior and posterior but that he ought to have done so, since countenancing forms here violates Plato's own view that there are forms corresponding only to property-names. (Perhaps *EN* 1096a17–23 can be construed along similar lines.) Plato would of course protest that Aristotle is wrong to deny that goodness, for example, is a genuine property.

30. See Armstrong, ii. 23–9, for a parallel account and criticism of negative universals.

31. J. L. Ackrill, *Aristotle's Categories and De Interpretatione* (Oxford, 1963), 117–18. In *DI* (16a31), Aristotle denies that 'not-man' is a negation; but that is because he is using 'negation' for negative statements, and 'not-man' is not a statement.

32. So just as Socrates accepts (some of) the premisses but not the conclusion of the Arguments from the Sciences, so he accepts a one over many argument, though he is not committed to the conclusion of the One over Many Argument.

33. Cherniss, *Aristotle's Criticism*, 260 n. 170. (Cherniss does not explicitly say that the passage means to establish the existence of a form for every predicate; but I think that is what he means.) Cherniss also cites *So.* 243de and *Phil.* 34e3–4. The *So.* passage is indeterminate. The *Phil.* passage reads: 'What was the common feature, then, that we had in mind to persuade us to call these very different things by the same name?' However, Plato does not say that the fact that there is a name shows that there is a corresponding form; he says that we apply names only when we believe there is a shared property. The direction of fit is from property to name, not from name to property. Notice that all three of the passages that Cherniss cites are from late dialogues.

34. I discuss the Third Man Argument in Ch. 15. In Ch. 16 I ask whether Plato is vulnerable to it.

35. Cornford, *Plato and Parmenides*, 87, translates 132a1 as follows: 'I imagine your ground for believing in a single Form in each case (*hekaston*) is this.' Even on this translation, the passage need not be taken to assert that there is a form for every predicate. Plato might mean only that there is a single form in each case *in which there is a form*, in which case he says nothing about how

many predicates have corresponding forms. But for reasons given in Ch. 15 n. 8, I think the translation I supply in the text is to be preferred.

36. One might argue, however, that we need not try to make 130cd consistent with 132, on the ground that this part of *Parm.* considers different accounts of forms, without meaning to suggest that they all add up to a consistent package that Plato ever bought. One might also argue that although 130cd is unsure about acknowledging forms for every predicate, 135ac overcomes the hesitation.

37. Cf. 81. 5; 79. 10. This use of '*apeiron*' is obviously very close to the one in AS II.

38. '*Barbaros*' is not a negation in the technical sense I have specified, since it is not the complement of being Greek: it does not apply to everything that fails to be Greek including e.g. the sun or circles. (It does, however, apply to more than non-Greek people, as in '*barbaros gē*', a foreign country.) Nor is it clear that being Greek is a genuine property; if it is not, then that is yet a further reason for saying that '*barbaros*' is not a negation. It is sometimes thought that Plato objects to the division into *barbaroi* and other peoples on the ground that every division must be genuinely dichotomous, in the sense that it must divide any given class into two, each division containing equal numbers of members. But his point is rather that if we want to understand the nature of human beings, the division into Greeks and *barbaroi* is not explanatory. (He suggests that the division into male and female would be more appropriate.)

39. See the references cited in n. 2. In Ch. 7.4 we saw that despite the fact that Plato sometimes focuses on narrow compresence, he sometimes focuses on a broader sort of imperfection that requires the existence of further forms. I return to the Imperfection Argument below, but for the moment I focus on the one over many.

40. The Greek is *eidos gar pou ti hen hekaston eiōthamen tithesthai peri hekasta ta polla hois tauton onoma epipheromen*. The standard translation has been challenged by J. A. Smith, in 'General Relative Clauses in Greek', *Classical Review*, 31 (1917), 69–71. He suggests the following alternative translation: 'We are, as you know, in the habit of assuming [as a rule of procedure] that the Idea which corresponds to a group of particulars, each to each, is always one, in which case [*or*: and in that case] we call the group, or its particulars, by the same name as the *eidos*.' On this translation, 596a6–7 says nothing about how many predicates have corresponding forms. It says only that (i) there is exactly one form of *F* corresponding to every predicate for which there is a form (this is the *Uniqueness Assumption* (U), which is relevant both to the Third Man Argument and to the so-called Third Bed Argument; see Chs. 15 and 16, and below, sect. 7); and (ii) if there is a form of *F*, then the particulars that have it are called *F*.

   A. Nehamas, 'Plato on Imitation and Poetry in *Republic* 10', in J. Moravcsik and P. Tempko (eds.), *Plato on Beauty, Wisdom, and the Arts* (Totowa, NJ, 1982), 47–78 at 72–3 n. 32, says that Smith's construal is 'not implausible'. M. F. Burnyeat, 'The Practicability of Plato's Ideally Just City', in K. Boudouris (ed.), *On Justice: Plato's and Aristotle's Conception of Justice in Relation to Modern and Contemporary Theories of Justice* (Athens, 1989)

95–104 at 102 n. 4, thinks that the passage 'can equally well be construed either way', though 'Smith's construal fits the context much better'. I do not agree with Burnyeat on the second point. It is true that Plato goes on to defend U. But his defence involves a one over many thesis. So both a one over many and U fit the context. Nor does Smith's construal seem as natural as the standard one. I shall therefore assume that the standard translation is correct.

It is worth noting that even on Smith's translation, the passage should give pause to those who think that in the middle dialogues Plato restricts forms to predicates whose sensible instances exhibit narrow compresence. For *Rep.* 10 has a form of bed, and one of table; yet narrow compresence does not show that there are such forms.

41. For this view, see Frede, *Prädikation*, 92–4; Annas, 'Forms and First Principles', 277, 279; and S. M. Cohen, 'The Logic of the Third Man', *Philosophical Review*, 80 (1971), 448–75 at 473 n. 41.

42. Frede, *Prädikation*, 93, notes the similarity between Aristotle's criticism of the One over Many Argument and *Pol.*; but he seems to think Plato's criticism precedes Aristotle's (cf. 'bereits' and 'dann').

43. For a similar suggestion, see I. M. Crombie, *An Examination of Plato's Doctrines* (London, 1963), ii. 282.

44. I discuss *Crat.* on names in more detail in 'Plato on Naming'. On the date of *Crat.*, see Ch. 6 n. 32.

That *Crat.* uses 'name' for property-names is suggested by 386a ff. At 387d4–8, for example, Plato says that in order to name, one must name things as they are by nature (i.e. as they really are); otherwise, one does not succeed in naming at all. At 388b7–8, he asks what we do when we name, and he goes on to say (388b13–c1) that to name is to teach and to distinguish *ousia*, essences or natures.

A more moderate version of my suggestion that *Crat.* restricts names to property-names would be the following. *Crat.* distinguishes between correct and incorrect names: 'n' seems to count as a correct name just in case it is a good description of the property or kind to which it refers; 'n' seems to be an incorrect name just in case, although it refers to a real property or kind, its descriptive content is less rich or informative. If so, then both correct and incorrect names demarcate properties or kinds, and so all names are, as on my view, property-names. But assume for the sake of argument that incorrect names do not need to demarcate properties or kinds, in which case not all names are property-names. Then one could say that *Rep.* 596a uses 'name' for *true* or *correct* names.

45. For example, both passages are unusual in explicitly mentioning artefact forms. Further, both passages distinguish between users and makers of artefacts; Plato claims that the maker looks to the relevant form in fashioning his creation, although the user directs the maker in so far as he knows what features artefacts should embody. It is a curious fact about both contexts that the user is accorded knowledge, even though he is not said to look to forms. See n. 67.

46. In terms of the more moderate interpretation of *Crat.*, Plato posits a form of *F* only if he thinks that '*F*' is a correct name. The account I have been

suggesting restricts forms to (at most) property-names because (i) Socrates' one over many argument so restricts forms; (ii) usually Plato appeals only to narrow compresence, which does not establish forms even for every property-name; (iii) forms are supposed to carve at the natural joints, but not every predicate does that; (iv) the broader version of IA likewise requires forms at most for every property-name; (v) none of the passages we have explored appeals to semantic considerations, or to anything else that might require forms for every predicate. (Although *Phd.* is sometimes thought to introduce forms for semantic reasons, it is not committed to the existence of forms for every predicate. I consider *Phd.* in more detail esp. in Ch. 9.5; see also Ch. 10, and Ch. 11 n. 26. I argue in Ch. 9 and in Ch. 11 that *Phd.* does not conceive forms as meanings.)

47. See White, *Plato on Knowledge and Reality*, 9, 27 n. 49.
48. I follow Aristotle in taking a one over many argument to be an argument that posits universals by appealing to the fact that many things are *F* (or share the predicate '*F*'); see Ch. 4 n. 20.
49. See Ch. 4.4.
50. We have not yet looked at *Phd.*, but see n. 46.
51. See e.g. 16a19–21, 16a26–9, 17a1–2. In his second commentary on *DI* (ed. Meiser, ii. 93–4; I owe the reference to N. Kretzmann, 'Plato on the Correctness of Names', *American Philosophical Quarterly*, 8 (1971), 126–38 at 129 n. 9), Boethius links the last passage to *Crat.* and develops the connection between naturalism and tools. Plato discusses the difference between names and animal noises at *Crat.* 423 ff.; and of course the debate between nature and convention theories of the correctness of names is a central topic of *Crat.*
52. Does Aristotle misinterpret Plato if 596a6–7 should be construed as Smith (see n. 40) construes it? Perhaps not. True, there would then be no passage in the middle dialogues that explicitly says that every name has a corresponding form. But neither does Plato explicitly say that there are forms corresponding at most to every property-name; nor is he ever especially clear about the precise range of forms. Perhaps Aristotle's point would then still be that Plato does not do enough to tell us how many predicates have corresponding forms, and that point is certainly correct.
53. Plato countenances forms of *opposites*: there is a form not only of beauty but also of ugliness, not only of equality but also of inequality, and so on. But opposites are not negations. The negation of the beautiful is not the ugly, but the not-beautiful. I discuss forms of opposites further in Ch. 13.3.
54. For the view that *So.*'s forms are meanings, see e.g. Frede, *Prädikation*, 92–4; Cornford, *Plato's Theory of Knowledge*, 293 and *passim*; Ackrill, 'Συμπλοκὴ εἰδῶν'. For further discussion of whether *So.*'s forms are meanings, see Ch. 9.5–6.
55. 'Not-being' and 'different' are generally thought to denote the same form; see e.g. Vlastos, 'Ambiguity', 289 n. 44. But Frede, *Prädikation*, 81–5, argues that not-being is only a part of the different. I shall write as though Vlastos is correct, although nothing I say turns on this dispute.
56. On the technical account I provided, not-being is a negation just in case it is the complement of being and being is a genuine property. One might argue

that since being is not a genuine property, not-being is not a negation. But I take it that Plato counts being as a genuine property; he would none the less deny that not-being is a negation on the ground that it is not the complement of being.

57. Cherniss, *Aristotle's Criticism*, 262, also argues that not-being is not a negation, but some of his reasons differ from mine. He also suggests that *Aristotle* may have thought that not-being was a negation, 'the contrary of the idea of existence' (p. 263). Quite apart from the fact that *'einai'* does not mean 'to exist' here, I do not think this is Aristotle's view. For some criticism of Cherniss, see D. J. Allan's review in *Mind*, 55 (1946), 263–72.

58. I discuss this aspect of Plato's epistemology briefly in 'Knowledge and *Logos* in the *Theaetetus*', *Philosophical Review*, 88 (1979), 366–97; see also 'Knowledge and Belief in *Republic* V–VII'.

59. This point is lucidly discussed by H. Putnam, 'On Properties', in id., *Philosophical Papers*, i. 305–22.

60. This suggests that Plato does not take the *Politicus'* argument against the existence of a form of barbarian to count against the existence of forms of being, different, and the like; contrast Frede, *Prädikation*, 94.

61. Here I agree with Cornford, *Plato's Theory of Knowledge*, 293; Cherniss, *Aristotle's Criticism*, 263–5; and Ross, *Plato's Theory of Ideas*, 167–8. Contrast Frede, *Pradikation*, 92–4. The issue is also discussed in R. S. Bluck, *Plato's Sophist: A Commentary* (Manchester, 1975), 165 ff.

62. Since it is controversial to deny that the not-beautiful and so on are forms, it is worth asking what we should say if, contrary to my view, they are forms. In this case, Plato seems to accept forms of negations. But it does not follow that he accepts (1*b*) or (1*c*). Frede, *Prädikation*, 92–4, for example, believes that *So.* has forms of negations but not forms for every general term, in which case (1*c*) is not in play. J. M. E. Moravcsik, 'Being and Meaning in the *Sophist*', *Acta Philosophica Fennica*, 14 (1962), 23–78 at 72, argues that although Plato countenances forms of negations, he takes them to be genuine properties; this suggestion could be used to provide an alternative to (1*b*). Plato's argument seems to be that in order to understand what it is to be beautiful, one needs to know what it is to be not-beautiful (whether or not it is a form), what being beautiful excludes as well as what it includes. Here as elsewhere he appeals not to semantic but to explanatory or epistemological considerations.

63. The curious appendix to the One over Many Argument (IV; 81. 10–22)— which, perhaps significantly, is omitted by F and not mentioned elsewhere by Aristotle (or by Asclepius, who generally follows Alexander rather closely)— suggests yet another reply to Aristotle's suggestion that the One over Many Argument commits Plato to forms of negations. In the One over Many Argument, Aristotle writes as though Plato treats 'not-*F*' as a predicate so that in saying, for example, that Socrates and Callias are not horses, Plato would take it that one affirms that they are not-horses. In IV, however, it is suggested that in saying that Socrates and Callias are not horses, one denies that they are horses. That is, saying that Socrates and Callias are not horses does not involve a special predicate, 'not-horse'; rather, it involves only the familiar predicate, 'horse'. If we understand negation in this way, then we can

avoid Aristotle's criticism in II. It is curious, to say the least, that having offered his objection in II, Aristotle (or someone) goes on to record an argument in IV that appears to vitiate his objection. Perhaps the author of IV thinks that although IV explains how one could in fact avoid the criticism in II, this escape-route is not available to Plato, since he does not understand negation in the appropriate way. In *So.*, however, Plato does treat negation in the appropriate way. But perhaps the author of IV thinks that this is an innovation in *So.*, whereas Aristotle's target is the middle dialogues. It is true that the middle dialogues do not explicitly explain negation in the way in which *So.* does; but I do not see that it is confused about it in a way that makes the suggested escape-route unavailable. But perhaps the author of IV would reply that since the middle dialogues do not explicitly provide an appropriate account of negation, he is under no obligation to assume that one is available. For an interesting discussion of IV, see Ackrill's review of Wilpert.

64. If (contrary to my view) Plato acknowledges forms of negations at least in *So.*, then we need a different explanation of Aristotle's claim that the Platonists did not want forms of negations. (We should then face a problem parallel to one we faced in connection with Aristotle's second criticism of the Arguments from the Sciences. He says there that the Platonists did not want forms of artefacts; yet it was difficult to understand why he said that, when Plato so plainly countenances some sort of artefact forms.) I think the best explanation of Aristotle's objection, on the assumption (which I reject) that *So.* countenances forms of negations, is that although Plato thinks that negations are genuine properties, Aristotle disagrees with him. His criticism would then be, not that Plato is internally inconsistent (both restricting forms to properties and also acknowledging forms of negations even though he does not count negations as properties), but that since Plato wants to restrict forms to properties, he *ought* not to admit forms of negations for, contrary to Plato, negations are not properties. As we shall see in Ch. 13, Aristotle's claim that the Platonists do not want forms of relatives also involves this strategy; see also above, n. 29.

65. Similarly, we saw that the premisses of the Arguments from the Sciences are recognizably Socratic, though its conclusion is Platonic. None the less, we saw that a good case can be made for the claim that their premisses are also, if more subtly, Platonic.

66. U is mentioned without argument at 596b2–4; it is defended at 597cd. I explore its defence in Ch. 16.4. On Smith's translation (see n. 40), 596a6–7 also asserts U.

67. At 601d8–602a2, however, Plato says that the craftsman has (not knowledge, but) true belief. He also says here that the craftsman acquires his true beliefs (not from consulting forms, but) from the user, who has knowledge (not from consulting forms, but) based on experience (601d8). Plato therefore leaves it unclear precisely what cognitive value looking to forms has.

68. 596e11 says that a pictured bed is an apparent (*phainomenēn*) bed. But the point seems to be that this explains the sense in which a pictured bed is a bed; Plato is not retracting the suggestion that it is a bed. 597d11–e2 qualifies the claim that a painter makes a bed; but the qualification seems to be to the

claim that he is a craftman and maker, rather than to the claim that what he 'makes' is (an apparent bed, and so) a bed. See Ch. 10.4 for a discussion of Plato's view of pictured *F*s.

69. See Ch. 7.4.

70. If this is right, then Aristotle thinks that at least sometimes Plato takes artefact forms to be separate. Still, he might view *Rep.* 10 as being aberrant in this respect. See Ch. 6, interpretation (vi).

NOTES TO CHAPTER 9

1. For the relevant passage from LF, see Ch. 1.

2. The text at this point mentions particulars as such, not particular *men*; the same is true in the text corresponding to (3). But I assume that particular men are the only relevant particulars in the case of thinking of man.

3. For '*nous*' and its cognates used for BT in Plato, see e.g. *Phd.* 73c8–9, d7. In *Rep.* 6–7, '*nous*' is sometimes used for the highest sort of knowledge (as at 511d8), sometimes for knowledge as such (as at 533e8–534a); in *Tm.* 51d3 it is used for knowledge as such. For '*nous*' used for BT (or, at any rate, not for an especially exalted cognitive condition) in Aristotle, see e.g. *EN* 1170a32–3. Aristotle also often uses '*nous*' and its cognates for practical, as opposed to theoretical, reason. In *APo.* 2. 19, however, '*nous*' is used for a cognitive condition more exalted than *epistēmē*.

4. Leszl, *Il 'De Ideis'*, ch. 8, however, suggests that the Arguments from the Sciences concern knowledge as such and that the Object of Thought Argument concerns the highest sort of knowledge. Cherniss, *Aristotle's Criticism*, 272, thinks that the Object of Thought Argument is the same as the second Argument from the Sciences. It might also be argued that although the Arguments from the Sciences and the Object of Thought Argument both concern knowledge, they appeal to different considerations about knowledge. But the *Peri ideōn* is more neatly organized if the Object of Thought Argument considers a different cognitive condition from one considered at an earlier stage. The next consideration mentioned in the text also counts in favour of BT.

5. See Ch. 5.3.

6. 'Only' should be included if we assume (1*g*) but not if we assume (1*h*). (I distinguish between (1*g*) and (1*h*) below.) (1) is more controversial if 'only' is included than it is if it is not included, though some would dissent from (1) even if it is not included.

7. For parallel considerations in another context, see Ch. 5.3.

8. Syntax allows (1) to concern thinking not of man but of a particular man, but this alternative seems less likely. First, II plainly considers thoughts about particulars (Socrates is mentioned as an example). If I also concerned such thoughts, Aristotle could easily have supplied a similar example; instead he uses man, footed, and animal—species, differentia, and genus. Secondly, if I concerned thoughts about particulars, it is not clear how it would differ from

II. But if I concerns (some) general thoughts, the transition from I to II has obvious point: the Platonists believe that (some) general thoughts require the existence of special objects, the forms; but they would be embarrassed to have to concede the existence of a form of Socrates no less than of man. II argues that they need to concede just this. That (1) concerns thinking of a particular man is defended by J. Annas, 'Aristotle and Plato on Objects of Thought' (unpublished paper). I thank Annas for allowing me to read and refer to this paper; it has influenced me at various stages in this chapter.

9. If they accept (1*d*) and (1*g*), they also accept (1*d*) and (1*h*). But in this case, *x* is the appropriate substitution for '*y*' in (1*h*).

10. At least, I think that both options are unattractive. Aristotle also thinks they are unattractive, since he allows one to think of non-existent things; see e.g. *Top.* 121b1–4; *Met.* 1047a32–b2; *De Mem.* 452b11; *APo.* 92b5–8. (In these passages, 'thought' is presumably BT. For Aristotle generally denies that one can know particulars, whether perished or not; see e.g. *Met.* 7. 15. He also denies that one can know fictional entities; see e.g. *APo.* 92b5–8.) In sects. 5 and 6 I ask whether Plato finds these options unattractive.

11. Cf. AS I(1), 79. 5–6: every science works by referring to some one and the same thing.

12. This means, not that if you think of man *qua* rational animal and I think of man *qua* warmonger, the complete content of our thoughts is exactly the same, but that in so far as we are thinking simply of man as such, the content is the same.

13. OAC does not explicitly say that (basic) objects of thought must be everlasting, but it seems to intend this claim. As often, LF makes the relevant point clearly: *touto de ouden an eiē heteron ē hē idea aphthartos ousa*, 82. 1.

14. 81. 27 says that when we think of (e.g.) man, we think of something other than *any* particular (*kath' hekaston*); so the (basic) objects of thought (which turn out to be forms) are not particulars. (As I say in n. 2, the text seems to mean that whenever we think of man, we think of something other than any particular man, though 'man' is not explicitly mentioned. But whether or not it is supplied, the Object of Thought Argument assumes that no particulars whatsoever are everlasting.) Since there are only particulars and universals (*DI* 17a38–b1), the (basic) objects of thought are universals. It is true that 81. 28 mentions *sensible* particulars (*kath' hekasta kai aisthēta*). So one might argue that 81. 27 means only that when we think of man, we think of something other than a sensible particular; this would leave open the possibility that we think of a non-sensible particular. But 'sensibles' seems to be a gloss, rather than a restriction, on *kath' hekasta*; as elsewhere in the *Peri ideōn*, the existence of non-sensible particulars is ignored. LF is again more explicit; cf. 82. 7–9. Cf. also (in OAC) 88. 7–8: *ho te gar apo tou noeisthai ti koinon epi pleiosi, noeisthai de kai mēketi ontōn tōn kath' hekasta.* Cf. Ch. 2 n. 27, and Ch. 5 n. 16.

15. The first Argument from the Sciences and the One over Many Argument conclude, respectively, that the basic objects of knowledge and what is predicated must be everlasting. But they do not say that all *kath' hekasta* fail to be everlasting: that is not the defect of *kath' hekasta* they have in mind.

16. I ask whether it is invalid when I discuss IV.

17. Of course, it is plausible (though not uncontroversial) to believe that two thoughts cannot have the same content if they are about different objects. But the present point is that two thoughts can have the same content even if there is no object they are both about.

18. As in Ch. 2, I restrict myself here to the version of a referential theory of meaning that is most often associated with Plato.

19. See M. Furth, 'Elements of Eleatic Ontology', *Journal of the History of Philosophy*, 6 (1968), 111–32, for a lucid explanation of how Parmenides seems to assume a referential theory of meaning. Among many who believe that Plato (at least prior to *So.*) assumes a referential theory of meaning, see the articles by Owen cited in Ch. 2 n. 15. For the classic refutation of the referential theory of meaning, see Frege, cf. Ch. 2 n. 24.

20. See e.g. *Phd.* 79. Souls are like forms in being everlasting and non-sensible; but there are many particular souls where there is only one form.

21. Asclepius, *in Met.*, 75. 13–16 thinks that Plato would not mind this result; he suggests that Plato allows *phantasia*, but not *noēsis*, of perishables. For a similar view, see Cherniss, *Aristotle's Criticism*, 272. (However, they both seem to assume that *noēsis* here is more than BT.) Note that just as there are questions about the level of *noēsis* in the Object of Thought Argument, so there are questions about the level of *epistēmē* in the Arguments from the Sciences; see the three interpretations discussed in connection with AS II in Ch. 5.3.

22. This is one reading of the outcome of the argument in the central books of *Met.* For one defence of this reading, see Irwin, *AFP*, esp. Chs. 10–12.

23. Plato raises similar difficulties, though about general descriptions rather than about forms, in *Tht.* 201c–210a. For some discussion, see my 'Knowledge and *Logos*'.

24. Annas, 'Aristotle and Plato on Objects of Thought', suggests that III is an insertion. It is true, as she points out, that Plato and Aristotle do not really discuss problems connected with the possibility of thinking about fictional entities. It is also worth noting that the capsule reference to the Object of Thought Argument in *Met.* 1. 9 does not repeat III. And whereas in the *Peri ideōn*, the Object of Thought Argument is said to establish forms from thinking quite generally, in *Met.* 1. 9 Aristotle instead mentions an argument concerning the thought of something perished (990b14 = 13. 4, 1079a10). Further, III's examples—hippocentaur and Chimaera—are not mentioned elsewhere in Aristotle, although cf. *APo.* 89b32 for 'centaur'. (I take it that 'Chimaera' in III refers to a fictional individual rather than to a fictional kind; when '*Chimaera*' is used as a common noun, as at *HA* 523a1, it refers to a she-goat, not to the fictional Chimaera.) Plato uses 'hippocentaur' in *Phdr.* 229d5, and 'the Chimaera' at *Phdr.* 229d6 and *Rep.* 588c3.

Although III is in some ways odd, I assume it is genuine. One point in its favour is that it makes a legitimate criticism of the Object of Thought Argument (if it is read with BT, and with (1e) or (1f)). Moreover, III occurs not only in LF but also in OAC. By contrast, the parallel criticisms of the One over Many Argument recorded in OAC do not mention hippocentaur or Chimaera; they are mentioned only in LF (80. 20–4). Asclepius, *in Met.*, 75. 12, retains III's examples, though (as is appropriate) he provides no examples of non-existent things in discussing the One over Many Argument (see Ch. 8 n. 27).

25. See n. 10.

26. Anyone who believes this should also, of course, be puzzled by Aristotle's criticisms of the Arguments from the Sciences and the One over Many Argument, which likewise assume that Plato does not want forms corresponding to every predicate. The point I make in the next paragraph is therefore relevant not only here but also in connection with the Arguments from the Sciences and the One over Many Argument. (However, unlike the Object of Thought Argument, these arguments do not even tacitly involve a referential theory of meaning. The relevant parallel is just that in criticizing all these arguments, Aristotle suggests that Plato does not want forms corresponding to every predicate.)

27. So just as the first Argument from the Sciences and the One over Many Argument fail to prove that forms are everlasting, so too does the Object of Thought Argument.

28. The Object of Thought Argument might seem to imply that forms are separate, since it might seem to assume that we can think of man (which is assumed to exist), whether or not there are any particular men, in which case (since man turns out to be the form of man) the form of man can exist whether or not there are any particular men. But the argument says only that our thought of man is unaffected by the fact that particular men come into and go out of existence, in which case there must be something besides particular men to ground our thought. This does not imply that man can exist whether or not there are any particular men. The argument might also seem to imply that forms are separate because (as Aristotle seems to say in his objection) it would prove that there is a form of e.g. centaur if it proved that there are any forms at all; but a form of centaur would be separate since it would never be instantiated. However, to generate a form of centaur we need to add to the argument the premiss that we can think of non-existent things. Of course, this premiss is plausible and Aristotle uses it in his objection. But not everyone accepts it; and in any case, the crucial point is that since it is not present in the argument, it does not by itself generate forms of fictional entities.

29. See n. 14, which is also relevant to the next sentence in the text.

30. One might object that it is not warranted on the ground that the inference to everlastingness is unwarranted, yet Aristotelian universals must be everlasting. But I am not sure whether Aristotle has this point in mind, and in any case not all Aristotelian universals need to be everlasting.

31. Although Aristotle takes the Object of Thought Argument to be unsound, it is not clear how well he can explain its unsoundness: see the curious passage in *APr*. 1. 33, 47b20–30, which considers an argument rather like the Object of Thought Argument (though it says that the argument is invalid). I owe the reference to Owen (in class).

32. I discuss *Rep*. 5 further in Ch. 7.2–3.

33. Contrast Owen, 'Plato on Not-Being', 106. Not every use of 'is' in the *Rep*. 5 argument is veridical. For example, 479ac uses 'is' predicatively, to claim that each of the many *F*s is *F* and not-*F*; returning what one owes, for example, is

both just and not just. But this does not bring the argument any closer to the Object of Thought Argument. It is sometimes thought that 478bc uses 'is' existentially. I am not sure that it does; but if it does, the claim would only be that like knowledge, belief must have content—one cannot believe, but believe nothing. Unlike the Object of Thought Argument, however, 478bc does not say that for belief to have content, it must be correlated with an actually existing object. For a more detailed (though still too brief) discussion of 478bc, see my 'Knowledge and Belief in *Republic* V', 130–1. If the suggestion made there is correct, then 478bc, like 477a, is quite different from *Tht.* 188e–189b, despite the fact that they are often assimilated. For the assimilation see e.g. McDowell, 200.

34. If the Object of Thought Argument is read with HLT and unrestricted (1*h*), then both it and *Rep.* 5 conclude that if one knows *x*, one knows some form or other. But the premisses of the two arguments would still differ. The premisses of the two arguments would also differ even if, as is often thought to be the case, *Rep.* 5 restricts knowledge to forms.

35. I discuss this argument in more detail in 'False Belief in the *Theaetetus*' *Phronesis*, 24 (1979), 70–80. My translation is adapted from McDowell and from Burnyeat–Levett.

36. For an interesting discussion of this argument, see Proclus, *in Parm.* 891–901, and M. F. Burnyeat, 'Idealism and Greek Philosophy: What Descartes Saw and Berkeley Missed', *Philosophical Review*, 91 (1982), 3–43. An alternative translation of 132b7–8 is: 'Then is each ⟨form⟩ one of these thoughts, and yet a thought of nothing?' For this translation, see Cornford, *Plato and Parmenides*, 91.

37. I discuss the Third Man Argument in Ch. 15.

38. I owe this way of putting the point to Robert Bolton.

39. Armstrong, i. 27.

40. Cornford, *Plato's Theory of Knowledge*, 99–100.

41. Although Cornford translates '*dialegesthai*' as 'dialectic', in his discussion he shifts to 'discourse'. That the passage concerns dialectic rather than discourse seems to be suggested by J. C. B. Gosling, *Plato* (London, 1973), 175 with 197.

42. Cornford, *Plato's Theory of Knowledge*, 99; cf. Cherniss, 'The Relation of the *Timaeus* to Plato's Later Dialogues', 356.

43. Plato might only argue, more weakly, that one cannot describe objects that are in complete flux; this would leave open the possibility that even in a world of complete flux one could use language in other ways—e.g. to express general claims that do not refer to particular objects in flux.

44. For further criticism of Cornford's and Cherniss's reading of *Tht.* 181–3, see M. F. Burnyeat, *The Theaetetus of Plato* (Indianapolis, 1990), esp. the brisk and apt footnote on p. 46 n. 58.

45. I discuss this passage further in 'Plato on Perception'. My account is indebted to M. F. Burnyeat, 'Plato on the Grammar of Perceiving', *Classical Quarterly*, NS 26 (1976), 29–51.

46. Cornford, *Plato's Theory of Knowledge*, 105–6, thinks that *koina* are forms. McDowell, *Plato: Theaetetus*, 189, argues that they are not. (If they are forms, they are presumably at most a subclass of forms, since *koina* are said

to belong to the objects of more than one sense. Hence hardness, for example, would not be a *koinon*, though in e.g. *Rep.* 523–5 Plato acknowledges a form of hardness.) Here as often in the late dialogues (and in assessing Aristotle's criticisms of Plato in the *Peri ideōn*), the answer turns in part on what one thinks it takes to be talking about forms. If countenancing properties is sufficient for countenancing forms, then *koina* are forms. If forms are not in the offing unless perfection, paradigmatism, and separation are mentioned, then *koina* are not forms. One might take the fact that *koina* are said to be unperceivable to be evidence that they are forms. But when Plato says, in the middle dialogues, that one cannot perceive forms, he means that forms cannot be defined in observational terms. When, on the other hand, he says that one cannot perceive *koina*, he means that unlike e.g. red, *koina* are not the proper objects of a given sense. Even if *koina* are unperceivable in the same sense in which forms are, it does not follow that they are forms, since being a non-perceivable universal is not sufficient for being a form.

Cornford takes *koina* to be not only forms but also meanings; for, he says, *koina* are common 'in the sense in which a name is common to any number of individual things'. It is true that *koina* belong to several things, but that does not turn them into meanings. They are common to many things in that they are properties of many things. Plato is not discussing how we come to understand the meanings of terms; he is asking how we identify the objects we perceive as being something or other. We do that by identifying them as being something or other—that is, by applying various properties to them.

47. See Ch. 5.3, interpretation (i).

48. Some of the considerations mentioned in n. 46 are relevant to deciding whether *So.* countenances forms of the same sort as those countenanced in the middle dialogues. According to Ackrill, 'Συμπλοκὴ εἰδῶν', 208, *So.*'s forms differ from those in the middle dialogues in that they are concepts but not ethical ideals or 'metaphysical objects of intuitive and perhaps mystical insight'.

49. At 249c7 Plato says that stable objects are necessary for *epistēmē ē phronēsis ē nous*. If '*ē*' is epexegetic, then presumably *nous* is HLT; if it is not, then *nous* might be BT. The context perhaps favours the epexegetic reading.

50. For the meaning view, see e.g. Ackrill, 'Συμπλοκὴ εἰδῶν'. For the truth interpretation, see R. E. Heinaman, 'Communion of Forms', *Proceedings of the Aristotelian Society*, 83 (1982–3), 175–90. Yet a further possibility is that '*logos*' means 'argument', in which case the point is perhaps that philosophical reasoning requires the existence of forms. If the passage makes this point, then it parallels one possible reading of *Parm.* 135 (discussed above).

51. Contrast Cornford, *Plato's Theory of Knowledge*, 314, who believes that according to the interweaving thesis, 'at least one Form enters into the meaning of any statement'. For cogent criticism of this interpretation, see Ackrill, 'Συμπλοκὴ εἰδῶν'.

52. 'Συμπλοκὴ εἰδῶν', esp. 207–8.

53. Aristotle pursues this theme in e.g. *Met.* 3 and 4; I discuss some of the

relevant passages in Ch. 5.3. This interpretation of the interweaving thesis also fits well with my account, in Ch. 8.6, of *So.* on negations, in so far as both take forms to be properties.

54. See e.g. R. E. Allen, *Plato's Parmenides: Translation and Analysis* (Minneapolis, 1983), 155.

55. At 439d3–4 Plato says: 'Let us then consider that very thing, not whether some face is beautiful or any of such things, and all these appear to be in flux.' As Irwin, 'Plato's Heracleiteanism', 2, notes, 'and all these . . .' seems to be part of the 'whether' clause. If so, Plato is not claiming that sensibles appear to be in flux; he leaves that question to one side.

56. I also discuss this passage briefly in Ch. 7 n. 8.

57. This is close to what Bostock calls the 'simple' version of the theory of recollection. The suggestion I discuss in the next paragraph corresponds to what he calls the 'more interesting' version. See *Plato's Phaedo*, 103–5.

58. Alternatively, one might argue that Plato would deny this by arguing that one cannot think of what does not exist. But we have not yet found any reason to suppose that he thinks this. (The claim is made in *Tht.* 188–9, but that passage does not express Plato's own views; see the discussion of that passage above, and also below, n. 65.)

59. This strategy also shows that Plato is not committed to the existence of forms of particulars. True, Plato says that I can recollect Cebes no less than the form of equal, and he speaks of recollecting 'the form of the boy' (*eidos tou paidos*, 73d8). But 'form' is used non-technically here—as the fact that it immediately drops out of the discussion suggests. It is true that Plato does not explicitly say that he is using 'form' non-technically; nor does he explicitly say that recollection involves forms at most for some general thoughts. But a sympathetic reading of the passage makes these points tolerably clear.

60. A similar view is (independently) defended by D. Scott, 'Platonic Anamnesis Revisited', *Classical Quarterly*, NS 37 (1987), 346–66.

61. The main objection I have heard to this interpretation is that it 'would limit the scope of the Recollection Argument to the souls of philosophers' (Gallop, 120; cf. Bostock, *Plato's Phaedo*, 67). But I do not think this is so. First, even if philosophers are the only ones who do any recollecting (of the sort that involves forms) in the example used in *Phd.*, Meno's slave recollects, and he is no philosopher. Secondly, as I go on to explain, Plato believes that everyone is capable of recollection, and he takes this to require everyone, not just philosophers, to have pre-natal knowledge of forms. Bostock is in rough agreement with my account of the *Meno*, but he rejects it for *Phd.*; on my view, the two contexts agree.

62. It is also worth noting that some of those who recollect forms have *de dicto* beliefs about forms. By contrast, the slave in the *Meno*, or in general those who move from *eikasia* to *pistis*, have only *de re* beliefs about forms. *De dicto* beliefs about forms emerge only at the third stage of the Divided Line.

63. To be sure, some people take concepts or beliefs to be capacities; and the theory of recollection postulates innate capacities. But as Aristotle points out in e.g. *DA* 2. 5, there are two different ways of construing capacities. A child has what Aristotle calls a first potentiality to become a general in that, in

suitable circumstances, she might become one when she grows up; I have a second potentiality to speak English in that I can do so immediately if I so choose (and nothing intervenes). Concepts and beliefs might plausibly be construed as second potentialities; but they are not plausibly construed as first potentialities. But the theory of recollection postulates only innate first potentialities.

64. Since, according to the theory of recollection, the possibility of moving from belief to knowledge requires the existence of forms, the existence of forms is necessary for more than knowledge and explaining the way things are. But this further motivation for positing forms does not suggest that forms are meanings.

65. Penner, *Ascent*, 383 n. 5, believes that *So.* 238d–239c, considered together with 258e and 263c, also says that one can think only of what exists. But 238d–239c is aporetic: Plato is raising various puzzles that he later dissolves. 258e and 263c express Plato's views; but it has been cogently argued that they do not say that one can think only of what exists; see e.g. Owen, 'Plato on Not-Being'. It is also worth noting that even those who think that Plato was at some stage committed to a referential theory of meaning believe that he rejects it at least by the time of *So.*; so e.g. Owen.

66. However, although the Object of Thought Argument can be read with HLT, unrestricted (1*h*) is inappropriate.

NOTES TO CHAPTER 10

1. 82. 11 mentions an argument *from* (*ek*) relatives; by contrast, *Met.* 1. 9 mentions an argument that *produces* ideas of relatives (990b15–17), where this is said to be an unwanted consequence. If it is an unwanted consequence of the argument that it produces forms of relatives, then it might seem unlikely that (as 82. 11 suggests) the argument self-consciously takes its start *from* relatives. Hence 'Argument from Relatives' might seem to be misleading. Moreover, Hayduck's apparatus records LF as having 'the argument which produces ideas even (*kai*) of relatives'. Perhaps LF is correct, and OAC ought to be emended? Or perhaps 'from' is an Alexandrian misunderstanding?

   However, Harlfinger's more recent apparatus shows that like OAC, LF has '*ek*', not '*kai*'; '*kai*' was a conjecture of Bonitz's that has no manuscript warrant. (It was no doubt influenced by the '*kai*' at 83. 17 (cf. 85. 7).) But we need not assume that the name is due to Alexander; at least, I argue in Chs. 12 and 13 that it is not misleading.

   Although both labels are apt, the difference between them is interesting. In *Met.*, Aristotle identifies the argument by mentioning what he takes to be one of its fatal flaws; in this it matches his description of the other more accurate argument as one that leads to the Third Man Argument. By contrast, his names for two of the less accurate arguments (the Arguments from the Sciences and the One over Many Argument) focus on a premiss of the argument rather than on an unwanted result of it; and in both cases, it is a premiss that, properly construed, Aristotle takes to contribute to a valid argument for the existence of *koina*.

Aristotle's *Met.* and *Peri ideōn* labels for the Object of Thought Argument differ in a way parallel to his different names for the Argument from Relatives, though in reverse. In *Met.* he mentions an argument from the thought of something that has perished (990b14)—he mentions a premiss of the Object of Thought Argument but not, in this case, a premiss he believes implies that there are *koina*. In the *Peri ideōn* he calls the Object of Thought Argument 'the argument from thinking'; and he believes that considerations about the nature of thought imply that there are *koina*. In this case, the *Peri ideōn*, but not *Met.*, identifies a less accurate argument by reference to a virtuous premiss. The facts that Aristotle names the Object of Thought Argument in two different ways (which are analogous to the two names for the Argument from Relatives) and that *Met.*'s name for the Object of Thought Argument parallels the *Peri ideōn*'s name for the Argument from Relatives support the suggestion that '*ek*' is due to Aristotle.

2. In this respect, the less accurate arguments stand with the other more accurate argument, which likewise does not distinguish between predicates like 'man' and those like 'equal'. Because of this difference between the Argument from Relatives and the less accurate arguments, Cherniss, *Aristotle's Criticism*, 278 (cf. n. 186), is wrong in saying that the Argument from Relatives is 'essentially the same as' the One over Many Argument. For unlike the Argument from Relatives, the One over Many Argument does not discriminate between equal and man.

3. The first Argument from the Sciences mentions paradigmatism, but this seems to be weak paradigmatism. The Accurate One over Many Argument again stands with the less accurate arguments in so far as it does not explicitly conceive forms as perfect self-predicative paradigms. (But in Chs. 15 and 16 I indicate a way in which self-predication may enter through the back door; and in Ch. 15 we shall see that, unlike Aristotle, Plato and Eudemus mention paradigmatism in connection with the Third Man Argument.)

4. As we saw in Ch. 5, the Arguments from the Sciences are often thought to advert to change in the sense of succession; but I argued that they do not do so. The One over Many Argument is also sometimes thought to advert to change; but as I interpret '*allassamenōn*', it does not do so. The Object of Thought Argument claims that particulars are not everlasting; but succession through time (MH, EH) is not at issue.

5. It is also often thought to refer to a phenomenon called 'incompleteness', which I discuss in Ch. 11.

6. There are at least two versions of the semantic interpretation of the Argument from Relatives. On one version, it assumes that '*F*' can be meaningful only if something is fully (*kuriōs*) *F*. On a second version, it assumes that we can understand '*F*' only if we are acquainted with something that is fully *F*—a perfect sample or example of '*F*'. For the first version, see White, *Plato on Knowledge and Reality*, 86 n. 57. (More precisely, he thinks that *Phd.* 74 involves this view, and that it is 'most likely' involved in the Argument from Relatives as well.) For the second version, see Owen in e.g. 'Proof'.

7. 'Proof', 177.
8. In the next chapter, I argue that incompleteness (see n. 5) is irrelevant to the argument.
9. In describing cases (*a*) and (*b*), Aristotle uses *hotan* with the subjunctive (*legōmen*, 83. 1; *katēgorōmen*, 83. 3). But in case (*c*), he uses *ei* with the optative (*legoimen*, 83. 6). For a guess about the significance of the shift, see n. 22.
10. Cherniss, by contrast, believes that when Plato uses 'homonymy' for the relation of sensibles to forms, it means 'having the same name and nature derivatively' (*Aristotle's Criticism*, 230–1 n. 137; cf. 178–9. n. 102). For, he argues, Plato says that sensibles are homonymous with forms (*Phd*. 78e; cf. *Phd*. 102b, *Parm*. 133d; *Met*. 987b10) and (Cherniss believes) sensibles have their names and natures derivatively from forms. But on this account, homonymy must implausibly be taken to be an asymmetrical relation: sensibles are homonymous with forms but forms are not homonymous with sensibles. Further, as Cherniss himself points out (n. 102; cf. Owen, 'Proof', 171), Plato uses 'homonymy' in cases that do not conform to this account (see e.g. *Laws* 757b; *Phil*. 57b). Cherniss thus seems committed to saying that Plato uses 'homonymy' in more than one sense. It seems better to say that Plato uses 'homonymy' in just one sense, to mean 'having the same name'; although he uses the word in the sorts of cases Cherniss describes, such cases do not fix a special meaning of the word. In commenting on *Met*. 987b9–10, Alexander, *in Met*. 51. 10–15, makes it plain that in his view, when Plato says that forms and sensibles are homonyms, he means not that sensibles have their names and natures derivatively from forms, but that forms and sensibles are synonyms in Aristotle's sense.
11. 'Proof', 167–72; cf. Mansion, 'Critique', 183 n. 42. Although I agree with Owen that the Argument from the Relatives uses 'homonymy' in its Aristotelian sense, I disagree with his account of Aristotelian homonymy; and this leads to further differences between us. I discuss Owen on homonymy more fully in 'Owen's Progress', sect. 3.

As Owen notes ('Proof', 167 n. 6), it is sometimes thought that Part I of the Argument from Relatives uses 'homonymy' not in its Aristotelian sense, but in an allegedly special Speusippean sense. For it is sometimes thought that Part I—allegedly like Speusippus but unlike Aristotle—counts words rather than things as homonyms. Owen replies that Aristotle himself sometimes counts words rather than things as homonyms; hence one ought not to conclude from the fact that Part I counts words rather than things as homonyms that it invokes a special Speusippean sense of homonymy. He also notes that Part III counts things rather than words as homonyms. So he concludes that the Argument from Relatives as a whole 'reflects a general academic usage' ('Proof', 167 n. 6; 'Aristotle on the Snares of Ontology', in id., *LSD* 259–78 at 262 n. 8)—Part I uses Speusppius' standard account of homonymy, an account Aristotle sometimes uses too; Part III uses Aristotle's standard account of homonymy. (It is somewhat awkward that Owen thinks Part I counts words as homonyms, whereas Part III counts things as homonyms. For he rightly criticizes Cherniss for positing a shift in the sort of homonymy at issue in Parts I and III. On his own view too there turns out to be a shift, though between two Aristotelian uses rather than between an Aristotelian and a Platonic use.)

Although I agree with Owen's conclusion, I would defend it differently. For contrary to Owen, Part I does not count words rather than things as homonyms. Rather, as in Aristotle's standard view, it counts things as homonyms in so far as they have certain names. (Perhaps this is all Owen means when he says that in Part I 'the vehicles of homonymy and its opposite seem to be not things but words'. But if so, it is misleading to contrast Part I with Part III on this score; and if so, it is misleading to describe this as a special Speusippean notion of homonymy.) Hence Part I, like Part III, uses 'homonymy' as Aristotle standardly does. (Hence we need not claim that the Argument from Relatives invokes different sorts of homonymy.) Further, as J. Barnes argues in 'Homonymy in Aristotle and Speusippus', *Classical Quarterly*, NS 21 (1971), 65–80, it is not clear that Speusippus standardly counts words rather than things as homonyms; rather, he too seems typically to count things as homonyms. (Owen might agree, for he expresses doubts about the traditional view of Speusippus; but he does not say what his doubts are or what view he prefers. Barnes's view is challenged by L. Tarán, 'Speusippus and Aristotle on Homonymy and Synonymy', *Hermes*, 106 (1978), 73–99). It is not clear, then, that there is any difference between Aristotle's and Speusippus' standard accounts of homonymy. If, as Owen says, the Argument from Relatives 'reflects a general academic usage', that is because it throughout uses Aristotle's standard account of homonymy, an account that seems to correspond to that favoured by some other members of the Academy as well.

12. The meaning view is favoured by e.g. Ackrill, *Aristotle's Categories and De Interpretatione*: 'Roughly, two things are homonymous if the same name applies to both but not in the same sense, synonymous if the same name applies to both in the same sense' (p. 71). See also Owen, 'Logic and Metaphysics', which is permeated with talk of meaning.

13. For the distinction between what I call the meaning and real-essence view, see Irwin, 'Homonymy' and 'Aristotle's Concept of Signification'; and S. MacDonald 'Aristotle and the Homonymy of the Good', *Archiv für Geschichte der Philosophie*, 71 (1989), 150–74. They both defend the real-essence view, and my discussion is indebted to theirs. On this view, the relevant sort of *logos* is the *horismos*, the definition that signifies the real essence; see e.g. *Top.* 107a36.

14. See the articles cited in n. 13. Irwin and MacDonald both explain in detail that the real-essence view is not only possible but also makes many of Aristotle's claims more plausible. For example, on the meaning view, Aristotle is committed to the implausible claim that 'good' has different senses in 'Socrates is good' and in 'This is a good knife'. On the real-essence view, he is committed only to the much more plausible claim that the nature of a person's goodness differs from the nature of a good knife.

15. For a full discussion, see Irwin, 'Homonymy'. Irwin defends the moderate view.

16. The phrase is due to Irwin, 'Homonymy', 531. In 'Proof', Owen uses 'has a common factor'; in various later works he uses 'focal meaning' (thereby

suggesting his allegiance to the meaning view of homonymy). 'Focal connection' is preferable if, with me, one believes that focally connected cases involve not different meanings but different real natures or essences—that is, if one favours the real-essence interpretation of homonymy.

17. On the meaning view, Aristotle implausibly claims that 'being' has different lexical definitions or is ambiguous. On the real-essence view, he more plausibly claims that substances and qualities, for example, are different kinds of beings. Here, then, is another example that illustrates the fact that the real-essence view is more plausible than the meaning view.

18. Irwin, 'Homonymy', 531 and n. 12.

19. See e.g. *DA* 412b17–22; *Meteor.* 389b23–390a16; *Pol.* 1253a20–5; *PA* 640b30–641a6; *GA* 734b25–7. This claim also makes more sense on the real-essence than on the meaning view. 'Hand' presumably has the same lexical definition as applied to an organic, functioning hand and as applied to either a detached, non-functioning hand or to a pictured hand. But it is plausible to suppose that an organic hand has a different nature from dead or pictured hands. For in the case of things like hands, real natures are functional; since in Aristotle's view detached and pictured hands cannot perform the function of an organic hand, they have not the same nature as an organic hand.

20. See 'Homonymy'. Owen, by contrast, favours the extreme view. He believes, that is, that the division between homonymy and synonymy is not exhaustive, and that focal connection counts as a *tertium quid*. Although Owen sometimes counts focal connection as a *tertium quid*, he sometimes counts it as a case of (or as an 'extension of') synonymy instead. Contrast e.g. 'Logic and Metaphysics', 193 with 198; cf. 183. Interestingly enough, in his later 'Aristotle on the Snares of Ontology', Owen abandons the extreme view in favour of the moderate view. Here he says that focal connection is a 'sophisticated variant on the idea of homonymy' (pp. 261–2). Unfortunately, Owen never explained how he would revise his account of the Argument from Relatives in the light of his later view of homonymy. See my 'Owen's Progress', sect. 3.

21. 'Proof', 167. Note that in using 'sense', Owen again suggests the meaning view.

22. I mentioned in n. 9 that although Aristotle uses the subjunctive in describing cases (*a*) and (*b*), he switches to the optative in describing case (*c*). Perhaps he does so because he finds case (*c*) puzzling in the way just mentioned.

23. See e.g. Robin, 19–21, 603–5, 607; Wilpert, *ZaF* 41–4; Cherniss, *Aristotle's Criticism*, 229–33, esp. n. 137; and Mansion, 'Critique', 181–3, esp. n. 42.

24. 'Proof', 168. I discuss Owen's two solutions in 'Aristotle and the More Accurate Arguments', 175 and n. 31; see also D. Devereux, 'The Primacy of *Ousia*: Aristotle's Debt to Plato', in D. O'Meara (ed.), *Platonic Investigations* (Washington, DC, 1985), 226–32. Although I focus on Owen's discussion in 'Proof', the same inconsistency that I go on to describe infects 'Logic and Metaphysics'; contrast e.g. p. 195, which appeals to 'the same sense' (and so to synonymy), with pp. 196–7, which invokes focal meaning.

25. 'Proof', 168; cf. n. 10. On p. 178 Owen writes of 'the treatment of "equal" in P [i.e. in the Argument from Relatives] and its sources as applying synonymously to earthly things and to the Form'. Isnardi Parente, 138, denies

that Plato treats forms and sensibles as synonyms; but she thinks Xenocrates does, and so she suggests that the Argument from Relatives is Xenocratean rather than Platonic. But her account of synonymy implausibly requires forms and sensibles to share not only the same name and definition but also such features as being substances, universals, and so on.

26. 'Proof', 168 n. 10. His only reference, however, is to *de Lin. Insec.* 968a9–10, a work that, he says, is 'Aristotelian though not by Aristotle' ('Logic and Metaphysics', 188 n. 28). But 'Logic and Metaphysics', 195 ff., gives further (and plausible) reasons for thinking that Aristotle takes forms and sensibles to be synonymously related.

27. One might attempt to save Owen from inconsistency by appealing to his occasional view that focal connection is an 'extension of synonymy'. But, first, that view is untenable; for in synonymy, the definitions are just the same whereas in focal connection they are not. Secondly, it does not absolve Owen from all inconsistency, since he often counts focal connection, not as a type or extension of synonymy, but as a *tertium quid* between homonymy and synonymy.

28. Curiously, *Phd.* 73–4, which the Argument from Relatives plainly has in view, does not explicitly say that forms and the corresponding sensibles are similar; see esp. 74a2–3, c13–d2. Further, although *Phd.* 73–4 discusses pictured *F*s and *F*s, on the one hand, and sensible *F*s and the form of *F*, on the other, it does not explicitly order pictured *F*s, sensible *F*s, and the form of *F* on a scale of increasing perfection. The Argument from Relatives thus makes more precise and explicit claims that, in *Phd.* 73–4 at any rate, are tacit.

29. Cf. *Cat.* 11a12–13; *Top.* 107b17–19; *Phys.* 249a3–8 (on which see 'Proof', 168 n. 10); *Met.* 993b24–7; *Pol.* 1259b36–8.

30. Alexander, *in Met.* 50. 19–51. 25 (a discussion of *Met.* 987b9–10), agrees that Aristotle correctly takes Plato to believe that forms and sensibles are synonymously related. He speculates that Aristotle none the less refrains from using 'synonymy' here because Plato uses 'homonymy' rather than 'synonymy' to describe the relation between forms and sensibles. But, Alexander suggests, though Plato uses 'homonymy' here, he means that forms and sensibles are synonymously related (see n. 10). (Unfortunately, Alexander's speculation does not explain why the Argument from Relatives uses 'non-homonymy', since Plato does not use that term to describe the relation between forms and sensibles.) LF also assumes the moderate view, and makes the point clear by using 'synonymy' in crucial places.

One might argue that Aristotle offers Plato focal connection as a more plausible alternative than synonymy, on the ground that focal connection avoids, but synonymy gives rise to, the Third Man Argument. Some later Platonists invoked focal connection to avoid the Third Man Argument; see e.g. Syrianus, *in Met.* 111. 31–112. 4. I argue in Ch. 16 (see esp. sect. 3 and n. 27), however, that focal connection does not fare better with respect to the Third Man Argument than synonymy does.

31. Here it is important to note that in Aristotle's view, synonymy does not imply class membership. For example, in his view, animal is synonymously predicated in 'Socrates is an animal' and in 'The mammal is an animal', but

'is' functions differently: in the first case it indicates class membership; in the second case it indicates class inclusion. So even if man is predicated synonymously of men and of pictured men, in Aristotle's view that does not by itself imply that pictured men are members of the class of men—it all depends on how 'is' is used. If I am right to say that in Aristotle's view synonymy does not imply class membership, then even if he takes particular *F*s and the species *F* to be synonymously *F*, he is not thereby committed to the claim that the species *F* is itself a member of the class of *F*s, and so he is not thereby committed to SP. In 'Platonism', however, Owen seems to commit Aristotle to SP on the ground that in some cases Aristotle takes particular *F*s and the species *F* to be synonymously *F*. I discuss this issue further in 'Owen, Aristotle, and the Third Man', *Phronesis*, 27 (1982), 13–33. I return to questions about synonymy in Chs. 15 and 16.

I am not sure whether the Argument from Relatives, in violation of Aristotle's own views, takes synonymy as such to imply class membership, or whether it considers only those cases of synonymy that it takes to involve class membership. Either way, the Argument from Relatives involves a claim Aristotle rejects. For in both cases, it takes pictured men to be members of the class of men. Presumably the Argument from Relatives involves this non-Aristotelian view because it is a Platonic, not an Aristotelian, argument. Now, I said in Ch. 2.7 that Aristotle takes the Argument from Relatives to be valid but unsound. If so, he must reject at least one of its premisses. We have just discovered a premiss of the argument that he rejects; see n. 56 for another rejected premiss.

32. In Act I, Scene 14 (Dover edn.) of *The Magic Flute*, Papageno notes that the Pamina in the picture lacks hands and feet; this seems to involve (*c*). Pamina, on the other hand, seems to intend (*b*), for she thinks that she is the Pamina in the picture ('Ja, ich bin's!').

33. See the references cited in n. 19. Owen seems to intend (*a*) when he writes that 'an eye or a doctor in a painting cannot see or heal, a stone hand or flute cannot grasp or play' ('Logic and Metaphysics', 198); for these remarks are true of (*a*), but not of (*b*) or (*c*)—a doctor in a picture in sense (*c*) can heal, if he is depicted as doing so; and actual doctors do heal. In 'Plato on the Undepictable' in id., *LSD* 138–47 at p. 144 and n. 18, Owen writes that '[o]f course a picture or model of a lion is not in vital respects as enlightening as the live beast'. He adds in a note: 'Though Aristotle, thinking of the material picture rather than what it can be taken to portray, arguably overpressed this contrast.' Perhaps he means that Aristotle favours (*a*) but should favour (*c*).

34. One might argue that this line of reasoning could equally well be used to explain why *ho gegrammenos* in sense (*a*) is a man; but the claim seems more reasonable (though still controversial) if we assume (*c*). In *Rep.* 597a, Plato considers someone who is tempted to say that the only real bed is the work of a carpenter; the reply is that 'anyone versed in this kind of reasoning (*logos*)', i.e. in Plato's generous ways with the extensions of predicates, will resist that temptation, wanting to say instead that the form of bed is the 'most real' bed. Perhaps Plato thinks that the line of reasoning that shows that 'ordinary' beds are inferior to the form, although they are none the less beds, also shows that pictured beds, although they are even more inferior to forms, are none the less beds.

35. Barford, 'A Proof from the *Peri Ideon* Revisited', favors the reverse strategy from LF: in his view, AR consistently takes equal to be homonymous. He is well answered, on this point, by Rowe, 'The Proof from Relatives'.

36. Cherniss, *Aristotle's Criticism*, 230–2 n. 137, retains the OAC reading but argues that 'homonymy' is now being used in a Platonic, rather than in an Aristotelian, sense. Since something can be homonymously *F* in Plato's sense(s) (as both Cherniss and I understand that sense: see n. 10) and nonhomonymously *F* in Aristotle's sense, the alleged inconsistency is dissolved. But this solution is also unsatisfactory. First, we have seen that Cherniss misunderstands Plato's notion of homonymy. Secondly and more importantly, it is undesirable for a key term of the argument to shift sense in mid-stream.

37. I discuss Owen's interpretation of the Argument from Relatives in more detail in Ch. 11. For the moment, I focus only on his solution to the second puzzle.

38. See also Mansion, 'Critique', 183 n. 42. I agree with Owen that when II says that when we predicate the equal itself of things here, we do so homonymously, 'we' are we non-Platonists, since the Platonists do not identify the equal itself with anything sensible. So although the surface grammar of the sentence is not counter-factual, its sense is, in so far as its sense is that equality would be homonymous if it were sensible (as it is erroneously taken to be by non-Platonists). For criticism of Owen's construal, see Barford and Rowe.

39. Owen does not explicitly say that '*auto*' and '*kuriōs*' have the same sense, and perhaps he intends something weaker. But he certainly shifts between the two terms in a way that suggests that he takes them to have the same sense; see e.g. 'Logic and Metaphysics', 196. Similarly, in 'Proof' he writes that '[i]nstead of asking in set terms whether "equal" can, without ambiguity, be predicated *strictly* of such things, II seems to introduce the compound predicate "strictly equal" and ask whether this can, without ambiguity, be predicated of such things. This comes to the same thing' (p. 170 n. 11). But Part II has '*autoison*', not '*kuriōs ison*'. The fact that Owen translates '*auto*' as 'absolutely', rather than as 'itself', also suggests that he takes it to be somehow equivalent to '*kuriōs*' (fully, strictly).

40. 'Proof', 170.

41. Owen records David Furley as making the similar but weaker objection that II*a* is designed to rule out I*b* as well as I*a* ('Proof', 170 n. 12); I am objecting, more strongly, that II*a* rules out *all* of I*a–c*. Owen objects that if Furley were right, '(1) the conclusion of II would contradict V, (2) as well as being a thesis foreign to Plato' (n. 12; arabic figures added). I reply to these objections below.

42. But since, as I have just indicated, the question raised in Parts II and following can be put in predicative terms—what has the property of being the property of equality?—we need not say that whereas Part I concerns predication, Parts II and following turn to identity. We therefore need not see any shift in the sense or use of 'predication' (though even if there were a shift, that would not by itself be troubling). But since it is often easier and more natural to speak in terms of identifying or defining equality, I shall often do so.

43. I ask later about the criteria for being fully *F*.

44. For a similar suggestion, see Leszl, *Il 'De Ideis'*, 194, 198. Rowe, 'The Proof from Relatives', 276, objects that if Aristotle were restricting our attention to sensibles, he would have indicated the restriction but, according to Rowe, he does not do so. But, contrary to Rowe, Aristotle *does* indicate the restriction, by replacing Part I's ontologically neutral 'of many things' with 'of things here'. Aristotle uses *'pleiō'* broadly elsewhere in the *Peri ideōn* too, reserving other phrases (here, *'entautha'*, elsewhere *'kath' hekasta'* or *'aisthēta'*) for a narrower range of entities. For further discussion, see Ch. 14 and 'Aristotle and the More Accurate Arguments'. (It is true that 81. 11, 16, and 83. 30 use *'pleionōn'* where we might have expected a more restricted phrase. But the first two passages may be suspect; see Ch. 8 n. 63. Perhaps Aristotle is careful about his use of these terms only when something specifically hangs on their difference, as it does not in these passages.)

45. Since Aristotelian homonymy is involved, the relevant sort of account is a definition; see n. 13. Notice, in support of the moderate view, that the Argument from Relatives infers directly from a difference in definition to homonymy. This move is legitimate on the moderate view, but not on the extreme view, according to which not every difference in definition imports homonymy.

46. Owen's second objection to Furley is therefore disarmed; see above, n. 41.

47. 'Proof', 177.

48. Ibid. 176. Owen says that II*b* 'seems' to add this rider, but I assume he thinks that II*b* *does* add this rider, for otherwise he gives no account of II*b* at all. If sensibles are constantly changing their dimensions, then the phrase 'having the same size as A' has no fixed *extension*; but, contrary to Owen, it does not follow that it has no fixed *meaning*. Once again, a concern with meaning is irrelevant.

49. Owen does not interpret being fully *F* as I do, nor does he think that the sensible equals at issue here are sensible properties; but it is just as true on his interpretation as it is on mine that if II*b* invokes succession, it does not fit the surrounding context; see Ch. 11.3, second objection. Devereux, 'The Primacy of *Ousia*', also interprets II*b* in terms of succession. He accepts the lack of fit between II*b* and the rest of the Argument from Relatives, arguing that it matches the dialogues where (he thinks) concern with being fully *F* and with succession also sit together uncomfortably.

50. I discuss this passage from *Phd.* in Ch. 11.4, third criticism.

51. This is not to say that Plato never adverts to succession. It is only to say that he does not do so, in arguing that there are forms, in the contexts the Argument from Relatives has in mind. Owen agrees; see 'Proof', 175.

52. Though Alexander does not spell out the sort of flux he takes the Argument from Relatives to involve, his discussion of the flux argument recorded in *Met.* 1. 6 makes it clear that he believes that sensible properties undergo the flux at issue there (see *in Met.* 50. 7–16); so perhaps, like me, he believes that the Argument from Relatives likewise ascribes change to sensible properties, in which case the change at issue should be compresence rather than succession since, although properties undergo flux in the sense of compresence, they do not undergo flux in the sense of succession.

53. Being *F* without also being not *F* in the sense of narrow compresence seems to be necessary but not sufficient for being fully *F*. For if it were both necessary and sufficient, we would face the following problem. According to Part I, pictured men are not fully men; but they are not both men and not men in the sense of narrow compresence. If escaping narrow compresence with respect to *F*-ness were sufficient for being fully *F*, then pictured men would be fully men—a result we plainly do not want. (Pictured men are both men and not men in the sense of broad compresence; but that cannot be what is wanted here, since sensible men are men and not men in the sense of broad compresence, yet they are fully men.) Unfortunately, the Argument from Relatives does not explicitly say what else is involved in being fully *F*. It cannot be necessary that *x* be a paradigm of all other *F* things—for Socrates is fully a man, but he is not a paradigm of all other men. Perhaps the Argument from Relatives is deliberately vague here, since Plato focuses on narrow compresence, says that pictured beds are not fully beds (though they do not suffer narrow compresence), yet does not tell us what single set of conditions is true of pictured beds and sensible equals but not of sensible men.

54. In Ch. 7.5, however, we saw that the Arguments from the Sciences might be concerned with broad compresence.

55. However, in *Met.* Aristotle seems to think that the flux argument yields more forms than narrow compresence does. Perhaps he is thinking of broad compresence.

56. So here is one (suppressed) premiss of the argument that Aristotle rejects; in n. 31 I mentioned another premiss that he rejects.

57. For a more accurate way of putting the relevant point, see Ch. 4 n. 36.

58. Alexander, *in Met.* 51. 20–5, esp. 23–5, says that sensible men do not receive the definition of man—rational animal—*kuriōs*; yet according to the Argument from Relatives, sensible men are *kuriōs* men. (Note that the argument speaks of receiving a definition *akribōs*, and of various things' being *kuriōs F*, whereas Alexander speaks of receiving a definition *kuriōs*. I think his shift is quite legitimate: '*akribōs*' is not restricted to definitions or linguistic entities, and '*kuriōs*' is not restricted to things.) Perhaps the explanation is that the Argument from Relatives counts sensible men as *kuriōs* men at least partly because they are not both men and not men in the sense of narrow compresence, whereas 51. 20–5 (which is not explaining the Argument from Relatives) debars them from being *kuriōs* men because they are both men and not men in the sense of broad compresence, or are at any rate in some way imperfectly men for the purpose of understanding what it is to be a man.

59. In his account of first philosophy in *Met.* 4, Aristotle seems to think that even if *F*s are focally (and so homonymously) connected, they can be known (cf. 1004a22–5, 1005a5–11), though he presumably still thinks that focal connection precludes demonstration. For some discussion, see T. Irwin, 'Aristotle's Discovery of Metaphysics', *Review of Metaphysics*, 31 (1977–8), 210–29, and *AFP*, sect. 93.

60. Owen, 'Proof', 170, takes Part IV to be 'concessive because it forestalls an objection: the objection that the talk of ambiguity in II is misleading and may be taken to apply to *ison*, not *to ison auto*'. However, Part IV simply repeats

a point already made, that paradigms and their likenesses are not homonymous. If there is any concession here, presumably it is Aristotle's, in the sense that he concedes what he does not believe but what the Argument from Relatives assumes, that paradigms and their likenesses are not homonymous but synonymous. But '*ei de kai*' need not be concessive: cf. Denniston, *Greek Particles*, 299–305, esp. 303–4, sect. (*c*).

61. Although the Argument from Relatives posits forms only for predicates like 'equal', it does not preclude the existence of further forms. Similarly, in the dialogues Plato sometimes offers arguments that (if successful) establish only a limited range of forms; but it does not follow that he admits only such forms. Contrast Owen, 'Proof', 175 *fin.*, who concludes more sweepingly that the Argument from Relatives (and its Platonic antecedents) 'exclude' forms for predicates like 'man'.

62. Interestingly enough, the equal itself and so on are not explicitly called forms in *Phd.* 74; but see 102b2, where it is also said that forms and the corresponding sensibles are homonymous, i.e. have the same name, for which see also 78e2.

63. 'Proof', 177.

64. See n. 6; I return to this view in the next chapter.

65. I have already argued that forms are conceived as universals in the Arguments from the Sciences, the One over Many Argument, and the Object of Thought Argument. I argue in Ch. 14 that they are also conceived as universals in the Accurate One over Many Argument.

66. In *Met.* 7. 15, for example, Aristotle conceives forms as particulars; he does not say that they are also universals. Elsewhere, as in *Met.* 13. 9, he says that they are both particulars and universals.

67. Owen agrees that '*auto*' is used in the same way in 83. 7 and 15 ('Proof', 170), but he denies that it indicates a property in either place. So my argument that the Argument from Relatives conceives forms as properties depends not only on the claim that '*auto*' is used in the same way in 83. 7 and 15—a claim Owen accepts—but also on my previous argument that, in 83. 7, it is used to indicate a concern with property identification and not, as Owen believes, only with *kuriōs* predications.

68. In his objections, though, Aristotle explains only why the Platonists should not countenance forms of relatives—that is, he attacks a consequence of the argument. He does not say which premiss(es) of the argument he rejects. But since he takes the argument to be valid but unsound, he must reject at least one of its premisses; and we have already uncovered two premisses he rejects (see n. 31 and 55).

69. 83. 18–22 is usually thought to be Alexandrian rather than Aristotelian. (So e.g. Wilpert, 'Reste', 383; Cherniss, *Aristotle's Criticism*, 275–7. Neither Ross nor Harlfinger prints it.) Wilpert takes the fact that the passage contains three occurrences of '*dokei*' to be evidence of Alexandrian authorship. But '*dokei*' can be otherwise explained: Alexander might be citing or paraphrasing an Aristotelian passage but be unsure about whether it is apposite; or the hesitation might be Aristotle's own, expressing his uncertainty about what to say about the Argument from Relatives. It is true that '*charaktēristikon*' is Alexandrian rather than Aristotelian. But it does not

follow that the entire passage is in Alexander's words. Even if it is, he could be paraphrasing Aristotle accurately. That Alexander is, at the minimum, paraphrasing accurately is supported by the fact that the passage fits so well not only with the Argument from Relatives but also with Aristotle's general account of how the less and more accurate arguments differ.

70. Cherniss, *Aristotle's Criticism*, 27, seems to assume something like the following translation of 83. 19–21 (he paraphrases but does not quote): 'For this argument does not, like the preceding ones, seem to prove simply that the common thing is something besides the particulars, but rather that the common thing is some paradigm which is related to things here and is fully'; cf. also Allen, *Plato's Parmenides*, 305 n. 69. On this translation, the passage explicitly says that the Argument from Relatives proves that there are universals that are perfect paradigms, in which case it is reasonable to assume that the point is that it is a valid argument for the existence of forms. But although this translation captures something I think Aristotle believes, it seems less natural than the translation I supply in the text. For *to paradeigma* is presumably the subject, not the predicate.

71. Contrast Cherniss, *Aristotle's Criticism*, 275–6. See also 'Aristotle and the More Accurate Arguments', 156–9; 172–3.

NOTES TO CHAPTER 11

1. Unless otherwise noted, all references to Owen in this chapter are from 'Proof', and they are generally cited in the text rather than in the notes.

2. In the last chapter, we saw that Owen takes '*auto*' and '*kuriōs*' to be synonymous (or at any rate interchangeable); the passages just cited suggest that he also takes '*akribōs*' and '*haplōs*' to be synonymous (or interchangeable). He also seems to believe that '*kath' hauto*' is sometimes used interchangeably with '*akribōs*' and '*haplōs*'. But it is less clear what relation he thinks obtains between these last three terms and the first two. He explains the last three in terms of completeness; but it is difficult to believe that he thinks '*auto*' or '*kuriōs*' should be *translated* as 'completely'. Perhaps he believes that '*akribōs*', '*haplōs*', and '*kath' hauto*' should be translated as 'completely', and that to be *auto* or *kuriōs* F consists in being completely F? Owen does not spell out what if any differences he intends between these terms—consisting in, synonymy, or something else again—but he shifts pretty freely between them, and I shall feel free to follow his lead. He tends, however, to use '*akribōs*' and '*haplōs*' only of predicates, '*kuriōs*' only of things, and '*kath' hauto*' of both predicates and things. I do not know whether this is significant.

3. At 83. 15 and 16, '*pros*' is used for sensibles generally, in their relation to forms; the claim is that sensibles are somehow derivative from the corresponding forms. This is not helpful for Owen's purposes (nor does he suggest that it is). He needs an example where e.g. a particular stick is said to be equal in relation to (*pros*) another particular stick.

4. VIII speaks of '*autoison*', but Owen does not rely on this.

5. Indeed, Owen may rely on different accounts in different places, and the differences are significant. But it will help if we start with a fairly precise account; as we proceed, we will see how Owen may occasionally deviate from it.

6. p. 229. (For Strang's remark, see his 'Plato and the Third Man', in Vlastos (ed.), *Plato I*, 197.) See also 'Logic and Metaphysics', p. 196: '*must* be supplemented'; 'the supplement *required*' (emphases added). Owen and Strang use 'unambiguously' where I use 'non-homonymously'.

7. See e.g. 'Logic and Metaphysics', 196, where he contrasts cases that require a supplement with cases where 'a supplement . . . is not required'.

8. 'Being in the *Sophist*: A Syntactical Enquiry', *Oxford Studies in Ancient Philosophy*, 4 (1986), 49–70. She is discussing Owen's account of incomplete uses of 'to be', rather than of predicates; but parallel remarks apply to his account of incomplete predicates.

9. However, not everything I say requires (*b*) rather than (*a*). If completeness is construed in way (*b*), the division between completeness and incompleteness would still be exhaustive if an incomplete predicate were taken to be one that admits but does not require a complement. At one point (p. 176) Owen may have this account of incompleteness in mind, but he sees that it is not the one at issue in the Argument from Relatives; see n. 10. But at another point (p. 174), Owen may slide into this account; see n. 22.

10. Owen suggests that Plato came to think that 'man' was incomplete, indeed that all predicates are incomplete, on the ground that 'all apply at one time and not at another' (p. 176). This seems to mean that 'man', for example, is incomplete because it was true of Socrates when he was alive but is no longer true of him since he no longer exists. I am not sure I should want to say that it was once true, but is no longer true, that Socrates is a man. But even if we do say this, 'man' does not seem to be incomplete, if an incomplete predicate is one that *requires* a complement. So perhaps Owen means that it is incomplete because it *admits* a complement? If so, he is sliding into a broader notion of incompleteness. In any case, Owen sees that the sense in which 'man' allegedly came to be viewed as incomplete (however we explicate that sense) is different from the sense in which 'equal' allegedly is; for he says that 'equal' is incomplete in a 'narrower sense' (p. 176) than 'man' is. Owen also sees that his interpretation of the middle dialogues and of the Argument from Relatives requires the narrower sense; for the broader sense generates more forms than he believes are countenanced in the middle dialogues or the Argument from Relatives. So the suggestion that an incomplete predicate is one that requires a complement seems reinforced. For discussion of incompleteness in connection with temporal qualifications, see White, *Plato on Knowledge and Reality*, 67.

11. This third contrast is a subcase of the first, but it is useful to discuss it separately.

12. Owen does not himself speak in this way; he speaks instead of an incomplete predicate applying completely to a form, in which case he says that the form exists *kath' hauto*. But I do not think it is misleading as an interpretation of Owen to say he believes that in such cases the form of *F* is completely *F*. Alexander speaks of objects as being not only *kuriōs* but also *akribōs F* (see Ch. 10 n. 58).

13. 'Notes', 88. The fact that Owen speaks interchangeably of relative and incomplete predicates is another sign that he has not a univocal account of incompleteness in mind, for relative and incomplete predicates differ—at least, this is so if we think of Aristotle's category of relatives. Slave, for example, is an Aristotelian relative, but 'slave' is not an incomplete predicate. 'Epictetus was a slave', for example, is semantically complete; no complement is required.

14. For a similar point, see W. Leszl, *Logic and Metaphysics in Aristotle* (Padua, 1970), 189. Owen might agree that 'to *y*' and so on are not part of the definition of equal, but argue that that is irrelevant. For he sometimes seems to suggest that the *logoi* at issue are not different definitions of equal but different explanations of particular cases of equality—what *x* is equal to, what *z* is equal to, and so on. However, this sort of *logos* is irrelevant to homonymy (on both the meaning and real-essence view). For *x* and *z* to be homonymously *F*, *F* must have different definitions in the two cases. The mere fact that *x* is equal to *y*, *z* to *w*, and so on does not show that they are homonymously equal.

15. Owen, 176, thinks *Tm.* and *Symp.* are 'preoccupied' with succession; but he does not think they are among the Argument from Relatives' sources; rather, the argument 'ignores this extension of the theory'. In Ch. 10.6 I mentioned further difficulties with Owen's interpretation of II*b*. Here are two further ones. First, Owen believes that it follows from the fact that sensibles are constantly changing their dimensions that '*x* is the same size as *y*' has no 'fixed meaning'. But then II*a* and II*b* (as Owen interprets them) are at odds with one another. II*a*, on his account, says that we can avoid homonymy only by saying what *x* is equal to. But on his account of II*b*, it emerges that the dimensions of sensibles are changing so rapidly that we can never say what *x* is equal to, and so we can never be in a position to complete the *logos* so as to avoid homonymy. Maybe homonymy does not in fact obtain; but we would never be in a position to know. Yet the Argument from Relatives assumes we do know this.

    Secondly, Owen attempts to make II*b*'s claim that sensibles are always changing an irrelevant parenthesis. However, the claim explains (*gar*, 83. 8) why sensible equals are not true equals, i.e. are not fully equal. The claim about change is therefore more integral to the Argument from Relatives than Owen allows; the fact that he has to discount it is therefore a further difficulty for his interpretation.

16. Possible exceptions: *Crat.* 386e3–4; *Rep.* 476b11; *Meno* 100b. But the first and third of these passages do not clearly refer to forms. The second speaks not of a form's *existing* in itself, but of *thinking* of (actually, of seeing; but I take it he means thinking of) a form in itself; Plato seems to mean only that one can think of a form without thinking of anything else, one can isolate it in thought.

17. Interchangeable or not, I argue in the next chapter that Plato does not use '*kath' hauto*' to indicate completeness.

18. I am not sure that Plato uses '*auta kath' hauta*' of forms to indicate *only* freedom from compresence; but he uses it to indicate at least that, and not to indicate completeness. (Though Plato may use '*auta kath' hauta*' of forms to

express more than their freedom from comprecence, I do not think he uses it to express their separation; see Ch. 4 n. 69.) I am unsure whether Owen intends to claim that it indicates only freedom from comprecence.

19. Contrast 'Notes', 88: it was 'that favoured set of incomplete predicates which seems to have provoked Plato to invent Forms as quasi-ostensive samples for them because the world, understandably, offers no such samples'.

20. It is quite surprising that Owen goes to such lengths to avoid importing comprecence into the Argument from Relatives—for importing it avoids some of the difficulties his own account is vulnerable to. He does consider interpreting IIc (though, curiously, not IIb) in terms of comprecence—though only briefly in a footnote, and only to reject it (p. 176 n. 40). He raises two objections to interpreting IIc in terms of comprecence: (i) it would make Aristotle's objections to the Argument from Relatives irrelevant; and (ii) it would ignore a parallel passage in *EE* 7. 2. I respond to (i) in Ch. 13. I respond to (ii) in the third criticism below.

21. Owen does say that Plato's 'earlier accounts of Forms are dominated by a preoccupation with incomplete predicates' (p. 176). But at least sometimes in 'Proof', he seems to think that Plato is preoccupied with them not in so far as they are incomplete predicates, but only in so far as their instances exhibit comprecence. I pursue this point further below.

22. But perhaps he ought not to mean this, for the mere fact that x is F in some relation or other does not show that 'F' applies to x incompletely. At least, the fact that x is F in some relation does not imply that 'F' is ambiguous. But on p. 174 Owen seems to assume that if x is F in some relation, then 'F' applies to it incompletely; and I shall follow his lead. Perhaps here he conceives of incompleteness as admitting a complement?

23. Owen writes that 'where the Idea is overtly or covertly a comparative it can as well be represented as *superlatively* X, X in comparison with everything; so that here the predicate would retain its "relative" character even when used of the Idea' (p. 179). So at least in these cases, Owen allows that a form of F can be F in some comparison or other without also being not F. Although Owen concedes the general point that some forms of F can escape comprecence even if 'F', as applied to them, admits a complement, he may not agree with me that (as I go on to say) the form of beauty illustrates the point. For the quotation cited in the last paragraph continues as follows: 'Between these alternatives the treatment of *auto to kalon*, "the beautiful itself", in *Symposium* 210e–211a seems to be ambiguous' (p. 179). In saying that Plato's treatment of the form of beauty is 'ambiguous', Owen seems to mean that it is unclear whether Plato means (*a*) the form is more beautiful than anything else; or (*b*) the form is beautiful without qualification (completely). But whichever Plato means, the form of beauty can in fact be beautiful in some comparison or other without also being ugly, since it is more beautiful than anything else.

24. Owen could avoid this problem by saying that although Plato need not have made forms into complete instances of their predicates in order for them to avoid comprecence, he did not see this. At some stages Owen seems to suggest this, as when he says that 'Plato talks as if it is true' that incompleteness always imports comprecence (p. 174)—sc. though it is not in

fact true. But elsewhere he seems to say instead that Plato's main concern is not so much completeness as compresence, and that incompleteness does not always give rise to compresence—as when he says that when Plato says that forms are *kath' hauta* (more exactly, *auta kath' hauta*), he 'evidently means rather to exclude the opposite of X than to exclude the relativity that gives entry to an opposite' (p. 178).

25. p. 178. Cf. also 'Dialectic and Eristic', 229–30.

26. Plato says that although sensible equals 'sometimes, being the same, appear equal to one but not to another' (*eniote tauta onta tō(i) men isa phainetai, tō(i) . . . d' ou*, 74b8–9), 'the equals themselves' (that is, the form of equal) never 'appeared unequal to *you*' (*auta ta isa estin hote anisa soi ephanē*, expecting a 'no' answer, 74c1). Owen takes Plato to mean that a given stick, for example, is equal to one thing but not to another, whereas the form of equal is equal without being equal to anything. In defence of this interpretation, he says that 'the argument of *Phaedo* 74b–c is probably better-construed on these lines, taking the *tôi men . . . tôi d'ou* of 74b8–9 (despite the then misleading dative in 74c1) as neuter and governed by *isa. . . .* Otherwise it turns directly on relativity to different observers' (p. 175 n. 35).

Now even if the passage says that any given stick, for example, is equal to one thing but not to another, whereas the form of equal is not at all unequal, it does not follow that Plato adverts to incompleteness and completeness; for the very same words could be used to advert only to compresence and its absence. But I doubt whether we should follow Owen in taking the datives to be neuter. Owen characteristically notes one difficulty for his interpretation: the masculine dative in 74c1 is then misleading. Since the dative in 74c1 is clearly masculine, it seems reasonable to take the datives in 74b8–9 to be masculine too. If they are masculine, then sensible equals appear equal to one *person* but unequal to another, rather than (as on Owen's view) equal to one *thing*, unequal to another. On this reading, the passage does not advert to incompleteness or completeness directly; they are at best an underlying, but unexpressed, explanation of what Plato explicitly says. (We have seen that even if the datives are neuter, the passage need not advert to incompleteness; it could advert to compresence instead.)

Owen is no doubt reluctant to construe the datives in 74b8–9 as masculine, because he thinks that if they are, then 'appears' must be construed nonveridically (assuming a suppressed *einai*). And if 'appears' is nonveridical, the argument would go as follows: (i) sensible equals appear equal to one person, unequal to another (although they might not really be equal and unequal); (ii) the form of equal never appeared unequal to *you* (although it might be both equal and unequal); (iii) therefore, the form of equal and sensible equals are different. But this argument involves an illegitimate substitution into an intensional context, and so it is invalid.

However, even if the datives are masculine, 'appears' can be veridical (assuming a suppressed *onta* rather than a suppressed *einai*); on this reading, the argument is valid. For it then in effect says that since sensible equals evidently are both equal and unequal, whereas the form of equal is not at all unequal, sensible equals and the form of equal are different.

One might wonder how the passage could be so read if the datives are masculine. Perhaps Plato's thought is that Jones, focusing on the fact that this three-inch thing is equal to that one, infers that three inches is equal, whereas Smith, focusing on the fact that this three-inch thing is unequal to that five-inch one, infers that three inches is unequal. What appears to each of them to be the case—that three inches is equal, and that it is unequal—evidently is the case; both appearings are veridical.

I agree with Owen, then, that 'appears' is veridical; but I none the less favour construing the datives as masculine. So read, the argument is valid; but it adverts to compresence rather than to completeness. Perhaps in the Argument from Relatives Aristotle uses 'is' rather than 'appears' to make it clear that he takes 'appears' to be veridical.

Interestingly enough, Owen cites no passages besides *Phd.* 74ac in which Plato allegedly recognizes this alleged consequence of his argument. Indeed, Owen seems to deny that the verbally quite similar *Symp.* 211a4–5 should be so read: cf. p. 175 n. 35.

For a recent discussion of the passage that agrees with Owen's reading of it, see Bostock, *Plato's Phaedo*, ch. 4, sects. C–E. Owen's interpretation was anticipated by N. R. Murphy, *The Interpretation of Plato's Republic* (Oxford, 1951), 111 n. 1. (Their accounts were arrived at independently.)

27. But even this can be challenged. For a brief discussion, see Ch. 13 n. 24.
28. That is to say, on BSP, as on Owen's account, Plato takes the form of equal to be equal without being equal to anything. But on Owen's view, Plato's claim rests on a misunderstanding of the logic of certain predicates, whereas on my view it rests on his generous and heterodox view of the extensions of predicates.
29. See n. 3.
30. If Owen could establish that the key terms used in the Argument from Relatives ('*auto*', '*kuriōs*', '*akribōs*') and in the criticisms (e.g. *kath' hauto*) are synonymous, then he could argue that *if* the criticisms concern completeness, so too does the Argument from Relatives. But in the next chapter we shall see that Aristotle's criticisms do not concern completeness, in which case even if all the relevant terms were synonymous, this would not help Owen's attempt to import completeness and incompleteness into the Argument from Relatives.
31. Though see my discussion of Diogenes in Ch. 13.4 for a qualification of this claim.
32. Owen may disagree. At least, he sometimes writes as though relative and incomplete predicates are the same; see n. 13.
33. See also the discussion of '*haplōs*' and '*ti*' in Ch. 5.4.
34. The *APo.* passage contrasts *akribesteron* and *kata prosthesin*; *Met.* 982a25–8 contrasts *akribes* and *ek prostheseōs*; *Met.* 1078a9–13 equates *akribes* and *haploun*; the *EN* passage contrasts *haplōs* and *kata prosthesin*.
35. My basic point here and in what follows is unaffected by which account of completeness Owen intends—not admitting, or not requiring, a complement. For my point is that being *F haplōs* and being *F ti* (etc.) both involve complements—there is a difference in degree but not in kind. But neither of Owen's accounts of being completely *F* allows this degree of similarity between being completely and incompletely *F*.

36. See 'Logic and Metaphysics', 181 and n. 3; 'Aristotle on the Snares of Ontology', 264.

37. Owen appeals to the *EE* account of friendship on behalf of his view that IIc adverts to completeness rather than to compresence. But the *EE* passage does not advert to Owenian semantic completeness, and so it should not persuade us to interpret Part IIc in such terms either. It is also important to note that, as Owen agrees, the *EE* passage concerns focal connection; whereas on my view (and on one of Owen's views), the Argument from Relatives concerns synonymy. So even if, as Owen says, 'the similarity of language is very striking', the two passages are in fact importantly different. Leszl, in *Logic and Metaphysics*, 396–405, also challenges Owen's claim that the Argument from Relatives and *EE* 7. 2 are strikingly parallel.

38. For a parallel point, see the discussion of Protagoras in Ch. 13.2.

39. I say more about some relevant Platonic contexts in Ch. 12.

NOTES TO CHAPTER 12

1. 'Proof', 173. If Owen thinks the Academy inherited the distinction from Plato, then presumably he thinks it was a Platonic distinction. According to Annas, 'Plato shows some interest in the dialogues in the difference beween *kath' hauto* and *pros ti* items, and this becomes developed into something like an "Academic theory of categories"' ('Forms and First Principles', 266). S. Mansion, 'Deux écrits de jeunesse d'Aristote sur la doctrine des idées', *Revue philosophique de Louvain*, 48 (1950), 398–416 at 405, also takes the distinction to be Platonic.

2. 'Proof', n. 27; for discussion of the *Phil.* passage, cf. also p. 175. Annas discusses some of these passages in 'Forms and First Principles', 266–8; cf. also her *Aristotle's Metaphysics, Books M and N*, 57.

3. This passage contrasts '*auta kath' hauta*' and '*pros alla*', not '*kath' hauto*' and '*pros ti*'; it is not clear that the two sets of phrases are interchangeable. For example, it is unclear that Plato uses '*auto kath' hauto*' and '*kath' hauto*' interchangeably (see Ch. 11.4, criticism (*b*)). Most of the other Platonic passages we shall be discussing do not contrast '*kath' hauto*' and '*pros ti*' either, although they use very similar terminology. As we shall see, there are also terminological variations in the passages Owen cites as evidence for an Academic use of the terms. Although is not clear that the variations are significant, they are worth noting; none the less, I shall not always pause to comment on them.

4. For the view that the passage distinguishes between complete and incomplete predicates (e.g. 'man' and 'equal'), see R. E. Heinaman, 'Being in the *Sophist*', *Archiv für Geschichte der Philosophie*, 65 (1983), 1–17 at 14, 16. For the view that it distinguishes between a complete and an incomplete use of 'be', see Moravcsik, 'Being and Meaning in the *Sophist*', 48; D. Bostock, 'Plato on "Is Not" (*Sophist*, 254–9)', *Oxford Studies in Ancient Philosophy*, 2 (1984), 89–119. Brown, pp. 68–9, argues that 'itself by itself' is complete, in the sense that it does not require a complement; but she then argues that this does not help Owen, since he requires complete uses to be ones that do not

admit a complement. She also rightly challenges the framework within which this debate has generally been carried on.

5. 'Snares', 260 and n. 2; 'Plato on Not-Being', 125–6, 127; 'Dialectic and Eristic', 225 n. 13. See also Frede, *Prädikation*, 12–29. Annas, 'Forms and First Principles', n. 33, agrees with Owen's later view of the *So.* passage, but, unlike later Owen, she thinks it expresses a relevant complete/incomplete distinction.

6. Owen cites only *Charm.* 168bc, which uses not '*pros*' but the genitive ('*tinos*'). '*Pros*' is first used at 168d1, for something's being F in relation to itself—so it is used where, on Owen's view, we might expect *kath' hauto*.

7. Annas, 'Forms and First Principles', n. 33, accepts a similar interpretation of the *Charm.* passage; but unlike me she none the less thinks it draws a relevant complete/incomplete distinction.

8. *Meno* 73e also uses '*haplōs*' and '*tis*' to distinguish between a genus and its species. AS III uses '*haplōs*' and '*tode*' to draw this distinction, and it then argues that since there must be something that is *haplōs F*, there must be such a thing as *auto to F*, and so a form of F.

9. This fits nicely with my claim in Ch. 11.4, criticism (*c*), that '*haplōs*' and '*ti*' both involve complements. For even though the genus knowledge is knowledge *haplōs*, it is essentially of something. It is knowledge *haplōs* not because it is not of anything, but because it lacks the particular sort of qualification that species of knowledge have. Notice that my point here holds good whether we take incompleteness to be admitting or requiring a complement, and whether we take completeness to be not admitting or not requiring a complement. For my point is that what is *haplōs F* and what is *F ti* both involve complements in just the same way.

10. I assume that 'of something' and 'in relation to something' indicate not that e.g. if x is equal, it is equal to something, but that a person perceives only if she perceives something. Just as an object is F only if someone perceives it to be F, so someone perceives only if she perceives something. Acts of perception are as relational as are the properties perceived.

11. He no doubt believes that if I perceive, I perceive something. But he does not believe that objects have properties only if they are perceived to have them.

12. As Owen, 'Proof', 175, notes, Plato here allows that some sensibles are *kath' hauta* beautiful; contrast R. Hackforth, *Plato's Examination of Pleasure (the Philebus)* (Cambridge, 1945), 99. However, Owen thinks that in allowing this, *Phil.* is a step beyond *Rep.*, whereas I think that *Rep.* allows some sensibles to be *kath' hauta* beautiful, as *Phil.* uses that phrase.

13. J. C. B. Gosling, *Plato's Philebus* (Oxford, 1975), 121.

14. 'Proof', 173–4.

15. Cf. also *Met.* 1079a15–17 (cf. 990b18–21; 1092b19–20). But there is a textual problem in 1079a15–17: on the reading adopted by Annas in her translation, number is not clearly called '*pros ti*'. Unfortunately, Annas does not say why she favours her reading (presumably it is because she does not think Aristotle should classify number as *pros ti*). Owen thinks that 1079a15–17 classifies number as a relative; he then says that 'relative' does not refer to the Aristotelian category; rather, Aristotle subsumes 'number under *pros ti* as a general class contrasted with *to kath' hauto*' ('Proof', 174). But the account I go on to give of 86. 5–6 also explains 1079a15–17.

16. For his reasons, see below, and Ch. 13.1. Similarly, when Aristotle describes the Object of Thought Argument as an argument from the thought of something that has perished (*Met.* 990b14), he does not mean that it produces forms *only* for such things; he describes the argument by hinting at one of its difficulties. (However, Aristotle believes that if it generated any forms at all, it would generate them for *all* perishable things; by contrast, the Argument from Relatives is not meant to generate forms for all relatives since it is not meant to generate a form of e.g. slave.)

17. Aristotle himself realizes that his first account has unwelcome results. He admits, for example, that it seems to make some secondary substances relatives even though, in his view, no substance can be a relative. One might object that if Aristotle had the category of relatives in mind, he would have used, not his problematical first account of relatives, but his favoured second account. However, his second account is no more satisfactory than his first one. (Ackrill, *Aristotle's Categories and De Interpretatione, ad loc.*, well documents some of the difficulties.) And anyway, as Aristotle or Alexander goes on to note, such refinements are unnecessary here. For even if number were classified as a quantity rather than as a relative, the same objection could still be made (86. 11–12). (Owen, 'Proof', 173–4 and n. 29, takes the remark to be Alexandrian; Wilpert, *ZaF* 109, thinks it is Aristotelian. Whoever makes the point, it seems apt.) For it would in that case turn out that quantity is prior to substance; but substance is supposed to be prior to quantity no less than to relative. If the basic point stands no matter which of the two accounts of relative we use, then there is no reason to turn to a more cumbersome, and still deficient, account.

18. Cf. also 86. 10, where Alexander says that 'relatives are like appendages, as he says in the *Ethics*'. The passage is not recorded in Harlfinger. For relatives described as appendages, see Elias' report of Andronicus (see sect. 4 and n. 33).

19. However, Owen, 'Logic and Metaphysics', 186, believes that although Aristotle mentions his own categorial scheme in 1096a20, he suddenly shifts to a different, allegedly Academic, one in 1096a20–1. He then suggests that 'the subsequent conflation of the Platonic "categories" with the Aristotelian in, e.g., Albinus ..., may derive from Aristotle himself (*EN* 1096a19–21)' (p. 173 n. 27). (See also Annas, 'Forms and First Principles', 268, who remarks that 'the passage is unique in this regard'.) However, Owen's only reason for thinking that 1096a20–1 shifts to an Academic categorial scheme seems to be the belief that it takes *kath' hauto* and *pros ti* to be exhaustive. But it seems more likely that Aristotle picks out relatives (in his narrow sense) as an especially clear example of something that is posterior to substance. That this is what he is doing is suggested by a parallel passage, *Met.* 1088a22–5, which I go on to discuss in the text. If this is right, then the *EN* passage involves only Aristotle's familiar categorial scheme. Spengel excises '*en tō(i) poiō(i)*'. If we follow him, then it is less clear that 1096a20 adverts to Aristotle's own categorial scheme, in which case my reply to Owen is weakened. But if I can provide a plausible reading of the passage without the excision, then we need not follow Spengel.

20. I assume that 'affection', 'appendage', and 'coincident' are used interchangeably. The main difference between the two passages is that in *EN*

relatives are said to be appendages and coincidents of *being*, whereas in *Met.* they are said to be affections of *quantity*. In Aristotle's view, (i) every member of a category is a being, and (ii) every relative is an affection of something in some category other than the category of relatives, although (iii) not all relatives are affections of quantity in particular (slave, for example, is not). The *EN* passage expresses (ii) (thereby using '*tou ontos*' to indicate that every relative is an appendage of something in some category or other). By contrast, in the *Met.* passage, which focuses on the great and the small, Aristotle illustrates (ii) with an example from the category of quantity. The two passages therefore illuminate one another—the *Met.* passage makes it clear why relatives are posterior to everything else; the *EN* passage makes it clear that not all relatives are appendages of quantity in particular.

21. Aristotle does not mean that a man, for example, cannot be a slave. He means that a slave is a slave by being, among other things, a man, whereas a man is not a man by being anything in another category. A similar point is made in *APo.* 83a30, although there the contrast is between substance and non-substance rather than between relative and non-relative.

22. Owen, 'Proof', 173 n. 26, says that the relevance of the Academic dichotomy was pointed out by D. G. Ritchie. According to Ritchie, *Plato* (Edinburgh, 1902), in VII Aristotle means either: '(1) that we, the Platonists, do not attempt to bring things that are merely relative to something else (*ta pros ti*) into the same class with things that have their meaning *per se* (cf. *Eth. Nic.* i.6 sect. 8, 1096b,8); or rather, perhaps, (2) that we do not seek to bring co-relatives under the *same* idea' (p. 214 n. 13). Presumably Owen takes (1) (which Ritchie does not actually seem to favour; he certainly does not elaborate on it) to anticipate his own view. Ross, *Aristotle's Metaphysics*, *ad loc.*, by contrast, seems to favour (2), for he suggests that Aristotle's point in X is that relatives—e.g. equal things, fathers, slaves, and so on—do not collectively constitute a genuine kind. (2) gives Aristotle a true point; but it has no anti-Platonic force and it is irrelevant to our context.

23. 'Proof', 173 n. 27; 176 n. 38.

24. Moraux, 84–6; see also H. Mutschmann's preface to his Teubner edition and Rose, *Ar. Ps.*, pp. 677–8. Rose gives 145 BC as the latest the *Div. Ar.* could have been written; he does not say how much earlier it might be. Owen does not say when he believes the work was composed. Moraux seems to think it may date from Aristotle's lifetime.

25. The last three passages (especially the Sextus passage) are often thought to describe Plato's so-called unwritten doctrines. Their value as evidence for the so-called unwritten doctrines has been demolished by G. Vlastos, in 'On Plato's Oral Doctrine', in id., *PS* 379–98; see also Ackrill's searching review of Wilpert, *ZaF*. The considerations Vlastos and Ackrill adduce should make us equally wary about relying on these passages as evidence for an alleged Academic distinction between complete and incomplete predicates.

26. One might take Hermodorus to say that Plato himself used '*kath' hauto*' and '*pros heteron*' to distinguish between (e.g.) man and (e.g.) good. If so, he relies on a source other than the dialogues—sometimes, it is thought, on the so-called unwritten doctrines (see e.g. J. Dillon, *The Middle Platonists: 80 BC to AD 200* (Ithaca, NY, 1977), 8, 133). However, it is at least as reasonable to

suppose that Hermodorus is reporting Plato using not Plato's terminology but his own. Nor do we know whether he describes Plato's views accurately. For some discussion of the Hermodorus fragment, see Cherniss, *Aristotle's Criticism*, 169–70 n. 96; C. J. de Vogel, 'Problems Concerning Later Platonism I', *Mnemosyne*, 4th ser., 1 (1948), 197–216.

27. So Owen seems to believe; see 'Proof', 176; 'Dialectic and Eristic', 225. But Owen ought not to believe this, since, as I go on to say, the broader division does not correspond to the division between complete and incomplete predicates.

28. Hermodorus' category of *pros ti* (like Aristotle's, as we saw above) may also be too broad for Owen's purposes. For Hermodorus counts the arranged as a *pros ti* item (*to hērmosmenon*, 248. 9), but it is not clear that the Argument from Relatives is supposed to produce a form in its case.

29. In *Met.* 7. 1, for example, Aristotle says that only substance is separate, i.e. only it exists independently; everything else depends for its existence on the existence of some substance or other. He also says there that the definitions of non-substances all need to mention substance, whereas substance is in some way definitionally independent. In *APo.* 73b5–10 he characterizes substances as being what they are without being something else, whereas all non-substances are of something else.

   J. Annas and J. Barnes, *The Modes of Scepticism* (Cambridge, 1985), 131–2, seem to think that Hermodorus' distinction is not between substance and non-substance, but epistemological. At least, they so interpret Philo, and they suggest that Philo is relying on a Platonic division, for which they cite Hermodorus. I myself do not think Hermodorus' distinction is epistemological; nor do I agree with their suggestion that Plato's notion of *pros ti* is (always) epistemological. But if Annas and Barnes were right, it would not support Owen, nor do they think it would; indeed, they distinguish between epistemological relatives and semantic incompleteness.

30. However, Hermodorus does not say that all *pros heteron* items are of substance in particular; he makes only the less committal claim that they are all of something.

31. Andronicus is not an Academic, and he is too late to be a source on whom Aristotle could draw; but Xenocrates is relevant.

32. In the famous footnote in 'Snares' (p. 260 n. 2) in which Owen retracts the suggestion that *So.* 255c distinguishes between complete and incomplete (uses of) predicates, in favour of the view that it distinguishes between two incomplete uses of 'be', he also says that his new interpretation 'explains some Aristotelian terminology (e.g. *Posterior Analytics* I, 73b5–10)'. This suggests that he takes the *APo.* passage to distinguish not between complete and incomplete (uses of) predicates, but between two incomplete uses of a single predicate. But the *APo.* passage is very similar to the Simplicius one. So perhaps Owen came to agree that the Simplicius passage does not after all advert to a relevant complete/incomplete distinction.

33. Elias, *in Cat.*, 201. 18–23. (The work is sometimes ascribed to David rather than to Elias; see Busse's preface to *CAG* 18.) Elias says that Andronicus made *pros ti* the last category on the ground that, unlike the other categories, '*pros ti* has no matter of its own (for it seems to be an appendage)'. We have

seen that Aristotle also uses 'appendage' for relatives. One might argue that Elias is right about Andronicus, and that Simplicius is right about Xenocrates but wrong to say that Xenocrates' and Andronicus' divisions are the same.

34. In the alternative recension recorded by Rose, *Ar. Ps.*, and Mutschmann, the examples of *pros ti* items are double and knowledge. Unlike Diogenes' examples, these are not explicit comparatives; but like his examples, they are Aristotelian relatives. The account of *pros ti* items given in the recension is similar to the one given in the *Peri ideōn* to explain why number is a relative—because they are of something, take a genitive.

35. Interestingly, he explains what it is to be *pros ti* in terms of being *pros heteron*: cf. 265 with the Hermodorus fragment discussed above.

36. Annas and Barnes, *Modes*, 132.

37. Annas and Barnes, *Modes*, 131, agree that the Pythagorean and Hermodoran divisions differ. But they do not say what the difference is, and they take both divisions to be epistemological. Although I agree that the Pythagorean division is epistemological, on the account I gave above of Hermodorus his division is not epistemological; see also n. 29.

38. If (contrary to my view) VII and X use an Academic distinction, the best option seems to be that they distinguish between Aristotelian relatives and all the other categories. (In this case, the operative distinction would be the one Elias ascribes to Andronicus.) For VII says that *pros ti* items have their being in their relation *to one another*, which strongly suggests Aristotelian relatives. '*Kath' hauto*' would then indicate a feature that items in all other categories have, and that forms must therefore have since, being substances, they cannot (in Aristotle's view) be relatives. But this interpretation does not help Owen, since the distinction between Aristotelian relatives and all the other categories is not the distinction between the incomplete and the complete; and for reasons already given, this interpretation also seems less plausible than Alexander's.

NOTES TO CHAPTER 13

1. In *Met.* 990b15–17 Aristotle says that the Argument from Relatives 'produces ideas of relatives'; Alexander writes that it 'establishes ideas *even* (*kai*) of relatives. At least (*goun*) . . .' (83. 22; cf. 83. 17, 85. 7; cf. *goun* at 83. 23). Owen ('Proof', 173) speculates that *kai* and *goun* are Alexandrian additions, motivated by the thought that the Argument from Relatives posits forms for more than relatives, in the strict sense in which 'relative' names one of Aristotle's ten categories. Even if Owen's speculation were correct, it would not follow (nor does Owen think it follows) that the criticism is not due to Aristotle.

2. So in saying that 'they used to ˌsay that there were no ideas of relatives', Aristotle means, not that the Platonists explicitly used to say this, but that they are committed to this view. It is not unusual for Aristotle to use 'they say' in this way. He also does so in recording various Presocratic views in e.g. *Met.* 1. 3; see also the discussion of (iii) in Ch. 8 n. 29.

3. See Ch. 4.2. In a complicated argument in *Met.* 1. 9, 990b27–991a1 (cf. 13. 4, 1079a19–34), Aristotle argues that the Platonists can admit forms corresponding at most to substance predicates; he seems to infer that such forms must themselves be substances. (The argument is difficult. For discussion, see the references cited in Ch. 6 n. 7.) But he is unlikely to have this argument in mind here. For here he seems to think that it is uncontroversial to claim that the Platonists count forms as substances—and so it is if he has in mind the suggestion given in the text. But it would not be uncontroversial if he had in mind the argument from 990b27–34, which aims to commit the Platonists to an unwelcome conclusion.

4. The terminology is Owen's in e.g. 'Dialectic and Eristic' (though he uses 'predicate' where I generally use 'property').

5. See e.g. *Cat.* 8a13 ff.; *Met.* 1088a21–b4. For a brief discussion of the second passage—which, interestingly enough, discusses equality in particular—see Ch. 12.3.

6. Contrast Cherniss, *Aristotle's Criticism*, 283.

7. In Ch. 12 I argued that '*kath' hauto*' refers to a feature special to substances, and that '*pros ti*' indicates the category of relatives. But this does not by itself explain precisely why no substance that exists in itself can be a relative.

8. '*Huphestanai*' (83. 25) probably indicates existential independence, but the word seems to be due to Alexander rather than to Aristotle, so I take it to be his interpolation, explaining his view of the force of '*kath' hauto*'. For although Aristotle uses '*huphistasthai*', he does not use it in a relevant way, whereas Alexander standardly uses it for existential independence. For Alexander's use of the word, see *De Mixt.* 217. 33–4 with 228. 13–14 and 24, along with R. B. Todd, *Alexander of Aphrodisias on Stoic Physics: A Study of the De Mixtione with Preliminary Essays, Text, Translation, and Commentary* (Leiden, 1976).

9. See e.g. the passages from *Met.* 13. 4 and 9, translated in Ch. 4.2. However, Aristotle sometimes uses '*para*' for separation; see Ch. 8.2; cf. also Ch. 6 n. 31. As we have seen, Vlastos thinks that Plato uses *auta kath' hauta* of forms to indicate separation, though I disputed this view; see Ch. 4.6.

10. See e.g. Owen, 'Notes'; White, *Plato on Knowledge and Reality*, ch. 3. This is part of the view that Plato accepts 'semantic atomism', according to which the form of *F* is only *F*, in which case it can function as a paradigmatic example of *F*-ness, so that by looking at it we can understand '*F*'. This dovetails with Owen's view (discussed in Ch. 11) that Plato takes forms to be complete instances of their predicates, so that they can function as 'standard cases'. If, as I go on to suggest, Plato does not view forms as isolated atoms, that is yet another count against Owen's semantic interpretation of Plato.

11. Contrast White, *Plato on Knowledge and Reality*, 79 n. 16.

12. I discuss this passage in more detail in 'Forms as Causes' and 'Immanence'.

13. One might argue that, for Aristotle, particulars cannot, strictly speaking, be defined; but they at least have formulae or *logoi* in some weaker sense.

14. Owen, 'Platonism', and M. Woods, 'Substance and Essence in Aristotle', *Proceedings of the Aristotlian Society*, 75 (1974–5), 167–80, in effect argue that in the *Met.* Aristotle believes that Socrates is identical with the species man, in which case he is not distinct from it. For some criticism of this view, see my 'Owen, Aristotle, and the Third Man'; and J. Kung, 'Aristotle on

Thises, Suches, and the Third Man Argument', *Phronesis*, 26 (1981), 207–47.
15. However, it is not clear that Aristotle can defend this claim satisfactorily. In *Cat.*, for example, definitions of Aristotelian substances mention differentiae, which in that work are not substances. To avoid this complication, one could put the second possibility by saying that, in Aristotle's view, one can define substances without referring to anything in any non-substance category; for in *Cat.* differentiae belong neither in the category of substance nor in any other category.
16. I ask below whether the fact that the form of equal is a paradigm requires its definition to refer to something sensible, even if the fact that it is equal does not require this.
17. In the next section, I ask whether the equality of the form of equal requires it to be equal to something distinct from itself. In *Top.* 147a Aristotle suggests that some forms have definitions that refer to other forms; but he does not suggest that definitions of forms ever need to refer to something other than a form.
18. I discuss this issue in more detail in 'Relational Entities', *Archiv für Geschichte der Philosophie*, 65 (1983), 225–49, and in 'Plato and Aristotle on Form and Substance'.
19. At *Rep.* 509b Plato says that the form of the good is not *ousia*. If he means that it is not a substance, then Aristotle could urge that Plato himself believes that all forms depend on something that even in his own view is not a substance. But I do not think Plato means to say that the form of the good is not a substance. For a brief account of what I think he means, see my 'Knowledge and Belief in *Republic* V–VII', 97–8.
20. So, contrary to Owen, VII is not irrelevant to the Argument from Relatives if that argument is interpreted as I interpret it; see Ch. 11 n. 20. VII might well be irrelevant to the Argument from Relatives (as I interpret the argument) on Owen's interpretation of VII. For he believes that VII objects that the form of equal is, impossibly, a complete (*kath' hauto*) instance of an incomplete (*pros ti*) predicate—it is equal without being equal to anything. (Owen believes this shows that VII involves a one-level paradox between two B-level predicates; see 'Dialectic and Eristic', 229.) Since in my view the distinction between complete and incomplete (uses of) predicates is irrelevant to the Argument from Relatives, it would be irrelevant to mention it in VII. However, in Ch. 12 I argued that '*pros ti*' and '*kath' hauto*' should not be interpreted as Owen interprets them.
21. So on my account, VII and VIII are different objections. By contrast, Owen, 'Proof', 178, seems to think that VII and VIII level the same objection. I discuss Uniqueness in more detail in Ch. 15 (esp. sects. 1 and 2); cf. also Ch. 8.7 and Ch. 16.4.
22. At *Parm.* 132bc, Plato argues that if forms are thoughts, then for every predicate for which there is even one form, there will be two forms: the form-thought, and what the form-thought is of. Once again, there are two forms corresponding to a given predicate, though no larger regress is in the offing. See Ch. 9.5.
23. Several people have suggested to me that even if Plato accepts (1)–(3), he can still evade the argument by rejecting (4); for presumably the form of equal is equal to itself. However, Aristotle begins *Cat.* ch. 7 by saying that

relatives are what they are of (or than) *other things* (*heterōn*, 6a37); so perhaps he treats equality in such a way that one thing can be equal only by being equal to something else. This seems confirmed by *Met.* 5, which says that numerical relatives essentially involve reference to something else (1021a26–9), and equality is a numerical relative (1021a8–14). (Plato also conceives of equality in quantitative terms; for in *Parm.* 140b6–8 he says that *a* is equal to *b* just in case they are of the same measures (i.e. have the same number of units).) And in *Cat.* 6a26, Aristotle says that equality is the *idion* of quantity; only quantities, that is, are called equal or unequal (6a30–1). So things that lack measures—e.g. colours—cannot be equal to one another. Aristotle says that they are similar to one another (6a33–4).

24. At least, it seems more reasonable to say this if we do not want to say that the form of equal is equal by being equal to itself; see n. 23. To say that Aristotle's objection seems more successful if it is aimed against NSP than against BSP is not to say that it succeeds against NSP. And in fact the issue is quite complicated, partly because there are different ways of explaining how the form of equal could be NSP-equal. Owen offers one explanation: in his view Plato takes the form of equal to be a single object that is NSP-equal all on its own. If this were Plato's view, then Aristotle would certainly be right to protest against it, in so far as it rests on misunderstanding the logic of relative or incomplete predicates. In 'The Third Man Again', however, in Allen (ed.), *Studies in Plato's Metaphysics*, 265–77, P. T. Geach suggests that the form of equal consists of two perfectly equal parts; to say that the form of equal is equal is to say that its two parts are perfectly equal to one another. On this view, Plato does not misunderstand the logic of relative or incomplete predicates. Nor does Aristotle's objection succeed if it is aimed against this view; for on this view, the form of equal can correctly be said to be equal without our needing to invoke a second form of equal. I do not think Geach's view is correct—for on it, forms are particulars that enjoy NSP, whereas on my view they are properties that enjoy BSP. But his view is not vulnerable to all the objections that have been levelled against it, and it is worth considering it, to see whether NSP can be made more intelligible than it is on Owen's view. (For some objections to Geach, see Owen, 'Proof', 174–5. n. 34; and 'Dialectic and Eristic', 230–1.)

25. In Chs. 15 and 16 we shall see that Aristotle may believe that Plato is also committed to NSP for other reasons.

26. But see n. 24.

27. For this objection, though it is not directed to the present context, see Gallop, 125: 'sensible unequals could hardly be held to "fall short" of Inequality in the way that sensible equals may be held to fall short of Equality'.

28. See e.g. *Rep.* 475e9–476a7 (just and unjust; good and bad); 523–4 (hard and soft; thick and thin); *Phd.* 101 (large and small) and, possibly, 74bc (equal and unequal); also *Parm.* 128e6–130a2 (like and unlike); *So.* 254e14–255e1 (same and different). Another reason for denying that Plato wants forms for all opposites is that forms are supposed to be objects of supreme value; they are perfect and ideals aimed at. But then how could there be forms of e.g. ugly and bad?

Cherniss, *Aristotle's Criticism*, 278 n. 185, takes the unequal to be a negation; and we know from Aristotle's criticisms of the One over Many Argument that he believes that Plato does not want forms of negations. But unequal is not a negation. The negation of P is the complement of P. The negation of equal is not 'unequal' but 'not equal'. ('Not equal' differs from 'unequal' if we assume that only things that have measures, or are quantities, can be equal or unequal to one another. In this case, colours, for example, are not equal or unequal to one another, any more than rocks, for example, are either sighted or blind. See n. 23.)

29. If Plato accepts NSP, would he need to introduce a second form of unequal to explain how the first form of unequal is unequal? Here we can raise some of the same questions that we raised above, about how the form of equal could be NSP-equal (see n. 24). For example, one might argue that the form of inequality consists of two unequal parts so that, in saying that it is unequal, one is saying that its two parts are unequal to one another. But perhaps Aristotle would argue that the form of unequal could be NSP-unequal only by being unequal to a second form of inequality because, for example, it is a relative and relatives have their being in relation to something distinct from themselves. I leave it to others to say how Plato might avoid postulating a second form of inequality if, contrary to my view, he accepts NSP.

30. It is disputed whether this passage is from the *Peri ideōn*; see Ch. 3, n. 24. Even if it is not, there is no reason to doubt that it is Aristotelian. Whether or not it is Aristotelian, the objections it raises are interestingly enough related to the ones just considered that it is appropriate to discuss them here.

31. However, it is not clear that (1) should be so read. For one thing, it seems somewhat awkward for Aristotle to use 'substances' here to refer to his candidate substances. But later stages of the argument perhaps suggest that he is doing so; and certainly elsewhere in the *Peri ideōn* he uses terminology in his own way even when he aims to articulate a Platonic argument (cf. e.g. his use of 'homonymy' in the Argument from Relatives). It might be a second count against reading (1) as I do that it seems to make (5) question-begging; but perhaps later stages of the argument also explain why Aristotle feels entitled to (5) even if it is so read.

Three other possible readings are worth mentioning:

(a) Forms are principles of the entities *Plato* views as substances. But as against (a), one would expect Plato to claim, not that forms are the principles of his own substances, but that they are the substances themselves. Of course, he might believe that some forms are principles of others—e.g. the form of the good is in some way a principle of all other forms (see e.g. *Rep.* 509b6–10). But (1) claims, not that some forms are principles of some substances, but that forms as such are principles of substances as such. But perhaps Plato believes that something can be a principle of itself?

(b) Aristotle might be thinking of the one and the indefinite dyad, which may be of concern in surrounding passages.

(c) Aristotle might mean that forms are the principles of the basic beings, whatever they turn out to be. On this reading, 'substances' refers neutrally to the basic beings, whatever they are; but it takes no stand on what they are.

32. For references, see Ch. 4 n. 83. In Ch. 4.7 I also say something about the connection between perfection and paradigmatism.

33. However, (3) raises various difficulties, for not everything that is in some way

of something seems to be a relative in the sense of being an entity that falls into Aristotle's category of relatives; see Ackrill, *Aristotle's Categories and De Interpretatione*, 99; Ch. 12 n. 17. But I shall ignore such difficulties here, in order to focus on what if any difficulties Plato faces if he concedes that in so far as forms are paradigms they are relatives.

34. In VII and X Aristotle claims that no relative can be a substance, i.e. a basic being. He believes, however, not only that relatives are not basic beings but also that they are the least important beings there are, since every relative is what it is by also being something else in another category, whereas no non-relative is what it is by also being something else in another category; see *Met.* 1088a22–5. For a brief discussion, see Ch. 12.3.

35. I say 'may' because, as I go on to explain briefly, I am not altogether sure that it does succeed from his own metaphysical perspective.

36. Aristotle seems to use 'natural priority' here to indicate definitional or explanatory priority; elsewhere (e.g. *Met.* 5. 11) he uses the same phrase for ontological priority.

37. I discuss this matter further in 'Forms as Causes' and 'Plato and Aristotle on Form and Substance'.

38. For helpful discussion, see Ackrill, *Aristotle's Categories and De Interpretatione*, nn. on *Cat.* ch. 7.

39. This is not to say that Plato accepts both views. It is to say that they are compatible.

40. Cf. 83. 15–16, where sensibles are said to be *pros* forms.

41. This point is well made by Annas, 'Forms and First Principles', 269–70. The rest of my discussion in this section is also indebted to Annas.

42. Alexander explains that the notion of 'a paradigm is borrowed from painters, who are said to paint by referring to a paradigm. He ⟨i.e. Aristotle⟩ shows that those who say that the ideas are paradigms are speaking empty words by his question, "For what is it that works by looking towards ideas?" For if the ideas are paradigms, there must be something that works by referring to them, as we see painters painting by referring to paradigms' (*in Met.* 101. 5–10).

43. Or perhaps it is even worse than a metaphor, for in *Top.* 140a7 ff. he says that calling a law a likeness (*eikōn*) is 'not using the word in a proper sense . . . and with worse effect than any kind of metaphorical language'.

44. See Ch. 4 n. 85.

45. For example, even if Aristotle conceded to Plato that the demiurge looked to forms in creating natural kinds, he would still object that particular instances of natural kinds do not involve any craftsmen looking to forms; as he is fond of saying, a man produces a man (see e.g. *Met.* 7. 7–9). Plato would agree that instances of natural kinds are not directly created by the demiurge. But he does not think this shows that forms are not paradigms; for a full causal explanation of how members of natural kinds come into being would refer to the demiurge's activity, which is therefore causally relevant, though not causally sufficient, for their production. For some discussion, see my 'Forms as Causes', esp. sect. 11. The issue is interestingly discussed by Alexander, in his comments *in Met.*, on 991a20–b8; see also the passage quoted by Simplicius, *in Phys.* 310. 25–311. 37 (in which Alexander comments on Aristotle's *Phys.* 194b26).

NOTES TO CHAPTER 14

1. Aristotle writes as though there are more than two more accurate arguments, but see Ch. 2 n. 37.
2. Robin, 21; Cherniss, *Aristotle's Criticism*, 275; cf. Leszl, *Il 'De Ideis'*, 183 ff.
3. Ch. 2.7; Ch. 10.9. Robin, 19 n. 16, accepts this account of 'more accurate', but he none the less says that the One over Many Argument is the second more accurate argument. Cherniss, *Aristotle's Criticism*, 276–7, sees that on this account of 'more accurate', the One over Many Argument is not a more accurate argument. He therefore rejects this account of 'more accurate' in favour of Ross's account, according to which Aristotle means only that such arguments are more 'abstractly logical'. (For Ross's account, see his *Aristotle's Metaphysics*, ii. 424, n. on 1080a10; and i. 194, n. on 990b15.)
4. Aristotle says that more accurate arguments of the second sort *legousi* the Third Man. Alexander substitutes '*eisagonta*' (83. 34; 85. 7–8), indicating that he takes '*legousi*' to mean that the premisses of these arguments give rise to the Third Man Argument. I think Alexander is right about this. However, it is sometimes thought that the second more accurate argument is not an argument introducing or leading to the Third Man Argument, but the Third Man Argument itself; see e.g. Jackson, 'Plato's Later Theory of Ideas', 255–6 n. 2 (criticizing Zeller and Bonitz who, however, have the right view); Ross, *Aristotle's Metaphysics*, i. 194–5, note ad loc. Ross bases his view partly on the belief that '*legousi*' must mean 'mention' rather than 'introduce' in the sense of 'lead to' or 'give rise to'. This view is well criticized by Cherniss, *Aristotle's Criticism*, 276 n. 184.
5. Mansion, 'Critique', 192–3, seems to see that the second more accurate argument is not the One over Many Argument (though cf. p. 187). However, her account of how the two arguments differ is not satisfactory.
6. I insert named steps for ease of reference. 'AOM' stands for 'accurate one over many'; 'NI' stands for 'non-identity'; 'G-Sep' stands for 'generalized separation'. I discuss these claims shortly.
7. This formulation of premiss (4) of the One over Many Argument is slightly different from that in Ch. 8. The present formulation suits the present context better; but I intend no difference in content.
8. '*Pleiō*' and '*kath' hekasta*' can be used interchangeably, but they are not used interchangeably here. For as we saw in Ch. 8, in the One over Many Argument *kath' hekasta* are only sensible particulars; but since (as we shall see in Ch. 15) the Third Man Argument requires forms over groups that contain both particulars and forms, '*pleiō*' should not be restricted to sensible particulars. Further, the difference between the One over Many Argument and the Accurate One over Many Argument is obscured if the two words are not distinguished in the way I suggest. Notice that '*pleiō*' is used, as it should be, at 84. 22 and at 84. 26; '*kath' hekasta*' is used at 84. 25, 84. 26–7, and 85. 1, where its use is appropriate. 85. 1 makes it plain that forms are not *kath' hekasta*, although they fall within the scope of '*pleiō*'. The other more accurate argument, the Argument from Relatives, also uses '*pleiō*' broadly (82. 12); it is again appropriate to do so, since forms must fall within its

scope. (This is because the Argument from Relatives begins by describing the ways in which something can be predicated non-homonymously; it turns out that some things can be predicated non-homonymously only if forms bear the corresponding predicate fully.) When the Argument from Relatives wishes to discuss sensibles, it uses '*entautha*' (83. 6, 10) or '*aisthēta*' (83. 9). See also Ch. 10 n. 44.

9. Premiss (5) of the One over Many Argument does not mention forms, but the argument concludes that separated forms are what is predicated. Until now, I have used an initial lower case in 'separation' (unless the word began a sentence!). But it will be convenient if, in the rest of this chapter and occasionally hereafter, I use an initial capital when I am speaking of existing independently of sensible particulars. For it will then be clear precisely which separation assumption, out of various alternatives that we shall be looking at, I have in mind.

10. This inference is made at 84. 22–4. 84. 28 mentions both G-Sep and NI, but it does not infer NI from G-Sep. Interestingly, 84. 28 uses '*kat' idean huphestōs*' (rather than any form or cognate of '*chōrizein*'). I assume that the phrase is due to Alexander (see Ch. 13 n. 8). Alexander might be correctly paraphrasing Aristotle; but perhaps he uses the phrase, not to paraphrase Aristotle, but as an independent insertion, in an effort to make 84. 28 parallel 84. 22–4 (though if so, he does not quite capture the parallel since he omits the inferential link). That Alexander inserted the phrase is perhaps suggested by the fact that LF has nothing corresponding to 84. 28.

11. However, the Accurate One over Many Argument and the One over Many Argument involve different separation claims (G-Sep and Sep, respectively) and different difference claims (NI and premiss (4) of the One over Many Argument, respectively). I return to these points in Chs. 15 and 16.

12. Since Aristotle takes the Accurate One over Many Argument to be valid but unsound, he must reject at least one of its premisses. He presumably rejects G-Sep. For since in Aristotle's view universals are what is predicated, G-Sep in effect involves the claim that universals are separate. But in Aristotle's view universals cannot exist uninstantiated and so they cannot be separate.

13. As we saw in Ch. 4.6, in *Met.* 13. 9 Aristotle gives Plato yet another valid argument for separation.

NOTES TO CHAPTER 15

1. See e.g. Owen, 'Platonism'. I discuss Aristotle's response to the TMA in 'Owen, Aristotle, and the Third Man'; I shall not consider it further here.

2. OAC records four arguments, each of which is called a Third Man Argument. The first is ascribed to Eudemus (in *Peri lexeōs*), the fourth to Aristotle. The second and third arguments are ascribed to the sophists (84. 8, 17); they are importantly different from the other versions and will not concern us here. They seem to be due not to Alexander but to a later hand; see Ch. 3 n. 22, and Cherniss, *Aristotle's Criticism*, App. 4. Interestingly enough, however,

OAC suggests that the first of these two arguments 'is given encouragement by those who separate what is common from the individuals' (84. 15–16). I explore the relevance of separation to the TMA in sect. 4.

3. Or perhaps I should say 'at least one', since it has been doubted whether the Third Man Argument recorded in the *Peri ideōn* is the same as the one Aristotle has in mind elsewhere; see A. E. Taylor, 'Parmenides, Zeno, and Socrates', *Proceedings of the Aristotelian Society*, 16 (1915–16), 234–89, esp. 268–70 (for his reasons, see below, n. 79).

4. For the force of the parenthesis, see Ch. 4 n. 17.

5. At least, he believes that if there is a form of *F*, then one can know that something is *F* only if one knows the form of *F*. As we have seen, he sometimes seems committed to the existence of a form for every property; but sometimes the range of forms is less clear.

6. See Vlastos, 'TMA I', 240 n. 1, for a similar account of why the regress is troubling. This account obviously involves attributing some highly controversial claims to Plato. Notice, though, that the claim that explanation requires the existence of something that is self-explanatorily *F*, *F* in virtue of itself, is compatible with the view that the justification that is necessary for knowledge consists in some sort of coherence; for it does not follow from the fact that the possibility of explanation requires the existence of something that is *F* in virtue of itself that one can justify any of one's beliefs independently of others. My own view is that Plato is a coherentist about justification who also believes that the possibility of explanation requires the existence of some entities that are *F* in virtue of themselves. (For a brief discussion, see my 'Knowledge and *Logos* in the *Theaetetus*' and my 'Knowledge and Belief in *Republic* V–VII'.)

    To regain the possibility of knowledge, one need not establish U; perhaps showing that there are, say, five forms of *F* (or however many one could know), at least one of which is *F* in virtue of itself and explains the others, would do. So just as the regress proves more than is needed to prove U false (since proving that there are as many as two forms of *F* if any at all would do that), so U is a stronger claim than is needed to avoid the conclusion that knowledge is impossible.

7. The literature on P-TMA is vast. Like everyone else who works on this topic, I am indebted to Vlastos's classic article, 'The "Third Man" Argument in the *Parmenides*' (= 'TMA I'). I am also indebted to Peterson and, especially, to Cohen, 'The Logic of the Third Man'. (In this chapter all references to Cohen are to this article.)

8. Step (1) is sometimes instead translated as 'that there is in every case a single form' (see 'TMA I', 232; Cornford, *Plato and Parmenides*, 87). This translation suggests that Plato is explaining why he believes that forms exist, whereas my translation (which takes *hekaston* as subject and *hen* as predicate) suggests that he is explaining why there is just one form for any predicate that has a form. Though both translations are possible when step (1) is considered on its own, the argumentative context favours my construal.

9. The uniqueness assumption is sometimes instead formulated as: (U') There is exactly one form corresponding to every predicate. (See e.g. Peterson, 451.) I argued in Ch. 8, however, that Plato is not committed to U'. But he accepts

U. Since the TMA is a more serious threat to Plato if it challenges a claim he accepts, U should be preferred to U'.

10. Here, in contrast to the Second Argument from the Sciences, '*apeira*' clearly means 'infinitely many'. Allen, *Plato's Parmenides*, 139, believes that P-TMA argues, not that there are infinitely many forms of F if there are any at all, but that (*a*) each form has infinitely many parts and that (*b*) there are infinitely many forms of large. On this view, P-TMA aims to show, not that U is false for every form, but that U is false for the form of large.

11. 'TMA I', 236.

12. Ibid. 236, 237.

13. Vlastos says instead: 'in virtue of which we apprehend *a*, *b*, and *c* as *F*'. I shall ignore this difference.

14. 'TMA I', 239. As Geach, 'The Third Man Again', 265–6, points out, SPV and NIV are actually formal contradictories.

15. 'TMA I', 254, and also sect. II *passim*.

16. Cohen, 451–2.

17. 132a6 (cf. 132a10–11) uses only 'the large itself', but the phrase plainly denotes a form. For 132a10 says that *another* form (*eidos*) besides the large itself will appear.

18. In subsequent writings, Vlastos himself formulates the relevant self-predication assumption in a way closer to SP than to SPV. (Indeed, the last two sentences of SPV require no more than SP.) See Vlastos, 'TMA II', 351.

19. See Ch. 4 n. 35; Vlastos, 'TMA II'; below, n. 72.

20. That BSP is adequate as the self-predication assumption of the TMA is in effect a main theme of Peterson's article. (I say 'in effect' because her version is not exactly BSP; cf. Ch. 4 n. 78.) In saying that BSP is adequate as the self-predication assumption of the TMA, I mean that it satisfies SP (the claim that any form of *F* is *F*) and that it allows us, in conjunction with the other premises of the TMA, to engender the regress from consistent premises. (To say that BSP is consistent with the other premises of the TMA is not to say that they all fit naturally together, that one would be tempted to believe them all. I take up this issue in Ch. 16.4.)

21. 'TMA I', 238, 260. Vlastos uses 'particulars' where I use 'sensibles', and 'full-strength' where I use 'strong'. In this and the next chapter, I sometimes speak as though Plato recognizes only sensibles and forms. This is not accurate, since he also recognizes non-sensible particulars, e.g. souls. The fastidious reader might therefore like to substitute 'non-forms' where I have 'sensibles'. Cf. Ch. 2 n. 27.

22. The One over Many Argument has weak non-identity. For it argues that there is a form of *F* for every predicate, so that if *x* is *F* (where substituends for '*F*' are restricted to sensibles) it is *F* in virtue of the form of *F*, and so in virtue of something distinct from itself. Cf. 80. 10–12: each of the sensible men, for example, is a man in virtue of something that is not itself a sensible man—as it turns out, in virtue of a separated, everlasting form of man. I discuss Plato and weak identity further in Ch. 16.1.

23. I assume that '*para*' at 132a10, and '*epi*' at 132a11, indicate difference, not Separation. In saying that Separation is not involved in P-TMA, I may disagree with Cornford, *Plato and Parmenides*, 90; and Vlastos, 'TMA I',

254. (I do disagree with them if they interpret separation as I do.) As we shall see, Aristotle mentions a separation assumption in connection with his Third Man Argument.

24. I now leave off explicit detailed discussion of 'TMA I', since it does not discuss (2) in any detail. My discussion of different formulations of (2) is indebted to Cohen.

25. (2) does not use either 'in virtue of some one form' or 'by participating in some one form'; but see 132a7–8 and b1 for the former, and 132a11 for (almost) the latter. I shall use the two phrases interchangeably. A. Nehamas, 'Participation and Predication in Plato's later Thought', *Review of Metaphysics*, 36 (1982), 343–74, in effect argues that the two phrases are not interchangeable. But I do not mean to build a lot of theoretical baggage into the phrase 'by participating in some one form'. Those who favour Nehamas's view might like to substitute 'in virtue of some one form' wherever they find 'by participating in some one form' inappropriate.

26. See e.g. 'TMA II', 348.

27. Vlastos seems to believe that Plato accepts not only U but also U'; I shall ignore this complication here. (On the difference between U and U', see n. 9.)

28. Vlastos freely admits that his 'TMA II' formulation of the premisses makes them an inconsistent triad; see 352–3 and n. 40.

29. One might argue that we should reformulate not (2a) but the self-predication or non-identity assumptions. But my second objection to (2a) shows that (2a) is defective whether or not my formulations of the self-predication and non-identity assumptions are defective. See also Cohen, 457 n. 21.

30. (2b) is in effect endorsed by W. Sellars, 'Vlastos and the "Third Man"', *Philosophical Review*, 64 (1955), 405–37, Strang, and Peterson. There are important and subtle differences between their formulations of the argument, but I shall largely ignore them here. For a more detailed discussion of Sellars and Strang, see Cohen.

31. These objections may be found in 'TMA II', 354–8. He does not distinguish between them in exactly the way in which I do.

32. For the phrase 'transparent fallacy', see 'TMA II', 355. I am not sure why Vlastos is moved by this consideration when he is not moved by the consideration that, on his account, P-TMA has inconsistent premisses. Perhaps his reply would be that the move from 'at least one' to 'just one' is a transparent fallacy, whereas the contradiction between SPV and NIV (or between his alternative formulations of the premisses in 'TMA II') is not transparent. Peterson, 452 n. 4, agrees with Vlastos that with (2b) the inference to (3) is a transparent fallacy; but she does not view that as an objection to (2b).

33. For example, as Peterson notes, 453 n. 4, when Plato speaks of 'one and the same day' (*Parm.* 131b3–4), he does not mean 'the one unique day'. Sometimes when Plato speaks of 'one form', he means that it is uniform, not mixed up with other features, in contrast to sensibles, which are multiform; see e.g. *Phd.* 78d.

34. In *Rep.* 5, for example, Plato uses 'is' both veridically and predicatively; but this does not vitiate his argument. On the contrary, there is an illuminating

connection between the two uses. I discuss this in the articles cited in Ch. 7 n. 15.

35. Cohen says that (2c) is 'unobjectionable as a Platonic truth' (p. 460). But if Plato believes that every form of *F* is *F* in virtue of itself, then (2c) is *not* unobjectionable as a Platonic truth. (I argue in Ch. 16.4 that Plato believes that every form of *F* is *F* in virtue of itself). What would be unobjectionable is (2c′) All large sensibles are large in virtue of exactly one form of large. Unlike (2c), (2c′) leaves open the possibility that every form of *F* is *F* in virtue of itself. But like (2c), (2c′) is not an adequate one over many assumption for the regress, since it does not posit forms over groups that contain forms.

   (2c′) is an instance of the One over Many Argument's one over many assumption (= OM), which says that whenever many *F*s are *F*, they are *F* in virtue of having one form of *F* predicated of them. I said in Chs. 8 and 14 that the One over Many Argument is not vulnerable to the regress. We can now see why this is so: its one over many assumption does not posit forms for groups that contain forms.

36. Alternatively, one might say that (2c) is the correct reading of (2) (or that (2) is in some way restricted to sensibles), and then argue that, in addition to (2c), P-TMA relies on a more general but tacit one over many assumption that, coupled with the other relevant assumptions, generates the regress. (One might argue that the generalization is conveyed by '*hōsautōs*' in 132a6.) In this case, not only are SP and NI tacit, but so too is the relevant one over many assumption. In 'TMA I', Vlastos restricts '*poll' atta megala*' to sensibles; in 'TMA II', 344–5 n. 10, he retracts the restriction. Both readings seem possible, but the one I assume in the text is simpler.

   Cohen, 460, argues that '*poll' atta megala*' refers to any old set of large things; that is, it is not restricted to *all* large sensibles. He may well be right about this. But in order to deal with non-maximal sets, he is then forced to introduce additional complexity into the argument that I would prefer to avoid here, since it is not necessary for our purposes. (I explain 'maximal set' below.) For an account of how the argument goes if '*poll' atta megala*' refers to any old set of large things, see Cohen, 464–9.

37. In saying that 'we need' such a one over many assumption, I do not mean that Plato must have formulated it himself; on the other hand, although the account I go on to give sounds more technical than Plato does, its basic notions are not foreign to his thought, and in that sense they are not anachronistic. I am trying to provide a relatively precise formulation of a one over many assumption that meets the various desiderata we have mentioned: it should tempt one to accept U though it should not actually imply U; it should be consistent with NI and SP; it should posit forms for groups that contain forms; and so on. Let us say that any one over many assumption that satisfies these various desiderata is an *adequate* one over many assumption for the TMA. The account I go on to give is a simplified version of Cohen's.

38. I take it to be an assumption of the argument that there is at most one form of *F* per level. In Ch. 16.4 we shall see how Plato might justify this assumption. On my account, then, P-TMA explains how, even if there is at

most one form of F per level, it does not follow that there is at most one form per predicate.

39. So for a set to be a maximal set, it must be at a level. It follows that if there are Fs at infinitely many levels, there is no maximal set that consists of all the Fs there are. For if there are infinitely many levels, then a maximal set of all the Fs there are could not contain a highest-level member; see Cohen, 469 n. 33, and below, n. 42. Although every maximal set is at the level of its highest-level member, not every member of the set needs to be at that level. If a maximal set consists of sensible Fs and a form of F that is at level 1, then the maximal set is at level 1 but sensible Fs are at level 0.

40. Note that OM-TMA implies NI. None the less, it is useful to state NI as a separate assumption, and so I shall continue to do so. Note too that on OM-TMA, the 'over' relation is a one–one relation between forms and maximal sets. But although for any maximal set there is just one form over it, the TMA tries to show that the members of any given maximal set are F in virtue of more than one form. So, for example, the form of F at level one is the only form over the maximal set of sensible Fs, which is at level 0. But the members of this maximal set are also members of the maximal set of Fs at level 1. The form of F at level 2 is the only form over the maximal set of Fs at level 1. But since sensible Fs are members of this maximal set, they are F not only in virtue of, by participating in, the form of F at level 1 but also in virtue of the form of F at level 2, and so on.

41. For what I mean by 'adequate', see n. 37.

42. They are consistent if every maximal set is at a level (see n. 38). Without this assumption, there could be a maximal set of all the Fs there are even if there are Fs at infinitely many levels. But if there is a maximal set of all the Fs there are, then according to OM-TMA there is a form of F at the next-highest level. If this form is at the next-highest level, it is not a member of the maximal set. But if the set consists of all the Fs there are, it would have to include the form that is over it. We might say that I assume at the outset that a maximal set must be at a level; the TMA then argues that there cannot be a maximal set of all the Fs there are. See Cohen, 469 n. 33; Peterson, 454 n. 8.

43. OM-TMA implies this as well. Of course, we do not need NI or OM-TMA to tell us this, since no form is a sensible.

44. However, the force of 'one' is 'exactly one over each maximal set', not 'exactly one *tout court*'. I am not sure whether this is sufficient to forestall Vlastos's worry about equivocation (if one is worried by it). Cohen thinks it is sufficient to forestall that worry (see e.g. 455 n. 18); indeed, the desire to forestall it is one of the main factors motivating his account.

45. So e.g. Cohen, 468.

46. The suggestion that OM-TMA can be restricted to property-names goes along with my suggestion (see n. 9) that the relevant uniqueness assumption should be U rather than U'. In Ch. 16.2 I explain why restricting the predicates to which OM-TMA applies does not affect the logic of the argument.

47. See n. 42.

48. I discuss this passage in Ch. 9.5.

49. I discuss the whole and part models of participation, and their relation to paradigmatism, in 'Immanence'.

50. I retain '*eidous*' at 132e1.
51. '*Ta alla*' at 132d2 seem to be only sensibles: forms are paradigms and the other things—i.e. non-forms, i.e. sensibles (see n. 21)—are likenesses of them. (The fact that the Resemblance Regress so clearly begins by considering just sensible Fs (and not Fs as such) might suggest that '*poll' atta megala*' in step (2) of P-TMA is restricted to sensibles, and that the generalized one over many assumption that P-TMA requires is tacit; see n. 36.) However, '*ti*' at 132d5 seems to be more general: if a thing—*any* thing—is a likeness of a form, then the form is like it. Hence in my formulation I assume that substituends for '*a*' are not restricted to sensibles.

    Unlike P-TMA, the Resemblance Regress does not say what property of *a* it has in mind. Further, whereas P-TMA asks what *many* F things have in common, the Resemblance Regress begins by considering a *single* F thing. However, it is of course a single F thing rather than the set of F things that is like a form of F (if anything is) or participates in it, so perhaps Plato assumes that *a* is a member of some suitable set. Suppose, however, that he allows that even if there is just one F sensible, it participates in a form of F. Aristotle defines a universal as what is naturally predicated of *many* things, where this might mean that x is not a universal unless it is multiply instantiated (see Ch. 2 n. 28). If Aristotle means this, then he would say that if *a* is the only F sensible there is at t_1, and it none the less participates in a form of F at t_1, then at t_1 the form of F is not a universal. But if Plato accepts separation, then he would disagree, saying that universals need not be instantiated at all, let alone be multiply instantiated, in order to exist. He might agree, however, that for a form to be a universal, it must be such that it *can* be multiply instantiated.
52. So e.g. Vlastos, 'TMA I', 242. On an alternative account, suggested but not endorsed by Allen, *Plato's Parmenides*, 161, *a* and the form of large are similar in virtue of having property P; *a*, the form₁ of large, and property P are similar in virtue of having some further property, Q, and so on. On this account, the Resemblance Regress generates infinitely many forms, but no more than one form per predicate. If this reading were correct, then the Resemblance Regress would differ from P-TMA. (Allen curiously seems to suggest that on this reading, the Resemblance Regress would be the same as Aristotle's version of the TMA.) My schematization of the Resemblance Regress assumes that this reading is false.
53. One might think that the fact that the Resemblance Regress conceives forms as paradigms shows that NSP is required. But we have seen (in e.g. Ch. 4.7) that forms can be paradigms even if they enjoy BSP rather than NSP. I return to this point below.
54. If *a* and the form₁ of large are alike in both being large, then presumably this likeness is to be explained by the fact that they both participate in a form₂ of large. Participation only in e.g. the form of likeness (as favoured by Allen, *Plato's Parmenides*, 158–62) would not explain why *a* and the form₁ of large are alike in being large; see n. 52.
55. Perhaps some assumption other than NI would also validate the inference to (6); but NI is the most reasonable assumption to supply in the context.
56. Contrast Allen, *Plato's Parmenides*, 160.

57. Although Vlastos formulates P-TMA and the Resemblance Regress differently from me, he agrees that they are 'similar in logical structure' and that they both involve self-predication and non-identity; see e.g. 'TMA I', 242. ('TMA I' does not focus on the one over many assumption.)

58. I have also mentioned two further differences that I shall not pursue further. First, P-TMA focuses on 'large'; the Resemblance Regress does not say what predicate it has in mind. Secondly, P-TMA posits a form of *F* only over *many F* things, whereas the Resemblance Regress may posit an initial form of *F* over a *single F* thing; see n. 51.

59. He writes that the moral of P-TMA is 'that the common run of a thing's properties are not to be assigned to themselves'. Plato 'had, in Ryle's words, spoken as though universals could be instances of themselves, and he now proves, by ascribing largeness to itself, that to credit anything with both functions generates a regress'. Or again (more hesitantly), 'if the first [regress, P-TMA] can (but with reservations) be constructed as confusing bigness with what is big, the second [the Resemblance Regress] requires only that the Form should have the character it represents. If the first forces a choice between two possible functions of a form, the second reduces one of them to absurdity'. The first two quotations are from 'Notes', 102; the third is from 'Proof', 168 n. 9. Cf. also 'Platonism', 207 n. 9; 'Place', 70 n. 29. 'Place' may suggest that, in Owen's view, the Resemblance Regress takes forms to be both universals and particulars; it at least suggests that, in his view, Plato is unclear about the differences between universals and particulars.

60. Unfortunately, Owen does not say why he thinks P-TMA takes forms to be (not only particulars but also) universals. Note that Owen's reasons for believing that P-TMA and the Resemblance Regress take forms to be particulars match his reasons for thinking that the Argument from Relatives takes forms to be particulars. Not surprisingly, my reasons for thinking that, in P-TMA and the Resemblance Regress, forms can be viewed as universals that are not also particulars parallel my reasons for thinking that in the Argument from Relatives forms can be viewed as universals that are not also particulars.

61. For my account of the way in which Platonic forms are paradigms, see esp. Ch. 4.7.

62. However, Aristotle does not explicitly say that the TMA challenges U; indeed, he does not say why the regress is troubling.

63. I speak of Plato's regress in the singular since I have argued that P-TMA and the Resemblance Regress are logically the same argument.

64. I begin by formulating the premisses as I did in Ch. 14, so that they are fairly close to the text. I then attempt to formulate them more precisely, so as to bring out their real force.

65. Hence the third man is the second form of man; the second man is the first form of man. The first man is 'the particulars'; 'the first man' and so on thus seem to be used for all the men at a given level—at the first level (of sensibles), at the next level (of the first form), and so on. This way of speaking has Platonic licence. Not only does Plato speak of different degrees or levels of reality but in *Rep.* 10 he also speaks of 'three beds', by which he means that there are three sorts of beds, or beds at three different levels of

reality. Owen, in 'Platonism', 208–9, seems to think that the first and second men are e.g. Callias and Socrates, and that the third man is the first form. But if Owen were right, Plato would welcome, rather than reject, a third man.

66. However, as Aristotle phrases NI, it says that what is predicated of a *plurality* of things is different from any of them. One might argue that this leaves open the possibility that something can be *F* in virtue of, or be predicated of, itself so long as it is not also predicated of anything else. For if it is predicated only of itself it is not predicated of a plurality of things. For a somewhat related point in connection with the Resemblance Regress, see n. 51. I doubt, however, whether Aristotle intends to allow this possibility; for if he did, the regress would not proceed as he takes it to.

67. On Aristotle's use of '*ho anthrōpos*', see n. 75.

68. However, Aristotle may take the connection between the TMA's one over many and non-identity assumptions to be closer than I have made it appear to be. For he states them together in the text as two clauses of a single sentence (84. 22–3). I have separated them as I do because that makes it easier for me to bring out the fact that in his formulation NI is inferred from G-Sep; but this obscures the fact that AOM and NI may not be thus independent for Aristotle. A. Code, 'On the Origins of Some Aristotelian Theses about Predication', in J. Bogen and J. E. McGuire (eds.) *How Things Are: Studies in Predication and the History of Philosophy* (Dordrecht, 1983), 105 and n. 14, formulates A-TMA's one over many assumption so that it does not include NI. For further discussion of Code's account of A-TMA, see nn. 69 and 72. Penner, *Ascent*, 408 n. 6, says that in 'Alexander's paraphrase of Aristotle's *On the Ideas*, NI is made part of OM'; but on p. 250, he numbers A-TMA's one over many and non-identity assumptions as though they were separate assumptions.

69. That is to say, of the different possible readings of AOM (plus NI), the one that makes it come out equivalent to OM-TMA is to be preferred, since it best meets the various desiderata a one over many assumption that is adequate for A-TMA should meet, such as allowing us to generate a regress from consistent premisses, and so on. I do not mean that Aristotle consciously formulated OM-TMA, any more than I suggested that Plato did so; see n. 37. On the other hand, we have seen that some of the crucial features of OM-TMA are vivid to Aristotle; to the extent that they are, OM-TMA does not go beyond him. Code, 124 n. 13, takes A-TMA's one over many assumption to be an at least one assumption. But an at least one assumption has the same defects here as in P-TMA; since it is not required in either place, it should be avoided.

70. I said above that Aristotle indicates that '*ho anthrōpos*' is a property by saying that it is predicated of things. Despite the definite article, I say '*a* property' rather than '*the* property' because according to A-TMA there is more than one property of being a man. There is, however, only one property at any given level—hence Aristotle's use of the definite article, and hence the Platonists' alleged temptation to infer U from a one over many thesis. See n. 75.

71. Strictly speaking, then, the premisses of the Accurate One over Many Argument do not imply that there is a Third Man, since SP is needed as well. In just the same way, though, strictly speaking Plato never believed that a

one over many assumption on its own both implied U and led to the regress; he believed that a one over many assumption led to the regress only when it was combined with further claims about forms, one of which is SP.

72. Vlastos, however, argues that:

> Some scholars...⟨take 84. 29⟩...to imply that Aristotle had identified self-predication as an assumption in the TMA. But 'predication' is used by Aristotle much more broadly than we now use it in our debates over self-predication in Plato. For Aristotle every case in which the verb *to be* connects two terms in a sentence will count as a predication, including cases of (*a*) class-membership ('Socrates is [a] man'); (*b*) identity ('man is man'); (*c*) class-inclusion ('man is [an] animal'); (*d*) class equivalence ('man is [a] two-footed animal'). The claim that SP is a tacit premiss of the TMA has in view only (*a*). ('TMA II', 350–1 n. 35; cf. 'TMA I', 250 n. 3.)

I agree that Aristotle uses 'predication' more broadly than for class membership, and that SP involves class membership. But even though Aristotle uses 'predication' in ways (*a*)–(*d*), a given context might make it clear that he has a particular use in mind. And as I indicate in the text, a good case can be made for supposing that Aristotle intends class membership here.

Code, 105–6, argues that instead of SP, A-TMA involves the following assumption:

(Alex-OM) If each member of a plurality of objects is a man, then there is an
  X such that:
  (1) X is a man,
  (2) X is separable,
  (3) X is predicable of each member of that plurality.

He then writes that the 'so-called "Self-Predication" assumption is not a premiss of the TMA. Owen's SP does not play any role in this argument. Alex-OM does have built into it the idea that the postulated item is a man; but since it does not say that this item is predicable of itself (it says that it is a man, but not how or why), it would be quite misleading to label Alex-OM$_1$ "Self-Predication"'. But as we have seen (in Ch. 4 n. 35), 'the so-called Self-Predication assumption' just is the assumption that any form of *F* is *F*; it does not say how or why it is *F*. (Code also says that the assumption that *Owen* calls 'self-predication' is not involved in A-TMA. *That* might be true; but that is because Owen does not always use 'self-predication' in the usual way. But Code should put this by saying, not that A-TMA does not involve self-predication as usually understood, but that it does not involve Owen's unusual formulation of self-predication.)

Others who agree that A-TMA involves a self-predication assumption include Owen, 'Platonism' (although, as just noted, he sometimes understands SP in an unusual way; see my 'Owen, Aristotle, and the Third Man', and the next note); Peterson; and Strang. Kung thinks that A-TMA uses what she takes to be a version of self-predication, but not one that requires class membership.

73. Relatedly, although the One over Many Argument has weak non-identity, it is not committed to strong non-identity. (It is not committed to SP either, but then neither does the Accurate One over Many Argument involve SP; see n. 71. But if we add SP to the premisses of the Accurate One over Many

Argument, the TMA arises; whereas if we add it to the premises of the One over Many Argument, it does not arise.)

74. But see nn. 42 and 75.

75. My account of A-TMA is, however, open to challenge. It is sometimes doubted whether (Aristotle sees that) A-TMA involves self-predication; see n. 72. Owen issues a different challenge. In 'Platonism', he argues that A-TMA's self-predication and non-identity assumptions conflict. (So just as Vlastos believes that the premises of P-TMA conflict, so Owen believes that the premises of A-TMA conflict.) On my account, however, they do not conflict. Owen formulates A-TMA's self-predication and non-identity assumptions as follows:

(NIO) What is predicated of a number of things is always something different from the subjects of which it is predicated.

(SPO) What is predicated of a number of things is itself a subject of that same predicate.

In explaining A-TMA, he writes that:

Plato is accused of misconstruing the logic of such a statement as 'Socrates is a man' by making two quite incompatible assumptions about it. He thinks (*a*) that what is predicated, in this case man (not the expression but what it stands for), is always something different from the subjects of which it is predicated; for if it were identical with its subjects these would become identical with each other. Plato is a man, Socrates is a man: if these statements have the form of '*a* = *c*, *b* = *c*', *a* will be *b* and Plato will be Socrates. But also Plato thinks (*b*) that what is predicated is itself a subject of that same predicate; for it seems undeniable even if truistic that man is man or a man is a man. (p. 207.)

(*b*) is ambiguous. The form of man 'is itself a subject of that same predicate' (i.e. of man) in that it is a man. But if this is all Owen means, then (*a*) and (*b*) do not conflict. Incompatibility requires the form of man to be 'itself a subject of that same predicate' by being predicated of itself. But the text of A-TMA does not require the form of *F* to be *F* in virtue of itself; it requires only that it be *F*. Hence A-TMA's self-predication assumption need not be read so as to be incompatible with its non-identity assumption.

That only SP (and not the claim that any form of *F* is *F* by being predicated of itself) is required can be seen by considering more carefully what '*ho anthrōpos*' at 84. 25 and at 84. 29–85. 1 refers to. I suggested that the first occurrence of '*ho anthrōpos*' refers to the property of being a man that is over the maximal set of particular sensible men. *Ho anthrōpos* is then promoted into a form of man—*autoanthrōpos* at 84. 25. What, then, is the *ho anthrōpos* at 84. 29–85. 1? If it is the same *ho anthrōpos* as that at 84. 25—which was promoted into the first form of man (*autoanthrōpos*, Man-itself₁) and of which the *ho anthrōpos* of 84. 29–85. 1 is predicated—then a form of man is predicated of itself, and inconsistency does arise. But the second *ho anthrōpos* need not be man-itself₁. Another possibility, which I assumed in the text, is that it is a second property of being a man, one the Platonists believe is predicated both of the first form (man-itself₁) and of particular sensible men—a second property that is then promoted into a second form of man, man-itself₂. On this reading, the two occurrences of '*ho anthrōpos*' refer to two different properties of being a man, properties that (as NI requires) are predicated of different ranges of things. This reading is consistent with the text, and it avoids making the premisses inconsistent; it is therefore preferable to Owen's reading. For as we have seen, an inconsistent premiss set is not necessary for the regress; and if Plato does not use one, it is surely undesirable for Aristotle to saddle him with one. My reading of the text is thus not only possible but also fairer to Aristotle.

Owen's account of A-TMA also differs from mine in that it does not involve a one over many assumption. But we have seen that, as in P-TMA, a one over many assumption is quite explicit.

Mansion, 'Deux écrits', 405, also denies that A-TMA is the same as P-TMA.

76. In the next chapter I consider the possible significance of this difference.

77. I describe the differences between Separation and G-Sep in Ch. 14. Code takes the relevant separation assumption to involve, not existential, but logical, separation. For cogent criticism of his account of separation and its alleged role in A-TMA, see F. Lewis, 'Plato's Third Man Argument and the "Platonism" of Aristotle', in Bogen and McGuire (eds.) *How Things Are*, 133–74. Kung also discusses the role of separation in A-TMA; her account of separation, like Code's, differs from mine.

78. We have seen that at least one reason for mentioning G-Sep is independent of the TMA: G-Sep implies Separation, which Aristotle takes to be a key feature of forms; indeed, this helps to explain why he says that the Accurate One over Many Argument is a more accurate argument for the existence of forms.

79. '*Tode ti*' need not indicate particularity, but it plainly does so in these passages. A. E. Taylor, 268–70, believes that the Third Man Arguments mentioned in *SE* 22 and in *Met.* 7. 13 differ from Plato's and from the one mentioned in the *Peri ideōn*; for he thinks that the claim that universals are thises is irrelevant to the regress argument. He cites Alexander's commentary on the *SE* as evidence that Alexander likewise does not take the *SE*'s Third Man Argument to be the regress recorded by Plato and in the *Peri ideōn*.

80. This is not to say that Aristotle thinks that NSP is necessary for the regress. But he may think that if one accepts NSP rather than BSP, one will find it psychologically more difficult to avoid the regress.

81. In Aristotle's view, both G-Sep and Sep imply particularity.

82. G-Sep commits Plato to NI. In Aristotle's view, both Sep and G-Sep make forms particulars and so (given SP) suggest NSP.

83. The range is narrower on the reasonable assumption that property-names are not restricted to substance predicates. Although A-TMA uses 'man' as its sample predicate, its one over many assumption is not restricted to such predicates.

84. Hence E-TMA, like the Resemblance Regress, begins by mentioning a restricted class of entities (Aristotelian primary substances in E-TMA, sensibles in the Resemblance Regress), but it then mentions things quite generally.

85. I assume that like '*pleiō*', '*tina*' is ontologically neutral, covering things quite generally, irrespective of their level. The assumption is justified by the fact that it is needed for the regress.

86. Otherwise put, NI is not built into E-TMA (2). In this respect, it parallels AOM as well premiss (4) of the Resemblance Regress. But we have seen that this by itself does not mean that a different regress is in the offing.

87. More precisely, (3) says that if *x* is predicated of *things* (plural), then it is different from any of the things it is predicated of. So one might take (3) to leave open the possibility that if *x* is predicated of only one thing, that thing could be itself, in which case (3) would fall short of NI. For a parallel point about A-TMA, see n. 66.

88. Again, I mean only that OM-TMA best meets the various desiderata that any one over many assumption that is adequate for E-TMA should meet. I do not mean that every detail of it is required by the logic of the argument (though some of them are), or that no other reading is consistent with the text, or that Eudemus must have 'had it in mind'. See n. 37.

89. However, Eudemus curiously neglects to say that there is also a fourth man, and so on *ad infinitum*; he makes only the weaker point that there is a 'third man' (84. 5–6)—in contrast to Aristotle's '*ep' apeiron*' (85. 3), and Plato's '*apeira*' (132b2; cf. 133a1–2). (Or perhaps Alexander has abbreviated Eudemus' account.)

90. It may be significant that whereas E-TMA uses '*homoia*', the Resemblance Regress also uses '*homoiōmata*' (132d3); the latter word suggests being made to be similar to something rather than (like the first word) simply being similar. The Resemblance Regress uses not only '*homoiōmata*' but also '*homoion*' (132d6, 7, 8, e3, 133a1). I speculate about the significance of the shift in Ch. 16.3.

91. See Ch. 8.2.

92. This should be qualified in two ways. First, E-TMA says only that there is a third man; it does not explicitly say that there is a regress (see n. 89). Still, although Eudemus does not say so, the premisses of E-TMA imply the regress. Secondly, the texts do not unambiguously require OM-TMA and, indeed, not all the versions of the regress build NI into the relevant one over many assumption. None the less, we have seen that it seems best to read each regress with OM-TMA.

93. This is so because (3) encapsulates NI, whereas (1) and (2) are more directed at SP and OM-TMA even though, as we have seen, (2) does not fully state OM-TMA.

NOTES TO CHAPTER 16

1. Since I argued in the last chapter that the four regress arguments are logically the same, I shall generally simply ask whether Plato is vulnerable to the TMA. But I shall occasionally discuss some of the differences between the various versions. Further, here as elsewhere, I shall generally focus on the middle dialogues, although I shall occasionally discuss some passages in the late dialogues, as seems appropriate (primarily in notes).

2. Owen, 'Place', 70, and Strang, 193, argue that Plato is committed to NSP in the middle but not in the late dialogues, and that Plato is therefore

invulnerable to the TMA in the late dialogues. (In 'Place', 69–70, Owen seems to suggest that since (in his view) Plato is committed to NSP in the middle dialogues, he is vulnerable to the TMA in the middle dialogues. But in e.g. 'Platonism', he sees that NSP is not sufficient for the regress.) But since BSP is adequate as the self-predication assumption of the TMA, rejecting NSP is not sufficient for avoiding the TMA. (So although BSP avoids some of the difficulties NSP is subject to, it does not by itself extricate him from the TMA.) One late dialogue relevant to the question of whether Plato revised his views about self-predication is *So*. For the view that it has something like NSP, see R. E. Heinaman, 'Self-Predication in the *Sophist*', *Phronesis*, 26 (1981), 55–66. Vlastos, 'Ambiguity', argues that at least some of its self-predications should be interpreted as Pauline Predications. (For a brief account of Pauline predication, see Ch. 4 n. 80).

Cherniss believes that Plato was never vulnerable to the regress because he never accepted any version of SP: 'Plato, then, believed that since the idea *is* that which the particular *has* as an attribute, the "third man" is illegitimate as an argument against the ideas because idea and particular cannot be treated as homogeneous members of a multiplicity' (*Aristotle's Criticism*, 298).

3. A. Nehamas, 'Predication and Forms of Opposites in the *Phaedo*', *Review of Metaphysics*, 26 (1973), 461–91, 474, argues that Plato believes that there are forms corresponding only to some properties, and that where sensibles are *F* and there is no form of *F*, sensibles are *F* in virtue of themselves. On the other hand, on 479, he says that 'Plato is certainly committed to (NI) for all values of "x," if "x" ranges over particulars.' I am not sure how to square this claim with that made on 474, from which it would follow that Plato is not committed to weak non-identity. We have seen that Plato is vague about the range of forms; but we have not uncovered any argument that precludes the existence of forms for every property, and we have seen that he sometimes seems committed to the existence of forms for every property. When he is so committed, he is also committed to weak non-identity. In order to give myself the harder case, I shall assume that he is committed to weak non-identity.

4. The difference between weak and strong non-identity is sometimes obscured. Annas, for example, writes:

> If, however, Forms are universals, as in Book 10 ⟨of the *Republic*⟩, then the Form F will be what makes particulars F, in the sense that it is the item, not identical with any of them, which legitimizes our calling them all F. This is often called the 'non-identity' assumption; the Form of F can't be identical with any particular F thing, or it couldn't be what makes it right to call them all F. But this raises the possibility of a regress. For if the form of F is F in the same sense as the particulars (by self-predication), then it is (by non-identity) another F thing to add to the F things. So won't there have to be another Form, call it F′, which is what makes Form and particulars all F? (*An Introduction to Plato's Republic*, 231.)

But what Annas calls the non-identity assumption is only weak non-identity; the TMA requires strong non-identity, i.e. NI.

Owen also seems to confuse weak non-identity and NI. For he says that Plato:

> thinks (*a*) that what is predicated, in this case *man* (not the expression but what it stands for), is always something different from the subjects of which it is predicated; for

if it were identical with its subjects these would become identical with each other. Plato is a man, Socrates is a man: if these statements have the form of '$a = c, b = c$', a will be b and Plato will be Socrates. ('Platonism', 207.)

If this is Plato's argument, it is invalid; for it does not follow from the fact that man cannot be identical with *everything* of which it is predicated that it cannot be identical with *anything* of which it is predicated. If man is predicated of and identical with itself, but is not identical with either Plato or Socrates, then Plato and Socrates are not identical even though man is not different from everything of which it is predicated. (For this point, see Code, 102.) Plato can avoid the view that Plato and Socrates are identical without endorsing NI; weak non-identity will do.

5. Vlastos, 'TMA I', 253–4, argues that separation implies NI. But in this article he does not take separation to be Separation. In *Socrates*, 264–5, Vlastos retracts the account of separation he favoured in 'TMA I' in favour of my account; so presumably he would no longer defend the view that separation implies NI.

6. Contrast Cornford, *Plato and Parmenides*, 90. Both Kung and Code think that some sort of separation assumption is crucial in Aristotle's version of the TMA, but they do not discuss Plato's version of the TMA. (See Ch. 15 n. 77.) If rejecting separation were sufficient for avoiding the TMA, and if (as is sometimes thought) Plato accepts separation in the middle dialogues but rejects it in the post-*Parm.* dialogues, then one might argue that he rejects it in response to the TMA. K. M. Sayre, *Plato's Late Ontology* (Princeton, N.J. 1983), argues that in *Phil.* Plato rejects separation and thereby avoids various of *Parm.*'s objections, but he does not quite say that Plato responds to the TMA by rejecting separation (and in any case, he construes both the TMA and separation quite differently from me); see e.g. pp. 14–15, 180, 184. But rejecting separation is not sufficient for avoiding the TMA (if separation is taken to be Separation); nor am I convinced that Separation is rejected in the late dialogues. Indeed, we have seen that Plato is more clearly committed to it in *Tm.* (and so in one post-*Parm.* dialogue) than in any of the middle dialogues (see Ch. 4.6).

7. 'Logic', 473.

8. See Ch. 8.5.

9. This question is relevant not only to OM-TMA but also to NI. If I am right about what the crucial question is, then it is an understatement to say that OM-TMA can be restricted to property-names. For even if OM-TMA applies to just one predicate, the TMA would arise in its case if SP and NI also obtain. If 'one over many' arguments posit forms at least for every property (see Ch. 4 n. 20), then a one over many assumption is not necessary for the regress. However, Plato seems to say that he accepted U because he accepted some sort of one over many argument; so even if we can generate a regress without a one over many assumption, doing so would not capture Plato's actual reasoning.

10. I discuss some of what follows in 'Aristotle and the More Accurate Arguments', sect. 6. There, however, I vacillate between saying that the Imperfection Argument 'avoids' and that it 'rejects' OM-TMA and NI.

11. In the Imperfection Argument, 'a group of things' need not be a maximal set.

(For an explanation of 'maximal set', see Ch. 15.2.) Note that the argument says that *all* the members of a given group participate in a given form, not that *only* such things do.

12. As we have seen, to say that the Imperfection Argument does not posit a form of man is not to say that it precludes its existence. So even if it posits only a limited range of forms, it is not incompatible with weak non-identity, though if it posits only a limited range of forms, it does not imply weak non-identity.

13. Alternatively, one might hold that although imperfectly *F* things are *F* in virtue of something distinct from themselves, perfectly *F* things are not *F* in virtue of anything. This would not be sufficient for rejecting NI, according to which nothing is *F* in virtue of itself. I argue below, however, that Plato believes that any perfectly *F* thing is *F* in virtue of itself.

14. *Rep.* 10 explicitly mentions a form of bed, and so it presumably also has one of man. *Tm.* countenances forms of natural kinds; *Phil.* 15a explicitly mentions a form of man. (In Ch. 7, we saw that Plato may also be committed to a form of man elsewhere; it depends on how often he assumes the broader version of the Imperfection Argument.) It has been argued that the forms in *Phil.*, and perhaps also in *Rep.* 10, are different from the forms in e.g. *Rep.* 523–5. If (as is sometimes supposed) the relevant difference is separation, then that does not affect the regress. If (as Owen, 'Place', 71 n. 33, believes) *Phil.*'s forms are not paradigms, then that might be relevant to the Resemblance Regress. I consider paradigmatism and the Resemblance Regress briefly below.

15. When I say that a form is over a group, I mean that a form corresponds to the group and that the form is not a member of the group. I am no longer using 'over' in the technical sense accorded it in Ch. 15.2.

16. On the connection between perfection and paradigmatism, see Chs. 4.7 and 7.3.

17. Owen, 'Place', 69–71; see also Strang, 199.

18. On the dating of *Tm.*, see Ch. 3 n. 42.

19. In 'Proof', Owen sees that the Argument from Relatives, which treats forms as paradigms, avoids the regress. So at least in this article he presumably does not think that paradigmatism is sufficient for the regress.

20. See Ch. 15 n. 55.

21. In Ch. 14 I speculated that in Aristotle's view, Plato posits forms not to explain particularity but to explain similarity. If this is Aristotle's view, it is consistent with the present suggestion, which says not that only sensibles need to be explained by reference to forms, but rather that only sensibles need to be explained by reference to something distinct from themselves.

I noted before (Ch. 15 n. 90) that the Resemblance Regress uses both '*homoiōmata*' and '*homoion*'. We can now see why it does so. Plato begins by suggesting that forms are paradigms of which sensibles are likenesses. If so, then forms and sensibles are similar to one another. He then formulates the regress focusing on the similarity claim, ignoring the fact that sensibles are likenesses of paradigmatic forms. But once we recall the fact, we can see that it provides an escape-route from the Resemblance Regress. For not every group of similar things is similar in virtue of something distinct from anything in the group; if the group contains a perfect form of *F* and deficient *F* sensibles, then all the members of the group are *F* in virtue of the form in the group, and so one member is *F* in virtue of itself.

22. Cherniss, *Aristotle's Criticism*, 297, suggests something like my account, saying that paradigms and their likenesses are not alike 'in the way in which two particulars may be'. But he then jumps to the quite different, and false, claim that for Plato paradigms and their likenesses are not alike at all: Plato, he writes, 'must have rejected the argument [i.e. assumption] on which [the Resemblance Regress] rests, namely that the idea has to be "like" the particular if the latter is a likeness of the idea'. I am not claiming that Plato denies that forms and sensibles are alike. Proclus, *in Parm.* 912, seems to say that although sensibles are like forms, forms are not like sensibles—likeness is not symmetrical. I am not claiming this either. Sometimes, however, Proclus seems to say only that the explanation of how sensibles are like one another is different from the explanation of how sensibles are like forms (912). If this means that the form of *F* and sensible *F*s are both *F*, but in different ways, then I agree.

23. 'TMA I', 253.

24. We saw in Ch. 10.4 that Plato, both in fact and in Aristotle's view, takes the form of *F* and sensible *F*s to be synonymously *F*, in which case they are *F* in the same sense of 'F'. (On the real-essence view of synonymy, which I favour, 'synonymy' does not *mean* 'same sense'. However, on the real-essence view, if *x* and *y* are synonymously *F*, they are *F* in the same sense of 'F'; it is just that on the real-essence view the converse is not true.) See also Ch. 4.7.

25. See the references cited in Ch. 10 n. 29.

26. Owen, 'Logic and Metaphysics', 193; cf. 181–90, esp. 185–6. (Although Owen sometimes says that synonymy gives rise to the TMA, he sometimes sees that this is not so. I discuss this issue in 'Owen's Progress'.) See also Rowe, 'The Proof from Relatives', 277–9. Owen seems to think that synonymy gives rise to the TMA because he thinks that synonymy implies SP, which is sufficient for the TMA. But as Aristotle understands synonymy, it is not sufficient for SP; see Ch. 10 n. 31. (Nor is SP sufficient for the TMA.)

27. Those who believe that synonymy gives rise to the TMA sometimes suggest that the TMA can be avoided if sensibles and forms are focally connected; and they sometimes suggest that Plato takes sensibles and forms to be focally connected. See e.g. Allen, *Plato's Parmenides*, 143–4; Owen, 'Logic and Metaphysics', 193–9. I have argued, however, that Plato takes sensibles and forms to be synonymously, not focally, connected. If synonymy did give rise to the TMA, then so too, I think, would focal connection. For we could then say that although sensible *F*s and the form of *F* are *F* in different senses of 'F', the different definitions corresponding to 'F' have a common core that requires a further form. Of course, since I do not think that synonymy by itself gives rise to the TMA, neither do I think that focal connection does. The point is that one ought not to be tempted by focal connection on the ground that it, but not synonymy, affords an escape-route from the TMA.

28. In this section, I am indebted to Sydney Shoemaker for helpful discussion.

29. Cohen, 'Logic', 473 n. 43. More precisely, he believes that the TBA has the same one over many assumption as the TMA; but he does not formulate this

assumption as I do. However, this difference between us does not affect anything I say here.

30. 'TMA I', Addendum 1963, p. 263.

31. p. 193. Peterson, 464 n. 22, says that nothing in the TBA prevents the infinite regress. J. Adam, *The Republic of Plato*, 2 vols. (Cambridge, 1902), vol. ii, n. ad loc., says that the TMA 'rests on the same basis' as the TBA.

32. Cherniss, *Aristotle's Criticism*, 295–7, and 'The Relation of the *Timaeus*', 371–3. See also Strang, 193; Cornford, *Plato and Parmenides*, 90. Cherniss and Cornford believe that Plato deliberately and consciously denies SP; Strang believes that 'Plato failed to see, or glimpsed only momentarily, the point of his own argument', so that 'one cannot quote it, as Cherniss does, to show that he had a clear insight into the fallacy of the TMA'.

33. Plato also defends U in *Tm.* 31.

34. I insert numbers into the text for ease of reference. The numbers correspond to the numbered steps in my first schematic formulation of the argument, not to the numbered steps in the final formulation that I provide at the end of this section.

35. Plato says not just that there are two forms of bed, but that god made them; but since this further claim does not matter for anything I shall be saying, I shall ignore it here. Note that whereas P-TMA assumes that there is at most one form of F per level (though not one per predicate), the TBA assumes (for the purpose of reductio) that there are two forms of bed at a given level.

36. See n. 15.

37. Cohen, 'Logic', 473 n. 43, says that '[t]here is almost an overwhelming temptation to think that the TBA depends upon a restricted one-over-many principle, for it appears that Plato is assuming, in that argument, that anything which requires a Form over it (to make it what it is) is not a Form'. He then argues that 'this temptation should be resisted'. My account of the TBA's one over many assumption resists it.

38. Or, perhaps better, OM-TMA posits exactly one form of F over every maximal set of Fs such that 'F' is a property-name. But in this section I shall ignore questions about the range of predicates that have corresponding forms.

39. However, OM-TMA says that all and only the members of the maximal set of Fs are F in virtue of exactly one form of F at the next highest level; OM-TBA omits the 'only' claim.

40. See Cornford, *Plato and Parmenides*, 90, and Cherniss, *Aristotle's Criticism*, 297, for a similar suggestion. We can see why OM-TBA might appeal to Plato. First, as befits a one over many assumption that might tempt one to believe U, it is an exactly one, rather than at at least one, one over many assumption. Secondly, Plato believes that sensible Fs and the form of F are F in different ways; this might lead him to believe that a group consisting of sensible Fs and a form of F are not F in virtue of a further form of F. But he might none the less believe that a plurality of things, all of which are F in the same way, are F in virtue of something that is not a member of the plurality. For if they were all F in virtue of one of the members of the set, say in virtue of F_1, then they would not all be F in just the same way, since F_1, but nothing else in the plurality, would be F in virtue of itself. Further, what grounds would there be for singling out just one member of a plurality, all of which

are *F* in the same way, as the one thing in virtue of which they are all *F*? Alternatively, if each member of the set is *F* in virtue of another member of the set (*x* is *F* in virtue of *y*, *y* in virtue of *z*, and so on, with no single entity's explaining the *F*-ness of more than one member of the set), then again they are not all *F* in the same way, since they are not all *F* in virtue of the same thing.

41. OM-TBA implies NI-TBA, just as OM-TMA implies NI. But it is again useful to mention the relevant non-identity assumption separately.

42. Vlastos, 'TMA I', 263, writes that the TBA requires NI for '[w]ere it not for this assumption there would be no reason why there would have to be a *third* Form, i.e. why the required Form should not be identical with either the first or the second of the supposed Forms'. But although NI-TBA falls short of NI, it explains why the required form cannot be identical with either the first or the second of the supposed forms. That the TBA does not require NI is also argued by R. D. Parry, 'The Uniqueness Proof for Forms in *Rep.* 10', *Journal of the History of Philosophy*, 23 (1985), 133–50 at 142–3.

43. p. 193. As we have seen (n. 33), Cherniss and Cornford also believe that the TBA denies SP.

44. Plato says e.g. that there are three beds—pictured beds, sensible beds, and the form of bed. In saying that the form of bed is a (type of) bed, Plato assumes SP. See Ch. 10.4.

45. I first mentioned this assumption in Ch. 4 n. 35, saying that I should defer discussion of it until Ch. 16. We saw before (n. 37) that the TBA's one over many assumption should not include SE. Nor should the version of self-predication assumed in the move from (1) to (2) include it, or else the conclusion that the first two forms are not forms will be too easily won. But to say that the TBA does not assume SE as early as the inference to (2) is not to say that the TBA nowhere assumes it. SE is compatible with NI. (Here I am indebted to correspondence with Marc Cohen.) For SE does not say that there are any forms, and so it does not say that there is something that is *F* in virtue of itself. If NI and SE are both true, then there are no forms. Conversely, if SE is true and if there are forms, then NI is false. I return to these two conditionals below.

46. In Ch. 15.2 (see also Ch. 15 n. 38) I suggested that P-TMA assumes that there is at most one form of *F* per level. We have now seen how Plato might justify that assumption. So we can say that P-TMA gives Plato one conclusion of the TBA—that there is at most one form of *F* per level—but challenges its further conclusion that there is at most one form per predicate.

47. At least, Plato believes that this is so if there is a form of *F*; and, as I said (n. 3), I am assuming that Plato accepts weak non-identity. This is especially reasonable in the present context, since *Rep.* 10 seems to be committed to the existence of a form corresponding to every property.

48. See my 'Knowledge and Belief in *Republic* V–VII' and 'Knowledge and *Logos* in the *Theaetetus*'.

49. In arguing that the first two forms of bed are not beds, Plato assumes that every form of *F* is *F* in virtue of itself. It now emerges that he also assumes that only a form of *F* can be *F* in virtue of itself.

50. More exactly, it has been argued that there must be a level accessible to us at

which there is exactly one form of bed. For the sake of simplicity, Plato assumes that this is the level of the third form of bed; I shall follow his lead, although the assumption is not necessary.

51. Cohen writes: 'suppose we add our Third Bed, TMA style, to the beds already collected. The one-over-many principle will produce a Fourth Bed, and it, not the Third, will be the Form' ('Logic', p. 470). But unlike OM-TMA, OM-TBA does not require us to add the third form of bed to the first two, since it is at a different level.

52. Earlier I disputed Vlastos's claim that the TBA requires NI (see n. 42). I am now suggesting, more strongly, that the TBA actually rejects NI. If the TBA rejects NI, then it also rejects OM-TMA.

53. Sensible beds cannot be beds in virtue of either of the first two 'forms' of bed, since they are not really forms, but if sensibles are F they are F in virtue of a form of F. So the first real form of bed that we come to must be the form that explains why all the beds below it are beds; we are assuming that this is the third form of bed.

54. The TMA argues that there are infinitely many forms of F, though it assumes that there is at most one form of F at any given level.

55. I assume that Plato rules out the possibility of over-determination.

56. If forms are Separate, then there might be forms that do not actually explain anything besides themselves, since there might be some forms that are uninstantiated by sensible particulars and whose explanatory role is limited to them. But forms must still be such that they *can* explain some phenomena besides themselves. That helps to explain why there are forms corresponding at most to every property-name. For if there were forms corresponding to predicates that are not property-names, they could not explain anything (besides themselves). But there cannot be any such forms.

57. Cohen, 'Logic', 470, says that: '[i]f the TBA shows that one-over-many reasoning does yield the uniqueness thesis, then either the TMA is invalid or my account of it is mistaken. Fortunately, the TBA does not establish the uniqueness thesis; hence it cannot provide an answer to the TMA'. He then argues that what the TBA shows is (not U, but) 'that there is not *more* than one Form of Bed; it cannot show that there is exactly one unless it can show that the regress ... will stop. But, according to the TMA, this is precisely what it cannot do. So while the TBA shows only that there is not more than one Form, the TMA shows that there is not exactly one Form. And if neither exactly one nor more than one, then none. The surprising conclusion of the TMA together with the TBA is that there are no Forms.' However, the conditional in the first sentence quoted from Cohen is true only if the TBA's one over many assumption is the same as the TMA's; I have argued that it need not be. I have also argued that the TBA shows that the regress will stop, and so it can show that there is exactly one form of bed.

Ross, *Plato's Theory of Ideas*, 87 (cf. 230–1), says that '[t]o show that if there were two Ideas of bed there would have to be a third does nothing to disprove the contention that if there is one Idea of bed, related to particulars as Plato supposes, there must be a second'. Ross's conditional is true. However, the TBA argues more than that if there were two forms of bed there would have to be a third; and the more it argues does 'disprove the contention that if there is one Idea of bed, related to particulars as Plato supposes, there must be a second'.

58. G. Vlastos, 'Self-Predication and Self-Participation in Plato's Later Period', in id., *PS* 335–41 at 340 n. 13, and C. Stough, 'Two Kinds of Naming in the *Sophist*', *Canadian Journal of Philosophy*, 20 (1990), 355–81 at 362–3, argue that at least by the time of *So.*, Plato believes that any form of *F* is *F* in virtue of itself. This claim is challenged by Nehamas, who writes:

> If the very nature of the Different guarantees its distinctness from every Form, then simply naming it 'the Different' would ensure that it was so distinct. At most, we would need an existence proof to the effect that there is such a thing as the Different and the rest would follow. We would not need what we get—a series of complicated arguments of dubious soundness distinguishing the Different from the other Forms by showing that not drawing the distinction has unwelcome consequences. ('Participation and Predication', 354.)

But this argument is unconvincing. The complicated arguments Plato gives are intended to be (among other things) proof that the form of the different exists; existence proofs need not be simple and straightforward. In any case, although Nehamas denies that the form of the different is different in virtue of itself, he allows that it is different by participating in itself; and even that seems incompatible with NI. So one way or the other, at least *So.* seems to deny NI. But, as I go on to suggest, the middle dialogues (and not just the TBA) also seem to reject NI.

59. This is not to say that BSP is inconsistent with NI. BSP does not say or imply that any form of *F* is *F* in virtue of itself. It says that any form of *F* is *F* because of its explanatory role. Hence even if we take the TMA's self-predication assumption to be BSP, its premises are consistent; see Ch. 15 n. 20. However, although BSP and NI are consistent, it is not clear why anyone should accept them both. But perhaps that is part of Plato's point in formulating the TMA. For he formulates it with SP; nothing he says requires BSP or NSP, though both are adequate for the regress. But once we see that his actual self-predication assumption is not just the bare SP, but BSP, we shall see that NI is no longer tempting, and so we shall see how to avoid the regress. If this is Plato's point, then we can say not only that Plato's actual self-predication assumption is best interpreted as BSP (see Ch. 4 n. 74), but also that he intends BSP.

60. See Ch. 4 n. 35. The remark made there applies to Plato as well as to Socrates.

61. We have also seen that various attempts to commit Plato to NI fail; see sect. 1. Is Aristotle then wrong to suggest that Plato is committed to G-Sep and so to NI? But perhaps Aristotle need not be taken to mean that Plato is really committed to G-Sep. Rather, he sees that Plato's actual separation assumption is only Sep. But he is bothered by the fact that Plato never argues for Sep; so he gives Plato a valid argument for Sep, which includes G-Sep as a premiss, and he then asks what results. But Plato can reply that that is not how he does or would ground Sep. I return to Aristotle's reasons for suggesting that Plato is vulnerable to the TMA in the next section.

62. I have focused on his rejection of NI. But if he rejects NI, then he also rejects OM-TMA.
63. I discuss Aristotle's objections to the Argument from Relatives in Ch. 13.
64. 'Logic and Metaphysics', 193–9.
65. Owen, 'Logic and Metaphysics', 197–8, also considers this possibility.
66. Owen, 'Logic and Metaphysics', 198, makes something like this point, although he phrases it in terms of focal connection rather than in terms of synonymy.
67. For this debate between Plato and Aristotle, see Ch. 13.4.

BIBLIOGRAPHY
OF WORKS CITED

Note: When more than one source is cited for a given work, I have used the pagination of the first source cited.

ACKRILL, J. L., review of Wilpert's *Zwei aristotelische Frühschriften über die Ideenlehre*, *Mind*, 61 (1952), 102–13.

—— 'Συμπλοκὴ εἰδῶν', in Vlastos (ed.), *Plato I*, 201–9. From *Bulletin of the Institute of Classical Studies*, 2 (1959), 31–5.

—— *Aristotle's Categories and De Interpretatione* (Oxford: The Clarendon Press, 1963).

ADAM, C., and TANNERY, D. (eds.), *Œuvres de Descartes* (Paris: Cerf, 1897–1913; repr. Paris: J. Vrin, CNRS, 1964–76). Cited as AT.

ADAM, J., *The Republic of Plato*, 2 vols. (Cambridge: Cambridge University Press, 1902).

ALLAN, D. J., review of Cherniss' *Aristotle's Criticism of Plato and the Academy*, *Mind*, 55 (1946), 263–72.

—— 'Aristotle and the *Parmenides*', in Düring and Owen (eds.), *Aristotle and Plato in the Mid-Fourth Century*, 133–44.

ALLEN, R. E., 'Participation and Predication in Plato's Middle Dialogues', in id. (ed.), *Studies in Plato's Metaphysics*, 43–60. From *Philosophical Review*, 69 (1960), 147–64.

—— *Plato's Euthyphro and the Earlier Theory of Forms* (London: Routledge and Kegan Paul, 1970).

—— *Plato's Parmenides: Translation and Analysis* (Minneapolis: University of Minnesota Press, 1983).

—— (ed.), *Studies in Plato's Metaphysics* (London: Routledge and Kegan Paul, 1965).

ANNAS, J., 'Forms and First Principles', *Phronesis*, 19 (1974), 257–83.

—— *Aristotle's Metaphysics, Books M and N* (Oxford: The Clarendon Press, 1976).

—— 'Aristotle on Substance, Accident and Plato's Forms', *Phronesis*, 22 (1977), 146–60.

—— *An Introduction to Plato's Republic* (Oxford: The Clarendon Press, 1981).

—— 'Aristotle and Plato on Objects of Thought' (unpublished).

—— and BARNES, J., *The Modes of Scepticism* (Cambridge: Cambridge University Press, 1985).

ANSCOMBE, G. E. M., and GEACH, P. T., *Three Philosophers* (Ithaca, NY: Cornell University Press, 1961).

ARMSTRONG, D. M., *Universals and Scientific Realism*, 2 vols. (Cambridge: Cambridge University Press, 1978).

BARFORD, R., 'A Proof from the *Peri Ideon* Revisited', *Phronesis*, 21 (1976), 198–219.

BARNES, J., 'Homonymy in Aristotle and Speusippus', *Classical Quarterly*, NS 21 (1971), 65–80.
—— *Aristotle's Posterior Analytics* (Oxford: The Clarendon Press, 1975).
—— 'Editor's Notes', *Phronesis*, 30 (1985), 99–110.
—— (ed.), *The Complete Works of Aristotle: The Revised Oxford Translation*, 2 vols. (Princeton: Princeton University Press, 1984). Cited as *ROT*.
BERTI, E., *La filosofia del primo Aristotele* (Padua: CEDAM, 1962).
BLUCK, R. S., 'Aristotle, Plato, and Ideas of *Artefacta*', *Classical Review*, 61 (1947), 75–6.
—— *Plato's Sophist: A Commentary* (Manchester: Manchester University Press, 1975).
BOGEN, J., and McGUIRE, J. E. (eds.), *How Things Are: Studies in Predication and the History of Philosophy* (Dordrecht: Reidel, 1983).
BOLTON, R., 'Plato's Distinction between Being and Becoming', *Review of Metaphysics*, 29 (1975), 66–95.
BONITZ, H. (ed.), *Alexander in metaphysica commentaria* (Berlin: Reimer, 1847).
—— *Index Aristotelicus* (Berlin: Küniglich Prenßische Akademie der Wissenschaften, 1870) (= *Aristotelis Opera*, v, ed. I. Bekker (Berlin, Reimer)).
BOSTOCK, D., *Plato's Phaedo* (Oxford: The Clarendon Press, 1986).
—— 'Plato on "Is Not" (*Sophist*, 254–9)', *Oxford Studies in Ancient Philosophy*, 2 (1984), 89–119.
BRANDIS, C. A. (ed.), *Aristotelis et Theophrast: Metaphysica*, 2 vols. (Berlin: Reimer, 1823–37)
BRANDWOOD, L., 'The Dating of Plato's Works by the Stylistic Method: A Historical and Critical Survey', Ph.D thesis (University of London, 1958).
—— *A Word Index to Plato* (Leeds: W. S. Maney and Sons, 1976).
—— *The Chronology of Plato's Dialogues* (Cambridge: Cambridge University Press, 1990).
BROWN, L., 'Being in the *Sophist*: A Syntactical Enquiry', *Oxford Studies in Ancient Philosophy*, 4 (1986), 49–70.
BROWNSTEIN, D., *Aspects of the Problems of Universals* (Lawrence, Kan.: Kansas University Press, 1973).
BURNYEAT, M. F., 'Plato on the Grammar of Perceiving', *Classical Quarterly*, NS 26 (1976), 29–51.
—— 'Examples in Epistemology: Socrates, Theaetetus, and G. E. Moore', *Philosophy*, 52 (1977), 381–98.
—— 'Aristotle on Understanding', in E. Berti (ed.), *Aristotle on Science: The Posterior Analytics* (Padua: Antenore, 1981), 97–139.
—— 'Idealism and Greek Philosophy: What Descartes Saw and Berkeley Missed', *Philosophical Review*, 91 (1982), 3–43.
—— 'Platonism and Mathematics: A Prelude to Discussion', in Graeser (ed.), *Mathematics and Metaphysics in Aristotle*, 213–40.
—— 'The Practicability of Plato's Ideally Just City', in K. Boudouris (ed.), *On Justice: Plato's and Aristotle's Conception of Justice in Relation to Modern and Contemporary Theories of Justice* (Athens: Greek Philosophical Society, 1989), 95–104.
—— introduction to *The Theaetetus of Plato*, trans. M. J. Levett (Indianapolis: Hackett Publishing Company, 1990).

Butchvarov, P., *Resemblance and Identity* (Bloomington, Ind., and London: Indiana University Press, 1966).

Calvert, B., 'Forms and Flux in Plato's *Cratylus*', *Phronesis*, 15 (1970), 26–47.

Cherniss, H. F., *Aristotle's Criticism of Plato and the Academy* (Baltimore: The Johns Hopkins Press, 1944; repr. New York: Russell and Russell, 1962).

—— *The Riddle of the Early Academy* (Berkeley and Los Angeles: University of California Press, 1945).

—— 'The Relation of the *Timaeus* to Plato's Later Dialogues', in Allen (ed.), *Studies in Plato's Metaphysics*, 339–78. From *American Journal of Philology*, 78 (1957), 225–66.

Code, A., 'On the Origins of some Aristotelian Theses about Predication', in Bogen and McGuire (eds.), *How Things Are*, 101–33.

Cohen, S. M., 'The Logic of the Third Man', *Philosophical Review*, 80 (1971), 448–75.

—— 'Plato's Method of Division', in J. M. E. Moravcsik (ed.), *Patterns in Plato's Thought* (Dordrecht: Reidel, 1973), 181–91.

Cooper, J. M., 'The *Magna Moralia* and Aristotle's Moral Philosophy', *American Journal of Philology*, 94 (1973), 327–49.

—— *Reason and Human Good in Aristotle* (Cambridge, Mass.: Harvard University Press, 1975).

—— 'Plato's Theory of the Human Good in the *Philebus*', *Journal of Philosophy*, 74 (1977), 714–30.

Cornford, F. M., *Plato's Theory of Knowledge* (London: Routledge and Kegan Paul, 1935).

—— *Plato and Parmenides* (London: Routledge and Kegan Paul, 1939).

Cottingham, J., Stoothoff, R., and Murdoch, D. (eds.), *The Philosophical Writings of Descartes*, 3 vols. (Cambridge: Cambridge University Press, 1984–91). Cited as CSM.

Cousin, V. (ed.), *Procli Commentarium in Platonis Parmenidem*, in *Procli Opera Inedita* (Paris: Durand, 1864), 617–1258.

Crombie, I. M., *An Examination of Plato's Doctrines*, 2 vols. (London: Routledge and Kegan Paul, 1963).

Dancy, R., *Sense and Contradiction* (Dordrecht: Reidel, 1975).

—— *Two Studies in the Early Academy* (Albany: State University of New York Press, 1991).

Denniston, J. D., *The Greek Particles* (2nd edn., Oxford: The Clarendon Press, 1954).

Devereux, D., 'The Primacy of *Ousia*: Aristotle's Debt to Plato', in D. O'Meara (ed.), *Platonic Investigations* (Washington, DC: Catholic University of America Press, 1985), 226–32.

—— 'Particular and Universal in Aristotle's Conception of Practical Knowledge', *Review of Metaphysics*, 39 (1986), 483–504.

Diels, H., and Kranz, W. (eds.), *Die Fragmente der Vorsokratiker*, 6th edn. (Berlin: Weidmann, 1952). Cited as DK.

Dillon, J., *The Middle Platonists: 80 BC to AD 200* (Ithaca, NY: Cornell University Press, 1977).

Dooley, W. E. (tr.), *Alexander of Aphrodisias: On Aristotle, Metaphysics I* (London: Duckworth, 1989).

DÜRING, I., 'Aristotle and Plato in the Mid-Fourth Century', *Eranos*, 54 (1956), 109–20.

—— *Aristotle in the Ancient Biographical Tradition* (Göteborg: Studia Graeca et Latina Gothoburgensia, 5, distributed by Almqvist & Wiksell, 1957).

—— *Aristotle's Protrepticus: An Attempt at Reconstruction* (Göteborg: Studia Graeca et Latina Gothoburgensia, 12, distributed by Almqvist & Wiksell, 1961).

—— *Aristoteles: Darstellung und Interpretation seines Denkens* (Heidelberg: Carl Winter, Universitätsverlag, 1966).

—— and OWEN, G. E. L. (eds.), *Aristotle and Plato in the Mid-Fourth Century* (Göteborg: Studia Graeca et Latina Gothoburgensia, 11, distributed by Almqvist & Wiksell, 1960).

EVERSON, S. (ed.), *Companions to Ancient Thought*, i: *Epistemology* (Cambridge: Cambridge University Press, 1990).

FINE, G., 'Plato on Naming', *Philosophical Quarterly*, 27 (1977), 289–301.

—— 'Knowledge and Belief in *Republic* V', *Archiv für Geschichte der Philosophie*, 60 (1978), 121–39.

—— 'False Belief in the *Theaetetus*', *Phronesis*, 24 (1979), 70–80.

—— 'Knowledge and *Logos* in the *Theaetetus*', *Philosophical Review*, 88 (1979), 366–97.

—— 'The One over Many', *Philosophical Review*, 89 (1980), 197–240.

—— 'Owen, Aristotle, and the Third Man', *Phronesis*, 27 (1982), 13–33.

—— 'Aristotle and the More Accurate Arguments', in Nussbaum and Schofield (eds.), *Language and Logos*, 155–77.

—— 'Plato and Aristotle on Form and Substance', *Proceedings of the Cambridge Philological Society*, 209 (1983), 23–47.

—— 'Relational Entities', *Archiv für Geschichte der Philosophie*, 65 (1983), 225–49.

—— 'Separation', *Oxford Studies in Ancient Philosophy*, 2 (1984), 31–87.

—— 'Immanence', *Oxford Studies in Ancient Philosophy*, supplementary volume (1986), 71–97.

—— 'Forms as Causes: Plato and Aristotle', in Graeser (ed.), *Mathematics and Metaphysics*, 69–112.

—— 'Plato on Perception', *Oxford Studies in Ancient Philosophy*, supplementary volume (1988), 15–28.

—— 'Owen's Progress: A Review of *Logic, Science and Dialectic*', *Philosophical Review*, 97 (1988), 373–99.

—— 'Knowledge and Belief in *Republic* V–VII', in Everson (ed.), *Companions to Ancient Thought*, i: *Epistemology*, 85–115.

—— review of Penner's *The Ascent from Nominalism*, *Nous*, 25 (1991), 126–32.

—— 'Inquiry in the *Meno*', in R. Kraut (ed.), *Cambridge Companion to Plato* (Cambridge, 1992), 200–226.

—— 'Ancient Metaphysics: A Critical Notice of R. M. Dancy's *Two Studies in the Early Academy*', *Canadian Journal of Philosophy* 22 (1992), 393–410.

FRANK, D. H., 'A Disproof in the "Peri Ideon"', *Southern Journal of Philosophy*, 22 (1984), 49–59.

—— *The Arguments 'From the Sciences' in Aristotle's Peri Ideon* (New York: Peter Lang, 1984).

FREDE, M., *Prädikation und Existenzaussage* (Göttingen: Hypomnemata, 1967).
—— 'An Empiricist View of Knowledge: Memorism', in Everson (ed.), *Companions to Ancient Thought*, i: *Epistemology*, 225–50.
FREGE, G., 'On Sense and Reference', in id., *Philosophical Writings*, trans. and ed. P. T. Geach and M. Black (Oxford: Blackwell, 1952). Originally published 1892.
FURTH, M., 'Elements of Eleatic Ontology', *Journal of the History of Philosophy*, 6 (1968), 111–32.
GALLOP, D., *Plato's Phaedo* (Oxford: The Clarendon Press, 1975).
GEACH, P. T., 'The Third Man Again', in Allen (ed.), *Studies in Plato's Metaphysics*, 265–77. From *Philosophical Review*, 65 (1956), 72–82.
—— *God and the Soul* (London: Routledge and Kegan Paul, 1969).
GIGON, O. (ed.), *Aristotelis Opera*, iii: *Librorum deperditorum fragmenta* (Berlin and New York: Walter de Gruyter, 1987).
GOODMAN, N., *Fact, Fiction, and Forecast* (Indianapolis: Bobbs-Merrill, 1965).
GOSLING, J. C. B., *Plato* (London: Routledge and Kegan Paul, 1973).
—— *Plato's Philebus* (Oxford: The Clarendon Press, 1975).
GRAESER, A. (ed.), *Mathematics and Metaphysics* (Berne: Haupt, 1987).
HACKFORTH, R., *Plato's Examination of Pleasure (the Philebus)* (Cambridge: Cambridge University Press, 1945).
—— *Plato's Phaedo* (Cambridge: Cambridge University Press, 1955).
HARLFINGER, D., 'Edizione critica del testo del "De Ideis" di Aristotele', in Leszl, *Il 'De Ideis'*, 15–39.
HARTMAN, E., *Substance, Body, and Soul* (Princeton, NJ: Princeton University Press, 1977).
HEINAMAN, R. E., 'Self-Predication in the *Sophist*', *Phronesis*, 26 (1981), 55–66.
—— 'Being in the *Sophist*', *Archiv für Geschichte der Philosophie*, 65 (1983), 1–17.
—— 'Communion of Forms', *Proceedings of the Aristotelian Society*, 83 (1982–3), 175–90.
—— 'Self-Predication in Plato's Middle Dialogues', *Phronesis*, 34 (1989), 56–79.
HEINZE, R., *Xenokrates: Darstellung der Lehre und Sammlung der Fragmente* (Leipzig: Teubner, 1892).
HEITZ, E., *Fragmenta Aristotelis* (Paris: Didot, 1869).
IRWIN, T. H., 'Plato's Heracliteanism', *Philosophical Quarterly*, 27 (1977), 1–13.
—— *Plato's Moral Theory* (Oxford: The Clarendon Press, 1977). Cited as *PMT*.
—— *Plato's Gorgias* (Oxford: The Clarendon Press, 1979).
—— 'Aristotle's Discovery of Metaphysics', *Review of Metaphysics*, 31 (1977–8), 210–29.
—— 'Homonymy in Aristotle', *Review of Metaphysics*, 34 (1981), 523–44.
—— 'Aristotle's Concept of Signification', in Nussbaum and Schofield (eds.), *Language and Logos*, 241–66.
—— (tr.) *Nicomachean Ethics* (Indianapolis: Hackett Publishing Company, 1985).
—— *Aristotle's First Principles* (Oxford: The Clarendon Press, 1988). Cited as *AFP*.
ISNARDI PARENTE, M., 'Le *Peri Ideōn* d'Aristote: Platon ou Xénocrate?', *Phronesis*, 26 (1981), 135–52.

JACKSON, H., 'Plato's Later Theory of Ideas', *Journal of Philology*: I, 10 (1882), 253–98; II, 11 (1882), 287–331; III (1885), 1–40; IV, ibid. 242–72; V, 14 (1885), 172–230; VI, 15 (1886), 289–305.

JAEGER, W., *Aristotle: Fundamentals of the History of his Development*, trans. R. Robinson (2nd edn., Oxford: The Clarendon Press, 1948).

—— review of Wilpert's *Zwei aristotelische Frühschriften über die Ideenlehre*, *Gnomon*, 23 (1951), 246–52.

JONES, B., 'Introduction to the First Five Chapters of Aristotle's *Categories*', *Phronesis*, 20 (1975), 146–72.

KAHN, C. H., 'Language and Ontology in the *Cratylus*', in Lee *et al.* (eds.), *Exegesis and Argument*, 152–76.

KARPP, H., 'Die Schrift des Aristoteles Περὶ ἰδεῶν', *Hermes*, 68 (1933), 384–91.

KIRWAN, C., *Aristotle's Metaphysics, Books Γ, Δ, and E* (Oxford: The Clarendon Press, 1971).

KRAUT, R., *Socrates and the State* (Princeton, NJ: Princeton University Press, 1984).

KRETZMANN, N., 'Plato on the Correctness of Names', *American Philosophical Quarterly*, 8 (1971), 126–38.

KUNG, J., 'Aristotle on Thises, Suches, and the Third Man Argument', *Phronesis*, 26 (1981), 207–47.

LACEY, A. R., review of Leszl's *Il 'De Ideis'*, *Mind*, 87 (1978), 281–3.

LEE, E. N., MOURELATOS, A. P. D., and RORTY, R. M. (eds.), *Exegesis and Argument* (Assen: Van Gorcum, 1973).

LESZL, W., *Logic and Metaphysics in Aristotle* (Padua: Antenore, 1970).

—— *Il 'De Ideis' di Aristotele e la teoria platonica delle idee* (Florence: Olschki, 1975).

LEWIS, D., *On the Plurality of Worlds* (Oxford: Basil Blackwell, 1986).

LEWIS, F., 'Plato's Third Man Argument and the "Platonism" of Aristotle', in Bogen and McGuire (eds.), *How Things Are*, 133–74.

LLOYD, A. C., *Form and Universal in Aristotle* (Liverpool: F. Cairns, 1981).

LOCKE, J., *An Essay Concerning Human Understanding*, ed. P. Nidditch (Oxford: The Clarendon Press, 1975). Originally published 1690.

LOUIS, P. (ed.), *Albinus: Didaskalikos* (Paris: Les Belles Lettres, 1945). (Ascribed in the manuscripts to 'Alcinous', which Louis, following Freudenthal, emends to 'Albinus'.)

LUCE, J. V., 'The Date of the *Cratylus*', *American Journal of Philology*, 85 (1964), 136–54.

—— 'The Theory of Ideas in the *Cratylus*', *Phronesis*, 10 (1965), 21–36.

MACDONALD, S., 'Aristotle and the Homonymy of the Good', *Archiv für Geschichte der Philosophie*, 71 (1989), 150–74.

MCDOWELL, J., *Plato: Theaetetus* (Oxford: The Clarendon Press, 1973).

MALCOLM, J., 'Vlastos on Pauline Predication', *Phronesis*, 30 (1985), 79–91.

MANSION, S., 'La Critique de la théorie des idées dans le ΠΕΡΙ ΙΔΕΩΝ d'Aristote', *Revue philosophique de Louvain*, 47 (1949), 169–202.

—— 'Deux écrits de jeunesse d'Aristote sur la doctrine des idées', *Revue philosophique de Louvain*, 48 (1950), 398–416.

MATTHEWS, G. B., and COHEN S. M., 'The One and the Many', *Review of Metaphysics*, 21 (1968), 630–55.

MORAUX, P., *Les Listes anciennes des ouvrages d'Aristote* (Louvain: Éditions universitaires de Louvain, 1951).

MORAVCSIK, J. M. E., 'Being and Meaning in the *Sophist*', *Acta Philosophica Fennica*, 14 (1962), 23–78.

MORRISON, D., 'Χωριστός in Aristotle', *Harvard Studies in Classical Philology*, 89 (1985), 89–105.

MORROW, G., and DILLON, J. (trans.; introduction and notes by Dillon), *Proclus' Commentary on Plato's Parmenides* (Princeton: Princeton University Press, 1987).

MURPHY, N. R., *The Interpretation of Plato's Republic* (Oxford: The Clarendon Press, 1951).

MUTSCHMANN, H. (ed.), *Divisiones Aristoteleae* (Leipzig: Teubner, 1908).

NEHAMAS, A., 'Predication and Forms of Opposites in the *Phaedo*', *Review of Metaphysics*, 26 (1973), 461–91.

—— 'Confusing Universals and Particulars in Plato's Early Dialogues', *Review of Metaphysics*, 29 (1975), 287–306.

—— 'Self-Predication and Plato's Theory of Forms', *American Philosophical Quarterly*, 16 (1979), 93–103.

—— 'Plato on Imitation and Poetry in *Republic* 10', in J. Moravcsik and P. Tempko (eds.), *Plato on Beauty, Wisdom, and the Arts* (Totowa, NJ: Rowman and Littlefield, 1982), 47–78.

—— 'Participation and Predication in Plato's Later Thought', *Review of Metaphysics*, 36 (1982), 343–74.

NUSSBAUM, M., and SCHOFIELD, M. (eds.), *Language and Logos* (Cambridge: Cambridge University Press, 1982).

OWEN, G. E. L., 'The Place of the *Timaeus* in Plato's Dialogues', in id,, *LSD*, 65–84. From *Classical Quarterly*, NS 3 (1953), 79–95.

—— 'A Proof in the *Peri Ideōn*', in id., *LSD*, 165–79. From *Journal of Hellenic Studies*, 77 (1957), 103–11.

—— 'Logic and Metaphysics in Some Early Works of Aristotle', in id., *LSD*, 180–99. From Düring and Owen (eds.), *Aristotle and Plato in the Mid-Fourth Century*, 163–90.

—— 'Aristotle on the Snares of Ontology', in id., *LSD*, 259–78. From R. Bambrough (ed.), *New Essays on Plato and Aristotle* (London: Routledge and Kegan Paul, 1965), 69–75.

—— 'The Platonism of Aristotle', in id., *LSD*, 200–20. From *Proceedings of the British Academy*, 51 (1966), 125–150.

—— 'Plato and Parmenides on the Timeless Present', in id., *LSD*, 27–44. From *Monist*, 50 (1966), 317–40.

—— 'Dialectic and Eristic in the Treatment of Forms', in id., *LSD*, 221–38. From id. (ed.), *Aristotle on Dialectic: The Topics* (Papers of The Third Symposium Aristotelicum; Oxford: Oxford University Press, 1968), 103–25.

—— 'Notes on Ryle's Plato', in id., *LSD*, 85–103. From G. Pitcher and O. P. Wood (eds.), *Ryle* (Garden City, NY: Doubleday, 1970), 341–72.

—— 'Plato on Not-Being', in id., *LSD*, 104–37. From Vlastos (ed.), *Plato I*, 223–67.

—— 'Plato on the Undepictable', in id., *LSD*, 138–47. From Lee *et al.* (eds.), *Exegesis and Argument*, 349–61.

OWEN, G. E. L., 'Philosophical Invective', in id., *LSD*, 347–64. From *Oxford Studies in Ancient Philosophy*, 1 (1983), 1–25.

—— *Logic, Science, and Dialectic*, ed. M. Nussbaum (Ithaca, NY: Cornell University Press, 1986). Cited as *LSD*.

—— Unpublished manuscript on the *Peri Ideōn* (Classics Library in Cambridge University).

PARRY, R. D., 'The Uniqueness Proof for Forms in *Republic* 10', *Journal of the History of Philosophy*, 23 (1985), 133–50.

PEARS, D., 'Universals', *Philosophical Quarterly*, 1 (1950), 218–27.

PENNER, T., 'The Unity of Virtue', *Philosophical Review*, 82 (1973), 35–68.

—— *The Ascent from Nominalism* (Dordrecht: Reidel, 1987).

PETERSON, S., 'A Reasonable Self-Predication Premise for the Third Man Argument', *Philosophical Review*, 82 (1973), 451–70.

PHILIPPSON, R., 'Il Περὶ ἰδεῶν di Aristotele', *Rivista di filologia e d'istruzione classica*, NS 14 (1936), 113–25.

PRAECHTER, K., review of *Commentaria in Aristotelem Graeca* (tr. V. Caston), in R. Sorabji (ed.), *Aristotle Transformed: The Ancient Commentators and their Influence* (Ithaca, NY: Cornell University Press, 1990), 31–54. Originally published as 'Die griechischen Aristoteleskommentare', in *Byzantinische Zeitschrift*, 18 (1909), 516–38.

PRIOR, W. J., *Unity and Development in Plato's Metaphysics* (London and Sydney: Croom Helm, 1985).

PUTNAM, H., 'How Not to Talk about Meaning', in id., *Philosophical Papers*, ii. 117–30. From R. Cohen and M. Wartofsky (eds.), *Boston Studies in the Philosophy of Science*, ii (New York: Humanities Press, 1965).

—— 'On Properties', in id., *Philosophical Papers*, i. 305–22. From N. Rescher (ed.), *Essays in Honor of Carl G. Hempel* (Dordrecht: Reidel, 1970).

—— *Philosophical Papers*, 2 vols. (Cambridge: Cambridge University Press, 1975).

QUINE, W. V. O., *Word and Object* (Cambridge, Mass.: MIT Press, 1960).

RAVAISSON, F., *Essai sur la métaphysique d'Aristote*, i (Paris: Vrin, 1837).

RITCHIE, D. G., *Plato* (Edinburgh: T. & T. Clark; The World's Epoch Makers' Series, 1902).

ROBIN, L., *La Théorie platonicienne des idées et des nombres d'après Aristote* (Paris: Félix Alcan, 1908).

ROSE, V., *Aristotelis qui ferebantur Librorum Fragmenta* (Leipzig: Teubner, 1886). Cited as *Ar. Fr.*

—— *Aristotelis Pseudepigraphus* (Leipzig: Teubner, 1863). Cited as *Ar. Ps.*

—— *De Aristotelis Librorum ordine et auctoritate commentatio* (Berlin: Reimer, 1854).

ROSS, W. D., *Aristotle's Metaphysics*, 2 vols. (Oxford: The Clarendon Press, 1924).

—— 'The Socratic Problem', *Proceedings of the Classical Association*, 30 (1933), 7–24.

—— *Plato's Theory of Ideas* (Oxford: The Clarendon Press, 1951).

—— *Aristotelis Fragmenta Selecta* (Oxford: The Clarendon Press, 1955). Cited as *Ar. Fr.*

ROWE, C. J., 'The Proof from Relatives in the *Peri Ideon*: *Further Reconsideration*', *Phronesis*, 24 (1979), 270–81.
—— review of Leszl's *Il De ideis di Aristotele e la teoria platonica delle idee*, *Classical Review*, NS 29 (1979), 77–9.
RYLE, G., *Plato's Progress* (Cambridge: Cambridge University Press, 1966).
SACHS, D., 'Does Aristotle have a Doctrine of Secondary Substances?', *Mind*, 57 (1948), 221–5.
SAYRE, K. M., *Plato's Late Ontology* (Princeton, NJ: Princeton University Press, 1983).
SCOTT, D., 'Platonic Anamnesis Revisited', *Classical Quarterly*, NS 37 (1987), 346–66.
SELLARS, W., 'Vlastos and the "Third Man"', *Philosophical Review*, 64 (1955), 405–37.
SHOEMAKER, S., *Identity, Cause, and Mind* (Cambridge: Cambridge University Press, 1984).
SHOREY, P., *The Unity of Plato's Thought* (Chicago: University of Chicago Press, 1903).
SMITH, J. A., 'General Relative Clauses in Greek', *Classical Review*, 31 (1917), 69–71.
STOUGH, C., 'Two Kinds of Naming in the *Sophist*', *Canadian Journal of Philosophy*, 20 (1990), 355–81.
STRANG, C., 'Plato and the Third Man', in Vlastos (ed.), *Plato I*, 184–200. From *Proceedings of the Aristotelian Society*, supplementary volume 37 (1963), 147–64.
STRAWSON, P. F., 'Particular and General', *Proceedings of the Aristotelian Society*, 14 (1953–4), 233–60.
TARÁN, L., 'Speusippus and Aristotle on Homonymy and Synonymy', *Hermes*, 106 (1978), 73–99.
TAYLOR, A. E., 'Parmenides, Zeno, and Socrates', *Proceedings of the Aristotelian Society*, 16 (1915–16), 234–89.
TAYLOR, C. C. W., *Plato: Protagoras* (Oxford: The Clarendon Press, 1976).
TELOH, H., *The Development of Plato's Metaphysics* (University Park, Pa., and London: Pennsylvania State University Press, 1981).
TODD, R. B., *Alexander of Aphrodisias on Stoic Physics: A Study of the De Mixtione with Preliminary Essays, Text, Translation, and Commentary* (Leiden: Brill, 1976).
TOOLEY, M., *Causation: A Realist Approach* (Oxford: The Clarendon Press, 1987).
VLASTOS, G., 'The "Third Man" Argument in the *Parmenides*', in Allen (ed.), *Studies in Plato's Metaphysics*, 231–63. From *Philosophical Review*, 63 (1954), 319–49. Cited as 'TMA I'.
—— 'On Plato's Oral Doctrine', in id., *PS* 379–98. From *Gnomon*, 35 (1963), 641–55.
—— 'Plato's "Third Man" Argument (*Parm*. 132a1–b2): Text and Logic', in id., *PS* 342–65. From *Philosophical Quarterly*, 19 (1969), 289–381. Cited as 'TMA II'.
—— 'Self-Predication and Self-Participation in Plato's Later Period', in id., *PS* 335–41. From *Philosophical Review*, 78 (1969), 74–8.

VLASTOS, G., 'The Unity of the Virtues in the *Protagoras*', in id., *PS* 221–69. From *Review of Metaphysics*, 25 (1972), 415–58.

—— 'A Note on "Pauline Predications" in Plato', *Phronesis*, 19 (1974), 95–101.

—— 'What did Socrates Understand by His "What is F?" Question?', in id., *PS* 410–17.

—— 'An Ambiguity in the *Sophist*', in id., *PS* 270–322.

—— 'The "Two-Level Paradoxes" in Aristotle', in id., *PS* 323–34.

—— *Platonic Studies* (2nd edn., Princeton: Princeton University Press, 1981). Cited as *PS*.

—— '"Separation" in Plato', *Oxford Studies in Ancient Philosophy*, 5 (1987), 187–96.

—— 'Socrates', *Proceedings of the British Academy*, 74 (1988), 89–111.

—— *Socrates: Ironist and Moral Philosopher* (Ithaca, NY: Cornell University Press, 1991).

—— (ed.), *Plato: A Collection of Critical Essays*, i: *Metaphysics and Epistemology* (New York: Doubleday, 1971). Cited as *Plato I*.

VOGEL, C. J. DE, 'The Legend of the Platonizing Aristotle', in Düring and Owen (eds.), *Aristotle and Plato in the Mid-Fourth Century*, 248–56.

—— 'Problems Concerning Later Platonism I', *Mnemosyne*, 4th ser., 1 (1948), 197–216.

WHITE, N. P., 'A Note on Ἔκθεσις', *Phronesis*, 16 (1971), 164–8.

—— *Plato on Knowledge and Reality* (Indianapolis: Hackett Publishing Company, 1976).

WHITING, J., 'Aristotelian Individuals' (unpublished MS).

WIGGINS, D., *Sameness and Substance* (Oxford: Basil Blackwell, 1980).

WILPERT, P., 'Reste verlorener Aristotelesschriften bei Alexander von Aphrodisias', *Hermes*, 75 (1940), 369–96.

—— *Zwei aristotelische Frühschriften über die Ideenlehre* (Regensburg: Druck und Verlag Josef Habbel, 1949). Cited as *ZaF*.

WILSON, M., *Descartes* (London: Routledge and Kegan Paul, 1978).

WITTGENSTEIN, L., *The Blue and Brown Books* (Oxford: Blackwell, 1958).

—— *Philosophical Grammar*, trans. A. Kenny (Oxford: Blackwell, 1974).

WOODS, M., 'Substance and Essence in Aristotle', *Proceedings of the Aristotelian Society*, 75 (1974–5), 167–80.

INDEX LOCORUM

INDEX NOMINUM

References to ancient authors are given in the Index Locorum and the General Index.

GENERAL INDEX

form, forms (*cont.*):
  of not-being 113–14
  and numbers 35, 38, 260, 263
  form as one 48, 58, 67, 92, 106, 151, 155,
    189–90, 222, 300
  of opposites 190–1, 306
  as paradigms, *see* paradigms
  Parmenides on 111
  and participation 132
  as particulars 21, 25, 59, 61, 63, 127, 143,
    155–6, 160, 214, 245, 274, 326, 352
  perfection of 63, 86, 98, 102, 118–19,
    143, 193, 278, 295, 341, 360
  Platonic and Socratic 36, 38, 44, 46–54,
    62–4, 85–91, 94, 245, 248, 295
  v. predicates 51, 99, 106, 109–10, 231
  and predication 199, 201, 221, 226, 300
  prior to substances 193
  and properties, *see* properties
  range of 40, 83, 97–8, 111, 127, 155, 211,
    225–7, 231, 273, 288, 293, 300, 303,
    339, 341, 358–60
  and recollection 137, 315–16
  as relatives 171, 183, 191
  Republic 10 on 20, 87, 98, 118, 119
  as self-explanatory 204, 234, 270
  self-predication of, *see* self-predication
  separation of, *see* separation
  and souls 127
  Speusippus' view 259
  as standard cases 167
  as standards 53
  must be substances 184–6
  of substances 274, 300, 339
  synonymous with sensibles 147, 230,
    320–1
  and thought 132–3, 211, 340
  two-level paradoxes 192
  uninstantiated 269
  uniqueness 231
  as universals 25, 54, 60, 64, 73, 76, 78,
    105, 124, 127–9, 142, 156, 157–60, 214,
    218–19, 221–2, 240, 245, 247–8, 252,
    296, 326, 352
forms, arguments for the existence of:
  Aristotle on 26
  from change in sensibles 60, 295
  from compresence 58
  epistemological 50, 59
  from explanation 59
  from imperfection 98–9, 118–19,
    227–30, 238, 239, 299, 360
  metaphysical 50
  from one over many 267
  semantic 24, 50, 103, 107, 110–13, 126,
    143, 145, 155, 160, 169–70, 306, 317,
    339
forms, separation of 36, 51, 54, 60, 87, 96,

102, 105, 116, 187–8, 201, 207, 218,
  225, 251, 260, 268–9, 274, 294, 297,
  300, 312, 347, 359, 364
  and compresence 60
  and non-sensible forms 85
  and the One over Many Argument 110,
    116, 118
  and perfection 117, 119
  Plato's argument for 60, 297
  Plato's attitude to 96, 245
  Plato's late dialogues on 275, 359
  Plato's middle dialogues on 60–1, 275,
    359
  Plato's Socratic dialogues on 36, 51
  relatives cannot have 195
  Republic 10 on 294
  Timaeus on 60
  and the Third Man Argument 207, 215,
    218, 359
  see also G-Sep
forms, theory of:
  origin 35, 44–5, 56; *see also* Socrates
  not systematic 20

G-Sep, *see* separation, generalized
genesis 57, 68, 96, 271, 283
genus 77, 186
good, form of 186, 303, 340
Gorgias on forms of artefacts 91
grue, v. genuine properties 107, 213, 247

haplōs, unqualifiedly 77, 81, 90, 287, 327
  Aristotle on 169
  v. coincidents 78
  and explanation 78
  and genus 77
  and incompleteness 168–9, 334
  v. *kata prosthesin* 169
  and knowledge 93
  and *kuriōs* 169
  Plato's use 77
  v. *pros ti* 169
  and substance 77
  and universals 77
Heracleiteanism:
  and change 44–5
  and compresence 57, 271
  moderate and extreme 54
  Plato on 54, 271
  in the *Theaetetus* 134
Heracleitus, and Plato 260
Hermodorus, on *kath' hauto* and *pros ti*
  176–8, 336–8
Hesychius, catalogue 30
homonymy:
  in the Argument from Relatives 264, 318
  Aristotle on 70, 319, 323
  of being 320